D0459723

THE STATISTICAL IMAGINATION: ELEMENTARY STATISTICS FOR THE SOCIAL SCIENCES

Ferris J. Ritchey
Department of Sociology
University of Alabama at Birmingham

 **McGraw-Hill College**

Boston • Burr Ridge, IL • Dubuque, IA • Madison, WI • New York •
San Francisco • St. Louis • Bangkok • Bogotá • Caracas • Lisbon • London • Madrid •
Mexico City • Milan • New Delhi • Seoul • Singapore • Sydney • Taipei • Toronto

McGraw-Hill Higher Education

A Division of The McGraw-Hill Companies

THE STATISTICAL IMAGINATION
ELEMENTARY STATISTICS AND THE SOCIAL SCIENCES

This book is printed on acid-free paper.

2 3 4 5 6 7 8 9 0 DOC/DOC   0 9 8 7 6 5 4 3 2 1 0

ISBN 0-07-289123-8

Editorial director: *Phillip A. Butcher*
Sponsoring editor: *Sally Constable*
Developmental editor: *Kate Purcell*
Marketing manager: *Leslie A. Kraham*
Project manager: *Jim Labeots*
Production supervisor: *Rose Hepburn*
Freelance design coordinator: *Laurie J. Entringer*
Supplement coordinator: *Craig S. Leonard*
Compositor: *ElectraGraphics, Inc.*
Typeface: *10/12 Times Roman*
Printer: *R. R. Donnelley & Sons Company*
Cover image: *© 1995 Digital Art/Corbis*

Library of Congress Cataloging-in-Publication Data

Ritchey, Ferris Joseph.
   The statistical imagination: elementary statistics for the social
sciences/Ferris Ritchey.
     p.   cm.
   ISBN 0-07-289123-8
   1. Social sciences—Statistical methods.   2. Statistics.
I. Title.
HA29.R666 2000
519.5—dc21   99–17717

http://www.mhhe.com (McGraw-Hill web site)
http://www.mhhe.com/socscience/sociology (Sociology division, McGraw-Hill)

Dedication

To Wanda, Daniel, Sarah, Kitty, Dorrance, and Agnes
for their love and encouragement.

To Daniel O. Price and P. Neal Ritchey
for their generous assistance.

In loving memory of Phillip Ritchey.

BRIEF CONTENTS

CONTENTS

PREFACE

We all use statistical thinking—the calculation of likelihoods or probabilities—as we go about our daily lives. The simple decision about whether to carry an umbrella involves estimating the likelihood of rain. Probabilities come into play when one makes important life decisions such as whether to marry, take a job, invest in a stock, or change lanes in traffic. Even a moderate amount of statistical expertise in the workplace provides an employee with a competitive advantage. For students in scientific fields, statistical thinking is an essential ingredient for a clear understanding of the natural world, the social order, and human behavior. On a lighter note, statistical thinking underlies games of chance; just as gaming and gambling are fun, statistics is fun.

Unfortunately, students do not always appreciate how much fun a statistics course can be. Social science majors typically have a limited background in mathematics and resent being forced to take this required course. Some statistics texts disregard this fact by presenting complex formulas and thus cause unnecessary math anxiety. Other texts are "dumbed down" to reduce math anxiety, but usually by sacrificing basic statistical principles. This text attempts to teach the difficult concepts of statistics without sacrificing essential mathematics and calculations. However, it is designed to convince students that mathematics is only a tool for—not the essence of—learning statistics.

I learned that statistics can be taught thoroughly without overemphasizing mathematics when I had the great fortune of working as a graduate student assistant with Daniel O. Price, to whom this text is dedicated. His enthusiasm for the subject, along with his clear explanations of logical processes, caused me to fall in love with the subject matter. Like Dan, I have strived in over 20 years of teaching statistics to develop techniques to share this enthusiasm with students. In particular, I have targeted several conceptual hurdles with the idea of easing students past them. The course design of this text follows four basic principles:

- Statistics is not about mathematics. Instead, it is a learned way of thinking about things.
- Early assignments should be designed to build students' confidence.
- Mastery of the basic elements of statistical reasoning facilitates mastery of the more complex elements; therefore, the learning process is a cumulative one.
- Statistics is learned by doing. There will be many assignments, but the subject matter is inherently interesting and enjoyable. Whistle while you work.

Let me describe these principles in a little more detail. The first is that statistics is not about mathematics per se but about proportional thinking: the visualization of a part to a whole. This view on reality I call *the statistical imagination*. This concept parallels C. Wright Mills's idea of the sociological imagination, which defines the relationship of the individual to the larger society. Similarly, the statistical imagination calls for viewing data in a number of larger contexts. First, observations of individual behavior are viewed within the context of the larger social structure. Second, conclusions about a large population of subjects based on a sample of those subjects are viewed as only one of many sets of conclusions, because a second sample will produce slightly different results. Third, interpretations of statistical data must take into account practical circumstances and cultural realities that provide the essential meaning of the numbers.

The second principle of this text is that the course design should allow students to succeed early on in building confidence and allaying fear of failure. Thus, in the very first pages of the text simple but essential statistical calculations of fractions, proportions, and percentages are introduced. These calculations are presented as ways to quantify proportional thinking, reinforcing the idea that mathematics is only a tool for—not the essence of—learning statistics. Moreover, statistical abstractions that appear as hurdles to many students (for example, the standard deviation, standardized scores, sampling error, and sampling distributions) are given plenty of attention. The theme of error control is emphasized to convey the importance of diligence in statistical work and to encourage students to develop a sense of competence.

The third principle is that for students to grasp the logic of inferential statistics and hypothesis testing successfully, the basic elements of the testing procedure must be well mastered. Part of this objective is achieved through text design. Lots of coverage is given to working with areas under a bell-shaped graphical curve called the normal distribution curve. Considerable time is allowed for actually producing sampling distributions: descriptions of the outcomes that occur when, say, 10 coins are repeatedly tossed or samples of beans are repeatedly drawn from a boxful. Through actual repeated sampling, students learn that the statistics of any single sample are only one set of many possible estimates for the larger group from which the sample came. This hands-on approach will demystify this concept, which is at the core of statistical reasoning. Students learn that sampling distributions are real, not abstract, conjectures. The text also presents the logic of hypothesis testing in six steps, one of which requires drawing sampling distribution curves. This attention to detail fosters proportional thinking. The other part of the objective of mastering basic ideas is that students must apply themselves and keep up with course material and assignments.

The fourth principle is related to the previous ones: Statistics is learned by doing. Each chapter has pencil and paper questions and exercises that encourage the proportional thinking that underlies statistical analysis. For classes using computers, the *Computer Applications for The Statistical Imagination* compact disk provides *SPSS for Windows* software, chapter exercises, detailed illustrations on interpretating output, and a variety of data sets chosen to stimulate interest as well as expose students to real-world research. The disk has a point and click design that requires no prior experience in the use of computers.

To the Student

Through years of teaching statistics I have learned that students must be willing to work and keep up with this course. Attention to and success with early assignments make later, more abstract assignments much easier to grasp. Succeeding in a statistics course is much like an airliner taking off. A great deal of energy is used reaching altitude (Chapters 1 through 9), but then the plane can cruise the rest of the way (Chapters 10 through 16). This text is designed for early success to allay students' fears and reveal how enjoyable and interesting the subject is. Even an average student who is willing to put in the time and effort can earn an A in this course and have fun doing it. To borrow a line from a Walt Disney animated movie tune, a successful attitude for this course is "whistle while you work."

If you fear that this course will doom you because of your perceived weaknesses in math, put those fears aside. The course starts with simple calculations and builds on them. If you work hard and keep up, the math will not be an issue. Start by reviewing the basic mathematical procedures in Appendix A. Here are some study guides:

- Organize your study notes, assignments, returned papers, and the like, in a three-ring binder. This allows you to insert corrected materials and returned papers in their proper place and makes exam preparation highly efficient.
- Use proper reading technique. That is, look over a chapter for 20 to 30 minutes before reading it in detail. Read chapters before they are presented in class.

- Never miss a class or lab session. The material in this course is cumulative. Everything learned early on is applied in later chapters. Each chapter is a link in a chain, and a chain is only as strong as its weakest link. Keep up and this course is fun. Get behind and it becomes unnecessarily troublesome.

- In this course, do not be afraid to give back what is in the book. Complete sample exercises are provided for all procedures, and there is a summary of formulas at the end of each chapter. Exercises and tables distinguish between "givens" (information provided by a research problem) and "calculations" (what must be done to complete the problem). Follow the form of these exercises and "show the work" as well as the answer. In fact, answers to some of the problems are provided in Appendix C so that you may check your progress at home. A lifeless computer also can generate answers. Proper interpretation of the answer is what is important, and detailed work is necessary for learning the logic behind a procedure.

- Turn in work on time. Go over returned assignments and correct them immediately.

- Ask for assistance when needed. There is no such thing as a stupid question in this course, but failing to ask *is* stupid.

- Accept the fact that this course is fun. Concentrated effort will be rewarded not only in terms of earning a grade but also in terms of learning valuable job skills.

To the Instructor

This course is designed to cover basic elements of hypothesis testing in such a way that when inferential statistics are approached (Chapters 9 and beyond), the abstract concepts are easily achievable. The Instructor's Manual and the Test Bank and Solutions Manual that accompany this text provide details of the pointers listed below, along with lecture ideas, sample problems to present in class, multiple forms of assignments, quizzes, exams, and grading keys. Chapter exercises have a parallel, odd number–even number setup so that the odd-numbered exercises are assigned one term and the even-numbered are assigned the next.

While most instructors have developed their own effective techniques, I have found that the following pedagogical regimen maximizes students' success. This regimen has been class tested over 20 times, and it is based on the idea that assignments and quizzes are rehearsals for major exams. In my experience, major exams should be given "closed-book" (except for formulas and statistical tables). Open-book exams foster poor study habits. I alleviate the pressures of a closed-book exam, however, by providing students with ample opportunity to learn from mistakes on assignments.

- Require weekly assignments that are due on the class day after the completion of a lecture on a chapter's material.

- Return graded assignments at the next class and make assignment keys (from the Test Bank and Solutions Manual) available on reserve or provide multiple copies in a lab box. Since keys are to be made available, grading of assignments does not require extensive "red marking." (I have found that the availability of assignment keys does not compromise the next term's work. Moreover, exercises are designed with an odd-even format for alternating terms.)
- At the next class or in lab, quiz students on that chapter's material. Collect the quizzes five minutes after the first completed quiz is turned in. Distribute clean copies of the quiz and present or have students present the answers immediately.
- Give two or three in-term exams as well as a final exam (all closed-book except for formulas and statistical tables).

In my experience, several topics in the course must be given sufficient attention when presented or much time will be lost later attempting to fill in gaps.

- To eliminate math anxiety, allow students to enjoy early success with assignments on proportions, frequency distributions, and graphing. Moreover, a thorough review of proportions and percentages facilitates instruction on probability theory, sampling distributions, p-values, type I and type II errors, and so on.
- To foster linear thinking and proportional thinking skills, take plenty of time to explain the standard deviation and standardized scores and have the students work many problems partitioning areas under the normal curve.
- Actually generate at least two sampling distributions in class. Thereafter, when the concept is addressed, students will fully understand what a sampling distribution is.
- Require students to produce the details of the six steps of statistical inference—especially drawing the sampling distribution curve in step 2—on every hypothesis test on assignments, quizzes, and exams. Repeating this procedure will bring all students along. Some will grasp the details immediately (Chapter 9). By Chapter 11, every student who is truly working hard will have grasped the logic. Thereafter, you will be able to cruise because the pedagogical aspects of the six steps will be second nature to the students. Thus, in later chapters on bivariate analysis, you may concentrate on conceptual issues related to hypothesis testing and research ideas.

Special Features

- **Readability.** The text has been class tested many times.
- **Conceptual themes to spark interest.** The text is designed around

several conceptual themes that make statistics an enjoyable endeavor. First, statistics is about proportional thinking, and mathematical calculations are simply tools to assist in this process. Second, when the statistical imagination is used, statistical estimates are interpreted in relation to the larger pictures of not only a population of subjects but also a "population" of ideas, values, normative forces, practical circumstances, and theories. Distinctions are made between statistical significance and practical/theoretical significance. Third, the theme of error control emphasizes the importance of precision, diligence, and professionalism in the conduct of research.

- **Targeting results to the proper audience.** Discussions are included on how to present results to both scientific and public audiences, along with examples of tabular presentation.

- **Overcoming conceptual hurdles.** Conceptual hurdles are identified, and many devices learned by the author through long years of instruction are employed to get students past them. Such devices include a thorough delineation of the standard deviation, extensive coverage of standardized scores and sampling distributions, and a clear explanation of degrees of freedom.

- **A separate chapter on sampling distributions.** Sampling distributions are presented and illustrated to provide the essential ingredient of proportional thinking.

- **Six steps of statistical inference.** The logical procedures of hypothesis testing are consistently presented as "the six steps of statistical inference." Every statistical test is illustrated within this framework. Illustrations are preceded by a "Brief Checklist of the Six Steps of Statistical Inference."

- **The statistical hypothesis.** To avoid the vagaries and inconsistencies of the term *null hypothesis,* the straightforward term *statistical hypothesis* is substituted. In every situation, the statistical hypothesis is the one that generates the sampling distribution. It is noted where the term *null hypothesis* may be used correctly.

- **The four aspects of a relationship.** The interpretations of bivariate statistical tests follow four aspects of a relationship: existence, direction, strength, and nature.

- **Complete examples of each statistical procedure.** By adhering to the six steps of statistical inference and the four aspects of a relationship, complete examples keep students informed about what is expected on assignments and exams. Distinctions between "givens" and "calculations" facilitate problem solving.

- **Guidelines on choosing the proper statistical test.** Each hypothesis test is preceded by a box describing when to use a test (i.e., number of samples, level of measurements of variables, sample size). A cumulative decision-tree diagram at the end of each hypothesis testing chapter further reinforces the test selection process.

- **Highlighting of important terms and formulas.** Concepts and formulas are boxed throughout for easy review, and each chapter has a summary of formulas. The index is thorough. Symbols and formulas are listed inside the book cover.
- **Conceptual diagrams.** To teach students to think proportionally, all hypothesis tests are presented with conceptual diagrams that distinguish populations and parameters from samples and statistics.
- **Varied chapter exercises.** Pencil and paper exercises present a good mix of practical, everyday life problems and scientific problems from a variety of social science and health journals. Exercises are ordered from simple to complex. Answers to selected exercises are provided in Appendix C.
- **Optional computer applications.** Whether or not a class is using computers, throughout the text the utility of computers is described. The optional *Computer Applications for The Statistical Imagination* compact disk contains *SPSS for Windows* software and varied data sets, such as the General Social Survey, an ecological data set extracted from U.S. Census population data and U.S. Department of Justice crime data, and surveys on homelessness and physicians' fears of malpractice litigation. Updates of the compact disk are periodically made available. With its point and click design, no prior experience with computers is required.
- **Statistical follies and fallacies.** Consistent with the error control theme, each chapter presents common (and often comical) misinterpretations of statistics in everyday life and by the mass media and researchers.

Acknowledgments

Many family members were of special help to me in preparing this text. Thanks to Wanda for her love, help, and patience. Sarah and Kitty were especially helpful in editing early drafts, and Daniel assisted in mathematical formulations and computer applications. Gail provided advice on graphics. Alice, Ron, Linda, Terry, Alan, Annette, Cheryl, Chris, Dunia, Jim, and Joey provided encouragement, as did Dorrance and Agnes Anderson and my friends Timothy Crippen, Douglas Eckberg, Chuck Esary, Allen Martin, Jim and Debra Phillips, Lois Webber, and many more too numerous to mention. Lynn Harper Ritchey, a fellow sociologist, provided both encouragement and assistance. And thanks to Jack Brown, Chuck Bullock, Joe Casey, Paul Ritchey, and Terri Staples, members of Poppa Jack, a rock and roll group, for allowing me to keep my sanity by jamming with them.

I am especially appreciative of the help of two persons. First is Daniel O. Price, who was my mentor when I was a student at the University of Texas at

Austin. Dan coauthored a statistics text with Margaret Hagood in the 1950s and taught Hubert M. Blalock, whose text *Social Statistics* (McGraw-Hill) was a mainstay for so many graduate students in the 1960s and 1970s. Many of the ideas and pedagogical devices of this text—the emphasis on reifying sampling distributions, the six steps of statistical inference, the four aspects of a relationship—I learned from Dan. In fact, he first suggested that I write a text as his coauthor. As it turned out, time passed and he retired before the project moved very far, but he has been helpful since. Second, special thanks to P. Neal Ritchey, my brother and fellow sociologist at the University of Cincinnati. When I encountered conceptual challenges, he was always there with the correct insights and answers. As this text went through drafts, he suspended his very busy schedule to read, critique, and edit for me, and he assisted in compiling data sets for the computer applications. I truly appreciate the advantages of having an older brother in the same field. My love and thanks go to Neal, who has guided me in so many endeavors over the years.

I extend heartfelt thanks to the following who were generous in giving their time and assistance: Levi Ross and Lynn Gerald for compiling the computer applications diskette; Lucy Lewis for writing and assembling the instructor's accessories; Michael Foti for extensive editing; Takayo Ashford, Christine Lindquist, Nicole Liddon, Chris McDougal, Jeffrey Mullis, Marilyn Raney, David Sommers, Victoria Smith, and Marilyn Wright for helping with assignments. Sara Chamberlin, *SPSS, Inc.;* Grant Blank, University of Chicago; and Thomas A. Petee, Auburn University, provided information on software packages. Mary Laska assisted in the preparation of data files. Jackie Skeen, Tamalyn Peterson, Helen Dees, and Shirley Cottman helped with typing and the assembly of materials.

I wish to thank the following and several anonymous reviewers for their comprehensive and constructive suggestions: A. Troy Adams, Eastern Michigan University; Jay Alperson, Palomar College; Frank D. Beck, Illinois State University; William Feinberg, University of Cincinnati; Robin Franck, Southwestern College; and Surendar S. Yadava, University of Northern Iowa. My appreciation is extended also to my colleagues Kevin Fitzpatrick, Sean-Shong Hwang, and Mark LaGory for their advice and criticisms and to Jeffrey Clair, David Coombs, Thomas Edmonds, Guenther Lueschen, Bronwyn Lichtenstein, Earnest Porterfield, George Reinhart, Joe Schumacher, Ken Wilson, Michelle Wilson, Michael Wrigley, and Bill Yoels for encouraging words. And thanks to William Cockerham and Tennant McWilliams for their support, encouragement, and advice.

Finally, I very much appreciate the guidance and cooperation of the wonderful people at McGraw-Hill. My editor, Sally Constable, and her diligent assistants, Kate Purcell and Amy Smeltzley, were gracious with their time and energy and made the task fun, as did Kathy Shackleford, who was a great help locally. Phil Butcher, Jim Labeots, Leslie Kraham, Jill Gordon, and others helped bring this project to fruition.

Ferris J. Ritchey

THE STATISTICAL IMAGINATION

Introduction

One day when Chicken Licken was scratching among the leaves, an acorn fell out of a tree and struck her on the tail. "Oh," said Chicken Licken, "the sky is falling! I am going to tell the King."

From *Tomie dePaula's Favorite Nursery Tales* by Tomie dePaula. Copyright © 1986 by Tomie dePaula. Used by permission of G. P. Putnam's Sons, a division of Penguin Putnam Inc.

Chicken Licken did something everyone does from time to time: blow things out of proportion. While this is a normal reaction for storybook animals and many human beings, statisticians must not react to situations too quickly and emotionally. A statistician must step back and dispassionately observe so that a clear sense of balance and proportion is maintained.

The **field of statistics** is *a set of procedures for gathering, measuring, classifying, coding, computing, analyzing, and summarizing systematically acquired numerical information.* A course in statistics generally is perceived as one that involves lots of formulas and calculations. Indeed, some mathematical operations are involved, but this is not the thrust of statistics, and computers typically handle that part anyway. Statistics is truly about learning a new way of seeing things, acquiring a vision of reality based on careful analysis of facts rather than emotional reactions to isolated experiences.

The Field of Statistics

A set of procedures for gathering, measuring, classifying, coding, computing, analyzing, and summarizing systematically acquired numerical information.

Not all pursuits require accurate, objective portrayals of reality.[1] Popular entertainment media—movies, television, romance novels, and so on—are by definition fiction and fantasy, with imaginary characters and events. They are designed to excite, humor, sadden, or inspire us. Similarly, product advertising enters the world between fact and fantasy, appealing not only to reason but also to emotions to convince us that a purchase will *feel* good. Political campaigns appeal to the emotions of pride, patriotism, fear, and hatred. While most candidates are dedicated public servants, not all politicians stick to facts, and they are not legally required to do so. Many politicians hire "spin doctors" to dress up their images.

The political arena provides a strong contrast to science, an endeavor specifically designed to produce a clearer understanding of nature. Science is practiced, to the greatest extent possible, independently of political or ideological influence. Statistical analysis is a vital part of the scientific method. There is a great difference between the objective statistics of independent scientific polls and the biased opinions of pollsters hired by ambitious politicians. While the goal of a political campaign staff is to bolster support, independent firms attempt to gauge public opinion. For example, to show that a congressional representative is ahead in the polls, the campaign staff may hire a polling firm that is willing to ask loaded questions and survey only voters who have donated money. Of course, such a poll will reveal strong support, but the staff may neglect to mention to the media that the sample was not representative of all voters. Such manipulation of numerical information calls to mind Mark Twain's saying: "There are lies, damned lies, and statistics."

If a professional statistician conducted the same poll, the survey would not shade facts or include loaded questions. Instead, a statistician follows carefully controlled procedures and samples the entire population of voters. The results are presented as having a known range of error and a known degree of confidence, say, plus or minus 3 percentage points with 95 percent confidence. Statistics is about having a balanced perspective and using exacting precision in the gathering and presentation of information.

The major theme of this book is that the field of statistics is about obtaining an accurate sense of proportion in regard to reality. To acquire a sense of proportion is to see things objectively, to make fair judgments about events and behavior, to give the correct amount of attention to things that really matter and not be distracted by irrelevant events. A sense of proportion helps rein in subjective feelings, biases, and prejudices that can distort perceptions of reality. Learning to put things in the proper perspective requires imagination, and therein lies the potential for seeing statistical analysis as an interesting and enjoyable endeavor.

Proportional Thinking

The term *proportion* is a mathematical concept related to fractions and percentages. A good sense of proportion about a phenomenon requires more than having a good feel for what that phenomenon is about. Understanding proportions requires proportional thinking: weighing the part against the whole and calculating the likelihood of the phenomenon occurring over the long run. Having a sense of proportion and calculating mathematical proportions are essentially the same thing. Mathematical proportions are simply precise expressions of our intuitions about the significance of certain facts. Computing a proportion is a way to measure and evaluate a sense of likelihood and significance about the observations we make.

To get started properly, we will briefly review basic calculations of fractions, proportions, and percentages. (Additional review is provided in Appendix A.) Every aspect of statistical work—from measurement and graphical presentation to the computation of statistical probabilities—involves working with mathematical proportions; therefore, this review provides a good orientation to statistical calculations.

Mathematical proportions are simply *division problems which weigh a part (the numerator) against a whole (the denominator)*. To compute a proportion, we start with a **fraction,** *a way of expressing what part of the whole (or total number) a category of observations constitutes.*

$$\text{Fraction} = \frac{\text{numerator}}{\text{denominator}} = \frac{\text{part}}{\text{whole}}$$

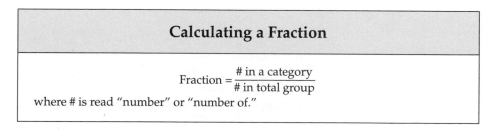

Calculating a Fraction

$$\text{Fraction} = \frac{\text{\# in a category}}{\text{\# in total group}}$$

where # is read "number" or "number of."

For example, in a study of the inmates occupying the Washington County jail, we determine that among the total jail population of 149 inmates, 112 have been charged with drug-related offenses (DROs) such as the possession or sale of an illegal substance. Is this a large part of the jail population? If so, what does this say about the nature of crime and law enforcement in Washington County? To have a good sense of proportion, the two figures, 112 and 149, should be constructed into a fraction:

$$\text{Fraction of Washington County jail inmates charged with DROs} = \frac{\text{\# charged with DROs}}{\text{total inmate population}} = \frac{112}{149}$$

An easier interpretation of this fraction can be found by transforming it into a proportion. **Proportion** means *part of a whole, or part of the total amount or number of observations, expressed in decimal form.* Fractions are reduced to proportions (or "decimalized") by dividing a fraction's numerator by its denominator to obtain a quotient. (A quotient is *the answer to a division problem.*) Thus:

$$p\,[\text{of Washington County jail inmates charged with DROs}] = \frac{\text{\# charged with DROs}}{\text{total inmate population}} = \frac{112}{149} = .7517$$

where p stands for proportion, the bracketed information describes the targeted population total (the denominator) followed by the targeted characteristic (the numerator), and the pound symbol (#) is read as "number."

Proportion

Part of the total amount or number of observations, expressed in decimal form.

Calculating a Proportion

$$p\,[\text{of total group in a category}] = \frac{\text{\# in a category}}{\text{\# in total group}} = \text{quotient}$$

where p = proportion of and the quotient is rounded to four decimal places (i.e., the nearest ten-thousandth). The quotient will always have a value between zero and 1.

This proportion for Washington County is correctly—but awkwardly—stated as "point seven-five-one-seven" or "seven thousand five hundred and seventeen ten-thousandths." For a general audience, then, we go a step further and transform this proportion into the more recognizable expression *percentage.* Percent means "per hundred," and a **percentage** is equal to *a proportion* *multiplied by 100.* The percentage tells us how many out of every 100 inmates are charged with DROs. Thus,

% [of Washington County
  jail inmates charged $= p\,(100) = (.7517)\,(100) = 75.17\%$
  with DROs]

Calculating a Percentage

% [of total group in a category] $= p\,(100)$

where p = proportion of total group in a category. The quotient will always have a value between 0 percent and 100 percent.

At this point we should have a sense that substance abuse is a serious problem for law enforcement in Washington County. Indeed, more than 75 of every 100 inmates are jailed on DRO charges. Clearly, *it is very likely and usual* for an incarcerated person to have gotten into trouble with drugs. The justice system in this county is heavily burdened by these cases.

Proportions and percentages are preferred ways of expressing "the part to the whole." Proportions will always have answers between 0 (none) and 1 (all). Similarly, percentages always range between 0 percent and 100 percent. Aside from their simplicity compared to the fractional form, proportions and percentages are useful for quickly producing common denominators for two or more fractions. Proportions provide the common denominator 1.00, while percentages provide the common denominator 100. For instance, suppose we compare the DRO cases of Jefferson County's and Washington County's jails. Jefferson County has only 42 DRO cases in a total jail population of 45 inmates. Which fraction is larger, then, 112 out of 149 or 42 out of 45? We obtain a common denominator by computing proportions and percentages. For Jefferson County, then:

p [of Jefferson County
  jail inmates charged $= \dfrac{\text{\# charged with DROs}}{\text{total inmate population}} = \dfrac{42}{45} = .9333$
  with DROs]

% [of Jefferson County
  jail inmates charged $= p\,(100) = (.9333)\,(100) = 93.33\%$
  with DROs]

The percentages allow us to see that in fact, Jefferson County's jail population is more heavily populated by drug-related offenders than is Washington County's (93.33 percent versus 75.17 percent, respectively), even though there are more DRO cases in Washington County.

We can observe from these calculations that to change a fraction into a proportion, we divide the numerator by the denominator to obtain the "decimalized" quotient. To change a proportion into a percentage, we multiply the proportion by 100 by moving the decimal point two places to the right. To transform a percentage into a proportion, we move the decimal point two places to the left, which is simply a matter of dividing by 100. To express a proportion as a fraction, we must have good mastery over decimal places. If necessary, review decimal place locations in Appendix A. Finally, as a general rule (with only a few exceptions) we round proportions to four decimal places to the right of the decimal point and round percentages to two decimal places to the right.

A percentage is a very common way to standardize statistics from different groups. Sometimes, however, percentages do not convey a meaningful sense of proportion. For example, what is the likelihood of being killed by lightning? From data for 1990, we find the U.S. population to be 248,709,873 (U.S. Bureau of the Census 1990). From a meteorologist we determine that 74 people were killed by lightning during that year.[2] The proportion and percentage of the population killed by lightning would compute as

$$p \text{ [of 1990 U.S. population killed by lightning]} = \frac{\text{\# killed by lightning}}{\text{total population size}} = \frac{74}{258,709,873} = .00000029$$

$$\% \text{ [of 1990 U.S. population killed by lightning]} = (p)(100) = .000029\%$$

Thus, assuming that 1990 is a typical year, the likelihood of being killed by lightning is 29 hundred-thousandths of a percent. This is difficult to conceive of even for the mathematically astute. A denominator of 100 is confusing when fewer than one in a hundred are at risk. The statistical imagination beckons us to find another way to convey this risk.

Another way to standardize is to compute a **rate,** *the frequency of occurrence of a phenomenon in relation to some specified, useful "base" number of subjects in a population.* The base number is placed in the denominator so that the rate may be stated as cases per thousand, per ten thousand, per hundred thousand, per million, and so forth. A useful base number is one that clearly specifies the "population at risk" for a phenomenon. With a large group such as the population of the United States, a larger base number is needed in place of the "per 100" used with percentages. Recall that when we transform a proportion into a percentage, we multiply by 100. Similarly, we can multiply a proportion by other multiples of 10 to get rates with larger denominators.

Calculating a Rate

Rate of occurrence = (p) (a useful base number)

where p = proportion of total group in a category and the useful base number is a multiple of 10.

A useful base number for a rate is one that conveys the counting of a phenomenon. In this example we count persons killed. Our rate, then, should be presented in whole persons with numbers to the left of the decimal point. Observing our proportion of .00000029, to get to a count of persons, we must move the decimal point seven places to the right. A review of decimal place locations in Appendix A shows that this is equivalent to multiplying by 10,000,000. Thus,

Rate of lightning deaths per ten million population = (p) (10,000,000)

= (.00000029) (10,000,000) = 2.9 lightning deaths per 10,000,000 people

This calculation is explicit and useful. It states that only about three out of 10 million people are killed by lightning each year. We can conceive of 10 million as the population of a large city (such as New York City). Imagining a city and thinking proportionately, we get a sense that the risk of a lightning death is very tiny. Only about three persons in an entire large city are likely to be killed each year. (In fact, if we were in a desert city where it seldom rains, we could adjust this figure downward.)

Another quick calculation allows us to set the numerator of this rate to one person rather than 2.9. This gives us the number of persons in the population per each lightning death. A ratio of 2.9 to 10,000,000 is equal to a ratio of 1 to 3,448,276. This is obtained by dividing 10,000,000 by 2.9:

$$\frac{2.9 \text{ lightning deaths}}{10,000,000 \text{ people}} = \frac{1 \text{ lightning death}}{X \text{ people}}$$

$$X = \frac{10,000,000}{2.9} = 3,448,276 \text{ people}$$

where X is the number of people in the population for each person killed by lightning. Thus, our chance of being killed by lightning in a year is about 1 in $3^{1}/_{2}$ million, the population of, say, Houston, Texas. Hence, our chances of dying by a lightning strike are quite small.

To Compare Two or More Groups of Different Size

Standardize the fraction by using a common denominator:

Proportions have a common denominator of 1.

Percentages have a common denominator of 100.

Rates have a selected useful common denominator in multiples of 10.

We have not gotten very far in our introductory discussion of statistics, and we already have encountered the importance of accurate communication.

Mathematical formulas are rather strict in form. All of our formulas will have the following elements:

Presenting Answers in a Way That Encourages Proportional Thinking

Symbol = formula = contents of formula = answer

Observe these elements in our calculations of inmates with DROs.

These basic calculations are introduced early in this book because having a sense of understanding about reality and understanding the mathematics of proportions go hand in hand. Measures of "part of the whole" are typically the first calculations made in any statistical analysis. Proportional thinking is a basic feature of the statistical imagination.

The Statistical Imagination

As was mentioned earlier, the intent of this text is to provide a new vision of reality based on having a sense of proportion and using proportional thinking. We will call this vision the statistical imagination. The social scientist C. Wright Mills (1959) defined the **sociological imagination** as *an awareness of the relationship of the individual to the wider society and to history.* The *sociological* imagination is the recognition that individual behavior is conducted in relation to larger social structures, that most actions by individuals involve conformity to *society's* rules and not personal initiative, and that right and wrong are defined within a cultural context. The sociological imagination involves seeing an isolated detail (a part) in relation to a larger picture (the whole), seeing the forest as well as the trees.

Similarly, the statistical imagination involves seeing a part in relation to a whole. The **statistical imagination** is *an appreciation of how usual or unusual an event, circumstance, or behavior is in relation to a larger set of similar events, and an appreciation of an event's causes and consequences.*

The Statistical Imagination

An appreciation of how usual or unusual an event, circumstance, or behavior is in relation to a larger set of similar events and an appreciation of an event's causes and consequences.

To have the statistical imagination is to understand that most events are predictable (i.e., they have a probability of occurrence based on long-term trends and circumstances).[3] The statistical imagination is the ability to think through a problem and maintain a sense of proportion when weighing evidence against preconceived notions. The statistical imagination involves recognizing highly unusual events for what they are and not overreacting to them.

To be statistically *un*imaginative is to blow things out of proportion, to think in a reactionary rather than proportional way. For example, many people became upset over news that a highly troubled person had stooped to cannibalism, as in the notorious case of Jeffrey Dahmer. While this event understandably evoked rage, fear, and disgust, many saw it as a symbol of moral decline in America. Such a notion is reactionary. Cannibalism is just as rare now as it has ever been! The statistical imagination says: Look at this over the long run. Is it happening frequently? Do a lot of people engage in this behavior? Am I likely to become someone's lunch? In fact, the Jeffrey Dahmer incident was an isolated occurrence involving a single person out of 250 million people. Seeing this event in its proper proportion brings reason to arguments about the larger picture of cultural stability.

To acquire the statistical imagination is to open one's eyes to the broader picture of reality and overcome misunderstandings, prejudices, and narrow-mindedness. For example, public health officials report that more than 40,000 people are killed in vehicle crashes every year. They puzzle over the fact that Americans do not see this major cause of death as a public health problem, one related to road safety and automobile design and therefore one to be solved by government policies. Instead, the public sees traffic fatalities as individual misfortunes or failures. We assume that traffic deaths result from bad luck (the victim got in the way of a careless driver), stupidity, recklessness or carelessness (the victim was speeding or dozed off), miserliness (too cheap to buy new tires), or immorality (the victim should not have been drinking). Why does the public fail to look past individual explanations? One reason is that traffic deaths and injuries infrequently strike any particular family and therefore appear to occur to "the other guy." As long as we are convinced that the victim brought it upon himself or herself, we are reassured that it will not happen to us. We, of course, would never drink and drive, and we speed only where it is safe to do so.

The statistical imagination, however, allows us to recognize the large-scale effects of this mode of transportation. We look at the broad picture of how traffic crashes affect the population as opposed to individuals. We compute total deaths and rates of deaths per million miles driven by using data covering many years. We determine which unsafe road conditions result in fatalities when individuals *are* careless or stupid. For example, it is well known that more deaths occur on two-lane roads than on four-lane or interstate highways. In fact, taking into account increases in automobiles and drivers (i.e., millions of miles driven), traffic death rates have dropped greatly since the interstate highway system was built in the 1950s and 1960s. By focusing on the group and examining circumstances in addition to individuals, we place traffic deaths in the larger context of public health. Only then do we begin to consider the safety value of other modes of travel, such as buses and subways.

Linking the Statistical Imagination to the Sociological Imagination

Statistical Norms and Social Norms

A balanced view requires more than careful mathematical calculation. For example, even if we are aware of the number of yearly automobile crash deaths, we may be "prejudiced" in favor of this private form of transportation. We may resist efforts to substitute mass transit systems because automobiles embody the strongly held American social value of individual freedom. We are willing to chance injury or death for freedom and convenience.

When human beings use their illustrious brains to compute proportions, percentages, and other statistics, they are simply struggling to obtain a measure of reality. A statistic, however, does not mean much by itself. A key principle of the statistical imagination is that statistical interpretations must take into account the circumstances of a phenomenon, including the social values of the society or some group within it. Social values may work to limit, or perhaps enlarge, the human response to a statistic. In this sense, any statistic is culturally bound or **normative:** *Its interpretation depends on the place, time, and culture in which it is observed.* A **social norm** is *a shared idea of the behavior that is appropriate or inappropriate in a given situation in a given culture.* In a word, a norm is a rule, and norms are peculiar to a particular society, a period of history, and the specific situation in which the action occurs. What is considered right or wrong, a lot or a little, depends on the place and the time. For example, being naked in the shower is normal; in fact, it would be peculiar to shower with one's clothes on. Being naked in the classroom, however, is deviant (or nonnormal) behavior.

When Is a Little a Lot?   Any single statistic is meaningless if we do not establish some basis of comparison—a statistical norm. A **statistical norm** is *an average rate of occurrence of a phenomenon.* Such an average may differ from one society to another or from one group to another because any statistical norm is influenced by social norms. To illustrate statistical norms and their relationship to social norms, let us compare some national infant mortality rates (IMRs), the number of children who die in the first year of life per 1,000 live births. Table 1–1 presents the IMRs of selected countries for the year 1992. In the United States the IMR was approximately nine deaths per 1,000 live births.

Was this U.S. rate high or low compared to the statistical norm? It was low compared to the world's statistical norm of 70, but Americans should not feel reassured by this. IMRs are closely tied to economic development; therefore,

TABLE 1–1   **Infant Mortality Rates for Selected Nations in 1992**

Nation	Infant Mortality Rate (deaths to children under 1 year of age per 1,000 live births)
Already Industrialized	
Japan	4.4
Iceland	5.5
Sweden	6.2
Germany	6.7
Canada	6.8
Great Britain	7.1
United States	8.6
Former Soviet Union	20
Industrializing	
Mexico	38
People's Republic of China	53
India	91
Haiti	105
Ethiopia	127
Afghanistan	168
World	70

SOURCE: Haub and Yanagishita 1993.

the U.S. rate is more appropriately compared to the statistical norms of cultures and economies like our own, such as the industrialized countries of Japan and Western Europe. As it turns out, our IMR is rather high compared with the IMRs of these countries, and U.S. public health officials are greatly concerned about this. Taken in context, a little is a lot. Any single infant death is significant to the victim's family, but public health officials in a poor country with a high IMR may not view this with alarm (any more than Americans view traffic deaths with alarm). For one thing, high IMR rates have endured for centuries, making a country's statistical norm appear stable. Second, cultural circumstances—poor sanitation and medical care and lack of economic resources—may greatly challenge efforts to reduce this rate. Third, other causes of death, such as acquired immunodeficiency syndrome (AIDS) may be so great that they make the IMR appear rather low or simply part of a larger problem. How public officials or a society as a whole interprets a statistic depends on the state of affairs at a given time. As this rudimentary analysis of the IMRs in Table 1–1 suggests, cultural circumstances influence the interpretation of statistical findings.

For some measurements, such as those for cognitive or behavioral performance, health status, and academic achievement, statistical norms are necessary even to make sense of a score. For example, with intelligent quotient tests

(IQ tests), the scores are normed against the psychological research community's informed *judgment* about what constitutes *average intelligence*. Thus, IQ tests are often specifically designed with a statistical norm of 100, a number with which we are familiar and comfortable. A person of presumably average intelligence scores 100, while those scoring higher have an above-average IQ, and those scoring lower have a below-average IQ.

Statistical Ideals and Social Values

A discussion of infant mortality rates brings to mind another distinction that links statistics to social reality: that between statistical norms and statistical ideals. While a statistical norm is an existing average, a **statistical ideal** is *a socially desired rate of occurrence of a phenomenon*, an optimum target rate. Statistical ideals often reflect **social values**—*shared ideas among the members of a society about the way things ought to be.* Values are a society's common notions of what a truly good society would hold dear. In the United States, for example, freedom, equality, achievement, material comfort, efficiency, and nationalism are highly valued (Williams 1970: 452–500). These social values are only ideals and are never realized in a pure sense. For example, while individual freedom is highly valued, pure freedom—every individual making his or her own rules— is anarchy. Values are like lighthouses on rocky shorelines. We use these lights as guides, but to reach them completely would be hazardous.

In response to social values, statistical ideals (target rates of occurrence) often are substituted for statistical norms. For example, the infant death rate in the United States (8.6 deaths per 1000 live births) is a statistical fact, and this rate is higher than the norm for most *already industrialized* countries, such as Japan and Germany. Thus, U.S. public health officials may target the rates of these countries as a statistical ideal, a rate to shoot for. The public, however, may not be willing to accept the changes needed to bring this about, such as higher taxes and greater government involvement in health care. Debates over statistical ideals often reveal underlying conflicts and opinions on social values. Statistical ideals, then, are just that. They are greatly influenced and constrained by social values.

The meaning of any statistic sometimes depends merely on practical circumstances. For instance, biophysical-based statistical norms and ideals abound in competitive sports, reflecting the practical limitations of physics. For example, is four minutes a long time? It is a terribly long time to circle the track in an automobile race but a remarkably short time to run a mile. A professional basketball player with a free-throw percentage of 50 percent is taking a chance of losing a multimillion-dollar contract. However, a professional major league baseball player need hit the ball only about 33 percent of the time (a batting average of .333) to win the league's batting title and get a multimillion-dollar raise. Sometimes a little is a lot. The significance of a statistic depends on statistical norms (averages), statistical ideals (optimum target rates), and practical circumstances. The statistical imagination is employed to choose the appropriate statistical norms and ideals to which statistics and observations are compared.

The statistical imagination, with its awareness of the linkages between statistical measurements and social facts, requires a degree of skepticism—a critical and doubting attitude. Just as a statistician is skeptical of what is reported as fact by those with vested political or economic interests, skepticism must be applied to a statistician's work, especially scientific work.

Statistics and Science: Tools for Proportional Thinking

As has been noted, statistics is about observing and organizing systematically acquired numerical information. *Systematically acquired information that is organized by following the procedures of science and statistics* is called **data** (the plural of *datum*).

Statistics and the gathering of data are not casual activities but are enterprises that require maximum effort. Statistical analysis is about precision: following procedures and making precise measurements of and accurate predictions on how events in the world will occur. When statistical analysis is properly done, the analyst knows the limitations of reasoning and mathematical procedures and knows when predictions about events or behaviors are less than perfectly precise. Furthermore, a statistician can express the degree of confidence he or she has in a conclusion. In this regard, statistics is about controlling error. Statistical errors are not mistakes. Instead, **statistical error** refers to *known degrees of imprecision in the procedures used to gather and process information.* To control error is to be as precise as necessary to enhance confidence in the conclusions drawn from statistical findings.

Statistical Error

Known degrees of imprecision in the procedures used to gather and process information.

Error control (covered in detail in Chapter 7) is the second major theme of this book and another facet of the statistical imagination. The statistical imagination requires not only a sense of proportion on reality but also the diligence to keep track of details in order to minimize error.

Descriptive and Inferential Statistics

Data are gathered for different statistical purposes. One purpose of statistical analysis is to take a lot of data about a category of people or objects and summarize this information with a few accurate mathematical figures, tables, and/or charts. This first step in statistics is called descriptive statistics.

Descriptive statistics tell us *how many observations were recorded and how frequently each score or category of observations occurred in the data.* For example, data from 291 survey respondents may show that 40 percent are male and have an average age of 21 years, with the youngest being 19 and the oldest 51. Descriptive statistics are used by scientists as well as by pollsters, marketing analysts, urban planners, and those in many other occupations. These calculations inform the public about what products to purchase, which politicians to believe, what stocks to buy, what cars are the most reliable, at what age annual physical checkups are in order, and so on. Descriptive statistics also are computed by scientists as a first step in analyzing scientific research hypotheses, the task of inferential statistics.

A second purpose of statistical analysis is to draw conclusions about the mathematical relationships among characteristics of a group of people or objects. For example, we might investigate whether Americans who are better educated are less likely to believe that the devil exists. This type of analysis is called inferential statistics. **Inferential statistics** are computed to *show cause-and-effect relationships and to test hypotheses and scientific theories.* (To infer means *to draw conclusions about something*.) The bulk of this text deals with inferential statistics. Understanding the basic principles of science is essential to grasping inferential statistics; thus, we will review these principles.

What Is Science?

Science is *a systematic method of explaining empirical phenomena.* **Empirical** means *observable and measurable.* Phenomena (the plural form of the Latin word *phanomenon*) are facts, happenstances, events, circumstances, or, simply put, "things that exist naturally." Empirical phenomena, then, are things that can be observed and measured, such as natural conditions, processes, events, situations, objects, groups of people, behaviors, thoughts, beliefs, knowledge, opinions, emotions, and feelings.

Not everything is measurable and observable. For example, whether there is an afterlife is not readily observed, although over 70 percent of American adults assert a belief in it. Furthermore, many intangible things, such as emotions, feelings, and beliefs, must be measured indirectly. In the social sciences such indirect measurements include survey questionnaires that measure opinions, knowledge, attitudes, and even behavior. Physical scientists use indirect measures as well. For instance, physicists indirectly observe neutrinos, subatomic particles so tiny and fast that they typically pass through the earth without bumping into anything. (Millions are passing through you right now.) Occasionally a neutrino displaces a water molecule, releasing observable energy, and this effect can be measured. An important aspect of the expansion of science is finding new ways to accurately measure things that are not readily visible to the naked eye. Microscopes, computerized x-ray machines, and seismometers, as well as survey instruments, are the tools scientists use to extend the reach of their measurement capabilities.

The Purpose of Scientific Investigation.   The main objective of science is to explain things. A scientific explanation is one based on strict procedures, and it is called a theory. A **scientific theory** is *a set of interrelated, logically organized statements that explain a phenomenon of special interest and that have been corroborated through observation and analysis.* Theories describe situations and how they work or proceed. The collection of ideas that constitute a theory is tested against observed facts. A theory is "corroborated" when its ideas successfully predict these observable facts. A theory is not a fact in and of itself; rather, it is a well-organized explanation of facts. As a phenomenon is better understood, a theory is modified and refined to improve its predictability. Thus, theory development is a cumulative process that occurs over a long period.

An adequate scientific theory accomplishes two things. First, it provides a sense of understanding about a phenomenon: how, when, why, and under what conditions it occurs. Simply put, it makes sense of things. Second, a theory allows us to make empirical predictions, to answer the question of under what conditions and to what degree a phenomenon will occur. Such predictions are possible because changes in one phenomenon are related to changes in other phenomena. For instance, we predict a greater chance of rain when atmospheric moisture (humidity) increases and predict an increase in the crime rate of a community when economic times are tough.

Scientific Skepticism and the Statistical Imagination

Science *requires* that its ideas withstand the test of being able to predict observations. Well-trained scientists are skeptics; they have a critical and doubting attitude. They are willing to tolerate uncertainty and are not too quick to draw conclusions. A skeptic is hesitant to believe something simply because it is reported to be true by trusted friends, the mass media, or people in positions of authority, such as government leaders and even parents. A look at popular culture, especially the ideas thrown about in the mass media, suggests that most people are highly credulous—inclined to believe things—even in the absence of evidence and even in the presence of contradictory evidence. The late renowned scientist Carl Sagan, a spokesperson for the value of science, observed that many people are very slow to "suspend *dis*belief." He noted, for example, how gullible people were in falling for the "crop circles" hoax, believing for 15 years that huge elegant pictograms discovered in English grainfields were left there by space aliens. (A couple of rogues named Bower and Chorley eventually confessed to the hoax.) Sagan argued that we are not skeptical enough of much that is only alleged to be fact. He beckoned us to take science more seriously because the scientific process is especially designed to separate fact from fiction (Sagan 1995a, 1995b). He made a good case that a society that encourages the learning of science will produce better-informed citizens. He noted:

In College . . . I began to learn a little about how science works . . . how rigorous the standards of evidence must be . . . how our biases can color our interpretation of the evidence, how belief systems widely . . . supported by the political, religious and academic hierarchies often turn out to be not just slightly in error but grotesquely wrong . . .

The tenets of skepticism do not require an advanced degree to master . . . All science asks is to employ the same levels of skepticism we use in buying a used car . . .

But the tools of skepticism are generally unavailable to the citizens of our society. They're hardly ever mentioned in the schools, even in the presentation of science, its most ardent practitioner . . . Our politics, economics, advertising and religions (New Age or Old) are awash in credulity. Those who have something to sell, those who wish to influence public opinion, those in power, a skeptic might suggest, have a vested interest in discouraging skepticism.* (Sagan 1995b:10–13)

Scientific explanations based on observation, strict procedures, and the collective scrutiny of the scientific community often contradict common sense as well as the ideas put forth by political leaders. This does not mean that science forgoes common sense. Instead, science uses **informed common sense,** *that which is weighed and double-checked against carefully gathered data.* Uninformed common sense is all too common! Scientific skepticism requires learning procedural skills and developing a questioning attitude. Similarly, having the statistical imagination involves learning skills (e.g., how to compute probabilities and think proportionally) and being ready to ask whether an observed phenomenon is reasonable.

At the same time, science has limitations. First, it is restricted to examining empirical—observable and measurable—phenomena. Faith, not science, must resolve, for example, the question of whether God and heaven exist. Second, many sound, factually based scientific arguments lack political or taxpayer support. For example, research reveals that poverty in the United States could be reduced by expanding government family assistance programs such as employment training and child care services. These "workfare" measures, however, are costly and typically lack taxpayer support, and so recent legislation simply gives public assistance recipients a limited time to solve these issues for themselves. A third limitation of science is that it creates ethical dilemmas and resistance to its application. For instance, an economist could make a convincing argument that euthanasia or "mercy killing" would save billions of dollars in medical expenses incurred by the terminally ill. Obviously, many would question this argument not on a factual but on a moral basis. There is more to human existence than cost accounting.

Science does not have all the answers, and scientists must be skeptical of the answers they have. When it comes to explaining empirical reality, however, the scientific method is the best approach. A key feature of the scientific method is statistical analysis.

*From Carl Sagan, *The Demon-Haunted World.* Copyright © 1995 by Random House. Reprinted by permission of the publisher.

Conceiving of Data

Variables and Constants.   *Measurable phenomena that vary (change) over time or that differ from place to place or from individual to individual* are called **variables.** Variables are features of the subjects (students, the homeless, the people of St. Louis, lab rats) or objects (buildings, trees, floods, bacteria, crimes) under study. (From here on, we will use the term *subject* to mean people *or* objects.) For instance, in studying individuals, we might note differences in the variables of age, weight, height, personality traits, race, and socioeconomic status.

A Variable

A measurable phenomenon that varies (changes) over time or that differs from place to place or from individual to individual.

We use the term **variation** to refer to *how much the measurements of a variable differ among study subjects,* and we compare differences in variation between groups. For example, there is much variation in ages among students on commuter college campuses in large cities, ranging perhaps from 17 to 70 years. In contrast, the variation in ages on traditional, day-class colleges in small "campus towns" is typically much smaller, say, 17 to 25 years.

Some variables exhibit little variation or do not vary at all within a group, such as the ages of first-grade pupils. *Characteristics of study subjects that do not vary* are called **constants.** Sometimes we intentionally "hold variables constant." For instance, in an experiment on the effects of alcoholic beverages on driving behavior, we would use subjects of about the same weight because lighter people are known to get drunk more quickly than heavier people. This way, reduced reaction time in driving can be attributed to the amount of alcohol consumed rather than to differences in weight. By "holding weight constant," we eliminate its effects on driving behavior; since weight did not vary, a variation in weight cannot possibly explain the results of the experiment. By holding weight constant and holding constant any other variables that affect drunkenness, we are able to isolate the effects of alcohol consumption on driving behavior.

The Dependent Variable and Independent Variables That Explain It. Typically, in gathering data, our purpose is to research a single variable that is of special interest to us. We want to know what causes an increase or decrease in the amount of this variable. What causes "variation" in it? What are its scores dependent on? This variable of main interest is called the **dependent variable,** *the variable whose variation we want to explain.* For example, the 1960s were characterized by urban strife, with rioting in over 40 cities in a three-year period. In an effort to understand and prevent riots, a National Advisory Commission on Civil Disorders (1968) was formed to conduct a scientific study. The incidence of riot behavior was the dependent variable. The commission wished to explain why riots occurred in some cities but not in others.

Variables suspected of being related to an increase or decrease in riot behavior also were measured. These variables included the rate of poverty in communities, the number of complaints of police brutality, racial disturbances in the weeks before a riot, and the number of known "Communist sympathizers" in a city. These *predictor variables that are related to or predict variation in the dependent variable* are called **independent variables**.[4] Table 1–2 distinguishes the characteristics of independent and dependent variables.

The Commission on Civil Disorders examined cities as its subject of investigation. The commission's research team found that the incidence of riots (the dependent variable) was related to independent variables such as the percentage of households living in poverty, the adequacy of welfare programs, the degree of governmental participation by minorities, the occurrence of "tension heightening incidents," and, especially persistent reports of police brutality. To say that a relationship exists between the incidence of police brutality and the incidence of riots is to say that cities with lots of police brutality tended also to have lots of riots. This statement and similar ones involving the other independent variables constituted a *protest theory of riot behavior.* This theory advanced the argument that people riot in response to oppressive police actions and because of frustration with poor government services. The ideas and data stimulated by this theory ultimately led to changes in local government policies and a reduction in civil disorders (Johnson 1973: 376).

The findings of the Commission on Civil Disorders disproved some common **myths,** *widely held beliefs that are false.* Specifically, it discredited the *Com-*

TABLE 1–2   **Possible Relationships between Independent and Dependent Variables**

Independent Variable		Dependent Variable
Cause	⟶	Effect
Predictor	⟶	Outcome
Stimulus	⟶	Response
Intervention (action taken)	⟶	Result
Correlation: change in one variable	⟶	Associated change in another variable

munist conspiracy theory, a political argument that the riots were part of an organized revolution aimed at overthrowing the U.S. government (Johnson 1973: 376). Why were people so quick to believe that the riots were Communist-inspired? Myths often arise from commonsense explanations reinforced by isolated or sporadic events and by political rhetoric aimed at stoking the fears of the electorate. The urban strife of the 1960s occurred during a period of rapid social change and uncertainty. On the domestic front there was a civil rights movement with racial minorities, especially African-Americans, demanding the elimination of discrimination in hiring, schooling, and the use of public facilities. At the same time, on the world scene there was a "Cold War" between the capitalist countries of the West and Communist countries, especially the former Soviet Union and the People's Republic of China. These Communist governments made open calls to arms and vowed to infiltrate the United States with spies who would encourage the poor and "repressed minorities" to revolt. Occasionally, small homegrown socialist organizations distributed pamphlets calling for an armed uprising to eliminate racial oppression. These isolated but emotionally charged protests made it easy for politicians to play on public fears. Many politicians tried to discredit their opponents who supported racial change by accusing them of having Communist leanings. In this atmosphere, the occurrence of riots in poor minority neighborhoods throughout the United States seemed to many people a plausible result of a Communist conspiracy. The public's tendency to believe this explanation so quickly was bolstered by racial politics and the uncertainty and fear that accompanied rapid social changes.

As it turned out, the facts showed that Communists among the riot participants were extremely hard to come by. Furthermore, there was no difference in the number of Communist sympathizers in cities where riots occurred and cities where they did not. The Communist conspiracy argument was disproved, it was not supported by data and did not withstand the scrutiny of statistical analysis.

A scientific theory is an organized argument that must be corroborated by empirical evidence. A theory is "corroborated" when its ideas successfully predict observable measurements.[5] As more data are acquired, theories are modified and refined to improve their predictability and sense of understanding.

The Research Process

The research process involves organizing ideas into a theory, making empirical predictions that support that theory, and then gathering data to test the predictions. The research process is a cumulative one, a continual process of accumulating knowledge. The research process for scientific investigation involves seven steps. Steps 1 through 3 are the major themes of social science theory courses, step 4 and 5 are covered in methodology courses, and steps 6 and 7 are covered in statistics courses. The seven steps are as follows:

1. *Specify the research question.*   We raise a question and identify the dependent variable. For example, we may ask: Why are riots occurring in some cities?

2. *Review the scientific literature.*   We do this to make sure that time and money are not wasted collecting data that already exist. We seek the "frontier of knowledge," the outer limits of what has already been learned, for example, about riots. Enlightened and publishable research extends knowledge beyond this frontier.

3. *Propose a theory and state hypotheses.*   Theory involves organizing ideas into a logical form that can explain variation in the dependent variable. In developing a theory, we identify independent variables and make predictive statements about how we think they affect the dependent variable, assuming the theory is meaningful. Such predictions are called hypotheses. A **hypothesis** is *a prediction about the relationship between two variables, asserting that changes in the measure of an independent variable will correspond to changes in the measure of a dependent variable.* [As we will discuss in later chapters, a hypothesis also indicates the direction of a relationship, whether the independent variable is related to an increase (positive direction) or a decrease (negative direction) in the dependent variable.]

Hypotheses are generated or "motivated" by theory—established ideas found in the scientific literature, with innovative modifications of the researcher. The theory directs us to expect certain observed outcomes from data. If these outcomes are then found to occur, the theory is corroborated. For example, the protest theory of riot behavior motivates the following hypothesis:

H_1: Cities with a high incidence of police brutality (independent variable) are likely to have a high incidence of civil disorders (dependent variable).

In contrast, the Communist conspiracy theory of riot behavior motivates the following hypothesis:

H_2: Cities with a large number of Communists (independent variable) are likely to have a high incidence of civil disorders (dependent variable).

In addition to testing hypotheses, theorizing involves the logical organization of ideas and philosophies. The theory, based on the literature review, also guides us in selecting "control" variables. For example, in measuring civil disorders, we must control for the crime rate. This assures us that cities with a large incidence of riots are not simply high-crime cities, in which case crime rate, not simply police brutality, would explain part of the incidence of civil disorders. The concept of statistical control is discussed in Chapter 2.

We should also note that not all scientific studies employ theory. Much *research is done simply to solve immediate practical problems or explore new phenomena about which so little is known that formulating a theory is impossible.* Such studies are called **exploratory studies.** For example, someone exploring privacy issues on the Internet may begin with loosely organized ideas and questions.

A Hypothesis

A prediction about the relationship between two variables, asserting that changes in the measure of an independent variable will correspond to changes in the measure of a dependent variable.

---

4. *Select a research design.*   The research design details how data are to be measured, sampled, and gathered. Common social science methods include direct observation of behavior, laboratory experiment, survey, content analysis of media, and analysis of existing or "secondary" data (such as police reports and the census of the population).

5. *Collect the data.*   This is usually the most expensive part of research. it involves "going into the field" to inform people about the study and gathering data by using the plan developed in step 4. This is also one of the most enjoyable parts of research. Data collection allows the researcher to get out of the office and meet new and often interesting people.

6. *Analyze the data and draw conclusions.*   This involves statistical analysis, the main topic of this text. Hypotheses are tested by comparing observations to theoretical predictions. In the riot example, the data collected by the Commission on Civil Disorders supported hypothesis 1 and disproved hypothesis 2, giving greater creditability to the protest theory.

7. *Disseminate the results.*   To disseminate means to scatter widely and thus share. Scientific findings are shared with two "audiences": the public and the scientific community.

Public audiences include not only citizens but also politicians and business, church, charity, and educational groups. Researchers may speak at public forums such as press conferences, talk shows, city council meetings, community organization meetings, and high school classes. Such talks must be kept conceptually and statistically simple.

For the scientific audience, dissemination of research findings involves presenting findings at scientific conferences and publishing books or, more commonly, short articles in professional journals. Research publication is a strenuous process of peer review—a system of checks and balances—that ideally maximizes the chance that a published work will be accurate and unbiased. A scientific manuscript follows a strict form. When completed, it is submitted to the editor of a journal in the field. The editor sends copies without author identification to similarly trained scientists. This "blind" review minimizes personal bias. Reviewers, however, are obliged to be highly skeptical of the manuscript. They scrutinize every detail, searching for faulty logic, biased interpretations, unsound sampling, poor measurement or analysis, and misguided conclusions. If several reviewers agree that the research is sound and would advance knowledge, the editor may accept it for publication if print space is available. Leading journals in most fields are extremely selective, publishing as few as 1 of every 10 submissions. This screening process ensures that the research selected for publication meets professional standards. Researchers who publish on a regular basis are highly skilled practitioners of science.

Manuscript reviews are, and should be, highly critical not of the individual researcher but of the quality of the scientific procedures he or she followed. Scientists, serious marketing researchers, pollsters, and others who digest carefully conducted statistical work learn to appreciate and respect the scrutiny of fellow analysts. Carl Sagan expressed his concern for the lack of skepticism many people exhibit, but he also pointed with pride to the outstanding efforts of those committed to doing the job of science right. Chapter 2 focuses on error control and how this requires a conscientious commitment to make the best effort when conducting statistical work.

☹   STATISTICAL FOLLIES AND FALLACIES   ☹

The Problem of Small Denominators

Care must be taken in interpreting proportions and percentages based on extremely small groups. Small baseline numbers in reports of percentage change are a particular source of confusion. Table 1–3 presents a fictional example of what typically occurred early in the AIDS epidemic.

TABLE 1–3   Percentage Change in the Number of New AIDS Cases Reported in a County from 1988 to 1989 by Gender (fictional data)

Gender	Number of New Cases in 1988	Number of New Cases in 1989	Percent Change from 1988 to 1989
Men	78	104	33%
Women	4	7	75%
Total	82	111	35%

Percentage change is calculated as follows:

$$\text{Percentage change} = \frac{\text{\# at time 2} - \text{\# at time 1}}{\text{\# at time 1}} \times 100$$

The table shows that the *percentage increase* in the incidence of AIDS was much higher for women than for men between the two years. Such statistics were often reported as evidence that the epidemic was spreading much more rapidly among women than among men, suggesting that AIDS had suddenly become a "female" disease. In fact, in 1989 only 7 new cases appeared among women

compared with 104 new cases among men. The apparent "female" phenomenon was due to the problem of a small denominator. In such a situation, a
good statistician would simply report that there were too few female cases to
make meaningful comparisons.

Formulas in Chapter 1

Showing the work when making calculations:

$$\text{Symbol} = \text{formula} = \text{contents of formula} = \text{answer}$$

Calculating a fraction:

$$\text{Fraction} = \frac{\text{numerator}}{\text{denominator}} = \frac{\text{part}}{\text{whole}}$$

Calculating a proportion:

$$\text{Proportion} = p \ [\text{of total group in a category}] = \frac{\text{\# in a category}}{\text{\# in total group}} = \text{quotient}$$

Calculating a percentage:

$$\text{Percentage} = \% \ [\text{of total group in a category}] = p \ (100)$$

Calculating a rate:

$$\text{Rate of occurrence} = (p) \ (\text{a useful base number})$$

Calculating percentage change:

$$\text{Percentage change} = \frac{\text{\# at time 2} - \text{\# at time 1}}{\text{\# at time 1}}$$

Questions for Chapter 1

1. An interviewer in a survey misunderstood a respondent and incorrectly
   recorded that respondent's age. Was this a mistake or a statistical error?
   Explain.
2. Mary Jones is upset about natural disasters, noting that in a single year
   there were floods in the Midwest, drought in the South, and major
   earthquakes in the West. She believes that these events are proof that the
   end of the world is near. While Mary has a vivid imagination, explain why
   she lacks the statistical imagination.
3. In a study of college *seniors* at a major university, you measure major
   curriculum (psychology, sociology, chemistry, English, art, and so on) and
   year of schooling (first year, sophomore, junior, senior). In your study,
   which of these measurements is a variable, and which is a constant?

4. In a study of college seniors, you measure grade point average (GPA) and alcohol consumption in the previous month. State a hypothesis for these two variables and indicate which is the independent variable, and which is the dependent variable. Could the results of your study of college *seniors* be "generalized" to *the entire student body* of the college? Why or why not?

5. For a sample of homeless persons, you are interested in the relationship between gender and types of sleeping places (where the subject spent the previous night). Which variable is the independent variable, and which is the dependent variable?

6. Bob owns a book and computer store named InfoManiacs. He calculated the proportion of his profits that result from selling computer software and got an answer of 2.49. Could this be correct? Explain.

7. What is the essential feature of science that separates it from other forms of inquiry into nature?

8. Identify a commonly held belief that you suspect is a myth. Suggest what types of data might be collected to expose the myth. How might proportional thinking be applied to challenge this widely believed falsehood?

9. To get an idea of how organized scientific procedures are, go to the library and page through several scientific journals, such as the *American Sociological Review*, the *American Journal of Sociology*, the *Journal of the American Psychological Association*, the *Journal of Health and Social Behavior*, *Administrative Science Quarterly*, *Criminology*, *Social Services Review*, *American Journal of Psychology*, *American Political Science Review*, *Review of Public Administration*, and *Political Science Quarterly*. Note the abundance of statistical tables and graphs in these articles. Note also that all articles in the various volumes have similar section headings.

   a. List the headings of at least five articles from at least three different journals.
   b. Compare these lists to the seven stages of the research process and comment.

10. Suppose one state in the United States had an infant mortality rate of 8.6 deaths per 1,000 live births in 1998. In the year 2000 the state public health department holds a conference called Goals 2010, in which policy makers and government officials vow to improve public health in the new millennium. They set a target rate of 6.0 infant deaths per 1,000 live births to be reached by the year 2010. This target rate is a _____ .

11. In most states the interstate speed limit is 70 miles per hour. Random samples of vehicle speed are made with a speed detector radar gun. The average speed is found to be 74 miles per hour. The set speed limit is a statistical _____ , while 74 miles per hour is a statistical _____ .

Exercises for Chapter 1

1. Fill the blanks in the following table (see Appendix A for review):

	Fraction	Proportion	Percentage
a.	$\dfrac{86}{211}$	.4076	_____
b.	$\dfrac{1}{656}$	_____	_____
c.	$\dfrac{28}{10,000}$	.0028	_____
d.	_____	.1711	
e.	_____	_____	23.22%
f.	_____	_____	89.20%

2. Fill the blanks in the following table (see Appendix A for review):

	Fraction	Proportion	Percentage
a.	$\dfrac{39}{192}$	.2031	_____
b.	$\dfrac{18}{423}$	_____	_____
c.	$\dfrac{441}{10,000}$	.0441	_____
d.	_____	.0877	_____
e.	_____	_____	45.50%

3. In a casual conversation after class, Jane and Anne discover that they have a common habit. To relieve stress, they keep tabs on how frequently they can ring the recycle bin when throwing away a ball of paper. Jane brags that in 250 tosses, she rang the bin 128 times. In 265 tosses, Anne made 157 "baskets." Who is the better tosser? Why?

4. As the statistician for a local high school basketball league, you are in charge of keeping points-scored statistics. In the games so far, Antonio "Hot Shot" Johnson has attempted 73 shots and made 34 while Clarence "Slam Dunk" Williams has attempted 52 shots and made 28. Which player has the higher scoring percentage?

5. In order to meet Environmental Protection Agency (EPA) guidelines, the quantity of particulate matter in the city's air can exceed 69 parts per million only 15 percent of the days in the year without incurring cautions. How many days is this?

6. Scott, Sam, and Sid, three friends who sack groceries at the local market, decided to pool their tips one afternoon to buy a gift for their friend Cindy, who was in the hospital. Scott put in $15, Sam $12, and Sid $10. What proportion of the gift money was contributed by each one?

7. Better Bodies Health Spa is to select 100 members to attend the Winter Olympics, half male and half female. Age groups are to be represented according to their proportional membership. In other words, if the membership is made up mostly of 31- to 40-year-olds, mostly this age group will make the trip. The chart below gives the membership breakdown by age and gender. Fill in the proportion (p) and number (# to attend) for each age group for each gender. Show the general formula and an example of the computation for at least one age group.

Age Group	Males	p	# to Attend	Females	p	# to Attend
21–30	49			80		
31–40	170			217		
41–50	169			176		
51–60	84			91		
61+	22			48		
Totals	494		50	612		50

8. A corporation with offices in Los Angeles and New York will train its administrative assistants in a new software program. Each training session accommodates 40 persons. So that some employees in every department will receive training right away, participants are chosen by using quotas for department and city. For instance, if 10 percent of the administrative assistants are in the marketing department in Los Angeles, 10 percent of the trainees will come from that department. The chart below gives the membership breakdown by department and city. Fill in the proportion (p) and number (# to attend) for each department and city. Show the general formula and an example of the computation for at least one department-city category.

Department	Los Angeles	p	# to Attend	New York	p	# to Attend
Personnel	36			43		
Marketing	81			93		
Shipping	65			78		
Management	24			31		
Accounting	25			38		
Totals	231		40	283		40

9. You are interested in the phenomenon of personalized license plates, plates on which the owner has his or her name or a saying. In a random sample of 341 plates, you find that 73 are personalized. What proportion is *not* personalized?

10. There are 768 frogs in Noisy Pond. Sixty-one percent are male. Seventy-five percent of the frogs have warts. All things being equal (i.e., male and female frogs have an equal chance of being "warted"), how many male frogs would you expect to have warts?

11. Complete the following table by calculating the rate of institutionalization (prisons and mental hospitals) per hundred thousand population. Show the general formula and the computation for Anderson, Indiana.

City	Population	Number of Persons Institutionalized	Rate per 100,000 Population
Anderson, Indiana	130,669	3,981	
Bellingham, Washington	127,780	1,602	
Duluth, Minnesota	239,971	4,610	
Modesto, California	370,522	4,456	

12. Complete the following table by calculating the rate of institutionalization (prisons and mental hospitals) per hundred thousand population. Show the general formula and the computation for Bakersfield, California.

City	Population	Number of Persons Institutionalized	Rate per 100,000 Population
Bakersfield, California	543,477	10,808	
Burlington, North Carolina	108,213	1,158	
Great Falls, Montana	77,691	787	
Poughkeepsie, New York	259,462	11,082	

13. Turner (1995) investigated the effects of unemployment. He contacted 5,612 persons whom he deemed eligible for study because they had been unemployed at least once since joining the labor force. Of these eligible persons, 3,617 were actually interviewed, among whom 1,252 were tagged for long-term study. In the long-term study group, 154 were "recently unemployed," having lost their jobs in the past three years. Of the recently unemployed, 45 remained unemployed.

    a. What proportion of eligible subjects was interviewed?
    b. What percentage of those interviewed was *not* accepted for long-term study?
    c. What percentage of the long-term study group became unemployed in the past three years?
    d. What percentage of the recently unemployed had returned to work?

14. Turner (1995) investigated the effects of unemployment. He contacted 5,612 persons whom he deemed eligible for study because they had been unemployed at least once since joining the labor force. Of these eligible persons, 3,617 were actually interviewed, among whom 1,252 were tagged for long-term study. Imagine that of the 1,252 persons in the long-term study group, 732 were males and 520 were females. Among the 154 recently unemployed, 80 were males and 74 were females. Among the 45 still unemployed, 25 were males and 20 were females.

    a. In this long-term study group, which gender had the higher proportion of recent unemployment?
    b. Among the recently unemployed, were men or women more successful in returning to the workforce?

15. It is homecoming weekend, and the campus elected a homecoming king and queen. When the results were announced for the queen's crown, Natalie won with 526 votes. The runner-up got 510 votes, and the next four candidates received 482, 325, 200, and 150 votes, respectively. The remaining 10 contestants received a total of 1,140 votes. At the victory party, you discover that Natalie comes from a large family and that 28 of her relatives attend college with her, all of whom voted for her.

    a. What percentage of the 15,000-member student body voted in the election?
    b. What percentage of the votes did Natalie receive?
    c. What proportion of the student body does Natalie's family constitute? Simplify this answer by computing a rate.
    d. Was family support a critical element in Natalie's victory?

16. In an international study of religious affiliation, a researcher obtained the following data from 2,465 randomly selected respondents (fictional data). Complete the table for the proportion (*p*) and the percentage (%) of respondents for each religion.

Religion	Number	*p*	%
Christians	814		
Muslims	444		
Hindus	320		
Buddhists	148		
Other religions	345		
Nonreligious persons	394		
Totals	2,465		

17. For the U.S. Bureau of the Census a Metropolitan Statistical Area (MSA) is a county with a central city of 50,000 or more population plus adjacent counties whose economies are closely tied to the central city. The following 1990 U.S. Census data present MSA populations broken down by residential location within the MSA.

   a. Complete the "Totals" column in the table.
   b. Fill in the proportion (*p*) for each residential area in each MSA. Show the general formula and an example of the computation for at least one calculation.
   c. Which MSAs appear more rural than others?

Metropolitan Statistical Area (MSA)	Residential Distribution						
	Urban	*p*	Rural Nonfarm	*p*	Rural Farm	*p*	Totals
Abilene, TX	107,052		11,620		983		
Bakersfield, CA	455,300		84,870		3,307		
Bellingham, WA	75,697		48,487		3,596		
Duluth, MN	167,424		71,271		1,276		
Poughkeepsie, NY	146,526		111,748		1,188		

18. For the U.S. Bureau of the Census a Metropolitan Statistical Area (MSA) is a county with a central city of 50,000 or more population plus adjacent counties whose economies are closely tied to the central city. The following 1990 U.S. Census data presents MSA populations broken down by residential location within the MSA.

   a. Complete the "Totals" column in the table.
   b. Fill in the proportion (*p*) for each residential area in each MSA. Show the general formula and an example of the computation for at least one calculation.
   c. Which MSAs appear more rural than others?

Metropolitan Statistical Area (MSA)	Residential Distribution						
	Urban	p	Rural Nonfarm	p	Rural Farm	p	Totals
Abilene, TX	107,052		11,620		983		
Anderson, IN	87,438		40,634		2,597		
Battle Creek, MI	95,188		37,967		2,827		
Burlington, NC	71,289		35,439		1,485		
Great Falls, NY	63,531		12,341		1,819		

19/20. Solve this ancient riddle.

As I was going to St. Ives, I met a man with seven wives.
Every wife had seven sacks, every sack had seven cats,
Every cat had seven kits.
Kits, cats, sacks, and wives; how many were going to St. Ives?

Optional Computer Applications for Chapter 1

If your class uses the optional computer applications that accompany this text, follow the simple directions on the *Computer Applications for The Statistical Imagination* compact disk to access the information on it. No prior experience with computers is required. The disk includes the *Statistical Package for the Social Sciences (SPSS)* software package, *SPSS for Windows, Student Version*. In addition, there are a variety of data sets with complete descriptions of data, chapter exercises tied to these data sets, and detailed illustrations of how to interpret computer output. Earlier *SPSS* versions may be used, but the output will appear different.

SPSS for Windows, Student Version is more than adequate for learning basic statistics. If you want to conduct your own research, however, you may wish to gain access to the full base system of the regular (nonstudent) version of *SPSS for Windows* or the *SPSS for Windows Graduate Pack*. (The latter, which sells for less than $200, was available on campuses with full version site licenses when this text went to print.) These versions of *SPSS* have several advantages, including a "Syntax Editor" window that pastes and saves mouse commands for later use and no limitations in the data files on the number of variables or sample size.

The data sets on the *Computer Applications for The Statistical Imagination* compact disk have been modified in minor ways to facilitate instruction and therefore do not suffice for true research purposes. You may request the unmodified original data sets from the sources listed on the disk. Other data sets are available with Internet access from government agencies and research foundations such as the Inter University Consortium for Political and Social Research (ICPSR) and the National Opinion Research Center (NORC).

To access Chapter 1 exercises, insert the compact disk in the CD-ROM drive, click Chapter Exercises, then click Chapter 1. This first exercise involves an orientation to *SPSS for Windows* statistical software with instructions on how to retrieve files from the compact disk. Once *SPSS for Windows* is activated, click <u>H</u>elp and then <u>T</u>utorial. Follow the tutorial to become familiar with basic windows, icons, and menus.

Notes

1. When someone makes an objective statement about an object (or person or situation), the statement describes a characteristic that is truly part of the object, for example, the statement "The stop sign is red." When someone makes a subjective statement, the statement actually describes a characteristic of the "subject" observer rather than the object. Subjective statements therefore are personal views or opinions which reflect the biases, distortions, personal opinions, or prejudices of the person making the statement. For example, someone who is color-blind might say. "The stop sign is gray." The "grayness" is not part of the sign but instead is only the perception of the subject observer.
2. This datum was provided by Jerry Tracey, meteorologist of WVTM Television, Birmingham, Alabama.
3. The Latin abbreviation *i.e.* means "that is" (*id est*); *e.g.* means "for example" (*exempli gratia*).
4. The term *independent* comes from laboratory science, where predictor variables are manipulated independently of outcomes. For example, in a study of the effects of a drug on rats, the drug is given to some rats (the experimental group), while a placebo (or fake drug) is given to a matched group of rats (the control group). The choice of which rats are assigned to each group is done independently of measuring which rats get well.
5. The term *theory* is often used to mean an uncorroborated idea, as in "That is just a theory." This is a nonscientific use of the term. Scientific theories are based *not* on conjecture or opinion but on objective analysis of carefully gathered data.

STATISTICAL ANALYSIS: ERROR MANAGEMENT AND CONTROL

Introduction

Whether done for scientific investigation, product marketing, weather forecasting, or placing a bet, attempting to predict the future is a common pastime. Scientists make empirical predictions to test the accuracy of their ideas. For example, what are your chances of being a victim of a crime at your workplace? Madriz (1996) found three predictive factors based on the idea that the risk of victimization can be reduced by means of the careful study of routine activities. One risk factor is exposure—situational vulnerability—such as working alone in a convenience store late at night. A second is proximity to potential offenders, such as working at a store in a high-crime area. A third is target attractiveness, the desirability of a victim's property, such as having large amounts of cash on hand.

If a store owner put his or her employees at unnecessary risk, a robbery or murder would not be a random occurrence or mistake; it would be an error. In Chapter 1 we noted that **errors** are *known degrees of imprecision*. Knowing the relationship between circumstances and the likelihood of robbery allows one to institute preventive measures that reduce the calculated chances that "errors" will occur. Risk reduction measures might include having at least two employees present, closing at 11:00 P.M., locating in a high-traffic area, keeping only small amounts of cash on hand, and installing alarm systems. Error reduction hinges on understanding the predictive relationships among variables.

As we briefly noted in Chapter 1, statistics is about the precise understanding and control of **statistical error,** *known degrees of imprecision in the procedures used to gather and process information.* Errors are not mistakes. Errors are known amounts of imprecision that can be calculated and reduced by careful, informed selection of sampling designs, measurement instruments, and statistical formulas.

Statistical Error

Known degrees of imprecision in the procedures used to gather and process information.

Statistical analysis typically involves sampling: observing only a small part of the group under study. For example, to learn about all convenience stores, we might study a sample of 20 stores. Can the data from a sample of 20 stores accurately reveal how all convenience stores operate? Research also involves observation and measurement. Can we assume that our measurements are completely accurate? Sampling and measurement are two potential sources of error in drawing conclusions in research. **Sampling error** is *inaccuracy in predictions about a population that results from the fact that we do not observe every subject in the population.* **Measurement error** is *inaccuracy in research which derives from imprecise measurement instruments, difficulties in the classification of observations, and the need to round numbers.* After discussing each of these types of error, we will show how they are related.

Controlling Sampling Error

To analyze means to pick something apart and examine it in fine detail in an organized way. In doing statistical work, we analyze groups of persons, objects, or events and measure variables to get averages, tendencies, or percentages. *Measurement of a single person,* say, recording Mary Smith's age as 19 years, does not provide a statistic; this is simply an **observation.** However, determining that the average age of a class of 30 students is 19.5 years is computing a statistic based on a set of observations. The field of statistics involves **summary calculations** of many observations, *the summing up of a group of measurements.* Our interests are in observing many cases, gathering precise information about them, and making summary statements about the group, not about individuals.

The group of subjects we observe is usually quite small. Our purpose is to study the small number of subjects to draw conclusions about the larger population from which those subjects came. Studying every instance of a phenomenon is impractical, costly, and unnecessary. For example, we do not have to poll every likely voter to determine candidate A's support. Instead, we can poll a cross section of likely voters, perhaps 500. This smaller group is called a sample, while the larger, complete group from which it came is called a population or universe.

Figure 2–1 depicts the notion of sampling. The **population** (or universe) is *a large group of people of particular interest that we desire to study and understand.* Commonly studied populations include the people of a country, state, or community; the inmates at a state, correctional facility; currently enrolled students at a college; families with school-age children; hospital patients; head chefs in New York City restaurants; and corporation executives. A **sample** is *a small subgroup of the population; the sample is observed and measured and then used to draw conclusions about the population.*

A Population (or Universe)

A large group of people (or objects) of particular interest that we desire to study and understand.

A Sample

A small subgroup of the population; the sample is observed and measured and then used to draw conclusions about the population.

Sampling is something we do all the time. We taste a spoonful (a sample) to decide whether to add more chili powder to the pot (the population). To explore an academic major, say, sociology, we may take one or two courses (a sample) to determine whether the universe of ideas and activities of sociology appeals to us. A first date with someone is a sampling of that individual's personality, a first exposure to the universe of his or her behavioral and attitudinal tendencies. Sampling is a common and efficient human behavior.

Our interest, however, is not in the sample per se. Instead, we want to learn about the entire population. To acquire absolutely correct information about an entire population, we would ideally measure *all* of its members and

FIGURE 2–1

The relationship of a population (universe) of measurements to sample of measurements

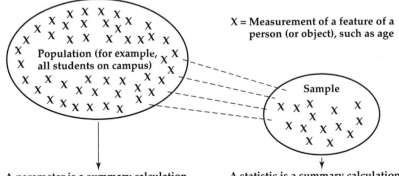

X = Measurement of a feature of a person (or object), such as age

Population (for example, all students on campus)

Sample

A parameter is a summary calculation of measurements made on all subjects in a population (for example, the true average age of all students on campus)

A statistic is a summary calculation of measurements made on a sample to estimate a parameter (for example, the average age of the student sample)

summarize the results in mathematical terms, reporting percentages, rates, and averages. *A summary calculation of measurements made on all subjects in a population* is called a **parameter.** For example, the average age of inmates at Sharpwire Prison is a parameter. The percentage of executives who are female at the Menrule Plastics Corporation is a parameter. Unfortunately, most populations are so large that we cannot afford the time and expense of measuring all members. For example, it would be absurd to measure the heights of all American adults. Because of the high costs of measuring every subject in a population, the true values of parameters are typically unknown.

Fortunately, sampling allows us to accurately *estimate* parameters. With samples we compute statistics rather than parameters. A **statistic** is *a summary calculation of measurements made on a sample to estimate a parameter of the population.* For instance, in a sample of 800 registered Republicans in New Jersey we might find that 74 percent support the governor. This percentage constitutes a statistic, only an estimate of the governor's true support. A sample and the statistics computed on it are simply tools for drawing *conclusions about a population in general*—the population as a whole. Such conclusions, if made by following proper statistical procedures, are called statistical generalizations.

A Parameter

A summary calculation of measurements made on all subjects in a population.

A Statistic

A summary calculation of measurements made on a sample to estimate a parameter of the population.

We must never lose sight of the fact that it is the population that is of concern to us. For example, an "exit poll" sample of voters (taken as people leave a voting place) may suggest that candidate A is the winner. This, however, is an estimate, an approximation of the true level of support. The true winner will be known only after all the votes are counted, that is, when the entire population of voters has been measured.

One way to remember that a single sample only provides estimates is to compare the results of several samples from the same population. If a statistics professor sent each of 30 class members out to gather a sample of 10 fellow students and estimate average student age, each class member would get a slightly different result. (If you are not convinced, draw two samples yourself.) This variability in sampling outcomes simply reflects the fact that a statistic from a single sample is only an estimate of the true population parameter.

How, then, are we to trust the results of a single sample? The answer to this question presents good news and bad news. The bad news is that statisticians must acknowledge that conclusions from a sample are not absolutely correct, that statistics are only estimates of parameters. The good news is that statistical procedures and the logic of probability theory allow statisticians to specify a known degree of error in predictions and therefore stipulate the degree of confidence we may place in a conclusion based on statistics. Put simply, although statistical estimates are not perfect, we know how close to perfect they are.

Careful Statistical Estimation versus Hasty Guesstimation

The statistical imagination emphasizes understanding a point of detail in its proper context, taking care not to draw simplistic or fantastic conclusions. Statistical estimation is different from commonsense "guesstimation," which is often biased. A **statistical estimate** is *the report of a summary measurement based on systematic sampling and precise measurements and reported with known degrees of error and confidence.* A **guesstimate** is *a report of a summary measurement based on limited and usually subjective personal experiences, anecdotal evidence, or hasty casual observations.*

Guesstimation might occur when a news reporter picks candidate A as the sure winner because an exit poll reports support by 52 percent of likely voters. In contrast, taking note of the sample size, a statistician would be more cautious and emphasize that 52 percent means 52 plus or minus 5 percentage points; therefore, support lies somewhere between 47 percent and 57 percent. Candidate A's victory is not assured because support could be *as low as* 47 percent. Moreover, the statistician provides a degree of confidence for the estimate, such as 95 percent. (We cannot claim 100 percent confidence until all the votes are in.) Careful statistical estimation is different from even a good guess. Statisticians differ from other prognosticators in two important ways: Statisticians (1) control and manage the degree of error in reported statistics and (2) precisely state confidence in their conclusions.

A particularly insidious type of guesstimation is a prejudicial **stereotype,** *a false generalization that implies that all individuals in a category share certain, usually undesirable, traits.* For example, there is the racist stereotype that African-Americans are too ignorant, lazy, or immoral to support their families and that this is the cause of poverty in America. In fact, nearly 7 of every 10 poor Americans are white and most poor people are employed. Guesstimates are often guided by feelings that reinforce stereotypes, feelings such as hate, fear, and superiority. In contrast, statistical generalizations are interpreted with caution and within the larger context of scientific testing with its safeguards against subjectivity. Table 2–1 compares guesstimates to statistical estimates.

Sampling Error and Its Management with Probability Theory

Because the only way to know a true parameter is to survey the entire population, each statistic computed from a sample is an estimate. Just by chance, the

TABLE 2–1   Commonsense "Guesstimates" versus Statistical Estimates

Commonsense Guesstimates	*Statistical Estimates*
The idea is based on limited and usually subjective personal experiences, anecdotal evidence, or hasty observations.	The idea is based on systematic sampling and measurement.
Produces conjectures and mistaken conclusions.	Produces reliable estimates with known degrees of error and confidence.
Produces and reinforces stereotypes.	Produces statistical generalizations.
Usually a matter of opinion.	Usually a matter of fact.

statistics of some samples are closer to the true parameter value than are those of others. **Probability theory** (Chapter 6) is *the analysis and understanding of chance occurrences*. It provides a set of rules for determining the accuracy of sample statistics and computing the degrees of confidence we have in conclusions about a population.

To successfully manage sampling error we must focus on its specific sources: sample size and sample representativeness. **Sample size** refers to *the number of cases or observations in a sample: the number of persons or objects observed*. Generally speaking, the larger the sample, the smaller the range of error. Suppose a researcher sent two assistants out to determine the average age of the student body. One asked 3 students for their ages, while the second asked 1,000. Intuition leads us to place greater trust in the results from the larger sample because the smaller sample could more easily bunch up with all young or all old students. In a later chapter we will learn to compute and report statistics with a "confidence interval" of plus or minus an exact amount of error for any given sample size. With a sample of 1,000 we may find that the average age on campus is 22.4 years plus or minus 0.3 year, which asserts that the average age lies between 22.7 years (i.e., 22.4 + 0.3) and 22.1 years (i.e., 22.4 − 0.3). The computation of "plus or minus some sampling error" is based on mathematical probabilities or probability theory.

Probability theory also allows us to say exactly how often a statistic will incorrectly predict the parameter, that is, how often errors may cause a wrong answer. For example, we may note that 5 percent of the time our procedures produce a false conclusion. By noting this level of error, however, we are also noting our level of confidence. If our estimate is wrong only 5 percent of the time, then it is correct 95 percent of the time; thus, we are 95 percent confident in it.

A second factor affecting sampling accuracy is the extent to which all segments of a population actually land in the sample—sample representativeness. A **representative sample** is one in which *all segments of the population are included in the sample in their correct proportions in the population*. For example, if a campus population is actually 54 percent male and 46 percent female, a representative sample will have close to these percentages of men and women.

Representative Sample

A sample in which all segments of the population are included in the sample in their correct proportions in the population.

A **nonrepresentative sample** is *one in which some segments of the population are overrepresented or underrepresented in the sample.* This is a dangerous type of sampling error because it can lead to totally bogus results. Suppose, for instance, the campus administration wishes to poll students on their support for expanding the football stadium. Nursing Student Association volunteers do the polling and are told to poll every tenth student, but instead they poll every tenth student coming out of the nursing building. Unsurprisingly, the results show that only 23 percent of students favor the expansion. Why? Because the association members actually surveyed the population of nursing students, which is disproportionately female and not representative of the campus as a whole. We would say that this sample is *biased* by a disproportionately high share of females. This nonrepresentative sample allowed one segment of the population to have more than its fair share of "votes" on an issue.

There are a variety of sampling designs, but one of the most commonly used is a simple random sample. A **random sample** is *one in which every person (or object) in the population has the same chance of being selected for the sample.* (In technical terms, we say that everyone in the population has *an equal probability of inclusion* in the sample.) This design is like a raffle or lottery in which every person in the population may enter only once. A random sample of sufficient size usually will produce a representative sample.

Random Sample

A sample in which every person (or object) in the population has the same chance of being selected for the sample.

Sample size and sample representativeness, however, are separate concerns. A large sample does not guarantee a representative sample. A systematic, repetitious mistake in sampling can produce a large but biased sample. A classic case of systematic sampling error occurred in the 1936 presidential campaign, in which *Literary Digest* magazine selected a large sample from telephone directories and automobile owners. The results showed overwhelming support for the Republican candidate, Alf Landon, over Franklin D. Roosevelt, the Democratic candidate. When election day rolled around, it was not Landon but Roosevelt who won the election—and by a landslide no less! The *Literary Digest* poll systematically ignored voters without telephones or automobiles and thus failed to adequately poll the poor, who constituted the bulk of Roosevelt's support (Babbie 1992: 192–93). There are methods to verify the representativeness of a sample, and we will cover them in Chapter 10. Suffice it to say here that a small representative sample is better than a large nonrepresentative one. A teaspoonful of chili with all the ingredients constitutes a better taste test than does a cupful drawn from only the top of the pot.

Controlling Measurement Error

In addition to avoiding sampling errors, we must precisely define how measurements are to be made and carefully code the responses once the data are acquired. *The set of procedures or operations for measuring a variable* is called its **operational definition.** For example, suppose we use U.S. Census data to conduct a study of urban poverty with a sample of 300 cities. There are various ways to *operationalize* a measure of poverty. The challenge is to select the way that most accurately depicts how many of a city's households are occupied by poor families. One measure is the percentage of households receiving food stamps. A second is the city's unemployment rate. A third is the percentage of households living below the federally defined poverty level (a specific income adjusted for household size). In fact, the third option generally is recognized as the best approximation of poverty for a community, and so we would choose this as our operational definition. The choice of an operational definition is guided by identifying common types of measurement error and doing everything possible to minimize them. In general, measurement error has to do with the precision, validity, and reliability of an operational definition.

A **precise measurement** is *one in which the degree of measurement error is sufficiently small for the task at hand.* Precision depends on practical circumstances and is controlled by specifying rounding error (a topic that will be discussed shortly). For instance, in cutting two-foot-long fireplace logs, a small degree of precision will suffice because we can afford a large degree of error, say, "give or take a half foot." By contrast, for a quality test of microcomputer circuit boards, a precision of one-thousandth of an inch may be required. The degree of precision is a question of tolerance. We ask: How much measurement error can we tolerate (or put up with) without encountering practical problems or drawing faulty scientific conclusions?

A **valid measure** is *one that measures what is intended.* Validity pertains to the question: Does an operational definition measure what it is supposed to? For example, measuring waist size as an operational definition of the variable weight would not be valid, but the use of a properly balanced weight scale would be. Perfectly valid measures are hard to come by. For instance, education is typically operationalized as years of schooling, but there are other ways to become educated, such as military or on-the-job training. The validity of a measure is seldom known with complete certainty.

Reliability has to do with *the consistency of measurements from subject to subject and from time to time.* With a reliable weight scale, two sample subjects who truly weigh the same will have the same readings. Moreover, if the weight scale is unreliable, it is not truly measuring weight. In other words, an unreliable scale is useless and not valid.

In social surveys, reliability depends primarily on whether a question is worded so that all the respondents interpret it the same way. For example, to measure *annual income* in a door-to-door survey, it would be unreliable and not valid to simply ask: "What is your total income?" Does this mean just the respondent's income or that of all in the household who work? Does it include dividends and other income besides salary? Might respondents fib about this private matter? Although not perfect, a better way to measure household income is to show a card with income categories and ask: "In which of these groups did your total family income, from all sources, fall last year, before taxes, that is? Just tell me the letter" (National Opinion Research Center 1994; www.icpsr.umich.edu/gss/codebook/income.htm).

Levels of Measurement: Careful Selection of Statistical Procedures

Measurement

Measurement is *the assignment of symbols, either names or numbers, to the differences we observe in a variable's qualities or amounts. The measurement of a particular sample subject on a single variable* is that subject's **score** for that variable or, to use computer terminology, a code. Suppose for a moment that your statistics class is a sample. We could score the variables age, class level, gender, grade point average (GPA), and race. For one student, Joanie, these scores are 20 on age, junior on class level, female on gender, 3.25 on GPA, and white on race; for another, Ron, the respective codes are 19, sophomore, male, 3.48, and African-American. We will use the terms *score* and *code* interchangeably. The *value* of a score is its amount.

As this simple illustration reveals, not all variables are measured in the same way. Some are scored with names or categories that identify differences in kind or quality, such as African-American and white for the variable race. Other variables allow for distinctions of degree or distance between quantities, such as the variables age and GPA. These variables have a **unit of measure,** a *set interval or distance between quantities of the variables.* We score them numerically, like the numbered marks on a ruler or meter stick. The unit of measure for a temperature scale is a degree; for weight, a pound; for height, an inch, and so on.

To capture the fine distinctions among the measurement properties of variables, we use a scheme called levels of measurement. The **level of**

measurement of a variable *identifies its measurement properties, which determine the kind of mathematical operations (addition, multiplication, etc.) that can be appropriately used with it and the statistical formulas that can be used with it in testing theoretical hypotheses.* These levels are called nominal, ordinal, interval, and ratio. The level of measurement of a variable is an important guide for selecting statistical formulas and procedures.

Level of Measurement of a Variable

Identifies the variable's measurement properties, which determine the kind of mathematical operations (addition, multiplication, etc.) that can be appropriately used with it and the statistical formulas that can be used with it in testing theoretical hypotheses.

Nominal Variables

Nominal variables are those for which *codes merely indicate a difference in category, class, quality, or kind.* The word *nominal* comes from the Latin word for *name*, and these variables have named categories. Examples include place of birth (Chicago, Atlanta, Portland, etc.), favorite flavor of ice cream (vanilla, chocolate, cookies and cream, etc.), make of automobile (Ford, Lexus, Pontiac, etc.), and academic major (psychology, chemistry, electrical engineering, etc.).

Nominal variables do not allow for meaningfully ordered numerical scores. Nonetheless, because computers more efficiently process numbers, we sometimes number the categories of these variables in computer codes. For instance, with the variable *gender* we may set the codes as 0 = male and 1 = female. The choice of numbers for such codes is arbitrary; we could just as well have coded 0 = female and 1 = male. Additionally, the categories of a nominal variable cannot be meaningfully ranked in magnitude (from high to low) even if ordered numbers are assigned as codes. For example, to code female as 1 and male as 0 does not imply that females are a score of 1 higher than males. There is no sense of degree with nominal variables. A person is either male or female, not one or the other to some degree. Even some apparently numerical scores are actually nominal variables. For example, social security number is actually a category, and there is no point in computing its average.

Since many nominal variables have only two categories, there is a special name for them. A **dichotomous variable** is *one with only two categories.* A common dichotomous survey variable is any with the answers "yes" and "no" and, in laboratory research designs, one that distinguishes "presence" (the experimental group) or "absence" (the control group). For example, in testing the effectiveness of a new hay fever medication, the experimental group is administered the new drug and scored 1. The control group is given an imitation drug (or placebo) and scored zero. In the computer we name this variable

LABGROUP. When we desire to isolate the experimental group for analysis, we instruct the computer to search the codes of LABGROUP and pull out those cases with a code of 1.

Ordinal Variables

Like nominal variables, **ordinal variables** *name categories, but they have the additional property of allowing categories to be ranked* from highest to lowest, best to worst, or first to last. Typical ordinal variables include social class ranking (upper, middle, working, poverty), educational class level (senior, junior, etc.), and quality of housing (standard, substandard, dilapidated). Survey questions that measure attitudes and opinions often employ ranked scores. For example, the variable "attitude toward legal abortion" might rank the extent of agreement using the response categories: *strongly agree, agree, don't know, disagree, strongly disagree.* This widely used set of codes is called Likert scoring after its originator, Rensis Likert (1932).

Interval Variables

Interval variables have the characteristics of nominal and ordinal variables, plus *a defined numerical unit of measure.* Interval variables identify differences in amount, quantity, degree, or distance and are assigned highly useful numerical scores. Examples include temperature (scored to the nearest thermal degree) and intelligence quotient (IQ) score, ranging from zero to 200 points. With interval variables, the intervals or distances between scores are the same between any two points on the measurement scale. For example, with the variable temperature, the difference between 10 degrees and 11 degrees Fahrenheit is the same as that between 40 degrees and 41 degrees. A set, ordered unit of measure provides the ability to add, subtract, multiply, and divide scores and compute averages.

Interval variables give a sense of "how much" or "what size," such as how hot, how opinionated, how conservative, how depressed, how long, and how heavy. With interval variables we think in terms of distances between scores on a straight line. For example, if the average test grade in a class is 80, and Carl got an 85 and Brett got a 90, then Brett's score was twice as far above average as Carl's. Furthermore, the ranges of error with interval variables are more definite and easier to manage because, for instance, numerical scores can be rounded.

Comparing the properties of interval and ordinal variables is informative. Unlike interval variables, ordinal variables lack the property of a set unit of measure even if the ordered categories are numbered. For instance, position of finish in a horse race (1, 2, 3, etc.) is merely ordinal; it simply says which horses crossed the finish line first, second, third, and so on, but not how far apart they finished. For this ordinal variable to be treated as an interval variable, the horses would have to finish in single file order and equal distances apart. Furthermore, subtraction of the ranked numbers of an ordinal variable provides only differences in rank, not distance between scores. For example, if One Leg Up and Trouble at the Gate finished third and sixth, respectively, then One Leg Up came in three positions ahead. These horses could have been separated by a few inches or hundreds of yards. While ordinal variables do allow some calculations, such as differences in rank and average rank, they have limited mathematical usefulness. Interval variables have much greater mathematical usefulness than do ordinal variables.

Interval-Like Ordinal Variables.   Because interval level statistical procedures are more thorough and informative than are ordinal procedures, efforts frequently are made to force ordinal variables into interval techniques. This exception is justified sometimes because interval level statistics are robust (see Chapter 16). When can we treat an ordinal variable as if it has an interval level of measurement? First, the ordinal variable must have at least seven ranked categories or scores; the more, the better. Second, the score distribution cannot be skewed or bimodal. This means the scores can be either normally distributed (see Chapter 5) or rectangularly distributed (i.e., evenly distributed across their range with about the same frequency at each score). When these circumstances apply, we can refer to an ordinal variable's level of measurement as "interval-like." However, caution must still be used in the interpretation of computations with such variables. The application of this exception to the four conventional levels of measurement will be apparent in later chapters.

Ratio Variables

Ratio variables have the characteristics of interval variables plus *a true zero point, where a score of zero means none.* Weight, height, age, distance, population size, duration of time, and GPA are examples of ratio variables.

Comparing ratio variables to interval variables is informative because both have set intervals in their unit of measure, but only ratio variables have a meaningful zero point. Some *interval* variables may have a score of zero, but the zero point is arbitrary; that is, it could be set at any point in a variable's possible score range because the zero does not mean none. For instance, zero temperature does not mean no temperature. Thus, on the Fahrenheit scale it is set at 32 degrees below the freezing point, while on the Celsius scale it is set at the freezing point itself.

The true zero points of ratio variables allow even greater flexibility in computations and statistical analysis. Like interval variables, ratio variables can be multiplied and divided, but we can also compute ratios, hence the name. A **ratio** is *the amount of one observation in relation to another.* For example, if John eats three slices of pizza and Jessica eats one, the ratio is three to one, written as 3:1. With a ratio level variable the answer for a computed ratio makes sense, while with an interval level variable it does not. For example, an

80-pound boy is twice as heavy as a 40-pound boy, a ratio of 2:1. But it makes no sense to say of the interval level variable *temperature* that it is four times warmer in Miami, where it is 80 degrees, than in New York, where it is 20 degrees. In New York it is not warm at all! One way, then, to determine whether a variable has a true zero is to attempt to interpret a ratio. If the ratio is meaningless, the variable is at best interval level and its zero point is arbitrary.

Because of the similarities of statistical procedures applied to interval and ratio variables, we often lump these distinctions together by referring to interval/ratio variables. Similarly, we often refer to nominal/ordinal variables. Table 2–2 summarizes the properties of the four conventional levels of measurement.

To take advantage of set units of measure, scientists often devise ways to change nominal/ordinal variables into interval/ratio forms. Table 2–3 lists several nominal variables that have been transformed into a ratio level variable called the Index of Health Risk Behavior. The nominal variables are scored zero for no and 1 for yes. This is called dummy coding because the numerical scores are artificial; zero and 1 do not distinguish amounts or quantities. Instead, zero means the risk factor is not present, and 1 means that it is. The ratio variable RISKIND is an individual's total number of risk factors, and this variable has a true zero point. If Jeremy smokes, drinks, drives drunk, and

TABLE 2–2   Characteristics of the Four Levels of Measurement

Level of Measurement	*Examples*	*Qualities*	*Mathematical Operations Permitted*
Nominal	Gender, race, religious preference, marital status	Classification into categories; naming of categories	Counting of the number of cases (i.e., the frequency) of each category of the variable; comparing the sizes of categories
Ordinal	Social class rank, attitude and opinion questions	Classification of categories; rank ordering of categories from low to high	All the above plus judgments of greater than and less than and computations of differences and averages of ranks
Interval	Temperature, summary indexes, attitude and opinion scales	All the above plus distances between scores have a fixed unit of measure	All the above plus mathematical operations such as addition, subtraction, multiplication, division, square roots
Ratio	Weight, income, age, years of education, size of population	All the above plus a true zero point	All the above plus the computation of meaningful ratios

---

TABLE 2–3   Creating an Index to Transform Several Nominal Variables into a Ratio Variable

Variable Number and Name	Operational Definition (how the variable is measured)	Level of Measurement	Codes (how scored)
1. SMOKES	Current smoker?	Nominal	0 = no 1 = yes
2. BINGE	Has consumed five or more alcoholic beverages on a single occasion in the past month.	Nominal	0 = no 1 = yes
3. EXERCISE	Does not exercise regularly.	Nominal	0 = no 1 = yes
4. DRUGS	Has used an illicit drug in the past month.	Nominal	0 = no 1 = yes
5. DROVEDR	Has driven while intoxicated.	Nominal	0 = no 1 = yes
6. RISKIND	Number of risk behaviors reported.	Ratio	Sum of yeses for variables 1 through 5

---

takes drugs while Adam only smokes, then Jeremy experiences four times as many risky behaviors as Adam, a ratio of 4:1. We hope your own RISKIND score computes low.

The fields of survey methods and psychometric analysis are dedicated to constructing interval/ratio indexes and measurement scales from large sets of survey questions of the nominal/ordinal level. An **index** is *a summing up of objective events, behaviors, knowledge, and circumstances.* A **measurement scale** is *a summing up of subjective responses on attitudes, feelings, and opinions.* Among the common attitude and social scales are spirituality (how religious a person is), self-esteem, social distance (perceived difference in social status between persons), and liberalism-conservatism.

Coding and Counting Observations

Once data collection is complete, the next step in managing data is to code and record all measurements on a spreadsheet or in a computer data file. Table 2–4 is an example of a simple **codebook,** *a concise description of the symbols that signify each score of each variable.* These data come from a survey of students at the fictional college Apple Pond Institute. In this codebook we substitute number symbols for the categories male and female and for class levels. This is done because computers have an easier time counting and sorting numbers (in computer lingo, *numeric* symbols) than they do sorting words (*character* or *string* symbols).

TABLE 2–4   **Codebook for Questionnaire Responses of Criminal Justice Majors at Apple Pond Institute**

Variable Name	*Description of Variable Codes*
STUDENT NAME	Record first name, middle initial without period, and last name; blank = missing.
AGE	Record self-reported age up to 97 years; 98 = 98 years or more; 99 = missing.
GENDER	0 = male, 1 = female, 9 = missing.
GPA	Grade point average on a four-point scale = number of quality points earned per credit hour earned (rounded to two decimal places); 9.99 = missing.
CLASS LEVEL	1 = first year, 2 = sophomore, 3 = junior, 4 = senior, 8 = other, 9 = missing.

In a codebook, care is taken to be very precise because response coding may introduce measurement error. Every variable is coded by following two basic principles: inclusiveness and exclusiveness. The **principle of inclusiveness** states that for a given variable *there must be a score or code for every observation made*. Simply put, did we include a response category or score for every possible answer? For example, with the nominal variable *race*, we might list the categories White, African-American, Native American, Asian-American, Hispanic, and Other. The response category Other avoids the need to waste questionnaire space for categories expected to get few responses in a given study locale (such as Eskimo in Kansas). Other is a *residual category* that picks up the leftovers (think of the word *residue*).

Even if we ignore the issue of how to code persons of mixed heritage, if we merely use White and African-American, the tabulation of race will not be inclusive of, say, Asian-Americans. Without their own or an Other category, we cannot assume that all Asian-Americans will score themselves the same way. Some may check white, but others may leave the question blank. After computing totals, we would not be able to say exactly how many we have of *any* race. We missed Asian-Americans who left the question blank, and some of our "whites" are Asian-Americans, but we have no idea how many. Such a careless loss of control over measurement error can make the data on race useless.

The **principle of exclusiveness** states that for a given variable *every observation can be assigned one and only one score*. Simply put, each category must exclude scores that do not belong there, and any two categories must not share a response. For example, with the variable *religious affiliation in childhood*, the response categories Protestant, Baptist, Catholic, Jewish, and Other would not be mutually exclusive because one Baptist may check Baptist, while another may check Protestant. When the totals for each category were summed, we could not say how many Baptists were in the sample. Some might have checked "Protestant," but we have no way of telling who did and how many. Table 2–5 presents the results of the 1994 General Social Survey for this variable. Exclusiveness is assured by asking Protestants a "probe" or follow-up question to determine their specific denominations. (To aid your understanding of table information in this text, we modified tables to stipulate "Givens" [i.e., the data available] and "Calculations." In published reports of these tables these terms would not appear.)

Return to the codebook of Table 2–4 and note that the principle of inclusiveness is met by supplying *codes for missing data,* called **missing values.** We say, for example, that gender and class level have a missing value of 9. In surveys, missing values occur when an interviewer accidentally skips a question or a respondent does not answer. When we compute statistics for a variable, we disregard cases that score a missing value.

Table 2–6 is a simple spreadsheet of the results of a questionnaire survey

---

TABLE 2–5   **Distribution of Religious Affiliation in Childhood, Response to Questions: In What Religion Were You Raised? If Protestant: What Specific Denomination Is That, if Any?**

	Givens	Calculations
Response Category	*(a)* *Number*	*(b)* *Percent of Total Sample*
Protestant		
Baptist	706	23.73%
Methodist	319	10.72
Lutheran	220	7.39
Presbyterian	139	4.67
Episcopalian	68	2.29
Other	309	10.39
No denomination or		
nondenominational church	69	2.32
Total Protestant	1,830	61.51%
Catholic	882	29.65
Jewish	55	1.85
None	127	4.27
Other	74	2.49
No answer	7	0.23
Total	2,975	100.00%

SOURCE: National Opinion Research Center, General Social Survey 1994.
www.icpsr.umich.edu/gss/codebook/relig16.htm.
www.icpsr.umich.edu/gss/codebook/denom16.htm.

TABLE 2–6   **Computational Spreadsheet of Questionnaire Responses of 10 Criminal Justice Majors at Apple Pond Institute (fictional data)**

		Givens		
Student Name	*Age*	*Gender*	*Grade Point Average*	*Class Level*
Jessica A Cortland	19	1	3.21	2
Mark E Pippin	22	0	2.75	4
Stayman V Winesap	19	0	2.43	1
Barry D McIntosh	21	0	3.39	3
Harriet G Smith	20	1	3.87	3
Antonio B Rome	22	0	2.32	3
Robert J Cox	18	0	3.25	1
Rodney I Greening	20	0	9.99	2
Thomas R York	22	0	2.47	4
Goldie D Licious	19	1	3.68	2

administered to 10 criminal justice majors at Apple Pond Institute. A spreadsheet is a matrix listing the scores of all variables, organized in columns, and all cases, organized in rows.

A spreadsheet is useful for summarizing data in an efficient way. For example, we can quickly count the number of females in the sample by summing the ones listed under "Gender." From this simple spreadsheet we can quickly see that the sample is composed of seven males and three females; there are two first-year students, three sophomores, three juniors, and two seniors; ages range from 18 to 22 years; and GPAs range from 2.43 to 3.87 with one unreported case. Of course, for a large sample, an efficient procedure involves entering these spreadsheet codes into a computer data file and allowing computer software to handle the computations. Computer data files are organized like spreadsheets.

Frequency Distributions

Once all the data are organized onto a spreadsheet or computer file, the next step in the analysis is to focus separately on each variable and answer the question: How many subjects fall into each category or score? We organize the data of each variable into a **frequency distribution,** *a listing of all observed scores of a variable and the frequency (f) of each score (or category).* We use capital English letters to represent a variable. If X is defined as the variable *gender,* the frequency distribution of X simply shows how many men and women are in the sample. Table 2–5 above provides the frequency distribution for religious affiliation in childhood.

Frequency Distribution

A listing of all observed scores of a variable and the frequency (*f*) of each score (or category).

Standardizing Score Distributions

Knowing the frequency of a category is not very informative by itself. For example, someone may note that there are five millionaires living in a city. Five is not many for New York City, but is a lot for a town of 800 people. Thus, it is more informative to report a category frequency as a proportion or percentage of the total number of subjects in the sample. The statistical imagination beckons us to express a category frequency in a larger context, as a part in relation to a whole. We address the question: Five millionaires out of how many people? As we noted in Chapter 1, fractions, proportions, and percentages provide common denominators or "standard measures" for easy comparison of categories and samples. For a sample as a whole, the **proportional frequency distribution** is *a listing of the proportion of responses for each category or score of a variable*. The **percentage frequency distribution** is *a listing of the percent of responses for each category or score of a variable*.

Proportional Frequency Distribution

A listing of the proportion of responses for each category or score of a variable.

Percentage Frequency Distribution

A listing of the percent of responses for each category or score of a variable.

To obtain these distributions for each response category or score of a variable, we write a fraction and then divide it to obtain the proportion and percentage. For ease of interpretation, the percentage frequency distribution is the one usually reported. For example, with data from the spreadsheet in Table 2–6, the percentage of the Apple Pond Institute sample that are males is

$$p \text{ [of student sample that are males]} = \frac{\# \text{ males}}{n} = \frac{7}{10} = .7000$$

$$\% \text{ [of student sample that are males]} = (p)(100) = (.7000)(100) = 70.00\%$$

where *p* stands for proportion and *n* is the sample size. After doing the same for females, we have the percentage frequency distribution of the variable *gender* as in the rightmost column of Table 2–7. This table also provides the frequency and proportional frequency distributions. The total of all proportions

TABLE 2–7   **Frequency, Proportional Frequency, and Percentage Frequency Distributions of the Variable Gender for a Sample of 10 Apple Pond Institute Students**

Givens		Calculations	
Gender (X)	Frequency (f)	Proportional Frequency	Percentage Frequency
Male	7	.7000	70.00%
Female	3	.3000	30.00
Total	10	1.0000	100.00%

and percentages for a distribution will equal 1.0000 and 100.00 percent, respectively, within rounding error.

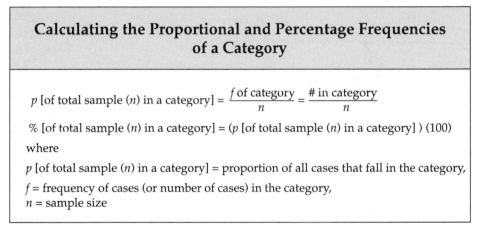

Calculating the Proportional and Percentage Frequencies of a Category

$$p \text{ [of total sample } (n) \text{ in a category]} = \frac{f \text{ of category}}{n} = \frac{\# \text{ in category}}{n}$$

$$\% \text{ [of total sample } (n) \text{ in a category]} = (p \text{ [of total sample } (n) \text{ in a category]})(100)$$

where

p [of total sample (n) in a category] = proportion of all cases that fall in the category,

f = frequency of cases (or number of cases) in the category,

n = sample size

Table 2–5 (on page 48) provides both the frequency and percentage frequency distributions for the variable religious affiliation in childhood.

Comparing the Frequencies of Two Nominal/Ordinal Variables

Another common device for presenting data is a **cross-tabulation** (or cross-classification) **table** that *compares two nominal/ordinal variables at once*. Such "crosstab" tables are essential for testing a hypothesis about the relationship between those variables (see Chapter 13). For example, is there a relationship between gender (X) and church attendance (Y) among college students? The (fictional) results of a campus study are presented in Table 2–8.

For the data in Table 2–8, Table 2–9 presents the conventional language used to describe parts of a crosstab table. The numbers in cells represent the frequency of joint occurrences (or simply "joint frequency") of categories of

TABLE 2–8   **Church Attendance in the Past Month by Gender among College Students, *n* = 440 (fictional data)**

	Givens		
	Gender (X)		
Church Attendance (Y)	*Men*	*Women*	*Total*
Attended	66	94	160
Did not attend	134	146	280
Total	200	240	440

the two variables. A joint occurrence is the combination of categories *for a single individual*. For example, say Charles attended church; then he is counted as part of the joint frequency of the "men-attended" cell, in which there are 66 subjects. The joint frequency of men who did not attend is 134; of women who attended, 94; and of women who did not attend, 146. The sums in the table margins are called marginal totals. The column total for men tells us that altogether there are 200 men in the sample; similarly, there are 240 women. The row totals for attended and did not attend are 160 and 280, respectively. The grand total is the sample size (*n*), which is presented in the bottom right corner. Note that both column and row totals add to the grand total.

TABLE 2–9   **Crosstab Table Language: Church Attendance in the Past Month by Gender among College Students, *n* = 440**

Church Attendance (Y)	**Gender (X)**		*Totals*
	Men	*Women*	
Attended	**66**	**94**	160
		Cells (Contain Joint Frequencies)	Row (Marginal) Totals
Did not attend	**134**	**146**	280
Total	200	240	440
	Column (Marginal) Totals		Grand Total (*n*)

If there is a relationship between gender and church attendance, one or the other gender has a much higher frequency of church attendance. The raw numbers in the table can be confusing, however, because there are more women than men in the sample. We must ask, Out of how many? Thus, we use marginal totals to compute *percentages* of men and women who attended church:

$$p \text{ [of men attending church in past month]} = \frac{\text{\# men attending}}{\text{total \# of men}} = \frac{66}{200} = .3300$$

$$\% \text{ [of men attending church in past month]} = (p)(100) = (.3300)(100) = 33.00\%$$

Similarly, the percentage of women attending church in the past month is 94/240 (100) = 39.17 percent. After calculating these percentages, we clearly see that a higher percentage of women attended church in the past month. These percentages, incidentally, are called column percentages because they are based on column marginal totals. That is, a **column percentage** is *a cell's frequency as a percentage of the column marginal total*. Similarly, a **row percentage** is *a cell's frequency as a percentage of the row marginal total*. For example, the row percentage of church attenders who are men is 66/160 (100) = 41.25 percent. These simple crosstab tables provide important descriptive statistics and help determine whether a relationship exists between two nominal/ordinal variables.

Calculating Column and Row Percentages of Cells in a Crosstab Table

$$\text{Column \% [of joint occurrence]} = \frac{\text{\# in a cell}}{\text{total \# in column}} (100)$$

$$\text{Row \% [of joint occurrence]} = \frac{\text{\# in a cell}}{\text{total \# in row}} (100)$$

Coding and Counting Interval/Ratio Data

Variables with interval/ratio levels of measurement are distinguished from nominal/ordinal variables by their numerical qualities, especially their set units of measure, such as miles, kilometers, inches, seconds, and pounds. Such "quantitative" variables allow us to picture a ruler and think linearly, in terms of distance between points on a straight line. Moreover, we can make very precise measurements, with the level of precision being determined by practical circumstances. For example, is it practical to measure distance to school to the nearest tenth of a mile or the nearest hundredth of an inch? Precision also is confined by the limitations of measuring instruments. For instance, the measurement of distance in hundredths of an inch came only after the microscope was invented. With interval/ratio variables, the degree of precision is specified by how far we round numbers.

Rounding Interval/Ratio Observations

An observation of an interval/ratio variable may not give us the true score because its measurement often can be made endlessly more precise. For example, we can measure distances to the nearest kilometer, meter, centimeter, and so on. Therefore, we round interval/ratio scores to some specified, chosen degree of precision. In doing so, we acknowledge that the recorded code for the score has some measurement error in it. **Rounding error** is *the difference between the true or perfect score (which we may never know) and our rounded, observed score.* Rounding error depends on what *decimal place we choose as our level of precision—our rounding unit.* (If necessary, review decimal place locations in Appendix A.) If we decide to measure time to the nearest hundredth of a second, such as in Olympic track events, then our rounding unit is the hundredths place.

The procedure for rounding a score of an interval/ratio variable is as follows:

1. Specify the rounding unit according to its decimal place.
2. Observe the number *to the right* of the rounding unit and follow these rules.
   A. If it is 0, 1, 2, 3 or 4, round down.
   B. If it is 6, 7, 8, or 9, round up.
   C. If it is 5, look at the next decimal place to the right, and, if the number in it is 5 or greater, round up. If there is no number in this next decimal place, round to an even number.

Think of rounding as moving to the nearest point on a line. For instance, if we are rounding to *the nearest integer* (the ones place), we are simply moving to the nearest integer.

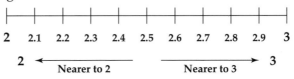

Here, for example, 2.1, 2.2, 2.3, and 2.4 are rounded down to 2 simply because they are closer to 2 than to 3. Additional examples are provided in Appendix A.

The Real Limits of Rounded Scores

Once we are presented with rounded scores, the numbers *in the rounding unit's decimal place* must be recognized as estimates. A score's true value could be any of the scores that are rounded to get the recorded score. Suppose, for example, we measure Jonathan's height to the nearest inch and record 69 inches. Several hours later, with Jonathan absent, Alan asks us how tall Jonathan is. We look at our data spreadsheet and see a code of 69 inches. At this instant, all we can say is that Jonathan's true height is somewhere between 68½ and 69½ inches, or 69 plus or minus one-half inch. This *range of possible true values of an (already) rounded score* is called the **true limits** or **real limits** of the score.

The real limits of a rounded score specify the range of numbers that could have been rounded to get the recorded score. In this sense, computing the real limits is the reverse of rounding. For example, suppose we score how long it takes each of 150 students to complete a chemistry lab project and round to the nearest hour. Suppose also that 56 of these students receive a score of two hours. Some of them took a little less than two hours, and some took a little more. Precisely, a student scoring two hours could have taken as little as 90 minutes (1½ hours), the *lower real limit*, or as much as 150 minutes (2½ hours), the *upper real limit*. A score of two hours *really* means between 1½ and 2½ hours, and so we call this range of times the real limits.

Lower real limit		Upper real limit
of two hours		of two hours
1½ hours ←	—— 2 hours ——	→ 2½ hours
(90 minutes)	(120 minutes)	(150 minutes)

We calculate real limits by moving a half rounding unit in each direction, using the following procedure:

Calculating Real Limits of an Interval/Ratio Score

1. Focus on the "rounding unit," the decimal place to which the score was rounded. Divide this rounding unit by 2. (Caution: Do not divide the number in the rounding unit's decimal place by 2.)
2. Subtract the result of (1) from the observed rounded score to get the lower real limit.
3. Add the result of (1) to the observed rounded score to get the upper real limit.

For example, for the 56 students who scored two hours on the chemistry lab project, we rounded to the nearest hour (the ones place). We divide *this rounding unit of one hour* by two to get one-half hour. Then we subtract this result from the observed rounded score of two hours to get the lower real limit (1½ hours) and add it to the observed score of two hours to get the upper real limit (2½ hours). It is unlikely that even one of these 56 students took exactly two hours to complete the project; two hours is a rounded estimate. We can rest assured, however, that each of the 56 finished somewhere between 1½ and 2½ hours. Our degree of precision is the rounding unit of one hour.

The principles of inclusiveness and exclusiveness also apply to interval/ratio variables. For a variable such as age, sticking to the principle of inclusiveness would appear straightforward; we simply record "age at last birthday." To ensure inclusiveness, however, a survey question should include the responses "refused" and "don't know." Exclusiveness is straightforward as long as all measurements are made the same way, in this case, age to the last birthday. If a respondent says she or he is 26 years old, then record 26, not 27 or 25.

Proportional and Percentage Frequency Distributions for Interval/Ratio Variables

Proportional and percentage frequency distributions for interval/ratio variables are calculated the same way as they are for nominal/ordinal variables except that in place of categories we have scores. For instance, if Smithville University has 10,000 students and 3,000 are 19 years old, the proportional and percentage frequencies for the score of 19 years is

$$p \text{ [of 19 year olds at Smithville University]} = \frac{f \text{ of 19 year olds}}{n} = \frac{3,000}{10,000} = .3000$$

$$\% \text{ [of 19 year olds at Smithville University]} = (p)(100) = 30.00\%$$

If these calculations are made for all ages, the results are presented as the percentage frequency distribution of the variable *age* for the population of Smithville University students.

Cumulative Percentage Frequency Distributions

Table 2–10 presents the frequency, percentage frequency, and cumulative percentage frequency distributions of the education levels of 20 caregivers—relatives who accompany Alzheimer patients to a clinic (Clair, Ritchey, and Allman 1993). These three pieces of information are standard parts of computer output because together they generate quick answers to a series of questions. Obviously, the raw score frequency (f) provides an answer for how many subjects received a specific score and the percentage frequency standardizes the frequency for sample size. The additional piece of information in Table 2–10, the cumulative percentage frequency, is a valuable way to view the frequency of scores in a distribution up to and including a score of interest. This is the **cumulative percentage frequency,** *the percentage frequency of a score plus that of all the scores preceding it in the distribution.* For example, for the caregivers in Table 2–10, what percentage has an education up to and including the high-school level? To obtain the cumulative percentage frequencies we list scores from lowest to highest and calculate the percentage frequency of each score. Then

TABLE 2–10   **Illustration of a Cumulative Percentage Frequency Distribution: Years of Formal Education among Elderly Caregivers of Alzheimer Patients**

Givens		Calculations	
Years of Formal Education (X)	*Frequency (f)*	*Percentage Frequency*	*Cumulative Percentage (f)*
5	1	5%	5%
6	1	5	10
7	1	5	15
9	2	10	25
10	1	5	30
11	1	5	35
12	10	50	85
14	2	10	95
16	1	5	100
Total	20	100%	100%

we add the percentage frequencies of a target score and all lesser scores. In Table 2–10, 85 percent had 12 years of schooling or less. By subtracting this cumulative percentage frequency from 100 percent, we can promptly see that only 15 percent of the sample went beyond high school.

Percentiles and Quartiles

We often visualize a distribution of scores as being broken or "fractured" into groups above and below a score or into groups with equal percentages of cases. Cumulative frequency distributions provide the tool for identifying **fractiles,** *scores that separate a fraction of a distribution's cases.* Percentile ranks (or, simply, percentiles) are one common fractile. *Among the cases in a score distribution,* a **percentile rank** is *the percentage of cases that fall at or below a specified value of X.* For example, from the cumulative percentage frequencies in Table 2–10, we see that a caregiver with 14 years of education has a level of education equal to or exceeding 95 percent of the sample, a percentile rank of 95. Percentiles often are used in education circles as a way to rank grades or test scores. For instance, on a college admissions test a student who scores at the 90th percentile or better may qualify for admission to an exclusive college.

Quartiles are *fractiles that identify the score values that break a distribution into four equally sized groups (i.e., 25 percent of the cases in each group).* When a distribution has a large range of scores, quartiles are easily obtainable from cumulative percentage frequency distributions. The first quartile, Q_1, is the 25th percentile; the second, Q_2, is the 50th percentile; and the third, Q_3, is the 75th percentile. Computer statistical software typically is programmed to identify quartiles and other fractiles, such as deciles, which break a distribution into 10 equally sized groups.

Table 2–11 presents the distribution of grades on a midterm exam (X) and illustrates the utility of quartiles. In this class of 20 students, the lowest 25 percent (or the five lowest grades) are from $X = 69$ and below, the next quarter of students are from $X = 72$ to 84, the third quarter are from $X = 85$ to 91, and the highest quarter are from $X = 93$ and above. We can also see that one-fourth of the students scored 69 or below, failing to make a C; one-half scored above 84, three-fourths scored 91 or below, half scored between 72 and 91, and so on. As we shall see in Chapter 3, a graph called a boxplot uses quartiles to reveal much about the way a distribution of scores is shaped.

Fractiles

Scores that separate a fraction of a distribution's cases.

Percentile Rank

Among the cases in a score distribution, the percentage of cases that fall at or below a specified value of X.

Quartiles

Fractiles that identify the score values that break a distribution into four equally sized groups.

Grouping Interval/Ratio Data

Sometimes, for clarity of presentation in a table or graph, interval/ratio distributions are grouped or "collapsed" into a smaller number of ordinal categories. For example, in a study of adults in the United States, the variable age will vary from 20 to about 100, providing 80 scores. It is confusing to present a table listing the frequency and percentage frequency of all 80 ages. For clarity, we combine ages into 10-year categories, as in Table 2–12.

There is an important thing to note about grouping interval/ratio data. When we group data, we throw away detail, which results in *grouping error*. For instance, Table 2–12 shows that there were 106 respondents between 40 and 49 years of age. But were most of them closer to 40 or to 49? We have no way of knowing by observing the grouped scores. If the ungrouped data are available, we can use them to obtain more precise computations of averages. In general, any time we move from a "higher" level of measurement to a

---

TABLE 2–11   Quartiles of a Distribution of Midterm Exam Grades

	Givens		Calculations		
	Exam Grade (X)	f	Percentage f	Cumulative Percentage f	Location of Quartiles (Q)
	31	1	5.0%	5.0%	
	58	1	5.0	10.0	
	63	1	5.0	15.0	
	68	1	5.0	20.0	
$Q_1 \longrightarrow$	69	1	5.0	25.0	$\longleftarrow$ Q_1 = 25th percentile
	72	1	5.0	30.0	
	76	1	5.0	35.0	
	77	1	5.0	40.0	
	82	1	5.0	45.0	
$Q_2 \longrightarrow$	84	1	5.0	50.0	$\longleftarrow$ Q_2 = 50th percentile
	85	1	5.0	55.0	
	86	2	10.0	65.0	
	88	1	5.0	70.0	
$Q_3 \longrightarrow$	91	1	5.0	75.0	$\longleftarrow$ Q_3 = 75th percentile
	93	2	10.0	85.0	
	94	1	5.0	90.0	
	95	1	5.0	95.0	
	97	1	5.0	100.0%	
	Total	20	100.0%		

TABLE 2–12   The Ratio Variable Age Grouped into 10-Year Ordinal Categories

Givens			Calculations
Ordinal Code	Age Group	f	Percent
1	20–29	47	10.49%
2	30–39	68	15.18
3	40–49	106	23.66
4	50–59	96	21.43
5	60–69	53	11.83
6	70–79	45	10.04
7	80–89	24	5.36
8	90 and over	9	2.01
	Total	448	100.00%

"lower" level (i.e., from ratio to interval, from interval to ordinal, or from ordinal to nominal), we lose information and this limits what can be done mathematically.

Nonetheless, in reading the work of others, we may be presented grouped data without the accompanying statistics. In these situations, attempt to contact the author for descriptive statistics. If this is not possible, then averages and other statistics can be computed from the grouped data, but these statistics will include grouping error. See Freund and Simon (1991: 70) for a discussion of computing statistics with grouped data.

☹   STATISTICAL FOLLIES AND FALLACIES   ☹

Failing to Reduce Both Sampling and Measurement Error

To properly manage error we must minimize both sampling error and measurement error. Even if we have a representative sample and it is large, this by itself does not assure accurate results; we must also have good measurements. For example, in measuring income in a household survey, a failure to distinguish single- from dual-earner households cannot be made up for by increasing the sample size. No matter how large the sample, and thus how small the sampling error, our data on income are worthless. A common statistical fallacy is the belief that large sample size makes up for poor measurements.

By the same token, precise measurement will not make up for poor sample size or a nonrepresentative sample, either of which will result in a large sampling error. For example, suppose we wish to determine the average weight of men on campus and use a precise weight scale to obtain a small measurement error. Suppose, however, that we inadvertently obtain a nonrepresentative sample with a disproportionate share of large men. The precise measure of weight is compromised by the large sampling error, leading us to believe that the average weight of campus men is greater than it truly is. The study's results are worthless.

It is essential that both measurement and sampling errors be minimized in order to obtain correct, dependable conclusions. The relationships among sampling error, measurement error, and total study error are illustrated with the Pythagorean theorem in Figure 2–2. The Greek mathematician Pythagoras discovered that the squared length of a hypotenuse (C), the side of a right triangle opposite the right angle, is equal to the sum of the squares of the lengths of the other two sides (A and B); that is, $C^2 = A^2 + B^2$. This means that the hypotenuse is large if either A or B is large. Figure 2–2A shows that total error is small *only when both* measurement and sampling errors are small. Figure 2–2, B through D, shows how failure to minimize one or both types of error results in a large total error (Blalock 1979: 573–74).

FIGURE 2–2

The relationship of sampling and measurement errors to total error

A. Ideal relationship: Both sampling and measurement error are minimized, resulting in small total error.

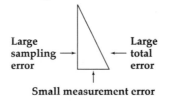

B. Unacceptable situation: Both sampling and measurement error are great, resulting in large total error.

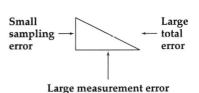

C. Unacceptable situation: Although measurement error is small, large sampling error results in large total error.

D. Unacceptable situation: Although sampling error is small, large measurement error results in large total error.

To a truly dedicated statistician, the statistical imagination and error control offer challenges that make the enterprises of science and statistics exciting journeys in well-designed vehicles. The statistical imagination requires having the intuition and clarity of thought to foresee the larger routes the journey may take. Error control and management involve keeping the vehicle safely on course so that the proper destination is reached. The journey is fun and, if successfully completed, highly rewarding.

Formulas in Chapter 2

Calculating the proportional frequency of a category or score:

$$p \text{ [of total sample } (n) \text{ in a category]} = \frac{f \text{ of category}}{n} = \frac{\text{\# in category}}{n}$$

Calculating the percentage frequency of a category or score:

$$\% \text{ [of total sample } (n) \text{ in a category]} = (p \text{ [of total sample } (n) \text{ in a category] }) (100)$$

Calculating column and row percentages of a cell in a crosstab table:

$$\text{Column } \% \text{ [of joint occurrence]} = \frac{\text{\# in a cell}}{\text{total \# in column}} (100)$$

$$\text{Row } \% \text{ [of joint occurrence]} = \frac{\text{\# in a cell}}{\text{total \# in row}} (100)$$

Calculating real limits of an interval/ratio score:

1. Focus on the "rounding unit," the decimal place to which the score was rounded. Divide this rounding unit by 2. (*Caution:* Do not divide the number in the rounding unit's decimal place by 2.)
2. Subtract the result of (1) from the observed rounded score to get the lower real limit.
3. Add the result of (1) to the observed rounded score to get the upper real limit.

Calculations for percentiles and quartiles:
Set up a spreadsheet with the following headings:

Score (X)	f	Percentage f	Cumulative Percentage f

The percentile of a score is its cumulative frequency. Quartiles are located at the 25th, 50th, and 75th percentiles.

Questions for Chapter 2

1. Discuss the difference between an observation and a statistic.
2. Discuss the difference between a statistic and a parameter.
3. What is a good way to prove that the statistics from a single sample are only estimates of a population's parameters?
4. Although brought up far removed from any minority neighborhood, Karen fancied herself an open-minded individual without prejudices. She became a social worker and got a job at the human resources department tracking minority children who were abused by substance-addicted parents. Karen developed overwhelming feelings of racism and is now convinced that minorities are morally inferior. In terms of sampling bias, what has happened to Karen?
5. A self-proclaimed expert on female sexuality reports that three-fourths of women state that they hate men. Talk show hosts challenge this statistic. The expert responds by noting that her sample of over 6,000 is the largest sample ever collected on the subject and that her results have a range of error of less than one-tenth of 1 percent. Her sampling method was a mail-in questionnaire inserted in a popular women's magazine. Name the ways in which her sample might be biased.
6. By way of a telephone survey, you want to assess the public's opinion on the mayor's proposal for raising taxes to build a new zoo. If you randomly selected every 100th number from the area telephone directory, would you obtain a representative sample? Explain in terms of sample bias.

7. Dr. Burnett tests a new antidepressant drug at a mental hospital. The drug is found to be quite effective. Will the drug necessarily have the same effectiveness for all persons suffering from depression? Explain in terms of sample bias.

8. Schizophrenia is a mental illness characterized by delusions and a general loss of touch with reality. Would counting the number of times a person lashes out at family members be a valid measure of schizophrenia? Explain.

9. Religiosity is a measurement of how religious a person is. On his questionnaire, Tom attempts to measure it by asking respondents how often they attend church services. Would this be a valid and reliable measure? Explain.

10. Suppose we are measuring weight among a sample of body builders and record Sam the Ham's weight as 246 pounds. He actually weighs between $245\frac{1}{2}$ and $246\frac{1}{2}$ pounds, this range of weights being the _____ and _____ limits of a score of 246 pounds.

11. Holly and Cheryl both conducted studies of social science majors at their colleges, asking them how many expected to be employed in industry after graduation. Holly, with a sample of 650, got an estimate of 31 percent. Cheryl, with a sample of 45, got an estimate of 23 percent. Which estimate can we place more "faith" in, and why? In terms of controlling sampling error, what else do we need to know about Holly's and Cheryl's samples? Why?

12. Bob bought firewood for his 36-inch-wide fireplace. To make sure the pieces would fit, he took a two-foot-long stick with him and made sure each piece of wood was roughly within six inches of the length of the stick. Shara designs microcomputer circuits. Her measurement instrument measures to the nearest tenth of an inch, but this instrument is less precise than Bob's stick. Explain.

13. Brian surveyed 5,000 respondents for his health survey. His operational definition of the level of health is "physician visits," the number of times a respondent went to a physician in the past year.

    a. Would this be a valid and reliable measure for the level of health? Explain.
    b. Would it be wise of him to boast of his small sampling error? Explain.

Exercises for Chapter 2

1. Indicate the level of measurement of the following variables.

Variable Number and Name	Operational Definition and Coding (how the variable is measured and scored)	Level of Measurement
a. GPA	Grade point average: the number of academic quality points earned divided by the number of earned credit hours	
b. HEIGHT	Physical height in inches	
c. CPUNISH	10-item attitude scale on support for the death penalty with summary scores ranging from 0 to 40	
d. AUTOTAG	Automobile license plate number: 7-digit number with county identifiers	
e. LABORSTA	Labor status: 1 = unskilled, 2 = semiskilled, 3 = skilled	
f. CITYPOP	Population within the city limits	
g. CARMAKE	Make of automobile: Ford, Buick, Toyota, etc.	

2. Indicate the level of measurement of the following variables.

Variable Number and Name	Operational Definition and Coding (how the variable is measured and scored)	Level of Measurement
a. WEIGHT	Physical weight in pounds	
b. DENSITY	Population (number of people residing in a defined area) per square mile of area	
c. IMRATE	Infant mortality rate: number of deaths in the first year of life per 1,000 births	
d. STUDENT	Student status: 1 = undergraduate, 2 = graduate, 3 = special	
e. ESTEEM	Self-assessment of self esteem: 15-item summary scale with scores ranging from 0 to 60	
f. JOBSAT	Satisfaction with job: 0 = very dissatisfied, 1 = dissatisfied, 2 = satisfied, 3 = very satisfied	
g. LIFEEXP	Life expectancy: average number of years newborns may expect to live (usually sex- and age-adjusted)	

3. In a study of caregivers of elderly family members, 293 women are interviewed concerning the stresses of caregiving and maintaining employment at the same time. Identify the levels of measurement of each of the following variables from the study:

Caregiver Variables	Care Recipient Variables
a. Distance between home and work	d. Gender
b. Age	e. Weight
c. Occupation	f. Severity of condition

4. In a study of caregivers of disabled children, 141 women are interviewed concerning the stresses of caregiving. Identify the levels of measurement of each of the following variables from the study:

Caregiver Variables	Child Variables
a. Perceived quality of care provided (excellent, good, fair, poor)	c. Medical diagnosis or condition
	d. Can he or she bathe self?
b. Income	e. Body temperature

5. Imagine that caregivers are asked the following items on a questionnaire. With the provided response categories, does each variable follow the principles of both inclusiveness and exclusiveness? If not, how can they be improved to be in accordance with these principles?

a. Do you have a religious preference? If so, what is it? (Please check one space.)

_____ Protestant   _____ Catholic   _____ Jewish
_____ Baptist   _____ None

b. What is your marital status? (Please check one space.)

_____ Single   _____ Married

c. Please check the category that most closely fits your total annual family income from all sources.

_____ $0–10,000   _____ $41,000–50,000
_____ $11,000–20,000   _____ $50,000 and above.
_____ $21,000–30,000

d. Are you currently employed outside the home? (Please check one space.)

_____ Full-time   _____ Part-time   _____ Unemployed
_____ Employed

6. Sibckey et al. (1995) studied empathetic concern as a motivation for helping behaviors. With the provided response categories, does each variable follow the principles of both inclusiveness and exclusiveness? If not, how can they be improved to be in accordance with these principles?

    a. Were you motivated to help by (check one):

    _____ Warmth   _____ Compassion   _____ Sympathy

    b. Are you:

    _____ Over 25 years of age   _____ Under 25

    c. How many times would you be willing to help the same person?

    _____ 0–4   _____ 6–10   _____ 11–15   _____ None

7. Round the following numbers to the stipulated rounding unit:

    a. 28.349 to nearest tenth
    b. 31.666 to nearest hundredth
    c. 587 to nearest hundred
    d. 25.6388 to nearest thousandth
    e. 25.6388 to nearest hundredth
    f. 25.6388 to nearest tenth
    g. 25.6388 to nearest ten

8. Round the following numbers to the stipulated rounding unit:

    a. 5.456 to nearest tenth
    b. 5.456 to nearest hundredth
    c. 20.821 to nearest hundredth
    d. 381 to nearest hundred
    e. 467,988 to nearest thousand
    f. 467,988 to nearest hundred thousand
    g. .00051 to nearest thousandth

9. Specify the real limits of the following rounded numbers:

    a. 4.0 inches
    b. 4 inches
    c. Age 5 rounded to last birthday
    d. Age 5 rounded to nearest birthday
    e. 3,300 rounded to nearest hundred
    f. 3,360 rounded to nearest 10
    g. .0030
    h. .068

10. Specify the real limits of the following rounded numbers:

    a. 5.00 kilograms
    b. 5 kilograms
    c. Age 9 rounded to last birthday
    d. Age 9 rounded to nearest birthday
    e. 71,000 rounded to nearest hundred
    f. 9,680 rounded to nearest ten
    g. .01605
    h. .248

11. The following is the distribution of family caregivers' relationships to Alzheimer patients. Calculate the ratio of female to male caregivers.

Family Caregiver's Relationship to Patient	f
Wife	114
Husband	17
Daughter	37
Son	4
Sister	8
Brother	1
Mother	2
Daughter-in-law	13
Other female relative	24
Other male relative	2

12. The following is the distribution of workers by position title in a communications firm (fictional data). Calculate the ratio of other employees to managers.

Position in Firm	f
Management positions	
President	1
Chief executive officer	1
Vice president	3
Assistant vice president	8
Administrative assistant	8
Chief of floor staff	12
Other positions	
Secretary	16
Sales associate	42
Office clerk	18
Technical/professional	14
Housekeeping	3

13. The following are data on the number of vehicles registered for a random sample of 20 households in Madison County.

   a. Compile the data into a frequency distribution table with columns for the frequency, the proportional frequency, the percentage frequency and the cumulative percentage frequency. (No need to show formulas.)

   b. If a household has three registered vehicles, what is that household's percentile rank? Interpret your answer.

   2, 1, 2, 4, 2, 3, 4, 2, 1, 4, 2, 1, 0, 3, 2, 4, 3, 4, 2, 2

14. Pearson et al. (1997) showed that when a grandmother lives with a family, she is likely to become involved in parenting activities. Suppose the

following data represent the number of parenting commands given to 25 children by their grandmothers.

   a. Compile the data into a frequency distribution table with columns for the frequency, the proportional frequency, the percentage frequency, and the cumulative percentage frequency. (No need to show formulas.)
   b. If a grandmother gave two commands, what is her percentile rank? Interpret your answer.

5, 4, 3, 3, 6, 5, 3, 2, 4, 7, 5, 6, 2, 3, 4, 8, 7, 5, 6, 4, 2, 1, 5, 7, 3.

15. A random sample of 1,888 public health professionals from four countries was surveyed on how important they felt it was for the European Community to formulate and oversee a European national health policy. The results are in the following crosstab table.

   a. Overall, what percentage of respondents consider a health policy to be very important?
   b. What percentage consider a health policy to be very unimportant?
   c. Complete the table by inserting column percentages. Show the formula for and calculation of one entry.
   d. Comment on any result that stands out.

Response	Belgium (col.%)	France (col.%)	Germany (col.%)	Netherlands (col.%)
Very important	88	49	234	194
Important	226	41	375	355
Unimportant	16	51	53	56
Very unimportant	3	2	3	7
Don't know	47	13	21	54

16. A random sample of 641 first-year college students is studied to determine ways in which economic background is an advantage for succeeding in college. The following crosstab table presents social class ranking by ownership of a personal computer (fictional data).

   a. Overall, what percentage of respondents own a personal computer?
   b. Complete the table by inserting row percentages. Show the formula for and calculation of one entry.
   c. Comment on any result that stands out.

| | Has Own Personal Computer | |
Social Class Level	No (row %)	Yes (row %)
Lower (poverty)	62	2
Working	79	33
Lower middle	83	148
Upper middle	36	142
Upper	1	55

17. As a quality control manager of a new ice cream parlor chain, you visit the two local stores and randomly record the ice cream flavor selections of every fifth customer by checking (✓) the following list.

   a. Compile the data into a frequency distribution table with columns for the frequency, the proportional frequency, and the percentage frequency. (No need to show formulas.)

   b. Would it make sense to include the cumulative frequency? If not, why not?

Vanilla	✓✓✓✓✓✓✓✓✓✓✓✓✓✓✓✓✓✓
Chocolate	✓✓✓✓✓✓✓✓✓✓✓✓✓
Strawberry	✓✓✓✓✓✓✓✓
Cookies and cream	✓✓✓✓✓✓✓✓
Other	✓✓✓✓✓✓✓✓✓✓✓✓✓✓✓✓✓

18. A polling official at a voting place for a primary election is tabulating political party participation. As voters request their ballots, she keeps a tab of which party's ballot they requested by checking (✓) a party name list.

   a. Compile her data into a frequency distribution table with columns for the frequency, the proportional frequency, and the percentage frequency. (No need to show formulas.)

   b. Would it make sense to include the cumulative frequency? If not, why not?

Democratic party	✓✓✓✓✓✓✓✓✓✓✓✓✓✓✓✓✓✓✓✓✓✓✓✓
Republican party	✓✓✓✓✓✓✓✓✓✓✓✓✓✓✓✓✓✓✓✓✓
New Independent party	✓✓✓✓✓✓

19. The following data records provide names of subjects and an indication of whether they have seen an eye doctor in the past year. Compile the data into a crosstab table and answer the questions that follow (show formulas).

   a. What percentage of the subjects are men?

   b. What percentage of the subjects saw an eye doctor in the past year?

      c. What percentage of men saw an eye doctor in the past year?

      d. What percentage of women saw an eye doctor in the past year?

David—Yes	Pedro—No	Christine—No	Maria—Yes
Elizabeth—No	Anthony—No	Sean—Yes	Manuel—No
Mike—No	Samuel—Yes	Arthur—No	Cynthia—No
Eudora—Yes	Leroy—No	Bernadette—Yes	Vanessa—Yes
Henry—No	Paula—Yes	Ernest—No	Sabrina—No
Gary—Yes	Helen—No	Mark—Yes	Kevin—No
Barbara—No	Sonya—Yes	Robert—No	Cathy—Yes
Andrea—No	Andrew—Yes	Nancy—No	Laura—Yes
Donald—Yes	Carolyn—No	Rebecca—Yes	Renee—No
Kimberly—No	Ginger—Yes	Debra—No	Ralph—No

20. Smetana (1989) notes that minor but persistent conflict between American adolescents and their parents is a normal part of growing up. Suppose the following data are from a survey of adolescents asking them if they had a conflict with a parent in the previous 48 hours. Compile the data into a crosstab table and answer the questions that follow (show formulas).

    a. What percentage of the respondents are females?

    b. What percentage of respondents had a conflict with parents?

    c. What percentage of males had a conflict with parents?

    d. What percentage of females had a conflict with parents?

Peggy—Yes	Jason—Yes	Christie—No	Mark—Yes
Jeremy—Yes	Patsy—Yes	James—Yes	Andy—No
Anita—No	Kyle—Yes	Julie—Yes	David—No
Linda—Yes	Alex—No	Donna—No	Mary—Yes
Beth—Yes	Wes—No	Janice—No	Rhonda—Yes

21. For one of your moderate-size classes other than this statistics class, compile a data spreadsheet with the variables gender, race, and predominant color of shirt, blouse, or sweater. Compile frequency and percentage frequency distributions for these variables. Construct a crosstab table of gender by race.

22. For one of your moderate-size classes other than this statistics class, compile a data spreadsheet with the variables gender, race, and proximity to front of room (front or back half of rows). Compile frequency and percentage frequency distributions for these variables. Construct a crosstab table of gender by proximity to front of room.

Optional Computer Applications for Chapter 2

If your class uses the optional computer applications that accompany this text, open the Chapter 2 exercises on the *Computer Applications for The Statistical Imagination* compact disk. The exercises involve (1) creating and saving data (*.SAV) files using *SPSS for Windows*, (2) producing frequency distributions, quartiles, and percentiles, and (3) managing and saving output files.

Quality control of data coding and entry is very important for minimizing mistakes. To meet scientific and ethical standards, a researcher must be able to look colleagues in the eye and honestly assure them that the data set has no random mistakes in it. Aside from ethics, poor data entry wastes time and energy in the later stages of analysis. An ethical but careless researcher may spend months analyzing a data set and then find incorrect data entries. The discovery of a single incorrect entry requires a complete reanalysis of data. Thus, we must diligently check the accuracy of a data set before analysis begins.

Here are some guidelines for the detection of coding and entry mistakes for self-coded data or existing data files.

Quality Control Guidelines for Data Entry

1. Make sure entered code values are consistent with the codebook and measurement instruments (such as questionnaires).
2. If your typing skills or eyesight is poor, have an assistant read and double-check data entries. Alternatively, use an especially designed data-entry program, such as *dBase©*. *SPSS* will readily accept *dBase* files as well as data files from spreadsheets such as *Lotus 1-2-3©*, *Excel©*, *Quattro Pro©* and *Multiplan©*.
3. Double-check codes on a printout which lists all variables and their codes.
4. Use frequency distribution printouts to check for stray codes (i.e., codes that should not be present in the data).

Specific quality control procedures are described in the Chapter 2 computer application exercises on the *Computer Applications for the Statistical Imagination* compact disk.

CHARTS AND GRAPHS: A PICTURE SAYS A THOUSAND WORDS

Introduction: Pictorial Presentation of Data

To convey a sense of proportion, we describe the score distribution of a variable numerically with percentage frequencies as we did in Chapter 2. Numerical distributions, however, make sense only if a person tends to think proportionately. Therefore, we often substitute graphs and "pictorial" drawings such as pie charts to encourage proportional thinking directly. Graphs provide strong support for the maxim "A picture says a thousand words." When some of those words are numerical, a picture clarifies a thousand words and calculations.

With today's user-friendly software, the mass media bombard us with graphs, pie charts, and pictographs (pictures of objects, stick figures, or shaded maps). Sometimes the software takes on a life of its own and draws a graph incorrectly. In terms of error control, it is important to know the mathematical computations behind graph construction and not rely solely on software programmers.

Graphical and pictorial designs are chosen on the basis of (1) the level of measurement of a variable, (2) the study objectives and points to be made, and (3) the targeted audience. For public audiences, colorful, uncluttered graphs work best, providing an overview of descriptive statistics such as percentages and averages. In contrast, professional audiences are accustomed to inferential statistics—those designed to explain and test hypotheses. Along with statistical tables, graphs may assist us in discerning the shapes of frequency distributions. Even descriptive graphs can alert an analyst to potential sources of error that may influence additional analysis.

Graphing Guidelines

Graphical presentations must follow some simple rules and guidelines which also apply to tables and report construction.

Graphing Guidelines

1. Choose the design on the basis of (*a*) the level of measurement of a variable, (*b*) the study objectives, and (*c*) the targeted audience.

2. Above all, a good graphical presentation should be clear and understandable. It should simplify, not complicate.

3. A graph or chart should be self-explanatory and convey information without reference to a text or speaker. Careful selection of titles, scale designations, captions, and other legend material accomplishes this objective. Submit each graph or table to the "lost in the parking lot" test. Ask: If this graph were dropped in the parking lot, could a complete stranger pick it up and interpret it?

Graphing Guidelines continued

Graphing Guidelines concluded

4. Before deciding on the type of pictorial presentation (e.g., pie chart versus bar chart), produce rough drafts of several options. Computer software makes this relatively easy. To broaden the choices, seek advice and peruse other materials, such as organizational reports.
5. Adhere to the principles of inclusiveness and exclusiveness (Chapter 2). Footnote any exceptions.
6. If the data are not your own, indicate the source at the bottom of the table.

Graphing Nominal/Ordinal Data

Pie Charts

A simple style of presentation for nominal/ordinal data is the pie chart. A **pie chart** is *a circle that is dissected (or sliced) from its center point with each slice representing the proportional frequency of a category.* All of us have sliced pies, and sometimes we fail to get a fair share. When a researcher wants to provide a sense of proportion in regard to a nominal/ordinal variable, pie charts are especially useful. They convey fairness, relative size, or inequality among the categories. The relative size of a pie slice is a form of proportional thinking with which everyone is familiar.

Pie Chart

A circle that is dissected (or sliced) from its center point with each slice representing the proportional frequency of a category of a nominal/ordinal variable. It is especially useful for conveying a sense of fairness, relative size, or inequality among categories.

Figure 3–1 portrays the distribution of marital status in a sample of 161 homeless persons. The area within the entire circle represents 100 percent of the subjects in the sample. The area of a slice represents the percentage in a specific category. It is easy to see that over half the homeless respondents had never been married and that a substantial portion had divorced. The most striking revelation is the small piece dedicated to "married."

While a computer program readily produced the pie chart in Figure 3–1, to relate the pie to the frequency distribution of marital status, let us construct it by hand. The first step in producing any graph is to determine the variable's

FIGURE 3–1

Pie chart of marital status of homeless adults, n = 161

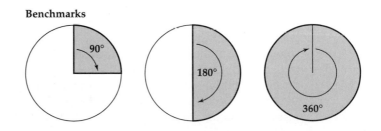

FIGURE 3–1

Pie chart of marital status of homeless adults, n = 161

frequency distribution. In addition, for pie charts we compute the proportional frequency and percentage frequency of each category. The proportional frequencies, together with knowledge about the dimensions of a circle, are used to compute the sizes of the slices.

Correct slicing of the pie depends on knowing that the angles that dissect a circle from its center are measured in degrees with a protractor (a half-moon-shaped circular ruler). Regardless of the size of a circle, its circumference is defined as having a total distance around of 360 degrees (°). A half circle is 180° around, or a proportion of .5 times 360 degrees. A quarter circle is 90° around, or one-fourth of 360 degrees. These benchmarks of a circle are illustrated in Figure 3–2. Any part of the pie can be sliced by multiplying the proportion in a category by 360 degrees.

Table 3–1 provides calculations for the pie chart shown in Figure 3–1. How is each category awarded its portion of the pie? A category's portion is the proportional frequency p times 360°, the total circumference of the pie. If .51 (51 percent) of the respondents had never married, they should "get" 51 percent of the pie—185° worth—or just over one-half. Once the 360 degrees are awarded for all categories, a protractor is used to cut the pie into correctly proportioned pieces. Percentages are placed on the pie chart for the sake of clarity. If the chart is presented to a public audience, we round to a whole percentage (i.e., the ones place).

FIGURE 3–2

Degrees of a circle for one-quarter circle, one-half circle, and full circle

Benchmarks

TABLE 3–1   **Computational Spreadsheet for Constructing a Pie Chart: The Distribution of Marital Status for a Sample of 161 Homeless Persons**

Givens		Calculations		
Marital Status	*f*	*p*	*(p) (360°)*	*%*
Never married	83	.5155	185°	51%
Divorced	43	.2671	96	27
Separated	22	.1366	49	14
Married	7	.0435	16	4
Widowed	3	.0186	7	2
No answer	3	.0186	7	2
Totals	161	.9999*	360°	100%

*Total did not add to 1.0000 because of rounding error.

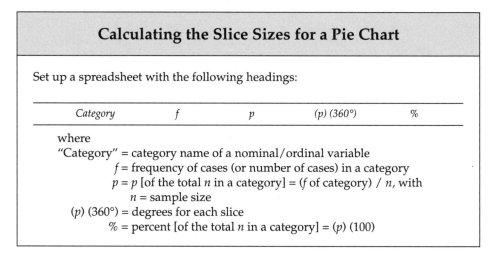

Calculating the Slice Sizes for a Pie Chart

Set up a spreadsheet with the following headings:

Category	*f*	*p*	*(p) (360°)*	*%*

where
"Category" = category name of a nominal/ordinal variable
   f = frequency of cases (or number of cases) in a category
   $p = p$ [of the total n in a category] = (f of category) / n, with
       n = sample size
$(p) (360°)$ = degrees for each slice
   $\%$ = percent [of the total n in a category] = $(p) (100)$

Note in Table 3–1 that the percentage in the "Never married" category is rounded down to 51 percent instead of up to 52 percent. Moreover, we award this category 185° instead of 186°. These adjustments for rounding error are necessary to keep the total degrees of the circle from exceeding 360, since a circle has a defined space of that amount. Adjusting the "Never married" category has the smallest effect on error compared with adjusting other categories.

Computer software packages (such as the *SPSS for Windows,* which is an option with this text) provide a wide range of pie chart styles. One or more slices can be brought out in relief or "exploded," and pairs of pie charts can be presented for comparison of groups or time periods.

Bar Charts

Another way to graph nominal/ordinal data is to use a bar chart. A **bar chart** is *a series of vertical or horizontal bars with the length of a bar representing the percentage frequency of a category of a nominal/ordinal variable.* Like a slice of a pie chart, the area of a bar—which is determined by its length—conveys a sense of the proportional frequency of a category. Bar charts are especially good at conveying competition among categories ([i.e., which category finishes with the greatest frequency (longest bar)]. Bar charts are constructed on two axes: one lying flat, or horizontal (the *abscissa*), and the other standing straight up, or vertical (the *ordinate*). In other words, the two lines are joined at a 90°, or "square," angle. The categories of a variable are situated on one axis, and markings for percentages are made on the other axis. We need only compute the percentage frequency of each category to construct a bar chart.

Bar Chart

A series of vertical or horizontal bars with the length of a bar representing the percentage frequency of a category of a nominal/ordinal variable.

Bar charts are especially useful for conveying a sense of competition among categories.

Calculating the Bar Heights for a Bar Chart

Set up a spreadsheet with the following headings:

Category	f	p	%

where

"Category" = category name of a nominal/ordinal variable

f = frequency of cases (or number of cases) in a category

$p = p$ [of the total n in a category] = (f of category) / n, with

n = sample size

% = percent [of the total n in a category] = (p) (100)

Figure 3–3 shows a bar chart of the percentage frequency distribution of employment among homeless adults in the week before an interview. The similarity of bar heights quickly conveys that almost as many homeless adults work as not.

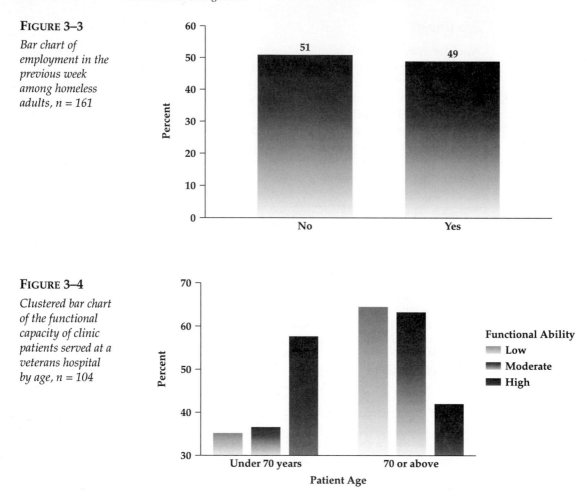

FIGURE 3–3

Bar chart of employment in the previous week among homeless adults, n = 161

FIGURE 3–4

Clustered bar chart of the functional capacity of clinic patients served at a veterans hospital by age, n = 104

Figure 3–4 shows a "clustered" bar chart, which is good for comparing two or more groups for a nominal/ordinal variable. This figure compares the functional ability of 104 clinic patients at a veterans hospital and reveals how low functional capacity is very characteristic of ill veterans over age 70.

Pictographs

Pictographs are *object-shaped figures that are arranged so that the number or size of objects represents the proportional frequency of a category.* Pictographs often are used in newspapers and magazines. Desktop publishing software provides a variety of pictographs, the choice of which depends on the topic.

Graphing Interval/Ratio Variables

Histograms

Again, the first step in producing any graph is to organize scores into a frequency distribution. The calculation spreadsheet in Table 3–2 presents the frequency distribution of the interval level variable Academic College Testing Service (ACT) test scores, a college admissions test. These fictional data consist of a sample of 110 college applicants, and f is the frequency of students for each ACT score. Our interest is in how the scores are clustered and how they are spread out. We can readily see that the ACT scores tend to cluster around 24 and vary from a minimum of 17 to a maximum of 32. By graphing the data, we get an even better sense of proportion about how ACT scores are distributed.

Figure 3–5 presents these ACT scores in a frequency histogram, a type of graph used with interval/ratio variables. A **frequency histogram** is *a 90-degree plot presenting the scores of an interval/ratio variable along the horizontal axis and the frequency of each score in a column parallel to the vertical axis.* A histogram is

TABLE 3–2   **Computational Spreadsheet for Constructing Histograms and Polygons: Frequency Distribution of ACT Scores for 110 College Applicants to State University, 1998 (fictional data)**

Givens		Calculations
ACT Score	*f*	*Real Limits of Score*
17	1	16.5–17.5
18	1	17.5–18.5
19	3	18.5–19.5
20	6	19.5–20.5
21	9	20.5–21.5
22	9	21.5–22.5
23	13	22.5–23.5
24	18	23.5–24.5
25	15	24.5–25.5
26	11	25.5–26.5
27	10	26.5–27.5
28	7	27.5–28.5
29	4	28.5–29.5
30	2	29.5–30.5
31	0	30.5–31.5
32	1	31.5–32.5
Total	110	

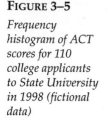

FIGURE 3–5

Frequency histogram of ACT scores for 110 college applicants to State University in 1998 (fictional data)

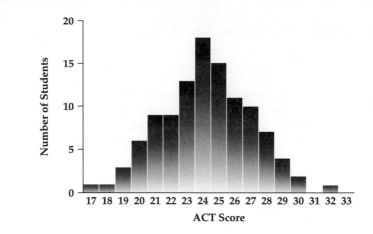

similar to a bar chart except that the columns of a histogram touch one another (unless a score has a frequency of zero cases, in which case there will be a column missing). The width of each column of the histogram is the same. The columns touching one another account for the real limits of each score. For example, the scores in Table 3–2 are rounded to the nearest integer; in other words, not everyone making, say, a 24 got exactly the same number of questions correct. With the columns widened to touch one another, the principal of inclusiveness is met. This histogram conveys the message that the most frequently occurring score is 24 and that the bulk of the applicants score between 20 and 28.

Frequency Histogram

A 90-degree plot presenting the scores of an interval/ratio variable along the horizontal axis and the frequency of each score in a column parallel to the vertical axis.

Calculations for Histograms

Set up a spreadsheet with the following headings:

Score	f	Real Limits of Score

where
Score = score of an interval/ratio variable
  f = frequency of cases (or number of cases) for a score
Real limits of score as calculated in Chapter 2.

Polygons and Line Graphs

Another graphing technique for interval/ratio variables is the frequency polygon or *line graph*. A **frequency polygon** is *a 90-degree plot with interval/ratio scores plotted on the horizontal axis and score frequencies depicted by the heights of dots located above scores and connected by straight lines.* The axes of a polygon are designed like those of a histogram, with the values of a variable on the horizontal axis and the frequencies plotted up the vertical axis. However, to establish the frequency of the variable at a particular score, we use dots in place of columns. While histograms convey volume and draw attention to the horizontal axis, polygons convey peakedness and draw attention to the vertical axis. Polygons also communicate a sense of trend or movement. For example, in Figure 3–6 the message is that as one moves up the range of ACT scores, there is a tendency for frequencies to increase up to a score of 24 and then to decline.

Frequency Polygon

A 90-degree plot with interval/ratio scores plotted on the horizontal axis and score frequencies depicted by the heights of dots located above scores and connected by straight lines.

Frequency polygons are especially useful for comparing two or more samples. For example, let us compare the distributions of ACT scores for applicants to both State and Crosstown universities. Suppose Crosstown has 204 applicants, while State has only 110. Since the sample sizes differ, we use a common denominator for the distributions of ACT scores for each school: the percentage frequencies. Table 3–3 provides the computations, and Figure 3–7 presents the two polygons. Once these two distributions are graphically depicted, their differences become quite clear. Applicants to both schools tend to score between 15 and 32, but Crosstown applicants are more likely to score below 22 while State University applicants tend to score above 22. The peaks convey a difference in central tendency or average, the topic of Chapter 4.

FIGURE 3–6

Frequency polygon of the distribution of ACT scores for 110 college applicants to State University in 1998 (fictional data)

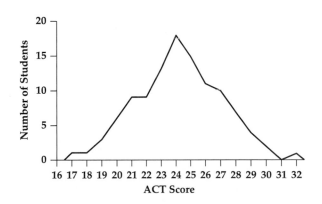

TABLE 3–3   **A Comparison of ACT Scores at State University and Crosstown University in 1998 (fictional data)**

	State University		Crosstown University	
ACT Score	f	Percent	f	Percent
16	0	0.0%	9	4.4%
17	1	0.9	11	5.4
18	1	0.9	14	6.9
19	3	2.7	18	8.8
20	6	5.4	27	13.2
21	9	8.2	34	16.7
22	9	8.2	22	10.8
23	13	11.8	17	8.3
24	18	16.4	12	5.9
25	15	13.6	11	5.4
26	11	10.0	9	4.4
27	10	9.1	7	3.4
28	7	6.4	4	2.0
29	4	3.6	3	1.5
30	2	1.8	4	2.0
31	0	0.0	2	1.0
32	1	0.9	0	0.0
Totals	110	99.9%*	204	100.1%*

*Total percentages do not add to 100 because of rounding error.

FIGURE 3–7

A comparison of the distributions of ACT scores for 110 applicants to State University and 204 applicants to Crosstown University in 1998 (fictional data)

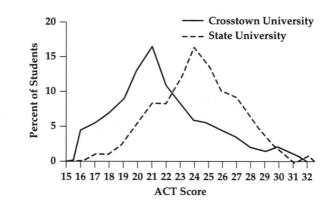

Crosstown applicants typically score around 21, and State University applicants score around 24.

Histograms with Grouped Data

As was noted in Chapter 2, for clarity of presentation in a table or graph, interval/ratio distributions sometimes are grouped or "collapsed" into a smaller

TABLE 3–4   **Computational Spreadsheet for Graphing the Interval/Ratio Variable *Age* Grouped into 10-Year Ordinal Categories**

Givens			Calculations			
Ordinal Code	Age Group	*f*	Real Limits of Group	Midpoint of Group	Percentage *f*	Cumulative Percentage *f*
1	20–29	47	19.5–29.5	24.5	10.49%	10.49%
2	30–39	68	29.5–39.5	34.5	15.18	25.67
3	40–49	106	39.5–49.5	44.5	23.66	49.33
4	50–59	96	49.5–59.5	54.5	21.43	70.76
5	60–69	53	59.5–69.5	64.5	11.83	82.59
6	70–79	45	69.5–79.5	74.5	10.04	92.63
7	80–89	24	79.5–89.5	84.5	5.36	97.99
8	90–99	9	89.5–99.5	94.5	2.01	100.00%
Total		448			100.00%	

number of ordinal categories. For example, the variable *age* might range from 1 to 100, and a 100-column histogram would clutter a single page. Thus, we collapse this interval/ratio variable into ordered age groups with a set interval of years in each group. In this process care must be taken to follow the principle of inclusiveness; in other words, no age should be left out. To accomplish this, we compute the real limits *of each group's interval of scores* so that the columns of a histogram will touch.

Table 3–4 (which uses fictional data) is a reproduction of a table from the previous chapter (Table 2–12) with the real limits of each interval of scores added. (Additional calculations in the table are addressed below.) The real limits of a group are all scores that fall in that group, keeping in mind that individual scores are rounded before being grouped. Thus, those in the 20- to 29-year group could be as young as 19.5 years—the lower real limit of the lowest score in the group—because that age would round to 20. Similarly, subjects in this group could be as old as 29.5—the upper real limit of the highest score in the group. The real limits *of each group* are computed by taking the lower real limit of the lowest score in a group and the upper real limit of the highest score in that group.

Figure 3–8 presents a histogram of this distribution of age groups.

Polygons with Grouped Data

To draw a polygon for grouped data we must identify points on the horizontal axis above which to situate dots. We use the midpoint of a group's interval of scores for this dot location because this minimizes grouping error. First, we determine the width of the interval of scores in a group. This is equal to the width of columns on a histogram: the distance from the lower real limit of the

FIGURE 3–8

Histogram of ages grouped into 10-year ordinal categories

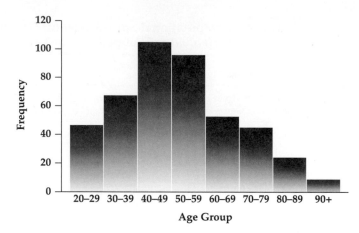

lowest score in the group to the upper real limit of the highest score in the group. Then we divide the interval width by 2 and add the resulting quotient to the lower real limit of the lowest score in the group. In other words, the **midpoint of a grouped data category** is *the point halfway between the upper and lower real limits of the interval of scores in the group*. This conveys the notion that the midpoint of an interval of scores is computed in the same way that one finds the midpoint of distance between two towns. If Larksville is 20 miles from Rocky City and we wish to drive to the midpoint between them, we drive 10 miles from Larksville toward Rocky City or 10 miles from Rocky City toward Larksville. Here is a shortcut, computational formula for locating the midpoint: Simply add the upper and lower real limits and divide by 2.

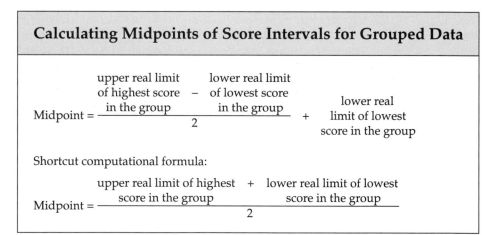

Calculating Midpoints of Score Intervals for Grouped Data

$$\text{Midpoint} = \frac{\begin{array}{c}\text{upper real limit} \\ \text{of highest score} \\ \text{in the group}\end{array} - \begin{array}{c}\text{lower real limit} \\ \text{of lowest score} \\ \text{in the group}\end{array}}{2} + \begin{array}{c}\text{lower real} \\ \text{limit of lowest} \\ \text{score in the group}\end{array}$$

Shortcut computational formula:

$$\text{Midpoint} = \frac{\begin{array}{c}\text{upper real limit of highest} \\ \text{score in the group}\end{array} + \begin{array}{c}\text{lower real limit of lowest} \\ \text{score in the group}\end{array}}{2}$$

Now let us see that the midpoint is a geographic center of an interval of scores. The age group 20 to 29 years has an interval width of 10 years and a midpoint of 24.5 years:

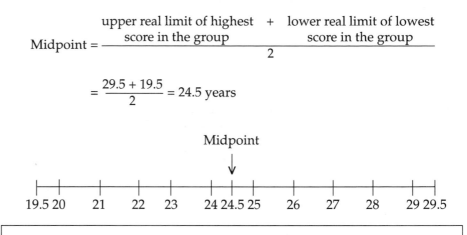

$$\text{Midpoint} = \frac{\text{upper real limit of highest score in the group} \quad + \quad \text{lower real limit of lowest score in the group}}{2}$$

$$= \frac{29.5 + 19.5}{2} = 24.5 \text{ years}$$

Midpoint of a Grouped Data Category

The point halfway between the upper and lower real limits of the interval of scores in the group.

To construct the polygon (not shown), we move along the horizontal axis to the midpoint of the group's interval of scores and place the dot above that point at the height of the frequency for that group. Specifically, we place the first dot above 24.5 years at a frequency of 47, the second dot above a score of 34.5 at a frequency of 68, and so on. The ends of the polygon tie to the horizontal axis at the lower real limit of all ages (i.e., 19.5 years) and the upper real limit of all ages (i.e., 99.5 years).

Graphing Cumulative Frequency Distributions

Ogives

Recall from Chapter 2 that a **cumulative percentage frequency** is *the percentage frequency of a score plus that of all scores preceding it in the distribution.* Cumulative percentage frequencies indicate what percentage of a sample's scores fall below a particular value of X. For example, on an examination we may be interested in what percentage of students scored 69 or below (i.e., failed to get a C). *A cumulative frequency polygon (or cumulative frequency line graph) is called an* **ogive.**

Ogive

A cumulative frequency polygon.

FIGURE 3–9

Ogive (cumulative percentage frequency polygon) of the age groups presented in Table 3–4

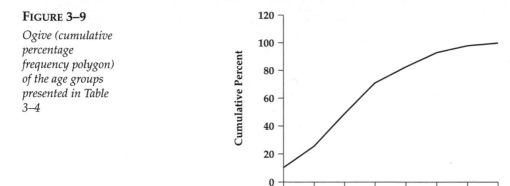

Figure 3–9 shows an ogive that uses the grouped data of ages in Table 3–4 and *SPSS for Windows* software. The graph gives us the cumulative percentage frequencies on the vertical axis, and these data are from the rightmost column of Table 3–4. Note, however, that for age on the horizontal axis, the locations of marks (called ticks) are not group midpoints. Instead, the ticks are the rounded scores of the lower real limits of age groups. This makes sense. If we want to know what percentage of ages fall below 40, we use the cumulative percentage frequency of age groups up to and including 39. We are asking what percentage is below 39.5 years, but we use 40 years on the graph for clarity. In Figure 3–9 we see that the graph begins to flatten at about 80 years, indicating that a small percentage of cases falls above this age.

Using Graphs with Inferential Statistics and Research Applications

Graphs are used primarily for descriptive purposes with public audiences. In scientific research and inferential statistics, however, we sometimes graph a variable to become familiar with its distribution and to prepare it for later analysis. To expedite this preparation phase, we computer-generate histograms and polygons (line graphs). In inferential statistics, these graphics are especially useful for detecting atypical scores in a distribution. For example, a graph depicting divorce rates in the 50 states reveals that Nevada, with its liberal divorce laws, is markedly different. Such an atypical case is called a **deviant score or outlier,** *a score that is markedly different from the others in the score distribution.* As we will learn later, outliers distort statistical calculations such as averages. If the distortions are great, it is necessary to discard or adjust these deviant scores. For example, in the case of divorce rates the appropriate procedure might be to discard the Nevada data. We inform the reader that it is an exceptional state that is worthy of a case study (individualized analysis) and stipulate that our conclusions apply only to the other 49 states. Another way to modify the distorting effects of outliers is to mathematically adjust extreme scores. One method involves taking the logarithm of the scores, a mathematical transformation that compresses scores into a smaller range. A second method is simply to reduce the value of the outlier to the next lowest or highest score, a procedure called truncating. A final caution: It is inappropriate to omit or adjust outliers simply because they do not fit the expected pattern. The researcher must clearly explain the theoretical and practical reasons for such adjustments. More will be said about outliers in later chapters.

Deviant Score or Outlier

A score that is markedly different from the others in the score distribution.

Boxplots

A graphical technique that is very useful for detecting outliers is a boxplot (or box-and-whiskers plot). A boxplot displays quartiles as well as the minimum and maximum scores in a distribution. It also identifies outliers (scores that are over 1.5 box lengths to one end of the distribution) and extreme scores (scores that are over three box lengths to one end of the distribution). Figure 3–10 presents a boxplot of the data from Table 2–11 in the previous chapter. The leftmost mark is an outlier, the grade of 31, with a 1 next to it indicating the case number of the outlier. The mark on the left "whisker" is the minimum score in the distribution aside from any outliers, a grade of 58. The mark on the end of the right whisker is the maximum score, a grade of 97. The ends of the box are the first and third quartiles, and the mark inside the box is the second quartile.

The boxplot in Figure 3–10 tells us as much as or more than the data table itself does. Focusing on Q_2 we can see that the grades are bunched toward the top of the score distribution; the upper half of the class scored above about 85

FIGURE 3–10

Boxplot of a distribution of midterm examination grades

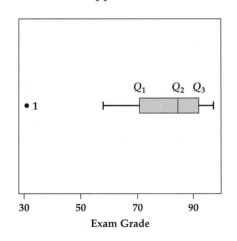

FIGURE 3–11

*Boxplots
comparing the ages
of male and female
physicians*

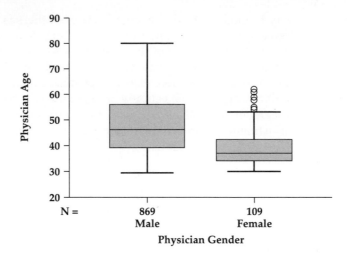

up to the maximum score of 97, a spread of only 12 exam points. Looking to the left of Q_2, we see that the bottom half of scores has a wide spread of about 30 points, discounting the single outlier. In other words, the boxplot conveys the information that the grades leaned toward the upper end. In general, the class did quite well on the examination.

While boxplots may be constructed by hand, they are best generated by computer. SPSS for Windows provides many options for boxplots, including comparisons of the spreads of scores for two categories. For example, Figure 3–11 compares the spread of the distributions of ages for male and female physicians. The plot quickly reveals that on the whole female physicians are markedly younger than males. There are so few females over age 55 that these cases appear as outliers.

☹   STATISTICAL FOLLIES AND FALLACIES   ☹

Graphical Distortion

Graphs and charts provide mental maps of large sets of data. The procedures for designing graphs are normative; that is, different people have different ideas about what is pleasing to the eye. In other words, pictorial presentation is part art.

Since the norms of the presentation of data are aesthetic as well as technical, often they are unclear. For example, how wide should the bars in a bar chart be? Should we paint the bars a variety of colors? The conventions that apply to these and similar questions are flexible and often follow fashion. Art inspires creativity and individuality.

When the rules are unclear, however, they are easy to break, intentionally or unintentionally. For example, with the assortment of computer graphics

FIGURE 3–12

Poster presented to Mortimer Mainstreet by his campaign staff to report the results of the most recent gubernatorial campaign poll

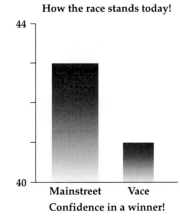

programs available today, users are often willing to leave the details of graphing to the unknown individual who designed the software. As a result, popular (as opposed to scientific) media assault us with rapidly conceived computer-generated graphs and charts. As you become astute in statistical thinking, you will begin to see that many if not most of these "quickies" are at best unreliable (i.e., open to multiple interpretations) and at worst misleading.

The following parable depicts a common graphical distortion. Fictional gubernatorial candidate Mortimer Mainstreet had a comfortable two-to-one margin in early electoral polls over the only serious contender, Harry Vace. For Mortimer, however, it has been downhill ever since. Rumor has it that he is about to scrap his campaign staff, whose members are beginning to fear that their dreams of ruling the state and their jobs are in peril.

The latest poll has come out, and it shows that Mortimer's lead has dwindled to 2 percentage points, 43 to 41 percent, with 16 percent undecided and a margin of error of plus or minus 3 percent. The race has become too close to call. In an attempt to avoid losing their jobs, the staff members inform Mortimer of the poll results with the poster above (Figure 3–12). (If Mortimer Mainstreet lets this get by, he does not deserve to be governor!) Can you identify all the things wrong with this chart?

Formulas in Chapter 3

Calculations for pie charts:
Set up a spreadsheet with the following headings:

Category	f	p	(p) (360°)	%

Calculations for bar charts:
>   Set up a spreadsheet with the following headings:

Category	f	p	%

Calculations for histograms and polygons:
>   Set up a spreadsheet with the following headings:

Score	f	Real Limits of Score	Midpoint

Calculations for histograms and polygons with grouped data:
>   Set up a spreadsheet with the following headings:

Score	f	Real Limits of Group	Midpoint of Group

Calculations for ogives and boxplots:
>   Set up a spreadsheet with the following headings:

Score	f	Percentage f	Cumulative Percentage f

For ogives, use real limits to locate heights of dots. For boxplots, identify maximum and minimum scores and quartiles.

Questions for Chapter 3

1. What are three things to consider in choosing a graphical style or design?
2. What is the foremost objective of graphing data?
3. What is the "parking lot" test?
4. Pie charts and bar charts are used with variables of what levels of measurement?
5. Histograms and polygons (line graphs) are used with variables of what levels of measurement?
6. Under what circumstances is a pie chart especially useful?
7. Under what circumstances is a bar chart especially useful?
8. Explain the relationship between rounded scores and the real limits of scores.
9. Mrs. Barker is on a bus with the 24 pupils in her fifth-grade class. She is chatting with the bus driver, Kevin Braughn. If you were to construct a frequency histogram of ages of the bus's occupants, how would it appear? What would be peculiar about Mrs. Barker's and Kevin's ages? What statistical term is used to describe these two scores?

Exercises for Chapter 3

1. In his budget proposal for the upcoming fiscal year, the governor of a Midwestern state indicates that the percentages of revenue from various sources are expected to be as follows (fictional data). Construct a pie chart.

Tax	Percent
Income	30%
Gasoline	12
Sales	21
Other taxes and fees	24
Other sources	13

2. As an employee of a home health care company, Charlotte is required to catalog the time spent on various tasks while at the homes of her elderly clients. The following is a typical eight-hour day (fictional data). Construct a pie chart depicting the percentage allocation of time spent on various tasks.

Task	Time (hours)
Cooking and feeding	1.6
Bathing and dressing	1.0
Reading and conversation	2.5
Shopping and errands	1.8
Housekeeping	1.1

3. For European countries, Lueschen et al. (1995) examined 1990 health care expenditures as a percentage of gross domestic product (GDP). Construct a bar chart and comment on their findings.

Country	Percentage of GDP Spent on Health Care in 1990
Belgium	7.6%
France	8.8
Germany	8.3
Netherlands	8.2
Spain	6.6

4. Lueschen et al. (1995) analyzed alcohol consumption for five European countries. Construct a bar chart of their data and comment on their findings.

Country	Liters Consumed per Person over 24 Years of Age in 1990
Belgium	12.4
France	16.7
Germany	12.3
Netherlands	9.9
Spain	15.5

5. You are conducting a historical comparison of tax expenditures of local and state governments for 1975 and 1995. The source of your (fictional) data is the U.S. Bureau of the Census. State and local governments spent their revenues as follows for those two years.

  a. Construct a clustered bar chart of type of expenditure by year.
  b. Comment on how revenue expenditures changed over two decades.

Type of Expenditure	Distribution by Year	
	1975	1995
Education	35%	24%
Highways	9	18
Health and welfare	18	32
Other expenditures	38	26

6. In a study of the factors that influence adolescent deviance, parents' levels of education are used to measure social class. Create a clustered bar chart comparing the percentages of fathers and mothers at each level of education (fictional data).

Highest Level of Education	Mother	Father
Less than high school	12.5%	14.5%
High school graduate	59.7	46.6
College graduate	27.8	38.9

7. Alba, Logan, and Crowder (1997) examined the makeup of white ethnic neighborhoods in the New York City. One area of interest is migration from the central city from 1980 to 1990. The following table presents ethnic group populations for a neighborhood for those two years.

  a. Construct a pie chart for these two years (on the same page) to depict the population of each ethnic group.

   b. Construct a clustered bar chart for these two years to depict the population of each ethnic group.

   c. Compare the two types of charts. In general, what do the charts convey? Which graphical style is better at depicting the phenomenon? Explain your choice.

	1980			1990		
	Germans	*Irish*	*Italians*	*Germans*	*Irish*	*Italians*
Population	46,920	9,570	50,773	18,300	9,436	41,429

8. A content analysis of weight-control advertisements in *Ladies Home Journal* reveals the following types of ads for two five-year periods (fictional data).

   a. Construct pie charts (on the same page) to portray changes in percentage frequencies of types of diets advertised in the two periods.

   b. Construct a clustered bar chart to portray changes in percentage frequencies of these ads.

   c. Compare the two types of charts. In general, what do the charts convey? Which graphical style is better at depicting the phenomenon? Explain your choice.

	Number of Times it Appeared	
Type of Weight-loss Advertisement	*1984–88*	*1989–93*
Quick weight loss	78	47
Fat free/light	129	487
Sugar free	94	138
Cholesterol free	108	262
Other	52	32

9. The following are the ages of students on a college debate team: 20, 19, 20, 21, 20, 21, 22, 24, 23, 22, 19, 20, 21, 21, 22, 23, 22, 20, 21, 21, 23, 29.

   a. Construct a frequency histogram of these (fictional) data.

   b. Construct a frequency polygon of these data.

   c. Which of the two graphs would you choose to present to a public audience? Why?

   d. One of the scores is peculiar. What is this peculiarity called?

10. A small college is interested in increasing participation in campus activities. A random sample of students was asked to check events they

attended on a checklist for the previous term. The numbers of events attended were as follows (fictional data): 2, 2, 4, 8, 5, 2, 3, 1, 6, 5, 4, 12, 1, 4, 2, 7, 6, 3, 2, 4, 7, 4, 2, 3.

   a. Construct a frequency histogram of these data.
   b. Construct a frequency polygon of these data.
   c. Which of the two graphs would you choose to present to a public audience? Why?
   d. One of the scores is peculiar. What is this peculiarity called?

11. The following are frequency distributions of distances (in kilometers) traveled daily by high school students in suburban and rural school districts (fictional data).

   a. Construct frequency polygons for the two distributions on the same graph. *Caution:* The sample sizes differ.
   b. What is the obvious conclusion drawn in comparing distance traveled for the two school districts?

Kilometers	Suburban f	Rural f
1	2	0
2	4	1
3	9	0
4	13	3
5	14	5
6	8	6
7	6	9
8	5	13
9	4	17
10	2	24
11	0	15
12	0	8
13	0	7
14	0	2
15	0	1

12. The following are frequency distributions of the ages of inpatients at a substance abuse treatment hospital by the major diagnoses of cocaine addiction and alcohol addiction (fictional data).

   a. Construct overlying frequency polygons of these data. *Caution:* The sample sizes differ.
   b. What does the graph reveal?

Age	Cocaine Addicts f	Alcohol Addicts f
26	2	1
27	5	2
28	6	2
29	11	3
30	13	5
31	8	6
32	4	9
33	4	15
34	0	17
35	1	15
36	0	7
37	0	5
38	0	2

Optional Computer Applications for Chapter 3

If this course utilizes the optional *Computer Applications for The Statistical Imagination* compact disk, open the Chapter 2 exercises. These exercises describe how to produce graphs and charts using *SPSS for Windows* and how to choose appropriate graphical styles.

MEASURING AVERAGES

Introduction

Everyone is familiar with the general concept of an average in situations such as an average grade, an average income, a bowling average, and a batting average. If someone is "average" in some way—average height, weight, intelligence, and so forth—this person is not unusual. To be average is to be like most other people.

In a distribution of scores, an average will fall between the extreme scores—somewhere in the middle area of the score distribution. For instance, most men are not too tall or too short; they are "about average." We call this typical, average score the central tendency of the variable. A **central tendency statistic** *provides an estimate of the typical, usual, or normal score found in a distribution of raw scores.* For example, the heights of American males tend to cluster around five feet, eight inches, and healthy infants weigh around seven pounds at birth. If Bob has a bowling average of 165, we do not expect him to bowl that exact score every game but to bowl around that score most of the time.

Central Tendency Statistic

A statistic that provides an estimate of the typical, usual, or normal score found in a distribution of raw scores.

There are three common central tendency statistics: the mean, the median, and the mode. Why three? Because each has strengths but also potential weaknesses, depending on the particular shape of a variable's score distribution. Depending on a distribution's shape, one measure of average may be more accurate than another, and sometimes reporting any central tendency statistic alone may mislead or fail to provide enough information.

The Mean

The arithmetic mean of a distribution of scores (or, simply, the mean) is a central tendency statistic that is familiar to any student who has calculated the average of examination grades for a course. The **mean** is *the sum of all scores* *divided by the number of scores observed (i.e., the sample size).* To compute the mean of a variable, we simply add all scores and divide by the sample size.

The Mean

The sum of all scores in a distribution divided by the number of scores observed (i.e., the sample size).

The mean is the most useful central tendency statistic. With a quick mathematical calculation, it furnishes a summary of the typical or average scores in a distribution. Because it uses the mathematical operation of division, the mean applies to interval/ratio variables. It also may be calculated for interval-like ordinal variables, but caution must be used in the interpretation of results.

In mathematical formulas, the conventional symbol used to represent a variable name is a capital English letter. The letters X and Y are fashionable here. For example, we might set X to stand for age and set Y to stand for height. Often, Y is used for a dependent variable and subscripted X's are used for a set of independent variables. For example, we might set Y = college grade point average (GPA), with the following set of predictor variables: X_1 = high school GPA, X_2 = college admissions test score, X_3 = reading comprehension ability, and X_4 = year of schooling.

For a variable X, whatever we define it to be, the symbol for the mean *computed on sample data* is $\bar{X}$, which is stated "X-bar." For example, if X = age and the mean age of a statistics class is 20.5 years, we say, "X-bar equals 20.5 years." Remember to state the units of measure of the variable, in this case, years. The mean is calculated as follows (Σ is read as "the sum of").

Calculating the Mean

$$\bar{X} = \frac{\Sigma X}{n}$$

where

$\bar{X}$ = the mean of the interval/ratio variable X computed on sample data
ΣX = the sum of all the individual scores for the variable X
n = the number of observations (i.e., the sample size)

If there are 12 children in a sample, ages 6, 12, 5, 10, 9, 10, 8, 7, 9, 11, 8, and 10 years, their mean age is

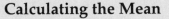

$$\bar{X} = \frac{\Sigma X}{n} = \frac{6+12+5+10+9+10+8+7+9+11+8+10}{12}$$

$$= \frac{105 \text{ years}}{12} = 8.75 \text{ years}$$

Technically, the mean is 8.75 years *per child*, but we leave off the unit of the denominator. Conceptually, the value of the mean tells us what the *X*-scores in a sample would be *if* every sample subject had the same score. In the example above, 8.75 years (i.e., eight years, nine months) would be the age of every child if all the children had the very same age. It is useful, then, to think of the mean as a measure of "equal share." For example, if we wanted to know the mean amount of pocket cash among students in a classroom, we would put all the cash in a pot and divide it equally. (Any volunteers?) The amount each person received would be the mean value of pocket cash. The mean also can be viewed as a balance point, the point at which *differences between* the mean of *X* and the individual *X*-scores in the distribution balance out. In Chapter 5 we will pursue this notion further.

Finally, in calculating central tendency statistics, particularly the mean, care must be taken not to include the scores coded as missing cases. Only "valid" cases are included in the calculation of the mean. For example, if in a sample of 49 persons, 2 failed to report their ages, the sum of ages would be divided by 47—the number of valid scores—instead of the sample size of 49. Moreover, with computer files, care must be taken not to add the "missing value" codes (such as 99) to the sum of scores.

Proportional Thinking about the Mean

Combining the Means of Two Different-Size Samples.   The mean is the most widely used central tendency statistic. Thus, it is important that we have a good sense of proportion about its calculation. First, let us examine a situation where a common mistake is made: combining the means of two groups by adding the two means and dividing by 2. [The only time this is not a mistake is when the two groups have the same sample sizes (i.e., when the *n*'s are equal).] For example, observe the mean number of vacation days per year (*X*) for group 1, the eight secretaries of a local bank, and group 2, the three vice presidents. For the eight secretaries:

$$\bar{X}_{(group1)} = \frac{\Sigma X_{(group1)}}{n_{(group1)}} = \frac{7 + 10 + 7 + 12 + 16 + 7 + 14 + 10}{8}$$

$$= \frac{83 \text{ days}}{8} = 10.38 \text{ vacation days}$$

For the three vice presidents:

$$\bar{X}_{(group2)} = \frac{\Sigma X_{(group2)}}{n_{(group2)}} = \frac{60 + 30 + 30}{3}$$

$$= \frac{120 \text{ days}}{3} = 40.00 \text{ vacation days}$$

If we *incorrectly* calculated the mean of the entire office by summing these two means and dividing by 2, we would obtain the erroneous answer of 25.19 vacation days. The correct calculation for the combined mean is

$$\bar{X}_{(groups\ 1\ plus\ 2\ combined)} = \frac{\Sigma X_{(group1)} + \Sigma X_{(group2)}}{n_{(group1)} + n_{(group2)}}$$

$$= \frac{83 + 120}{8 + 3} = \frac{203}{11} = 18.45 \text{ vacation days}$$

With a moment's thought we can see that this formulation is equivalent to treating all 11 employees as one sample. Additional illustrations of mistakenly "averaging" group means are provided in "Statistical Follies and Fallacies" at the end of this chapter.

Locking into an Average.   We all encounter situations in which our average for a performance seems to become stuck at some level. No matter how much we improve, the average seems to be locked in. For example, the mean is used to calculate bowling averages, which range from zero to 300. Brian bowls weekly in league play, and after 100 games his average is 150 pins per game. What score must he bowl in the next game to raise his average 1 point?

Proportional thinking about a "moving average" directs our calculations of the mean. Let us first focus on the denominator, n. After the 101st game, it will have increased from 100 to 101. The numerator, ΣX, will increase by the amount of Brian's score in game 101. The question is: How much must ΣX increase to raise his mean to 151 pins per game?

Brian may be disappointed to learn that he must bowl a score of 251 in the 101st game to raise his average a mere point! Why so much? Let us determine the total pin count Brian had accumulated through game 100 with his average of 150. This is calculated by solving for ΣX in the equation for the mean:

$$\text{Since } \bar{X} = \frac{\Sigma X}{n}, \text{ then } \Sigma X = (n)(\bar{X})$$

Brian's total pin count after 100 games is

$$\Sigma X_{(through\ game\ 100)} = (n)(\bar{X}) = (100)(150) = 15,000 \text{ pins}$$

If his average is to rise to 151, his ΣX after game 101 must be

$$\Sigma X_{(needed\ after\ game\ 101)} = (n)(\bar{X}) = (101)(151) = 15,251 \text{ pins}$$

The score he needs in game 101 is the difference between these two sums of X:

Score Brian needs to boost bowling average to 151 after 101 games

$$= \Sigma X_{(needed\ after\ game\ 101)} - \Sigma X_{(through\ game\ 100)}$$
$$= 15,251 - 15,000 = 251 \text{ pins}$$

What this amounts to is that in order for Brain to raise his average 1 point, he must bowl 1 point higher in game 101 *plus an extra point for all the previous 100 games*. Indeed, if there are only a few weeks of league play left, Brian's bowling average is well fixed at this point.

With a moving average, the sample size (*n*) increases steadily over time in small increments, such as three bowling games per week or three times at bat per game for major league ball players. To move an average up, a player must equal his or her previous average plus some value. As the season moves along, the amount of this "plus some" continues to grow. By the same token, however, it is easy to improve an average early in the season. For example, if Brian bowls 150 in the very first game of the league season, how much will he have to bowl in the second game to move his average up to 151? Finally, this highlights an important point about accurately assessing someone's performance at a given point in time: It is more appropriate to use the mean of recent games instead of the entire season.

Potential Weaknesses of the Mean: Situations Where Reporting It Alone May Mislead

When a central tendency statistic is reported, we tend to presume that its value is representative of typical scores in the middle of a distribution. There are times, however, when reporting the mean can mislead in this regard. This is the case because the calculation of the mean can be inflated (pulled up) or deflated (pulled down) by extreme scores, or outliers. Extremely high scores, or positive outliers, inflate the value of the mean by "boosting up" the sum of X (i.e., ΣX) in the numerator of the formula. Extremely low scores in a distribution, or negative outliers, deflate the value of the mean by "shrinking" ΣX. For example, suppose we compute the mean amount of pocket cash for 10 students. Ideally, this mean should tell us what the typical amount is. But suppose one student cashed a $400 paycheck and our calculation comes out as follows, where X = amount of cash on each student (for simplicity, rounded to the nearest dollar):

$$\bar{X} = \frac{\Sigma X}{n} = \frac{5 + 2 + 6 + 10 + 8 + 3 + 9 + 11 + 5 + 400}{10}$$

$$= \frac{\$459}{10} = \$45.90 \approx \$46$$

Obviously, this computed mean of $46 does not represent the typical, average, or central tendency amount of pocket cash. Most students have less than $10, and to report a mean of $46 is misleading. The calculation of the mean is distorted by the presence of an outlier. To obtain a sense of proportion about how the formula for the mean is calculated, examine the relationship between the numerator (ΣX) and the denominator (*n*). When ΣX is large and *n* is small, the mean will be large. If ΣX is large because of the presence of one or two high-value outliers, the mean will "inflate" to a large value.

Keep in mind that our objective is to use sample statistics to estimate the parameters of a population. If an inflated or deflated *sample* mean is reported, this will present a distorted summary of how subjects *in a population* score. This limitation of the mean is a special problem with small samples; the smaller the sample, the greater the distortion resulting from an outlier. For example, compute the mean age of the following sample of five college students at Crosstown University, where one student in the sample has an extremely high age: 19, 19, 20, 21, and 54 years. The answer will leave the impression that this sample is quite above the typical college age when in fact four of the five students *are* of the typical age. See also what happens when there is an extremely low score as with this sample of ages: 8, 19, 19, 20, and 21 years. In such cases, the outlier should be removed and the mean should be recalculated without it. In reporting this "adjusted mean," we note why the adjustment was made.

Any time we compute a mean, especially with a small sample, we first examine the raw score frequency distribution for outliers. One handy device for this is a boxplot (Chapter 3). Because the mean is more useful than the median and the mode are, we often adjust the scores in a distribution to reduce the effects of outliers on the computation of the mean. The distorting effects of outliers are noted throughout the text.

The Median

The **median** (Mdn) is *the middle score in a ranked distribution*—that value of a variable which divides the distribution of scores in half, *the score for which half of the cases fall above and half fall below*. For example, if the median income of households in Cornbelt City is $26,000, half the households in that city have incomes higher than $26,000 and half have incomes lower than $26,000. Conceptually, the median is a location point—the middle position score. The median brings to mind a geographic location between equal areas, such as the median of a highway. The median score is also equal to the 50th percentile, the point at which 50 percent of the observations fall below it. Among the three central tendency statistics, the median is most useful when a distribution is skewed (i.e., has a few scores to one side). For example, the median price of recent housing sales is preferable to the mean price because a few high-price sales inflate the value of the mean.

The Median

For an ordinal or interval/ratio variable, the middle score in a ranked distribution, the score for which half of the cases fall above and half fall below.

To compute the median of a distribution, the scores for a variable X must first be ranked; that is, the scores must be arranged in order of size from the smallest to the largest or from the largest to the smallest. Divide the sample size n by 2 to get near the middle score in the distribution. If n is an odd number, the median will be an actual case in the sample. Suppose, for instance, we have a sample of five families with the following monthly household incomes (X):

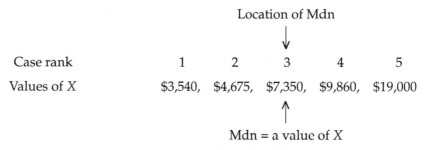

The median income is $7,350, the value of X for the third-ranked score.

If n is an even number, the median is located between two middle scores and is calculated by taking the mean of those two scores. For example, if a sixth family with an income of $20,000 is inserted into the above sample,

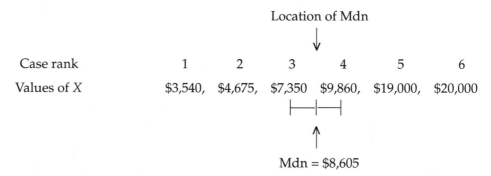

The median is situated between the third and fourth cases. It is calculated by summing the scores of $7,350 and $9,860 and dividing by 2.

With a small sample, locating the median is a straightforward task. With a large sample (and in computer software), the median is mathematically located by dividing the sample size by 2 and adding .5. Note that this result gives *the ranked location* of the median, not the median itself. Rank the scores, then count to this position. The X-score in this position is the median. After finding the median, double-check by seeing whether your answer indeed splits the cases in half. The median can be used with interval/ratio variables as well as ordinal variables. Finally, do not confuse the median with another statistic called the *midrange*, the halfway point between the minimum and maximum values of X.

Calculating the Median (Mdn)

1. Rank the distribution of scores from lowest to highest.
2. Locate the position of the median. Divide the sample size, n, by 2 to get near the middle score in the distribution. If n is an odd number, the median will be an actual case in the sample. If n is an even number, the median will be located between two middle scores and is calculated by taking the mean of those two scores. (Mathematically, the rank position of the median is found by dividing the sample size by 2 and adding .5.)

Potential Weaknesses of the Median: Situations Where Reporting It Alone May Mislead

The median is based on the ranked location of scores in a distribution. It is *insensitive to the values of the scores* in a distribution; that is, regardless of the values of the X's around it, the median is the middle score determined by the number of scores (n) in the sample. For example, the following two distributions of exam scores have the same median even though they are composed of markedly different scores.

Classroom 1: 39, 51, 77, 78, 81

↑

Mdn

↓

Classroom 2: 74, 75, 77, 94, 98

To say that the average examination grade in both classes is 77 is misleading because it suggests that the two classes performed equally. (In fact, classroom 2 did much better with a *mean* of 83.6 compared with a *mean* of 65.2 for classroom 1.) The median is not affected by the values of X.

While insensitive to score values, the median is sensitive to (or affected by) a change in sample size. For example, suppose that in classroom 1 two students take the examination late; they do poorly, which is typical of students who take a test late. When their scores are included in the distribution, the median shifts drastically from 77 to 51:

Classroom 1 (including late scores): 34, 36, 39, 51, 77, 78, 81

↑

Mdn

The median, then, has two potential weaknesses: (1) It is *in*sensitive to the values of the scores in a distribution, and (2) it is sensitive to (or affected by) a change in sample size. Before reporting the median make sure that neither of these potential weaknesses will lead to faulty conclusions.

The Mode

The **mode** (Mo) is *the most frequently occurring score in a distribution*. Conceptually, the mode is the "most popular" score. Table 4–1 presents the distribution of ages for a sample of college students. The mode is 19 years because more people (49 of them) scored this age than any other. Note that the mode is an *X*-score (19 years), *not* a frequency, *f* (49 cases).

TABLE 4–1   **The Distribution of Ages for a Sample of 125 College Students**

	Givens		Calculations
	Age	*f*	*Percent*
	18	31	24.8%
Mo $\longrightarrow$	19	49	39.2
	20	20	16.0
	21	18	14.4
	22	7	5.6
	Total	125	100.0%

The Mode

The most frequently occurring score in a distribution.

Calculating the Mode (Mo)

1. Compile the scores into a frequency distribution.
2. Identify Mo = value of *X* with the most cases (i.e., the greatest frequency, *f*).

A cautionary note is in order. Do not confuse the mode (the "most frequently occurring score") with the "majority of scores." A simple majority would be "more than half" or 50 percent of the cases in a sample plus at least one. Note that in this distribution, although the most frequently occurring score is 19 years, the majority of the sample is not 19 years old; only 39.2 percent of the sample is that age. No age in this distribution has a majority.

The mode is useful with variables of all levels of measurement. The mode is easy to spot in charts. In a pie chart, it is the category with the largest slice; in a bar chart, the tallest bar; on a histogram, the tallest column; and on a polygon, the score for the highest point, or peak.

Potential Weaknesses of the Mode: Situations Where Reporting It Alone May Mislead

Generally speaking, *by itself* the mode is the least useful central tendency statistics because it has a narrow informational scope. While it identifies the most

FIGURE 4–1

Variously shaped score distributions with the same mode

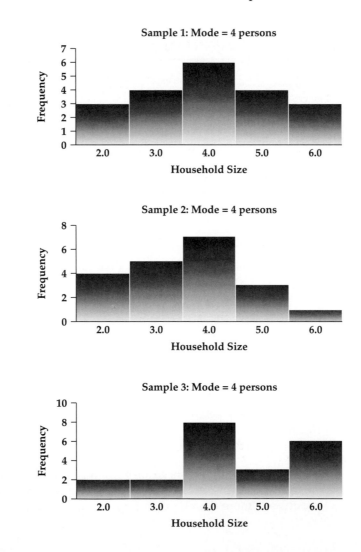

frequently occurring score, it suggests nothing about scores that occur around this score value. Thus, the mode is most useful when it is reported in conjunction with the median and the mean. As we will see below, reporting all three central tendency statistics is quite informative.

The mode can be misleading when it is used alone because it is insensitive to both the values of scores in a distribution and the sample size. This means that you may have any number of totally different shaped distributions, yet all could have the same mode, as is depicted in Figure 4–1.

There is at least one situation in which the mode is an appropriate central tendency statistic by itself and reporting the mean and the median is misleading. This occurs when the scores of X are essentially of the same value for all cases except a few. An example is the wage structure of a fast-food restaurant where everyone except the managers is paid the same low wage. This distribution is shown in Table 4–2, where X is the hourly wage and f is the frequency of scores. The mean here is $7.17, and it is "pulled up" by the extreme scores of the managers' wages. To a job seeker, this mean leaves the false impression that the restaurant on average provides quite a bit more than the minimum wage. The median is $5.75, the same as the mode, but reporting this median leads to the incorrect interpretation that half the employees make above that amount, which is not the case. To report the mode, $5.75, is to say that lots of the employees are paid this low salary. This is the most accurate depiction of this distribution of wages.

TABLE 4–2   **Distribution of Wages in a Fast-Food Restaurant**

Wage ($)	f	Employee Classification
5.75	13	Regular employees
10.50	2	Night managers
18.90	1	Head manager
Total	16	

Central Tendency Statistics and the Appropriate Level of Measurement

Recall from Chapter 2 that the level of measurement of a variable tells us what mathematical formulas and statistics are appropriate for that variable. The mean and the median are clearly appropriate with interval/ratio variables. It makes sense to talk about mean weight, height, or income. These statistics also may be used with interval-like ordinal variables if the frequencies are not bunched at one end of the distribution or split between the two ends. Novice statisticians, however, should avoid using the mean and the median with ordinal variables. With nominal variables, means and medians are meaningless. The nominal variable *gender* is a case in point. A person cannot be an average of so much male and so much female; he or she is one or the other. Recall Table 2–5, which gives the distribution of religious affiliations in childhood for a sample of U.S. adults. It makes no sense to ask what the mean religion is.

While the mean and the median apply best to interval/ratio variables, the mode can be used with variables of all levels of measurement. From Table 2–5 we could report that the modal religion is "Total Protestant" for major religions, "Catholic" for any single denomination, or "Baptist" for any single Protestant denomination.

Frequency Distribution Curves: Relationships among the Mean, Median, and Mode

Given that each of the three central tendency statistics has potential weaknesses, it is worthwhile to view them as a set of statistics to be interpreted together. These three statistics are especially useful when they are examined graphically. An imaginative way to understand the relationship among these three statistics is to locate the values of each one on a frequency distribution curve.

A **frequency distribution curve** is *a substitute for a frequency histogram or polygon in which we replace these graphs with a smooth curve.* This substitution is appropriate because the smooth curve is viewed not so much as a depiction of the sample distribution but more as an estimate of the way scores are distributed *in the population.* As with a histogram, the scores of a variable are depicted from left (lowest) to right (highest); that is, the scores are ranked on the horizontal axis. The area under a frequency distribution curve represents *the total number of subjects in the population and is equal to a proportion of 1.00 or a percentage of 100 percent.* Our concern is with assessing the shape of a distribution, *examining the relative locations of the mean, median, and mode to estimate the shape of a frequency distribution.*

Frequency Distribution Curve

A substitute for a frequency histogram or polygon in which we replace these graphs with a smooth curve. The area under the curve represents the total number of subjects in the population and is equal to a proportion of 1.00 or a percentage of 100 percent.

Figure 4–2 shows three very common shapes of score frequency distribution curves. As with our histograms, the horizontal axis of the curves represents the scores of a variable X. The vertical axis (which we often do not bother to draw) represents the proportional frequency or percentage frequency; thus, the height of the curve at any value of X represents the proportion of a sample or population with that score.

FIGURE 4–2

*Common frequency
distribution curves
and the relative
locations of the
mean, median, and
mode, where X is
an interval/ratio
variable (fictional
data)*

A. The Normal Distribution or Normal Curve

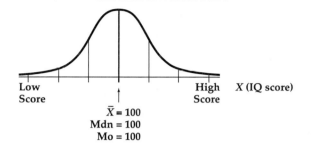

Low
Score

High
Score   X (IQ score)

$\bar{X}$ = 100
Mdn = 100
Mo = 100

B. Positively Skewed Distribution or Right Skew

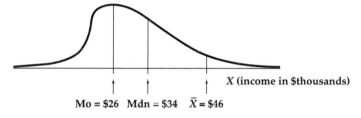

X (income in $thousands)

Mo = $26   Mdn = $34 $\bar{X}$ = $46

C. Negatively Skewed Distribution or Left Skew

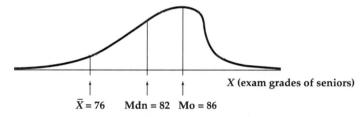

X (exam grades of seniors)

$\bar{X}$ = 76   Mdn = 82   Mo = 86

The Normal Distribution

A **normal distribution** is one in which *the mean, median, and mode of a variable
are equal to one another and the distribution of scores is bell-shaped.* We also refer to
this as "a normal curve." Figure 4–2A depicts IQ scores, which are normally
distributed with a mean of 100. A normal distribution is symmetrical (i.e., balanced on each side). Its mean, median, and mode are located in the center of
the distribution. The presence of the median there assures symmetry because,
by definition, the median splits a ranked distribution of scores in half. Since
the mode is at the center point of a normal distribution, the peak of the curve
is located there.

A Normal Distribution

A frequency distribution curve in which the mean, median, and mode of a variable are equal to one another and the distribution of scores is bell-shaped.

Skewed Distributions

A **skewed distribution** is *one in which the mean, median, and mode of the variable are unequal and many of the subjects have extremely high or low scores.* When this is the case, the distribution stretches out in one direction like the blade of a sword or barbecue skewer; hence, the name *skewed* (Figure 4–2B and C).

Skewed Distribution

A frequency distribution curve in which the mean, median, and mode of the variable are unequal and many of the subjects have extremely high or low scores.

The positions of the mean, median, and mode are predictable for skewed distribution curves. A **right (or positive) skew** is *one with extreme scores in the high or positive end of the score distribution* (Figure 4–2B). For example, household income in the United States is positively skewed; most households make only so much money, but a few are extremely wealthy. The high extreme scores inflate the mean, "pulling" it in the positive direction. The mode is the central tendency measure with the lowest computed score. The median will equal either the mean or the mode or, most likely, will fall between them.

A **left (or negative) skew** is *one with extreme scores in the low or negative end of the score distribution* (Figure 4–2C). For example, test scores in a senior-level college course tend to be left-skewed. Most seniors get high scores, but a few tail off in the negative direction. These few extreme low scores deflate the mean, pulling it in the negative direction. The mode is the highest computed score, and the median falls between the mean and the mode.

With either a left or a right skew, if the median does not fall between the mean and the mode, this suggests that the distribution is oddly shaped. One such oddly shaped distribution is a bimodal distribution, one with two modes or peaks. For example, the variable weight for a sample that includes both men and women may produce a bimodal distribution, with the higher mode resulting from the fact that men are heavier on average (Figure 4–3).

FIGURE 4–3

Bimodal distribution of the weights of men and women

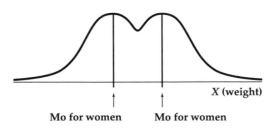

Using Sample Data to Estimate the Shape of a Score Distribution in a Population

In computing central tendency statistics and histograms for *sample* data, the data for a variable often appear slightly skewed. This does not guarantee, however, that the variable's scores are skewed in *the population* from which the sample was drawn. The skew in the sample data may be due to sampling error. In other words, a second sample from the population may appear normal or skew slightly in the other direction.

Skewness statistics are used to determine whether sample data are so skewed that they suggest that the population scores are skewed. We will not compute a skewness statistic by hand. Computer programs, however, provide skewness statistics, and a common one is available with the optional computer applications that accompany this text. When this skewness statistic's absolute value (its value ignoring the plus or minus sign) is greater than 1.2, the distribution may be significantly skewed, depending on the shape of the distribution as well as the sample size. A few outliers in a large sample will have little effect on statistics. If this skewness statistic's absolute value is greater than 1.6, however, regardless of sample size, the distribution probably is skewed; then reporting the sample mean of X as an estimate of the population mean can be misleading because of the mean's potential distortion by extreme scores. Aside from the issue of accurately describing the shape of a distribution, skewness is a concern with inferential statistics. As we shall see in later chapters, in testing a hypothesis about the relationship between two variables, a skewed variable requires extra work to avoid incorrect conclusions. Such instances will be identified as they are encountered.

As we will see in Chapter 5, when a distribution is not skewed or otherwise oddly shaped, the mean is the central tendency statistic of choice. This is especially true for reports to public audiences whose members may be overloaded by more than one statistic. However, if a distribution is skewed, the median is the statistic to report. The median minimizes error in describing a skewed distribution because it falls between the mean and the mode, as is depicted in Figure 4–2, B and C. As the most central of the three statistics, the median is the best of three poor choices for a skewed distribution when only one statistic is to be reported.

For scientific audiences, skewed distributions are noted by reporting all three central tendency statistics and perhaps including a graph to convey the distribution's shape accurately. Sometimes a skewed distribution is very informative. For example, *hospital stays* is positively skewed. In a given year, most people stay no days or very few days in the hospital. But a substantial percentage stays longer, and a few "skew out," spending weeks or months in the hospital. Such a skew stimulates thinking about predictors of long stays. Can you think of hypotheses that explain the skew of hospital stays?

As we shall see in Chapter 5, overall the mean is the most valuable central tendency statistic. It allows much greater flexibility in mathematical

TABLE 4–3   Characteristics, Strengths, and Potential Weaknesses of the Mean, Median, and Mode

Central Tendency Statistic	Definition	Strengths and Applications	Potential Weaknesses
Mean	Value of X if all scores are the same	Open to mathematical operations; preferable when distribution is normally shaped; useful with interval/ratio and interval-like ordinal variables.	Its calculation is distorted by outliers or a skew in the distribution curve.
Median	Middle score in a ranked distribution; score for which half the scores fall above and half fall below	Preferred when the distribution is skewed; useful with interval/ratio and interval-like ordinal variables.	Insensitive to the values of X in the distribution but sensitive to changes in sample size.
Mode	Most frequently occurring score in a distribution	Preferred when virtually all scores in the distribution are the same; useful with all levels of measurement.	Insensitive to the values of X and insensitive to how scores are distributed around it.

calculations. For the most part, the median and the mode are dead-end streets because they offer no additional worthwhile mathematical operations. Little is gained beyond reporting them. Whenever possible, the mean is the summary measurement to use, especially with inferential statistics. Because of this, we often adjust skewed distributions to "bring them down to normal" so that we can use the mean. The specifics of this type of error control are discussed later in this text. Table 4–3 summarizes the properties of the three central tendency statistics.

Organizing Data for Calculating Central Tendency Statistics

There are two common formats for organizing data and computing central tendency statistics on those data. One format is a spreadsheet of the raw score distribution. As was indicated in Chapter 2, a spreadsheet format typically is used for computer data entry or input, but spreadsheets also are commonly used by business, government, and community groups to maintain organization records. Spreadsheet computer software programs such as *Lotus 1-2-3,*

Excel, and *Corel Quattro Pro,* are especially designed for this purpose. Spreadsheet formats evolved from the logical way to do problems by hand—simply listing the scores of a variable in a vertical column.

The second common format for calculations is a frequency distribution format. In this format, the scores of a variable are listed in one column and the frequency of each score is listed in another (like the frequency distributions in Chapter 2). This format is typical of computer output. Now let us do a simple problem using both formats.

Spreadsheet Format for Calculating Central Tendency Statistics

Suppose we are interested in how often film students in a college communications department study their art by going to new-release movies. We collect a random sample of 19 students. We ask each one to name the new movies he or she saw in the past month at theaters and record the following results: 2, 6, 4, 5, 2, 3, 4, 3, 6, 4, 3, 3, 5, 4, 5, 2, 3, 4, 3. Table 4–4 presents these data in a spreadsheet format with the calculations necessary for computing the mean. The scores are ranked to facilitate calculation of the median and the mode.

TABLE 4–4   Data Organized in a Spreadsheet Format: Number of New-Release Movies Seen in Past Month (X)

	Givens	
Subject's Number	*Subject's Initials*	*X*
1	BH	2
2	KP	2
3	JN	2
4	TW	3
5	JD	3
6	WA	3
7	KM	3
8	BC	3
9	CR	4
10	ML	4
11	MW	4
12	MF	4
13	JS	4
14	BY	4
15	LL	5
16	WF	5
17	CM	5
18	BL	6
19	SH	6
$n = 19$		$\Sigma X = 72$ movies

First, let us calculate the mean:

$$\bar{X} = \frac{\Sigma X}{n} = \frac{72}{19} = 3.79 \text{ movies}$$

Second, let us calculate the median. We have already ranked the scores, something necessary for computing the median. The sample size ($n = 19$) divided in half is about nine cases, and since n is odd, we determine that the tenth case is the median. On the spreadsheet, we count down to the tenth case and find that the median is four movies:

$$\text{Mdn} = 4 \text{ movies}$$

Finally, we calculate the mode. Observation of the ranked data in Table 4–4 reveals that the most frequently occurring score is 4:

$$\text{Mo} = 4 \text{ movies}$$

Obviously, using a spreadsheet for doing calculations by hand would be cumbersome with a large number of cases. A more succinct way to organize the data is to use a frequency distribution format.

Frequency Distribution Format for Calculating Central Tendency Statistics

Table 4–5 presents the same data on the 19 film students, but it uses a frequency distribution format. Working off of the spreadsheet of Table 4–4 (as a computer would), in Table 4–5 we see that there is a frequency of three students who score two movies, five who score three movies, and so on.

First, let us calculate the mean. To do so, we multiply each score by its frequency. This is equivalent to adding the individual scores listed in the spread-

---

TABLE 4–5   **Data Organized in a Frequency Distribution Format: Number of New-Release Movies Seen in Past Month (X)**

Givens		Calculations	
X	f	$f(X)$	*Cumulative f*
2	3	6	3
3	5	15	8
4	6	24	14
5	3	15	17
6	2	12	19
	$n = 19$	$\Sigma f(X) = 72$ movies	

sheet format of Table 4–4. In both formats, the sum of scores is 72 movies, and thus the mean computes to 3.79 movies:

$$\bar{X} = \frac{\Sigma f X}{n} = \frac{72}{19} = 3.79 \text{ movies}$$

Second, let us calculate the median. The scores in the frequency distribution are already ranked. The rank position is determined in the same manner as it is in the spreadsheet format and remains the tenth case. To locate the tenth case, we calculate the cumulative frequency, the number of cases at or below a score of the distribution (Chapter 2). We see that the tenth case in the distribution is one of the six students who scored four movies. Thus:

Mdn = 4 movies

Finally, calculation of the mode is quite easy with the frequency distribution format. In Table 4–5 we simply observe the column listing frequencies (i.e., the *f* column) and see which score occurred with the highest frequency. More students (six of them) saw four movies than any other number of movies for the month:

Mo = 4 movies

☹   STATISTICAL FOLLIES AND FALLACIES   ☹

Mixing Subgroups in the Calculation of the Mean

Because the mean is susceptible to distortion by outliers and extreme scores, we must clearly describe which cases or subjects are included in its calculation. Organizations such as businesses and school systems, intentionally or not, commonly report means that are unrealistic. For example, a public school district may report that the mean salary of its teachers is $45,000. When this occurs, teachers are likely to congregate in the faculty lounge and ask one another: Who around here makes that much money? Of course, teachers are not stupid. They know right away that whoever did the calculations "mixed the status ranks" by including higher-paid personnel—such as student counselors, assistant principals, and principals—all of whom are certified to teach but seldom do. These administrators might have been included because the "statistician" simply asked the computer to calculate the mean salary for all certified teachers without regard to rank. When these higher-paid personnel are included, their high salaries skew the mean. To avoid such statistical follies, means should be reported separately for distinct subgroups.

Mixing status ranks sometimes results in a mean that fits no group at all. For example, a company may have only two ranks of employees: blue-collar workers averaging about $30,000 per year, and managers averaging about $70,000. If these two groups are about the same size, the mean salary for the entire company will come out to about $50,000. Interestingly, not a single employee in the company earns a salary near that amount.

Another example is the mean age of attendees of parents' night at a third-grade class at an elementary school. The mean age will calculate to about 20 years, yet everyone there will be either eight or nine years old (the kids) or in his or her thirties (the parents). The mean is certainly inappropriate for summarizing this distribution of ages.

Formulas in Chapter 4

Calculating the mean:

Working from a spreadsheet: Working from a frequency distribution:

$$\bar{X} = \frac{\Sigma X}{n} \qquad\qquad\qquad \bar{X} = \frac{\Sigma f X}{n}$$

Calculating the combined mean of two groups (given individual scores):

$$\bar{X}_{(groups\ 1\ plus\ 2\ combined)} = \frac{\Sigma X_{(group1)} + \Sigma X_{(group2)}}{n_{(group1)} + n_{(group2)}}$$

Calculating the combined mean of two groups (given group means):

$$\text{Since } \bar{X} = \frac{\Sigma X}{n}, \Sigma X = (n)(\bar{X})$$

Substitute to obtain:

$$\bar{X}_{(groups\ 1\ plus\ 2\ combined)} = \frac{n_{(group1)}\ \bar{X}_{(group1)} + n_{(group2)}\ \bar{X}_{(group2)}}{n_{(group1)} + n_{(group2)}}$$

Calculating the median:

1. Rank the distribution of scores from lowest to highest.
2. Locate the position of the median. Divide the sample size, n, by 2 to get near the middle score in the distribution. (If working from a frequency distribution, calculate the cumulative frequency to compute the median's location.) If n is an odd number, the median will be an actual case in the sample. If n is an even number, the median will be located between two middle scores and is calculated by taking the mean of these two scores. (Mathematically, the rank position of the median is found by dividing the sample size by 2 and adding .5.)

Calculating the mode:

1. Compile scores into a ranked raw score spreadsheet or frequency distribution format.
2. Identify Mo = value of X with the greatest frequency.

Questions for Chapter 4

1. For each central tendency statistic, variables of what levels of measurement are appropriate?

2. Define the mean, the median, and the mode. Specify the potential limitations of each one.

3. Why is it better to compute all three measures—the mean, median, and mode—than to rely on one?

4. As a general rule, it is incorrect to calculate the mean for two groups combined by simply dividing their separate means by 2. What is the exception to this rule?

5. If a score distribution is skewed, what single central tendency statistic is most appropriate for a public audience? Why?

6. In general, the mode of a distribution is the least useful central tendency statistic. Under what circumstances, however, is it the most appropriate central tendency statistic to report?

7. If the modal age of a distribution is 22 years, does this mean that a majority of the persons in this population is 22 years old? Explain.

8. How is the mode located on a histogram, a polygon, and a frequency distribution curve?

9. On a frequency distribution curve, what do the horizontal and vertical axes represent?

10. Describe the characteristics of a normal frequency distribution curve.

11. State in general terms how a left skew in a frequency distribution affects the three common averages: mean, median, and mode.

12. State in general terms how a right skew in a frequency distribution affects the three common averages: mean, median, and mode.

13. Suppose a distribution of ages has a mean of 55 years, a mode of 28 years, and a median of 34 years. What is the likely shape of the frequency distribution curve of this variable?

14. The highest score a person can bowl is 300. Fred has tracked his average over 310 games, and it is currently 179. Without making any calculations, explain why it is impossible for Fred to raise his average to 180 in a single game.

15. As illustrated in "Statistical Follies and Fallacies" in this chapter, a variable's mean can be a poor measure of central tendency when there is a mixture of status ranks within a population. Provide an example of how mixing status ranks can result in a mean that fits no rank at all.

Exercises for Chapter 4

Remember to include the formula, stipulate the units of measure, and answer the question.

1. Given the following, calculate the modal age, median age, and mean age. X = age.

X	X
14	14
15	17
19	19
19	22
22	28

2. The following data are for the variable Y = distance from workplace (in miles) for the employees of a copy machine retailer. Calculate the mode, median, and mean of Y.

Y	Y
13	10
9	11
6	14
3	5
12	7

3. That annoying guy who zooms around the parking lot on in-line skates also participates in in-line competition. In the last 11 races he has placed 2, 4, 1, 5, 3, 3, 1, 3, 2, 3, and 4.

   a. Find the mode, median, and mean of his typical position of finish.
   b. Although position of finish is an ordinal variable, why is it reasonable to calculate central tendency statistics on it?

4. The university's Scholar Bowl team participated in eight competitions last year with the following positions of finish: 4, 3, 2, 2, 3, 1, 2, 1.

   a. Find the mode, median, and mean of the team's position of finish.
   b. Although position of finish is an ordinal variable, why is it reasonable to calculate central tendency statistics on it?

5. Seven office workers entered a weight-loss competition. After a few weeks of dieting their weight losses (in pounds) were as follows: 5, 7, 3, 0, 2, 4, and 3. Calculate the modal, median, and mean weight loss.

6. Scores on the analytical portion of the GRE (Graduate Records Examination) of five candidates to a graduate program were as follows: 700, 625, 640, 590, and 600. Compute the mean and median scores.

7. Paul drives like a bat out of you know where. He is known to run it and gun it even on short drives and spends about half his income on tires and brake linings. At least on short trips, his brother, Terry, just moseys along at a casual pace. They both leave their mother's house to drive to a local bar just two miles away through city streets. Terry takes four minutes to get there.

   a. In miles per hour (mph), what speed did Terry average over the two-mile drive?
   b. How fast would Paul have to drive to get to the bar in two minutes and "save time" compared to Terry?
   c. Does it make sense to try to save time by speeding on short trips?

8. Coming into this week's league play, Lisa has bowled 56 games and has an overall average of 163 pins per game.

   a. What would Lisa have to average for her three games tonight to raise her overall average to 165?
   b. Given her past performance, is Lisa likely to raise her overall average two points tonight?

9. Demographers study the populations of various states, communities, and countries. One subject of interest is the growth or decline in a population's size, which is affected by how quickly people are being born, how long they live (i.e., longevity), and at what ages they typically die. One variable is age of mortality (i.e., age of death). Suppose in nation A, the modal age of mortality is 55, the median is 60, and the mean is 65. In nation B, the mean is also 65, but the mode is 75 and the median is 70.

   a. From this information, construct the frequency curves for each nation.
   b. Which nation appears better off in terms of longevity?

10. In evaluating crime rates between two cities a criminologist calculates that X = the average number of vehicles stolen per day (over a six-month period). For city A, the mode of X is 15 vehicles, the median is 20, and the mean is 25. For city B, the mean is also 25, but the mode is 35 and the median is 30.

    a. From this information, construct the frequency curves for each city.
    b. In which city would you feel safer parking your car on the street?

11. All five members of a family work. Their hourly wages are $30, $10.50, $5.15, $12, and $6.

    a. Compute the mean and the median.
    b. Compared to the other scores, what would we call the $30 rate?
    c. What is its effect on the calculation of the mean?
    d. Adjust for this peculiarity by recalculating the mean without it.

12. The following are grade point averages (GPAs) of the students in a tutorial program: 1.7, 2.6, 2.3, 3.9, 2.2, 1.9, 2.1. Set Y = GPA.

    a. Compute the mean and the median.
    b. Compared to the other scores, what would we call the GPA of 3.9?
    c. What is its effect on the calculation of the mean?
    d. Adjust for this peculiarity by recalculating the mean without it.

13. The mean age of the 47 men in the Sparkesville Bridge Club is 54.8 years. The mean age of the 62 women in the club is 56.4 years. What is the mean age of all 109 members?

14. The following are the mean ages of substance-addicted patients at a local treatment facility separated out by type of primary addiction (fictional data). Calculate the mean age of all substance-addicted patients at the facility.

	Primary Addiction			
	Cocaine *(n = 44)*	*Crack Cocaine* *(n = 29)*	*Heroin* *(n = 24)*	*Alcohol* *(n = 69)*
Mean age (years)	29.8	23.4	34.6	42.9

15. In an experiment to see whether chickens can distinguish colors, rewards of corn kernels are supplied when a chicken correctly pecks a pad with matching colors. Reaction times are measured to the nearest one-hundredth of a second. Flossy's reaction times are as follows: 1.32, 1.45, 1.21, 1.05, .97, .91, .93, .93, .96, .93, .88, .94, .98.

    a. Organize the data into a frequency distribution table.
    b. Calculate Flossy's mean, median, and modal reaction times.
    c. Describe the shape of the distribution of Flossy's reaction times.

16. The batting averages of the starting lineup of the little league team, the Fastball Dodgers, are as follows: .360, .200, .350, .355, .230, .345, .360, .380, and .400.

    a. Organize the data into a frequency distribution table.
    b. Calculate the team's mean, median, and modal batting averages.
    c. Describe the shape of the distribution.

17. Given the following statistics and what we know about how they are related within a distribution of scores, indicate the shape of the distribution for each variable listed.

Variable	$\bar{X}$	Mdn	Mo	Shape of Curve
Age (years)	30	35	39	
Household size	4.1	3.0	2.0	
Years employed	11	8	7	
Weight (pounds)	160	132	134	

18. Given the following statistics and what we know about how they are related within a distribution of scores, indicate the shape of the distribution for each variable listed.

Variable	$\bar{X}$	Mdn	Mo	Shape of Curve
Height (inches)	70	68	66	
Exams this semester	10	13	15	
Spirituality score	30	30	30	
Grocery budget	$130	$109	$104	

Optional Computer Applications for Chapter 4

The optional computer exercises for Chapter 4 are found on the *Computer Applications for The Statistical Imagination* compact disk. These exercises include generating central tendency statistics using *SPSS for Windows* and using central tendency statistics to gain a sense of proportion about the shapes of score distributions.

5

MEASURING DISPERSION OR SPREAD IN A DISTRIBUTION OF SCORES

Introduction

Reporting a central tendency statistic by itself is not enough to convey the shape of a distribution of scores. Two samples with the same means can have radically different shapes. Figure 5–1 shows two distributions of ages: for a sample of elementary school pupils (grades kindergarten through six, or K–6) and for a third-grade class from a second school. The mean age of the pupils in both schools is 8.5 years. In the K–6 school, however, children are as young as 5 and as old as 12. In the third-grade class of the other school, none of the pupils is under 7 or over 10 years of age. Although these two distributions of ages have the same central tendency, their scores are dispersed very differently, with a greater spread of ages at the K–6 school.

The topic of this chapter is **dispersion,** *how the scores of an interval/ratio variable are spread out from lowest to highest and the shape of the distribution in between.* (As a memory aid, recall that Johnny Appleseed *dispersed* apple seeds.) There are an infinite number of possible distribution shapes for a variable with

FIGURE 5–1

Comparison of the spreads of ages of pupils in two samples with the same means

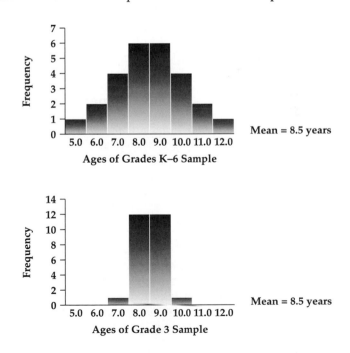

a given mean. All scores could be lumped around the mean with the distinct shape of a bell curve, but the curve could be of different sizes, depending on the sample size. Or scores could be slightly or greatly skewed to one side. Furthermore, a single variable may have very different spreads from one population to another. For example, yearly household income for residents of the United States ranges from zero to tens of millions of dollars while the household income of the poor living in housing projects ranges from zero to a few thousand dollars.

Dispersion

How the scores of an interval/ratio variable are spread out from lowest to highest and the shape of the distribution in between.

Dispersion statistics *describe how the scores of an interval/ratio variable are spread across its distribution.* Dispersion statistics allow precise descriptions of the frequency of cases at any point in a distribution. For instance, if the federal government decides to increase taxes for "the rich," by using dispersion statistics, we can identify the income level of the wealthiest 5 percent of all households. Similarly, if a public welfare program is budgeted to cover only 10,000 city households, we can establish what household income level qualifies for assistance. Studying dispersion is like taking a walk back and forth across the X-axis of a histogram and observing where cases are concentrated. Do most cases fall around the mean, or are they off to one side? How many cases fall between any two points? What value of the variable lops off the top 10 percent of cases? The two most used dispersion statistics are discussed below: the range and the standard deviation.

Dispersion Statistics

Statistics that describe how the scores of an interval/ratio (or interval-like ordinal) variable are spread across its distribution.

The Range

The **range** is *an expression of how the scores of an interval/ratio variable are distributed from lowest to highest*—the distance between the minimum and maximum scores found in a sample. It is computed as the difference between the maximum and minimum scores plus the value of the rounding unit. The value of the rounding unit (e.g., 1 if scores are rounded to the nearest whole number, 0.1 if scores are rounded to the nearest tenth, and so on) is added to account for the lower real limit of the lowest score and the upper real limit of the highest score.

Computing the Range of an Interval/Ratio Variable X

1. Rank the scores in the distribution from lowest to highest.
2. Identify the minimum and maximum scores.
3. Identify the value of the rounding unit (see Appendix A for a review).
4. Calculate the range:

Range = (maximum score – minimum score) + value of rounding unit

The Range

An expression of how the scores of an interval/ratio variable are distributed from lowest to highest.

Let us compute the range for a sample problem. Suppose X = age (rounded to the nearest year) and we have the following distribution of scores:

$$21, 23, 43, 26, 20, 21, 25$$

Start by ranking the scores:

$$20, 21, 21, 23, 25, 26, 43$$

Identify the minimum and maximum scores of 20 and 43, respectively, and identify that the rounding unit is 1.
Compute the range:

Range = (maximum score – minimum score) + value of rounding unit
= (43 – 20) + 1 = 24 years

As a result of rounding, the individual who scored 20 could be as young as 19.5 years and the 43-year-old could be as old as 43.5 years. The range of 24 years is the distance between these lower and upper real limits of the scores; that is, 43.5 years – 19.5 years = 24 years.

Often it is more informative to report the minimum and maximum scores themselves by saying that these ages range from 20 to 43. This way we indirectly show that there is no one in the sample under about 20 years of age or over about 43 years of age.

Limitations of the Range: Situations Where Reporting It Alone May Mislead

Since the range uses the most extreme scores of the distribution, an outlier will greatly inflate its calculation. This happened for the seven ages shown above. The 43-year-old made the range appear to be spread out over 24 years. Reporting this would give the impression that the sample has a considerable number

Figure 5–2

*Comparison of two
differently shaped
distributions that
have the same
range*

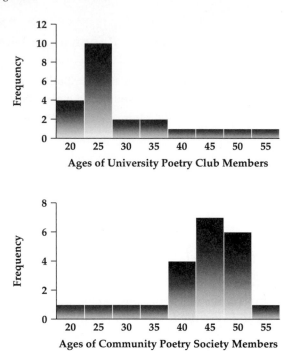

of 30- and 40-year-olds. A more accurate report would stipulate that with the exception of the 43-year-old student, the ages had a range of 7 years (26 – 20 + 1 = 7). Removing the outlier and noting it as an exception is a reasonable way of adjusting for this limitation of the range.

The range also is limited by its narrow informational scope. It tells us nothing about the shape of the distribution between the extreme scores. For example, the two distributions depicted in Figure 5–2 have the same range, suggesting similar shapes, but in fact their shapes are radically different. Finally, there is little one can do mathematically with the range. In sum, the range has limited usefulness, especially when reported alone.

The Standard Deviation

The standard deviation is another summary measurement of the dispersion or spread of scores in a distribution. This dispersion statistic is fundamentally different from the range. By focusing on the extremes of the distribution, the range approaches dispersion from the "outsides" or ends of the distribution. Viewing the range is like watching a basketball game from high in the stands; the court appears boxed in by the goals at each end. In contrast, the **standard deviation** *describes how scores of an interval/ratio variable or interval-like ordinal are spread across the distribution in relation to the mean score.* The mean is a central tendency statistic and as such provides a point of focus that is centered "inside" the distribution. Viewing spread from the mean with its standard deviation is like watching from center court; the focus is on distance from center court to other points in either direction. Like the mean, the standard deviation is most appropriate with interval/ratio variables and interval-like ordinal variables.

The Standard Deviation

Describes how scores of an interval/ratio (or interval-like ordinal) variable are spread across the distribution in relation to the mean score.

Proportional and Linear Thinking about the Standard Deviation

The standard deviation is computed by determining how far each score is from the mean—how far it *deviates* from the mean. In this sense, the standard deviation is a derivative (or offspring) of the mean, and the two measures are always reported together. In fact, the phrase "the mean, and standard deviation" is the one most often used by statisticians. The standard deviation—as a summary measurement of all the scores in a distribution—tells how widely scores cluster around the mean. As we shall see shortly, the standard deviation also is useful in conjunction with the normal curve.

Before computing a standard deviation, let us study its formula. The following is the formula for directly computing the standard deviation:

Direct Method of Computing the Standard Deviation

$$s_X = \sqrt{\frac{\Sigma(X - \bar{X})^2}{n - 1}}$$

where

s_X = standard deviation for the interval/ratio variable X

$\bar{X}$ = mean of X

n = sample size

It is worthwhile to take a step-by-step approach to the computation of the standard deviation. This removes the mystery from the formula (with its Σ, square, and square root symbols) and helps us appreciate that the standard deviation is an essential part of the normal curve.

Identify Givens.   We start by identifying the information given.

Given: X = an interval/ratio (or interval-like ordinal) variable, n = sample size, and the distribution of raw scores for X.

Compute the Mean.   We compute the mean because the standard deviation is designed to measure spread around the mean.

$$\bar{X} = \frac{\sum X}{n}$$

Compute Deviation Scores: Linear Thinking.   Next we determine how far each subject's score falls from the mean. The difference between a score and its mean is called a **deviation score,** *how much an individual score differs or "deviates" from the mean:*

$$X - \bar{X} = \text{deviation score for a value of } X$$

Think of a deviation score as a measure of distance on the X-axis. What does the deviation score tell us? Suppose X is the variable weight and the mean weight for a sample of women volleyball players from Elmstown University is 138 pounds. The star player, Sandra "Soul Spiker" Carson, weighs 173 pounds; this is her raw score or "X-score." Her deviation score is plus 35 pounds:

$$\text{Deviation score} = X - \bar{X} = 173 - 138 = 35 \text{ pounds}$$

The deviation score tells us two things about a score in the distribution: (1) the amount or distance the X-score falls from the mean and (2) the direction of the X-score: whether it is below or above the mean. When an X-score is greater than the mean, the deviation score will compute to a positive value, like Sandra's, meaning that the X-score lies to the right on a distribution curve. When an X-score is less than the mean, the deviation score will compute to a negative, meaning that the X-score lies to the left of the mean. Sandra's deviation score of +35 pounds tells us that she is 35 pounds *above* the mean weight of the team.

Deviation Score

How much an individual score differs or "deviates" from the mean.

The deviation score is the central mathematical computation in computing the standard deviation. As a summary measurement for the whole sample, the standard deviation is a summation and average of these deviation scores squared, as in the steps below.

Sum the Deviation Scores.   The next step in computing the standard deviation is to sum the deviation scores. This sum will always equal zero (within rounding error):

$$\sum(X - \bar{X}) = 0 = \text{sum of the deviation scores}$$

The summation of deviation scores is a check on the accuracy of computations because the sum of deviation scores will *always* equal zero (within rounding error). We spoke in Chapter 4 of how the mean is a balance point in the distribution. What the mean does is balance the deviations so that they cancel one another out and result in a sum of deviation scores of zero. In fact, another mathematical definition of the **mean** is *that point in a distribution where the deviation scores sum to zero.*

Square the Deviation Scores and Sum the Squares.   The dispersion of a variable is often compared for two or more samples. Summing the deviation scores will not detect a difference in spread between two samples because the sum for both will be zero. This potentially leaves us on a dead-end street. If one sample's scores are widely spread out and the other's are only narrowly spread out, what good is it to report that both have a sum of deviation scores of zero? None! Therefore, in comparing two samples, we must find a way to sum the deviation scores so that the sum is larger for a sample with a greater spread. The most useful solution is to square each deviation score and then sum the squares. Squaring eliminates negative signs in deviation scores. *The sum of squared deviation scores* is the **variation** (often referred to as the **sum of squares**), *a statistic that summarizes deviations for the entire sample:*

$$\Sigma(X - \bar{X})^2 = \text{the variation (or "sum of squares")}$$

The Variation or the Sum of Squares

The sum of squared deviation scores; a statistic that summarizes deviations for the entire sample.

Divide the sum of squares by $n - 1$ to Adjust for Sample Size and Error: Proportional Thinking.   The sum of squares, or variation, is a good measure of the spread of a distribution, but this statistic presents two problems. First, suppose we wish to compare distributions from two samples of different sizes. For instance, we may compare the distributions of grade point averages (GPAs) for student samples from Crosstown University ($n = 88$) and State University ($n = 104$). When we sum the squares for each sample, we may find a higher sum for State University simply because we summed more numbers—104 cases rather than a mere 88. Each X-score adds some amount to the computation. In other words, everything else being equal, the more observations, the larger the sum of squares. To make a balanced comparison of two different-size samples, then, we need to adjust for the number of observations in each sample by dividing each by its sample size (n). This gives us the average variation (the mean of the sum of squares) in each sample. In this manner we adjust the sum of squares in proportion to the number of cases in the sample.

A second consideration regarding sample size is that it will encompass sampling error; the larger the sample, the less the sampling error. Statisticians have determined that if we subtract 1 from n, this slight adjustment results in a sample statistic that more accurately estimates the parameter of the population. Put simply, by subtracting 1 from the sample size, we make an adjustment for sampling error. (Note that with large samples, this adjustment would have very little effect on the calculation, whereas with small samples, it would have a great effect.)

In summary, we divide the variation (sum of squares) by $n - 1$ to account for the effects of sample size on the sum and to account for sampling error. The result is called the variance, and its symbols is s_X^2:

$$s_X^2 = \frac{\Sigma (X - \bar{X})^2}{n - 1} = \text{variance of a sample}$$

The **variance** is *the average variation of scores in a distribution*. To avoid confusing variance and variation, note the accented n sound in "variance" and note that n is in its denominator. (Finally, we should note that if the standard deviation is computed for the scores of an entire population, sampling error is not an issue. Therefore, we do not need to subtract 1 from n to obtain the variance of a population, which would be symbolized as σ_X^2.)

The Variance

The average variation of scores in a distribution (i.e., the mean of the sum of squares).

Take the Square Root of the Variance to Obtain the Standard Deviation. A final step is required to produce a good measure of spread. The variance is perfectly acceptable for calculations, but it is not directly interpretable because the units of measure are squared. Thus, we might compute the variance of weight for Crosstown University's football team and find it to be 1,391.45 squared pounds. Well, what is a "squared pound"? It is a pound times a pound, but who knows what that really means except perhaps a mathematician? We need a directly interpretable unit of measure—pounds instead of squared pounds. To "get back to" pounds, we take the square root of the variance. (The square root of a squared unit of measure is the unit of measure itself.) The result is the standard deviation:

$$s_X = \sqrt{\frac{\Sigma(X - \bar{X})^2}{n - 1}} = \sqrt{s_X^2}$$

In the case of the Crosstown team's weight, the standard deviation would be 37.30 pounds:

$$s_X = \sqrt{\frac{\Sigma(X - \bar{X})^2}{n - 1}} = \sqrt{s_X^2}$$

$$= \sqrt{1391.45} = 37.30 \text{ pounds}$$

The steps outlined above involve a direct computation of the standard deviation. The elements of the equation—deviation scores, the sum of squares or variation, and the variance—are important in and of themselves. These elements appear by themselves in many statistical formulas (see, for example, Chapter 12). The steps for directly calculating the standard deviation are summarized in Table 5–1 which you will find useful in later chapters.

It is a good practice to set up a spreadsheet for these computations. Table 5–2 presents a spreadsheet for computing the standard deviation of the weights of 12 of the 98 players on Crosstown's football team. (Column 5 of the

TABLE 5–1   Understanding the Standard Deviation through Its Direct Computation

Step in Computing the Standard Deviation	*What the Step Accomplishes*
1. Identify the givens.	1. X must be an interval/ratio (or interval-like ordinal) variable.
2. Compute the mean: $$\bar{X} = \frac{\Sigma \bar{X}}{n}$$	2. Because the standard deviation is based on deviations from the mean.
3. Compute deviation scores: $$X - \bar{X}$$	3. To determine each score's distance from the mean.
4. Sum the deviation scores: $$\Sigma(X - \bar{X})$$	4. Make sure that $$\Sigma(X - \bar{X}) = 0$$
5. Square the deviation scores and sum them to obtain the variation or sum of squares: $$\text{Variation} = \Sigma(X - \bar{X})^2$$	5. The deviation scores are squared to remove negative signs and obtain a sum other than zero.
6. Compute the variance: $$s_X^2 = \frac{\Sigma(X - \bar{X})^2}{n - 1}$$	6. Divide the sum of squares by $n - 1$ to adjust for sample size and sampling error.
7. Compute the standard deviation, s_X: $$s_X = \sqrt{\frac{\Sigma(X - \bar{X})^2}{n - 1}} = \sqrt{s_X^2}$$	7. Take the square root of the variance to obtain directly interpretable units of measure (units instead of squared units).

TABLE 5–2   Spreadsheet for Computing the Standard Deviation Using the Direct and Shortcut Methods of Computation: Weight of Crosstown Football Players ($n = 12$)

Givens		Calculations		
(1) Player	*(2)* X	*(3)* $X - \bar{X}$	*(4)* $(X - \bar{X})^2$	*(5)* X^2
1	165	−73	5,329	27,225
2	200	−38	1,444	40,000
3	216	−22	484	46,656
4	217	−21	441	47,089
5	226	−12	144	51,076
6	236	−2	4	55,696
7	239	1	1	57,121
8	244	6	36	59,536
9	261	23	529	68,121
10	268	30	900	71,824
11	283	45	2,025	80,089
12	301	63	3,969	90,601
$n = 12$	$\Sigma X = 2{,}856$ pounds	$\Sigma(X - \bar{X}) = 0$	$\Sigma(X - \bar{X})^2 = 15{,}306$ squared pounds	$\Sigma X^2 = 695{,}034$ squared pounds

table is used with a shortcut computational method that will be described shortly.)

To compute the deviation scores, $X - \bar{X}$, we calculate the mean and subtract each score from it to produce the third column of the spreadsheet:

$$\bar{X} = \frac{\Sigma X}{n} = \frac{2856}{12} = 238 \text{ pounds}$$

Finally, we square the deviation scores in column 3 to obtain column 4. The sum in column 4 of Table 5–2 and the sample size n are all we need to compute the standard deviation:

$$s_X = \sqrt{\frac{\Sigma(X - \bar{X})^2}{n - 1}} = \sqrt{\frac{15{,}306}{11}} = \sqrt{1391.45} = 37.30 \text{ pounds}$$

Shortcut Method of Computing the Standard Deviation

Our purpose in doing the direct computation of the standard deviation is to gain a sense of proportion about how it measures deviations from the mean. On a day-to-day basis, however, directly computing the standard deviation is cumbersome and error-prone. It requires computing the mean and then doing lots of error-prone subtraction, something that is especially troublesome with decimal numbers. Fortunately, there is a shortcut or "computational" method of calculation, which is arrived at by substituting $\Sigma X/n$ for the mean of X and expanding the direct formula equation:

$$s_X = \sqrt{\frac{\Sigma(X - \bar{X})^2}{n - 1}} = \sqrt{\frac{\Sigma[X - (\Sigma X/n)]^2}{n - 1}} = \sqrt{\frac{\Sigma X^2 - \frac{(\Sigma X)^2}{n}}{n - 1}}$$

Shortcut Method of Computing the Standard Deviation

$$s_X = \sqrt{\frac{\Sigma X^2 - \frac{(\Sigma X)^2}{n}}{n - 1}}$$

where

s_X = standard deviation for the interval/ratio variable X
n = sample size

This shortcut formula does not require computing the mean and deviation scores. In Table 5–2, we simply square *each raw score* in column 2 to obtain column 5. The sums of columns 2 and 5 are then plugged into the shortcut formula:

$$s_X = \sqrt{\frac{\Sigma X^2 - \frac{(\Sigma X)^2}{n}}{n - 1}} = \sqrt{\frac{695,034 - \frac{(2,856)^2}{12}}{11}} = 37.30 \text{ pounds}$$

One cautionary note: Be careful to distinguish between $(\Sigma X)^2$, the same sum (from column 2) that is used to compute the mean, and ΣX^2 from column 5. For the purpose of learning statistics, calculating the standard deviation with both methods is a good way to check for computational errors. If the two answers are not the same within a small amount of rounding error, recheck all calculations.

Limitations of the Standard Deviation

Since the standard deviation is computed from the mean, like the mean it is inflated by outliers. Outliers produce large deviation scores. When squared, these large deviations, whether positive or negative, produce a large positive, inflated result. Thus, the standard deviation can be very misleading when reported for a skewed distribution in which a few scores are strung out in one direction. To convince yourself of the effect of extreme scores on both the mean and the standard deviation, complete the spreadsheet in Table 5–2 but add the following two cases to obtain a new sample with $n = 14$: player 13 who weighs 115 pounds and player 14 who weighs 125 pounds. Then compare the answers from the original and new samples.

The Standard Deviation as an Integral Part of Inferential Statistics

The features of the mean and the standard deviation make them highly useful for getting a sense of proportion about individual variables under study. The standard deviation and the deviation scores from which it is computed are also essential for examining the relationships between two variables. The focus of inferential statistics is to gain an understanding of why the individual scores of a dependent variable deviate from its mean.

Suppose, for instance, we are studying alcohol abuse. For a sample of adult drinkers, we find that the mean consumption of alcoholic beverages is 4.3 gallons per year. Gary consumed 7.3 gallons last year, 3 gallons over the mean. Sam consumed only 1 gallon, 3.3 gallons less than the mean. What accounts for these high and low deviations? Perhaps we could hypothesize some predictor (independent) variables we believe are related to this dependent variable. For example, the mealtime consumption hypothesis might explain part of Gary's positive deviation score: Drinkers from families that consume wine with meals have a higher mean alcohol consumption. There is also the social drinker hypothesis, which might explain part of Sam's negative deviation score: Drinkers who consume alcohol only when it is served at social functions have a lower mean alcohol consumption.

For an entire sample, our interest is in explaining the variation—the sum of squared deviation scores. Deviation scores, the variation, and the standard deviation are simply measures of differences in scores for a variable among the subjects of a population. Is the mean amount of yearly alcohol consumption higher for persons in some regions, among different age or religious groups, or between the sexes? The answers to such questions hinge on the mathematical properties of the mean, the standard deviation, and the normal curve.

Why Is It Called the "Standard" Deviation?

The standard deviation gets its name from the fact that it provides a *common unit of measure* (a standard) for comparing variables with very different *observed units of measure*. For example, imagine that Mary Smith and Jason Jones are both applying for a scholarship based on college admissions test performance. Mary took the Academic College Testing Service (ACT) test and scored 26 ACT points. Jason took the Stanford Admissions Test (SAT) and scored 900 SAT points. These two test scores have very different observed units of measure: ACT test points range from zero to 36, and SAT test points range from 200 to 1,600. Raw scores for the two tests cannot be compared directly. By using the means and standard deviations for both tests, however, we can devise a way of comparing them. With the following statistics, we find that in comparison to others taking these tests, Mary had the higher score:

$$X = \text{ACT test score} \qquad \bar{X} = 22 \text{ ACT points} \qquad s_X = 2 \text{ ACT points}$$

$$Y = \text{SAT test score} \qquad \bar{Y} = 1{,}000 \text{ SAT points} \qquad s_Y = 100 \text{ SAT points}$$

Mary's ACT score of 26 is 2 standard deviations above the mean for those taking the ACT test; that is, her score is 4 ACT points—2 times 2 standard deviations—above the average of 22. Jason scores *1 standard deviation below* the mean for those taking the SAT test; that is, his score is 100 SAT points—1 standard deviation—below the average of 1,000. Without hesitation we can award the scholarship to Mary. By using standard deviations as units of measure in place of "ACT test points" and "SAT test points," we have a common yardstick or standard of measure for these two variables—hence the name *standard* deviation. Who said you cannot compare apples to oranges?

Standardized Scores (Z-Scores)

The example above illustrates the fact that a research subject's score on any interval/ratio variable may be expressed in several ways. First, we can *express it in its original, observed units of measure* as a **raw score.** For example, Mary's raw score of X is 26 ACT points. Second, we can *express it as a deviation from the mean* (i.e., the deviation score $X - \bar{X}$); Mary's deviation score is +4, meaning that she scored 4 ACT points above the mean for those who took the ACT. Third, we can express her score as *a number of standard deviations from the mean* ACT score. We call this her **standardized score (or Z-score),** which is computed as follows for the variable X:

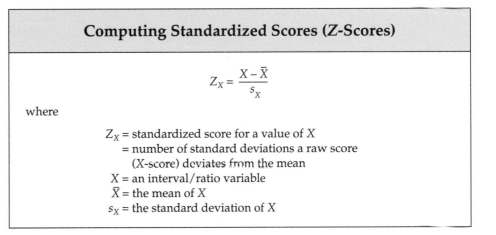

Computing Standardized Scores (Z-Scores)

$$Z_X = \frac{X - \bar{X}}{s_X}$$

where

Z_X = standardized score for a value of X
    = number of standard deviations a raw score
      (X-score) deviates from the mean
X = an interval/ratio variable
$\bar{X}$ = the mean of X
s_X = the standard deviation of X

If we set $X =$ ACT score with $\bar{X} = 22$ ACT points and $s_X = 2$ ACT points, Mary's Z-score is

$$Z_X = \frac{X - \bar{X}}{s_X} = \frac{26 - 22}{2} = \frac{4}{2} = 2.00 \text{ SD}$$

where SD means "standard deviations." A Z-score is an X-score's distance from the mean (i.e., its deviation score) divided into standard deviation unit distances.

A key to keeping track of these three ways of expressing score is to focus on the units of measure. Raw scores *and* deviation scores for a variable are presented in the original observed unit of measure, which of course is defined by a variable. For example, the observed unit of measure for age is years; for weight, pounds; for height, inches; and so on. But no matter what the unit of measure of a variable is, its Z-scores are measured in SD. Table 5–3 summarizes these distinctions.

Here are some examples from a random sample of women students at Crosstown University:

1. Where X = weight, $\bar{X}$ = 120 pounds, s_X = 10 pounds:

Case	X (weight)	X − X̄ (deviation score)	Z_X (standardized score)
Cheryl Jones	110 pounds	−10 pounds	−1 SD
Jennifer Smith	125 pounds	5 pounds	.5 SD
Terri Barnett	107 pounds	−13 pounds	−1.3 SD

2. Where Y = height, $\bar{Y}$ = 65 inches, s_Y = 3 inches:

Case	Y (height)	Y − Ȳ (deviation score)	Z_Y (standardized score)
Cheryl Jones	64 inches	−1 inch	−.33 SD
Jennifer Smith	65 inches	0 inch	0 SD
Terri Barnett	68 inches	3 inches	1 SD

TABLE 5–3   The Different Ways in Which a Variable's Scores Can Be Presented

Form of Score for a Variable and Its Symbol	Units of Measure of the Variable	Example: X = Height
Raw score (X-score): X	The variable's unit of measure	Inches
Deviation score = $X - \bar{X}$	The variable's unit of measure	Inches
Standardized score (Z_X) or "Z-score": $Z_X = \dfrac{X - \bar{X}}{s_X}$	Standard deviations of the variable (SD)	SD

Keep in mind that both deviation scores *and* Z-scores are measures of the distance from a variable's raw score to its mean. The deviation score is obtained by subtracting the mean from the raw score (i.e., $X - \bar{X}$). In dividing this deviation score by the standard deviation, we cut this deviation score into parts and multiples of standard deviations from the mean. Recall that after computing the mean, computing the deviation scores is the next thing we do when we calculate the standard deviation. The essence of the standard deviation is viewing an individual's raw score as a deviation from the mean.

To gain a good sense of proportion about the formulas for deviation scores and Z-scores, let us examine the relationships among the sizes of raw scores, deviation scores, and Z-scores. First, the farther from the mean an X-score is, the larger are its deviation score and Z-score. Moreover, the sign of any deviation score and Z-score indicates the **direction of a score:** *whether that observation fell above the mean (the positive direction) or below the mean (the negative direction).* The sign "–"(minus sign) indicates that a raw score is below the mean; the sign "+" (plus sign) which is implied, not written, indicates that it is above the mean. In the examples above, Cheryl and Terri are below average on weight and Terri is above average on height. In fact, we can tell from these Z-scores that Terri is a tall, thin person—more than 1 SD below on weight but 1 SD above on height. Jennifer is the mean height; thus, her deviation score and Z-score for Y are zero: she deviates none from the mean height.

Since we will be using Z-scores or similar measures of deviation in every chapter in the remainder of this text, it is wise to practice computing deviation scores and Z-scores and to study the directions (signs) of those scores. A simple double check is in order. If a raw score is below the mean, its deviation and Z-scores are negative. Also keep in mind that Z-scores are just another way to express raw scores. Every raw score has a corresponding Z-score, and vice versa.

The Normal Distribution

In addition to providing a standard of comparison between different variables and samples, under the appropriate conditions the mean and the standard deviation provide a wealth of information. This is the case when a variable has a distribution of scores that is normal—shaped like the normal distribution curve. As we defined it in Chapter 4, a normal distribution is symmetrical, with its mean, median, and mode equal to one another and located in the center of the curve. Symmetry or balance in the curve is not the whole picture, however. The normal curve also has a distinct bell shape that is not too flat or too peaked. Many variables are normally distributed (such as height, weight, and intelligence). Regardless of which variable is examined, if it is normally distributed, it carries the properties of a normal curve.

What makes the standard deviation such a valuable statistical tool is that it is a mathematical part of the normal curve. As you follow the curve from its center (i.e., its peak) out in either direction, the curve changes shape to approach the *X*-axis. From the peak, the point at which the curve begins to shift outward is 1 standard deviation from the mean. This point is called the point of inflection, and it is highlighted in Figure 5–3. This indicates that the mean and the standard deviation are mathematical aspects of a natural phenomenon: the tendency for a bell-shaped, normal distribution to occur for many natural events.

Understanding the phenomenon of normality is an important aspect of the statistical imagination. Many naturally occurring phenomena have frequency distributions which take the bell shape of the normal curve. The normal curve depicts the fact that as we deviate farther from the mean, we can expect fewer and fewer cases. For many variables, there is an average around which most scores fall, and as we move away from this average, case frequencies diminish. For example, physical height is normally distributed; most people are about average, with just a few really tall people and really short people.

One of the best features of the naturally occurring phenomenon of normality is that it allows precise predictions of how many of a population's scores fall within any score range. As illustrated in Figure 5–3, *for any normally distributed variable:*

1. Fifty percent of the scores fall above the mean, and 50 percent fall below. This is due to the fact that the median is equal to the mean.

2. Virtually all scores fall within 3 standard deviations of the mean in both directions. This is a distance of 3 *Z*-scores below to 3 *Z*-scores above the mean, a width of 6 standard deviations across. The precise amount is 99.7 percent. The remaining .3 percent of cases (that is, 3 cases out of 1,000) fall outside 3 standard deviations, and theoretically the curve extends into infinity in both directions. (Practically speaking, the scores for some variables, such as personal weight, have finite limits.)

3. Approximately 95 percent of the scores of a normally distributed variable fall within 2 standard deviations distance in both directions from the mean. This is plus and minus 2 *Z*-scores from the mean.

4. Approximately 68 percent of the scores of a normally distributed variable fall within 1 standard deviation (plus or minus 1 *Z*-score) distance in both directions from the mean.

Keep in mind that the normal distribution has very predictable features. *If a variable is distributed in this peculiar bell shape,* we can use sample statistics and what we know about the normal curve to estimate how many scores *in a population* fall within a certain range.

To illustrate the utility of the normal curve, let us follow through on the example above, a sample of women students from Crosstown University, where X = weight, the mean weight is 120 pounds, and s_X = 10 pounds. First, we need to make sure that the distribution of scores is indeed normal, that is, that it is bell-shaped. This could be done by producing a histogram of the

FIGURE 5–3

The relationship of the standard deviation to the normal curve

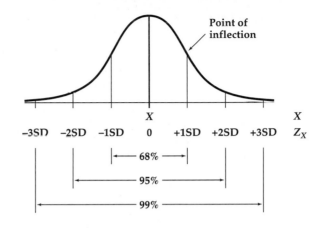

scores from a sample (not shown). If this graph appears roughly bell-shaped, we can assume that this variable is normally distributed not only in the sample but also in the population. We refer to this as "assuming normality." (The shape of a sample histogram can be slightly off from normal as a result of sampling error.) As is graphed in Figure 5–4, assuming normality, we can make the following estimates of the weights of the population of female students at Crosstown University:

1. Half these female students weigh over 120 pounds.
2. Approximately 68 percent of Crosstown University's female students weigh between 110 and 130 pounds.
3. Approximately 95 percent of Crosstown University's female students weigh between 100 and 140 pounds.
4. Very few weigh under 90 pounds or over 150 pounds.

FIGURE 5–4

Using the normal curve to estimate the weight (X) distribution of female students at Crosstown University

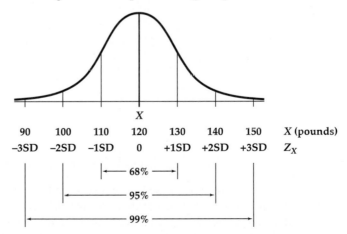

Remember, a Z-score is just another way to express a raw score (i.e., the X-score for an individual observation). If Susannah weighs 110 pounds, she is 1 SD below the mean weight and has a Z-score of –1.00 SD.

Using the Range to Estimate the Standard Deviation

If a distribution is normal, nearly all cases fall within 3 standard deviations distance from both sides of the mean (as shown in Figures 5–3 and 5–4). This means that a normally distributed variable is very close to exactly 6 standard deviations wide. In fact, 95 percent of scores in a normal distribution can be found within 2 standard deviations on both sides of the mean. Recall that the range provides a measure of the expanse of scores in a distribution: the distance from the lowest to the highest. If a variable is normally distributed, the size of the range should be about 4 to 6 standard deviations wide because this expanse of scores encompasses nearly 100 percent of the scores. Thus, to estimate the standard deviation, we can divide the range by 4 or 6, with the former being the conventional method:

Estimating the Standard Deviation Using the Range

$$\text{Estimate of } s_X \text{ based on the range} = \frac{\text{range}}{4}$$

where

s_X = the standard deviation for the variable X

Range = (maximum score – minimum score) + value of rounding unit

---

Before computing the standard deviation using either the direct method or the shortcut method of computation, it is a good idea to estimate it by dividing the range by 4. This estimate and the subsequent calculation of the standard deviation should be close in value. If they are not, this is a signal that the distribution may be skewed or that outliers are stretching the value of the range. In these situations, observation of a histogram provides insight into the discrepancy between the estimated and the calculated values.

With its mathematical ties to the mean and the standard deviation, the normal curve is a very useful device, particularly as a probability distribution, the topic of Chapter 6.

A Complete Illustration of Dispersion Statistics Calculations

Now that we have discussed the concepts behind the range and the standard deviation, let us a complete a problem to illustrate the basic organization of descriptive statistics. The three most commonly reported statistics for interval/ratio data are the mean, the standard deviation, and the range.

Using a Spreadsheet Format to Calculate the Standard Deviation

Table 5–4 presents a spreadsheet on the gasoline excise taxes charged by selected Western states; thus, X = gasoline tax per gallon, and we have ranked the scores.

First, let us calculate the range. With these ranked scores, we see that the minimum score is 17 cents and the maximum is 28 cents. Our rounding unit is a whole number.

$$\text{Range} = (\text{maximum score} - \text{minimum score}) + \text{value of rounding unit}$$
$$= (28 - 17) + 1 = 12\text{¢}$$

Second, we estimate the standard deviation using the range:

$$\text{Estimate of } s_X \text{ based on the range} = \frac{\text{range}}{4} = \frac{12}{4} = 3\text{¢}$$

Third, we compute the mean and use it to calculate deviation scores and to complete the sums in the spreadsheet (Table 5–4):

$$\overline{X} = \frac{\Sigma X}{n} = \frac{217}{10} = 21.7\text{¢}$$

TABLE 5–4   State Excise Taxes on Gasoline in Selected Western States in May 1996

	Givens	Calculations		
State	*Tax (¢) per Gallon* X	*Deviations* $X - \overline{X}$	$(X - \overline{X})^2$	X^2
New Mexico	17	−4.7	22.09	289
California	18	−3.7	13.69	324
Arizona	18	−3.7	13.69	324
Utah	19	−2.7	7.29	361
Colorado	22	.3	.09	484
Washington	23	1.3	1.69	529
Nevada	23	1.3	1.69	529
Oregon	24	2.3	5.29	576
Idaho	25	3.3	10.89	625
Montana	28	6.3	39.69	784

$\Sigma X = 217\text{¢}$ $\Sigma(X - \overline{X})^2 = 116.10$ squared ¢

$n = 10$ $\Sigma(X - \overline{X}) = 0$ $\Sigma X^2 = 4{,}825$ squared ¢

SOURCE: Tax rates from http://www.api.org/news/596sttax.htm. Copyright © 1996 by American Petroleum Institute. Reprinted by permission of the Institute.

Fourth, we calculate the standard deviation using the direct method of computation:

$$s_X = \sqrt{\frac{\Sigma(X - \bar{X})^2}{n-1}} = \sqrt{\frac{116.10}{9}} = 3.59\text{¢}$$

Fifth, we calculate the standard deviation using the shortcut method:

$$s_X = \sqrt{\frac{\Sigma X^2 - \frac{(\Sigma X)^2}{n}}{n-1}} = \sqrt{\frac{4{,}825 - \frac{(217)^2}{10}}{9}} = 3.59\text{¢}$$

Sixth, we check to see if both calculations of the standard deviation produced the same answer. This is the case. Finally, we compare the computed standard deviation to the estimate and see that they are relatively close. If the estimate had been half the size or twice the size of the calculated value, that would have warranted checking for outliers or other peculiarities in the distribution of scores. Now that we have the mean and the standard deviation, we can see that gasoline excise taxes average about 22 cents per gallon and that about two out of three states (about 68 percent) are within 3.59 cents of this average.

Using a Frequency Distribution Format to Calculate the Standard Deviation

In Chapter 4 we noted that a frequency distribution format is a more concise way to organize data. Using this format simply requires counting each score the number of times (f) it occurs. Table 5–5 presents the data on gasoline taxes as a frequency distribution. Let us calculate the standard deviation with formulas modified to account for the frequency (f) of each score.

First, let us calculate the range. In Table 5–5 the scores are ranked with a minimum score of 17 cents and a maximum of 28 cents. Our rounding unit is a whole number. Thus,

Range = (maximum score − minimum score) + value of rounding unit
= (28 − 17) + 1 = 12¢

Second, we estimate the standard deviation using the range, just as we did above:

$$\text{Estimate of } s_X \text{ based on the range} = \frac{\text{range}}{4} = \frac{12}{4} = 3\text{¢}$$

Third, we compute the mean and use it to calculate deviation scores and complete the sums in Table 5–5:

$$\bar{X} = \frac{\Sigma f(X)}{n} = \frac{217}{10} = 21.7\text{¢}$$

TABLE 5–5   **Calculation of the Standard Deviation Using a Frequency Distribution Format**
(State Excise Taxes on Gasoline for Selected Western States in May 1996)

Givens		Calculations						
X	f	$f(X)$	$(X - \bar{X})$	$f(X - \bar{X})$	$(X - \bar{X})^2$	$f(X - \bar{X})^2$	X^2	$f(X^2)$
17	1	17	–4.7	–4.7	22.09	22.09	289	289
18	2	36	–3.7	–7.4	13.69	27.38	324	648
19	1	19	–2.7	–2.7	7.29	7.29	361	361
22	1	22	.3	.3	.09	.09	484	484
23	2	46	1.3	2.6	1.69	3.38	529	1058
24	1	24	2.3	2.3	5.29	5.29	576	576
25	1	25	3.3	3.3	10.89	10.89	625	625
28	1	28	6.3	6.3	39.69	39.69	784	784

$\Sigma (fX) = 217¢$ $\qquad\qquad$ $\Sigma f(X - \bar{X})^2 = 116.10$ squared ¢

$n = 10$ $\qquad$ $\Sigma f(X - \bar{X}) = 0$ $\qquad\qquad$ $\Sigma f(X^2) = 4{,}825$ squared ¢

SOURCE: Tax rates from http://www.api.org/news/596sttax.htm. Copyright © 1996 by American Petroleum Institute. Reprinted by permission of the Institute.

Fourth, we calculate the standard deviation using the direct method of computation:

$$s_X = \sqrt{\frac{\Sigma f(X - \bar{X})^2}{n - 1}} = \sqrt{\frac{116.10}{9}} = 3.59¢$$

Fifth, we calculate the standard deviation using the shortcut method:

$$s_X = \sqrt{\frac{\Sigma f X^2 - \frac{[\Sigma f(X)]^2}{n}}{n - 1}} = \sqrt{\frac{4{,}825 - \frac{(217)^2}{10}}{9}} = 3.59¢$$

Sixth, we check to see if the two calculations are equal, which is the case. Finally, we compare the computed standard deviation to the estimate and see that they are relatively close.

Tabular Presentation of Results

In research articles, a basic descriptive statistics table is one that lists all variables and their means and standard deviations. Table 5–6 presents a descriptive statistics table from a study of the psychological well-being of homeless persons at two points in time.

TABLE 5–6 **Descriptive Statistics for Psychological Symptoms, Life Satisfaction, and Self-Mastery**

Subscales	Follow-Up 1		Follow-Up 2	
	M	*SD*	*M*	*SD*
Psychological symptoms				
Anger	4.17	.80	4.14	.85
Anxiety	3.97	.79	3.97	.80
Depression	3.60	.76	3.68	.77
Mania	3.59	.87	3.68	.90
Psychoticism	4.51	.72	4.52	.72
Life satisfaction				
Clothing	4.33	1.59	4.49	1.60
Food	4.79	1.53	4.98	1.42
Health	4.81	1.38	4.77	1.41
Housing	4.37	1.49	4.51	1.54
Leisure	3.74	1.53	3.84	1.56
Money	2.98	1.57	3.19	1.67
Social	4.42	1.44	4.51	1.79
Self-mastery				
Mastery-1	3.21	.85	3.24	.84
Mastery-2	3.36	.87	3.28	.85

NOTE: *n* = 298. Higher scores reflect greater subjective well-being.
SOURCE: Modified from Marshall et al., 1996: 49.

☹ STATISTICAL FOLLIES AND FALLACIES ☹

What Does It Indicate When the Standard Deviation Is Larger Than the Mean?

As we noted in Chapter 4, the mean is susceptible to distortion by the presence of extreme scores, outliers, and skewed distributions. Because it is based on deviations from the mean, the standard deviation is susceptible to the same problem. The distortion is compounded by the fact that the deviation scores are squared.

A common type of skewed distribution is a positive (or right) skew in which most people score low but a few score high. For example, "hospital stays," or the number of times a random sample of persons over age 65 have stayed in a hospital in the past year, is right skewed. Most persons will score zero stays, a few will score one stay, slightly fewer will score two stays, and a few severely ill persons will score frequent stays. This type of distribution is presented in Table 5–7.

TABLE 5–7   **The Skewed Distribution of Hospital Stays in the Past Year among People over 65 Years of Age (fictional data)**

Givens		Calculations		
(1) Case	(2) X	(3) $X - \bar{X}$	(4) $(X - \bar{X})^2$	(5) X^2
1	0	−2.41	5.81	0
2	0	−2.41	5.81	0
3	0	−2.41	5.81	0
4	0	−2.41	5.81	0
5	0	−2.41	5.81	0
6	0	−2.41	5.81	0
7	0	−2.41	5.81	0
8	0	−2.41	5.81	0
9	1	−1.41	1.99	1
10	1	−1.41	1.99	1
11	1	−1.41	1.99	1
12	2	− .41	.17	4
13	2	− .41	.17	4
14	5	2.59	6.71	25
15	9	6.59	43.43	81
16	10	7.59	57.61	100
17	10	7.59	57.61	100

$\Sigma X = 41$ times $\Sigma(X - \bar{X})^2 = 218.15$ times

$n = 17$ $\Sigma(X - \bar{X}) = .03^*$ $\Sigma X^2 = 317$ squared times

*Did not sum to zero because of rounding error.

Even without a histogram, the relative values of the mean and standard deviation for this distribution provide a signal that the distribution is skewed. These statistics compute as follows:

X = hospital stays = for the past year, the number of times a person is admitted to a hospital and stays at least one night

$$\bar{X} = 2.41 \text{ times} \qquad s_X = 3.69 \text{ times} \qquad n = 17 \text{ cases}$$

Note that the standard deviation is larger than the mean. This suggests that one or more extreme scores inflated the mean and the standard deviation. Moreover, since numbers are squared in the standard deviation, a few extreme scores can quickly "explode" its value. Note, for instance, the large contribution to the sum of squares the three largest cases made with their stays of 9, 10, and 10 times.

Why should a standard deviation larger than the mean indicate a skew? Recall that if a distribution is not skewed (i.e., it has a normal bell shape), its range will be about 4 to 6 standard deviations wide. When the curve is drawn,

2 or 3 standard deviations' width will fit on each side of the mean. If the lower limit of a variable's X-scores is zero, at least 2 standard deviations distance should fit between an X-score of zero and the mean. When the standard deviation is larger than the mean, as in the case of hospital stays, not even a single width of the standard deviation can make this fit. Another way to put it is that the standard deviation should be about half the size of the mean or less.

Two general rules apply to the relative sizes of the mean and the standard deviation:

1. If the standard deviation is larger than the mean, this probably indicates a skew, the presence of outliers, or another peculiarity in the shape of the distribution, such as a bimodal distribution.
2. If the standard deviation is not half the size of the mean or less, care should be taken to examine the distribution for skewness or outliers.

As we will discuss in later chapters, when a skewed variable is correlated with other variables, the results may be misleading (Chapter 14). In such cases, adjustments must be made to statistics to avoid such mistakes.

Formulas in Chapter 5

Organize a spreadsheet with cases in rank order:

Givens		Calculations		
(1) Case	(2) X	(3) $X - \bar{X}$	(4) $(X - \bar{X})^2$	(5) X^2
•	•	...	...	...
•	•	...	...	...
•	•	...	...	...
	$\sum X = ...$		$\sum(X - \bar{X})^2 = ...$	
$n = ...$		$\sum(X - \bar{X}) = 0$		$\sum X^2 = ...$

Or organize data in a frequency distribution with cases in rank order:

Givens		Calculations						
X	f	$f(X)$	$(X - \bar{X})$	$f(X - \bar{X})$	$(X - \bar{X})^2$	$f(X - \bar{X})^2$	X^2	$f(X^2)$
•	•	...	...	...	...	...	...	...
•	•	...	...	...	...	...	...	...
•	•	...	...	...	...	...	...	...

$$\Sigma(fX) = ... \qquad\qquad \Sigma f(X - \bar{X})^2 = ...$$

$$n = ... \qquad\qquad \Sigma f(X - \bar{X}) = 0 \qquad\qquad \Sigma f(X^2) = ...$$

Calculating the range:

1. Rank the scores in the distribution from lowest to highest.
2. Identify the minimum and maximum scores.
3. Identify the value of the rounding unit (see Appendix A).
4. Calculate the range:

Range = (maximum score − minimum score) + value of rounding unit

Estimating the standard deviation using the range:

$$\text{Estimate of } s_X \text{ based on the range} = \frac{\text{range}}{4}$$

Direct method of calculating the standard deviation:

1. Start by computing the mean of X and completing a spreadsheet similar to the one in Table 5–2.
2. Calculate the standard deviation:

Working with a spreadsheet   Working with a frequency distribution

$$s_X = \sqrt{\frac{\Sigma(X - \bar{X})^2}{n - 1}} \qquad\qquad s_X = \sqrt{\frac{\Sigma f(X - \bar{X})^2}{n - 1}}$$

Shortcut method of calculating the standard deviation:

Working with a spreadsheet   Working with a frequency distribution

$$s_X = \sqrt{\frac{\Sigma X^2 - \dfrac{(\Sigma X)^2}{n}}{n - 1}} \qquad\qquad s_X = \sqrt{\frac{\Sigma f X^2 - \dfrac{[\Sigma f(X)]^2}{n}}{n - 1}}$$

Calculating standardized scores (Z-scores):

$$Z_X = \frac{X - \bar{X}}{s_X}$$

Questions for Chapter 5

1. Dispersion statistics are computed only on variables of what levels of measurement?
2. Both the range and the standard deviation are measures of the dispersion of scores within a distribution. Explain the differences in perspective between these two statistics.
3. What effect does an extreme score or outlier have on the computation of the range?
4. The standard deviation is "derived from" the mean. What does this mean?
5. In computing the range, the value of the rounding unit of the variable is added to the difference between the maximum and minimum scores. Why is the value of the rounding unit added?
6. In computing the standard deviation, why is it necessary to square the deviation scores?
7. In computing the standard deviation for sample data, why must we divide by $n - 1$?
8. In computing the standard deviation, why must we take the square root?
9. What is the mathematical relationship between the variance and the standard deviation?
10. What is another name for the variation?
11. What is the significance of the word *standard* in the term *standard deviation?*
12. An expression of how far a raw score is from the mean of a distribution in the original units of measure of the variable X is called a _____ score.
13. An expression of how far a raw score is from the mean of a distribution in units of measure of standard deviations (SD) is called a _____ score.
14. What are the properties of a normal distribution?
15. In a normal distribution, approximately what percentage of scores fall within 1 standard deviation of the mean in both directions? Within 2 standard deviations of the mean in both directions? Within 3 standard deviations of the mean in both directions?
16. In a normal distribution, exactly what percentage of scores falls above the mean? What central tendency statistic besides the mean accounts for this phenomenon?

17. In a normal distribution, the curve peaks at the value of the mean. What central tendency statistic besides the mean accounts for this phenomenon?

18. If a raw score falls below the mean in a distribution, will the sign of its Z-score be positive or negative? Illustrate your answer by using the formula for calculating a Z-score.

19. In any interval/ratio score distribution, there is a score for which the deviations from it sum to zero. What central tendency statistic is located at this point?

20. For his age group, Charles is 1 standard deviation below the mean height but 1.5 standard deviations above the mean weight. Describe his general body build.

21. Daniel is 3 standard deviations above the mean in terms of his intelligence quotient (IQ). Describe his general intellect.

22. Explain why a distribution probably is not normal when the standard deviation is larger than the mean.

Exercises for Chapter 5

1. Use the formula for the standard deviation to complete the blanks in the following table. The table presents calculations on interval/ratio variables from different samples of size n.

Sum of Squares	n	Variance	Standard Deviation
11,828.52	88	135.96	———
3,120.00	21	———	———
893.49	———	30.81	———
———	347	124.65	11.16

2. Use the formula for the standard deviation to complete the blanks in the following table. The table presents calculations on interval/ratio variables from different samples of size n.

Sum of Squares	n	Variance	Standard Deviation
38.76	7	———	———
347,295.92	1,041	———	18.27
———	91	40.89	———
5,865.04	———	17.56	———

Use the following data for exercises 3 through 8.

Demographic and Social Service Characteristics of 15 Clients of Eldergarden

(I) Age	(II) Physician Visits in Past Year	(III) Monthly Income	(IV) Case Contacts in Past Year	(V) Gender
74	8	$ 2,347	10	M
81	7	2,434	8	M
83	11	1,636	13	F
77	4	1,963	7	M
76	5	2,358	6	F
79	13	1,968	15	F
79	7	2,683	6	M

3. Suppose you are a caseworker for Eldergarden, an agency that provides social services to the elderly. You are assigned to provide some descriptive statistics for the agency's caseload for the month.

    a. Compute the mean, median, and modal age (column I of the table).
    b. Compute the range of ages and use it to estimate the standard deviation.
    c. Compute the standard deviation of ages using both the direct and shortcut methods.
    d. Compare the answers to parts (*b*) and (*c*) and comment.

4. Do (*a*) through (*d*) of exercise 3 for physician visits in the past year (column II of the table).

5. Do (*a*) through (*d*) of exercise 3 for monthly income (column III of the table).

6. Do (*a*) through (*d*) of exercise 3 for case contacts in past year (column IV of the table).

7. What percentage of the Eldergarden sample is female (column V of the table)?

8. What percentage of the Eldergarden sample is over age 80 (column I of the table)?

9. It's homecoming week, and things are happening around campus. One of those things is a footrace among sororities. A random sample of racing sisters and pledges produces the following ages: 19, 18, 20, 19, 29, 18, 20, 18, 22, 21.

    a. Organize the data into a frequency distribution table.
    b. Using this frequency distribution format, calculate the mean and the standard deviation (using the direct method).
    c. Is there something peculiar in this distribution? Adjust for it by recalculating the statistics.

     d. Comment on the differences between the original statistics and the adjusted statistics.

10. The following are grade point averages (GPAs) for a sample of students in a scholarship competition: 3.6, 3.8, 3.6, 3.9, 2.6, 3.8, 3.8, 3.9.

     a. Organize the data into a frequency distribution table.
     b. Using this frequency distribution format, calculate the mean and the standard deviation (using the direct method).
     c. Is there something peculiar in this distribution? Adjust for it by recalculating the statistics.
     d. Comment on the differences between the original statistics and the adjusted statistics.

11. The following data are from a sample of 16- to 20-year-old smokers.

$$Y = \text{number of cigarettes smoked per day}$$

$$\bar{Y} = 15 \text{ cigarettes} \quad s_Y = 5 \text{ cigarettes}$$

     a. Complete the columns in the following table. Be sure to specify the units of measure.
     b. Who stands out as a heavy smoker?

Case	Y (cigarettes per day)	$Y - \bar{Y}$ (deviation score)	Z_Y (standardized score)
Bob Smith	17		
Spencer Byrd	30		
Sonya Turnham	4		
Chuck Martin	20		

12. The following are rates of hate crimes per 100,000 population covered by reporting agencies for a random sample of states (U.S. Department of Justice, http://www.fbi.gov/ucr/hatecm.htm).

Y – hate crime rate = number of hate crimes reported per 100,000 population covered by reporting agencies

$$\bar{Y} = 1.19 \text{ hate crimes per 100,000 population covered}$$

$$s_Y = .32 \text{ hate crimes per 100,000 population covered}$$

     a. Complete the columns in the following table. Be sure to specify the units of measure.
     b. What state stands out as having a relatively high rate of hate crimes?

State	Y (hate crimes)	Y −Ȳ (deviation score)	Z_Y (standardized score)
Florida	1.15		
Indiana	1.08		
Iowa	1.02		
Mississippi	.97		
Texas	1.75		

13. Suppose we are studying how eating and work habits affect weight among a sample of 250 men. We compute descriptive statistics on weight and get the following results:

$$X = \text{weight} \qquad \bar{X} = 169 \text{ pounds} \qquad s_X = 18 \text{ pounds}$$

   a. Draw and label the normal curve for these weights.
   b. The following table includes data for just a few of the observations. Complete it by estimating each Z_X by sight (i.e., by simply observing X on the curve).
   c. Now compute the exact Z-score for each X-score. (Show the formula and computation for X = 128 pounds.)

X (pounds)	Sight Estimate of Z-score (SD)	Computed Z-score (SD)
169		
128		
192		
177		
151		
109		

14. Suppose we are studying aggressive behavior among 13- to 16-year-old boys in a youth detention facility. The variable is operationalized as the number of aggressive acts—verbal insults and threats, acts of physical violence and destruction of property—committed over the past week. The acts are tabulated by observing videotapes of the facility's recreation rooms and grounds, library, rest rooms, and cafeteria. We compute descriptive statistics on this variable and obtain the following results:

$$X = \text{number of aggressive acts}$$

$$\bar{X} = 16.8 \text{ acts} \qquad s_X = 4.4 \text{ acts}$$

   a. Draw and label the normal curve for these acts.
   b. The following table includes data for just a few of the observations. Complete it by estimating each Z_X by sight (i.e., by simply observing X on the curve).

c. Now compute the exact Z-score for each X-score. (Show the formula and computation for X = 9 acts.)

X (acts)	Sight Estimate of Z-score (SD)	Computed Z-score (SD)
9		
12		
19		
26		
3		
14		

Optional Computer Applications for Chapter 5

If your class is using computers, open the Chapter 5 exercises on the *Computer Applications for The Statistical Imagination* compact disk. The exercises involve (1) using *SPSS for Windows* to compute the range, the standard deviation, and Z-scores and (2) using central tendency and dispersion statistics to discern the shapes of score distributions.

CHAPTER

6

PROBABILITY THEORY AND THE NORMAL PROBABILITY DISTRIBUTION

Introduction: The Human Urge to Predict the Future

Human mental capacity is distinguished from that of other animals by an ability to forecast the future—to conceive of what happens "in the long run." To predict future events is to understand them, and the development of human culture depends on prediction. The field of statistics is about making predictions with highly precise measurements. Statisticians gain status and authority from successful prediction and understanding. With its applications in the sciences, business, industry, weather forecasting, medicine, public health, public services, government, the gambling industry, entertainment, and sports, statistical work is an example of forecasting the future.

Human desires to forecast events are not new. From the earliest times of human social organization, "seers" (such as priest-doctor shamans) acquired great authority by predicting climactic cycles and important events such as rain. Applying mathematics to practical problem solving also has a long history. Measurement and computing techniques are as old as human culture and were very well established 4,000 years ago. The pyramids of ancient Egypt exemplify a precise mathematical organization of the physical world. In fact, many scholars argue that the extent of Egyptian knowledge is greatly underrated (Gillings 1972, Neugebaurer 1962, Struik 1948). As Tompkins (1971: xiv–xv) notes:

> Whoever built the Great Pyramid . . . knew the precise circumference of the planet, and the length of the year to several decimals—data which were not rediscovered till the seventeenth century.

Modern mathematics, trigonometry, and "exact sciences" such as physics have their origins in ancient Mediterranean cultures in which the systematic study of nature was revered. Underlying the development of science is the recognition that physical nature is highly cyclical and thus predictable to the extent that it follows strict scientific laws. For example, a physicist standing on the ground can rest assured that any object heavier than air will drop to the earth. Human behavior, however, is not quite as predictable. Therefore, social and behavioral scientists often must qualify their conclusions by noting that their predictions are based on limited *but calculable* degrees of accuracy. For instance, a social scientist studying the relationship of, say, high school grades to college grades may only be able to assert a correlation between them, stating that there is a calculable *chance* that an A student in high school will get A's in college. The laws of chance are tools for determining the degree of accuracy in social science predictions. We refer to *the analysis and understanding of chance occurrences* as **probability theory.**

Probability Theory

The analysis and understanding of chance occurrences.

Discovery of the laws of chance began in ancient times and perhaps was stimulated as much by leisure activities such as gaming as by work activities (David 1962: 4–10). Among the artifacts of Egypt's first dynasty (3500 B.C.) are board games, playing pieces, and animal *astralagi* (joint bones), the precursors of dice. In Egypt, cubical dice were in common use by 3000 B.C. Gaming was so common in Roman times that it was prohibited on certain days. In Roman literature there are references to a book by Claudius (10 B.C.–A.D. 54) entitled *How to Win at Dice*. Astute gamblers had the statistical imagination. They could think proportionately, recognizing that some "tosses of the bones" occurred a greater proportion of the time than did others. By successfully advising members of the ruling classes on how to increase their gambling winnings, these early statisticians gained high status. Successful stock market analysts and survey researchers as well as horse race handicappers are the modern equivalent of these highly respected statistical advisers.

We may surmise that human interest in predicting the outcomes of future events was not limited to games of chance. As far as humans are concerned, the forces of nature (especially climate) involve chance, and environmental adaptation is wrought with fate and good or bad luck. Cultural evolution is stimulated by a society's need to anticipate what will happen next. For example, by the middle dynastic period (circa 2000 B.C.) the ancient Egyptians had developed complex irrigation and canal systems to regulate the annual flooding of the Nile River. With data managed by a highly efficient bureaucracy, they monitored the river's depth with "nilometers" placed at strategic points along the Nile's vast 4,145-mile length. By studying and anticipating flows, they used floodwater advantageously for crop irrigation (David 1962). The accuracy of their predictions produced a stable economy that enhanced the political power of the ruling dynasties. Many ancient cultures had their share of empiricists: individuals who believed in the merits of observation and measurement. Empiricism and the popularity of gambling, religion, and fortune-telling attest to an innate human interest in betting on what will happen next and preparing for it. Everything from predicting enemy troop strength to deciding whether to carry an umbrella, invest in stocks, or propose marriage requires measurements and estimations of the likelihood of success or failure. Statistical analysis using probability theory is the tool by which predictions are made with a maximum degree of accuracy.

What Is a Probability?

A **probability (*p*)** is *a specification of how frequently a particular event of interest is likely to occur over a large number of trials (situations in which the event can occur).* We call the probability of this interesting event occurring the probability of success. Similarly, the probability of the event *not* occurring is called the probability of failure. Brackets are used to distinguish the targeted event of interest, and a lowercase *p* is used to indicate "the probability" of a specific calculation. Note that this symbol is the same one used in previous chapters for *proportion.* This is done because probabilities *are* proportions, as we will discuss shortly.

A Probability (*p*)

A specification of how frequently a particular event of interest is likely to occur over a large number of trials.

The general formula for presenting a probability is as follows:

Computing a Probability

$$p \text{ [of success]} = \frac{\text{\# successes}}{\text{\# trials}} = \frac{\text{\# possible successful outcomes}}{\text{total \# possible outcomes}}$$

where *p* [of success] = probability of "the event of interest."

For consistency in instruction, in this text answers to computations of probabilities will be rounded and presented to four decimal places. Of course, probabilities also may be presented as percentages by multiplying *p* by 100. Here are some examples which reveal how simple the notion of probability is:

Example A: When flipping a single coin, what is the probability of getting heads?

For a coin there are two possible outcomes, and heads is one of them. Thus:

$$p \text{ [heads]} = \frac{\text{\# heads}}{\text{\# of possible outcomes}} = \frac{1}{2} = .5000$$

Example B: When randomly drawing a single card from a standard deck of 52 playing cards:

$$a. \quad p \text{ [king]} = \frac{\text{\# kings in deck}}{\text{total \# cards in deck}} = \frac{4}{52} = .0769$$

    b. $p\,[7] = \dfrac{\#\ 7\text{'s in deck}}{\text{total \# cards in deck}} = \dfrac{4}{52} = .0769$

    c. $p\,[\text{heart}] = \dfrac{\#\ \text{of hearts in deck}}{\text{total \# cards in deck}} = \dfrac{13}{52} = .2500$

Example C: When randomly drawing a single marble from a box of 300 marbles in which 100 are red and 200 are green:

    a. $p\,[\text{red}] = \dfrac{\#\ \text{of reds in box}}{\text{total \# marbles in box}} = \dfrac{100}{300} = .3333$

    b. $p\,[\text{green}] = \dfrac{\#\ \text{of greens in box}}{\text{total \# marbles in box}} = \dfrac{200}{300} = .6667$

As these illustrations reveal, computing a probability is simply a matter of proportional thinking in regard to the long-term occurrence of an event of interest. To ask, What is the probability? is to wonder, out of all the times a category of events occurs, how many of those times we can expect a certain outcome. This expectation is then expressed as a proportion or percentage.

Basic Rules of Probability Theory

There are just a few basic rules to follow in computing any probability. All calculations of probabilities employ these essential rules.

Probability Rule 1: Probabilities Always Range between 0 and 1

Since probabilities are proportions, their lower numerical limit is zero (the event cannot happen) and their upper numerical limit is 1.00 (the event must happen). In other words, probabilities always calculate between 0.00 and 1.00 (or 0 percent and 100 percent). If this is not the case, a mathematical mistake has occurred.

    Some events do have a zero probability of occurring—they never occur (e.g., remaining alive underwater for 24 hours without life-support devices). Some events occur with a 100 percent probability—they always happen (e.g., the sun will rise tomorrow). Many events, however, are not so definite; their probabilities of occurrence are somewhere between never and always.

Probability Rule 2: The Addition Rule for Alternative Events

Sometimes we may desire to define "success" as more than a single characteristic event. For example, what is the probability of drawing a king *or* an ace from a deck of cards? Here we have two alternatives for success: a king or an ace. The **addition rule for alternative events** states that *the probability of alternative events is equal to the sum of the probabilities of the individual events.* Therefore,

$$p \text{ [king or ace]} = p \text{ [king]} + p \text{ [ace]}$$

$$= \frac{\text{\# kings in deck}}{\text{total \# cards in deck}} + \frac{\text{\# aces in deck}}{\text{total \# cards in deck}}$$

$$= \frac{4}{52} + \frac{4}{52} = \frac{8}{52} = .1538 \text{ (about 15\%)}$$

A simple trick to follow with the addition rule is to replace the word *or* with an addition sign, + .

Do not make this complicated. The addition rule is just a guide to help us calculate a probability when there are several ways to gain success. In the case of drawing an ace or a king, there are eight ways. (If you are not convinced, count the aces and kings in a deck of cards.)

In later chapters we will use the symbol P (capitalized) to represent the probability of success and Q to represent the probability of failure. (These symbols probably evoked the old adage "Mind your p's and q's.") The addition rule leads to an important point: The probability of success *or* failure must be 1.00; that is, $P + Q = 1$. It follows from this that if we know P, then Q can be computed quickly. That is,

$$Q = 1 - P$$

Similarly,

$$P = 1 - Q$$

For example, if $P = p$ [king or ace], then

$$Q = p \text{ [any card other than a king or ace]} = 1 - p = 1 - .1538 = .8462 \text{ (about 85\%)}$$

In other words, if we have about a 15 percent chance of drawing a king or ace, then we have about an 85 percent chance of not doing so.

Probability Rule 3: Adjust for Joint Occurrences

Sometimes success for an event is not straightforward because a single outcome is successful in more than one way. For example, in drawing a single card from a standard deck of 52, there is a problem in the following computation, which uses the addition rule:

$$p \text{ [king or queen or heart]} = p \text{ [king]} + p \text{ [queen]} + p \text{ [heart]}$$

Incorrect

$$= \frac{\text{\# kings + \# queens + \# hearts in deck}}{\text{total \# cards in deck}} = \frac{21}{52} = .4038$$

This answer is incorrect. If we take a deck of cards and count the "success cards" (kings, queens, and hearts), we will find 19, not 21. This is the case because when adding the separate probabilities, we counted both the king of hearts and the queen of hearts twice. By being a king *and* a heart, the king of hearts is successful in two ways (put another way, the characteristics are not mutually exclusive). Similarly, double success occurs for the queen of hearts.

When we have *an event that double counts success or joins two aspects of success*, we call this a **joint occurrence.** (This is the same thing as a joint frequency of occurrence of categories of the two variables in the cells of a cross-tabulation table; see Chapter 2.) To compute the correct probability, we must subtract every joint occurrence to eliminate these double counts. In this case, the queen of hearts and the king of hearts each is a joint occurrence. Thus:

$$p \text{ [king or queen or heart]}$$

$$= \{\, p \text{ [king]} + p \text{ [queen]} + p \text{ [heart]} \,\} - \{\, p \text{ [joint occurrences]} \,\}$$

$$= \frac{\text{\# kings + \# queens + \# hearts in deck}}{\text{total \# cards in deck}} - \frac{2 \text{ joint occurrences}}{\text{total \# cards in deck}}$$

$$= \frac{21}{52} - \frac{2}{52} = \frac{19}{52} = .3654.$$

Probability Rule 4: The Multiplication Rule for Compound Events

Some events have two or more parts to them. We call these *multiple-part events* **compound events** (from chemistry, where a *compound* such as water is defined as a substance composed of two or more elements, in this case hydrogen and oxygen). For example, we may define success as drawing a pair of aces from the deck, that is, drawing an ace, putting it back in, reshuffling (i.e., randomizing), and then drawing an ace again. The **multiplication rule for compound events** states that *the probability of a compound event is equal to the multiple of the probabilities of the separate parts of the event*. Thus,

$$p \text{ [ace then ace]} = p \text{ [ace]} \cdot p \text{ [ace]}$$

$$= \frac{4}{52} \cdot \frac{4}{52} = \frac{16}{2{,}704} = .0059$$

A simple trick to follow is to replace the word *then* (or *and*) with the multiplication sign, $\cdot$.

Do not make this complicated. Mathematically, the multiplication rule simply extracts the number of successes in the numerator of the fraction and the total number of possible events in the denominator. Accordingly, it turns out that if we spent months drawing a card, replacing it, reshuffling, drawing a second card, and recording the outcomes, we would discover that there are 2,704 possible combinations of two cards. And we would discover that there are 16 possible combinations of ace pairs, as is shown in Figure 6–1. Thank

FIGURE 6–1

Possible pairings of aces when randomly drawing a card, replacing it, and randomly drawing a second card

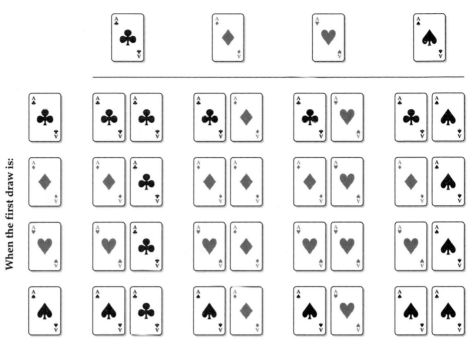

goodness for mathematicians! They astutely noticed that instead of having to sort these combinations out piecemeal, we need only multiply the separate probabilities.

A simple coin-flipping exercise will further reinforce the simplicity of the multiplication rule. Let us compute the probability of flipping a coin twice and getting heads both times:

$$p \text{ [heads then heads]} = p \text{ [heads]} \bullet p \text{ [heads]}$$

$$= .5 \bullet .5 = .2500 \text{ (or 1 out of 4)}$$

As is shown in Figure 6–2, flipping two coins (or flipping a single coin twice) results in four possible outcomes, and only one of those outcomes is heads then heads.

To really grasp this, make your own similar chart for the probability of getting all heads when tossing three coins. (Mathematically, the probabilities of dichotomous events are calculated by expanding the binomial distribution formula; see Chapter 13.)

Probability Rule 5: Account for Replacement with Compound Events

When we illustrated rule 4, the multiplication rule for compound events, we computed the probability of drawing a pair of aces and found that $p = .0059$.

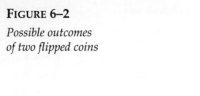

FIGURE 6–2

*Possible outcomes
of two flipped coins*

First Coin   **Second Coin**

We stipulated that the first card drawn was to be returned to the deck before the second card was drawn. This stipulation for calculating the probability of a compound event is called "with replacement." If we had not returned the first card, the calculation would have been done "without replacement" and the computed probability would have been different:

p [ace then ace] without replacement = p [ace] • p [ace]

$$= \frac{4}{52} \cdot \frac{3}{51} = \frac{12}{2,652} = .0045$$

The probability of the first ace is the same with or without replacement because the event begins with 52 cards and four aces. But if the first card drawn is an ace *and it is not replaced*, then for the second draw there are only 51 cards in the deck and only three are aces. Close attention must be paid to issues of replacement in compound events. Numerators and denominators are adjusted accordingly. For instance, let us compute the following:

p [ace then king then ace] without replacement = p [ace] • p [king] • p [ace]

$$= \frac{4}{52} \cdot \frac{4}{51} \cdot \frac{3}{50} = \frac{48}{132,600} = .0004$$

Finally, not all compound events involve issues of replacement. For example, replacement is not an issue with coin tossing. The calculated probabilities are the same for "heads then heads" in tossing two coins at once or tossing one coin twice.

The five rules of probability are fundamental; that is, they must be considered in computing the probability of any event, no matter how simple or complicated that event is. The simple examples presented in this chapter illustrate these basic principles. Much more complex formulations of probabilities are presented in advanced texts such as that of Lee and Maykovich (1995). Fortunately for students and scholars today, it is not necessary to have extensive mathematical skills to compute probabilities. Computer software writers require us to learn only which buttons to push or what table to read to obtain the answers to probability questions. A thorough understanding of basic probability theory, however, is necessary to avoid misinterpreting such computer output. Moreover, an understanding of probability theory is essential for acquiring the statistical imagination.

Using the Normal Curve as a Probability Distribution

Proportional Thinking about a Group of Cases and Single Cases

As we noted in Chapter 5, the standard deviation is used to examine the way scores in a distribution are spread out and to compare the spread of two or more samples. We can, however, do much more with the standard deviation. With a single interval/ratio variable *that we have reason to believe is normally distributed in its population,* we can compute standardized scores (Z-scores) and use them to determine the proportion (*p*) of a population's scores falling between any two scores in the distribution. Since the normal curve has a distinct shape, we can identify and measure areas because the areas represent a proportion of cases.

Recall from Chapter 5 that a Z-score tells us how many standard deviations away from the mean a raw (or X-score) lies:

$$Z_X = \frac{X - \bar{X}}{s_X} = \begin{array}{l} \text{number of standard deviations (SD)} \\ \text{from the mean} \end{array}$$

We noted that roughly 68 percent of the cases in a normally distributed population have X-scores within 1 standard deviation distance to both sides of the mean (i.e., between a Z-score of plus and minus 1). For example, suppose we have the following information where X = height for a sample of men at a health and fitness club:

$$\bar{X} = 69 \text{ inches} \qquad s_X = 3 \text{ inches} \qquad \text{Distribution is normal}$$

Since this distribution is normal, let us draw the normal curve to get a sense of proportion about how many of the men are how tall. Our basic knowledge of the normal curve tells us that roughly 68 percent are between 66 inches and 72 inches, as noted on the curve (page 164). Moreover, since the median is located at the mean, we know that half the men are below 69 inches (five feet, nine inches) and half are above. And since over 99 percent of a normally distributed population falls within three Z-scores to both sides of the mean, very few are shorter than 60 inches or taller than 78 inches.

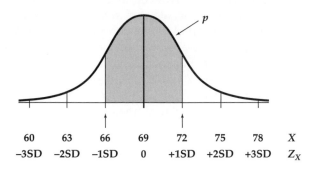

60	63	66	69	72	75	78	X
−3SD	−2SD	−1SD	0	+1SD	+2SD	+3SD	Z_X

Thus,

$$p \text{ [of } X = 66 \text{ to } X = 72] = \text{approximately } 68\%$$

In fact, with the help of a statistical table, we can compute Z-scores and use them to determine any area under the curve. This procedure is called partitioning areas under the normal curve, and we will do some partitioning shortly.

As it turns out, areas under the normal curve represent probabilities of occurrence. Notice that we use the symbol *p* to represent proportions *and* probabilities. Probabilities are proportions of time for which success occurs out of all possible occurrences. Knowing the proportion of success for the population as a whole gives us the probability of success for a single subject. In other words, a specified area under the normal curve provides the probability of occurrence of any single score falling between any two score values.

To illustrate this connection, suppose we are hanging out at the health and fitness club, killing time. To entertain ourselves, we play a whimsical game called "guess the height." The rules of the game are such that when we hear someone approaching from around the corner, we guess his height and then ask him when he appears. If we are within 3 inches of the correct height, we win.

How can we improve our chances of winning? We know that the fitness club members' heights are normally distributed around a mean of 69 inches with a standard deviation of 3 inches. This tells us that about 68 percent of the men are between 66 and 72 inches tall. Let us think probabilistically; that is, let us look at the long run. For every 100 men that approach, 68 will fall in the "success" range:

$$p \text{ [of next man being 66 to 72 inches tall]} = \frac{\# \text{ that tall}}{100 \text{ who approach}} = \frac{68}{100} = .6800$$

If we guess 69 inches, our chance of winning, then, is about 68 percent—not bad odds. To get a sense of proportion on this, imagine that the club members are 100 marbles in a box, with green marbles representing those with heights of 66 to 72 inches. There are 68 green marbles, and the probability of randomly drawing one is .6800, or 68 percent.

In a normal distribution of scores, (1) the proportion of cases between two scores, (2) the area under the curve between these two scores, and (3) the probability of randomly selecting a case between these scores *are all the same*. This is why we use p to represent all these ideas. For instance, the symbol p [of $X = 66$ to $X = 72$] can be stated and interpreted in three ways:

1. *A distributional interpretation that describes the result in relation to the distribution of scores in a population or sample.* Thus, roughly .6800 (or 68 percent) of the men in the club are between 66 and 72 inches tall.

2. *A graphical interpretation that describes the proportion of the area under a normal curve* (assuming the distribution is normal in shape). Thus, roughly 68 percent of the area under the normal curve falls between the X-scores of 66 and 72 inches.

3. *A probabilistic interpretation that describes the probability of a single random drawing of a subject from this population.* Thus, if a random member of the club approaches, there is about a .6800 chance that he is between 66 and 72 inches tall.

Three Ways to Interpret the Symbol p

1. A distributional interpretation that describes the result in relation to the distribution of scores in a population or sample.
2. A graphical interpretation that describes the proportion of the area under a normal curve (assuming the distribution is normal in shape).
3. A probabilistic interpretation that describes the probability of a single random drawing of a subject from this population.

These three interpretations are saying the same thing: About 68 percent of the men are between 66 and 72 inches in height. Because of its probabilistic interpretation, the normal curve often is referred to as a probability curve.

These distinctions also highlight an important point about the probabilities of events. Although stated for a single type of "success," any probability is based on the entire distribution of all possible events. A singular event is assessed relative to a larger set of occurrences. This type of proportional thinking is central to grasping the statistical imagination.

Partitioning Areas under the Normal Curve

To **partition an area under the normal curve** is *to identify part of the curve and compute the proportion (p) of the total curve this part represents.* We use the normal distribution table (Statistical Table B in Appendix B) when we do partitioning.

Where do the numbers in this table come from? Statisticians long ago discovered how the occurrences of many natural phenomena fit the bell shape of the normal curve. They worked out the mathematics of this phenomenon and came up with the mean, the standard deviation, and Z-scores. Then they formulated areas or proportions (p) under the curve. These areas are fixed and apply to any normally distributed variable because normality is a natural occurrence—just like gravity. The normal curve table provides precisely calculated areas under the curve. One thing must be emphasized here: Such partitioning of areas using the mean, the standard deviation, Z-scores, and the normal distribution curve *works only if we have reason to believe that the scores in a population are normally distributed*. If the distribution of scores is skewed or otherwise oddly shaped, the normal curve table cannot be used in calculations.

To Partition an Area under the Normal Curve

To identify part of the curve and compute the proportion (p) of the total curve this part represents.

The normal curve table provides what is needed to calculate exactly how much area is under the curve between any two scores or to the sides of any individual score. Remember that an area under the curve represents a proportion (p) of the population between the raw scores corresponding to that section of the curve. These p's are computed to four decimal places. The information in the normal curve table is depicted in Figure 6–3. As is noted in Figure 6–3A, column A of the normal curve table lists Z-scores, where: Z_X is the number *of standard deviations* an X-score deviates from the mean. Column A provides only *positive* Z-scores, or those that apply to the right side of the normal curve. But the curve is symmetrical (i.e., the left side is a mirror image of the right side). Therefore, column A can be used with negative Z-scores by simply imagining a negative sign in front of the entries.

Column B of the normal curve table gives the area from the mean out to a Z-score as depicted in Figure 6–3B. For example, observe in the normal curve table a Z-score of 1.00 in column A. The column B entry is .3413 (about 34 percent). For the fitness club we can state that 34 percent of members are between the heights of 69 and 72 inches. Similarly, we can view this Z-score as –1.00, and again, column B reads .3413, the proportion of members between the heights of 66 and 69 inches. Two times .3413 is .6826, or about 68 percent—the proportion between 66 and 72 inches—that we noted falls within 1 standard deviation to both sides of the mean. Similarly, we said that approximately 95 percent of the scores in any normal distribution fall within about 2 standard deviations of the mean. Actually, 95 percent fall within 1.96 SD (a Z-score) to both sides of the mean. Start learning how to use the table by finding these Z-scores in column A and comparing the areas in column B.

FIGURE 6–3

Information provided in the columns of the normal distribution table (Statistical Table B in Appendix B)

A. In column A: Computed Z-scores for one side of the curve or the other

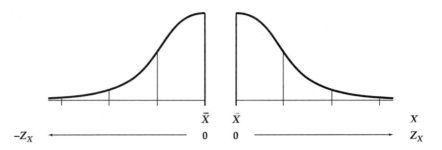

B. In column B: Area under the curve from the mean of X to the Z-score for a value of X

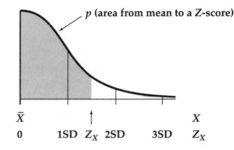

p (area from mean to a Z-score)

C. In column C: Area under the curve from the Z-score for a value of X and beyond

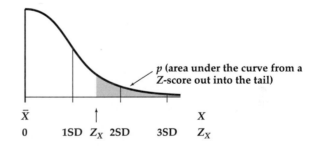

p (area under the curve from a Z-score out into the tail)

Column C of the normal curve table gives the area under the curve from a Z-score and beyond in the "tail" of the curve, as in Figure 6–3C. For example, .1587 (or 15.87 percent) of scores in a normal distribution fall to the right of a Z-score of 1.00 or to the left of a Z-score of –1.00. This is found by looking at a Z-score of 1.00 in column A and then observing the entry .1587 in column C.

We noted earlier that any normally distributed variable has a median equal to the mean. Thus, 50 percent of the scores in any normal distribution fall in either direction from the mean. Since the table provides half the curve, note that for any Z-score, columns B and C sum to .5000, or 50 percent. Finally, keep in mind that Z-scores may be positive or negative, depending on whether a raw score is above or below the mean, respectively. Z-scores can be infinitely large, although in practice they typically fall between about –3.00 and 3.00 because in a normal distribution nearly 100 percent of cases fall within 3 standard deviations to both sides of the mean. The *areas* in columns B and C of the normal curve table, however, are always positive; these areas depict space. Zero space is the smallest amount we can have, and 100 percent space is the largest.

Sample Problems Using the Normal Curve

To show the usefulness of the normal curve table, let us work some sample problems. Keep in mind that partitioning is based on the mean and the standard deviation; therefore, the variable must be interval/ratio (although an ordinal variable can be used under informed situations). In addition, to use the normal curve table we must be assured that the variable is normally distributed in the population. The distribution cannot be skewed, peaked, flat, bimodal, or otherwise shaped. Normality is best determined by observing the histogram of the variable to identify the distinctive bell shape. However, if the histogram of a variable is made *for a sample* and the score distribution is not perfectly bell-shaped, the variable still could be normally distributed *in the population*. The difference in shape could be due to sampling error. In this text we will not deal with this fine point. We will simply state that we assume that the variable is normally distributed in the population; in shorthand, we "assume normality."

Let us suppose that we have conducted interviews of 500 women who are receiving family assistance support payments. We will refer to these women as assistance recipients. (In common parlance such women are called welfare mothers, a somewhat politically biased term.) One interest we have in these women is how poverty affects self-esteem, an individual's feeling of "worthiness, adequacy, competence, and likeability" (Ensminger 1995: 351). Suppose we measure self-esteem with a 20-point attitude scale that has an interval level of measurement. The mean self-esteem score is found to be 8 with a standard deviation of 2. A histogram assures us that the distribution is normally shaped. We begin these exercises by taking an inventory of known information, that which is "given" in the problem.

Givens: An interval variable X = self-esteem and its raw scores (not shown). From these scores we obtain the following statistics:

$$\bar{X} = 8 \text{ self-esteem points} \qquad s_X = 2 \text{ self-esteem points}$$

$$n = 500. \qquad \text{Assume a normal distribution}$$

Study Hint: Draw the bell-shaped curve on all problems. It is a good practice always to draw the normal curve. Mark the mean and 3 standard deviations from it in both directions. Label the curve for X (in this case, self-esteem scores) and for Z-scores. *Remember:* X is a raw score with a unit of measure of self-esteem points, Z_X is a standardized or Z-score with units of measure of standard deviations (SD), and p is a proportion of the area under the curve.

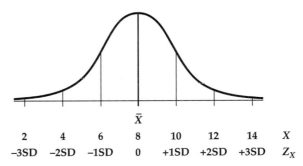

Our basic knowledge of the normal distribution readily tells us the following: (1) 50 percent of the assistance recipients score above 8, and 50 percent score below 8, (2) approximately 68 percent score between 6 and 10 on the self-esteem measure, (3) approximately 95 percent score between 4 and 12, and (4) nearly all—over 99 percent—score between 2 and 14.

We can use the normal curve table to answer several types of questions about the distribution of self-esteem among recipients of family assistance. **Important Study Hint:** The normal curve table requires Z-scores. When in doubt about how to start a problem, compute Z-scores.

Problem Type 1: p [of Cases from the Mean to an X-Score].   Find the proportion (p) of cases between the mean and some X-score.

Solution plan: Draw and label the normal curve for the variable X; shade the target area (p) from the mean out to the specified X-score; compute the Z-score for that X-score; locate the Z-score in column A of the normal curve table; get p from column B; report the answer in everyday terms.

Illustration: What percentage of assistance recipients have self-esteem scores between 5 and 8?

Identify this target area, p.

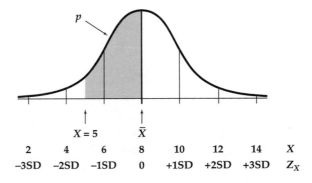

Column B in the normal curve table provides areas under the curve from the mean out to any Z-score. By drawing the curve, we can see that the target area (p) is bordered by the mean; thus, p is a "column B type" area.

The next step in solving problems is to transform a raw score into a Z-score:

$$Z_X = \frac{X - \bar{X}}{s_X} = \frac{5 - 8}{2} = \frac{-3}{2} = -1.50 \text{ SD}$$

Remember that a Z-score is just another way to express a raw score. An assistance recipient scoring 5 on self-esteem falls 1.50 SD *below* the mean, the *negative* Z-score of −1.50; she is among those with rather low self-esteem. In column A of the normal curve table, find 1.5 and treat it as −1.5. Look in column B and report the answer as follows:

$$p \text{ [of } X = 5 \text{ to } X = 8 \text{]} = .4332; \qquad \% = p \text{ (100)} = 43.32\%$$

Finally, answer the question in everyday terms: A little over 43 percent of assistance recipients scored between 5 and 8 on the self-esteem measure. (This is a distributional interpretation describing the result in relation to the distribution of scores of the population of recipients of family assistance.) If a randomly selected name is chosen from the case files, there is about a 43 percent chance that this person will score between 5 and 8 on the self-esteem measure. (This is a probabilistic interpretation, the probability of a single randomly drawn assistance recipient falling in the targeted area.) We compute percentages and substitute the term *chance* for *probability* for clarity of expression to a public audiene.

Problem Type 2: p [of Cases Greater Than an X-Score].   Find the proportion (p) of cases greater than a specified X-score.

Solution plan: Draw and label the normal curve for the variable X; shade the target area (p) from the X-score out into the tail in *the positive or "greater than" direction;* compute the Z-score and locate it in column A; get p from column C.

Illustration: What proportion of the assistance recipients score at or above 13 on the self-esteem scale?

Shade the target area, p:

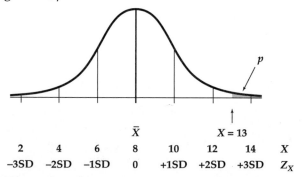

Compute the Z-score for $X = 13$:

$$Z_X = \frac{X - \bar{X}}{s_X} = \frac{13 - 8}{2} = \frac{5}{2} = 2.50 \text{ SD}$$

Find 2.50 in column A of the normal curve table. Look in column C and report the proportion of area greater than or equal to 13 as follows:

$$p \text{ [of } X \geq 13] = .0062$$

Answer the question in everyday terms: Only 62 of every 10,000 assistance recipients score 13 or above on the self-esteem scale. (In a sample of 500 this would be about three persons.) Very few assistance recipients have extremely high self-esteem. If a randomly selected name were chosen from case files, there would be less than a 1 percent chance that this person scored above 13.

Problem Type 3: p [of Cases between Two X-Scores on Different Sides of the Mean].   Find the proportion of cases between two X-scores, one below the mean and one above the mean.

Solution plan: Draw and label the normal curve; shade the target area (p) from one X-score to the other; compute the Z-scores for the two X-scores; locate them in column A of the normal curve table; get areas PA and PB (drawn below) from column B; compute the area (p) which will be the sum of PA and PB.

Illustration: What proportion of the assistance recipients score between 4 and 10 on the self-esteem scale? (*Study Hint:* Only by drawing the curve can we readily see that this problem involves two areas that adjoin the mean: two column B type areas.)

Shade the target area, p:

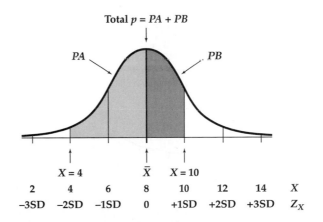

Compute the Z-scores for $X = 4$ and $X = 10$:

$$Z_X = \frac{X - \bar{X}}{s_X} = \frac{4 - 8}{2} = \frac{-4}{2} = -2.00 \text{ SD}$$

$$Z_X = \frac{X - \bar{X}}{s_X} = \frac{10 - 8}{2} = \frac{2}{2} = 1.00 \text{ SD}$$

Now use the normal curve table. In column A find each of the two Z-scores. Look in column B to get areas PA and PB and report the answer as follows:

$PA = p$ [of $X = 4$ to $X = 8$] $= .4772$
$PB = p$ [of $X = 8$ to $X = 10$] $= .3413$
p [of $X = 4$ to $X = 10$] $= PA + PB = .4772 + .3413 = .8185$
$\% = p\,(100) = 81.85\%$

Answer the question in everyday terms: About 82 percent of assistance recipients have self-esteem is scores between 4 and 10. If a randomly selected name is chosen from the case files, there is an 82 percent chance that this person will have a self-esteem score between 4 and 10.

Problem Type 4: p [of Cases between Two X-Scores on One Side of the Mean].   Find the proportion (p) of cases between two X-scores *on one side* of the mean.

Solution plan: Draw and label the curve; shade the target area (p) from one X-score to the other; compute the Z-scores and locate them in column A of the normal curve table; get areas PA and PB from column B; compute the area p, which is PA minus PB.

Illustration: What proportion of the assistance recipients scored between 11 and 13 on the self-esteem scale? In the sample of 500, *how many* assistance recipients is this?

Study Hint: By drawing the curve, we see that the target area p does not touch the mean. Therefore, it is *not* a column B type area in the normal curve table; neither is it a tail-shaped, column C type area. Thus, to solve this illustration, we must compute p indirectly.

Shade the target area p:

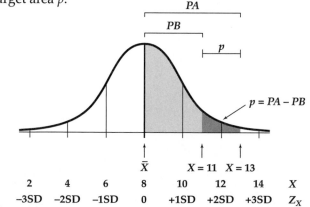

Compute the Z-scores for $X = 13$ and $X = 11$:

$$Z_X = \frac{X - \bar{X}}{s_X} = \frac{13 - 8}{2} = \frac{5}{2} = 2.50 \text{ SD}$$

$$Z_X = \frac{X - \bar{X}}{s_X} = \frac{11 - 8}{2} = \frac{3}{2} = 1.50 \text{ SD}$$

In column A find each of the two Z-scores. Look in column B to get areas *PA* and *PB* and report the answer as follows:

$PA = p$ [of $X = 8$ to $X = 13$] = .4938
$PB = p$ [of $X = 8$ to $X = 11$] = .4332
p [of $X = 11$ to $X = 13$] = $PA - PB$ = .4938 − .4332 = .0606
% = p (100) = 6.06%

Study Hint: Subtract *p*s (i.e., areas under the curve), not Z-scores.

To determine how many of the 500 assistance recipients score in this range, take the proportion of the sample size *n* as follows:

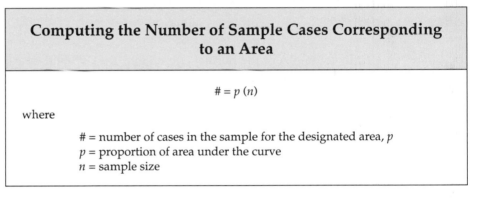

Computing the Number of Sample Cases Corresponding to an Area

$$\# = p\,(n)$$

where

$\#$ = number of cases in the sample for the designated area, *p*
p = proportion of area under the curve
n = sample size

The number of assistance recipients scoring between 11 and 13 on the self-esteem scale is

$$\# = p\,(n) = .0606\,(500) = 30.3 = 30 \text{ recipients}$$

Finally, answer these questions in everyday terms: Only 6 percent of assistance recipients have self-esteem scores between 11 and 13. This is only 30 of the 500 assistance recipients. If a randomly selected name were chosen from the case files, there would be only a 6 percent chance that this person would score between 11 and 13.

Problem Type 5: *p* [of Cases Less Than an X-Score That Is Less Than the Mean].   Find the proportion (*p*) of cases less than or equal to a specified X-score that is less than the mean.

Solution plan: Draw and label the normal curve; shade the target area (*p*) from the X-score out into the tail *in the negative direction;* compute the Z-score and locate it in column A of the normal curve table; get *p* from column C.

Illustration: If a randomly selected name were chosen from the case files, what is the probability that this assistance recipient would score at or below 6.5 on the self-esteem scale?

Shade the target area, *p*:

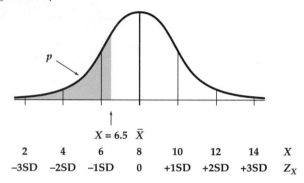

2	4	6	8	10	12	14	X
−3SD	−2SD	−1SD	0	+1SD	+2SD	+3SD	Z_X

Compute the Z-score for $X = 6.5$:

$$Z_X = \frac{X - \bar{X}}{s_X} = \frac{6.5 - 8}{2} = \frac{-1.5}{2} = -.75 \text{ SD}$$

In column A of the normal curve table, find .75 and treat it as though it were −.75. Look in column C and report the answer as follows:

$$p \text{ [of } X \le 6.5] = .2266$$
$$\% = p \,(100) = 22.66\%$$

Answer the question in everyday terms: The probability that a randomly selected assistance recipient scored at or below 6.5 on the self-esteem scale is about 23 percent.

Problem Type 6: *p* [of Cases Less Than an *X*-Score That Is Greater Than the Mean].   Find the proportion (*p*) of cases *less than* a specified X-score which is *greater than* the mean.

Solution plan: Draw the curve; shade the target area (*p*); compute the Z-score and locate it in column A; get *p* from column B and add .5000.

Illustration: What is the probability (*p*) that a randomly selected assistance recipient scores at or below 10.5 on the self-esteem scale?

Study Hint: Remember that the normal curve table gives areas only for one side of the curve. Remember also that a normal curve has a median equal to the mean; therefore, half (or a proportion of .5000) of the scores fall below the mean. This illustration is solved by working with the area above the mean and then adding the area below the mean. (Incidentally, to find the proportion (*p*) of cases *more than* a specified X-score which is *less than* the mean, work from the left side over. Calculate the area below the mean and then add it to .5000, which is the area above the mean.)

Shade the target area p:

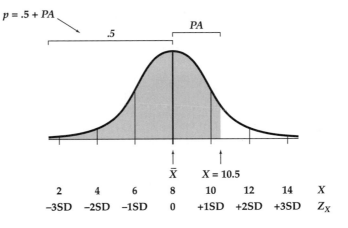

Compute the Z-score for X = 10.5:

$$Z_X = \frac{X - \bar{X}}{s_X} = \frac{10.5 - 8}{2} = \frac{2.5}{2} = 1.25 \text{ SD}$$

In column A of the normal curve table, find 1.25. Look in column B and report the answer as follows:

$$PA = p \text{ [of } X = 8 \text{ to } X = 10.5] = .3944$$
$$p \text{ [of } X \leq 10.5] = PA + .5000 = .3944 + .5000 = .8944$$

Answer the question in everyday terms: The probability that a randomly selected assistance recipient scored at or below 10.5 on the self-esteem scale is over 89 percent.

Problem Type 7: Find the X-Score That Has a Specified p [of Cases] above or below It.   Find the value of a raw score X for which a specified percentage of the sample or population falls above or below that value.

Solution plan: Whereas the previous problem types provided an X-score and asked for an area (p), this problem provides information on p and asks for an X-score. Draw and label the normal curve; *roughly* identify and shade the target area p; find this area in column B or column C of the normal curve table, whichever column is apparently appropriate from the drawing; read column A to get the Z-score; solve for X as follows:

$$Z_X = \frac{X - \bar{X}}{s_X}, \quad \text{thus, } X = \bar{X} + (s_X)(Z_X)$$

Illustration: The Department of Mental Health has a program designed to ward off episodes of acute psychological depression by building the self-esteem of assistance recipients. The program has funding for only 50 people among the

500 who were measured for self-esteem. Let us choose the 50 with the lowest self-esteem because they are presumably at the greatest risk of depression. What is the highest self-esteem score a recipient can have to qualify for the program?

To identify the target area p, we compute the proportion of assistance recipients who are to qualify:

$$p \,[\text{qualifying for program}] = \frac{\#\,\text{qualifying}}{n} = \frac{50}{500} = .1000$$

In drawing the target area, keep in mind that it will be a tail in the *negative* direction of scores because we are looking for the *lowest* 50 assistance recipients. Note that the target area is a column C type area.

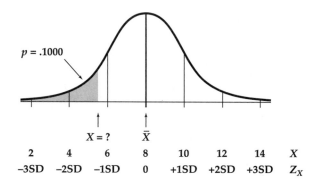

$p = .1000$

	$X = ?$	$\bar{X}$				
2	4	6	8	10	12	14	X
–3SD	–2SD	–1SD	0	+1SD	+2SD	+3SD	Z_X

Study Hint: At this point, estimate the answer from the graph. Our marking of the position of X should be close. We know by now that only 15.87 percent of cases fall below –1 SD, and so the 10 percent mark must be just below that. Thus, our X-score should be slightly below 6. Estimating the answer in this fashion not only encourages proportional thinking but also provides a warning if our calculated answer is incorrect.

Now use the normal curve table. In column C find .1000 or the nearest amount to it, in this case .1003. Look in column A to find the corresponding Z-score of –1.28 and solve for X:

$$X = \bar{X} + (s_X)\,(Z_X) = 8 + (2)\,(-1.28) = 8 - 2.56 = 5.44 \text{ self-esteem points}$$

Answer the question in everyday terms: Those assistance recipients who score less than or equal to 5.44 on the self-esteem scale fall in the lowest 10 percent and therefore qualify for the depression-avoidance program.

Study Hint: Problem Type 7 shows that as long as we know the mean and the standard deviation of a distribution and can assume that the distribution of scores in the population is normally shaped, only one additional piece of information is needed to solve any problem. This piece of information can be a raw X-score, a standardized Z-score, or an area under the normal curve (p).

Thus:

- If given an X-score, compute Z_X and use the normal curve table to get p.
- If given a Z-score, use the normal curve table to get p or solve for X, where $X = \bar{X} + (s_X)(Z_X)$.
- If given a percentage or area, p, use the normal curve table to get the corresponding Z-score and solve for X, where $X = \bar{X} + (s_X)(Z_X)$

Critical Values and Critical Regions under the Normal Curve

As we will see in later chapters, there are certain Z-scores and areas under the normal curve that are of critical (or great) importance in statistical procedures and therefore are used frequently. These are called critical Z-scores and critical regions of the curve. The critical regions are areas under the curve which, of course, can be viewed as probabilities. These critical probabilities are signified with the Greek letter alpha (α). Why do we call these scores and probabilities *critical*? Because statistical procedures are based on probability theory. These α-probabilities are decisive in determining the degree of confidence we may place in our reported results (Chapter 8) and also are important for testing hypotheses (Chapters 9 through 16). The notion of *critical* will become apparent later. For the time being let us focus on the relationship of these critical α-probabilities to the normal curve.

The most frequently used critical Z-score is ± 1.96. Ninety-five percent of the area under a normal curve falls between +1.96 and –1.96, leaving 5 percent of the area distributed in the two tails (2.5 percent in each tail). It is the area in the tails of the curve that constitutes the critical region or α-probability. Since the focus is on two tails, this is called a two-tailed critical region. A critical Z-score of ± 1.96, then, corresponds to the critical region "α = .05, two tails."

We can also have a critical region concentrated on one side of the curve—a one-tailed critical region. For example, the critical Z-score of 1.64 is a one-tailed critical region; 5 percent of the curve is beyond 1.64 on one side. A critical Z-score of 1.64, then, corresponds to the critical region "α = .05, one tail." These two critical scores and their critical regions are illustrated in Figure 6–4. Table 6–1 lists several commonly used Z-scores and the sizes of their critical regions (i.e., α-probabilities). Note that these critical regions are "comfortable" sizes (i.e., 5 percent, 1 percent, and 0.1 percent). For instance, if asked to rate the performance of the members of a rock and roll group, you might respond that the group rates in the top 5 percent or 1 percent. You are not likely to use an awkward percentage such as 4 percent.

Computing Percentiles for Normally Distributed Populations

Normal curve Problem Types 5, 6, and 7 deal with areas under the curve that are below a particular raw score X. These areas define **percentile ranks,** *the percentage of a sample or population that falls at or below a specified value of a*

FIGURE 6–4

*Critical Z-scores
for α = .05*

Illustration A: Critical two-tailed Z-score of ±1.96; critical region area totals .05 (5%) distributed in the two tails.

Designated: Critical region for α = .05, two tails.

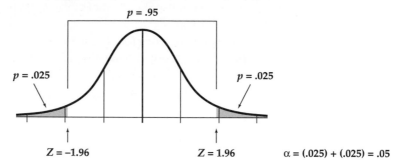

$\alpha = (.025) + (.025) = .05$

Illustration B: Critical one-tailed Z-score of 1.64; critical region area totals .05 (5%) in one tail.

Designated: Critical region for a = .05, one tail.

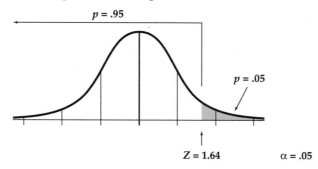

$\alpha = .05$

TABLE 6–1　**Commonly Used Critical Z-scores and α-Probabilities (p in the Critical Region)**

Critical Region (α)	Critical Z-score (Z_α)	In One Tail		In Two Tails		
		p	%	p	Σ% from Both Sides	(% on one side)
α = .05, 1 tail	1.64	.05	5%			
α = .01, 1 tail	2.33	.01	1%			
α = .001, 1 tail	3.08	.001	0.1%			
α = .05, 2 tails	1.96			.05	5%	(2.5%)
α = .01, 2 tails	2.58			.01	1%	(0.5%)
α = .001, 2 tails	3.30	.		001	0.1%	(.05%)

variable (see Chapter 2). For example, with regard to Problem Type 6, someone who scored 10.5 on the self-esteem scale scored higher than did 89 percent of the assistance recipients in the sample—a percentile rank of 89. Similarly, for Problem Type 5, someone who scored 6.5 has a percentile rank of 23. When a variable is normally distributed, we can use the normal curve table to quickly compute percentile ranks.

Many distributions, especially achievement, intelligence, and school admissions tests, are especially designed to produce a score distribution that is normally distributed. We all remember receiving percentile ranks in addition to the raw scores for such tests. The companies that distribute the tests intentionally "normalized" them so that score distributions would fit the normal curve. Once this normalization is accomplished, the normal curve table is used to generate percentile ranks.

Finally, we should mention that percentile ranks can be determined for distributions that are not normally distributed. All that is necessary to compute any percentile rank is to determine what percentage of a distribution falls below a specified X-score. Most computer programs provide this information as the "cumulative percentage" of a distribution (see Chapter 2).

The Normal Curve as a Tool for Proportional Thinking

Once we have gotten over learning the details of chopping the normal curve into areas, we should begin to truly appreciate its usefulness. As a descriptive tool, normalizing score distributions on tests is done because experience has shown that intelligence, learning, and achievement, are normally distributed; that is, most people are about average in intelligence and achievement, and this is why the normal curve "bells up" in the middle. Very few people are geniuses and very few are extremely below normal, and this is why the curve begins to hug the horizontal axis as we observe scores more than 1 standard deviation from the mean in either direction.

Working with the normal curve also makes us more cautious in the interpretation of data. We are now aware, for example, that scores from different tests (such as the ACT and SAT) can be compared by looking at the relative positions of scores within their own distributions; a simple way to do this is to compare percentile ranks.

After working with the normal distribution, we become aware that equal differences between scores do not always indicate that one score is just as far away from another in terms of how unusual it is. For example, suppose the 2,000 entering first-year students at State University had a mean ACT score (X) of 24 with a standard deviation of 4 and the distribution was normally shaped. Ronald made a 24, Barry made a 28, and Sophia made a 32. Observation of the raw scores suggest that Barry falls precisely between Ronald and Sophia in their ranks on these scores. Our sense of a normal distribution should convince us, however, that Barry is considerably above average although his score

---
TABLE 6–2   Comparing Raw Scores (X), Z-Scores, and Percentile Ranks to Gain a Sense of Proportion about Normally Distributed Variables

Givens		Calculations	
Student	X	Z_X	Percentile Rank
Ronald	24	0	50
Barry	28	1	84
Sophia	32	2	98

---

of 28 is only 4 points better than a 24. This is apparent when the raw scores (X), standardized scores (Z_X), and percentile ranks are compared, as they are in Table 6–2.

This illustrates the importance of knowing how a distribution of scores is spread. Barry is only 4 points better than Ronald on the raw score, but he is 34 percentage points better in terms of percentile rank. Barry, like Sophia, scored better than the great majority of entering students. Raw scores by themselves suggest otherwise and can be very misleading. The standard deviation as a unit of measure with normal distributions is a powerful tool for gaining accurate insight into the significance of a raw score.

Finally, the phenomenon of normality is the essence of statistical analysis. It is very important that we learn how to roam about the normal curve and develop the skills to partition areas under it. A quick look through the remainder of this text should convince you of the importance of mastering the problems in this chapter. Nearly every chapter after this one has depictions of the normal curve or similar probability curves.

Probabilities: Where Proportional Thinking and Error Control Intersect

The two major themes of this text are that statistics is about proportional thinking and that one can learn to control error in analysis. These themes come together in the concept of probability. By their very nature, probabilities provide information not about an isolated singular event but about the long-term occurrence of events. Probabilities answer questions about how usual or unusual the occurrence of some phenomenon is. With correctly gathered data these probabilities can be computed very precisely.

Many areas of life hinge on our reactions to events. Understanding that a single occurrence of an event has a calculable probability keeps us alert yet prevents us from overreacting and making poor decisions. For example, suppose our favorite stock investment drops 5 percent in value in one day. Has it become worthless as an investment? Is it time to sell? Look at it in the larger picture. Is it unusual for a stock to drop in price? (Of course not.) An examination of past fluctuations in value may reveal that every nine months the stock takes a slight drop, only to rebound with a 10–15 percent rise. This analysis of the long-term trend suggests that it is time to buy *more*, not sell.

Computing probabilities is an important aspect of everyday government and military policy making and decision making. For example, if a historically belligerent country moves massive numbers of troops to its borders, does this mean an invasion is imminent? Perhaps, but with good military "intelligence" (information gathered by spies and spy satellites) we may see that critical elements of an invasion are missing, such as long-term stores of ammunition. Thus, we conclude that if this country does start an invasion, the probability of its success will be low. Although our troops should be on alert, we know not to overreact with a preemptive strike. Government intelligence agencies such as the Central Intelligence Agency (CIA) employ vast numbers of statisticians whose jobs involve gaining a sense of balance and proportion by computing probabilities.

Because it so handily provides probabilities, the normal curve distribution and predictable curves similar to it are called probability distributions. As we shall see in Chapter 7, sampling events have predictable patterns of occurrence, and their probability curves are used to determine how usual they are. Probabilities in general and the normal probability distribution in particular are key elements in statistical analysis.

Finally, an interesting thought quiz about probabilities involves the matter of low-occurrence events. Any natural or human event has *some* probability of occurring. Occasionally, for instance, someone is struck by a meteorite. Most of us, however, do not check the sky constantly for these objects. We understand probabilities and know that "you just have to be really unlucky" for this to happen to you. Similarly, 40 million people enter a lottery. One person wins. He or she is very lucky! It snows in Florida once every five years, but it happens to snow on your wedding day. You are very unlucky! In terms of the ideas of probability theory, what does it mean to say someone is very lucky or unlucky? What is luck?

☹   STATISTICAL FOLLIES AND FALLACIES   ☹

The Gambler's Fallacy: Independence of Probability Events

Imagine that Bob and Terri are gambling by playing a coin-tossing game. Bob wins with heads, and Terri wins with tails. They take turns deciding how much the next flip will be worth, choosing an amount from 5 cents to 25 cents.

Bob just won three flips in a row at 10 cents a flip. Should Terri increase the bet to 25 cents for the next toss? Does the fact that heads fell three times in a row increase the chances that tails will come up next?

The answer is no. A common statistical mistake in computing probabilities involves the independence of the parts of compound events. Each coin is flipped independently of what happened to it in previous flips. If we flip a coin twice and get heads both times, this does not increase the probability of a third flip coming up tails. That probability remains .5000.

This tendency to imagine that independent events are tied together is one type of gambler's fallacy. When a gambler hits a streak of bad luck, he or she may start to believe that a streak of good luck must follow. In the long run, in-deed, good and back luck balance out. But what is the long run? Is it 3 tosses, 10 tosses, 1 million tosses? For a given gambler, is the long run longer than his or her money will hold out? Moreover, the balance between good and bad luck occurs among all gamblers, not within a single gambler. Thus, if 100 couples were playing this coin-tossing game, over the course of an evening, chances are great that about as many heads will be tossed as tails. But Bob and Terri may end up tossing more heads, while Joe and Maggie may toss more tails.

To assume that coin tosses are linked is to think mistakenly that we know the length of a "series," a sequence of tosses over the long run. Unfortunately, there are an infinite number of possible sequences, because each toss is inde-pendent of the next. For example, Bob's three heads in a row could be part of any of the following series in which heads and tails fall an equal number of times:

T, T, **H, H, H,** T, H, H, T, T

T, T, T, T, H, T, **H, H, H,** H, H, T

H, T, H, T, T, H, T, T, T, H, H, T, **H, H, H,** T

H, H, H, H, T, T, H, H, T, T, T, H, T, T, H, T, H, T, T, H

For a gambler to assume that he or she somehow knows the future sequence of outcomes is to assume that the future can be seen to a greater extent than what the basic probabilities of occurrence tell us. This obviously is not a sensi-ble way to gamble.

Formulas and Rules of Probability in Chapter 6

Calculating a probability:

$$p\ [\text{of success}] = \frac{\#\ \text{successes}}{\#\ \text{trials}} = \frac{\#\ \text{possible successful outcomes}}{\text{total}\ \#\ \text{possible outcomes}}$$

Calculating a Z-score:

$$Z_X = \frac{X - \bar{X}}{s_X}$$

Calculating a raw score (X) when Z_X is known:

$$X = \bar{X} + (s_X)(Z_X)$$

Computing the number of cases that correspond to an area under the normal curve:

$$\# = p(n)$$

Basic Rules of Probability Theory

1. Probability rule 1: Probabilities always range between 0 and 1.
2. Probability rule 2: The addition rule for alternative events: The probability of alternative events is equal to the sum of the probabilities of the individual events.
3. Probability rule 3: Adjust for joint occurrences, events that double count success or join two aspects of success.
4. Probability rule 4: The multiplication rule for compound events: The probability of a compound event is equal to the multiple of the probabilities of the separate parts of the event.
5. Probability rule 5: Account for replacement with compound events.

Questions for Chapter 6

1. What is probability theory?
2. Name three recent actions in your everyday life where you used probability theory (even though you did not calculate actual probabilities).
3. What does the denominator of a probability formula typically denote?
4. What does the numerator of a probability formula typically denote?
5. If someone reports a probability of 150 percent, what rule of probability has been broken?
6. Name two events that have a 100 percent probability of occurrence.
7. Name two events that have a 0 percent probability of occurrence.
8. State the addition rule of probability and specify when it is used. Give an example.
9. State the multiplication rule of probability and specify when it is used. Give an example.
10. When calculating a probability, an event that double counts success or joins two aspects of success is called a _____.
11. For a proportion of cases fitting success, what distinguishes a distributional interpretation from a probabilistic interpretation? Illustrate with an example.

12. The mean, standard deviation, and normal curve are used most appropriately with variables of what levels of measurement?

13. Why is it appropriate to use the same symbol *p* for proportion, probability, and area under a normal curve?

14. When a score of a normally distributed variable is to the right of the mean, it is in the _____ direction.

15. Explain why it is inappropriate to use Z-scores and the normal curve table for any distribution of scores that is not normally shaped.

16. What information does a percentile rank provide?

17. Explain what it means to be very lucky or very unlucky.

Exercises for Chapter 6

1. Compute the following probabilities for the roll of one gaming die:

   a. p [6]
   b. p [2 or 4]
   c. p [2 then 3 then 4]

2. Compute the following probabilities for the roll of one gaming die:

   a. p [5]
   b. p [5 then 6]
   c. p [1 or 3 or 6]

3. Suppose you have a box of 100 red marbles, 50 blue marbles, and 50 green marbles. Compute the probabilities of randomly drawing the following from the box:

   a. p [red then red then green] without replacement
   b. p [red then red then green] with replacement
   c. p [blue then red then green] with replacement of reds only

4. Suppose you have a box of well stirred dry beans: 150 red, 70 white, and 80 black. Compute the probabilities of randomly drawing the following from this box:

   a. p [white then red then black] without replacement
   b. p [red then red then black] with replacement
   c. p [white then black then white] with replacement of blacks only

5. For the toss of one coin (*H* = heads, *T* = tails), compute the following:

   a. p [*H*]
   b. p [*T* then *T*]
   c. p [*T* then *H* then *H*]

6. For the toss of one coin (H = heads, T = tails), compute the following:

   a. p [T]
   b. p [H then T]
   c. p [T then T then T]

7. Compute the following probabilities for drawing cards from a standard deck of 52 playing cards.

   a. p [ace]
   b. p [king or jack]
   c. p [queen or spade]
   d. p [ace then ace, or king then king] without replacement

8. Compute the following probabilities for drawing cards from a standard deck of 52 playing cards.

   a. p [10]
   b. p [7 or king]
   c. p [jack or diamond]
   d. p [king then king, or ace then ace] without replacement

9. With a standard deck of 52 playing cards, are your chances of drawing two aces in a row better with or without "replacement"? Illustrate with computations.

10. With a standard deck of 52 playing cards, are your chances of drawing an ace and then a king better with or without "replacement"? Illustrate with computations.

11. Frank is conducting a telephone poll of the residential households in Big Frog County. Foolishly, he uses the telephone book as a sampling frame and randomly draws phone numbers from it. As it turns out, 5 percent of county households have no telephone. Among households *with phones*, 30 percent have unlisted numbers. Moreover, 15 percent of the listed numbers are for businesses even though they are in the White Pages. What percent of Big Frog County households have any chance of being called by Frank?

12. The Melodious Lamp Shades is the hottest new popular music act touring, and it is booked to appear at the local coliseum in 14 days. Unfortunately, the concert sold out before your ticket order got in. Your only chance to go is to win a ticket in a local radio contest by being the first caller when a Lamp Shade hit song is played, which occurs six times each day. At any time, 20,000 people are listening to the station and 25 percent of them attempt to call. If you attempt a call at every opportunity between now and the concert, what is the probability that you will win a ticket?

13. We have the following descriptive statistics for a college admissions test. Use these data to answer the following questions. Draw the normal curve and label all target areas.

X = American College Testing (ACT) scores
$\bar{X}$ = 22 ACT points s_X = 2 ACT points
n = 441,574

The distribution is normal (i.e., normalized).

   a. What proportion of those who took this test scored *above* 26?
   b. What proportion of the scores fell *between* 17 and 19?
   c. What proportion of the scores fell *between* 18 and 23?
   d. Determine the score below which 90 percent of the scores fell.
   e. If an applicant had to make at least the 90th percentile rank to get into a college program, what score would he or she need to make (short answer)?

14. We have the following descriptive statistics for job performance scores where a high score indicates good work. Use these data to answer the following questions. Draw the normal curve and label all target areas.

Y = job performance score
$\bar{Y}$ = 78 points s_Y = 8 points
n = 480

The distribution is normal.

   a. What proportion of those rated scored *above* 90?
   b. What proportion of the scores fell *between* 88 and 98?
   c. What proportion of the scores fell *between* 70 and 90?
   d. Determine the score below which 95 percent of the scores fell.
   e. If an applicant had to make at least the 95th percentile rank to obtain bonus pay, what score would he or she need to make (short answer)?

15. You are an intake worker at a homeless shelter. When new clients arrive, you administer the Center for Epidemiological Studies Depression Scale (CESD), a community screening questionnaire, to determine who needs a doctor's care for acute psychological depression. Among homeless people, the mean CESD score is 23.5 with a standard deviation of 7.5, and the distribution is normal. Any client scoring 16 or higher is to be sent to a doctor. Draw a normal curve with the solution to each problem.

   a. What is the probability that your next client will be sent to a doctor?
   b. What is the probability that your next client will score 10 or below?
   c. If those homeless scoring in the highest 15 percent on the CESD are to be targeted for suicide prevention services, what score qualifies a client for these services?

16. You have a population of young adults with a mean age of 22 years and a standard deviation of 2 years. Ages in this population are normally

distributed. You are to randomly select an individual from this population. Compute the following probabilities. Draw the normal curve for each problem.

   a. p [of randomly drawing someone between the ages of 20 and 24].
   b. p [of randomly drawing someone (19 years old or younger) or (25 years old or older)].
   c. If the youngest 10 percent of the young adults are to be mailed a letter, below what age will the letters be targeted?

17. Draw and label a normal curve to answer each of the following questions.

   a. What critical value of Z has .01 of the area beyond it on one side of the mean?
   b. This critical value (Z_α) applies to what critical region (α)? (If necessary, review Table 6–1.)
   c. What critical value of Z has .01 of the area beyond it on both sides of the mean combined?
   d. This critical value (Z_α) applies to what critical region (α)? (If necessary, review Table 6–1.)

18. Draw and label a normal curve to answer each of the following questions.

   a. What critical value of Z has .001 of the area beyond it on one side of the mean?
   b. This critical value (Z_α) applies to what critical region (α)? (If necessary, review Table 6–1.)
   c. What critical value of Z has .001 of the area beyond it on both sides of the mean combined?
   d. This critical value (Z_α) applies to what critical region (α)? (If necessary, review Table 6–1.)

19. A statistician says that she rates the performance of a popular singing artist at 2.33 standard deviations above the mean performance of all artists she has seen. Percentagewise, how high does this statistician rate the performing artist? In other words, according to this statistician's judgment, what is the performer's percentile rank?

20. Jessica, Michele, and Caroline take an achievement test that is normalized—especially designed so that the score distribution fits a normal curve. The mean of the test is 1,000 with a standard deviation of 100. Jessica scores 1,000, Michele scores 1,200, and Caroline scores 1,400. Michele feels dejected because she believes she did not do much better than Jessica. Use the normal curve and percentiles to show why Michele is wrong to feel dejected.

Optional Computer Applications for Chapter 6

For classes using computers, on the *Computer Applications for The Statistical Imagination* compact disk open the Chapter 6 exercises. These exercises focus on using score frequency distributions as probability distributions and using Z-scores to compute probabilities with normally distributed interval/ratio variables.

CHAPTER

7

USING PROBABILITY THEORY TO PRODUCE SAMPLING DISTRIBUTIONS

Introduction: Estimating Parameters

To review briefly, a population is a large set of persons about whom we desire information. Typically, to save time and money, we sample rather than observe such a large group. Sample statistics provide estimates of the parameters of the total population. Suppose our population of interest is the 16,000 students in a four-year college. From this campus we select a random sample of 200 students. We are interested in parameters such as the following: What is the mean grade point average (GPA)? What percentage of students supports opening the campus library 24 hours a day? What is the mean age? Our interest, however, is not in the means or proportions of the 200 students in the sample. It is the entire student body of 16,000 for which we seek answers. The sample is merely a tool to obtain information about the parameters of this total campus population.

Point Estimates

Suppose we set X as GPA and for a sample of 200 students we find a mean of 2.46 "GPA points" (i.e., credits earned per credit hour taken). Does this assure us that the population mean is also 2.46? Of course not. There is sampling error to consider. By definition, sample statistics are merely estimates of parameters. If we report this single figure of 2.46, we are providing what is called a **point estimate,** *a statistic provided without indicating a range of error.* This is not much better than a best guess. Why? Because if we draw a second, a third, and a fourth sample, we are likely to get slightly different computed means from each one. In other words, there is variability in statistical outcomes from sample to sample.

Point Estimate

A statistic provided without indicating a range of error.

Predicting Sampling Error

It was the discovery of sample variability—the recognition that each sample's statistics differ slightly from those of the next—that underlies a basic understanding of sampling error. Like the ancient statisticians who repeatedly rolled dice, later statisticians learned about sampling error through **repeated sampling**—*drawing a sample and computing its statistics and then drawing a second sample, a third, a fourth, and so on*. These "bean-counting" statisticians learned two important natural facts about repeated sampling from a population. First, calculated results will differ from one sample to the next. Second, the calculations made on a sample—a group that is smaller than the entire population—are only estimates. That is, a sample's statistics will be slightly off from the true values of its population's parameters.

Repeated Sampling

Drawing a sample and computing its statistics and then drawing a second sample, a third, a fourth, and so on. Repeated sampling reveals the nature of sampling error.

Repeated random sampling and the resulting variability in statistical outcomes are illustrated in Figure 7–1, which presents a population of children whose ages range from zero (infant under one year) to nine years. For sample statistics—calculations made on sample data—we typically use English letter symbols such as $\overline{X}$ and s_X (with which we are already familiar). When feasible, we use Greek letters for population parameters. Specifically, we use the following symbols to represent population parameters for interval/ratio variables:

For the interval/ratio variable X

μ_X = the mean of a population (pronounced *mu*-sub-X)
σ_X = the standard deviation of a population (pronounced *sigma*-sub-X)

Mathematical Symbols Typically Used to Distinguish Populations and Samples

For sample statistics: English letters
For population parameters: Greek letters

In Figure 7–1, X = age and the mean age *in the population* of children is $\mu_X = 4.5$ years. Note that the depicted sample means $\bar{X}$'s in the smaller balloons vary around this population mean of 4.5 years. Each sample mean is slightly higher or lower than 4.5, reflecting sample variability caused by the natural occurrence of random sampling error.

A good way, then, to show that the sample statistics are not exact values of population parameters is to sample repeatedly. If you are unconvinced of this, draw a couple of random samples from the population (i.e., the large circle) of children's ages in Figure 7–1. Chances are great that you will come up with slightly different sample means. Each sample is a very small part of the larger population, and each is composed of a different set of six children. In one sample—just by chance—a few more older children may appear, resulting in a sample mean slightly higher than 4.5 years. In a second sample—just by chance—a few more younger children may appear, resulting in a lower sample mean. Repeated sampling results in varied statistical outcomes.

Over 100 years ago probability theorists recognized some "bad news": A statistic from a single sample is only an estimate of a population parameter. But through repeated sampling—many hours spent drawing one sample after another—these theorists discovered some good news: Sampling error is patterned and systematic and therefore is predictable.

FIGURE 7–1

Sampling variability with repeated sampling: X = ages of children, zero to nine years

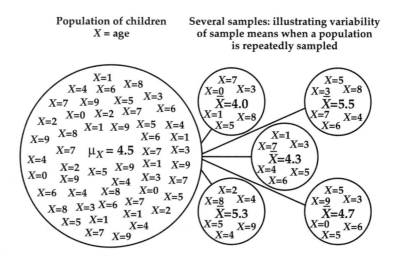

Population of children
X = age

Several samples: illustrating variability of sample means when a population is repeatedly sampled

The first predictable thing found from repeated sampling was that the resulting sample means were similar in value and tended to cluster around a particular value. Probability theorists suspected that this central value was the true value of the population parameter—the population mean itself (μ_X). Using models similar to Figure 7–1, they compared sample outcomes to known parameters and found that a distribution of sample statistics indeed centers on the actual population parameter. This makes sense. If the average age of a population of children is 4.5 years, the mean calculated on a truly random sample should be close to this value. Second, probability theorists discovered that sampling variability was mathematically predictable from probability curves. They took the results from repeated samples and plotted histograms. Most of their computed sample means fell very close in value to the population parameter, and as one moved away from this parameter in either direction, there were fewer and fewer outcomes. In other words, they discovered that statistical outcomes occur according to probability curves such as the normal curve. Finally, when comparing samples of different sizes, these theorists determined that the larger the sample size, the smaller the range of errors in repeated samples.

Sampling Distributions

When the distributions of statistics from repeatedly drawn samples are plotted on histograms, we get an informative picture of the predictability of sampling error. We call such a distribution a sampling distribution. *From repeated sampling,* a **sampling distribution** is *a mathematical description of all possible sampling event outcomes and the probability of each one.*

Sampling Distribution

From repeated sampling, a mathematical description of all possible sampling event outcomes and the probability of each one.

Sampling Distributions for Interval/Ratio Variables

To illustrate the particulars of a sampling distribution of means, let us see what happens if we sample repeatedly from a population *with a known mean.* Suppose we determine from licensing records that the mean age *of the population* of all licensed practicing physicians in the United States is 48 years. Since these data are for the entire population, this mean is a known parameter, symbolized as μ_X, where X = physician age. Suppose also that the standard deviation of this population is six years, symbolized as σ_X. The *raw score* frequency distribution of this *population* of ages is presented in Figure 7–2. Note that this distribution is close to a bell-shaped normal curve except that it is slightly flattened. We refer to such a distribution as an **approximately normal distribution,** *one that is like the normal curve in that it is symmetrical with equal mean, median, and mode, although the curve is slightly flattened or peaked.* Both normal and approximately normal curves have "tails" that swoop down on both sides. With a normal distribution we use the symbol Z for standardized scores (i.e., measuring the number of standard deviations from the mean). For reasons which will be made clear below, we use the symbol t to represent standardized scores for an approximately normal distribution.

It is important to keep in mind that on the horizontal axis of Figure 7–2 we plot raw scores (X-scores)—the actual ages of physicians.

Now let us move our focus away from the raw score distribution in Figure 7–2 and think about a sampling distribution of means. To determine all possible sampling outcomes, we must imagine repeatedly drawing samples from this population. Say we draw 10,000 samples of 37 physicians. For each sample, we compute the sample mean age, $\bar{X}$. A moment's thought should convince us that most sample means will calculate to around 48 years. But because of sampling error we would *not* be surprised if each sample mean were slightly off, say, 47.9 years or 48.2 years.

Now let us imagine that we plot the values of these 10,000 sample means on a histogram. That is, for each sample we treat the calculated mean age as a single observation. Thus, we plot $\bar{X}$'s in place of X's on the horizontal axis. Guess what shape this histogram will take? Yes, a normal distribution or very close to it. We will simply say that *a sampling distribution of means is approximately normal.* This approximation to normality is illustrated in the smooth curve in Figure 7–3. Most of the 10,000 sample means fall on or right around 48 years. As we move away from 48 years in either direction, the curve slopes downward, indicating fewer and fewer outcomes. Moreover, if we sum the values of all 10,000 sample means and divide by 10,000, this *mean of sample means* is 48 years—the mean age of physicians in the population. *The mean of a sampling distribution of means* is symbolized as $\mu_{\bar{X}}$ and will always equal the population mean (μ_X). Furthermore, as with any approximately normal curve,

FIGURE 7–2

Raw score frequency distribution of ages for the entire population of actively practicing physicians in the United States (fictional data)

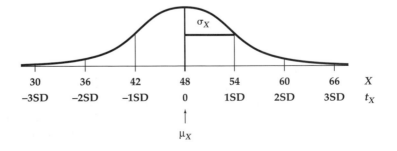

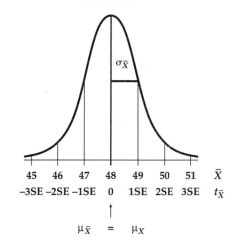

FIGURE 7–3

The sampling distribution of the mean age of physicians in the United States

the standard deviation is the distance to the point of inflection of the curve. In summary, the curve in Figure 7–3 is a sampling distribution of means (X-bars, not X's). It mathematically describes *all possible sampling event outcomes and the probability of each outcome.*

Approximately Normal Distribution

One that is like the normal curve in that it is symmetrical with equal mean, median, and mode, although the curve is slightly flattened or peaked.
Use the symbol t (rather than Z) to signify standardized scores on such a distribution. Sampling distributions are usually approximately normal.

What does this sampling distribution tell us? First, any sampling distribution (by definition) depicts all possible sampling outcomes. Figure 7–3 reveals all statistical outcomes that occur if we repeatedly draw samples of size 37 from the physician population and compute the mean of each sample. Second, since a sampling distribution of means takes an approximately normal shape, t-scores can be used like Z-scores with a table similar to the normal curve table to compute the probability of occurrence of any sample outcome. Thus, with this approximately normal distribution, about 68 percent of the observations fall within 1 standard deviation—in this case, 1 standard error—on both sides of the mean. Specifically, about 68 percent of the time our sample means ($\overline{X}$'s) will compute to between 47 and 49 years; approximately 95 percent of the time, between 46 and 50; and almost 100 percent of the time, between 45 and 51. In summary, this distribution provides a description of all possible sampling outcomes when $n = 37$ and the population mean is 48 years.

The Standard Error

The standard deviation of a sampling distribution has a special name—the standard error—because it is a measure of predictable sampling errors. The **standard error** is *the standard deviation of a sampling distribution.* Note that for the sampling distribution in Figure 7–3 the units of measure are labeled SE (standard errors) rather than SD (standard deviations). The standard error measures the spread of sampling error that occurs when a population is sampled repeatedly.

Standard Error

The standard deviation of a sampling distribution.
The standard error measures the spread of sampling error that occurs when a population is sampled repeatedly.

Mathematicians have determined that *the standard error of a sampling distribution of means* is equal to the population's standard deviation divided by the square root of the sample size (n), or

$$\sigma_{\bar{X}} = \frac{\sigma_X}{\sqrt{n}}$$

where

$\sigma_{\bar{X}}$ = the standard error of a sampling distribution of means for the variable X
σ_X = the standard deviation of the population
n = sample size

Seldom, however, do we know the population's standard deviation. (If we already knew it, we would not be sampling.) Therefore, we use the sample standard deviation to *estimate* the standard error. Mathematicians have discerned that the proper estimate is computed as follows. Note the English symbol which indicates that this estimated standard error is based on sample data:

Computing the Standard Error of a Sampling Distribution of Means When σ_X Is Unknown (for an interval/ratio or interval-like ordinal variable)

$$s_{\bar{X}} = \frac{s_X}{\sqrt{n-1}}$$

where

$s_{\bar{X}}$ = estimated standard error of means for the variable X
s_X = the standard deviation of a sample
n = sample size

For the sampling distribution of the mean ages of physicians depicted in Figure 7–3 the standard error is one year:

$$s_{\bar{X}} = \frac{s_X}{\sqrt{n-1}} = \frac{6}{6} = 1 \text{ year}$$

The Law of Large Numbers

A close look at the formula for the standard error of a sampling distribution of means reveals an important point about the spread of sampling error. *The larger the sample size, the smaller the standard error.* This principle, called the **law of large numbers,** makes sense. A big sample works better than a small one. This is apparent in the makeup of the formula for the standard error. When n is replaced with increasingly larger values, this increases the size of the denominator and reduces the size of the quotient. For samples of physicians, replace n with increasingly larger values and note how the calculated standard error decreases.

The Law of Large Numbers

The larger the sample size, the smaller the standard error (i.e., the smaller the range of error in the sampling distribution).

The Central Limit Theorem

To help us distinguish raw score and sampling distributions, note the similarities and differences between the curves in Figures 7–2 and 7–3. In both distributions the means are equal to the population mean, μ_X. In the sampling distribution of Figure 7–3, however, on the horizontal axis we plot *sample means* (*X*-bars, not raw *X*-scores), and the standard deviation is the standard error. Furthermore, the standard error in Figure 7–3 has a different formula and symbol than does the standard deviation in Figure 7–2.

Note also the differences in the size of the spread of these distributions. In the raw score distribution of Figure 7–2 the actual ages of the physicians range from about 30 to 66 years. In the sampling distribution of Figure 7–3 *the computed sample means* have a much narrower range, from a sample mean of about 45 years to one of about 51 years. This is highlighted in Figure 7–4, which superimposes the distributions. It makes intuitive sense that the sampling distribution has a smaller range. As a central tendency statistic, the mean for any sample is likely to compute within a central area of a raw score distribution. An average is likely to be average. Thus, when we plot a large number of means, they cluster *narrowly* around a center value that happens to be the mean of the population, μ_X. Mathematically, the narrower spread of a sampling distribution is apparent in the formula for the standard error. The standard deviation is in the numerator and thus is divided into smaller pieces. The

FIGURE 7–4

Comparison of the spreads of a distribution of raw scores to its sampling distribution: ages of physicians in the United States

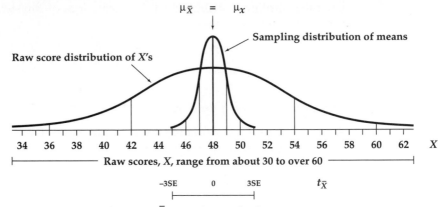

standard error will always calculate to a smaller value than will the standard deviation.

The tendency is strong for a sampling distribution to have a small range of values within the center of the raw score distribution. In fact, this tendency is so strong that it occurs even when the raw score distribution itself is not normal or even approximately normal. *Regardless of the shape of a raw score distribution, its sampling distribution will be approximately normal.* Among mathematicians this discovery is referred to as the **central limit theorem.**

The Central Limit Theorem

Regardless of the shape of the raw score distribution of an interval/ratio variable, the sampling distribution of means will be approximately normal in shape.

To illustrate the central limit theorem let us look at the random number table (Statistical Table A in Appendix B). Each single number in the table is called a digit. These "single random digits" range from zero to 9. Each digit can be viewed as a score of the variable X, such as the ages of children nine and under in Figure 7–1. How was this random number table generated? Let us imagine producing it by hand. We start by writing each of the digits (zero through 9) on separate slips of paper. We place these 10 slips into a hat, and stir them up—randomize them—so that each has an equal chance of being selected. We draw a slip, record the result, replace it in the hat, and repeat the process an infinite number of times. Since every digit has an equal chance of selection on each draw, over the long run we will record just as many zeros as 1's, 2's, and so on, through 9. The frequency distribution of these raw scores (i.e., X-scores) would appear as it does in Figure 7–5. This distribution is "rectangular" in shape; each column of the histogram is equal in height to all the

FIGURE 7–5

*Raw score
frequency
distribution of an
infinite set of single
random digits*

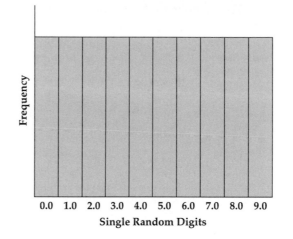

others. This is the case because all digits have an equal chance of selection and therefore each will occur with the same frequency. Thus, this distribution is *not* approximately normal. It is not even remotely normal—it lacks "tails."

Now let us imagine that we are taking *samples* from this random number table. We select a sample, compute the sample mean ($\bar{X}$), and repeat this process many times. Demonstrating the central limit theorem, the shape of a histogram of the resulting sampling distribution is approximately normal even though the raw score distribution is not remotely normal in shape. This is illustrated in Figure 7–6.

It is a good idea to gain a sense of this phenomenon by treating the random number table (Statistical Table A in Appendix B) as though it were a population of random digits and drawing repeated samples from it. (See the exercises at the end of the chapter.)

FIGURE 7–6

*Sampling
distribution of
means of samples of
single random
digits*

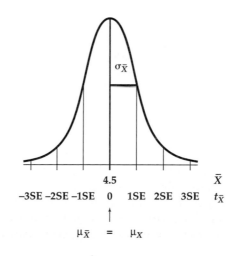

Fortunately, to determine the shape of a sampling distribution, we do not have to sample repeatedly. Probability theorists, the bean counters of the past, spent their time doing this and provided standard error formulas. We need only draw one sample and use its standard deviation to estimate the standard error of a sampling distribution.

The "Student's t" Sampling Distribution

As the law of large numbers asserts, for a sampling distribution of means, the larger the sample size *n*, the smaller the standard error. Conversely, especially small samples have standard errors so large that the probability curve is stretched and flattened. Such flat curves are only approximately normal. This flattening begins to appear with sample sizes less than 120 and is especially apparent when *n* is less than 30.

In addition to small sample size, a factor that introduces sampling error is estimation error—using a sample statistic to calculate a standard error. Remember, in everyday research situations we do not sample repeatedly. We simply use the standard deviation from a single sample to estimate the standard error. Estimates based on another sample's standard deviation would be slightly different. In other words, a calculation based on an estimate (i.e., the sample standard deviation) is necessarily an estimate itself. As with small samples, estimation error flattens the curve of a sampling distribution and prohibits the use of the normal distribution table (Statistical Table B in Appendix B) to calculate probabilities. As with especially small samples, the sampling distribution curve is only approximately normal.

The sampling distribution curve we use with especially small samples and/or when the standard error is estimated is called Student's *t*, or simply a *t*-distribution. This distribution curve is approximately normal. Like the normal curve, the *t*-distribution curve is symmetrical; that is, the mean, median, and mode are equal and one side of the curve is a mirror image of the other. But a *t*-distribution curve is flatter than the normal curve (i.e., a *t*-distribution is *platykurtic,* or flattened out like a plate). The standardized scores for this curve—a measure of distance on the horizontal axis as a number of standard errors—are symbolized by *t* instead of Z to indicate that the curve is only approximately normal.

To illustrate the flattening of a sampling distribution, let us focus on sample size. Figure 7–7 compares the sampling distributions for three sample sizes of 120, 20, and 10. If the standard error is estimated using the sample standard deviation, none of these curves is perfectly normal. With a sample size above 120, however, the curve will be perceptively normal, so close to normal that the eye will not see the difference. Below the sample size of 120, the smaller the sample size, the flatter the *t*-distribution. Thus, there is a separate *t*-distribution curve for every sample size below 120. As we have noted, flattening of the curve really shows up when *n* is less than 30.

The shape of a particular *t*-distribution curve depends on an adjustment

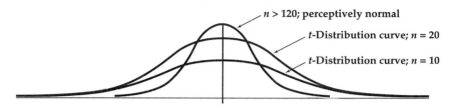

called degrees of freedom (*df*). For a sampling distribution of means, degrees of freedom are computed as the sample size minus 1.

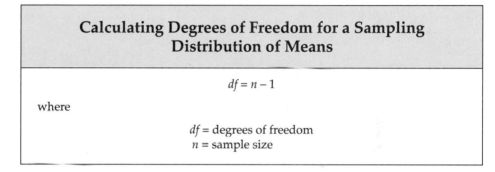

Calculating Degrees of Freedom for a Sampling Distribution of Means

where

$$df = n - 1$$

df = degrees of freedom
n = sample size

As Figure 7–7 indicates, the smaller the sample, the flatter the curve. To calculate probabilities from a *t*-distribution curve, we need over 120 *t*-distribution tables just like the normal curve table—one for each sample size from 121 down to 2. To save space, a single *t*-distribution table (Statistical Table C in Appendix B) consolidates information from all 120 curves. This table, however, is designed differently from the normal curve table; these differences are illustrated in Table 7–1.

The key difference is that the *t*-distribution table provides information only for the traditional *critical regions* of $\alpha = .05$, $\alpha = .01$, and $\alpha = .001$. Recall from Chapter 6 (Table 6–1) that we highlighted these critical regions under the normal distribution and identified the critical Z-scores (Z_α's) that correspond to each region. In the *t*-distribution table, the left column provides degrees of freedom (*df*) and the top row provides areas under the curve—but only for these critical regions. The body of the table contains critical *t*-scores (t_α's). In a *t*-distribution curve, these *t*-scores are used the same way as Z-scores.

Observe the two-tailed and one-tailed *t*-distributions on the right side of Table 7–1. For any number of degrees of freedom (*df*), as you move to the right across the table, the *t*-scores increase while the levels of α decrease from .05 to .001. This simply reflects the fact that the larger the value of the critical score, the smaller the area in the tail of the curve.

Notice that the t_α scores in the bottom row of Table 7–1 are essentially equivalent to Z_α scores. The differences are so small that they do not appear

TABLE 7–1   Locations of Information in the Normal Distribution and *t*-Distribution Tables

Statistical Table B in Appendix B The Normal Distribution Table		*Statistical Table C in Appendix B* The t-Distribution Table						
Column A	Column C		Two-Tailed			One-Tailed		
Z-scores	Area beyond Z	*df*	.05	.01	.001	*df*	.05	.01	.001

α-probabilities for critical regions are located here

Z-scores	Area beyond Z	df	.05	.01	.001	df	.05	.01	.001
1.64	.0505 (≈ .05) one-tailed								
•	•	5	2.571	4.032	6.869	5	2.015	3.365	5.893
2.33	.0099 (≈ .01) one-tailed								
•	•	10	2.228	3.169	4.587	10	1.812	2.764	4.144
3.08	.0010 one-tailed								
•	•								
1.96	.0250 (X 2 = .05) two-tailed								
•	•	20	2.086	2.845	3.850	20	1.725	2.528	3.552
2.58	.0049 (≈ .005 X 2 = .01) two-tailed								
•	•								
3.30	.0005 (X 2 = .001) two-tailed								
•	•	30	2.042	2.750	3.646	30	1.697	2.457	3.385
•	•	120	1.980	2.617	3.373	120	1.658	2.358	3.160
		∞	1.96	2.58	3.30	∞	1.64	2.33	3.08

Critical Z's (Z_α's) are in column A of the normal distribution table

Critical t's (t_α) are in these columns of the *t*-distribution table

when the *t*-scores are rounded. That is, Z-scores and *t*-scores are the same when the sample size (*n*) is 121 or more and, therefore, degrees of freedom compute to 120 or more. But going up any α-column of the *t*-distribution table, the *t*-score will always be larger than the Z-score that appears at the bottom of the table. This makes intuitive sense because both Z-scores and *t*-scores measure variability in sampling error—distance from the mean of the curve. When the sample size is small, calculated means have greater error because of the sensitivity of the mean to extreme scores of X. It is not unusual with a small sample to get sampling outcomes ($\overline{X}$'s) farther out in the tail of the curve— quite far removed from the parameter (μ_X). This "pushing" of a critical region farther from the mean (μ_X) of the sampling distribution for a small sample is illustrated in Figure 7–8, which shows the critical Z and *t* values at the .05 level, one-tailed when *n* > 120 and *n* = 20, respectively. With an *n* of 20, it would be just as unusual to draw a sample whose mean is 1.725 standard errors from μ_X as it would to draw a mean only 1.64 standard errors from μ_X when *n* is greater than 120.

FIGURE 7–8

Comparison of one-tailed critical regions and critical scores for sample sizes of 120 or more (a normal distribution) and 20 (a t-distribution)

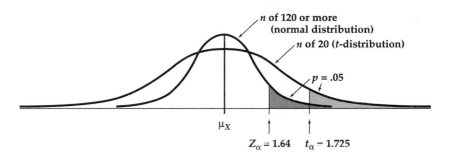

To sum up, for a sampling distribution of means, there are two sources of error that require adjusting for degrees of freedom and using a *t*-distribution in place of a normal distribution: sample size error and estimation error. We almost always have estimation error, and so we simply make a habit of using the *t*-distribution and its table. In fact, this is what computer programs typically do. Do not be thrown off by this. A *t*-distribution is simply an approximately normal curve—a normal curve that is flattened out by a greater spread of sampling error. The *t*-scores in the *t*-distribution table are like Z-scores except that they are for critical regions only. Calculated *t*-scores and Z-scores measure the same thing on these curves. In fact, the formula for a *t*-scores is the same as that for a Z-score except for the symbol. The different symbol simply indicates that we are aware that the distribution is only approximately normal.

Computing Standardized Scores (*t*-Scores) for the Approximately Normal *t*-Distribution

$$t_X = \frac{X - \bar{X}}{s_X}$$

where

t_X = standardized score for a value of X = number of standard deviations a raw score (*X*-score) deviates from the mean
X = an interval/ratio variable
$\bar{X}$ = mean of X
s_X = standard deviation of X

The Approximately Normal Sampling Distribution as a Probability Distribution.   In Chapter 6, we calculated probabilities by partitioning areas under the normal curve. In subsequent chapters, we will do the same using the approximately normal *t*-distribution and its table in place of the normal distribution table. The *t*-distribution is used as a probability sampling distribution. Our interest will focus on the probability of obtaining the sample mean we got for the one sample we drew (Chapter 10). For example, with a sample of physicians (Figure 7–3), what is the probability of drawing a single sample and getting a sample mean age greater than 49 years? The answer is found by following Problem Type 2 in Chapter 6 but using t in place of Z. In addition, we frequently wish to determine whether a sample outcome has a probability of occurrence less than a critical probability value such as .05 or .01. (See Chapter 6, Table 6–1, for a review of critical values.) For example, is the probability of drawing a sample with a mean age of 50 years less than 5 percent (or a proportion of .05)? The procedures for computing these probabilities from an approximately normal sampling distribution are detailed in later chapters.

Finally, the name *Student's t* has an interesting story behind it. The discovery and mathematical derivation of the t-distribution were made early in the 20th century by a mathematician named W. S. Gossett who worked for the Guinness Brewing Company in Dublin, Ireland. To protect its competitive advantage in the ale business, the company did not allow its employees to publish their work. His findings on dealing with small samples were so important for statisticians, however, that the company made an exception and allowed Gossett to publish under the pseudonym Student. Hence, he signed his work that way, and to this day statisticians refer to this sampling distribution as Student's t.

What Are Degrees of Freedom?

In gathering data and doing a statistical analysis on a sample, care must be taken to prevent research procedures from leading to inaccurate conclusions about the population. Every measurement instrument and statistical technique has limitations that potentially distort the interpretation of data. For example, the famous Hubble telescope (which rides on a satellite outside the atmosphere) provides distorted images because of a microscopic misalignment in the curvature of its lens. As a result, the photographic images appear blurred. The stars themselves are not blurred; the blurring is a function of the measurement instrument's limitations. The faulty telescope gets in the way of an accurate assessment of the true shapes of distant galaxies. On-site adjustments (via the space shuttle) have compensated for the bent lens up to a point, but the Hubble's images are still not pure. The telescope has a peak degree of accuracy, and this level is fixed. The conclusions drawn about the nature of its photographic subjects (stars, galaxies, quasars, etc.) are restricted by the tools and methods used to gather data. Even with computer enhancements, Hubble scientists inevitably confront a lack of flexibility in correcting the distortions of their measurement instrument. The picture they see is only a close approximation of what was really there. (We say "was" because when we observe a galaxy with an astronomical telescope, we are actually viewing light that was emitted billions of years ago.)

Similarly, statistical procedures have limitations that potentially get in the way of an accurate assessment of population parameters. To estimate the spread of a sampling distribution of means, we must consider the effects of the major limitation of the mean (Chapter 4): The calculation of the mean is affected by extreme scores or outliers. This distorting effect is especially troublesome with small samples. Being aware of this limitation, we adjust calculations to account for the sensitivity of the mean to outliers, just as Hubble scientists computer-enhance their photographic images. Any statistical procedure has limits: a lack of total freedom in how it is used. We use the term *degrees of freedom* to refer to how flexible a statistical procedure is. The more degrees of freedom we have, the better, because **degrees of freedom** are *the number of opportunities in sampling to compensate for limitations, distortions, and potential weaknesses in statistical procedures.*

Why are the degrees of freedom for the approximately normal *t*-distribution calculated as $n - 1$? For a variable, an extreme score in the sample can produce an inflated or deflated mean, one that does not reflect the true population parameter value of that variable. When the sample size is small, this distortion can be rather large. Once a high-value extreme score is randomly drawn into a small sample, there are not many opportunities left for a low-value case to be selected to pull the computed mean closer to the true population parameter. With a small sample, an extremely high score fixes or limits the calculation of the mean into the high-value end of the score range of the variable. The small sample is inflexible, not free of the mean's limitation of sensitivity to extreme scores. It has few degrees of freedom.

To illustrate these principles, we noted above that an infinite set of single random digits ranges from zero to 9 with a mean of 4.5 (as in Statistical Table A in Appendix B). That is, the true population parameter, μ_X, is 4.5. Suppose, however, we did not know this, and to get an estimate of this population parameter, we sampled these digits and computed the sample mean, $\bar{X}$. Ideally, this estimate would be close to the true parameter of 4.5. This is accomplished when in the random draw process each chosen score on the high side (e.g., 9, 8, 7, or 6) is balanced out by a score on the low side (e.g., 0, 1, 2, or 3). With a true parameter average of 4.5, a perfectly accurate random sample would in fact include as many 0's as 9's because the mean of these two scores is 4.5. Similarly, this perfect sample would include as many 1's as 8's, 2's as 7's, 3's as 6's, and so on. But suppose our sample size is small, say, $n = 5$. Imagine further that the first random digit drawn for the sample is a 9, an extreme score. When 9 is added to ΣX in computing the sample mean, it is likely to cause our estimate of the parameter to be on the high side. For example, the following sequence of sample draws could occur and result in a "high-side" sample mean of 6.2:

Sampling sequence: 9, 5, 3, 8, 6

$$\bar{X} = \frac{\Sigma X}{n} = \frac{31}{5} = 6.2$$

With this small sample, after we draw the 9, it is very likely that our estimate will be high because we have only four sampling opportunities left ($n - 1$) to pick up a zero to balance out the calculation of the mean. We would say that we have only 4 degrees of freedom. Drawing a 9 locks us into a high-side estimate. A sample of five is not very flexible once an extreme score enters the sample.

With a large sample, say, size 130, the drawing of a 9 early on is not as large a problem. We have 129 more chances to draw a zero to bring the sample calculation of the mean back into the 4.5 range. With a large sample there is greater freedom of adjustment in the sampling procedure. Having a lot of random draws increases the chance that any extreme score from one end of the variable's distribution will be balanced by the selection of a similarly extreme score from the other end.

Another way to look at the concept of degrees of freedom is to consider "independence of sampling events." For instance, suppose someone said he or she collected five random digits and computed a mean of 6.2, as in the illustration above. If this researcher told us the values of four of the digits, we could mathematically determine the fifth. That is, if the first four digits are 9, 5, 3, and 8, for the ΣX to add to 31 to produce a mean of 6.2, the last digit has to be 6. In other words, the last digit is not free to vary; its value is dependent on how the mean is calculated. Thus, in calculating the degrees of freedom for a mean, we subtract 1 from the sample size. In this example that leaves us 4 degrees of freedom. Four of the digits are "free to vary." Degrees of freedom, then, can be viewed as the number of independent sampling events—events that are independent of the limitations of the statistical formula used.

It is only with a sampling distribution of means that degrees of freedom are calculated as $n - 1$. With other statistical procedures, adjustments for degrees of freedom depend on the particular limitations of a procedure. In the remaining chapters, the limitations of various statistical procedures are discussed and degrees of freedom adjustments are made. It may be worthwhile to look through the remaining chapters for the symbol *df* to become familiar with the notion that sample statistics include this adjustment.

Degrees of Freedom (*df*)

The number of opportunities in sampling to compensate for limitations, distortions, and potential weaknesses in statistical procedures or the number of independent sampling events. Degrees of freedom are calculated in different ways for various statistical procedures.

Degrees of freedom calculations represent a recognition of the limitations of a procedure. We will use wording such as *"adjust* for degrees of freedom" and *"correct* for degrees of freedom." We often say that a particular limitation causes us to *"lose* degrees of freedom." For instance, the sensitivity of the mean to outliers causes us to lose 1 degree of freedom.

Adjusting for the degrees of freedom of a procedure is an essential part of error control. We must constantly be aware that to sample is to look through a narrow lens. We must ask: Are what we see and what is truly there one and the same? If we know our lens is blurred, we must take this into account, just as the Hubble scientists "correct" their digital photographic images with computer enhancements. The calculation of degrees of freedom is our mode of correction.

Sampling Distributions for Nominal Variables

With nominal variables we count the frequency of categories and calculate proportions. We often target a particular "success" category and wish to determine its parameter in the population. To obtain a sampling distribution of the proportion of success, we ask the question: What happens if we draw a sample, calculate the proportion for this category, and then repeat these procedures over and over? What shape will the distribution of sample outcomes take? As it turns out, a sampling distribution of proportions takes the shape of a normal distribution if the standard error is calculated with known parameter values and as long as *n* is sufficiently large (as we will discuss below). Just as with a sampling distribution of means, however, often we calculate the standard error for a sampling distribution of proportions by using sample data. This introduces additional estimation error, which flattens the normal curve into the approximately normal curve shape. Therefore, to simplify matters, we will simply say that a sampling distribution of proportions is approximately normal, and we will use the *t*-distribution table rather than the normal distribution table to obtain critical values.

To illustrate a sampling distribution of proportions, let us examine the proportion of female physicians among all physicians in active practice in the United States. Specifically, data from the American Medical Association's (1997) *Physician Characteristics and Distribution in the U.S., 1996–1997* reveal that in 1995 there were 720,325 physicians in active practice, of whom 149,404 were female. That is, the known population parameter of the proportion female was .2074 (approximately 21 percent). A moment's thought should convince us that if we draw, say, 10,000 random samples of, say, 300 physicians, the proportion female in each sample should come out to around .21. However, because of expected sampling error, for a given sample we would not be surprised if the calculated proportion was slightly off—say, .20 or .22—because of sampling error. We will find that the bulk of the 10,000 sample proportions fall right around .21, and as we move out in either direction, we will obtain fewer and fewer outcomes. A histogram of these outcomes is approximately normal in shape. Moreover, the mean of *these 10,000 sample proportions* is .21; that is, if we add all 10,000 proportions together and divide by 10,000, the result will be .21—the proportion of female physicians in the population. The standard deviation of this sampling distribution of proportions is called the standard error of proportions.

As with the sampling distribution of means, the sampling distribution of proportions has its own symbols. Since our interest is in the proportion of female physicians (a nominal variable), we will denote *the proportion of females among U.S. physicians* as P (i.e., success) and *the proportion of males among U.S. physicians* as Q (i.e., failure). Thus:

$$P = p \text{ [of U.S. physicians who are female]}$$

$$Q = p \text{ [of U.S. physicians who are male]}$$

We will use the following subscripted symbols to represent population parameters. To avoid nesting the letter p in the symbols, we use the subscript u for *universe,* another term for population. Thus:

$$P_u = p \text{ [of the population of U.S. physicians who are female]} = .21$$

$$Q_u = p \text{ [of the population of U.S. physicians who are male]} = 1 - P_u = 1 - .21 = .79$$

We will use a subscripted s to represent sample statistics. Thus:

$$P_s = p \text{ [of the sampled U.S. physicians who are female]}$$

$$Q_s = p \text{ [of the sampled U.S. physicians who are male]}$$

We want to know, based on the relative proportions of male and female physicians in the population, how much error is expected in repeated sampling. As with means, the size of the error is related to sample size: the larger the sample, the smaller the range of error. To determine sampling error, we compute the standard deviation of this sampling distribution—its standard error—for a sample size of 300 physicians. If the values of P and Q are known, as is the case with physicians, the standard error of proportions is symbolized by sigma-sub-p-sub-s (σ_{P_s}) with the following formula:

Computing the Standard Error of a Sampling Distribution of Proportions When P_u and Q_u Are Known (for a nominal variable)

$$\sigma_{P_s} = \sqrt{\frac{P_u Q_u}{n}}$$

where

σ_{P_s} = standard error of proportions for a nominal variable
    with $P = p$ [of the success category]
$P_u = p$ [of the success category in the population]
$Q_u = p$ [of the failure category in the population]
n = sample size

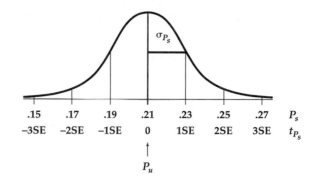

For the standard error of the proportion of female physicians with samples of size 300,

$$\sigma_{P_s} = \sqrt{\frac{P_u Q_u}{n}} = \sqrt{\frac{(.21)(.79)}{300}} = .02$$

Figure 7–9 shows the distribution of these samples, with P_s, the proportion female in a sample, plotted along the horizontal axis. As with any approximately normal curve, this one tells us what to expect if we repeatedly draw samples from the physician population: About 68 percent of the time our sample outcomes, P_s, will compute between .19 and .23 (i.e., .21 ± σ_{P_s}); about 95 percent of the time, P_s will compute between .17 and .25 (i.e., .21 ± 2 σ_{P_s}); and only a very small percentage of the time will any P_s be less than .15 or greater than .27 (i.e., .21 ± 3 σ_{P_s}). This sampling distribution, then, tells us how often to expect a sample outcome to miss the true parameter (P_u) and by how much. Moreover, since this distribution of sampling outcomes is approximately normal, we can mathematically describe its mean and a standard error (as in Figure 7–9). Finally, by calculating *t*-scores (like Z-scores in Chapter 6), we can partition the curve and compute the probability of the occurrence of any single sampling outcome or any range of sampling outcomes. Thus, this mathematically derived approximately normal distribution is a sampling distribution—a description of all possible sample outcomes and the probability of each one.

This illustration is unusual in that the true population parameters of the proportions of female and male physicians are known. In much research, the sample is the only source of data available and sample statistics are used to estimate the standard error of proportions. Thus, if P_u and Q_u are not known, σ_{P_s} is estimated as follows, using sample proportions P_s and Q_s.

> ## Computing the Standard Error of a Sampling Distribution of Proportions When P_u and Q_u are Unknown (for categories of a nominal variable)
>
> $$s_{P_s} = \sqrt{\frac{P_s Q_s}{n}}$$
>
> where
>
> s_{P_s} = estimated standard error of proportions for a nominal variable, with $P = p$
>   [of the success category]
> $P_s = p$ [of the success category in the sample]
> $Q_s = p$ [of the failure category in the sample]
> n = sample size

Rules Concerning a Sampling Distribution of Proportions

Repeated sampling and calculation of sample proportions (P_s) reveal the following qualities about a sampling distribution of proportions.

  1. The mean of a sampling distribution of proportions is equal to the population parameter, P_u.

  2. A sampling distribution of proportions will be approximately normal in shape when the smaller parameter (P_u or Q_u) times $n \geq 5$. (If the parameter is unknown, the sample estimates—P_s and Q_s—apply in making this judgment.) In the example above, P_u (the proportion of female physicians = .21) is smaller than Q_u (the proportion of males = .79). Thus, we set $p_{smaller}$ at .21. To see if an approximately normal distribution is appropriate, we must determine that $p_{smaller}$ times n is greater than or equal to 5:

$$(p_{smaller})\ (n) = (.21)\ (300) = 63 \quad 63 \geq 5$$

Thus, the sampling distribution of the proportion of female physicians where $n = 300$ is approximately normal. In general, for any value of P_u or Q_u (whichever is smaller), the minimum sample size needed to assume an approximately normal distribution is determined by using the following formula:

Computing the Minimum Sample Size Needed to Assume That a Sampling Distribution of Proportions Is Normally Shaped

$$\text{Minimum } n = \frac{5}{p_{smaller}}$$

where

Minimum n = minimum sample size needed to assume normality
$p_{smaller}$ = the smaller of P_u or Q_u (if these parameters are known) or the smaller of P_s or Q_s (if P_u and Q_u are unknown)

For example, when P_s = .1, the minimum n = 50; when P_s = .3, the minimum n = 17; and when P_s = .5, the minimum n = 10. These examples illustrate that when P_s is moderate (i.e., around .5) rather than extreme, a smaller sample will suffice to assure that the sampling distribution is approximately normal. Finally, when the minimum n is less than 5, the appropriate sampling distribution is called the binomial distribution, which is described in Chapter 13.

Bean Counting as a Way of Grasping the Statistical Imagination

Sampling distributions are depictions of what happens if we repeatedly draw samples from a population and compute statistics on a variable. Through this repeated sampling we discover all possible statistical outcomes and the probability of each one. The standard error, the size of which depends on sample size, gives us a ruler to compute these probabilities.

Sampling distributions are an essential feature of statistical analysis because they are useful as probability curves. Having discovered these predictable tendencies in sampling outcomes, probability theorists began to ask questions: Can we use knowledge about the predictability of sampling outcomes in a way that allows us to avoid having to "sample" the entire population to determine a variable's true mean? Can we, for instance, forgo the expense of interviewing all 16,000 students on a campus? Can we examine a single sample and simply estimate errors? For instance, if a single student sample has a mean GPA of 2.44, can we use our knowledge about the predictability of repeated samples to infer a range of error, say, plus or minus .1? Is there a way to compute the degree of confidence we have in the accuracy of a statistic from a single sample? We know that a sample statistic is an estimate—not 100 percent correct. But can we say that we are 90 percent, 95 percent, or 99 percent sure of our results?

You may realize by now that a sampling distribution is a probability distribution. For a given sample size, a sampling distribution tells us how frequently to expect any and all sampling outcomes when we draw random samples. This is no different from calculating, say, the probability of tossing heads and then heads with two coins, as we did in the previous chapter (Figure 6–2). In fact, some of the simple illustrations of probability distributions in that chapter are useful as sampling distributions. And our hard work in Chapter 6, partitioning areas of the normal curve, was done to prepare us for treating the sampling distribution as an approximately normal curve.

Producing sampling distributions by hand—through repeated sampling—is important for truly understanding the concept. This is what early statisticians did. First, they set out to determine what happens when a nominal variable is sampled repeatedly. To represent a category of a variable such as gender, they substituted a box of beans for the population, letting white beans represent men and red beans represent women. They repeatedly scooped samples from the box with a sample size of, say, 100 beans. For each sample they computed the proportion female (i.e., P_s, where $P = p$ [of beans that are red]). They plotted these sample proportions on a histogram and discovered the normal curve and the formula for the standard error. They tried various sample sizes ($n = 90, 80, 70$, etc.) and found that as long as the sample size is sufficiently large, a sampling distribution of proportions takes the bell shape of a normal curve.

For interval/ratio variables the early statisticians used random number tables such as Statistical Table A in Appendix B, treating the digits as though each represented a case for a variable such as age. After repeatedly drawing samples, computing the means, and plotting them on histograms, they discovered yet again the natural phenomenon of normality. Ultimately, these "bean-counting" mathematicians worked out standard error formulas and discovered the law of large numbers and the central limit theorem. Modern statisticians are thankful for the tireless efforts of these early mathematicians and statisticians. Today we need draw only one sample and use formulas to estimate the shape of a sampling distribution.

The central limit theorem essentially states that random sampling results in approximately normal curves: symmetrical distributions that bunch in the middle and tail out to the sides. This pattern occurs indirectly in the other major distributions in the statistical tables in Appendix B. The *F*-distribution table is composed of *t*-scores squared (Chapter 12) and the chi-square distribution table consists of *Z*-scores squared (Chapter 13). Normality in random sampling is a natural phenomenon that existed long before statisticians measured and formulated it, just as gravity existed long before Isaac Newton measured and explained it.

It is one thing for us to talk about how early statisticians learned about sampling distributions and another thing for us to experience the process of generating them for ourselves. The exercises and computer applications for this chapter provide simple ways to produce sampling distributions the old-fashioned way—by actually counting beans. *Bean counter* is a negative term that often is thrown at stingy bureaucrats who pinch pennies, but being a literal bean counter is not such a bad thing for gaining insight into the natural processes behind random sampling error. If you want for the remainder of the course to go smoothly, generate enough sampling distributions to gain a sense of mastery over the idea. Become a bean counter.

Distinguishing among Populations, Samples, and Sampling Distributions

It is helpful at this point to review some of the symbols and formulas we have used thus far. We have to use our imagination a lot in dealing with statistics because the only thing we touch is the sample. Meanwhile, we have to imagine what the larger population is like. Furthermore, we must imagine a sampling distribution and describe its shape mathematically and graphically.

Figure 7–10 provides a summary of the symbols used for sample statistics, population parameters, and sampling distribution statistics for means. From here on it will be very important to keep these ideas and symbols straight.

☹   STATISTICAL FOLLIES AND FALLACIES   .☹

Treating a Point Estimate as Though It Were Absolutely True

As we have learned in this chapter, no single statistic—a summary measure based on sample data—is the last word on estimating a parameter of the population. Repeated sampling shows that the next sample from the same population is likely to result in a slightly different statistical outcome. Yet it is not uncommon, especially in the mass media, for point estimates to be accepted quickly and then treated as though they were absolutely true.

Among political pollsters there may be advantages to having a less than perfect estimate. For instance, a single poll may show that just over 50 percent of the respondents—a simple majority—support a legislative bill. The pollster and the supporters of the legislation are likely to broadcast this result and then speak of it as though it were absolute fact. A second poll may show that considerably less than 50 percent support the bill. If the politicians are not interested in the absolute truth but simply want to support their positions, they are not likely to make an issue of the indefinite conclusions made with point estimates. A trained statistician or a skeptical citizen may not fall for this ruse, but many citizens may. Not only do such pollsters deceive us, they insult the intelligence of the populace. In Chapter 8 we will see that there is a way to specify the error in a point estimate and express the degree of confidence we have that it is an accurate estimate of a population parameter.

FIGURE 7–10

Distinguishing among measurements made on samples, populations, and sampling distributions (for the interval/ratio variable X)

	Sample	Population	Sampling Distribution
Symbols			
Mean	$\bar{X}$	μ_X	$\mu_{\bar{X}} = \mu_X$
Standard deviation	s_X	σ_X	$s_{\bar{X}} =$ (standard error estimated by s_X)

Description

Statistic = summary measurement of X computed on a sample of n (actual observation).

Parameter = summary measurement of X if every subject in the population is observed (usually unknown).

Hypothetical distribution of an infinite number of samples of size n. (Hypothetical implies that not even a large number of samples is usually drawn. This distribution is mathematically produced.)

Actual sample of size n Population of X's   Hypothetical infinite set of samples of size n

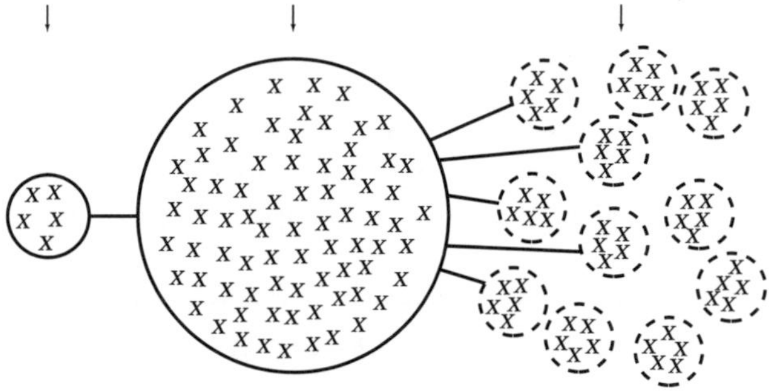

Description of distribution:

Raw scores (X's) in sample or the population may or may not be normally distributed.

OR

A sampling distribution of means ($\bar{X}$'s) will *always* be approximately normal and will appear normal if $n > 120$.

Formulas in Chapter 7

Computing the standard error of a sampling distribution of means (for the common situation where σ_X is unknown and s_X is used to estimate):

$$s_{\bar{X}} = \frac{s_X}{\sqrt{n-1}}$$

Computing the standard error of a sampling distribution of proportions (for a nominal variable):

When P_u and Q_u are known   When P_u and Q_u are unknown

$$\sigma_{P_s} = \sqrt{\frac{P_u Q_u}{n}} \qquad\qquad s_{P_s} = \sqrt{\frac{P_s Q_s}{n}}$$

Computing the minimum sample size needed to assume that a sampling distribution of proportions is normally shaped:

$$\text{Minimum } n = \frac{5}{p_{smaller}}$$

Thus, assume an approximately normal distribution when $(p_{smaller})\,(n) > 5$.

Questions for Chapter 7

1. What is the difference between a statistic and a parameter? Which one is usually unknown for the variable? Illustrate the symbols we use for the statistics and parameters of interval/ratio variables and nominal variables.
2. Define a sampling distribution. Distinguish it from a distribution of raw scores from a population.
3. How can we demonstrate that a statistic computed on a single sample only provides *an estimate* of a parameter?
4. If we draw a histogram to portray a *raw score* distribution, say, the distribution of ages for a sample of 200 students, what points are plotted along the horizontal axis of the histogram?
5. If we draw a histogram to portray the distribution of *mean ages* for 1,000 *samples* of 200 students, what points are plotted along the horizontal axis? What is this distribution called?
6. For an interval/ratio variable, provide the symbols for the standard deviation and the standard error. What does each dispersion statistic measure? How are the two related mathematically?
7. What are the similarities and differences in the shapes of the normal Z-distribution and the approximately normal *t*-distribution?
8. State and explain the law of large numbers.
9. Under what circumstances will a sampling distribution of proportions fit the normal distribution?
10. Match the symbols on the left with their definitions on the right.

    a. X _____ The standard deviation for a *sample* of raw scores X

    b. μ_X _____ The standard deviation for a *population* of raw scores X

    c. $\bar{X}$ _____ The symbol for an interval/ratio variable and its raw scores

    d. s_X _____ The standard error of a *sampling distribution* of means for the variable X, estimated from the sample standard deviation

    e. σ_X _____ The mean of a *sample* of raw scores of the variable X

    f. $s_{\bar{X}}$ _____ The mean of a *population* of raw scores of the variable X

11. The symbols in question 10 apply to variables of what levels of measurement?

12. Match the symbols on the left with their definitions on the right.

     a. P _____ The proportion in the "success" category in a *population* of subjects

     b. Q _____ p [of the success category]

     c. P_u _____ The proportion in the "success" category in a *sample* of subjects

     d. Q_u _____ The standard error of a distribution of sample proportions computed with known values of P_u and Q_u

     e. P_s _____ The standard error of a distribution of sample proportions estimated from the sample statistics P_s and Q_s

     f. σ_{P_s} _____ The proportion of the "failure" category in a *population* of subjects

     g. s_{P_s} _____ p [of failure], where "failure" is the absence of a defined category or characteristic of a variable

13. The symbols in question 12 apply to variables of what levels of measurement?

14. Explain and illustrate with formulas why a standard error of means will always be smaller than the standard deviation of that variable.

15. Erica has just driven 190 miles in a foggy drizzle that has caused her to run late. When the rain stops, she is within 10 miles of her home. She thinks to herself, "Now I can make up for lost time," and speeds up. In terms of degrees of freedom, why is it useless for her to speed up now?

Exercises for Chapter 7

1. As a marketing researcher at the Yeasty Feasty Bakery you conduct product purchase surveys. In your marketing area you find that the mean number of loaves of bread consumed per month per household is 5.3 loaves with a standard deviation of 1.5 loaves. These data are based on a sample of 200 households. Use these statistics to calculate the standard error of a sampling distribution of the mean loaves consumed per month.

2. You gather a random sample of 190 court records from the files of adults charged with assault over the past six months. You find that the mean age of those charged is 28.8 years with a standard deviation of 3.1 years. Use these statistics to calculate the standard error of a sampling distribution of ages.

3. The following data are from a random sample of 437 employees of a multinational corporation. Complete the following table by calculating standard errors.

Variable	Standard Deviation or P	Standard Error
A. Monthly salary	$1,200	
B. Age	4 years	
C. Proportion female	.39	
D. Years of service	2.7 years	
E. Proportion of workers in manufacturing divisions	.57	

4. A marketing firm has surveyed 395 households to assess television-watching habits. Complete the following table by calculating standard errors.

Variable	Standard Deviation or P	Standard Error
A. Age of household head	5 years	
B. Hours TV is on after 5:00 P.M.	1.5 hours	
C. Proportion of households owning their homes	.59	
D. Years of schooling	1.9 years	
E. Proportion of households with more than two TVs	.32	

5. Produce a sampling distribution of proportions. In a box (or large bowl), dump one pound of (dry, uncooked) red beans and one pound of northern white beans; mix thoroughly. This is a population of beans. Take a tablespoon and scoop a sample of beans from this population. To two decimal places, compute P_s, the proportion of red beans in the sample, where $P = p$ [of the beans that are red]. Do this 100 times and plot the resulting sampling distribution of P_s's as a histogram. Observe the sampling distribution and answer the following questions *without making calculations.*

   a. Give an estimate of the proportion of red beans in the population (i.e., the parameter for the entire box, P_u).

   b. Give an estimate of the standard error of this sampling distribution (i.e., σ_{P_s}).
   c. Use your basic knowledge of the normal curve to describe how often sample outcomes occur within 1, 2, and 3 standard errors to both sides.
   d. From this bean-counting experience, what did you learn about the dynamics of sampling nominal variables?

6. Follow the instructions for exercise 5, except take two scoops for each sample.

7. Produce a sampling distribution of the proportion of heads in the repeated tossing of 10 coins. Take 10 dimes. Toss them at once. Do this 100 times.

   a. With each toss, count the number of "heads" and record the result in the table below under column A with a slash or stem (i.e., /). This is called a stem plot.
   b. After the 100 tosses, count the stems and record the frequency of each combination of heads in column B (e.g., ⁄⁄⁄⁄ ⁄⁄ = 7 times).
   c. Plot the resulting distribution of sample tosses on graph paper as a frequency histogram.
   d. Compute the probability of each sample outcome and record it under column C as "p of outcome."
   e. Exhibit your statistical imagination by describing in everyday terms why the sampling distribution took the shape it did.

No. Heads	(A) Stem Plot of Frequency	(B) Recorded Frequency of Occurrence	(C) p of Outcome
0			
1			
2			
3			
4			
5			
6			
7			
8			
9			
10			

8. Follow the instructions of exercise 7 except toss 8 coins instead of 10.

9. Produce a sampling distribution of means for a sample size of 31. (*Note:* This problem is less cumbersome if done as a group project in the classroom or laboratory.)

    a. Using the random number table (Statistical Table A in Appendix B), randomly select 31 *single* random digits; that is, X = a single random digit. Compute the mean of this sample and record it to two decimal places. Do this 100 times to obtain 100 sample means ($\bar{X}$) of $n = 31$.

    b. On graph paper, draw a histogram of this sampling distribution.

    c. From observation (without computing) provide an estimate of the mean of the population of random digits (μ_X) of a random number table.

    d. From observation (without computing) give an estimate of the standard error ($s_{\bar{x}}$) of this sampling distribution.

    e. Use your basic knowledge of the approximately normal curve to describe how often sample outcomes occur within 1, 2, and 3 standard errors to both sides.

    f. From this repeated-sampling experience, what did you learn about the dynamics of sampling interval/ratio variables?

10. Follow the instructions of exercise 9 except use a sample size of 37 instead of 31.

11. To convince yourself that a sampling distribution of means for small samples is flatter than a normal distribution, repeat exercise 9, *a*, *b*, and *c*, except this time draw 100 samples of six single random digits (i.e., $n = 6$). Compare the shape of the distribution to that of exercise 9 and discuss the result in terms of degrees of freedom.

12. To convince yourself that a sampling distribution of means for small samples is flatter than a normal distribution, repeat exercise 9 or 10, *a*, *b*, and *c*, except this time draw 100 samples of four single random digits (i.e., $n = 4$). Compare the shape of the distribution to that of exercise 9 or 10 and discuss the result in terms of degrees of freedom.

13. Obtain a pair of six-sided gaming dice. Roll the dice 100 times. Calculate the frequency of each outcome by recording outcomes on a stem plot by using stem marks (e.g., ⫲⫲⫲ / = 6 times).

    a. Plot the resulting distribution of sample rolls on graph paper as a frequency histogram.

    b. Compute the probability of each sample outcome.

    c. Comment on the general pattern of outcomes.

14. Follow the instructions in exercise 13, except roll the dice 120 times instead of 100 times.

15. You want to describe the sampling distribution of the proportion of persons satisfied with services received from a stockbroker. You obtain a random sample of 40 of the broker's clients, survey them, and find that 36 are satisfied.

a. Would it be appropriate to use an approximately normal distribution to describe the sampling distribution? Why or why not?

b. Assuming that this sample proportion of those who are satisfied is a good estimate for the population of brokers, how large a sample is needed to use an approximately normal curve as a description of this sampling distribution?

16. You are to describe the sampling distribution of the proportion of persons satisfied with how quickly the Internal Revenue Service returned their tax refunds. You obtain a random sample of 20 persons who received refunds and find that 16 are satisfied.

a. Would it be appropriate to use an approximately normal distribution to describe the sampling distribution? Why or why not?

b. Assuming that this sample proportion of those satisfied is a good estimate for the population of those receiving refunds, how large a sample is needed to use an approximately normal curve as a description of this sampling distribution?

Optional Computer Applications for Chapter 7

If your class uses the optional computer applications that accompany this text, open the Chapter 7 exercises on the *Computer Applications for The Statistical Imagination* compact disk. These exercises involve producing sampling distributions by using the computer's random number generator. These exercises reinforce your understanding of sampling distributions and will help you achieve a sense of proportion on the relationship between sample size and sampling error.

CHAPTER

8

PARAMETER ESTIMATION USING CONFIDENCE INTERVALS

Introduction

Last night Kristi attended a rock concert at the campus stadium. Upon return-ing to her residence hall, she discovered that in the revelry of the event she had lost an inexpensive but sentimentally valuable ring, one passed down from her grandmother. She has spent most of today searching the stadium's ball field and is beginning to lose hope. It is getting late, and to make matters worse, the grass will be mowed in the morning; this is certain to destroy her ring and perhaps upset her grandmother. Finally, Kristi remembers that her friend Sarah has a metal detector and gives her a call. As it turns out, Sarah's metal detector is not very astute at pinpointing objects, but it is quite reliable within a span of error. Specifically, the detector beeps when it is within five yards of a metal object. Sarah arrives and walks the field with her metal detec-tor, and it beeps. But then she says that she must scoot to meet another friend for dinner. Kristi asks, "Where is my ring?" Sarah tells her to look a couple of yards to either side of the 50-yard line, near the far hash mark. Kristi asks: "Are you sure I will find it?" Sarah responds that her detector is precise to within five yards 95 percent of the time. Sarah is quite confident—95 percent—so she bets Kristi a dinner that she will find the ring. Sarah could not point to the ring's exact location, but she has a high degree of confidence that it is within the four-yard area she described. (Kristi, incidentally, found her ring within a few minutes and treated Sarah to a Mexican meal the next evening.)

Searching for the location of an object is similar to estimating the value of a population parameter by using the statistics from a sample. As we learned in Chapter 7, the statistics of a sample are estimates—calculations that only fall near the value of the true population parameter—just as Sarah's metal detec-tor only got Kristi close to the location of her ring. Can we do as Sarah did and not only point to a spot but also give a reliable span of area within which to look for a parameter? For example, can we take one sample of tenth-graders and estimate the mean height of all tenth-graders to within one inch—a point estimate give or take a half inch (say, 67.5 inches ± .5 inch)? Our conclusion would be that the mean height is between 67 and 68 inches—not exact but close. And can we, like Sarah, declare that we are 95 percent confident of this interval estimate? As we noted in Chapter 7, repeated sampling reveals that any single point estimate only gets us close when estimating a population pa-rameter, just as Sarah pinpointed a spot on the field. In this chapter we learn to say confidently just how close this single point estimate is to the true parameter *within a range of error,* just as Sarah sent Kristi to search within two yards to either side of the detector's beeping point. Such an estimation is called a confidence interval.

A **confidence interval** is *a range of possible values of a* **parameter** *expressed with a specific degree of confidence.* With confidence intervals we take a point estimate and couple it with knowledge about sampling distributions. We project a known, calculable span —or "interval"—of error around the point estimate. For example, where X = grade point average (GPA), suppose we take a sample of 300 Crosstown University students and compute a sample mean GPA($\bar{X}$) of 2.46. Our knowledge of repeated sampling and sampling distributions tells us that this sample statistic should be close to the true population parameter. How close? In Chapter 7 we saw that a sampling distribution of means, produced by repeatedly sampling a population, takes the shape of an approximately normal t-distribution curve. In fact, with 120 degrees of freedom or more (i.e., when $n > 121$), the sampling distribution is perceptively normal, essentially the shape of the normal curve. With a sample of 300 Crosstown students, we can report the results of repeated sampling in a distributional way and say, for example, that 95 percent of the samples fall within 1.96 standard errors of the true parameter. We may interpret this percentage in a probabilistic way and say that *if we draw only one sample,* there is a 95 percent probability that this single sample's mean falls within 1.96 standard errors of the parameter, whatever that parameter may be. This predictable error, the product of 1.96 times the standard error, is called the error term of a 95 percent confidence interval for this situation when n is greater than 121. This error term allows us to provide a probabilistic interpretation of a single-sample calculation.

Confidence Interval

A range of possible values of a parameter expressed with a specific degree of confidence.

In calculating confidence intervals, we do *not* repeatedly sample, plot, and compute areas under a sampling distribution curve. Instead, we draw only one sample and compute a point estimate such as the mean. We then compute a standard error and multiply it by 1.96 or another critical t-score that is chosen on the basis of the number of degrees of freedom. The result is a range of error based on knowing about the predictability of error from repeated sampling. Then we add and subtract this amount from the point estimate to obtain an interval within which the parameter is likely to fall. This error term is a "give or take some error" amount (just as Sarah said to look a couple yards to either side of the 50-yard line). For instance, if we calculate the 95 percent confidence interval of the mean GPA of Crosstown University students, our answer may take the form of an interval of values, say, 2.16 to 2.76 GPA points—the sample mean of 2.46 (a point estimate) plus or minus .30 (an error term). The result is an interval estimate of the true mean GPA (μ_X), a range of GPA values in which the true campus mean is likely to fall. While we do not say that we know the exact value of the mean GPA of the entire student body, we are 95 percent sure that this parameter is between 2.16 and 2.76. The calculated value of 2.16 sets the lower confidence limit (LCL), the smallest value we think μ_X could have. Similarly, 2.76 sets the upper confidence limit (UCL), the highest value we think μ_X could have. We acknowledge that the population mean GPA could be as low as 2.16 or as high as 2.76 or anywhere in between. That is, μ_X could be 2.16, 2.17, 2.18, 2.28, 2.34, or any value up to 2.76. We do not insist that we have found the exact value any more than Sarah insisted that she found the exact spot where Kristi's ring lay. But just like Sarah, we can bet with 95 percent confidence that the computed interval has the true population value within it. The objective of computing a confidence interval, then, is to estimate a population parameter within a specific span or "interval" of values.

Purpose of Computing a Confidence Interval

To provide an interval estimate of the value of an unknown population parameter and precisely express the confidence we have that the parameter falls within that interval.

Computing a confidence interval is like casting a fishing net into a pond in which there is only one fish. The location of the fish represents the unknown parameter. Is it 10 feet up shore, 20 feet, or 30 feet, and so on? We have one opportunity to cast the net and wish to feel 95 percent confident of catching the fish. A point estimate of the location provides some rough information, telling us in which part of the pond to cast the net, say, by a stump that is down the shore a ways. Computing the confidence interval tells us how wide to cast the net. Our stipulated level of confidence tells us our success rate—how often we will catch the fish if we use a net of a certain width: the width of the computed confidence interval. The **level of confidence** is *a calculated degree of confidence that a statistical procedure conducted with sample data will produce a correct result for the sampled population.*

Level of Confidence

A calculated degree of confidence that a statistical procedure conducted with sample data will produce a correct result for the sampled population.

Confidence Interval of a Population Mean

For any interval/ratio (or interval-like ordinal) variable X, such as GPA, we set out to estimate the mean of a population. The question we want to answer is: What is the value of μ_X? Sample statistics are the tools we use to obtain this estimate. This is depicted in Figure 8–1.

Suppose, for example, we are studying the wage structure of an industrial plant that employs several thousand computer assemblers but do not have access to all company files. We obtain a random sample of 130 personnel files with data on hourly wages, a ratio variable X. Our purpose is to use these sample data to make statements about the entire population of computer assemblers. Thus, we compute a confidence interval for the mean wage, μ_X, of all assemblers. Our research question is: Within a specified span of dollar amounts, what is the parameter μ_X, the mean hourly wage of *the population* of computer assemblers? Is it between, say, $9 and $10, or between $14 and $15, or what? With a 95 percent confidence interval, we will be 95 percent confident that the mean wage is within the span of dollar amounts we compute.

By relying on a sample, we know that there is error in our conclusion because we know about sampling error. In fact, the only way to be perfectly confident, or 100 percent confident, is to eliminate any sampling error by gathering data on the entire population and computing the correct parameter μ_X. This is too costly and time-consuming. Thus, we settle on using a sample, knowing that we will have some degree of error in our conclusion. Fortunately, the amount of this expected error is known. The **level of expected error** is *the difference between the stated level of confidence and "perfect confidence" of 100 percent.* In other words, if we are 95 percent confident about our stated conclusion, we are 5 percent unsure about it. Thus, we have a 5 percent level of expected error.

FIGURE 8–1

Using sample statistics to obtain an interval estimate of a population parameter for an interval/ratio variable X = GPA

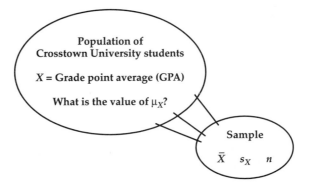

Conclusion about μ_X based on observing $\bar{X}$: We are 95 percent confident that the mean GPA of Crosstown University students is between 2.16 and 2.76.

In computing a confidence interval, we use the Greek letter *alpha* (α) to symbolize the level of expected error. This level of expected error also is called the level of significance, a term thoroughly covered in Chapter 9. Recall from Chapter 7 that α-probabilities are critical regions—important amounts of area in the tails of a sampling distribution curve. In computing the 95 percent confidence interval, our level of significance or expected error is 5 percent:

$$\text{Level of confidence} = 95\%$$

$$\text{Level of significance (expected error)} = \alpha = 100\% - \text{level of confidence}$$
$$= 100\% - 95\% = 5\%$$

In general, then, the level of confidence and the level of significance are inversely related; as one increases, the other decreases. Together, the level of confidence and the level of significance sum to 100 percent. Thus:

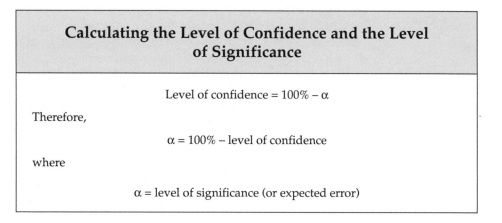

Calculating the Level of Confidence and the Level of Significance

$$\text{Level of confidence} = 100\% - \alpha$$

Therefore,

$$\alpha = 100\% - \text{level of confidence}$$

where

$$\alpha = \text{level of significance (or expected error)}$$

To calculate a confidence interval, we calculate a standard error. Then, from the *t*-distribution table (Statistical Table C in Appendix B), we obtain the critical *t*-score (the t_α) that corresponds to the number of degrees of freedom ($n - 1$) and a chosen level of significance or expected error (α). We multiply the t_α by the standard error to obtain an "error term." Then we add and subtract this error term from the sample mean. The resulting span of values is a confidence interval estimate of the population mean:

$$\text{Confidence interval} = \text{a point estimate} \pm \text{an error term}$$

Calculating the Standard Error for a Confidence Interval of a Population Mean

The purpose of a confidence interval is to determine an approximation of the population parameter. The parameter, then, is unknown. For an interval/ratio variable, both the mean and the standard deviation of the population are unknown. Therefore, we must use the sample standard deviation to estimate the standard error of the mean. Recall from Chapter 7 that this estimated standard error is as follows:

Computing the (Estimated) Standard Error of a Confidence Interval of a Population Mean

$$s_{\bar{x}} = \frac{s_X}{\sqrt{n-1}}$$

where

$s_{\bar{x}}$ = estimated standard error of means for an interval/ratio or interval-like ordinal variable X
s_X = standard deviation of a sample
n = sample size

In this formula, 1 is subtracted from n to adjust for estimation error—the fact that the standard error is estimated with sample data.

Selecting the Critical Probability Score, t_α

The particular t_α value depends on the number of degrees of freedom implied by the sample size, with $df = n - 1$. Since confidence intervals are always calculated by using both sides of the sample distribution curve, the t_α value is found in the four columns on the left side of the t-distribution table (Statistical Table C in Appendix B) under "Two-Tailed or Nondirectional Test." The t_α for confidence intervals at the 95 percent level are found in the ".05" column under "Level of Significance." This .05 is 5 percent of expected error. For a 99 percent confidence interval, the t_α is found under the .01 column (i.e., 1 percent expected error). Here are some example t_α values taken from the t-distribution table:

Example 1: We desire the 95 percent level of confidence and $n = 15$.

$$df = n - 1 = 14$$

The level of significance, $\alpha = 100\% -$ level of confidence
$$= 100\% - 95\% = 5\% = .05$$

Look under .05 and 14 degrees of freedom: $t_\alpha = 2.145$.

Example 2: We desire the 99 percent level of confidence and $n = 19$.

$$df = n - 1 = 18$$

The level of significance, $\alpha = 100\% -$ level of confidence
$$= 100\% - 99\% = 1\% = .01$$

Look under .01 and 18 degrees of freedom: $t_\alpha = 2.878$.

Example 3: We desire the 95 percent level of confidence and $n = 130$.

$$df = n - 1 = 129$$

On the t-distribution table, this is essentially an infinite number of degrees of freedom (∞).

The level of significance, $\alpha = 100\% -$ level of confidence
$$= 100\% - 95\% = 5\% = .05$$

Look under .05 and ∞ degrees of freedom: $t_\alpha = 1.96$.

The t_α of 1.96 is used very often. As we noted in Chapter 7, when we have over 120 degrees of freedom, the standardized scores of the approximately normal t-distribution curve are so close to the values of a normal distribution that the difference is unnoticeable. These "large-sample" t_α's are the same as the critical Z_α's of a normal distribution (review Table 7–1). Since it is not unusual to have samples larger than 121, the t_α's of 1.96 (95 percent level of confidence) and 2.58 (99 percent level of confidence) are used frequently.

Calculating the Error Term

Once the standard error is computed, it is multiplied by t_α to obtain the error term.

Calculating the Error Term of a Confidence Interval of a Population Mean

Error term = $(t_\alpha)\,(s_{\bar{X}})$

where

α = level of significance (or expected error)
t_α = critical t-score that corresponds to the stated levels of significance and confidence and number of degrees of freedom
$s_{\bar{X}}$ = estimated standard error of a confidence interval of the mean

---

Calculating the Confidence Interval

Keeping in mind that a confidence interval of a population mean is a sample mean plus and minus an error term, the general formula for computing the confidence interval of a population mean is as follows:

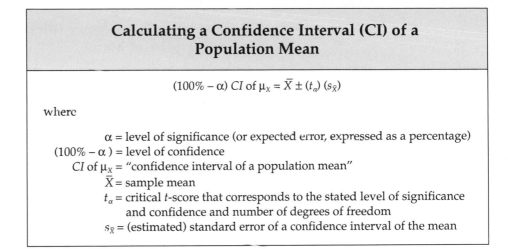

Calculating a Confidence Interval (CI) of a Population Mean

$$(100\% - \alpha)\ CI\ \text{of}\ \mu_X = \overline{X} \pm (t_\alpha)\ (s_{\overline{x}})$$

where

α = level of significance (or expected error, expressed as a percentage)
$(100\% - \alpha)$ = level of confidence
CI of μ_X = "confidence interval of a population mean"
$\overline{X}$ = sample mean
t_α = critical t-score that corresponds to the stated level of significance and confidence and number of degrees of freedom
$s_{\overline{x}}$ = (estimated) standard error of a confidence interval of the mean

Again, two very commonly reported confidence intervals are the 95 percent and 99 percent CIs. In the common situation of a sample size of n greater than 121—and therefore degrees of freedom greater than 120—the following formulas are used:

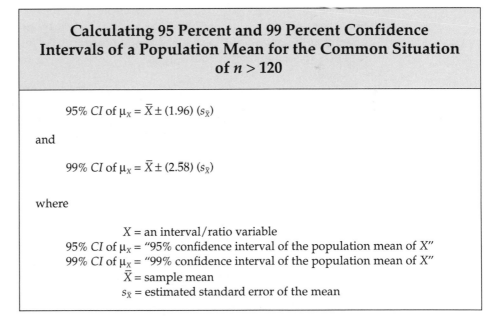

Calculating 95 Percent and 99 Percent Confidence Intervals of a Population Mean for the Common Situation of $n > 120$

$$95\%\ CI\ \text{of}\ \mu_X = \overline{X} \pm (1.96)\ (s_{\overline{x}})$$

and

$$99\%\ CI\ \text{of}\ \mu_X = \overline{X} \pm (2.58)\ (s_{\overline{x}})$$

where

X = an interval/ratio variable
$95\%\ CI$ of μ_X = "95% confidence interval of the population mean of X"
$99\%\ CI$ of μ_X = "99% confidence interval of the population mean of X"
$\overline{X}$ = sample mean
$s_{\overline{x}}$ = estimated standard error of the mean

When to Calculate a Confidence Interval of a Population Mean

1. The research question calls for estimating a population parameter.
2. The variable of interest (X) is of interval/ratio level of measurement (or an interval-like ordinal variable). Thus, we are to provide an interval estimate of the value of a population parameter μ_X.
3. We are working with a single representative sample from one population.

The Five Steps for Computing a Confidence Interval of a Population Mean, μ_X

We will compute confidence intervals by following these five steps: (1) State the research question, identify the level of measurement of the variable, list "givens," and draw a diagram (like Figure 8–1) representing the target population, its parameter to be estimated, the sample, and its statistics, (2) compute the standard error and the error term, (3) using the general formula for confidence intervals, compute the LCL and UCL, (4) provide an interpretation of findings in everyday language directed to individuals and groups that know little about statistics (e.g., college or company administrators, city officials, news reporters, and the public), and (5) provide a statistical interpretation illustrating the notion of "confidence in the procedure." The following checklist is handy for remembering these steps.

Brief Checklist of Five Steps for Computing Confidence Intervals

Step 1. State the research question, identify the level of measurement of the variable, list "givens," and draw a conceptual diagram of the target population and sample (as in Figure 8–1).

Step 2. Compute the standard error and the error term.

Step 3. Compute the LCL and UCL of the confidence interval.

Step 4. Provide an interpretation in everyday language.

Step 5. Provide a statistical interpretation illustrating the notion of "confidence in the procedure."

Sample Problem of a Confidence Interval of a Population Mean

Let us calculate a sample problem and discuss further what confidence intervals are and how they are interpreted.

Problem: We are conducting a study of the wage structure of an industrial plant that employs several thousand computer assemblers. We need to get a rough idea of the mean hourly wage of this population of assemblers. We randomly select 130 personnel files and record the hourly wages. In this sample we find a mean of $8.00 and a standard deviation of $1.70. Compute the 95 percent confidence interval for the mean hourly wage of the plant's assemblers. (In doing a problem, it is not necessary to state the instructions provided in parentheses.)

Step 1. Research question: Within a specified span of dollar amounts, what is the parameter μ_X, the mean hourly wage of the population of computer assemblers? *Givens:* X = hourly wage, interval/ratio level; target population = plant's computer assemblers. Sample statistics:

$$n = 130 \qquad \bar{X} = \$8.00 \qquad s_X = \$1.70$$

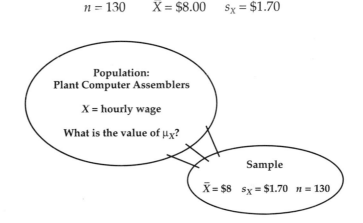

Step 2 (standard error, critical *t*-score, and error term)

$$s_{\bar{X}} = \frac{s_X}{\sqrt{n-1}} = \frac{1.70}{\sqrt{129}} = \$.15$$

$$df = n - 1 = 130 - 1 = 129$$

For 95 percent confidence, $t_\alpha = 1.96$.

(From the *t*-distribution table: level of confidence of 95 percent corresponds to a level of significance of .05; $df = \infty$; critical $t_\alpha = 1.96$.)

$$\text{Error term} = (t_\alpha)\,(s_{\bar{X}}) = (1.96)\,(\$.15) = \$.29$$

Step 3 (LCL and UCL)

$$95\% \; CI \; of \; \mu_X = \bar{X} \pm (1.96) \; (s_{\bar{x}})$$
$$= \text{sample mean} \pm \text{error term}$$
$$= \$8.00 \pm (1.96) \; (\$ .15) = \$8.00 \pm \$ .29$$
$$LCL = \$8.00 - \$ .29 = \$7.71$$
$$UCL = \$8.00 + \$ .29 = \$8.29$$

Step 4 (interpretation in everyday language)

"I am 95 percent sure that the mean hourly wage of the plant's computer assemblers is between $7.71 and $8.29."

Step 5 (statistical interpretation illustrating the notion of "confidence in the procedure")

"If the same sampling and statistical procedures are conducted 100 times, 95 times the true population parameter μ_X will be encompassed in the computed intervals and 5 times it will not. Thus, I have 95 percent confidence that this single confidence interval I computed includes the true parameter."

Proper Interpretation of Confidence Intervals

When we use the statement "I am 95 percent confident," we are *actually expressing confidence in our method.* For the example problem above, this is stated as the **statistical interpretation** of our results. For a 95 percent confidence interval of the mean, our statistical interpretation is: If the same sampling and statistical procedures are conducted 100 times, 95 times the true population mean μ_X will be encompassed in the computed intervals. Remember, since we did not gather data for every member of the population, we cannot declare an exact, true value of the population mean (the parameter). Therefore, there is a chance that the computed confidence interval does not include the true parameter. To return to our fishing analogy, we do not know exactly where the fish is located. We may cast the net and not catch the fish. With a 95 percent confidence interval, this chance of failure is 5 percent (100 percent – 95 percent = 5 percent), the level of significance (or expected error). While we are going to cast the net only once, our knowledge of sampling error and its predictability with an approximately normal curve assures us that if we cast it 100 times, we will net the fish 95 times. In the long run, a 95 percent confidence interval based on a single sample is correct 95 percent of the time.

To properly understand confidence intervals we must use the statistical imagination and employ what we know about repeated sampling, sampling distributions, and probability theory. Figure 8–2 portrays the notion of repeatedly sampling *and* computing confidence intervals for a sample size greater than 121. Ninety-five of every 100 sample means will compute to within 1.96 standard errors of the true population mean. Figure 8–2 conveys the notion

FIGURE 8–2

*The success rate of
a 95 percent
confidence interval
in providing an
interval estimate
that encompasses
the true population
parameter value*

μ_X = **unknown** mean of X in the population (i.e., the parameter)

LCL = lower confidence limit
UCL = upper confidence limit

Let us imagine drawing 100 samples with a sample size of, say, 122. We compute the $\bar{X}$ for each sample and plot the outcomes as a sampling distribution. This distribution will be approximately normal in shape, with sample means centering on the true population parameter value, μ_X (whatever its value may be). Since we have over 120 degrees of freedom, a critical t-score of ± 1.96 leaves 5 percent of the area in the tails of the curve and 95 percent in between. Thus, 95 percent of these means fall within 1.96 standard errors of the true parameter as it is depicted in the approximately normal curve below. Let us imagine also that we compute 95 percent confidence intervals for each of these 100 sample means. For the 95 means that calculate to within 1.96 standard errors, their confidence intervals will be spread widely enough to encompass (or "catch") the true parameter, μ_X. For the five sample means outside of 1.96 standard errors, their computed confidence intervals will *not* be spread widely enough to catch the true parameter. In other words, the procedure of calculating a 95 percent confidence interval works 95 percent of the time. The following diagram presents 20 of 100 samples with calculated confidence intervals. Ninety-five percent (19 of 20) encompass the population parameter (μ_X). Sample number 7 depicts the one of 20 (i.e., 5 percent) that fails to encompass the population mean.

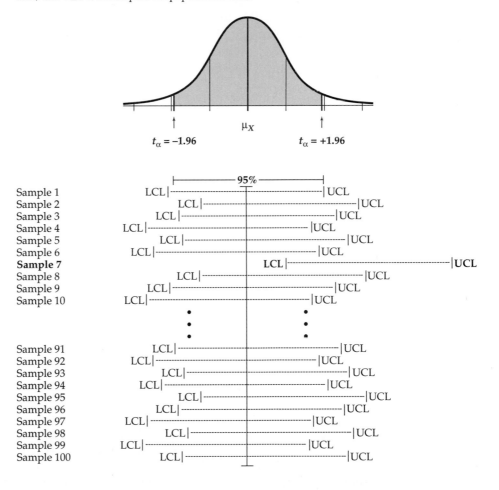

that the statistical procedure of repeatedly calculating confidence intervals results in the true population mean falling within the interval a predictable 95 percent of the time (19 times out of 20). This means, of course, that the computed confidence interval will miss the correct parameter a predictable 5 percent of the time (as is the case for sample number 7). Which samples hit and miss? *For the 95 means within 1.96 standard errors,* the computed confidence intervals will include the population's true parameter—its true mean. For the five means that calculate outside 1.96 standard errors, the computed confidence interval will miss the true parameter. In real life, we take only one sample and compute its confidence interval. We are banking on the probability that this single sample is one of the 95 that fall within 1.96 standard errors of the true parameter. If it does, the confidence interval encompasses the true parameter, μ_X. Of course, we still do not know the true parameter and our confidence interval is only an interval estimate; sometimes this estimate is quite broad. We will never know the true parameter μ_X unless we have the time and money to obtain data from every member of the population, but odds of 95 out of 100 are pretty good.

The Chosen Level of Confidence and the Precision of the Confidence Interval

For the sample of 130 computer assemblers, we chose the 95 percent level of confidence and used the critical *t*-score of 1.96 to compute the error term. The use of *t*-scores in computing confidence intervals is related to our knowledge of sampling distributions from repeated sampling. In Chapter 7 we learned that if we draw many samples and compute their means (as did our ancestral bean counters), the sampling distribution will be an approximately normal *t*-distribution. The *t*-scores (like the Z-scores in the normal distribution table) measure how far off a sample mean is from the true population mean. With the help of a *t*-distribution probability table, these scores determine the probability of occurrence of sampling outcomes.

In calculating a confidence interval, *once a sample has been drawn,* its mean, standard deviation, and sample size are "givens." That is, we are stuck with them. These givens determine the standard error of the confidence interval and therefore greatly influence the width of the calculated confidence interval. If the standard deviation is large or the sample size is small, the confidence interval is going to calculate widely; it will not be very precise. After the sample is "given," however, we may still influence the precision of a confidence interval through our choice of the level of confidence. The chosen level of confidence determines the size of the critical *t*-score (i.e., t_α from the *t*-distribution table). The greater the chosen level of confidence, the larger the t_α. Therefore, in the calculation of the confidence limits, a large t_α produces a large error term and a less precise (or broader) confidence interval.

For example, let us substitute a t_α of 2.58 in place of 1.96 in the example problem of the confidence interval of the mean wage of computer assemblers.

In the *t*-distribution table, this is the t_α that corresponds to a 99 percent confidence interval and with a sample of 130, essentially an infinite number of degrees of freedom:

$$99\% \; CI \; of \; \mu_X = \overline{X} \pm (2.58) \; (s_{\overline{x}}) = \$8.00 \pm (2.58) \; (\$ .15)$$

$$= \$8.00 \pm \$ .39 = \$7.61 \; to \; \$8.39$$

Comparing the two confidence intervals, we can see that we have greater confidence at the 99 percent level but that our estimate is less precise:

$$95\% \; CI \; of \; \mu_X = \$7.71 \; to \; \$8.29; \; this \; interval \; is \; \$.58 \; wide$$

$$99\% \; CI \; of \; \mu_X = \$7.61 \; to \; \$8.39; \; this \; interval \; is \; \$.78 \; wide$$

The greater the stated level of confidence, the greater the error term and therefore the less precise the confidence interval.

The Relationship between the Level of Confidence and the Degree of Precision

The greater the stated level of confidence, the less precise the confidence interval.

This makes sense. If we are going to place a lot of faith (or confidence) in an answer, we must play it safe by allowing for a lot of error. For example, we might say we are 99.9999 percent confident (and be willing to bet a $100 on our answer) that the mean wage of computer assemblers is between $3 and $100 per hour. In this absurd situation we are confident, but the degree of precision is so low that it is meaningless. On the other hand, if we provide an estimate with a high degree of precision of, say, 10 cents—$7.95 to $8.05—we will not bet too much on it. To return once again to the fishing analogy, someone might say that he or she is 100 percent confident that the fish is between one shore and the other, but this "help" is so imprecise that it is useless. On the other hand, if we asked whether the fish was between us and a dock 20 steps away, he or she might respond, "I'm not so sure."

Sample Size and the Precision of the Confidence Interval

There is a way to obtain a high degree of precision *and* maintain a high level of confidence: *Make sure before collecting data* that the sample size is sufficiently large to produce small standard errors and precise confidence intervals. To see how important a large sample is, let us see how a small sample size affects the width of a confidence interval.

As we noted in Chapter 7, because the mean is susceptible to distortion by extreme scores, sampling error is especially noticeable if $n \leq 120$ and is markedly so when $n \leq 30$. Let us recompute the 95 percent confidence interval for the population of computer assemblers but use a sample of 15 instead of 130. To determine the critical value of t_α we calculate degrees of freedom:

$$df = n - 1 = 15 - 1 = 14$$

Observe the *t*-distribution table for 14 degrees of freedom and $\alpha = .05$ to find the t_α-value of 2.145. This t_α is substituted in the equation in place of the t_α of 1.96 that we used above with the sample of 130. When we multiply this larger critical value by the standard error, we obtain a larger error term and a less precise confidence interval. This is compounded by the fact that even if the standard deviation is the same for this smaller sample, the standard error will calculate to a larger value. All told, a smaller sample inflates the error term and reduces the precision of the confidence interval.

$$s_{\bar{X}} = \frac{s_X}{\sqrt{n-1}} = \frac{170}{\sqrt{14}} = \$ .45$$

$$\text{Error term} = (t_\alpha)(s_{\bar{X}}) = (2.145)(\$ .45) = \$ .96$$
$$95\% \text{ CI of } \mu_X = \bar{X} \pm (t_\alpha)(s_{\bar{X}})$$
$$= \$8.00 \pm (2.145)(\$ .45)$$
$$= \$8.00 \pm \$ .96 = \$7.04 \text{ to } \$8.96$$

Comparing this sample of 15 to the sample of 130, we can see that the smaller sample estimate is less precise:

With $n = 130$, 95 percent CI of $\mu_X = \$7.71$ to $\$8.29$; this interval is $\$ .58$ wide

With $n = 15$, 95 percent CI of $\mu_X = \$7.04$ to $\$8.96$; this interval is $\$ 1.92$ wide

The more precise confidence interval for the sample of $n = 130$ makes intuitive sense and follows from the law of large numbers (Chapter 7). The larger the sample size, the smaller the sampling error and therefore the greater the precision of the confidence interval.

The Relationship between Sample Size and Degree of Precision

The larger the sample size, the more precise the confidence interval.

Large Sample Confidence Interval of a Population Proportion

With nominal/ordinal variables, confidence intervals provide an estimate of the proportion of a population that falls in the "success" category of the variable. Let us suppose that we are conducting election polling for a political candidate, Chantrise Jones. We wish to obtain an interval estimate of her support by conducting a telephone poll of likely voters two days before the election. We define: $P = p$ [of likely voters supporting Chantrise]. Of course, we cannot afford to poll all likely voters; thus, we sample them. The sample proportion, P_s, is used to estimate the population parameter, P_u, within an interval with a calculated sampling error. Just as in the case of confidence intervals of the mean, we use a sample statistic, P_s, as a point estimate of P_u and add and subtract an error term. The complete formula for computing the confidence interval of population proportion is

$$(100\% - \alpha) \; CI \; of \; P_u = P_s \pm (t_\alpha) \; (s_{P_s})$$

$$= \text{sample proportion} \pm \text{error term}$$

Here $P = p$ [of the success category] of a nominal/ordinal variable, α = the level of significance (or expected error), $(100\% - \alpha)$ = the level of confidence, CI of P_u is read as "the confidence interval of a population proportion," P_s = the sample proportion, t_α = the critical t-score (from the t-distribution table) that corresponds to the stated level of confidence and significance, and s_{P_s} = the estimated standard error of a confidence interval of a proportion.

Here are the circumstances in which calculating a confidence interval of a population proportion is appropriate:

When to Calculate a Confidence Interval of a Population Proportion (for a nominal/ordinal variable)

1. We are to provide an interval estimate of the value of a population parameter, P_u, where $P = p$ [of the success category] of a nominal/ordinal variable.
2. We have a single representative sample from one population.
3. The sample size (n) is sufficiently large that $(p_{smaller}) \; (n) \geq 5$, resulting in a sampling distribution that is approximately normal.

The requirement that the sample size (n) be sufficiently large that $(p_{smaller})$ $(n) \geq 5$ is the only restriction on sample size. Once this is established, we treat the sampling distribution curve as though it were based on an infinite sample size and therefore an infinite number of degrees of freedom. Thus, in calculating any confidence interval of a population proportion, the critical t-values are always taken from the "$df = \infty$" row of the t-distribution table. The critical t_α for a 95 percent confidence interval will always be ± 1.96, and for the 99 percent confidence interval it will be ± 2.58.

We compute an estimated standard error based on sample data (as in Chapter 7) and calculate the error term as follows:

Computing the Standard Error of a Confidence Interval of a Population Proportion (for a nominal/ordinal variable)

$$s_{P_s} = \sqrt{\frac{P_s Q_s}{n}}$$

where

s_{P_s} = estimated standard error of proportions for a nominal variable with $P = p$ [of the success category]

$P_s = p$ [of the success category in the sample]

$Q_s = p$ [of the failure category in the sample] $= 1 - P_s$

n = sample size

Calculating the Error Term of a Confidence Interval of a Population Proportion

$$\text{Error term} = (t_\alpha)(s_{P_s})$$

where

α = level of significance (or expected error)

t_α = critical t-score that corresponds to the stated level of confidence and significance with degrees of freedom = ∞

s_{P_s} = estimated standard error of proportions for a nominal/ordinal variable where $P = p$ [of the success category]

Since t_α will always come from the bottom line of the t-distribution table, we will always use one of the following two equations:

Calculating 95 Percent and 99 Percent Confidence Intervals of a Population Proportion when $(p_{smaller})$ $(n) \geq 5$ (for a nominal/ordinal variable)

$$95\% \ CI \ of \ P_u = P_s \pm (1.96) \ (s_{p_s})$$

and

$$99\% \ CI \ of \ P_u = P_s \pm (2.58) \ (s_{p_s})$$

where

$P = p$ [of the success category] of a nominal/ordinal variable
95% CI of P_u = 95 percent confidence interval of a population proportion
99% CI of P_u = 99 percent confidence interval of a population proportion
P_s = sample proportion
s_{p_s} = estimated standard error of a confidence interval of a proportion

---

As we noted in Chapter 7, a sampling distribution of proportions is approximately normally distributed only when the smaller of P_s and Q_s times n is greater than or equal to 5. This restriction accounts for both sample size and estimation errors. If $(p_{smaller})$ $(n) < 5$, the best solution is to increase the sample size.

Sample Problem of a Confidence Interval of a Population Proportion

Problem: We work for Chantrise Jones, who is running for the U.S. Senate. It is two days before the election. With 95 percent confidence, she wants to know if she is likely to win. What is her level of support among likely voters? In a telephone poll of 1,393 likely voters, 752 indicate that they intend to vote for her. We start by reviewing the checklist of the five steps for computing confidence intervals.

Brief Checklist of Five Steps for Computing Confidence Intervals

Step 1. State the research question, identify the level of measurement of the variable, list "givens," and draw a conceptual diagram of the target population and sample (as in Figure 8–1).

Step 2. Compute the standard error and error term.

Step 3. Compute the LCL and UCL of the confidence interval.

Step 4. Provide an interpretation in everyday language.

Step 5. Provide a statistical interpretation illustrating the notion of "confidence in the procedure."

Step 1. Research question: With 95 percent confidence, can we conclude that Chantrise Jones is likely to win the election? That is, does she appear likely to get more than .50 (50 percent) of the vote? Within a specified range of percentage of support, what is the parameter P_u, the proportion of the population of likely voters intending to vote for Chantrise Jones? *Givens:* One nominal variable from a single sample. *Target population* = likely voters.

$P = p$ [of likely voters supporting Chantrise]
$Q = p$ [of likely voters supporting someone else]
Sample: $n = 1{,}393$ likely voters   # supporting Chantrise = 752

$$P_s = \frac{\# \text{ supporting Chantrise}}{\text{total number polled}} = \frac{752}{1{,}393} = .54$$

$$Q_s = 1 - P_s = 1 - .54 = .46$$

[Check to see if n is large enough. See if $(p_{smaller})\,(n) > 5$.]

$$(p_{smaller})\,(n) = (.46)\,(1{,}393) = 640.78. \qquad 640.78 > 5$$

(Thus, we can use the critical t-score $t_\alpha = 1.96$)

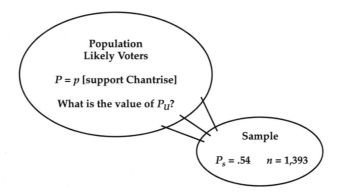

Step 2 (standard error and error term)

$$s_{P_s} = \sqrt{\frac{P_s Q_s}{n}} = \sqrt{\frac{(.54)(.46)}{1{,}393}} = .0134$$

For 95 percent confidence, $t_\alpha = 1.96$ (from t-distribution table, $\alpha = .05$, $df = \infty$).

$$\text{Error term} = (t_\alpha)\,(s_{p_s}) = (1.96)\,(.0134) = .0263$$

Step 3 (the LCL and UCL of the confidence interval)

$$95\% \ CI \ of \ P_u = P_s \pm (1.96) \ (s_{p_s})$$
$$= .54 \pm (1.96) \ (.0134)$$
$$= .54 \pm .0263$$
$$= \text{sample proportion} \pm \text{error term}$$
$$LCL = .54 - .0263 = .5137 = 51.37\%$$
$$UCL = .54 + .0263 = .5663 = 56.63\%$$

Step 4 (interpretation in everyday language)

"I am 95 percent sure that the percentage of likely voters supporting Chantrise Jones is between 51 percent and 57 percent." Chantrise's chances of winning are good. If the election were held today, she would get at least 51 percent of the vote. (*Note:* We rounded to a whole percentage for the benefit of a public audience.)

Step 5 (statistical interpretation illustrating the notion of "confidence in the procedure")

"If the same sampling and statistical procedures are conducted 100 times, 95 times the true population parameter, P_u, will be encompassed in the computed intervals and 5 times it will not. Thus, I am 95 percent confident that the single confidence interval I computed includes the true parameter."

Choosing a Sample Size for Polls, Surveys, and Research Studies

Sample Size for a Confidence Interval of a Population Proportion

A question that every researcher encounters is: How large a sample do I need? As we just learned, sample size is an important component in the size of a standard error. In the standard error equations for both means and proportions, the sample size (n) is in the denominator of the equations. Thus, a large sample size is better because it will produce a small standard error. Because of cost factors, however, we cannot simply choose an enormous sample size. Nevertheless, we can choose an *appropriate* sample size for the degree of precision we desire for the reported results. The degree of precision depends on the research objectives, the amount of time and money available for the research, and other considerations. For example, a political polling firm may use small samples early but increase the sample size to improve precision as the election approaches. Depending on these issues, we may choose to report results with plus or minus 1 percent error, 3 percent error, 5 percent error, and so on. The chosen precision hinges on the size of the error term of the confidence interval equation.

Let us demonstrate the choice of sample size for a confidence interval of proportions. Nominal/ordinal level variables, such as the proportion of likely voters favoring a candidate or supporting an issue, are used very commonly in political polling. A traditional standard in political polls as well as marketing surveys is to report results with 95 percent confidence and a 3 percent range of error (i.e., a 95 percent confidence interval with ± 3 percent). Once the size of the error term is chosen, the sample size required to reach that level of error is determined by solving for n in the error term equation. The error term for a confidence interval of proportions can be expanded as follows:

$$\text{Error term} = (t_\alpha)(s_{P_s}) = (t_\alpha)\sqrt{\frac{P_s Q_s}{n}}$$

Solving for n results in the following equation for calculating the needed sample size:

Calculating Sample Size for the Confidence Interval of a Population Proportion (for a nominal/ordinal variable)

$$n = \frac{(P_s\ Q_s)\ (t_\alpha)^2}{\text{Error term}^2}$$

where

n = sample size needed
t_α = t-score that corresponds to the stated level of confidence and significance (for example, $t_\alpha = 1.96$ for a 95% level of confidence)
$P_s = p$ [of the success category in the sample]
$Q_s = p$ [of the failure category in the sample]
Error term = desired precision in the results to be reported

To solve for n, all the other terms in the equation must be known or otherwise estimated. We *choose* the level of confidence which determines t_α, which is found at the bottom of the t-distribution table. If we choose the 95 percent level, $t_\alpha = 1.96$. We also choose the degree of precision—how large we want the error term to be. For example, we might choose the traditional ± 3 percent (i.e., $\pm.03$). Since we have not gathered data yet, we must estimate P_s and Q_s for the important variables in the study, such as the percentage supporting a candidate. These figures may be estimated on the basis of previous research. If such research is unavailable, a conservative estimate is to set P_s at .5. Since $Q_s = 1 - P_s$, then Q_s also will be estimated at .5. (These estimates are conservative in the sense that they will err on the large size; that is, the 3 percent error reported will be a worst-case scenario where error is overreported rather than underreported.) With all the previously unknown terms now specified, let us solve for the needed sample size when we desire ± 3 percent error at the 95 percent level of confidence:

$$n = \frac{(P_s\ Q_s)\ (t_\alpha)^2}{\text{Error term}^2} = \frac{(.5)\ (.5)\ (1.96)^2}{.03^2} = 1{,}067 \text{ survey respondents}$$

We can see that a considerable sample size is needed for a 3 percent reporting error at the 95 percent level of confidence. Because of the high cost of sampling, many polling firms have begun to settle for smaller samples and a larger error (such as ±5 percent). This is especially true of overnight telephone pollsters, whose costs have increased as a result of time delays caused by encountering answering machines and cellular phones.

Sample Size for a Confidence Interval of a Population Mean

Deciding on a sample size for confidence intervals of the mean is similar to the procedure for proportions; we solve the error term equation for n:

Calculating the Sample Size for a Confidence Interval of a Population Mean (for an interval/ratio variable)

$$n = \frac{(t_\alpha)^2 \, (s_X)^2}{\text{Error term}^2} + 1$$

where

n = sample size needed

t_α = t-score that corresponds to the stated level of confidence and expected error

s_X = standard deviation of a sample for the variable X

Error term = desired precision in the results to be reported

To solve for n in this equation, we must specify all terms except n. We are free to choose the level of confidence and obtain its critical value, t_α. This t-score, however, depends on the sample size itself and the number of degrees of freedom. It also is influenced by estimation error (i.e., using sample data to estimate standard errors). Thus, let us reduce estimation error by assuming that we are to use a sample of 121 or more. This gives us an infinite number of degrees of freedom on the t-distribution table with a critical t_α of 1.96 (for the 95 percent level of confidence) or 2.58 (for the 99 percent level of confidence). We also choose the size of the error term in accordance with the circumstances of the research. Since the research project is likely to have many interval/ratio variables, this estimate usually is made for an interval/ratio level *dependent* variable that is central to the research. Previous research usually reveals how small an error term can be tolerated. For example, if we are to sample adolescent girls with eating disorders and monitor their weight fluctuation, a four-pound difference in weight may be important for predicting a serious risk of other illnesses. Thus, to obtain practical results, we want an error term no larger than four pounds. Since we have not yet gathered data, we must estimate what the sample standard deviation (s_X) is likely to be. This estimate is also taken from previous research studies, which are likely to reveal a consistent mean and standard deviation. For example, such research may show that 25 pounds is a good estimate of the standard deviation. With these estimates in hand, we are ready to project a needed sample size for a 95 percent confidence interval with a ± four-pound error:

$$n = \frac{(t_\alpha)^2 \, (s_X)^2}{\text{error term}^2} + 1 = \frac{(1.96)^2 \, (25)^2}{(4)^2} + 1 = 151 \text{ study subjects}$$

This sample size would be a minimum. Other considerations may require additional cases.

When to Use a Confidence Interval Instead of a Hypothesis Test

A confidence interval is used to estimate a population parameter *when we have no idea* what the parameter value is. We are simply interested in using sample statistics to find and estimate the values of population parameters. For example, *with a confidence interval,* the central question might be: What is the mean GPA of State University's student body? With hypothesis tests, which are discussed in Chapter 9, we start with a target value for the parameter. *With a hypothesis test,* the central question might be: Is the mean GPA of State University's student body greater than 3.0 (or some other selected value)? This distinction will become more clear once we learn how to test hypotheses. For the time being, keep in mind that a confidence interval answers the research question: What is a good estimate of a parameter of a variable?

☹   STATISTICAL FOLLIES AND FALLACIES   ☹

A Cautionary Note on Interpreting Confidence Intervals

A confidence interval addresses the size of parameters, not individual scores. Thinking in terms of individual scores is a common misinterpretation of the nature of confidence intervals. In the example of a confidence interval of the mean wage of a plant's computer assemblers, we stated: "I am 95 percent sure that *the mean hourly wage* of the plant's computer assemblers is between $7.71 and $8.29." We are *not saying* that 95 percent of the computer assemblers earn hourly wages between those two figures! If our purpose had been to describe a score span in which 95 percent of the assemblers fall, we would have used the standard deviation of the sample—not the standard error—to make such a projection (as in Chapter 6). The confidence interval addresses issues of summary statistics, not individual scores.

We also must take care not to begin treating our sample mean as though it were the population mean itself. We learned in Chapter 7 that repeated sampling produces a sampling distribution with sample means centered on the population mean, μ_X. But it would be wrong to take the single sample mean, $\bar{X}$, of our study and treat it as though all other sample means centered on it. In other words, with a confidence interval, we are *not* saying that 95 percent of repeated samples will have means between the upper and lower confidence limits computed *from this single sample mean*. It is the unknown population mean around which these other samples fall. The confidence interval interpretation is based on our single sample, whose mean is unlikely to equal the population mean. In summary, the confidence interval simply gives us a span of possible values for the unknown population parameter.

Formulas in Chapter 8

Calculating a confidence interval of a population mean

Given: An interval/ratio (or an interval-like ordinal) variable X

Research question: What is the value of the population mean, μ_X?

$$95\% \ CI \ of \ \mu_X = \bar{X} \pm (t_\alpha = .05) \ (s_{\bar{X}})$$
$$99\% \ CI \ of \ \mu_X = \bar{X} \pm (t_\alpha = .01) \ (s_{\bar{X}})$$

$$s_{\bar{X}} = \frac{s_X}{\sqrt{n-1}} \qquad df = n - 1 \ (\text{Find } t_\alpha \text{ in } t\text{-distribution table})$$

Calculating confidence interval of a population proportion (when $[(p_{smaller}) \ (n)] \geq 5$)

Given: A nominal/ordinal variable with $P = p$ [of the success category]

Research question: What is the value of the population proportion, P_u?

$$95\% \ CI \ of \ P_u = P_s \pm (1.96) \ (s_{p_s})$$
$$99\% \ CI \ of \ P_u = P_s \pm (2.58) \ (s_{p_s})$$

$$s_{P_s} = \sqrt{\frac{P_s Q_s}{n}}$$

Calculating the sample size for a confidence interval of a population mean (for an interval/ratio variable):

$$n = \frac{(t_\alpha)^2 \ (s_X)^2}{\text{error term}^2} + 1$$

Sample size for the confidence interval of a population proportion (for a nominal/ordinal variable):

$$n = \frac{(P_s \ Q_s) \ (t_\alpha)^2}{\text{error term}^2}$$

Questions for Chapter 8

1. In plain language, what is a confidence interval?
2. What is the purpose of computing a confidence interval?
3. In computing a confidence interval, what two factors go into the size of the interval?
4. In computing confidence intervals, what is the relationship between sample size and the size of the standard error?
5. In computing confidence intervals, what is the relationship between the size of the confidence interval and the *t*-score used to compute it?
6. State the statistical interpretation of any confidence interval for which you have 99 percent confidence.
7. List the five steps in computing a confidence interval.
8. The level of significance (or expected error) in the computation of a confidence interval is symbolized by the Greek letter α. Mathematically, what is the relationship between α and the level of confidence?

Exercises for Chapter 8

1. Following the five steps for computing a confidence interval, compute and interpret the 95 percent confidence interval for the following data:

   X = age   *n* = 189 corporate executives
   Mean = 57 years   Standard deviation = 9 years

2. Following the five steps for computing a confidence interval, compute and interpret the 95 percent confidence interval for the following (fictional) data from a random sample of men in a national nutrition study:

   X = weight   *n* = 147 men
   Mean = 174 pounds   Standard deviation = 6 pounds

3. Redo the last three steps for computing a confidence interval to compute the 99 percent confidence interval for the data in exercise 1. Compare the results to the answer in exercise 1 and discuss.

4. Redo the last three steps for computing a confidence interval to compute the 99 percent confidence interval for the data in exercise 2. Compare the results to the answer in exercise 2 and discuss.

5. You need to compute an interval estimate of the mean incomes of city planners in 150 Metropolitan Statistical Areas (MSAs) in the Sun Belt. You obtain a random sample of 214 city planners and find a mean income of $43,571 with a standard deviation of $4,792. Following the five steps, construct the 99 percent confidence interval. As part of step 4, explain

your results to the head of the Urban Studies Department at the local university.

6. Dr. Latisia Latham, a marriage counselor, administers the Global Distress Scale (GDS), which measures overall marital discord. It consists of 43 true/false questions with a total score combined for the two partners (Snyder, Willis, and Grady-Fletcher 1991). She asks you to provide a rough estimate of the average score of her clientele. You obtain a random sample of 25 couples and find a mean GDS score of 59 with a standard deviation of 5.2. Following the five steps, provide a 95 percent confidence interval of the mean GDS score of Dr. Latham's clients.

7. It is the year 2010. You work for President Shirley D. Fendus as a pollster. She desires to know what proportion of her 8,469 party officials supports her legislative bill to increase defense spending. You poll 306 randomly selected party officials and find that 108 support her bill. To inform her, compute and interpret the 95 percent confidence interval. Follow the five steps.

8. Senator Daniel "Dandy" Barker is contemplating a run for the presidency. He has someone poll 90 randomly selected registered voters and finds that 51 percent support him against the incumbent. If the election were held today, could Senator Barker be assured of victory? Explain using a 95 percent confidence interval. Follow the five steps.

9. You are to conduct a survey to determine the percentage of registered voters currently supporting candidate A. The results are to be reported with 95 percent confidence and a 2 percentage point error term. What size sample should you obtain? *Hint:* P_s is unknown at this time, but assume it will be .5.

10. You are to conduct a survey to determine the percentage of a health maintenance organization's patients who are satisfied with their primary physicians. You wish to report the results with 99 percent confidence and a 3 percentage point error term. What size sample will you need to draw? *Hint:* P_s is unknown at this time, but assume it will be .5.

11. You are to conduct a survey to determine the mean age of patients of a health maintenance organization (HMO). You wish to report the results with 99 percent confidence with a plus or minus 3 year error term. What size sample will you need to draw? The standard deviation of ages of the general population of the city in which the HMO is located is 8.6 years. Use this as an estimate in calculating the needed sample size.

12. You are to conduct a survey to determine the mean number of cigarettes smoked per day by high school girls who smoke. You wish to report the results with 95 percent confidence with a plus or minus 1.5 cigarettes error term. What size sample will you need to draw? From previous studies, the standard deviation of cigarettes smoked per day is 4.1. Use this as an estimate in calculating the needed sample size.

13. Complete the following table, where $n = 1000$ and $P_s = .5$. Answer the questions that follow.

Level of Confidence	t_α	s_{P_s}	Error Term	LCL	UCL	Width of Confidence Interval
95%	1.96	.0158	.0310	.4690	.5310	.062
99%	____	____	____	____	____	____
99.9%	____	____	.0520	____	____	____

  a. What is the relationship between the size of the level of confidence and the width of the confidence interval? Explain.
  b. How is the width of the confidence interval computed?
  c. What is the relationship between the size of the level of confidence and the size of the error term? Explain.

14. Complete the following table, where $n = 225$ and $P_s = .6$. Answer the questions that follow.

Level of Confidence	t_α	s_{P_s}	Error Term	LCL	UCL	Width of Confidence Interval
95%	1.96	.0327	.0641	.5359	.6641	.1282
99%	____	____	____	____	____	____
99.9%	____	____	.1076	____	____	____

  a. What is the relationship between the size of the level of confidence and the width of the confidence interval? Explain.
  b. How is the width of the confidence interval computed?
  c. What is the relationship between the size of the level of confidence and the size of the error term? Explain.

Optional Computer Applications for Chapter 8

If your class uses the optional computer applications that accompany this text, open the Chapter 8 exercises on the *Computer Applications for The Statistical Imagination* compact disk. The exercises are on computing confidence intervals in *SPSS for Windows* with an emphasis on the importance of examining the effects of skewness on the computations.

HYPOTHESIS TESTING

Introduction: Scientific Theory and the Development of Testable Hypotheses

As was noted in Chapter 1, inferential statistics are computed to show cause-and-effect relationships and to test hypotheses and scientific theories. A theory is tested by making specific predictions about data. For example, in studying civil disorders such as riots, we might posit a "protest theory" that says that riot behavior is stimulated by the practice of suppressive authority, such as incidents of police brutality. This theory provides concepts (such as civil disorder, riots, suppression, and protest) as well as ideas about how the social world works (such as the idea that abusive state authority leads to protest). Most important, a theory steers our thoughts so that we are able to conceive of a set of propositions about relationships among measured variables. For instance, if suppressive authority leads to protest, measures of protest should be high (such as a high incidence of civil disorders and riots) in situations where state suppression is also high (such as lots of police brutality). In summary, a theory is a set of logically organized, interrelated ideas that explains a phenomenon of interest *and* allows testing of the soundness of those ideas against observable facts. The process of determining which facts are valid and which are not is called hypothesis testing, the topic of this chapter.

Before being regarded as an adequate scientific explanation a theory must accomplish two things: (1) It must make sense and improve understanding, and (2) it must provide empirical (i.e., observable and measurable) predictions. In other words, scientific propositions, no matter how reasonable they appear, are not simply accepted at face value. A scientist must establish the fact that a theory leads to useful predictions. The abstract ideas of a theory must have a practical side to them.

Relating the well-organized ideas of a theory to real events is the creative side of the statistical imagination. It requires "seeing the future," at least with regard to how a phenomenon of interest will behave. A theory "motivates" hypotheses by moving us to think in terms of proving our points. A **hypothesis** is *a prediction about the relationship between two variables that asserts that changes in the measure of an independent variable will correspond to changes in the measure of a dependent variable.* A hypothesis is a prediction in need of corroboration by observation and analysis of data. (The word *hypothesis* shares its root with *hypothetical*, a word meaning "let's imagine for the moment.") Hypotheses put theoretical ideas into practice by stipulating that given the logic of the theory, observable facts should appear in a certain way. The scientific process works on the notion that if data turn out as a theory suggests, that theory may be a worthwhile explanation of the phenomenon of interest. By contrast, if predictions are not supported by fact, that theory is not sound and must be rejected or greatly modified. In a broad sense, hypothesis testing serves the purpose of corroborating theory.

A Hypothesis

A prediction about the relationship between two variables that asserts that changes in the measure of an independent variable will correspond to changes in the measure of a dependent variable.

Corroborating a theory involves making predictions about how natural and social phenomena work. A hypothesis is stated *before* we gather data; thus, we must imagine how the data will turn out. For example, we may hypothesize that police brutality (an independent variable) stimulates riot behavior (our dependent variable). We then test this hypothesis by gathering data from a sample of cities of similar sizes and with similar economies. To corroborate our theory, we must show that cities with high rates of police brutality frequently have riots, while cities with little police brutality have few. If this pattern is found *not* to be the case, we will reject the protest theory of riot behavior. We accept a theory only after it is corroborated by empirical predictions.

Theoretical Purpose of a Hypothesis Test

To corroborate theory by testing ideas against facts.

Making Empirical Predictions

One challenge of scientific hypothesis testing is figuring out how to make empirical predictions. Actually, making such predictions is not difficult. We do so frequently in our everyday lives. Here are some questions you may raise and some hypotheses you may test today, along with the empirical observations you could make to test them.

Question 1. Should I carry an umbrella today?

Hypothesis: An increase in cloudiness (independent variable) is associated with an increase in rain (dependent variable).

Observation: Look out the window.

Question 2. Will I get better grades on my statistics quizzes if I study more for each one?

Hypothesis: The longer the study time (independent variable), the better the quiz grade (dependent variable).

Observation: Study more and see what happens.

Question 3. Will I suffer injury if I step in front of a moving bus?

1. *A physical science hypothesis:* Given the known physical laws that two objects cannot occupy the same space at the same time and that objects of greater mass moving at higher speeds will displace objects of lesser mass and speed, the massive bus should crush the less massive person.

Observation: Step in front of the bus.

2. *A behavioral science hypothesis:* There will be a greater incidence of head and body injuries (dependent variable) to victims of pedestrian bus crashes than to persons who have not experienced such crashes (independent variable).

Observation: Analyze hospital records. (This would be called a retrospective study, because we would be looking back at past experiences.)

Suggestion: Test this one with the retrospective data or crash dummies.

The last question illustrates the fact that we actually use tremendous amounts of empirically corroborated information as we go about our daily lives. We do not have to step in front of a bus to know that injuries will occur. In other words, some relationships between two variables can be accepted through mere "common sense." But most things require more than common sense. We extend common sense by observing data and maintaining a skeptical frame of mind (see "Statistical Follies and Fallacies" at the end of this chapter).

Statistical Inference

To infer is to draw a conclusion about something. **Statistical inference** entails *drawing conclusions about a population on the basis of sample statistics.* As was discussed in Chapter 2, statistical inferences must take into account sampling error. A measurement made on a sample can be expected to be slightly off from the true population parameter.

Statistical Inference

Drawing conclusions about a population on the basis of sample statistics.

An awareness of sampling error is important in making a statistical inference. For example, suppose we wish to compare grade performance for students on commuter (or drive-to) campuses to grade performance for those on residential (or live-on) campuses. Commuter campuses are located in large cities, where most students work and many are older, live at home, or raise children. In contrast, residential campuses are located in relatively small "college towns" where students are far from home and live in residence halls or private apartments. Most students on residential campuses do not work, and this leaves time for concentrated study and an enriched campus life. The differences in social context of the two types of campuses lead to a "role conflict" theory: Commuter students experience job and family pressures that interfere with study. This theory "motivates" the hypothesis that on average, students on commuter campuses get lower grades than do those at residential universities. In this hypothesis, type of campus is the independent variable and grade point average (GPA), is the dependent variable. We test the hypothesis by comparing the mean GPAs on the two types of campuses. If we sample 200 students from each type of campus, we may find that the mean GPA of the residential sample is 2.68 while that of the commuter sample is 2.64. The difference between these two sample mean GPAs is the *effect* of the type of campus on GPA. In this example, the observed effect is .04 (i.e., 2.68 minus 2.64). This calculation of sample statistics suggests that role conflicts affect grade performance in a way that reduces the commuter campus mean GPA by .04 points.

If we did not know better, we would immediately conclude that indeed commuter students on average do less well in school than do those on residential campuses. We are hesitant to draw this conclusion, however, because we did not compare the mean GPAs of all students, only samples of them. We observed sample statistics, not actual parameters (i.e., the true mean GPAs of the campus populations). Thus, it is possible that the .04 difference in sample means results from sampling error. While the theoretical purpose of hypothesis testing is to corroborate theory, hypothesis testing also has a more specific purpose: determining whether observed statistical effects calculated for a sample are real *in the population* or simply a result of sampling error. For instance, in comparing campus GPAs, is the .04 difference in mean GPAs a real effect of the type of campus or simply a reflection of sampling error?

Statistical Purpose of a Hypothesis Test

To determine whether statistical effects computed from a sample indicate (1) real effects in the population or (2) sampling error.

How do we measure sampling error and use it to make statistical inferences? The answer lies in our ability to predict sampling outcomes. To make a convincing case for a hypothesis, we must be able to stipulate—before observing sample data—exactly what the possible sampling outcomes can be. In other words, we must describe a sampling distribution by using probability theory. Only then do we actually draw a sample and gather data on its subjects. Sample results then are weighed against the predictions described by the sampling distribution.

In the GPA example we can make such a prediction. We can hypothesize that if there is *no difference* in the mean GPAs of the two campus *populations,* the difference between these mean GPAs is zero. This is the hypothesis that the variable *type of campus* has *no effect* on the variable GPA. If this is indeed the case, then once the sampling has been done, we can expect to find that the difference in the means of the *samples* should be zero or *very close* to zero. To say "very close" is to acknowledge that sampling error may cause the differences in the sample *statistics* to be slightly off from zero even when the population *parameters* are equal. We decide what is "slightly off" versus what is "significantly off" by computing probabilities of sampling outcomes. In this case we would evaluate the question: With samples of 200 students from each campus, *when both campuses have the same GPAs,* what is the probability of observing a .04 difference simply because of normal sampling error? What we do in a hypothesis test is determine whether the observed sampling effect (i.e., the .04 difference between mean GPAs *of the two samples*) is (1) due to a real difference between mean GPAs *in the two populations* or (2) simply due to sampling error.

To summarize this overview, to make a decision about the truth of a hypothesis, we must predict two things. First, we must mathematically predict a parameter outcome. In this GPA example, we predict that if the two campuses have the same mean GPAs, the difference in these two parameters is zero. Second, we must predict all possible sampling outcomes when sampling error is factored in; in other words, we use probability theory to describe the sampling distribution that would result with repeated sampling. Using these two predictions, we then specify the precise probability that our actual, single sampling outcome is significantly different from the predicted outcome. In this case, what is the probability of observing a .04 GPA point difference between the two campus *samples* when in fact there is "no difference" in the *population* means? The difference between what is observed (a difference of .04 GPA point) and what is expected (no difference between campuses) is called the *test effect* of the hypothesis testing procedure. The effect of the hypothesis test is the essential observation for drawing a conclusion. For a hypothesis test, common terms used to refer to the effect of the test are *statistical effect, test effect,* and *statistical test effect.* Precise calculations of test effects and their probabilities of occurrence depend on using the statistical imagination to project sampling distributions. Now we will proceed to learn the logic of hypothesis testing. Sampling distributions play a key role in this process.

The Logic of Hypothesis Testing

Let us suppose that we are sitting in class one day when a handsome stranger walks into the room dressed like a rodeo cowboy or country-and-western musician. He is wearing a feathered ten-gallon hat, a sequined western shirt, a turquoise-bejeweled string tie, a large belt buckle shaped like the state of Texas, and the shiniest pointy-toed boots we have ever seen. He introduces himself as Billy "Tex" Cooper from Dallas, Texas.

Tex says that he heard that statistics courses deal with predicting the future and that he would like to learn more about this because he wants to become a professional gambler. He pulls a pair of dice from his pocket and proposes a game. He says: "I'll tell you what. I will roll these dice four times. Each time they come up 7, all of you will pay me a dollar. Each time they come up any other combination—2, 3, 4, and so on—I will pay each of you a dollar." We ask to see his dice, and they appear legitimate.

Sounds like a very good deal. Why? Because our knowledge of probability tells us that we should have an advantage here. Probability theory allows us to figure out *what happens in the long run,* that is, when dice are rolled over and over again. If we can mathematically project how often each side of a die will come up, we can determine whether some combinations of two dice will come up more frequently than do others. Moreover, using the multiplication rule of probability, we can easily predict any combination of outcomes when dice are rolled four times. In other words, using practical experience and probability theory, we can produce the sampling distribution for the event of rolling two dice.

As we learned in Chapter 7, a sampling distribution is a mathematical description of all possible sampling event outcomes and the probability (p) of each one. Figure 9–1 is a matrix illustrating the sampling distribution for the roll of two dice, that is, all possible combinations and the probability of each combination. The matrix reveals that there are 36 possible outcomes. When the first die comes up 1, the second die can come up 1 or 2 or 3 or 4 or 5 or 6. When the first die comes up 2, the second die can again come up 1 or 2 or 3 or 4 or 5 or 6 and so on. Looking at the upper left-hand corner of the matrix, we see that when both dice come up 1, the combination is 2, the lowest possible outcome. This is the only way to obtain an outcome of 2, and there are 36 total possible outcomes; thus, the probability of rolling a 2 with two dice is 1 out of 36. The combination of 3 can occur in two ways: first die 1 and second die 2 and first die 2 and second die 1; thus, the probability of rolling a 3 is 2 out of 36. Looking at the lower right-hand corner of the matrix, we can see that when the first die rolls up 6 and the second die rolls up 6, the combination is 12, the highest possible outcome, with a probability of 1 out of 36. Observing the diagonal from the lower-left to the upper-right corners, we can see that the combination of 7 occurs more frequently than does any other, with a probability of 6 out of 36. The rest of the matrix gives the combinations for all other possible rolls, with each possible outcome (from 2 to 12) situated crosswise on the diagonals.

The matrix of Figure 9–1 is summarized in Table 9–1, which provides a clear description of the sampling distribution for the roll of two dice. It is a list of all possible outcomes and the probability (p) of each one. Note the familiar, approximately normal shape of the stargraph or "curve" of these outcomes.

FIGURE 9–1

Matrix of all possible combinations of side pairings for the roll of two dice

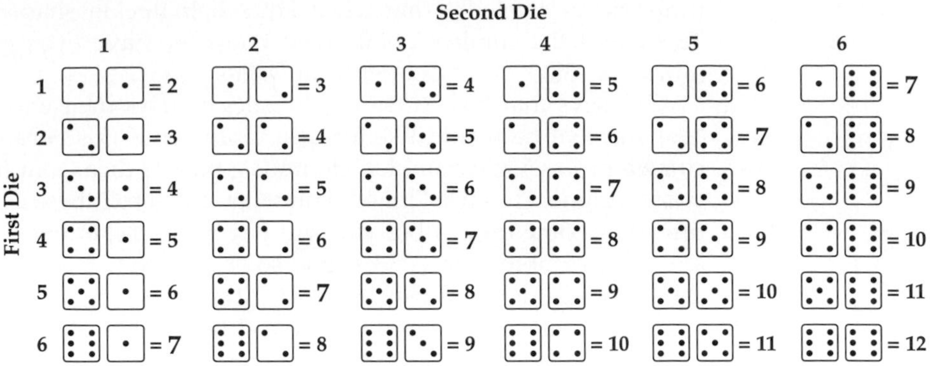

Like the means and proportions we produced with repeated sampling in Chapter 7, this distribution peaks (in this case at a score of 7) with gradually lower frequencies as we move into the "tails" of the curve. Taking note that 7 occurs 6/36 of the time, we can quickly calculate the probabilities of other outcomes by moving away from 7 and subtracting 1. Thus, the probability of rolling 6 is 5/36, that of rolling 8 is 5/36, that of rolling 5 is 4/36, and so forth. (Figure 9–1 and Table 9–1 are worth the cost of tuition for this course! They should be invaluable if you shoot craps or play Monopoly, backgammon, or any other game of chance that uses dice.)

Getting back to Tex, we should have an advantage. The probability of his winning a single roll with a 7 is 6/36, or .1667. Using the addition rule for alternative events, the probability of us winning a single roll is 30/36, or .8333— the probabilities of all other possible outcomes combined.

We should be feeling pretty good right now. Here's this charming guy, dressed elaborately, who says that he is rather ignorant about probability,

TABLE 9–1   The Sampling Distribution of the Roll of Two Dice

Possible Outcome	Fraction p	Stargraph
2	1/36 = .0278	*
3	2/36 = .0556	**
4	3/36 = .0833	***
5	4/36 = .1111	****
6	5/36 = .1389	*****
7	**6/36 = .1667**	******
8	5/36 = .1389	*****
9	4/36 = .1111	****
10	3/36 = .0833	***
11	2/36 = .0556	**
12	1/36 = .0278	*
Totals	36/36 = 1.0001*	

*Total does not sum to 1 because of rounding error.

which is the essence of gaming and gambling. (And we're thinking we are pretty smart right now because we have survived a statistics course to this point!)

But let's suppose he rolls the dice and 7 comes up. We pay the dollar, thinking of course that of any single combination, 7 has the greatest chance of coming up. He rolls the dice a second time and gets a 7, and we pay again. He rolls a third time and gets a 7, and we pay again. He rolls a fourth time and gets a 7, and we pay once more. Wait a minute! Something's not right here.

At this point we may suspect that Tex is a con artist and that the dice are loaded (weighted in such a way that only 7 will come up) or that he is using sleight of hand to switch to a loaded pair before he rolls. Why are our suspicions raised? Partly because his appearance in class is unexpected and we are prejudiced against people who dress differently and talk us out of our money. (Of course, if you are reading this in the western United States, he may not appear to be dressed differently.) But we are also suspicious because probability theory tells us what to expect from four rolls of two dice even before they are rolled. What is the probability that an honest pair of dice will come up 7 four times in a row? Using the multiplication rule for compound events:

$$p\ [7,7,7,7] = (.1667)\ (.1667)\ (.1667)\ (.1667) = .1667^4 = .0008$$

This is 8/10,000. In other words, if 10,000 gamblers had dropped by and rolled their dice four times *and all the dice were honestly marked and weighted*, only 8 of those gamblers would have rolled all 7's. We cannot be absolutely sure (Tex may be really lucky), but we suspect that we "got taken" and that Tex is a crook. We probably will conclude that rolling the four 7's was *the effect* of loaded dice, not the effect of very good luck in the random fall of honest dice.

Although we did not follow strict procedures, we tested the hypothesis that Tex is a crook. All hypothesis testing has the elements of this event. A question is raised, predictions are made on the basis of probability theory, an event is observed and its effects are measured, the probability of the test effect occurring is computed, and a conclusion is drawn.

When you decided whether to carry an umbrella today, you did the same thing:

Hypothesis: It is going to rain.

Prediction: If it is going to rain, there should be clouds in the sky.

Observation: The sky is a clear blue. This does not fit the prediction. The probability of rain with no clouds is extremely low.

Conclusion: Reject the notion that it is going to rain. Leave the umbrella home.

Essentially, the logic of hypothesis testing involves deciding whether to accept or reject a statement on the basis of observations of data.

Now we will proceed to learn the six steps of hypothesis testing. We also refer to these procedures as the six steps of statistical inference because they organize the logical processes involved in drawing a conclusion about a population on the basis of observing a sample.

The Six Steps of Statistical Inference

Hypothesis testing begins with a **research question,** *"a goal that can be stated in terms of a hypothesis"* (Bailey 1987:10). For "Tex the gambler" our research question is: Is Tex a crook? Hypothesis testing also ends with a focus on the research question, where we answer it in a straightforward, nontechnical fashion. All the statistical procedures between raising the research question and answering it are merely tools to achieve the theoretical goal of increasing understanding about a research question we have deemed important.

To conduct a hypothesis test, predictions must be made about observed empirical sampling events. Specifically, we must anticipate sampling outcomes by generating a sampling distribution. With regard to whether Tex is a crook, how can we do this? Can we predict how crooked dice fall? No, we cannot. Crooked dice can fall in any number of ways, depending on how the dice have been "juiced up." We do know, however, that an honest pair of dice will roll up in the predictable ways described in Table 9–1. Thus, we will turn the research question around and ask, "Is Tex *not* a crook?" because if he is not, we can predict what the dice will do. A hypothesis must be stated in such a way that sampling outcomes can be predicted. We call this hypothesis the statistical hypothesis because it predicts statistical results.

Once armed with these predictions, we can observe the actual sampling event—four rolls of Tex's dice—which represents a sampling of his behavior. As was noted above, our observation will reveal that Tex's four 7's in a row is a sampling event with a very low probability of occurring *with honest dice* (i.e., $p = .0008$). We must decide whether this unusual occurrence (1) was the effect of random sampling error (very good luck on Tex's part) or (2) was the effect of a nonrandom tampering with the dice. Random sampling error would imply honest dice with each side of a die having an equal chance of turning up on a roll. Nonrandom tampering would imply that the dice have been modified (such as by being loaded with lead to one side) to give some sides a greater than equal chance of turning up. A probability of .0008 seems unlikely with honest dice, and so we reject the statement that the outcome is an effect of random sampling error and conclude instead that Tex is a crook. The observations failed to fit the expected outcomes of an honest pair of dice.

What Each of the Six Steps of Statistical Inference Accomplishes

The six steps of statistical inference are summarized in Table 9–2. We get ready with test preparation by determining the research question, identifying the population of study and its variables and their levels of measurement, listing known information (or "givens") about population parameters and sample

---

TABLE 9–2   The Six Steps of Statistical Inference or Hypothesis Testing

---

Test Preparation
State research question; list givens, including variables (e.g., $X = \ldots$, $Y = \ldots$) and their levels of measurement, the population(s) under study, and sample(s) and sample size(s); select the statistical test; provide observations of statistics and parameters; and draw a conceptual diagram.

Six Steps
Using the symbol H for *hypothesis:*

1. State the statistical (or "null") hypothesis (Stat. H). State the alternative H (Alt. H) and stipulate the direction of the test (whether it is one-tailed or two-tailed).

The statistical hypothesis is one stated in such a way that you will know what statistical outcomes will occur in repeated random sampling *if this hypothesis is true.* The alternative hypothesis is accepted if the statistical hypothesis is rejected.

2. Describe the sampling distribution.

The sampling distribution is a projection of sampling outcomes that are likely to occur when the Stat. H is true. A sampling distribution consists of a listing of all possible sampling outcomes and a stipulation of the probability of each one.

3. State the chosen level of significance (α). Indicate again whether the test is one-tailed or two-tailed. Specify the critical test value.

Alpha (α) is the amount of sampling error we are willing to tolerate in coming to a conclusion. The critical test value is obtained from statistical tables in Appendix B.

4. Observe the actual sample; compute the test effects, the test statistic, and the *p*-value.

The *test effect* is the difference between what was observed in the sample and what was hypothesized (in step 1). The *test statistic* is a formula for measuring the likelihood of the observed effect. The *p-value* is the probability (p) of sampling outcomes as unusual as or more unusual than the outcome observed under the assumption that the Stat. H is true.

5. Make the rejection decision.

Compare the *p*-value to α:
If $p \leq \alpha$, reject the Stat. H and accept the Alt. H at the $1 - \alpha$ level of confidence.
If $p > \alpha$, do not reject the Stat. H.

6. Interpret and apply the results, and provide best estimates in everyday terms.

---

statistics, and selecting the appropriate statistical test. Let us examine the steps and discuss their interrelationships by using the Tex the gambler example.

Test Preparation.   First we determine the research question, which is: Is Tex a crook? We are to test this with the outcomes of the roll of two dice, a ratio level variable. The population will be all of Tex's gambling behavior. Our sample, however, is limited to observing four rolls of the dice, and we record four 7's. The test statistic is the calculation of probabilities using probability rules.

Six Steps
   Step 1. The first step in hypothesis testing is to state the **statistical hypothesis (Stat. *H*),** a hypothesis stated in such a way that we will know what

statistical outcomes will occur in repeated random sampling *if this hypothesis is true*. Thus, we will test the statistical hypothesis that Tex is honest because if this is true, we can predict the "honest dice" sampling outcomes in Table 9–1. The statistical hypothesis, then, is stated in such a way that a sampling distribution can be generated from it. Many texts use the term *null hypothesis* for the statistical hypothesis, but the two are not always the same. At the end of the chapter we will discuss when it is appropriate to use the term *null*.

In step 1, we also state an **alternative hypothesis (Alt. *H*)**, *the hypothesis we will accept if the statistical hypothesis is rejected*. In this case, the Alt. *H* is that Tex is a crook. If the dice roll up in unpredictable ways, we will in a later step of the process reject the idea that the dice are honest and accept this alternative. The statistical hypothesis is there to be rejected or not rejected. The alternative hypothesis is our conclusion in those cases where the statistical hypothesis is rejected.

The alternative hypothesis will be a reversal of the statistical hypothesis or vice versa. A hypothesis test is designed to provide two choices in a conclusion: the statistical hypothesis and its alternative. If difficulty is encountered in determining the statistical hypothesis, reverse the research question by putting *not* in its statement. Then observe both statements and see which leads to predictable sampling outcomes. As in the Tex the gambler case, it is often the alternative hypothesis that we wish to confirm. It is absolutely necessary, however, that we establish and state a statistical hypothesis so that we can generate a sampling distribution and complete the steps of the hypothesis test. Unless we can make empirical sampling predictions, we cannot proceed. It makes no difference whether the research question is supported by the statistical hypothesis or by the alternative hypothesis. The hypothesis test, however, hinges on the statistical hypothesis. Finally, in step 1 we also stipulate whether the alternative hypothesis is directional (one-tailed) or nondirectional (two-tailed). We will address this issue shortly.

Step 2. The second step in hypothesis testing is to describe the sampling distribution. The sampling distribution is a projection of all possible sampling outcomes and the probability of each outcome when the Stat. *H* is true. In other words, if Tex is honest, we should expect the outcomes and probabilities in Table 9–1, because this is what happens with honest dice. Table 9–1 shows the sampling distribution of the rolls of two honest dice.

Of course, we have produced sampling distributions before to calculate confidence intervals. In a hypothesis test, however, the sampling distribution is tied to the statistical hypothesis. It describes expected sampling outcomes assuming that the Stat. *H* is true.

Step 3. In step 3, we state a **level of significance** (symbolized by the Greek letter alpha, α). This is *the level of sampling error we are willing to tolerate in drawing our conclusion*. We expect a degree of sampling error because we know that sample statistics are estimates of parameters. Recall that in Chapter 8, in calculating confidence intervals, we referred to the level of significance as *expected error.* With hypothesis testing the principle is the same. The level of significance is the probability of making the error of rejecting the statistical hypothesis when in fact it is true and should not be rejected. We will discuss the level of significance in greater detail below. For the time being, let us just say that if Tex rolls "an outcome" that is so unusual that it occurs with honest dice fewer than 5 times out of 100, we will assume that this is not just from luck but from crooked dice. Thus, we set the level of significance α at .05.

Step 4. In step 4 we observe our actual sampling event and its statistical outcome, in this case Tex's four rolls of two dice. Then we compute the *p*-value, which is the probability of this sampling outcome under the condition that the Stat. *H* is true (i.e., the dice are honest, normal ones). Above, we found this to be .0008, a very unusual sampling outcome from honest dice, suggesting an effect of tampering with the dice. (The notion of "or more unusual than" in step 4 of Table 9–2 will be addressed later.)

Step 5. In step 5 we compare the p-value from step 4 with the level of significance (α) stated in step 3 (i.e., α = .05) and see that indeed, Tex's sampling event had a probability of .0008, which is less than .05. Thus, we reject our statistical hypothesis (Stat. *H*) that Tex is honest and accept the alternative hypothesis (Alt. *H*) that he is a crook. What we are asserting is that Tex's four 7's cannot reasonably be explained as the effect of normal, random, expected sampling error in four rolls of a pair of honest dice. Thus, we conclude that the dice must be dishonest, or "loaded."

This step of a hypothesis test is called the *rejection decision.* It is at the center of every hypothesis test. It is the step where we compare two probabilities: the α-probability from step 3 (the probability of error or of drawing an incorrect conclusion); and the *p*-value from step 4 (the probability of the observed outcome or test effect). The rejection decision highlights the importance of probability theory. Probability theory provides the projected sampling distribution from which to compute the *p*-value. The sampling distribution foresees the future and provides a ruler for evaluating the likelihood of our single sampling event. Probability theory is the essence of statistical analysis.

Step 6. Finally, in step 6, we interpret our results and apply them by providing best estimates in everyday terms (i.e., nontechnical English). Thus we would say: "We have reason to believe that Tex is a crook. We predict that his personal dice turn up 7 more often than expected with honest dice. We should probably ask him to leave quietly, but he may be carrying a gun, so let's discreetly call the campus police!

We will not try to digest all of the details of hypothesis testing at once, but the essential elements are illustrated by the simple Tex the gambler illustration. Corresponding to the six steps of statistical inference listed in Table 9–2, the following is a layout of this hypothesis test (with a few details missing and some abbreviated symbols). Before each sample problem in this text, a brief checklist of the six steps of statistical inference is provided.

Brief Checklist for the Six Steps of Statistical Inference

Test Preparation

State the research question; list givens, including variables (e.g., $X = \ldots$, $Y = \ldots$), their levels of measurement, the population(s) under study, and sample(s) and sample size(s); select the statistical test; provide observations of statistics and parameters; and draw a conceptual diagram.

Six Steps

Using the symbol H for *hypothesis:*

1. State the statistical H and the alternative H and stipulate the test direction.
2. Describe the sampling distribution.
3. State the level of significance (α) and specify the critical test value.
4. Observe the actual sample outcomes and compute the test effects, the test statistic and the p-value.
5. Make the rejection decision.
6. Interpret and apply best estimates in everyday terms.

Test Preparation

Research question: Is Tex the gambler a crook? *Givens:* Variable X = the outcomes of a pair of dice; ratio level. *Population:* The totality of Tex's gambling behavior. *Sample:* Four rolls of a pair of Tex's dice. *Statistical test:* Calculation of the probabilities of rolling two dice. *Observation:* Four 7s.

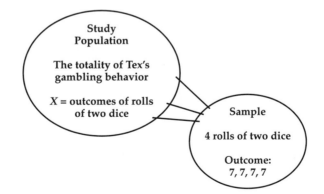

Six Steps

1. *Stat. H:* Tex and his dice are honest.

   Alt. H: Tex is a crook (i.e., he is not honest and his dice are loaded).

2. *Sampling distribution* (from Table 9–1): If the Stat. *H* is true and the dice are indeed honest, repeated rolling of the dice will result in the following outcomes:

Possible Outcomes	*p*	
2	.0278	
3	.0556	
4	.0833	The *p* of any compound event may be
5	.1111	computed by using these single-roll outcomes
6	.1389	and the multiplication rule of probability.
7	.1667	
8	.1389	
9	.1111	
10	.0833	
11	.0556	
12	.0278	

3. *Level of significance:* $\alpha = .05$ (specification of critical test value to be covered later).

4. *Observation:* Test effects, the test statistic, and *p*-value.

   Observation: Tex rolls four 7s in a row.

   Test effect: A big difference between what we observed and what we expected with honest dice.

   (Test effects and test statistics are covered more thoroughly in Chapter 10.)

   p-value: *p* [an outcome as unusual as four 7s in a row *when the dice are honest*] = *p* [7, 7, 7, 7] = .0008.

5. *Rejection decision:*

$$p < \alpha, \ .0008 < .05$$

   Reject the Stat. *H* and accept the Alt. *H* at the 95 percent level of confidence.

6. *Interpret and apply best estimates in everyday terms:*

   Conclusion: We reject that Tex is honest and conclude that he is a crook. It is highly unlikely that an honest pair of dice would come up four 7s. *Best estimate:* We can estimate that his dice produce an unusually high number of 7s.

Remember. All hypotheses tests follow the same logic as this one. If you begin to lose sight of the logic, refer back to this simple, straightforward example.

The Hypothetical Framework of Hypothesis Testing

Again, the word *hypothetical* means "let us imagine for the moment." Note that in steps 1 through 4 of the six steps of statistical inference, we make hypothetical or "if this is true" statements. In step 1 we state the statistical hypothesis "Imagine for the moment that Tex is honest." We do not assert that he is honest and in fact suspect the opposite. We simply imagine that this statistical hypothesis is true for the moment. In other words, we hypothesize.

In step 2 we continue to hypothesize by predicting sampling outcomes for "when the statistical hypothesis is true," when the dice and the person rolling them are honest. Tex may or may not be honest, but we describe what happens *if he is*, because this is a way for us to make mathematical predictions. Knowledge of the workings of honest dice provides us with a basis of comparison. The sampling distribution—which is hypothetical because we do not roll the dice an infinite number of times—provides a measuring stick against which to compare Tex's dice-rolling behavior.

In step 3 we state how unusual a sampling outcome must be, *when the statistical hypothesis is true*, for us to reject it. In step 4 we compute the probability of our sampling outcome *under the condition that the statistical hypothesis is true*. In other words, our calculation of Tex's four rolls of the dice is made on the basis of how honest dice behave. In each of the first four steps of the inference process, we do not assert that the statistical hypothesis *is* true but simply describe how the data should appear *if* the dice are honest ones. All four of these steps are imaginary in the sense that we use our statistical knowledge and imagination to foresee what happens in the natural world *if* the statistical hypothesis is true. Only in step 5 do we firm up a decision and decide what we really believe is true: the statistical hypothesis or the alternative. In testing a hypothesis, we say in each of steps 1 through 4: "Hold this thought. If the statistical hypothesis is true, here is what happens in repeated sampling."

Understanding the Place of Probability Theory in Hypothesis Testing

You should be convinced by now that computing probabilities is the essential mathematical operation in hypothesis testing. Note that in the six steps of statistical inference (Table 9–2) we discussed "probability" many times. First, in step 2, the sampling distribution is a prediction of all possible sampling outcomes and the probability of each outcome when the statistical hypothesis (from step 1) is imagined to be true. Second, in step 3, we set the level of significance (α), the critical probability level that may lead us to reject the statistical hypothesis. Third, in step 4, we compute the probability of our actual sampling outcome, still imagining that the statistical hypothesis is true. In step 5, we compare two probabilities: the one computed in step 4 and the one stated in step 3. This comparison leads us to a conclusion: We either reject the statistical hypothesis and accept the alternative hypothesis, or we "fail to reject" the statistical hypothesis and let it stand. *If you begin to lose sight of what hypothesis testing is about, remember that it is based on comparing two probabilities: that of what actually occurs in our single observed sample and that of what we expect to occur in repeated sampling.*

In the case of Tex the gambler, our ability to determine his crookedness depends on knowing the probabilities for a roll of two dice. For this introduction to hypothesis testing we purposely used a simple computation of a *p*-value. Other statistical tests of hypotheses require different sampling distributions and mathematical computations. For most statistical tests, the test statistic is a *t*-score or a similar formulation that measures probabilities on an approximately normal curve. The *p*-values are taken from the statistical tables in Appendix B.

A Focus on p-*Values*

In step 4, we compute *p* [of a sampling outcome as unusual as or more unusual than the one observed *assuming that Stat. H is true*]. This probability is called the *p*-value of the hypothesis test. The **p-value of a hypothesis test** is *a measurement of the unusualness of a sample outcome when the statistical hypothesis is true.*

The *p*-Value of a Hypothesis Test

A measurement of the unusualness of a sample outcome when the statistical hypothesis is true.

The *p*-value tells us how often in repeated sampling we are likely to obtain the observed difference between the "observed sampling outcome" and the "expected sampling outcomes." Again, *the difference between what is observed and what is expected* is called the **effect of the hypothesis test.** The hypothesis test hinges on deciding whether this effect is a real one that is significant and meaningful or is simply the result of sampling error. In step 5, the magnitude of the *p*-value determines whether we will accept the statistical hypothesis or reject it.

The Effect of a Hypothesis Test

The difference between what is observed in the sample (in step 4) and what is hypothesized (in step 1).

Understanding *p*-values is essential for grasping the logic of hypothesis testing. Let us apply some proportional thinking by asking these questions: What happens as the magnitude of a *p*-value increases? What does it mean when the *p*-value calculates small or large?

When the *p*-Value Is Large Relative to Alpha, That Is, When $p > \alpha$, We Do Not Reject the Statistical Hypothesis.   A large *p*-value tells us that our observed sample outcome is not much different or "far off" from the outcome predicted by the statistical hypothesis; in other words, the test effect is small. For example, suppose we hypothesize that the mean age of university students is 23 years. If this is true, the mean age of a sufficiently large, representative sample will calculate very close to 23 years. Suppose that we actually draw a sample and it has a mean age of 22.8 years. Our experience generating sampling distributions suggests that this small test effect—a difference of only .2 year—could very well be the result of normal sampling error. A sample mean so close to 23 is not an unusual outcome; it would have a high probability of occurrence if we were sampling repeatedly. The *p*-value measures this probability. When there is a small difference between the observed value of the statistic in step 4 and the value of a statistic as predicted by the statistical hypothesis in step 1, precise calculation of the probability of this outcome will produce a large *p*-value. This large *p*-value says: If the mean age of the population is 23, there is a good probability that a sample mean will be within .2 year of 23. A .2-year effect is not enough to reject the notion that 23 years is the mean age of the population. In scientific lingo we say: There is not "a statistically significant difference" between what is observed and what is hypothesized. The difference easily could have resulted from normal sampling error.

When the *p*-Value is Small Relative to Alpha, That is, When $p < \alpha$, We Reject the Statistical Hypothesis.   A small *p*-value tells us that *assuming* the statistical hypothesis is true, our sample outcome is unusual or "far off" from what we would expect. This large gap (or effect) suggests that the assumption of a true statistical hypothesis is wrong and should be rejected. For example, suppose that at a second university researchers hypothesize that the mean age of the student body is 23 years. They draw a sufficiently large, representative sample and calculate a mean of 29.3 years. This test effect is large (6.3 years), but the *p*-value will be small. The small *p*-value tells them: It is very unusual to draw a sample with a mean of 29.3 years from a population whose mean is 23, just as it is unusual to roll four consecutive 7s with an honest pair of dice. If this *p*-value is particularly small, that is, less than α, they no longer will accept 23 years as a reasonable estimate of the mean age of the university's student body. Their experience with repeated sampling and generating sampling distributions tells them that such a large test effect is unusual. The statistical hypothesis of 23 years will be rejected. Small *p*-values occur when the sample observation does not reasonably fit the hypothesized parameter. Recall the simple illustration. When no clouds are observed, reject the hypothesis that it will rain soon. The probability (or *p*-value) of getting rain from a cloudless sky is surely small, and so the hypothesis of rain is rejected.

In summary, there is an inverse relationship between the size of a test effect and its computed *p*-value; that is:

A small test effect $\longrightarrow$ A large *p*-value (in step 4)

(i.e., a small difference between the observed sampling outcome in step 4 and the hypothesized outcome of step 1)

(i.e., when the statistical hypothesis is true, there is a great chance that observed and expected outcomes will coincide; thus, in step 5 we probably will "fail to reject" the statistical hypothesis)

A large test effect $\longrightarrow$ A small *p*-value (in step 4)

(i.e., a large difference between the observed sampling outcome in step 4 and the hypothesized outcome of step 1)

(i.e., when the statistical hypothesis is true, a large difference between observed and expected outcomes is unusual; thus, in step 5 we probably will "reject" the idea that the statistical hypothesis is true)

The Relationships among Effect Size, *p*-Values, and Rejection Decisions

A small test effect $\longrightarrow$ a large *p*-value $\longrightarrow$ "fail to reject" the Stat. *H*

A large test effect $\longrightarrow$ a small *p*-value $\longrightarrow$ "reject" the Stat. *H*

The Meaning of "As Unusual As or More Unusual Than."   In step 4 of Table 9–2, the *p*-value is defined as the probability (*p*) of sampling outcomes *as unusual as or more unusual than* the outcome observed under the assumption that the statistical hypothesis is true. The word *or* is a cue for using the addition rule of probability, and what we do is add the probabilities. For simplicity, we did not follow this rule completely in the Tex the gambler example, although our conclusion would have been the same. If we had followed this rule, we would have added the probability of all consecutive rolls that had a lower probability of occurring than did the four 7s. For example, we would have summed the probability of rolling five 7s, six 7s, seven 7s, and so on, because each of these outcomes would have been more unusual than a roll of four 7s. Why include probabilities that are "more unusual"? Because if we are to call Tex a crook for rolling four 7s, we would surely do the same if he rolled five or more consecutive 7s. This is the case because the probabilities of these events are even lower than that of four 7s. In all remaining hypotheses tests we will compute the sum of all outcomes as unusual as or more unusual than the one observed. In Chapter 10 we will see that this simply involves computing areas in the tails of probability curves, as we did with the normal curve in Chapter 6.

The Level of Significance

How small does a *p*-value have to be before we reject the statistical hypothesis? This is where step 3 of the six steps of statistical inference comes into play: the stipulation of the level of significance, α. In simple terms, the **level of significance** is *the critical probability point at which we are no longer willing to say that our sample outcome resulted from random sampling error.* It states how extreme a sampling outcome must be before we begin to question whether the statistical hypothesis is true. For example, with our dice-rolling character Tex, do we call him a crook after he rolls two 7s in a row (p [7, 7] = .0278), three 7s in a row (p [7,7,7] = .0046), four 7s in a row (p [7, 7, 7, 7] = .0008), and so on? Just how unlikely and unusual does his "sampling event" have to be before we reject the hypothesis that he is using honest dice?

The Function of the Level of Significance in a Hypothesis Test

Specifies the critical probability point at which we are no longer willing to say that our sample outcome resulted from random sampling error.

We have referred to α-probabilities as critical regions. A critical region is an area of a probability curve that defines the point of likelihood where we become critical of the truth of the hypothesis. When the *p*-value is so small that it is equal to or less than α, we reject the statistical hypothesis.

The term *significance* implies that the α-probability level is a meaningful point. When we reject the statistical hypothesis, we say that there is a "statistically significant difference" between what we observed and what we hypothesized. This difference (or effect) is so large that we no longer believe that the statistical hypothesis is true. The difference between what Tex did and what honest dice do is so great that it signifies something—it throws up a red flag. We can no longer accept that his dice are honest; four 7s in a row are not likely to occur by chance.

It is essential that we decide how critical we are going to be *before* making our sample observation. That is, we must set α in step 3, before we look at the sample data (step 4). Why? If we waited until after we observed the sample outcome in step 4, we could set α to a level slightly larger than the computed *p*-value, and this would assure us of rejecting the statistical hypothesis. If we waited until after step 4, we could rig the hypothesis test to obtain the result we desire. For instance, suppose we do not like the way Tex dresses and want to teach him a lesson. We could frame him by making sure that we reject the hypothesis that he is honest. We would simply wait until he rolls the dice four times, calculate the *p*-value, and then pick a slightly larger α-value. Upon "finding" $p < \alpha$, we would reject the statistical hypothesis. From the standpoint of scientific integrity, however, this would be cheating. It would allow personal bias to enter into the scientific process. And aside from scientific integrity, this would be dishonest. We would become the con artists, and it would be we, not Tex, who should go to jail.

In analyzing data, it is tempting to peek at the results before setting the level of significance. In the world of scientific research, getting the results we desire may support the arguments of our theory, lead to publications in reputable journals, and make us famous. In the business world, getting the results we desire may enhance our status with the boss (by showing, for example, that there was a statistically significant increase in company profits). In political polling, getting the results we desire may sway undecided voters. Indeed, statistical analysis can be manipulated by setting an advantageous α level. But do not be tempted! Properly trained professional scientists view data tampering as unethical. Furthermore, as we discussed in Chapter 1, the scientific research process has checks and balances (such as blind reviews of journal article submissions) to catch unethical or careless behavior. These checks and balances minimize not only human error but also human vanity.

Another reason for setting α before looking at our sample data is that we want to be able to say exactly how confident we are in our conclusion. Our level of significance allows us to do so in precise mathematical terms. Recall from Chapter 8 that the level of significance and the level of confidence are inversely related. The lower the level of significance (or expected error), the greater the level of confidence. It is important to understand that unless we look at every subject in a population and compute the *parameter* for our variable, we can never be 100 percent confident in our conclusion. In other words, conclusions based on sample statistics are merely estimates of parameters. There is expected error for any conclusion based on a sample. We concluded that Tex was dishonest on the basis of a mere four rolls of the dice. There was a chance that we made a mistake, because we cannot be absolutely sure that he was not simply lucky. Unusual events do occur. Some unfortunate individuals are struck by lightning (the author of this book being one of them). Some lucky bloke wins the state lottery. We must decide beforehand what we consider "unusual," and this decision should be based on scientific procedures, not personal prejudices.

Choosing the Level of Significance.   It is in step 3 of the six steps of statistical inference that we set the level of significance, α. We come back to α in step 5, where we make the "rejection decision" by comparing the p-value to α. When $p < \alpha$, we reject the statistical hypothesis; when $p > \alpha$, we fail to reject the statistical hypothesis. As we noted above, unless we observe the entire population, our results are only estimates and the rejection decision and the conclusions made from it may be wrong. Any sampling-based conclusions have expected error, as we saw in Chapter 8, where we referred to α as expected error. We call this an error rather than a mistake because we are able to stipulate its chances of occurrence precisely. Setting the level of significance allows us to control the chances of making a wrong decision or "error."

TABLE 9–3   **Possible Results of Rejection Decisions**

	The Unknown Truth about Parameters	
Our Rejection Decision	*When the Stat. H Is Actually True*	*When the Stat. H Is Actually False*
We reject the Stat. *H*	Type I error	Correct decision
We fail to reject the Stat. *H*	Correct decision	Type II error

---

Table 9–3 depicts the relationship between true outcomes and the rejection decision and reveals four possible occurrences. Keep in mind that we will never know whether the statistical hypothesis is true or false *unless we "sample" the entire population and get the true parameter.* We conduct a statistical test with the knowledge that we may draw a wrong conclusion.

Although we will never know for sure when we do it, when we reject the statistical hypothesis when it is false, we have made the correct decision. Similarly, when we fail to reject the statistical hypothesis when it is true, we have made the correct decision. However, when we *reject a true statistical hypothesis,* we make a **type I error.** In any test where we reject the statistical hypothesis, there is a chance that we should not have rejected it. For example, could it be that Tex was simply lucky? Similarly, in any hypothesis test where we fail to reject the statistical hypothesis, there is a chance that we should have rejected it. This is a matter of *failing to reject a false statistical hypothesis,* and we call this error a **type II error.** This would have been the case of concluding that Tex was honest when in fact he was not.

We will never know for sure whether we made the correct decision or made an error. We can, however, manage and control the magnitude of such errors in a number of ways. First, if we reject the statistical hypothesis, we could not have made a type II error because a type II error involves *not* rejecting a hypothesis. Similarly, when we fail to reject the statistical hypothesis, we know we could not have made a type I error because this error involves *rejecting* a hypothesis. Second, we can easily control the amount of type I error we are willing to chance. This is the case because the level of significance α, which we set at our own discretion, is the probability of making a type I error. Thus,

$$\alpha = p \text{ [of making a type I error]}$$

Again, the statistical hypothesis is rejected when the *p*-value from step 4 is small. If we had chosen to set α low (say, .001), we would have made it difficult to reject the statistical hypothesis because the *p*-value would have had to be very small to "get under" .001. By making the statistical hypothesis difficult to reject at all, we make it difficult to reject in error. Thus, when we set α low, we reduce the chance of a type I error—of rejecting the statistical hypothesis when in fact it is true.

By contrast, if we choose to set α high (say, .10), we make it easier to reject the statistical hypothesis because the *p*-value from step 4 would not have had to compute very small to be less than an α of .10. By making it easy to reject the statistical hypothesis, we reduce the chance of making the mistake of not rejecting it when it is false (i.e., we reduce the chance of making a type II error).

We use the Greek symbol *beta* to signify the probability of a type II error. Thus,

$$\beta = p \text{ [of making a type II error]}$$

Unfortunately, controlling β is very difficult. Setting α is possible because it is based on the expected distribution of outcomes described by the sampling distribution—when the statistical hypothesis is true. Beta, however, depends on the statistical hypothesis being false. Since a hypothesis can be false in any number of ways, we have no easy mathematical basis for calculating the probabilities of these false outcomes. We can, however, indirectly control β when we set our alpha level. This is because α and β are inversely related; that is, as α increases, β must necessarily decrease, and vice versa. Although we typically do not calculate β, we know that when α is set high, this makes it easier to reject the statistical hypothesis. This lessens the chance of failing to reject it at all and therefore lessens the chance of failing to reject it *when it is false*.

Type I Error

Unknowingly making the incorrect decision of rejecting a true statistical hypothesis.

$$\alpha = p \text{ [of making a type I error]}$$

Type II Error

Unknowingly making the incorrect decision of failing to reject a false statistical hypothesis.

$$\beta = p \text{ [of making a type II error]}$$

Again, it is α, the level of significance, that we set. Deciding on its value is not troublesome, however, because scientists in a particular field follow conventions (traditions) that are based on the types of questions being studied and on what other scientists will accept. The four conventional α levels are presented in Table 9–4, which shows the relationship between these levels and the likelihood of rejecting a statistical hypothesis. The level of significance (α) should be set low when the consequences of a type I error are serious. For

TABLE 9–4   **Conventional Levels of Significance and the Likelihood of Rejecting a Statistical Hypothesis (Stat. *H*)**

Likelihood of Rejecting the Stat. H	Level of Significance* (α)	Typical Uses
High	.10	Exploratory research, where little is known about a topic.
Moderate	.05 and .01	Conventional levels in survey research and psychometric and educational assessment instruments.
Low	.01 and .001	Conventional levels in biological, laboratory, and medical research, especially when a type I error is life-threatening (such as testing the toxicity of drugs).

*These conventional levels apply to bivariate statistical analysis. In multivariate statistical modeling such as LISREL, model fit may be tested with an α set as high as .5. Such analysis is beyond the scope of this text.

instance, if our statistical hypothesis is that a new prescription drug is toxic (i.e., poisonous), we do not want to reject this hypothesis prematurely and make a type I error. Thus, we would set α low (say, .001). This would require strong evidence that the drug was safe before we would reject its toxicity. In social survey research the conventional α-level is .05, a moderate level. Unless you have a good reason to do otherwise, follow this convention.

The Level of Confidence

When we reject the statistical hypothesis at, say, the .05 level of significance, we have essentially decided that we are willing to take a 5 percent chance of rejecting the statistical hypothesis when it is in fact true. For example, we set α at .05 when we tested the hypothesis that Tex was honest. We rejected this and called him a crook, but we will never know for sure (he took his dice with him and got away). There was a 5 percent chance that he was simply very lucky and that we falsely accused him. But by the same token, there was a 95 percent chance that we made the correct decision and did not falsely reject his honesty. We call this the **level of confidence,** *the confidence we have that we did not make a type I error,* and it is equal to $1 - \alpha$.

The Level of Confidence

Level of confidence = 1 − level of significance = $1 - \alpha$

A .05 level of significance corresponds to a 95 percent level of confidence. Similarly, a .01 level of significance corresponds to a 99 percent level of confidence, and so on.

We defined these terms in Chapter 8 with regard to confidence intervals.

The mathematical properties are the same here. The level of confidence and the level of significance (or expected sampling error) are statements about the confidence we have in our sampling and statistical procedures. At the .05 level of *significance* we are asserting that *if the statistical hypothesis is actually true* and we conduct our procedures 100 times, we will *incorrectly* reject this true statistical hypothesis only 5 times. Therefore, we will make the correct decision 95 times. Thus, we are 95 percent confident in the conclusion we draw from this single hypothesis-testing procedure. Our level of confidence is inversely related to the chance we take of making a type I error. The less chance we take of rejecting the statistical hypothesis (i.e., the lower we set α), the more confident we are in our conclusion *when we do happen to reject it.*

The only time we have 100 percent confidence in a conclusion is when every subject in a population is observed. In this uncommon situation, the resulting computations are not estimates (i.e., statistics) but actual parameters. Also, sampling error is not an issue; that is, we have a zero probability of sampling error. For example, the records office of Crosstown University may use computerized records to provide an exact mean grade point average of its current student body, the actual population parameter. In most research, such as a telephone survey of households in the United States, we do not have access to every observation for a population. Fortunately, our ability to manage and control sampling error makes it unnecessary to spend large sums of money surveying entire populations.

Test Direction: One-Tailed and Two-Tailed Tests

Another thing that influences the size of the *p*-value, and therefore the likelihood of rejecting the statistical hypothesis, is whether we are able to predict in which *direction* our observed sample statistic will fall. That is, will the sample observation fall above or below the hypothesized parameter? For example, suppose we suspect that the mean American College Testing Corporation (ACT) admissions test score for State University students is higher than the national average of 21 because this school is very selective toward its applicants. In other words, we are predicting an outcome that is greater than the national average and in the positive direction. We must, however, state the statistical hypothesis as "equal to" the national average of 21 so that a sampling distribution may be predicted. Fortunately, we can add information on direction of outcome in the second part of step 1 of the six steps of statistical inference, the statement of the *alternative hypothesis*. Specifically, where X = ACT score and μ_X = the hypothesized mean of X for the population of State University:

Step 1: *Stat. H:* $\qquad \mu_{X \text{ (State University)}} = 21$

$\qquad\qquad$ *Alt. H:* $\qquad \mu_{X \text{ (State University)}} > 21$, one-tailed

We call this a one-tailed test because, as we shall see in subsequent chapters, the *p*-value for it will be computed using only one side (or tail) of the sampling distribution curve. For a hypothesis test such as this, there are actually three options for stating the alternative hypothesis.

Use Only One of These Three Options to State the Alternative Hypothesis:

  Option 1: We are asked to determine if State University's mean ACT score is *no different* from 21. We have no reason to assume beforehand whether it might be greater or lesser than 21. This is called a nondirectional test or a two-tailed test, and step 1 of our six steps of statistical inference would go as follows:

Step 1: *Stat. H:* $\mu_{X \text{ (State University)}} = 21$

   Alt. H: $\mu_{X \text{ (State University)}} \neq 21$, two-tailed

  Option 2: We are asked to determine if State University's mean ACT score is *greater than* 21. We have reason to believe beforehand that State University's students do better than the national average of 21. For example, perhaps we are aware that the university's admissions policies are tough and that it requires a high ACT score to get in. This is called a positive directional test, or a one-tailed test in the positive direction:

Step 1: *Stat. H:* $\mu_{X \text{ (State University)}} = 21$

   Alt. H: $\mu_{X \text{ (State University)}} > 21$, one-tailed

  Option 3: We are asked to determine if State University's mean ACT score is *less than* 21. We have reason to believe beforehand that State University's students do worse than the national average of 21. For example, perhaps we are aware that the university's admissions policies are not very tough and thus lots of applicants are admitted with relatively low ACT scores. This is called a negative directional test, or a one-tailed test in the negative direction:

Step 1: *Stat. H:* $\mu_{X \text{ (State University)}} = 21$

   Alt. H: $\mu_{X \text{ (State University)}} < 21$, one-tailed

Again, these are three options. We would use only one of them in a single hypothesis test.

Why Must Direction Be Stipulated before We Observe Data?   Direction is specified in step 1 of the six steps of statistical inference. As we will demonstrate later, it is easier to reject the statistical hypothesis with a one-tailed test. Most of the time, rejecting the statistical hypothesis and accepting the alternative hypothesis constitute the outcome that supports our theory. Using a one-tailed test, then, loads the procedure in our favor. Therefore, to avoid being accused of rigging our statistics, we must provide justification for using a one-tailed test and must make this decision independent of observing data (in step 4). Accordingly, we choose one of the three options prior to step 4. By no means do we look ahead to step 4 to determine the direction of our test.

When to Use a One-Tailed Test.   How, then, do we know whether to state the alternative hypothesis as a one-tailed or two-tailed test? This is a matter of deciphering the research question. In scientific research, a theory usually provides justification for a one-tailed test. For example, in a study of gender inequality in industry, the theoretical argument is that women are likely to suffer discrimination in pay levels and promotions. This is backed up by previous research findings. It would make sense, then, to state our research question as: Are women, compared to men of the same rank and time in service, being paid *less?* Perhaps we know that the mean annual salary of men is $31,000. Our theory tells us that if women truly suffer discrimination, their annual salaries will average *less than* $31,000. These conceptual arguments justify the advantage of a one-tailed test.

Direction is always stated in the alternative hypothesis. In this gender equity case, the research question would be: Is the mean annual salary of women less than $31,000? a prediction in the negative direction. While this expectation is stated in the alternative hypothesis, the statistical hypothesis *must be* stated as "equal to $31,000," because only this statement tells us what to expect of the sampling outcomes. The hypothesis test proceeds with a focus on whether the statistical hypothesis is true. Therefore, we project that the mean annual salary of *a sample* of women will fall around $31,000 within a computed range of error of, say, plus or minus $500. We could not state "less than $31,000" as the statistical hypothesis because if the mean of the population of women is indeed less than $30,000, what is it—$29,000, $28,000, $20,000? We do not know and cannot say what the alternative parameter is until the hypothesized parameter of $31,000 is ruled out. Just saying "less than" does not provide enough information to describe the sampling distribution in step 2. Thus, the direction "less than" is stated in the alternative hypothesis.

To establish the direction of a statistical test, examine the research question closely. If there are positive directional words (*greater than, more than, increase, heavier than, larger than, faster, gain*), a positive one-tailed test is in order. If there are negative directional words (*less than, decrease, lost, shorter than, slower than*), a negative one-tailed test is in order. Of course, when there is no stipulation of direction, we use a two-tailed test.

Deciding on the Direction of a Hypothesis Test: State the Alternative Hypothesis in One of Three Ways

1. One-tailed in the positive direction
Content of research question includes terms such as *greater than, more, increase, faster, heavier,* and *gain.*   ⟶   Use a positive one-tailed test in the alternative hypothesis and a $>$ sign.

2. One-tailed in the negative direction
Content of research question includes terms such as *less than, fewer, decrease, slower, lighter,* and *loss.*   ⟶   Use a negative one-tailed test in the alternative hypothesis and a $<$ sign.

3. Two-tailed, nondirectional
Content of research question includes no statements about direction or simply asserts inequality.   ⟶   Use a neutral two-tailed test in the alternative hypothesis and a $\neq$ sign.

Selecting Which Statistical Test to Use

How do we know the correct statistical formulas for a particular problem? The most difficult part of hypothesis testing is correctly stating the statistical hypothesis and choosing the proper sampling distributions and statistical formulas. These tasks are made easier if a systematic set of criteria are followed in making the choices. These criteria are presented in Table 9–5.

While each one of these criteria is important in determining the type of test to use, criterion 2 is especially useful. You may want to review the four

---

TABLE 9–5 Criteria for the Selection of a Statistical Test

---

1. Ask: How many variables are we observing for this test?
2. Ask: What are the levels of measurement of the variables? That is, are the variables nominal/ordinal (for calculating counts and proportions) or interval/ratio (for calculating means)?
3. Ask: Are we dealing with one representative sample from a single population or more?
4. Ask: What is the sample size, and/or how many degrees of freedom are available for the test?
5. Ask: Are there peculiar circumstances to consider?

---

levels of measurement (Chapter 2). One helpful point to remember is that the mean, deviation scores, variance, and standard deviation are computed only for interval/ratio or interval-like ordinal variables. Thus, statistical tests for these variables often carry the name *means test, differences of means,* or *analysis of variance.* In contrast, nominal/ordinal level variables typically involve counting frequencies, percentages, or proportions of cases in categories and often carry the name *proportions test* or *test of differences in rank.*

This basic statistics course covers the following statistical tests:

1. A "single-sample means test" or "*t*-test" (Chapter 10). This applies to a single interval/ratio or interval-like ordinal variable from one sample. For example, with a sample of 100 students, is the mean ACT score for entering Crosstown University students equal to the national average of 21? The sampling distribution is the approximately normal *t*-distribution with $df = n - 1$.

2. A "large single-sample proportions test" (Chapter 10). This applies to a single nominal/ordinal variable for a single sample, where $P = p$ [of a success category]. For example, is the proportion of females in medical schools equal to the proportion of females in the general population of the United States (52 percent)? A sample is sufficiently large if the smaller of P_u and Q_u times n is greater than or equal to 5 (i.e., $[(p_{smaller})(n)] \geq 5$ from Chapter 8). The sampling distribution is the approximately normal *t*-distribution with $df = \infty$.

3. A "small single-sample proportions test" or "binomial distribution test" (Chapter 13). This applies to a single dichotomous (i.e., two-category) nominal/ordinal variable for a single sample when $[(p_{smaller})(n)] < 5$. For example, is the proportion of females on a seven-member county commission equal to the proportion of females in the general population of the county (54 percent)? The sampling distribution is called the *binomial distribution.*

4. A "two-group difference of means test" (Chapter 11). This applies to two similar situations. The first is an interval/ratio or interval-like ordinal variable compared for two groups from different populations, such as, Is the mean GPA of Crosstown University students equal to that of State University students? The second is an interval/ratio or interval-like ordinal variable compared for two categories of a nominal/ordinal variable for a single sample and population, such as, For the students at Crosstown University is there a difference in the mean GPAs of men and women? In these tests, the focus is on the mean of the interval/ratio variable, which is typically the dependent variable. The sampling distribution is the approximately normal *t*-distribution.

5. An "analysis of variance" test of differences of means among three or more groups (Chapter 12). This is an extension of the two-group difference of means test (test number 4, above). Here we compare means for either (*a*) three or more samples from different populations

or (*b*) within a single sample, three or more groups of a nominal/ordinal variable, such as the nominal variable school of major, with categories arts and sciences, education, engineering, and so forth. For example, do the mean GPAs differ among Crosstown University, State University, and Uptown Community College? Or is there a difference in mean GPA by school of major at Crosstown University? The sampling distribution is called the *F*-distribution.

6. A "chi-square test" of a relationship between two nominal variables (Chapter 13). For example, is there a relationship between religious preference (Catholic, Protestant, Jewish, Other) and attitude toward abortion (pro-life, pro-choice, undecided)? The sampling distribution is called the chi-square distribution.

7. A "simple linear correlation" test of the relationship between two interval/ratio or interval-like ordinal variables (Chapters 14 and 15). For example, among college students, is there a correlation between high school GPAs and college GPAs? In other words, is high school GPA a good predictor of college GPA? The sampling distribution is the approximately normal *t*-distribution.

8. A "Spearman's rho rank-order correlation test" of the relationship between two ordinal variables (Chapter 16). For example, is there a relationship between high school class rank and order of finish in the schoolwide debating competition? In other words, did the top students in the class place at the top in that competition? The sampling distribution is called the Spearman's rho distribution.

9. A "gamma coefficient rank-order correlation test" of the relationship between two ordinal variables with few ranks (such as low, medium, and high) and many sample subjects in each of those ranks (Chapter 16). The sampling distribution is the normal distribution.

Table 9–6 provides a guide to assist in the selection of the appropriate test and formula.

Study Hints

The remaining chapters describe procedures for the hypothesis tests described above. Look through those chapters and notice the similarities and differences among the tests. All follow the logic of statistical inference. It would be wise to memorize the six steps in Table 9–2 now so that confusion about their wording will not get in the way of your understanding.

As you look through those chapters, note in the examples that the selection of a test depends especially on the level of measurement of variables. If you are still struggling with distinguishing levels of measurement, review that topic in Chapter 2.

Note also that for each hypothesis test, we deal with two probabilities: the α stipulated in step 3 and the *p*-value (the *p* [of sampling outcomes as unusual

TABLE 9–6   Statistical Tests, Their Applications, and Their Formulas

Name of Test	Test Statistic	No. Samples	Sample Size/ Degrees of Freedom	No., Type, and Level of Measurement of Variables	Peculiarities or Assumptions
Single-sample means test (Chapter 10)	$t_{\bar{X}} = \dfrac{\bar{X} - \mu_X}{s_{\bar{X}}}$	1	$df = n - 1$	One interval/ratio or interval-like ordinal variable	
Large single-sample proportions test (Chapter 10)	$t_{P_s} = \dfrac{P_s - P_u}{\sigma_{P_s}}$	1	$[(p_{\text{smaller}})\,(n)] \geq 5$	One nominal/ordinal variable	
Small single-sample proportions test (Chapter 13)	Expansion of the binomial equation: $(P + Q)^n$	1	$[(p_{\text{smaller}})\,(n)] < 5$	One dichotomous (i.e., two-category) nominal variable	
Two-group difference of means test, two samples, independent groups (Chapter 11)	$t_{\bar{X}_1 - \bar{X}_2} = \dfrac{\bar{X}_1 - \bar{X}_2}{s_{\bar{X}_1 - \bar{X}_2}}$	2	When group variances are equal, $df = n_1 + n_2 - 2$	One interval/ratio or interval-like ordinal dependent variable; means are compared for the two samples (i.e., groups)	Calculation of standard error hinges on whether the two groups have equal variances.
Two-group difference of means test, one sample, independent groups (Chapter 11)	$t_{\bar{X}_1 - \bar{X}_2} = \dfrac{\bar{X}_1 - \bar{X}_2}{s_{\bar{X}_1 - \bar{X}_2}}$	1	When group variances are equal, $df = n_1 + n_2 - 2$	One dichotomous nominal or ordinal independent variable and one interval/ratio or interval-like ordinal dependent variable	Calculation of standard error hinges on whether the two groups have equal variances.
Two-group difference of means test, one sample, nonindependent, matched-pair groups (Chapter 11)	$\bar{D} = \dfrac{\Sigma D}{n}$	1	$df = n - 1$	Two interval/ratio or interval-like ordinal variables with the same score design *or* a single interval/ratio or interval-like ordinal variable measured twice for the same subjects	
Analysis of variance (difference of means test for three or more groups) (Chapter 12)	$F = \dfrac{MSV_B}{MSV_W}$	1	n not radically different from group to group	One nominal or ordinal independent variable with three or more groups and one interval/ratio or interval-like ordinal dependent variable	Assumes all groups have equal variances.

(continued)

TABLE 9–6   Statistical Tests, Their Applications, and Their Formulas (concluded)

Name of Test	Test Statistic	No. Samples	Sample Size/ Degrees of Freedom	No., Type, and Level of Measurement of Variables	Peculiarities or Assumptions
Chi-square test of association (Chapter 13)	$\chi^2 = \sum \dfrac{(O-E)^2}{E}$	1	$df = (r-1)(c-1)$	Two nominal/ordinal variables	Requires at least five cases per cell.
Simple linear correlation and regression (Chapters 14 and 15)	$t_r = r\sqrt{\dfrac{n-2}{1-r^2}}$	1	$df = n-2$	Two interval/ratio or interval-like ordinal variables	Variables must be linearly related.
Spearman's rho rank-order correlation (Chapter 16)	$r_s = 1 - \dfrac{6\sum D^2}{n(n^2-1)}$	1	$n \geq 10$	Two ordinal variables	Requires few tied ranks.
Gamma coefficient rank-order correlation (Chapter 16)	$G = \dfrac{\sum f_a - \sum f_i}{\sum f_a + \sum f_i}$	1	Not applicable	Two ordinal variables	Accommodates many tied ranks.

as or more unusual than the outcome observed when the Stat. *H* is true]) computed in step 4. Finally, an understanding of normal and approximately normal curves is essential, because similar probability curves are the sampling distributions for most of the hypothesis tests.

You should be able to work statistical problems and produce the right conclusions even if you do not completely understand all six steps of statistical inference. Keep the faith. After working enough problems, you will become familiar with the wording and procedures of each step. At some point, things will fall into place and the overall process will become apparent.

A Word on Phrasing: The Conventional Term *Null Hypothesis*

In the design of statistical hypothesis testing procedures, many texts use the term *null hypothesis* in place of *statistical hypothesis*. A null hypothesis is one that is set up to be rejected or nullified. This phrasing brings attention to the fact that for many research questions we must test an opposite or neutral hypothesis. For example, suppose we believe the men in a company are being paid more than are women of equal rank (a directional statement). Since we do not know how much more, we must test the neutral, nondirectional statement—that men and women are paid equally—and we call this nullification of the research question a null hypothesis. The popularity of this term hinges on the fact that it is a device for identifying the statistical hypothesis when it is not apparent in the research question. For instance, with Tex the gambler we found the statistical hypothesis by nullifying the question, Is Tex a crook?

Unfortunately, however, the term *null* can be confusing because it is not conceptually consistent. Nullification implies that whatever the research question, it is proved by testing an opposite or nondirectional statement when in fact nullification is not always called for. Sometimes the research question is answered in failing to reject a null hypothesis, as with testing for sample representativeness (Chapter 10). This inconsistency is troublesome. In an attempt to determine the statistical hypothesis—a truly testable one—a researcher may routinely but wrongly nullify the research question. For example, what if a research question called for deciding whether men or women *are* paid equally? We cannot use the opposite of this as a statistical hypothesis. Moreover, attempts to nullify lead to confusing double negatives. If asked: "Is Tex dishonest?" do we test "Tex is not dishonest" or "Tex is honest"? Additional confusion develops in deciding whether to nullify means to nullify a statement, nullify the test effect, or nullify (i.e., falsify) a theory—philosophical issues that muddle research efforts. Students in particular sense the inconsistencies in the term *null hypothesis,* and this leads to frustration and diminished confidence.

In contrast, calling the testable hypothesis a *statistical hypothesis* is very consistent. It applies to all statistical tests in the same way. The statistical hypothesis is one that is *always* stated in such a way that statistical outcomes can be predicted. Whether this statistical hypothesis or its alternative hypothesis answers the research question is a separate issue. Moreover, without exception, this phrasing of the statistical hypothesis focuses attention on the requirement that a statement is testable only if we are capable of projecting sample outcomes from it (i.e., a sampling distribution).

Notwithstanding the problems presented by the term *null hypothesis,* its usage is conventional. Students in this course will encounter the term frequently in later methodology and survey courses. Thus, in this text we will note when the term *null* is consistent with the term *statistical hypothesis* so that students will not be left unaware in future methodology courses.

☹   STATISTICAL FOLLIES AND FALLACIES   ☹

Informed Common Sense: Going Beyond Common Sense by Observing Data

---

In both the social and the physical world much can be learned through common sense—applying a clear reasoning process to a situation. But scientists stay in business because many of the processes of nature are not so obvious. In fact, social scientists have long established that as humans, we are prone to prejudices and simplistic falsehoods that we come to believe because common sense tells us they are true. There are many myths and superstitions about reality, especially social reality. Science and the statistical imagination with its hypothesis testing procedure encourage us to question observations more closely, weigh them against predictable outcomes, and challenge myths and prejudices.

Common sense, for instance, leads many people to conclude that women are "obviously" physically and emotionally weaker than men. Clearly, on average, men have greater upper-body strength. But physical strength has many dimensions that challenge the male dominance claim. For instance, fewer females are stillborn, and girls have a lower infant death rate and greater life expectancy. Emotional strength is also hard to pin down. Many people assume that men are emotionally stronger than women because women are quicker to cry. But then, why do men commit over 90 percent of all emotionally charged violent crimes such as assaults and murders? Does the confusion lie with cultural restraints on how men and women express emotions? How can emotional strength be measured reliably and fairly? To fully understand physical and emotional strength, we must start with a clear definition of what strength truly is. While common sense explains much of reality, a greater understanding requires astute reasoning, meaningful prediction, and accurate observation and measurement. Methodical observation extends and *informs* common sense.

This is not to say that a given scientific report is the last word on an issue. Any scientific theory is always open to further modification. Nor is it to say that scientists are above creating and adhering to their own myths. For example, much scientific research in the late 1800s supported the notion that women were innately less intelligent than men. But in science such myths tend not to stand the test of time. The scientific research process has built-in systems of check and balances that increase the opportunities for exposing myths. Hypothesis testing is a key process in separating essential facts from apparent but prejudicial facts.

Questions for Chapter 9

1. A theory (a set of ideas about how the empirical world works) motivates hypotheses (specific predictions of which observations can be expected when a theory is true). Suppose we are testing a racial discrimination theory to account for residential segregation (i.e., the tendency for a neighborhood to be occupied by a single race). In regard to the behavior of real estate agents, what hypothesis is motivated by this theory?
2. Define and distinguish theoretical and statistical purposes for testing a hypothesis. Illustrate with an example.

3. In testing a hypothesis, we determine whether observed sample effects are due to real differences in population parameters or simply are due to sampling error. Mathematically, what two things must we predict in order to begin such a test?

4. Do we reject a statistical hypothesis when the *p*-value is large or small? Explain.

5. What is the relationship between the size of the effect of a statistical test and the *p*-value calculated for that test? Illustrate with an example.

6. In plain language, what is the level of significance of a hypothesis test and what is its function in the test?

7. Match the following:

    a. Type I error   _____ *p* [type I error]
    b. Type II error   _____ Rejecting the Stat. *H* when in fact it is
                                                         true
    c. Alpha (α)   _____ *p* [type II error]
    d. Beta (β)   _____ Failing to reject the Stat. *H* when in fact it
                                                        is false

8. A sampling distribution is hypothetical. What does this mean?

9. We use means tests for variables with what levels of measurement?

10. We use proportions tests for variables with what levels of measurement?

11. We use rank-order tests for variables of what level of measurement?

12. Why must we choose the level of significance before observing the statistical outcomes from our sample?

13. List the six steps of statistical inference.

14. List the criteria for the selection of a statistical test.

15. Now that you know the sampling distribution for the roll of a pair of dice (Table 9–1), use your statistical imagination to improve your strategy for the board game Monopoly. (You may wish to inspect the actual game to answer these questions.)

    a. Winning the game hinges on owning the more valuable properties and frequently collecting rent on them. Given this, if you could choose to own one color of properties (or streets) to start the game, what color would you choose? Why?

    b. What is the most foolish thing a player just sent to jail can do on the next turn if he or she does not own the purple or orange properties?

    c. The four railroads do not pay very much rent and thus often are not worth purchasing and holding. However, there are circumstances when it is advantageous to own them. When would this be? *Hint:* The addition rule of probability is helpful here.

Exercises for Chapter 9

1. Practice the art of identifying statistical hypotheses and conceiving of sampling distributions. In general terms, predict what sample outcomes may be expected to occur with repeated sampling when the following statistical hypotheses (Stat. *H*) are true (a review of Chapter 7 may be helpful).

    a. Stat. *H*: The mean age of students on campus is 21 years.
    b. Stat. *H*: Among the Fortune 500 corporations, the percentage of corporate board members that is female is only 20 percent.
    c. Stat. *H*: The mean weight of Lot-O-Chocolate candy bars is .75 ounces.
    d. Stat. *H*: The instructor is not biased toward men or women in awarding A's.

2. Practice the art of identifying statistical hypotheses and conceiving of sampling distributions. In general terms, predict what sample outcomes may be expected to occur with repeated sampling when the following statistical hypotheses (Stat. *H*) are true (a review of Chapter 7 may be helpful).

    a. Stat. *H*: Half the television-viewing public watches a network nightly news program.
    b. Stat. *H*: The mean speed of automobiles on the death alley stretch of the interstate is 80 miles per hour.
    c. Stat. *H*: Forty percent of high school seniors have illegally consumed alcohol.
    d. Stat. *H*: The mean age of corporate vice presidents is 49 years.

3. A research question is a project goal that can be stated in terms of a hypothesis. Practice the art of determining whether each of the following research questions will constitute the statistical hypothesis (Stat. *H*) or the alternative hypothesis (Alt. *H*). Explain your answer.

    a. On average, do the drivers on the death alley stretch of the interstate exceed the speed limit of 70 miles per hour?
    b. Using a sample of 30 of the 125 players, is the average weight of this year's football team the same as last year's, which was 224 pounds?
    c. Does this casino use loaded dice?

4. A research question is a project goal that can be stated in terms of a hypothesis. Practice the art of determining whether each of the following research questions will constitute the statistical hypothesis (Stat. *H*) or the alternative hypothesis (Alt. *H*). Explain your answer.

    a. On average there are over six acts of violence per week in every prime-time television drama series.

      b. On a bet, Elbert just flipped 10 coins and got all heads. Are his coins double-headed?

      c. Is the stereotype true that over 90 percent of homeless persons are addicted to alcohol or drugs?

5. The direction and sign of a hypothesis test are specified in the alternative hypothesis. Decide whether the following alternative hypotheses (Alt. *H*) are one-tailed in the positive direction, one-tailed in the negative direction, or two-tailed nondirectional. Also, indicate the mathematical sign and explain your choice.

      a. Alt. *H*: Over 50 percent of lung cancer victims are or have been smokers.

      b. Alt. *H*: The mean grade point average of male and female students is not the same.

      c. Alt. *H*: In the central city school district less than 60 percent of high school graduates go on to college.

6. The direction and sign of a hypothesis test are specified in the alternative hypothesis. Decide whether the following alternative hypotheses (Alt. *H*) are one-tailed in the positive direction, one-tailed in the negative direction, or two-tailed nondirectional. Also, indicate the mathematical sign and explain your choice.

      a. Alt. *H*: Over 80 percent of county jail inmates are imprisoned on drug-related charges.

      b. Alt. *H*: For the new drug Fixitall, the cure rate of the experimental group that received the drug is higher than that of the control group that received a placebo (i.e., a sugar pill).

      c. Alt. *H*: The percentages of Baptists and Methodists that believe that the Bible is free of errors is not the same.

7. Professor Smith is studying gender inequality in a large communications firm. On the basis of past experience and theories from the literature, she has reason to believe that the firm's women have a mean income below that of men. In the Stat. *H* she hypothesizes that the mean incomes of men and women are equal.

      a. Why does she state the Stat. *H* that way instead of saying that the mean for men is higher?

      b. In the Alt. *H*, should she use a one-tailed or a two-tailed test? Why?

      c. In step 3 of the test she states a level of significance (α) of .05. In step 4 of the test she computes a *p*-value of .03. In step 5 will she reject the Stat. *H* or fail to reject it?

8. In a study of work patterns among attorneys, a researcher hypothesizes that those specializing in corporate law work more hours per week than do those specializing in estate law. In the Stat. *H*, the researcher

hypothesizes that the mean number of hours worked per week for the two groups is equal.

    a. Why does she state the Stat. *H* that way instead of saying that the mean for corporate lawyers is higher?

    b. In the Alt. *H*, should she use a one-tailed or a two-tailed test? Why?

    c. In step 3 of the test she states a level of significance (α) of .05. In step 4 of the test she computes a *p*-value of .23. In step 5 will she reject the Stat. *H* or fail to reject it?

9. This exercise will familiarize you with the relationships among levels of significance, *p*-values, and rejection decisions. For the following levels of significance and *p*-values, indicate whether you would reject or fail to reject the statistical hypothesis.

	Level of Significance (α from step 3 of the six steps)	p-Value (from step 4 of the six steps)	Rejection Decision: Reject Stat. H or Fail to Reject Stat. H
a.	.05	.0476	
b.	.05	.3297	
c.	.01	.0476	
d.	.001	.0028	
e.	.01	.0006	
f.	.05	.4996	

10. This exercise will familiarize you with the relationships among levels of significance, *p*-values, and rejection decisions. For the following levels of significance and *p*-values, indicate whether you would reject or fail to reject the statistical hypothesis.

	Level of Significance (α from step 3 of the six steps)	p-Value (from step 4 of the six steps)	Rejection Decision: Reject Stat. H or Fail to Reject Stat. H
a.	.001	.0007	
b.	.05	.0650	
c.	.01	.0099	
d.	.05	.0399	
e.	.001	.0110	
f.	.01	.0101	

11. Compute the following probabilities for the rolling of *a pair* of dice *three times*.

    a. p [2, 12, 2]   *b. p* [7, 6, 7]   *c. p* [3, 7, 9]

12. Compute the following probabilities for the rolling of *a pair* of dice *three times.*

    a. p [4, 5, 10]   *b.* p [10, 10, 10]   *c.* p [2, 7, 2]

13. Compute the probability of rolling *a pair* of dice *twice* and getting a 12 (or boxcars) on both rolls.

14. Compute the probability of rolling *a pair* of dice *twice* and getting a 2 (or snake eyes) on both rolls.

Optional Computer Applications for Chapter 9

If your class uses the optional computer applications that accompany this text, open the Chapter 9 exercises on the *Computer Applications for The Statistical Imagination* compact disk. The exercises involve an orientation to bivariate statistical procedures in *SPSS for Windows.*

SINGLE-SAMPLE HYPOTHESIS TESTS: ESTABLISHING THE REPRESENTATIVENESS OF SAMPLES

Introduction

As we learned in Chapter 8, when we want to estimate an unknown parameter of a population, say, the mean age of managers of fast-food restaurants, we compute a confidence interval. With confidence intervals we address the question: *What is* the score value of the parameter? The confidence interval provides an interval or span estimate. In this chapter we address a different type of question. Rather than ask, *What is* the value of the parameter? we ask, *Is the parameter equal to some chosen target value?*

Where do these target values come from? There are several sources:

1. *A known population parameter from a comparison group.* For example, it is known that the mean intelligence quotient (IQ) score for all persons is 100. Where Stat. *H* is the statistical hypothesis and Alt. *H* is the alternative hypothesis, we can test the hypothesis that the mean IQ of a specific group, say, inventors, is higher:

$$\textit{Stat. } H: \mu_X \text{ (inventors)} \quad = \quad 100 \text{ IQ points (the known mean } (\mu_X) \text{ of all adults)}$$

$$\textit{Alt. } H: \mu_X \text{ (inventors)} \quad > \quad 100 \text{ IQ points (the known mean } (\mu_X) \text{ of all adults) One-tailed}$$

Note that on the left sides of these equations we subscript the name of the population under study and on the right we indicate the source of the target value.

2. *Known parameters from a past time period.* For example, 1990 U.S. Census data provide actual parameters, such as the proportion of the U.S. population living in households headed by women. Using a current national sample of

1,500 households, we can test the hypothesis that that proportion has changed since then:

Stat. H: P$_u$ (living in female-headed households today)   =   .16 (the known proportion (P_u) living in female-headed households in 1990)

Alt. H: P$_u$ (living in female-headed households today)   ≠   .16 (the known proportion (P_u) living in female-headed households in 1990) Two-tailed

3. *A statistical ideal.* For example, as the quality control manager of the Smellishou Perfume Company, you select a random sample of half-ounce bottles from store shelves and determine whether this desired volume was maintained throughout the production and delivery process.

Stat. H: μ$_X$ (bottles of Smellishou on store shelves)   =   .5 ounce (the desired target value)

Alt. H: μ$_X$ (bottles of Smellishou on store shelves)   <   .5 ounce (the desired target value) One-tailed

4. A *population is sampled, and the sample statistics are compared to some known population parameters to determine whether the sample is representative of the population.* For example, suppose we have sampled 250 nurses in the state. Complete state licensing records show that 64 percent of all state nurses are registered nurses (RNs). This is a known parameter for our sampled population. If our sample is representative, about 64 percent of the nurses in the sample will be RNs.

Stat. H: P$_u$ (sampled population)   =   .64 (the known parameter (P_u) of the targeted state nursing population)

That is, the sample *is* representative of state nurses with regard to the proportion of nurses holding RN licenses.

Alt. H: P$_u$ (sampled population)   ≠   .64 (the known parameter (P_u) of the targeted state nursing population)

That is, the sample *is not* representative of state nurses with regard to the proportion of nurses holding RN certificates.

Later in this chapter we will illustrate complete hypothesis tests for some of these source target values.

Purpose of a Single-Sample Hypothesis Test

To determine whether a parameter of a population is equal to a specified "target" value. Sources of target values: (1) comparison groups, (2) known parameters from a past time period, (3) statistical ideals, and (4) known parameters of a sampled population (for establishing sample representativeness).

The Single-Sample Means Test

A "single-sample means test," as the term *mean* implies, is used with one interval/ratio or interval-like ordinal variable. The sampling distribution is the *t*-distribution with degrees of freedom, $df = n - 1$. Specifically, we use a single-sample means test when the following criteria are met:

When to Use a Single-Sample Means Test
(*t*-distribution, $df = n - 1$)

In general: Useful for testing a hypothesis that the mean of a population is equal to a target value. Especially useful for testing the representativeness of a sample.

1. There is only one variable.
2. The level of measurement is interval/ratio or interval-like ordinal.
3. There is a single sample and population.
4. There is a target value of the variable to which we may compare the mean of the sample.

Let us first illustrate an example in which the target value comes from a comparison group. Suppose we are conducting a study of male high school athletes. We wish to examine whether the common stereotype that athletes are "dumb jocks"—all brawn and no brains—has any merit. The specific research question is: Do athletes have less intelligence than do students generally? Using our statistical imagination, we search for a way to compare these athletes to students in general. We obtain an IQ test that has a national average of 100, a target value to which high school athletes may be compared. Our research question is: Are athletes on average below this national average of 100? Having a target value also allows us to state a statistical hypothesis and predict sample outcomes. The statistical hypothesis is that the mean IQ of high school athletes is 100, *the same* as that of students on the whole. (In this instance, the statistical hypothesis can also be called a null hypothesis because we nullified the research question.)

To test the hypothesis, we will draw a sample of high school athletes and compare sample statistics to the target parameter IQ of 100. If the mean IQ of the sample is close to this parameter, give or take a little expected sampling error, we assert that our sample results are not significantly different from the hypothesized value. For instance, if the sample mean is 99, we probably will attribute the 1-point difference between this sample statistic and the hypothesized parameter to sampling error. However, if the sample statistic is not close to the hypothesized parameter, say, this statistic is 92, we will reject the statement that the mean IQ of athletes is 100. Like confidence interval problems, questions about whether a parameter equals a target value involve a single sample from a single population. Thus, these hypotheses tests are called single-sample tests.

All research questions involving single-sample hypothesis tests ask about a *specified target parameter*. This target value is necessary to formulate a statistical hypothesis in step 1 of the six steps of statistical inference. The target value serves as a hypothetically true value of a variable. In determining whether high school athletes are lower than average in intelligence, we must have a measure of average to which to compare them. For purposes of testing the hypothesis, we assert that the athletes do indeed score the national mean of 100. Given this target value, we are then able to predict sample outcomes in step 2 assuming that this target value is true. After observing the mean for the athletes, we decide whether it truly appears equal to 100 or is significantly different from 100. Without the target value, we would not have been able to state a statistical hypothesis and proceed to test it.

The Necessity of a Specified Target Parameter

To test a single sample hypothesis, we must specify a target value of a parameter of the variable.

Distinguishing between the Target Population and the Source Population

It is very important to conceive of this problem correctly, because two populations are discussed: the comparison group of the national high school population of IQ test takers (the source of the target parameter value) and high school athletes (the actual population under study). The national population simply provides the known target parameter. Our question, however, is about the population of high school athletes and whether its mean IQ test score is 100. It is this population from which we draw a sample and compute statistics. Figure 10–1 is a conceptual diagram of this example problem.

To determine whether high school athletes are less intelligent than other students, we administer the IQ test to a random sample of 150 high school athletes selected from all local school districts in a large metropolitan area. With X = IQ test points, the sample results are as follows:

$$\bar{X} = 98 \text{ IQ points} \qquad s_X = 16 \text{ IQ points}$$

$$n = 150 \text{ high school athletes}$$

We can see that the athlete sample has a mean IQ score 2 points lower than the national average. This 2-point difference, however, may be due to sampling error. We know from experience with repeated sampling that a second sample will provide a slightly different mean, a third yet a different mean, and so on.

FIGURE 10–1

Identifying the population of interest and a known target parameter

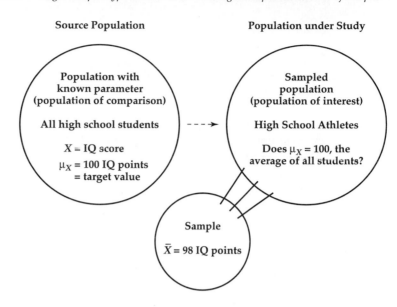

Source Population

Population with known parameter (population of comparison)

All high school students

X = IQ score

μ_X = 100 IQ points = target value

Population under Study

Sampled population (population of interest)

High School Athletes

Does μ_X = 100, the average of all students?

Sample

$\bar{X}$ = 98 IQ points

But we also know that such sample variability is predictable. Whatever the value of a population's mean (μ_X) is, most sample means from a large number of samples will compute very close to this parameter value. In other words, if the mean IQ of high school athletes is *no different* from the national average of 100, sample outcomes from the population of high school athletes will cluster around 100. We also have learned that the sampling distribution of means takes the shape of an approximately normal *t*-distribution. This sampling distribution tells us all possible sampling outcomes and the probability of each one when we draw samples of size 150 from a population with an IQ of 100.

To test any hypothesis we must state a statistical hypothesis (Stat. *H*), a hypothesis stated in such a way that we will know the shape of our sampling distribution, assuming that the statistical hypothesis is true. Thus, where X is the IQ test score and μ_X represents the mean of the designated population, step 1 of the six steps of statistical inference will be:

Stat. H: μ_X (high school athletes)   =   100 IQ points (the known mean (μ_X) of all high school students)

Alt. H: μ_X (high school athletes)   <   100 IQ points (the known mean (μ_X) of all high school students) One-tailed

Again, note that on the left side of these equations we subscript the name of the population under study and on the right we indicate the source population from which we took the target value. This is a one-tailed test because we want to confirm or dispel the negative stereotype that athletes are *less* intelligent.

This hypothesis test is designed to arrive at one of the following two conclusions. *If this statistical hypothesis is not rejected,* we will attribute the 2-point difference in IQ scores between the known national average and the observed sample mean of athletes to random sampling error; that is, we will state that athletes do not differ from others in intelligence and that the "dumb jock" stereotype is exactly that—a myth. However, *if we reject this statistical hypothesis and accept the alternative,* we will conclude that on average, athletes score lower on IQ tests.

The statistical hypothesis of all single-sample hypothesis tests will be that the population parameter of the sampled population is equal to some known "target" value:

Stat. H: parameter $_{\text{(sampled population)}}$ = known target parameter (from data on a source population or a statistical ideal)

The Sampling Distribution and the Test Statistic for a Single-Sample Means Test

In Chapter 7 we learned that if the mean (μ_X) of a population is in fact a known value, we may predict that repeated sampling from this population will produce an approximately normal *t*-distribution of sample means ($\bar{X}$'s) centered on this known population parameter μ_X. In this hypothesis test, however, we do *not know* for a fact that the mean IQ test score *of all athletes* is 100. The hypothesis test is designed, however, "to assume that this is true for the moment," and in steps 1 through 4 of the six steps we will proceed as though it were. This parameter is known in the sense that we know what will happen in repeated sampling when it is true.

The standard error of this sampling distribution was computed as was done in previous chapters and is repeated here for convenience:

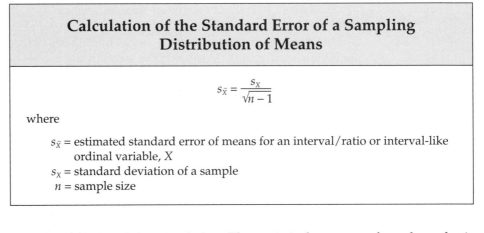

Calculation of the Standard Error of a Sampling Distribution of Means

$$s_{\bar{X}} = \frac{s_X}{\sqrt{n-1}}$$

where

$s_{\bar{X}}$ = estimated standard error of means for an interval/ratio or interval-like ordinal variable, X

s_X = standard deviation of a sample

n = sample size

The Test Effect and Test Statistic. The statistical purpose of any hypothesis test is to determine whether statistical effects computed from a sample indicate: (1) real effects in the population or (2) sampling error. In general, the "statistical effect" or "**test effect**" of the hypothesis test is the *difference between the observed sample statistic and what is expected (i.e., the hypothesized parameter).* Conceptually we ask: What is the effect on IQ of being an athlete? Our observation reveals a test effect of 2 IQ points. This is the difference between the observed sample mean and the hypothesized mean IQ of athletes assuming that theirs is equal to the national average (i.e., the test effect = $\bar{X} - \mu_X = 2$ IQ points). The hypothesis test is performed to determine if this effect is due to random sampling error (as asserted by the statistical hypothesis) or is the effect of low intelligence (as asserted by the alternative hypothesis).

The "Test Effect" of a Hypothesis Test

The difference between the observed sample statistic and what is expected (i.e., the hypothesized parameter).

A test effect is a deviation score. Recall from Chapter 6 that a deviation score is the difference (or distance) between the mean in the center of a normal curve and some point (i.e., score) on the horizontal or X-axis. Recall also that deviation scores are expressed in the original unit of measure of the raw score. With the example above, this would be IQ points. To calculate the probability of a test effect we must standardize the score—transform it into standard deviation units—so that we can use probability tables such as the approximately normal *t*-distribution table. (We do not have a table with IQ points in it!) For hypothesis tests, these standardized scores are expressed in standard error units. A **statistical test,** to be used in conjunction with probability curves and statistical probability tables, *is a formula for measuring statistical test effects in standard error units.*

A Statistical Test

A formula for measuring statistical test effects in standard error units. These formulas are used in conjunction with probability curves and the statistical tables in Appendix B.

For a one-sample means test whose sampling distribution fits an approximately normal curve, the test statistic is a *t*-score. The *t*-distribution table (Statistical Table C in Appendix B) is used to compute a *p*-value, the probability of the observed sample outcome when the statistical hypothesis is true. Statistical test effects usually are measured in the numerator of the test statistic and then standardized by dividing them by the standard error. This is the case for a single-sample test.

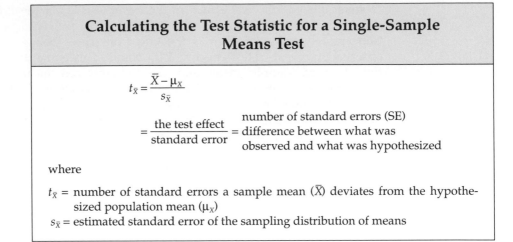

Calculating the Test Statistic for a Single-Sample Means Test

$$t_{\bar{X}} = \frac{\bar{X} - \mu_X}{s_{\bar{X}}}$$

$$= \frac{\text{the test effect}}{\text{standard error}} = \begin{array}{l}\text{number of standard errors (SE)}\\ \text{difference between what was}\\ \text{observed and what was hypothesized}\end{array}$$

where

$t_{\bar{X}}$ = number of standard errors a sample mean ($\bar{X}$) deviates from the hypothesized population mean (μ_X)

$s_{\bar{X}}$ = estimated standard error of the sampling distribution of means

A look at the terms of this formula in relation to the distribution curve is informative. Just like Z-scores (review Chapter 6), the *t*-score is a measure of the deviation ("how far off" the observed sample statistic falls) from an expected value. Any Z- or *t*-distribution curve has a mean and a standard deviation (SD) and an interval/ratio score measured across its horizontal axis.

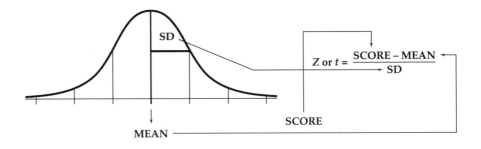

For instance, as we saw in Chapter 6, when the interval/ratio measurement is a raw score X, then Z_X is computed as follows:

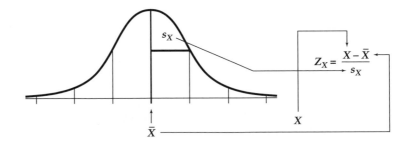

The parallel elements of an approximately normal *t*-distribution of sample means are as follows:

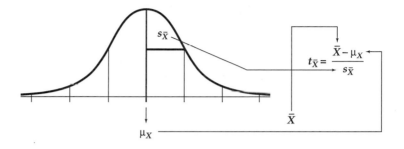

Take care to distinguish the standard error of this distribution of means from the standard deviation of the raw score distribution.

The Six Steps of Statistical Inference for a Single-Sample Means Test

The framework for understanding the logic of a large single-sample means test is revealed when we examine the six steps of statistical inference.

Brief Checklist for the Six Steps of Statistical Inference

Test Preparation

State the research question; list givens, including variables (e.g., $X =...$, $Y =...$), their levels of measurement, the population(s) under study, and sample(s) and sample size(s); select the statistical test; provide observations of statistics and parameters; and draw a conceptual diagram.

Six Steps

Using the symbol *H* for *hypothesis:*

1. State the statistical *H* and the alternative *H* and stipulate test direction.
2. Describe the sampling distribution.
3. State the level of significance (α) and specify the critical test value.
4. Observe the actual sample outcomes and compute the test effects, the test statistic, and the *p*-value.
5. Make the rejection decision.
6. Interpret and apply best estimates in everyday terms.

Test Preparation

Research question: Do athletes have less intelligence than do students generally? Is the "dumb jock" stereotype encouraged by facts? *Givens:* Variable: X = IQ score; interval level. *Population:* high school athletes. *Sample:* 150 randomly selected high school athletes. *Statistical procedure:* single-sample means test; t-distribution; target value = 100 IQ points, the known average IQ score of all high school students.

Observation:

$$\bar{X} = 98 \text{ IQ points}$$

$$s_X = 16 \text{ IQ points} \qquad n = 150 \text{ high school athletes.}$$

(The conceptual diagram for this test appears in Figure 10–1.)

Six Steps

1. *Stat. H:* μ_X (high school athletes) $=$ 100 IQ points (the known mean (μ_X) of all high school students)

   Alt. H: μ_X (high school athletes) $<$ 100 IQ points (the known mean (μ_X) of all high school students)
   One-tailed

2. *Sampling distribution:* If Stat. *H* is true and samples of size 150 are repeatedly drawn from the population of high school athletes, sample means ($\bar{X}$'s) will center on 100 as an approximately normal t-distribution, $df = n - 1 = 149$, with a standard error:

$$s_{\bar{X}} = \frac{s_X}{\sqrt{n-1}} = \frac{16}{\sqrt{149}} = 1.31 \text{ IQ points}$$

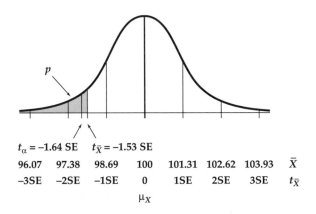

$t_\alpha = -1.64$ SE		$t_{\bar{X}} = -1.53$ SE					
96.07	97.38	98.69	100	101.31	102.62	103.93	$\bar{X}$
–3SE	–2SE	–1SE	0	1SE	2SE	3SE	$t_{\bar{X}}$
			μ_X				

3. *Level of significance:* α = .05. One-tailed. Critical test score $t_\alpha = -1.64$ SE.

4. *Observation:* $\bar{X} = 98$ IQ points $s_X = 16$ IQ points $n = 150$

Test effect $= \bar{X} - \mu_X = 98 - 100 = -2$ IQ points

Test statistic $= t_{\bar{X}} = \dfrac{\bar{X} - \mu_X}{s_{\bar{X}}} = \dfrac{98 - 100}{1.31} = -1.53$ SE

p-value: p [drawing a sample with a mean ($\bar{X}$) as unusual as or more unusual than 98 when the true population mean (μ_X) is 100] $> .05$. (This p-value is shaded on the curve in step 2.)

5. *Rejection decision:* $|t_{\bar{X}}| < |t_\alpha|$ (i.e., $1.53 < 1.64$). Thus, $p > \alpha$, (i.e., $p > .05$). Do not reject Stat. H.

6. *Interpretation:* High school athletes appear to have average intelligence. The 2-point difference between the mean IQ scores of the sample of high school athletes and the national average is due to normal, expected sampling error. *Best estimate:* We estimate that the mean IQ of athletes is 100—the same as that of other students. *Answer:* The "dumb jock" stereotype is wrong.

Some things of note about this hypothesis test:

- In step 1 we state the alternative hypothesis as a one-tailed test. To set this negative direction, we *do not* observe the sample mean to see if it is less than the target value. Instead, we choose the negative direction because the research questions asks whether athletes are *less* intelligent.
- In step 2 we describe the sampling distribution for the parameter hypothesized in step 1. In this instance, step 2 describes for any population having a population mean (i.e., parameter) of 100 what happens if we repeatedly sample with a sample size of 150: About 68 percent of the time the sample mean $\bar{X}$ will compute to between 98.69 and 101.31; about 95 percent of the time, between 97.38 and 102.62; and so on.
- In step 3 we observe the t-distribution table to find the critical t_α value for a one-tailed test at the .05 level of significance with $df = 149$ or "∞." This value is -1.64, with the minus sign indicating the negative direction or left side of the curve. This tells us that the critical region of the curve is below and to the left of -1.64 standard errors. That is, for us to reject the statistical hypothesis, the observed sample mean in step 4 must be at least 1.64 standard errors below the national mean IQ of 100. We will examine this further below.
- In step 4 the computation of the p-value tells us how unusual the observed sample outcome is *when the statistical hypothesis is true.* It answers the question: With repeated sampling, how often does a mean of 98 IQ points or less occur when the population mean is 100? We

determine this *p*-value by matching the test statistic $t_{\bar{x}} = -1.53$ to the *t*-distribution table (Statistical Table C in Appendix B). It's absolute value is less than the absolute value of the critical value of -1.64. Thus, the *p*-value is greater than .05. This indicates that a mean that is 2 points off from 100 is *not an unusual* occurrence in repeated sampling. It would occur more than 5 percent of the time. We decided in step 3 that our sample mean must occur *less than* 5 percent of the time in repeated sampling (i.e., $\alpha = .05$) before we would call it *unusual*. Thus, in step 5 we do not reject the statistical hypothesis because $p > \alpha$.

- In step 4 we could have used the normal curve table (Statistical Table B in Appendix B) and treated the *t*-score as a *Z*-score, because with a sample size over 120, the distribution curve is perceptively normal (i.e., the areas are precise to three decimal places). Using this table, a closer approximation of the *p*-value is .0630, which is greater than .05.

- In step 4 we return to step 2 and draw the *p*-value area on the sampling distribution curve. Whether the statistical hypothesis is true or not, in step 2 we predict what occurs in sampling "if the statistical hypothesis is true," and calculation of the *p*-value assumes this for the moment. Remember that steps 1 through 4 are predicated on the assumption that the statistical hypothesis is true.

- In step 5 take note of the careful wording of the rejection decision. We do not say that we *accept* the statistical hypothesis: we simply do not reject it. This is the case because in failing to reject the statistical hypothesis, we may have made a type II error; that is, the statistical hypothesis may be false and we failed to reject it. We have not, however, calculated the probability of such an error. Therefore, we cannot express a degree of confidence in this conclusion. Thus, we use conservative language: words that will not overstate our conclusion. On the other hand, in situations where the statistical hypothesis is rejected, we can *accept the alternative hypothesis* with a specified degree of confidence (which is equal to 1 minus the level of significance).

- In step 6 the interpretation focuses on the statistical hypothesis because we have not rejected it. At this point we can disregard the alternative hypothesis. Note that the tone of step 6 is substantive. This step involves a discussion of the research question and addresses concepts and variables. The earlier steps address technical aspects of the statistical procedure and focus on probability theory. Also keep in mind that step 6 reverts back to step 1. Therefore, in step 1 the statistical and alternative hypotheses must be stated properly and clearly. Otherwise, there will be confusion in stating step 6.

- Regarding step 6, if we fail to reject the statistical hypothesis, a public audience may desire to know why we did this when the sample data show that athletes average 2 IQ points lower than does the general high school student population. The audience may ask why we chose to ignore this effect and may even accuse us of bias or "political correctness." To answer, we must clearly explain the notion of random sampling error. For example, we can mention that a second sample could just as well have had a mean of 102—2 points higher rather than lower than the general mean.

Gaining a Sense of Proportion about the Dynamics of a Means Test

Critical Regions under a Probability Distribution Curve

As we noted in earlier chapters, statistical tests usually are conducted at the traditional levels of significance (or "alpha levels") of .05, .01, and .001. For a given hypothesis test, the test statistic score that corresponds to the stated alpha level is called the **critical test score,** *the one that is large enough to indicate a significant difference between the observed sample statistic and the hypothesized parameter.* On a probability curve, *the area in the tail(s) of the curve that is beyond the critical test score (t_α) of the stated level of significance (α) is* called the **critical region** of the curve. The critical region of a hypothesis test is simply the region under the sampling distribution probability curve, such as the *t*-distribution curve, where we become critical, or raise doubts, about the truth of the statistical hypothesis. It is the point where the observed outcome from our sample is so far removed from what we expected *when the statistical hypothesis is true* that we no longer believe that it is true. In other words, it is the point at which the computed effect of the test is so large that we do not think that it resulted from normal sampling error.

For a hypothesis test using the *t*-distribution curve, the critical test score is the specific *t*-score that is large enough to cause us to reject the statistical hypothesis. Again, we symbolize this critical score as t_α because it is the score that corresponds to a level of significance α. For the high school athletes, in step 3 we chose the level $\alpha = .05$ and specified a one-tailed test. Refer to the *t*-distribution table to see that the corresponding critical t_α is −1.64. This says that if our sample mean falls *1.64 standard errors or more below* the hypothesized mean of 100, the *p*-value is less than .05 and therefore we reject the statistical hypothesis.

Once we have selected this critical value in step 3, it is good practice to look back at the probability curve in step 2 and estimate what kind of sample outcome will reach the critical region. In other words, what would be the *value in IQ points* of a sample mean that is −1.64 standard errors below the hypothesized mean? We can estimate this critical mean value by observing the probability curve.

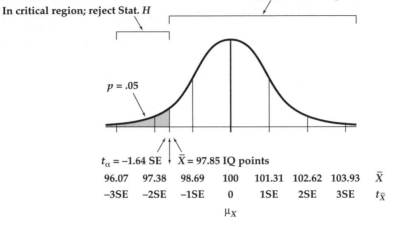

Outside critical region; do not reject Stat. H

In critical region; reject Stat. H

$p = .05$

$t_\alpha = -1.64$ SE $\bar{X} = 97.85$ IQ points

| 96.07 | 97.38 | 98.69 | 100 | 101.31 | 102.62 | 103.93 | $\bar{X}$ |
| -3SE | -2SE | -1SE | 0 | 1SE | 2SE | 3SE | $t_{\bar{X}}$ |

μ_X

A t_α of −1.64 standard errors is about "97 point something" *IQ points*. In fact, we can calculate this critical IQ score by following Problem Type 7 in Chapter 6. We solve for $\bar{X}$ and substitute the critical value of $t_\alpha = -1.64$ for $t_{\bar{X}}$:

$$t_{\bar{X}} = \frac{\bar{X} - \mu_X}{s_{\bar{X}}}$$

Thus,

$$\bar{X} = \mu_X + (t_{\bar{X}})(s_{\bar{X}}) = 100 + (-1.64)(1.31) = 97.85 \text{ IQ points}$$

We can see that the sample mean observed in step 4 would have to equal *97.85 IQ points or less* for us to have rejected the statistical hypothesis. This is our critical region: any sample outcome equal to or below 97.85 IQ points. Thus, in step 3 when we set the level of significance, before making the observation in step 4, we set it up so that the rejection decision in step 5 would leave us with one of two conclusions. First, in step 4, *if we observe a sample mean of 97.85 or below*, we will become critical of the idea that the mean IQ of the high school athletes is 100. We will assert that this sample mean is unusual—"a significant difference"—so far off from 100 that it probably did not come from a population with that mean. Thus, we will reject the statistical hypothesis that it came from a population with a mean of 100. By contrast, in step 4, *if we observe a sample mean above 97.85* (i.e., outside the critical region), we will assert that this is "close to the 100 IQ points we expected." It is not unusual and therefore easily could be due to sampling error. Thus, we will not reject the statistical hypothesis.

In the actual test we conducted above, of course, we settled on the conclusion that there is no significant difference between the mean IQs of regular students and athletes. Our observed mean of 98 IQ points fell short of 97.85, where the critical region begins. In other words, the spot on the horizontal axis of the curve at 98 IQ points is outside the critical region.

The Critical Test Score (t_α)

The statistical test score that is large enough to indicate a significant difference between the observed sample statistic and the hypothesized parameter.

The Critical Region of the Sampling Distribution Curve (t-distribution)

The area in the tail(s) of the curve that is beyond the critical test score (t_α) of the stated level of significance (α).

Relationships among Hypothesized Parameters, Observed Sample Statistics, Computed Test Statistics, p-Values, and Alpha Levels

It is important to have a sense of proportion about the relationships among the hypothesized parameter (μ_X), the observed sample statistic ($\bar{X}$), the computed test statistic ($t_{\bar{X}}$), the level of significance and its critical score (α and t_α), and the p-value. While this list of concepts may appear overwhelming, once their interrelationships are grasped, things fall into place and hypothesis testing appears quite simple. Let us think in terms of the likelihood of the statistical hypothesis (Stat. H) being rejected, after which the alternative hypothesis (Alt. H) is accepted. In other words, under what conditions are we no longer willing to accept that the statistical hypothesis is true? What sample observations lead to a rejection of the statistical hypothesis?

Rule 1: The Statistical Hypothesis Is Rejected When the Effect of the Test Is Large—Large Enough That the Test Statistic Value Is Greater Than the Critical Test Score.   Again, the effect of the test is the difference between the observed sample statistic and the hypothesized parameter. It is a deviation score on the curve. The statistical hypothesis will be rejected when the test effect is large. Recall the simple example of hypothesizing that it is going to rain soon. We expect to see dense dark clouds in the sky. If we observe a clear blue sky, this test effect is so different from what we expect that we reject the hypothesis of rain.

When the test effect is large, the test statistic value will be large. For the single-sample means test, the test statistic is $t_{\bar{X}}$, which is calculated in step 4 of the six steps. It measures the test effect *as a number of standard errors (SE)*. When the absolute value of this computed t-score reaches the absolute value of the critical t-score (t_α), the hypothesis is rejected. This is the case because the critical region has been reached. The area in the tail of the curve beyond $t_{\bar{X}}$ is the p-value. It will be less than the alpha level when $|t_{\bar{X}}|$ is greater than $|t_\alpha|$. Thus, when $|t_{\bar{X}}| > |t_\alpha|$, $p < \alpha$, and we reject the statistical hypothesis. When $|t_{\bar{X}}| < |t_\alpha|$, $p > \alpha$, we do not reject the statistical hypothesis. With a means test, for example, the test effect is calculated as $\bar{X} - \mu_X$, and this term appears in the numerator of the test statistic. In any division problem, when the numerator is large, the quotient will be large. Suppose we hypothesize that the mean grade point average (GPA) of students is greater than 2.6. This will be the alternative hypothesis, because we must state the statistical hypothesis as equal to 2.6 to produce a sampling distribution (i.e., Stat. *H:* $\mu_X = 2.6$ GPA points). Let us compare samples of students with large and small test effects, one sample from State University and another from Crosstown University. For simplicity's sake, let us imagine that the standard errors are the same and are equal to .2 GPA point and that the sample sizes are 500. The sample means from the two campuses differ as follows:

From State University (a large test effect and test statistic):

Step 1. *Stat. H:* $\mu_X = 2.6$ GPA points

  Alt. H: $\mu_X > 2.6$ GPA points   One-tailed

Step 4. Observed sample mean:

$$\bar{X} = 3.0 \text{ GPA points}$$

Test effect $= \bar{X} - \mu_X = 3.0 - 2.6 = .4$ GPA point

$$\text{Test statistic} = t_{\bar{X}} = \frac{\bar{X} - \mu_X}{s_{\bar{X}}} = \frac{3.0 - 2.6}{.2} = \frac{.4}{.2} = 2.00 \text{ SE}$$

From Crosstown University:

Step 1. *Stat. H:* $\mu_X = 2.6$ GPA points

  Alt. H: $\mu_X > 2.6$ GPA points   One-tailed

Step 4. Observed sample mean:

$$\bar{X} = 2.7 \text{ GPA points}$$

Test effect $= \bar{X} - \mu_X = 2.7 - 2.6 = .1$ GPA point

$$\text{Test statistic} = t_{\bar{X}} = \frac{\bar{X} - \mu_X}{s_{\bar{X}}} = \frac{2.7 - 2.6}{.2} = \frac{.1}{.2} = .50 \text{ SE}$$

The sample mean of State University misses by .4 GPA point—almost one-half of a letter grade. This is 2.00 standard errors away from the 2.6 GPA that we expect. This is a large difference between the observed sample GPA of 3.0 and the hypothesized parameter of 2.6. It is so large that we can confidently say that it is *not* due to random sampling error. We will reject the statistical hypothesis that the GPA at State University is 2.6 and conclude that it is higher. On the other hand, for the Crosstown University sample, the effect of the test was small—only .1 GPA point—and therefore $t_{\bar{X}}$ is small. The sample mean is only one-half a standard error from the expected mean. Our experience with sampling distributions suggests that this small difference could easily result from sampling error. To summarize rule 1, when the test effect and therefore the absolute value of the test statistic $t_{\bar{X}}$ are large, the likelihood of rejecting the statistical hypothesis goes up.

Rule 2: The Larger the Test Effect and the Test Statistic, the Smaller the *p*-Value. Large test effects and test statistic values are unusual when the statistical hypothesis is true. For example, if we hypothesized that it was going to rain soon but saw no clouds in the sky, rain would be unusual. As a precise probability statement, the *p*-value of the hypothesis test tells us how unusual an observed sample outcome is *if the statistical hypothesis is true.* The observed outcome is quite unusual (i.e., has a low probability of occurrence) when the test effect is large. For a means test, a large test effect is a big difference between the observed sample mean and the hypothesized mean. In the *t*-distribution curve, the low probability of a large test effect is apparent in the small area in the tail of the curve beyond a large $t_{\bar{X}}$.

The approximately normal *t*-distribution curve is useful for gaining a sense of proportion about the relationship between the value of the test statistic and the *p*-value. Since the *t*-distribution table provides areas in the curve only for critical regions, we can only estimate the probability of a particular test statistic value $t_{\bar{X}}$. Let us illustrate by examining the Crosstown and State University samples using a one-tailed test. In both samples, $df = n - 1 = 499$. The critical t_{α} values are found in the "∞" row of the *t*-distribution table.

For State University:

Stat. H: $\mu_X = 2.6$ GPA points

$$\bar{X} = 3.0 \text{ GPA points}$$

$$t_{\bar{X}} = 2 \text{ SE}$$

This is a relatively large test effect and test statistic value. The *p*-value is relatively small. To see this, observe the *t*-distribution table to get the *p*-value. The calculated *t*-value, $t_{\bar{X}} = 2$ SE, falls between the critical t_{α}-values of 1.64 and 2.33; thus, $p\ [t_{\bar{X}} = 2 \text{ SE}]$ is less than .05 but greater than .01.

The *p*-value is stated: *p* [drawing a sample with a mean ($\bar{X}$) as unusual as or more unusual than 3.0 GPA points when the true population mean (μ_X) is 2.6 GPA points] < .05.

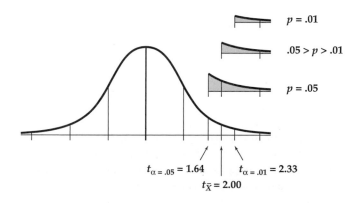

For Crosstown University:

Stat. H: $\mu_X = 2.6$ GPA points

$\bar{X} = 2.7$ GPA points

$t_{\bar{X}} = .5$ SE

This is a relatively small test effect and test statistic value. The *p*-value is relatively large. Observing the *t*-distribution table, the calculated *t*-value, $t_{\bar{X}} = .5$ SE falls to the left of the critical t_α-value of 1.64; thus, $p\,[t_{\bar{X}} = .5]$ is greater than .05.

The *p*-value is stated as *p* [drawing a sample with a mean $(\bar{X})$ as unusual as or more unusual than 2.7 GPA points when the true population mean (μ_X) is 2.6 GPA points] > .05.

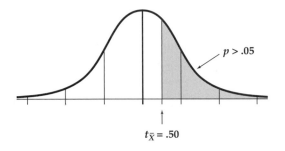

$t_{\bar{X}} = .50$

In this comparison, we can see for the Crosstown University sample that it would *not* be unusual to draw a sample mean of 2.7 GPA points from this population if its mean is 2.6 GPA points. In fact, if the population parameter is indeed 2.6 GPA points, in repeated sampling, a large proportion of the time we would draw sample means that are close to the hypothesized mean. The high probability of this outcome is apparent in the large shaded area of the Crosstown University curve. In testing at the .05 level of significance, we would not reject the statistical hypothesis for Crosstown University. In contrast, with the State University sample, we would conclude that it *is* unusual to draw a sample mean of 3.0 GPA points from a population with a mean equal to 2.6 GPA points. In fact, this effect of .4 GPA point seldom occurs as a result of chance sampling error—less than 5 times out of 100 samples. On the State University curve, this is apparent in the comparably small area beyond $t_{\bar{X}} = 2.00$ SE. In testing at the .05 level of significance, we would reject the statistical hypothesis for the State University case.

To summarize this second rule about the relationship of statistics and *p*-values, the larger the test effect and thus the larger the test statistic, the smaller the probability that the sample outcome occurred as a result of random sampling error. Now let us discuss levels of significance (alpha levels) in relation to test effects, test statistics, and *p*-values.

Rule 3: It Is Easier to Reject with a One-Tailed Test Than with a Two-Tailed Test. Another exercise that will help you gain a sense of proportion about hypothesis testing involves examining whether it is easier to reject the statistical hypothesis with a one-tailed test or a two-tailed test. As we mentioned in Chapter 9, the answer is a one-tailed test because with a one-tailed test the test effect—the difference between the observed sample outcome and the hypothesized parameter—does not have to be as great for the test statistic $t_{\bar{x}}$ to fall beyond the critical test statistic value t_α. When $t_{\bar{x}}$ falls beyond t_α into the critical region, the *p*-value will fall below α, and the hypothesis will be rejected. With a one-tailed test, the critical region is clustered to one side and the t_α is smaller (1.64 compared to 1.96 for the two-tailed test), placing the critical region closer to the hypothesized mean. Therefore, the test effect can be smaller to reach the area of the critical region.

To illustrate this, let us suppose that two researchers, Jerome and Charlotte, unbeknown to each other, are testing the hypothesis that State University's mean GPA is 2.6. Jerome has no reason to state a direction in his alternative hypothesis, and so he does a two-tailed test. Charlotte, however, is aware that State University, compared to other colleges in the area, has more scholarships to offer its students and thus attracts better students. Therefore, her alternative hypothesis states that State University's mean GPA is higher than 2.6, and she uses a positive one-tailed test. In step 1 of the statistics test, both Jerome and Charlotte state their statistical hypotheses as follows:

Step 1. *Stat. H:* μ_X (State University) $=$ 2.6 GPA points

Their alternative hypotheses, however, will be stated differently:

Jerome: *Alt. H:* μ_X (State University) $\neq$ 2.6 GPA points. Two-tailed

Charlotte: *Alt. H:* μ_X (State University) $>$ 2.6 GPA points. One-tailed.

Suppose that both of them collect samples of 122 and find sample means of 2.95 (i.e., $\bar{X}$ = 2.95 GPA points). Their sample standard deviations (s_X) are both 2.2 GPA points, and therefore their computed standard errors are .20 GPA point. Both of their sampling distributions would look like this:

$$s_{\bar{X}} = \frac{s_X}{\sqrt{n-1}} = \frac{2.2}{\sqrt{121}} = .20 \text{ GPA point}$$

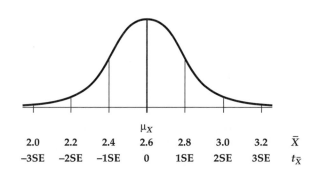

			μ_X				
2.0	2.2	2.4	2.6	2.8	3.0	3.2	$\bar{X}$
−3SE	−2SE	−1SE	0	1SE	2SE	3SE	$t_{\bar{X}}$

In step 3, although they both stipulate a level of significance (α) of .05, their critical (t_α) values will differ. Jerome will find his t_α to be 1.96 under the "two-tailed or nondirectional test" columns on the left side of the t-distribution table. Charlotte will find her t_α to be 1.64 under the "one-tailed or directional test" columns on the right side of the t-distribution table. In step 4 of their statistical tests, their calculated test effects and test statistics will be identical.

Step 4. *Observation:*

$$\bar{X} = 2.95 \text{ GPA points} \qquad s_X = 2.2 \text{ GPA points} \qquad n = 122$$

$$\text{Test effect} = \bar{X} - \mu_X = 2.95 - 2.6 = .35 \text{ GPA point}$$

$$\text{Test statistic} = t_{\bar{X}} = \frac{\bar{X} - \mu_X}{s_{\bar{X}}} = \frac{2.95 - 2.6}{.2} = \frac{.35}{.2} = 1.75 \text{ SE}$$

Their *p*-values (step 4) will differ, however, because they will be estimated from different columns of the *t*-distribution table. And in step 5 their rejection decisions will differ.

Jerome's *p*-value and rejection decision:

p [drawing a sample with a mean ($\bar{X}$) as unusual as or more unusual than 2.95 GPA points when the true population mean (μ_X) is 2.6 GPA points] > .05

Jerome's sample mean must be 1.96 SE from the hypothesized parameter to reject it, but the test statistic is only 1.75 SE, and so it falls short of the critical region.

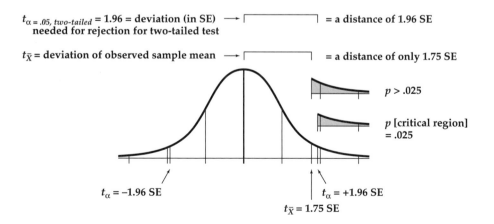

$t_{\alpha = .05,\ two\text{-}tailed} = 1.96 =$ deviation (in SE) $\longrightarrow$ [   ] = a distance of 1.96 SE
needed for rejection for two-tailed test

$t_{\bar{X}} =$ deviation of observed sample mean $\longrightarrow$ [   ] = a distance of only 1.75 SE

$p > .025$

p [critical region] $= .025$

$t_\alpha = -1.96$ SE $t_\alpha = +1.96$ SE

$t_{\bar{X}} = 1.75$ SE

Step 5. *Rejection decision:* $|t_{\bar{X}}| < |t_\alpha|$ (i.e., 1.75 < 1.96); thus, $p > \alpha$, (i.e., $p >$ .05). Do not reject Stat. *H*.

Charlotte's sample mean need be only 1.64 SE from the hypothesized parameter to reject it. Since the test statistic is 1.75 SE, it reaches her critical region for a one-tailed test.

Charlotte's *p*-value and rejection decision:

p [drawing a sample with a mean ($\bar{X}$) as unusual as or more unusual than 2.95 GPA points when the true population mean (μ_x) is 2.6 GPA points] < .05.

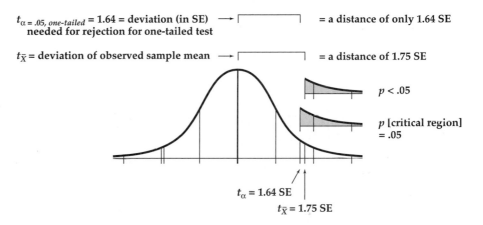

$t_{\alpha = .05,\ one\text{-}tailed}$ = **1.64 = deviation (in SE) needed for rejection for one-tailed test** $\longrightarrow$ = a distance of only 1.64 SE

$t_{\bar{X}}$ = **deviation of observed sample mean** $\longrightarrow$ = a distance of 1.75 SE

$p < .05$

p [critical region] = .05

$t_\alpha = 1.64$ SE

$t_{\bar{X}} = 1.75$ SE

Step 5. *Rejection decision:* $|t_{\bar{X}}| > |t_\alpha|$ (i.e., 1.75 > 1.64); thus, $p < \alpha$, (i.e., $p <$ .05). Reject the Stat. *H.* and accept the Alt. *H* at the 95 percent level of confidence.

For both Jerome and Charlotte, the *test effect*—the difference between what is observed in the samples and what is expected when the statistical hypothesis is true—is .35 GPA point. In step 5 of the six steps of the test, however, Jerome will not reject the statistical hypothesis while Charlotte will reject it. Charlotte's critical region is larger with its 5 percent area lumped to one side. This pushes her critical value ($t_\alpha = 1.64$) back toward the hypothesized mean, reducing the size of the test effect needed for rejection. Jerome's 5 percent critical region is split to both sides for his two-tailed test, leaving his critical value ($t_\alpha = \pm 1.96$) way out in the tail, and this requires a larger test effect to reach the critical region. What this amounts to is that by splitting the 5 percent area in two, Jerome's *p*-value must actually be less than .025 for him to reject the statistical hypothesis. The *p*-value of a two-tailed test is split to both sides, just like the area of the critical region. In other words, his test effect must be twice as unusual as Charlotte's before he can reject.

The selection of the direction of the test leads Jerome and Charlotte to different conclusions. Jerome, by not rejecting the statistical hypothesis that the mean GPA is 2.6, will conclude that State University's mean GPA could be that value, and he will attribute the test effect of .35 GPA point to sampling error.

Charlotte, however, by rejecting the statistical hypothesis, will conclude that the test effect of .35 GPA point is very unusual coming from a population with a mean GPA of 2.6; therefore, State University's mean GPA must not be 2.6. She will state that it is significantly higher than 2.6 GPA points. Charlotte increased her chances of rejecting the hypothesis by selecting a one-tailed test.

As we noted in Chapter 9, by selecting a one-tailed test we load the dice in favor of rejecting the statistical hypothesis and accepting the alternative hypothesis. If this is the result we desire to prove a theory or impress a boss, we must have good reasons for using a one-tailed test. Moreover, the choice of direction is not made by observing sample statistics. The direction of the test is determined by the research *question*, which pertains to parameters of the population. The direction of the test is *not* determined by the research answers that are found in sample statistics.

Rule 4: The Lower the Level of Significance, the Harder It Is to Reject the Statistical Hypothesis.   When the level of significance α is small, the critical region of the test will be smaller and its boundary on the probability curve will lie farther from the hypothesized parameter. This means that a test effect must be very large for the absolute value of the test statistic to reach the value of the critical *t*-score (t_α). For example, suppose a third researcher, Roger, is testing the hypothesis that State University's mean GPA is 2.6. His data are just like those of Charlotte and Jerome—a sample mean of 2.95 GPA points, and so on—and the test statistic $t_{\bar{x}}$ computes to 1.75 standard errors. Moreover, like Charlotte, Roger conducts a one-tailed test, *but he states his level of significance as .01*. His critical score from the *t*-distribution table is quite large: $t_\alpha = 2.33$. Thus, to reject the statistical hypothesis, his test effect must be large enough that his test statistic will equal at least 2.33 standard errors (SE). Let us look at Roger's *p*-value and rejection decision and compare it to Charlotte's above.

Roger's *p*-value and rejection decision:

Step 4. p [drawing a sample with a mean ($\bar{X}$) as unusual as or more unusual than 2.95 GPA points when the true population mean (μ_X) is 2.6 GPA points] < .05 but > .01.

Step 5. *Rejection decision:* $|t_{\bar{x}}| < |t_\alpha|$ (i.e., 1.75 < 2.33). Thus, $p > \alpha$, (i.e., $p > .01$). Do not reject Stat. H.

Both Roger and Charlotte have the same *test effects*, .35 GPA point, which is 1.75 standard errors distance from the hypothesized mean of 2.6. In step 5 of the hypothesis test, however, Roger *will not* reject the statistical hypothesis with $\alpha = .01$, while Charlotte *will* reject it with $\alpha = .05$. Roger will conclude that State University's mean GPA could be 2.6, but Charlotte will conclude that State University's mean GPA is significantly higher than 2.6 GPA points. While the test statistic value of 1.75 SE reached Charlotte's critical region of .05, it fell short of Roger's critical region of .01. It is harder to reject when the level of significance is low (say, $\alpha = .01$ or $.001$). Conversely, it is easier to reject when it is moderate to high (say, $\alpha = .05$ or $.10$).

While it is easier to reject a hypothesis at a high level of significance, when the statistical hypothesis is rejected, we are actually better off with a small alpha level. Why? Recall that a smaller alpha level results in a higher level of confidence because these two quantities are inversely related: The level of confidence is equal to 1 minus alpha. Also, remember that the level of significance is chosen neither to increase our chances of rejecting the statistical hypothesis nor to increase our level of confidence. The level of significance is chosen in step 3 of the six steps of statistical inference, prior to observing the sample outcomes in step 4. The level of significance is chosen for theoretical and practical reasons. (Review Table 9–4 for conventional levels of significance.)

Relationships among Hypothesized Parameters, Observed Sample Statistics, Computed Test Statistics, *p*-Values, and Alpha Levels

Rule 1. The statistical hypothesis is rejected when the test effect is large enough that the test statistic value is greater than the critical test score value, for example, with a single-sample means test when

$$|t_{\bar{x}}| > |t_{\alpha}|$$

Rule 2. The larger the test effect and the test statistic, the smaller the *p*-value.

Rule 3. It is easier to reject with a one-tailed test than with a two-tailed test.

Rule 4. The lower the level of significance is, the harder it is to reject the statistical hypothesis.

Using Single-Sample Hypothesis Tests to Establish Sample Representativeness

Single-sample hypothesis tests are especially useful in determining whether a sample is representative of the population from which it was drawn. In Chapter 2 we discussed the importance of a representative sample, one in which all segments of the population (such as males, females, whites, blacks, the young, the old, the wealthy, and the poor) are included in correct proportion to their representation in the population. For example, suppose a researcher in the fictional Delaney County conducts a telephone survey to see whether the citizens support a property tax increase. Her population of interest is all the adults in the county. To obtain a sample of adults (one from each of 456 households), the researcher uses a random dialing system that assures the inclusion of unlisted telephone numbers. Obviously, however, her poll excludes households without phones. Since most households without phones are occupied by poor people, she must determine whether using a phone survey unfairly excludes the poor. She therefore wishes to determine whether her sample is representative of the county's households with respect to *per capita income,* the mean income per person in households.

How can a nonrepresentative sample lead to an incorrect conclusion about support for the property tax increase? Suppose adults from wealthy households are more likely to own their homes. Homeowners directly see the amounts charged to their tax bills and are less inclined to support an increase. If homeowners are overrepresented in the sample, their responses will count more than will those of the members of poorer households. The results may indicate that the majority of county residents oppose a tax increase when in fact the poorer residents who are more in favor of it are not given a fair opportunity to voice their opinions.

Let us examine a small population to illustrate the consequences of under- and overrepresentation. Suppose a county has 10 households: 7 with phones and 3 without. Of the seven with phones, three support the tax increase and four oppose it. All three households without phones support it. Thus, the true support of the entire county is six *for* and four *against*. A correctly done poll, then, should show support for the tax increase. But what if those without phones were not polled? The poll results would make it appear incorrectly that county residents were against the increase four to three. Sample representativeness is an essential requirement for making statistical generalizations: statements about an entire population made on the basis of a sample.

Target Values for Hypothesis Tests of Sample Representativeness

To establish the representativeness of a sample, data must be acquired on some *known parameters* of the population. If we have a few known parameters, we can use them as hypothesized target values in a series of single-sample hypotheses tests. Demographic variables such as age, gender, marital status, income, and race typically are used as known parameters to evaluate the representativeness of a sample. This is the case because the U.S. Bureau of the Census provides these parameters by ZIP code area, census enumeration district, neighborhood, metropolitan area, county, or state. For groups and organizations such as companies, schools, clubs, and voluntary groups, organization records are a good source of such parameter data.

Returning to the researcher in Delaney County, to obtain a known parameter on income, she examines county population figures from the Census Bureau. She finds that the mean per capita income of all Delaney County households is $13,742 but that the standard deviation for the county is not supplied. If her sample is representative of Delaney County households with respect to per capita income, the mean of the survey sample households should also be $13,742, give or take a little sampling error. After completing all survey phone calls, her sample of 456 households reveals a mean per capita income of $14,174, with a standard deviation of $4,295. If she lets X = per capita income, the known county mean is μ_X = $13,742. The test effect of the sampling procedure on per capita income is the difference between the observed sample mean and this true county value. Thus:

Effect of sampling procedure on gauging per capita income =

$$\bar{X} - \mu_X = \$14,174 - \$13,742 = \$432$$

The one-sample means test is used to determine whether this test effect is: (1) due to random sampling error or (2) due to a failure to sample and represent poorer households adequately. From her experience with repeated sampling, the researcher knows that sample statistics vary slightly from known population parameters. Can this $432 difference be considered slight? The single-sample hypothesis test determines this. If the $432 difference is not statistically significant but simply is due to sampling error, she may say that the sample is representative. This means that the population group she sampled is the one she meant to sample: the targeted population of adults from all households, including poorer ones. It means that she tapped into all segments of the population in their correct proportions.

What is the significance of finding representativeness with regard to demographic variables? If the sample is representative of the demographic makeup of the county, she can safely *assume* that it is representative of other variables, such as support for the tax increase. Simply put, if her sample procedure correctly samples income levels, chances are that it correctly samples positive, negative, and neutral opinions on a tax increase. A correct balance of demographics suggests that the entire sampling procedure is correctly balanced. By contrast, if the demographic profile of the sample does not fit that of the population, the sample will be "biased" toward one segment of the population or another. Such response bias introduces errors into computations and leads to incorrect conclusions.

A challenge in testing sample representativeness is to properly conceive of the population. To test a hypothesis, of course, we must state it statistically—in such a way that we will know the shape of the sampling distribution *assuming that the hypothesis about the population is true*. Step 1 of the six steps of hypothesis testing is as follows:

Step 1: *Stat. H:*

$$\mu_X \text{ (sampled population)} = \$13,742 \text{ (the known parameter } (\mu_X) \text{ of the targeted Delaney County population)}$$

That is, the sample *is* representative of Delaney County households with regard to per capita income.

Alt. H: μ_X (sampled population) $\neq$ $13,742 (the known parameter (μ_X) of the targeted Delaney County population)

That is, the sample is not representative of Delaney County households. Two-tailed.

Picturing the notion of representativeness is a bit tricky. Note that we *do not* state the hypothesis with reference to the sample value (an often used but misleading device in some textbooks). That is, we do *not* hypothesize that the sample mean is equal to the population mean (i.e., that $\bar{X} = \mu_X$). *Hypothesis statements always pertain to a population.* Observed sample statistics should never appear in steps 1 through 3 of a hypothesis test. Samples and the statistics we compute from them are merely tools to address questions about a population.

For the Delaney County example, it is absurd for at least two reasons to state the hypothesis as "The sample mean per capita income is equal to the population mean." First, we can see that it is not; clearly, $14,174 \neq $13,742. Second, experience with sampling distributions tells us that if we draw another sample, its mean probably will differ from the $14,174 of the current sample. The real question of sample representativeness is: Did we actually sample the target population, or did we inadvertently obtain too many or too few sample subjects from some segment of this population?

The hypothesis test, correctly stated under step 1 above, would lead to *one of the following* conclusions: (1) If the researcher fails to reject the statistical hypothesis, she will conclude that there is no statistically significant difference between the mean per capita income of households in the population she actually sampled and that of the target population she set out to sample. Thus, the sample is a true representation of the population. She will note that the observed test effect—the $432 difference between the sample mean and the known county mean—is due to normal sampling error. (2) If, however, she rejects the statistical hypothesis, she will conclude that the sample is not representative of the population and that wealthy households were mistakenly oversampled. That is, the $432 effect is statistically significant—so large that she is 95 percent confident that it does not result from normal, expected sampling error. Since the sample mean is larger than the known population mean, she will conclude that the sample is biased toward wealthy residents. Let us use this example to illustrate the six steps of statistical inference for a single-sample means test of sample representativeness.

Illustration of a Single-Sample Means Test of Sample Representativeness

A researcher conducts a telephone poll of adults in Delaney County households. U.S. Census records show that the mean per capita income of the county's households is $13,742. Her sample of 456 households reveals a mean of $14,174 and a standard deviation of $4,295. Is her sample representative of the county with regard to per capita income? If it is not, speculate about why the sampling method failed.

Brief Checklist for the Six Steps of Statistical Inference

Test Preparation

State the research question; list givens, including variables (e.g., X =..., Y =...), their levels of measurement, the population(s) under study, and sample(s) and sample size(s); select the statistical test; provide observations of statistics and parameters; and draw a conceptual diagram.

Six Steps

Using the symbol H for *hypothesis:*

1. State the statistical H and the alternative H and stipulate test direction.
2. Describe the sampling distribution.
3. State the level of significance (α) and specify the critical test value.
4. Observe the actual sample outcomes and compute the test effects, the test statistic, and the p-value.
5. Make the rejection decision.
6. Interpret and apply best estimates in everyday terms.

Test Preparation

Research question: Is the sample of 456 households representative of Delaney County with respect to per capita income? *Givens:* Variable: X = household per capita income; ratio level. *Population:* Delaney County adults. *Sample:* 456 randomly selected adults from Delaney County households. *Statistical procedure:* single-sample means test; t-distribution; target value = $13,742, the known per capita income of Delaney County households (from U.S. Census data).

Observation:

$$\bar{X} = \$14,174 \qquad s_X = \$4,295 \qquad n = 456$$

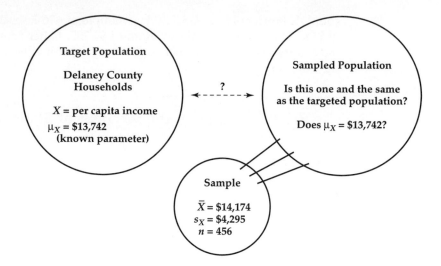

Six Steps

1. *Step 1: Stat. H:* $\mu_{X \text{ (sampled population)}}$ = \$13,742 (the known parameter (μ_X) of the targeted Delaney County population)

   That is, the sample is representative of Delaney County households with regard to per capita income.

   Alt. *H:* $\mu_{X \text{ (sampled population)}}$ ≠ \$13,742 (the known parameter (μ_X) of the targeted Delaney County population).

   That is, the sample is not representative of Delaney County households. Two-tailed.

2. *Sampling distribution:* If Stat. *H* is true and samples of size 456 are drawn repeatedly from the population of Delaney County households, sample means ($\bar{X}$'s) will center on \$13,742 as an approximately normal *t*-distribution, $df = n - 1 = 455$, with a standard error:

$$s_{\bar{X}} = \frac{s_X}{\sqrt{n-1}} = \frac{\$4,295}{\sqrt{455}} = \$201$$

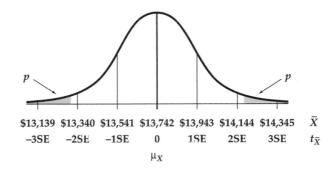

$13,139	$13,340	$13,541	$13,742	$13,943	$14,144	$14,345	$\bar{X}$
−3SE	−2SE	−1SE	0	1SE	2SE	3SE	$t_{\bar{X}}$

$$\mu_X$$

3. *Level of significance:* $\alpha = .05$. Two-tailed. Critical test value $= t_\alpha = \pm 1.96$.

4. *Observation:* $\bar{X} = \$14,174$ $s_X = \$4,295$
   $n = 456$.

   Test effect $= \bar{X} - \mu_X = \$14,174 - \$13,742 = \$432$

   Test statistic $= t_{\bar{X}} = \dfrac{\bar{X} - \mu_X}{s_{\bar{X}}} = \dfrac{\$14,174 - \$13,742}{\$201} = 2.15$ SE

   p-value: p [drawing a sample with a mean ($\bar{X}$) as unusual as or more unusual than $14,174 when the true population mean (μ_X) is $13,742] $< .05$. (This p-value is shaded on the curve in step 2.)

5. *Rejection decision:* $|t_{\bar{X}}| > |t_\alpha|$ (i.e., $2.15 > 1.96$); thus, $p < \alpha$, (i.e., $p < .05$). Reject Stat. *H* and accept Alt. *H* at the 95 percent level of confidence.

6. *Interpretation:* The sample appears not to be representative of Delaney County households. *Best estimate:* The population from which the sample came had a per capita income, on average, $432 higher than that of the county as a whole. *Answer:* The sampling method failed to include lower-income households in their correct proportion to the population as a whole. The researcher must state that the results apply only to households in Delaney County that have telephones and acknowledge that survey results on the tax increase are inconclusive.

Note the interpretation of this hypothesis test where the statistical hypothesis is rejected. We provide a best estimate of the parameter by describing the effect of the test: the $432 difference between the mean income of the sampled population and that of the targeted Delaney County population. It only makes sense to follow a rejection of something with an alternative explanation. If a public or professional audience is told that something is *not* a certain way, it is likely to ask: Then how is it? We respond with a best estimate based on our findings.

Finally, note that for a test of sample representativeness, it is confusing to look for a null hypothesis. The research question is: Is the sample representative? If we negate or nullify this research question, we get, "The sample is not representative." This statement does not provide us with a statistical hypothesis—one that directs us to the sampling distribution.

Large Single-Sample Proportions Test

A "large single-sample proportions test," as the word *proportion* implies, is used with one nominal/ordinal level variable, where $P = p$ [of the success category] of the variable and $Q = p$ [of the failure category(ies)]. This test is used when the smaller of P_u and Q_u times n is greater than or equal to 5 (i.e., $[(p_{\text{smaller}})\,(n)] \geq 5$).

When to Use a Large Single-Sample Proportions Test (t-distribution, $df = \infty$)

In general: With a sufficiently large sample that is useful for testing a hypothesis that the proportion of a category of a nominal/ordinal variable in a population is equal to a target value. Especially useful for testing the representativeness of a sample.

1. There is only one variable.
2. The variable is of nominal/ordinal level of measurement with $P = p$ [of the success category].
3. There is a single sample and population.
4. The sample size is sufficiently large that $[(p_{\text{smaller}})\,(n)] \geq 5$, where $p_{\text{smaller}} =$ the smaller of P_u and Q_u.
5. There is a target value of the variable to which we may compare the sample proportion.

The sampling distribution of proportions when $[(p_{\text{smaller}})\,(n)] \geq 5$ is the approximately normal t-distribution. Thus, the test statistic is a t-score, and the p-value is estimated by referring to the t-distribution table. As was noted in Chapter 7, the standard error of proportions is as follows:

Computing the Standard Error of a Sampling Distribution of Proportions When P_u and Q_u Are Known (for a nominal variable)

$$\sigma_{P_s} = \sqrt{\frac{P_u Q_u}{n}}$$

where

$\sigma_{P_s} =$ standard error of proportions for a nominal/ordinal variable with $P = p$ [of the success category], $Q = p$ [of the failure category]
$P_u =$ hypothesized p [of the success category in the population]
$Q_u =$ hypothesized p [of the failure category in the population]
$n =$ sample size

Note that the symbols in the numerator of this equation indicate population parameters (P_u and Q_u). This differs from the calculation of the standard error for confidence intervals, where sample statistics (P_s and Q_s) are used as estimates. Although P_u and Q_u are not truly known, in this hypothesis test the standard error is always computed in this manner. This is done because the sampling distribution describes sample outcomes assuming that the population parameters are equal to the *hypothesized* values. P_u and Q_u are known in the sense that we know what to expect in repeated sampling when their hypothesized values are true.

The test statistic is calculated as follows:

Calculating the Test Statistic for a Large Single-Sample Proportions Test

$$t_{P_s} = \frac{P_s - P_u}{\sigma_{P_s}}$$

$$= \frac{\text{the effect}}{\text{standard error}} = \frac{\text{number of standard errors (SE)}}{\text{difference between what was observed and what was hypothesized}}$$

where

t_{P_s} = number of standard errors a sample proportion (P_s) deviates from the hypothesized population proportion (P_u)

$P_s = p$ [of the success category in the sample]

$P_u = p$ [of the success category hypothesized for the population]

σ_{P_s} = standard error of the sampling distribution of proportions

---

The formula for t_{P_s} is derived from the dimensions of the approximately normal *t*-distribution curve as follows. Notice the similarity to other *t*- and *Z*-score calculations.

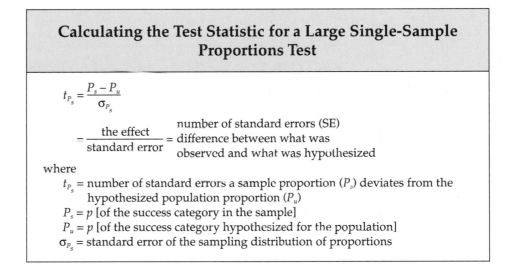

This test statistic, like the one we calculated for the means test, tells us how many standard errors (SE) an observed sample proportion falls from the

hypothesized population proportion. Now let us apply the six steps of statistical inference and discuss the particulars of this hypothesis test.

The Six Steps of Statistical Inference for a Large Single-Sample Proportions Test

Problem: The City University student records office has informed us that 27 percent of the student population is married. We draw a sample of 248 students from the campus and find that 20 percent of them are married. Is this sample representative of the City University student body with regard to marital status?

Brief Checklist for the Six Steps of Statistical Inference

Test Preparation

State the research question; list givens, including variables (e.g., $X = ...$, $Y = ...$), their levels of measurement, the population(s) under study, and sample(s) and sample size(s); select the statistical test; provide observations of statistics and parameters; and draw a conceptual diagram.

Six Steps

Using the symbol H for *hypothesis:*

1. State the statistical H and the alternative H and stipulate test direction.
2. Describe the sampling distribution.
3. State the level of significance (α) and specify the critical test value.
4. Observe the actual sample outcomes and compute the test effects, the test statistic, and the p-value.
5. Make the rejection decision.
6. Interpret and apply best estimates in everyday terms.

Test Preparation

Research question: Is this sample of 248 City University students representative of the City University student population with respect to marital status? *Givens:* Variable: marital status; nominal; $P = p$ [of City University students who are married]. $Q = p$ [of City University students who are not married]. *Population:* City University student body. *Sample:* 248 students. *Statistical procedure:* large single-sample proportions test; t-distribution; target value $= P_u = .27$

(the known, true proportion of married students in the City University student population). $Q_u = 1 - P_u = 1 - .27 = .73$.

Observations: $n = 248$; $P_s = .20$. $[(p_{smaller}) (n)] \geq 5$ (i.e., $(.27)(248) = 67$).

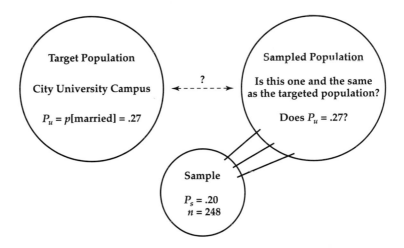

Six Steps

1. *Stat. H:* $P_{u\ \text{(sampled population)}}$ = .27 (the known proportion married (P_u) in the targeted City University population)

   That is, the sample *is* representative of the City University student population with regard to marital status.

   Alt. H: $P_{u\ \text{(sampled population)}}$ $\neq$ .27 (the known proportion married (P_u) in the targeted City University population). Two-tailed

   That is, there is a bias in our sampling procedure that results in the sample *not being* representative of the City University student population with regard to marital status.

2. *Sampling distribution:* If Stat. *H* is true and samples of size 248 are repeatedly drawn from the City University student population, sample proportions (P_s) will center on .27 as an approximately normal *t*-distribution and *df* = ∞, with a standard error:

$$\sigma_{P_s} = \sqrt{\frac{P_u Q_u}{n}} = \sqrt{\frac{(.27)(.73)}{248}} = .03$$

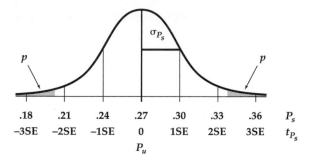

3. *Level of significance:* $\alpha = .05$. Two-tailed. Critical test score $= t_\alpha = \pm 1.96$.
4. *Observation:* $n = 248$; $P_s = .20$

   Test effect $= P_s - P_u = .20 - .27 = -.07$

   Test statistic $= t_{P_s} = \dfrac{P_s - P_u}{\sigma_{P_s}} = \dfrac{.20 - .27}{.03} = -2.33\ \text{SE}$

   p-value: p [of observing a sample proportion, P_s, as unusual as or more unusual than .20 when the true population proportion, P_u, is .27] $<.05$. (This *p*-value is shaded on the curve in step 2.)

5. *Rejection decision:* $|t_{P_s}| > |t_\alpha|$ (i.e., 2.33 > 1.96); thus, $p < \alpha$, (i.e., $p < .05$). Reject the Stat. H and accept the Alt. H at the 95 percent level of confidence.

6. *Interpretation:* There appears to be a bias in our sampling procedure. Married students appear to be underrepresented in the sample, while single students are overrepresented. *Best estimates:* Married students are undersampled by about 7 percent, an amount not likely to have resulted from random sampling error. *Answer:* The sample is not representative of the City University student population with regard to marital status.

Some things of note about this hypothesis test:

- In step 1 we state the alternative hypothesis as a two-tailed test. It would not be appropriate to examine the sample statistic P_s to determine the direction of the test. In general, tests of sample representativeness are done as two-tailed tests.
- In step 2, as with any hypothesis test, the test depends on describing the sampling distribution, which tells us what happens with repeated sampling. With this example, we are making a prediction for any nominal/ordinal variable having a population proportion (i.e., parameter) of .27 when samples of size 248 are repeatedly drawn: About 68 percent of the time the sample proportion P_s will compute to

between .24 and .30, and about 95 percent of the time it will compute to between .21 and .33. If you are unconvinced of this, put together a box of beans (i.e., a population) that are 27 percent red (to represent married students) and 73 percent white (to represent single students). Repeatedly draw, say, 300 random samples of size 248 (with replacement after each draw). Compute the proportion of red beans for each sample and plot these statistics on a histogram. This histogram will approximate a normal curve.

- In step 4 the difference between the observed sample proportion and the hypothesized proportion of married students (i.e., $P_s - P_u = .07$, or 7 percent) is "the effect" of the test. Essentially, the purpose of the hypothesis test is to determine whether this test effect is due to random sampling error (as asserted by the statistical hypothesis) or due to a bias in our sampling procedure (as asserted by the alternative hypothesis).

- In step 4 we determined that the observed sample proportion, $P_s = .20$, has a low probability of occurrence with repeated sampling of a population in which $P_u = .27$. This led us to conclude in step 5 that this observed P_s of .20 was due not to normal, random sampling error but instead was due to the fact that the population from which our sample came was not one and the same as the City University population. In other words, the sample is not representative of the population.

- In step 4, in computing the p-value, we are stating "how unusual" the observed sample outcome is "if the statistical hypothesis is true." Thus, if the population proportion, P_u, is indeed .27 and we have no reason beforehand to predict a direction, then it will be just as unusual to draw a sample proportion 2.33 SE above the mean as a sample proportion 2.33 SE below it. This is why we identify areas in *both tails* of the curve in step 2 for a two-tailed test. The purpose of including the area of the other tail in a two-tailed test is to acknowledge that when a direction is not expected beforehand, it is just as unusual for a particular sample to miss to one side as to the other. Essentially, the p-value is counted twice (or multiplied by 2) for a two-tailed test.

- In step 6 we focus on the alternative hypothesis and disregard the statistical hypothesis because it was rejected in step 5. Steps 1 and 6 of the six steps of statistical inference are substantive (they discuss the research question) as opposed to technical (a description of statistical procedures).

- Regarding step 6, with a public audience, the concept of representativeness may not resonate. Therefore, to bring substance to the answer, we provide a best estimate—some concrete numbers—that a public audience can relate to. We note that married students are undersampled by 7 percent [i.e., $(.27 - .20)(100) = 7$ percent]; that is, we know that married students constitute 27 percent of the campus population but account for only 20 percent of our sample.

What Does It Mean When a Sample Is Found Not to Be Representative?

With our sample of 248 City University students, we have now concluded that this sample is not representative with respect to marital status. When this situation occurs, three issues must be addressed. First, what defect in sampling design led to the undersampling of married students? Did mailed questionnaires not reach them as easily as they reached single students? Are married students harder to track because they live off campus, or are they too busy raising children to complete a questionnaire? Any number of things can cause faulty sample design.

Our second question is: In what ways will this biased sample change our conclusions? Clearly, a "single students" bias—an oversampling of them—can lead to the wrong conclusions about any opinion related to marital status. For example, suppose the questionnaire asks about support for university-provided child care services. Single students, the great majority of whom do not have children, are less likely to favor this, especially if fees are charged to all students to cover the cost. Our survey might reveal, for example, that only 40 percent of students support child care services. If single students are over-represented, however, their negative responses will pull down the overall student population estimate. The sample estimate, then, is lower than the real proportion of support (i.e., the parameter).

Our third question is: What adjustments are in order when a sample is not representative? Several things can be done to compensate for sample bias. First, additional subjects can be selected from the underrepresented categories. For instance, to avoid underrepresentation of poor households without telephones, telephone surveys often are supplemented with door-to-door interviews in poor neighborhoods. In fact, to assist in this endeavor, the U.S. Bureau of the Census provides neighborhood-based data on the percentages of households without telephones. Second, we can proceed with data analysis but stipulate that the population over- or underrepresents some groups. For example, with a telephone survey we may simply note that those without telephones—the poor—are underrepresented in the study. This, of course, opens the door to criticism. Finally, a nonrepresentative sample can be artificially adjusted mathematically by "weighting" sample categories to bring them up to their correct population proportions. Such sample weighting is complicated, must be done with great care, and is beyond the scope of this text. Suffice it to say that every effort should be made to design a sampling procedure that obtains correct proportions of meaningful segments of the population (review "Sampling Error and Its Management with Probability Theory" in Chapter 2).

Small Single-Sample Proportions Test

With a single sample, one nominal/ordinal variable, and $[(p_{smaller})\,(n)] < 5$, a "small single-sample proportions test" is used. This test takes into account the fact that the sampling distribution of sampled proportions will not take the shape of a smooth, approximately normal curve when $[(p_{smaller})\ (n)] < 5$. This test statistic is called the binomial distribution test. It is used most frequently in research on laboratory subjects or small groups. It has many applications in addition to testing the representativeness of a sample. This test is covered in Chapter 13.

Presentation of Data from Single-Sample Hypothesis Tests

It is in the area of sample representativeness that single-sample hypotheses tests are most frequently used. Table 10–1 comes from a scientific research journal article in which the author addressed the issue of sample representativeness. The sample consisted of 206 physicians in Jefferson County, Alabama, and the study was conducted from a local academic health science center. The table assesses whether the sample is representative of Jefferson County physicians and physicians in U.S. metropolitan areas. The percentages reported for these two *populations* are known parameters taken from medical directories. These known parameters were used as the target values in single-sample proportions tests. The probabilities reported under "p" are the p-values of each test, with "NS" indicating that there was not a significant difference between the population and the sample proportions at the .05 level of significance.

The table shows that for all four specialty categories the sampled physicians were representative of physicians in U.S. metropolitan areas. However, the sample was not representative of physicians in Jefferson County. Surgical specialties were underrepresented, and "other specialties" (such as nuclear medicine) were overrepresented. With additional analysis, it was determined that academic health science center physicians, many of whom were in the

---

TABLE 10–1   Comparison of Physician Specialty Categories for the Sample with the Population of Physicians in Jefferson County, Alabama, and in Metropolitan Areas of the United States

		Percentage of Physicians in			
Specialty Category	Sample (%)	Jefferson County (%)	p	U.S. Metropolitan Areas (%)	p
General practice	7.77	7.95	NS*	10.81	NS
Medical specialties	31.07	32.83	NS	28.46	NS
Surgical specialties	28.64	35.45	$p < .05$	24.35	NS
Other specialties	32.52	23.77	$p < .01$	36.38	NS

* NS = not significant at the .05 level of significance, two-tailed test.
SOURCE: Clair et al., 1993. Population data from *Physicians Characteristics and Distribution in the U.S.*, American Medical Association, Chicago, 1982.

"Other Specialties" category, were more likely to respond, perhaps because they felt compelled to cooperate with their campus colleagues who were conducting the study. To address the consequences of this sample bias, the authors stated that their results were more applicable to cities with academic health science centers. In other words, they acknowledged that the population to which their results were generalizable consisted not of all physicians but of those who reflected the makeup of their sample.

☹   STATISTICAL FOLLIES AND FALLACIES   ☹

Is a Mathematically Representative Sample Necessarily Representative in Other Respects?

The issue of sample representativeness concerns whether all the segments of a population are fairly represented in a sample. Because a test of representativeness requires a target value, we must rely on known parameters to state statistical hypotheses. It is *assumed* that if a sample is representative with respect to known parameters, that sample is representative with respect to the variety of opinions held by the members of a population. For instance, in our example of Delaney County residents we assume that if the researcher's sample procedure correctly samples income levels, chances are that it correctly samples residents with positive, negative, and neutral opinions on a tax increase. Such assumptions are not always realized. For one thing, if a sample is small, it may not have room for the variety of opinions that exists within the population. For example, if the researcher randomly selected only 10 households, even if they accurately represent proportions at each income level, with so few cases there is a good chance that not all opinions are represented. Suppose, for instance, that the median income of Delaney County's residents is $30,000 and the researcher's sample is size 10, with 5 residents above the median (i.e., high income) and 5 below it (i.e., low income). Mathematically this constitutes a representative sample. But could only five high-income residents represent the opinion of all the people in that income category? It is very possible that the chosen five lean in one direction or another on a tax increase. A second sample of five high-income residents may lean in the other direction. Establishing sample representativeness for a small sample is a shaky endeavor at best.

The analogy of tasting a pot of chili comes to mind here, where the pot represents a population with a variety of ingredients and nuances of flavors (or opinions). If we taste a large sample—an entire cup from a stirred pot—chances are that we will get a taste of every ingredient. If, however, we use a one-fourth-teaspoon measure—which lacks room for the beans and slices of rattlesnake meat—we are likely to sample only the broth.

In a small sample there may not be room for the expanse of opinions.

Imagine that you have been charged with a misdemeanor and are to appear before a three-judge panel. On a given day even a randomly selected panel may be loaded with two or three especially tough or especially forgiving judges. The disposition of your case may hinge on the luck of the draw. Small samples are inherently error-prone in terms of representativeness.

Statistical Procedures Covered to Here

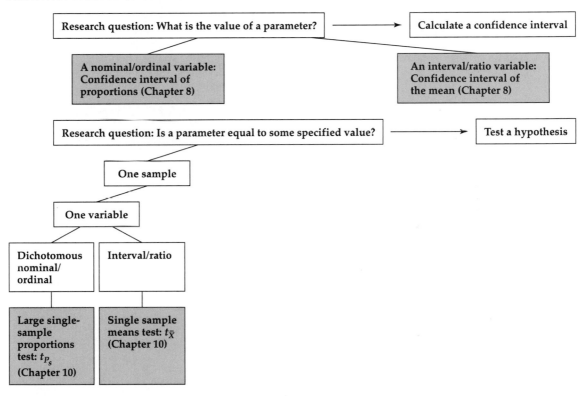

Formulas for Chapter 10

Single-sample means test (*t*-test):

Given: An interval/ratio variable X and a single sample and population

Research question: Is μ_X (i.e., the mean of X in the population) equal to a target value?

Stat. H: μ_X = a target value

Sampling distribution: *t*-distribution with $df = n - 1$; standard error estimated using the sample standard deviation.

Standard error =

$$s_{\bar{X}} = \frac{s_X}{\sqrt{n-1}}$$

Test effect = $\bar{X} - \mu_X$

Test statistic [for use with the approximately normal *t*-distribution table (Statistical Table C in Appendix B)]:

$$t_{\bar{X}} = \frac{\bar{X} - \mu_X}{s_{\bar{X}}}$$

$$df = n - 1$$

Large single-sample proportions test:

Given: A nominal/ordinal variable with $P = p$ [of the success category].

Use when: $[(p_{\text{smaller}})\,(n)] \geq 5$. (If $[(p_{\text{smaller}})\,(n)] < 5$, see Chapter 13.)

Research question: Is P_u (i.e., the p [of the success category in the population]) equal to a target value?

Stat. H: P_u = a target value.

Sampling distribution: t-distribution with $df = \infty$.

Standard error =

$$\sigma_{P_s} = \sqrt{\frac{P_u Q_u}{n}}$$

Test effect = $P_s - P_u$

Test statistic [for use with the approximately normal *t*-distribution table (Statistical Table C in Appendix B)]:

$$t_{P_s} = \frac{P_s - P_u}{\sigma_{P_s}}$$

Questions for Chapter 10

1. What is the purpose of a single-sample hypothesis test? What type of question does it answer with regard to a population?
2. For single-sample hypotheses tests, target parameter values come from four sources. Name each source and provide an example hypothesis for each one.
3. Describe the situation (i.e., the selection criteria) for using a "single-sample means test."

4. Describe the situation (i.e., the selection criteria) for using a "large single-sample proportions test."

5. Match the following:

   a. σ_{P_s} _____ The observed sample proportion
   b. P_u _____ The standard error of sample proportions
   c. t_{P_s} _____ The hypothesized population proportion
   d. P_s _____ The test statistic (i.e., the number of standard errors distance from the observed sample proportion to the hypothesized population proportion)

6. Match the following:

   a. $\overline{X}$ _____ The estimated standard error of sample means
   b. $t_{\overline{X}}$ _____ The hypothesized population mean
   c. $s_{\overline{X}}$ _____ The observed sample mean
   d. μ_X _____ The test statistic (i.e., the number of standard errors distance from the observed sample mean to the hypothesized population mean)

7. The statistics observed and calculated in step 4 of the six steps of hypothesis testing should never appear in steps 1 through 3. Why?

8. What is the relationship between the effect of a hypothesis test and the test statistic? Specifically, in what manner does the test statistic measure the test effect?

9. Is the statistical hypothesis more likely to be rejected when the test effect is large or small? Illustrate your answer by drawing an approximately normal t-distribution curve for a single-sample means test.

10. Is the statistical hypothesis likely to be rejected when the test statistic is large or small? Illustrate your answer by drawing an approximately normal t-distribution curve for a single-sample means test.

11. What is the relationship between the sizes of calculated values of test statistics and their p-values?

12. Is it easier to reject the statistical hypothesis with a one-tailed or a two-tailed test? Illustrate your answer by using an approximately normal t-distribution curve for a single-sample means test.

13. What does the word *critical* mean in the terms *critical region* and *critical test score?*

14. Provide an example of how a nonrepresentative sample can lead to faulty conclusions.

15. For a hypothesis test of sample representativeness, distinguish the sampled population from the targeted population. Are these populations the same or different when the sample is indeed representative of the target population?

16. In general, with a "single-sample means test," when the statistical hypothesis is true, the scores (i.e., sample means) in the sampling distribution will center on what value of X?

17. For a single-sample means test, when $t_{\bar{X}} > t_\alpha$, is the p-value greater than or less than α? Will we reject the statistical hypothesis or fail to reject it?

18. For a large single-sample proportions test, when $t_{P_s} < t_\alpha$ is the p-value greater than or less than α? Will we reject the statistical hypothesis or fail to reject it?

19. Like the normal curve, a t-distribution is symmetrical and its mean, median, and mode are equal. Why do we say, however, that a t-distribution is only *approximately* normal?

20. What underlying feature of the mean causes a loss of degrees of freedom when the mean is used in a statistical test?

21. What effect does an increase in sample size have on the size of the standard error of a sampling distribution?

Exercises for Chapter 10

General instructions: On all hypothesis tests, follow the six steps of statistical inference, including test preparation, a conceptual diagram, and probability curves. For consistency, round standard errors to two decimal places. Use $\alpha = .05$ unless otherwise stipulated.

1. For the following hypothesized target parameter values and observed sample statistics, compute the effect of the test. Show formulas.

Hypothesized Target Parameter Value (from step 1 of the six steps)	Observed Sample Statistic (from step 4 of the six steps)	Effect of Test
a. $\mu_X = 22$ years	$\bar{X} = 21.4$ years	
b. $P_u = .75$	$P_s = .69$	
c. $\mu_X = 146$ pounds	$\bar{X} = 138.8$ pounds	
d. $P_u = .56$	$P_s = .74$	

2. For the following hypothesized target parameter values and observed sample statistics, compute the effect of the test. Show formulas.

Hypothesized Target Parameter Value (from step 1 of the six steps)	Observed Sample Statistic (from step 4 of the six steps)	Effect of Test
a. $\mu_X = 100$ ears per bushel	$\bar{X} = 113$ ears per bushel	
b. $P_u = .50$	$P_s = .39$	
c. $\mu_X = 572$ stolen cars	$\bar{X} = 591$ stolen cars	
d. $P_u = .29$	$P_s = .34$	

3. Test your ability to correctly use the *t*-distribution table (Statistical Table C in Appendix B). Complete the following table, which presents the results of a series of *t*-tests of various sample sizes and levels of significance. For each test, stipulate (*a*) the "critical value" (t_α), (*b*) an estimate of the probability of obtaining a *t*-value as unusual as or more unusual than the one obtained ($t_{\bar{x}}$), and (*c*) whether you would reject or fail to reject the statistical hypothesis.

Sample Size (n)	Level of Significance (α)	Tails (direction of test)	Obtained t-value ($t_{\bar{x}}$)	Critical t-value (t_α)	Estimated p-value (p)	Reject or Fail to Reject the Stat. H
a. 15	.05	Directional	2.421			
b. 9	.01	Two-tailed	−3.081			
c. 37	.001	Two-tailed	1.986			
d. 19	.05	One-tailed	2.470			
e. 30	.05	Nondirectional	2.049			

4. Test your ability to correctly use the *t*-distribution table (Statistical Table C in Appendix B). Complete the following table, which presents the results of a series of *t*-tests of various sample sizes and levels of significance. For each test, stipulate (*a*) the "critical value"(t_α), (*b*) an estimate of the probability of obtaining a *t*-value as unusual as or more unusual than the one obtained ($t_{\bar{x}}$), and (*c*) whether you would reject or fail to reject the statistical hypothesis.

Sample Size (n)	Level of Significance (α)	Tails (direction of test)	Obtained t-value ($t_{\bar{x}}$)	Critical t-value (t_α)	Estimated p-value (p)	Reject or Fail to Reject the Stat. H
a. 23	.05	Nondirectional	1.720			
b. 9	.01	Directional	−3.081			
c. 13	.05	Directional	−1.133			
d. 22	.001	Two-tailed	3.141			
e. 11	.001	Two-tailed	13.462			

5. The proportion of married females in the labor force in 1980 was .54. You ask a random sample of 103 married women if they are working outside the home, and 62 say yes. Test a hypothesis to see if the proportion has changed since 1980.

6. The mean number of physician visits for persons in the United States over age 55 years is 5.2 per year, and the mean number of disability days (full days when unable to perform normal functions) is 7.5 days per year

(fictional data). Test the hypothesis that those over age 55 in your city have the national mean for physician visits. Your sample data:

$$n = 65 \qquad \bar{X} = 5.8 \text{ visits} \qquad s_X = 1.8 \text{ visits}$$

7. As the quality control supervisor of a soft drink canning company, Tasty Sip, Inc., you wish to test a hypothesis to determine whether there is a loss in the volume of 12-ounce drinks during the canning and delivery processes. To sample, you randomly remove four cans from each of six supermarkets from the previous delivery. Your findings:

$$\bar{X} = 11.7 \text{ ounces} \quad s_X = .8 \text{ ounce} \quad n = 24 \text{ cans}$$

8. A researcher found that two decades ago 53 percent of the population favored some form of handgun control. Test the hypothesis that the same proportion favors it today. Your sample data: 105 randomly selected adults among whom 66 favor control, 32 do not favor control, and 7 are undecided or have no opinion.

9. The proportion of nonwhites (African-Americans, Asians, Hispanics, and other non-Anglo persons) in a state population is .18. A random sample of 95 students at the state's major university reveals that 12 are nonwhite. Is the student population representative of the state population with respect to race?

10. Someone asks you if the average grade point average (GPA) of State University students is equal to a B (i.e., a GPA of 3.0). You do not think so and have reason to believe that it is less than 3.0. Test the hypothesis with the following sample data:

$$n = 140 \qquad \bar{X} = 2.87 \text{ GPA points} \qquad s_X = .8 \text{ GPA points}$$

11. When individuals feel disconnected from others in society, we say that they feel alienated. Dr. Conrad, a clinical psychologist, measures alienation with a survey scale that consists of 20 items, where the higher the score, the greater the feeling of alienation. The scale is normalized so that a score of 40 or below is considered healthy and not alienated. For 25 patients who are seeking care for anxiety, he finds a mean alienation score of 46 with a standard deviation of 13.2. Test a hypothesis to determine whether anxiety patients are above the healthy alienation score of 40.

12. You have a measurement index of happiness with scores ranging from 1 to 10. You wish to test the hypothesis that the mean score of the Elmsville area is higher than 6.5. You draw a random sample of 59 individuals and find a mean score of 5.9 with a standard deviation of 2.6. Test the hypothesis. Note that the observed sample mean of 5.9 is less than the hypothesized mean of 6.5. Take care in computing the *p*-value in step 4 of the six steps.

13. Using a random sampling technique, you conduct a health survey of 295 adults in the Bigcity metropolitan area. The following table provides known parameters about Bigcity's population from U.S. Census data as well as data from your sample.

   a. Is this sample representative of Bigcity's population with respect to age?

   b. Is this sample representative of Bigcity's population with respect to gender?

Comparison of Bigcity Population and Sample Data (n = 295)

Characteristic		Bigcity Parameters from U.S. Census Data	Sample Statistics
Gender (% female)		52.1%	54.0%
Age	Mean	27 years	26 years
	Standard deviation	Unknown	6
Years of residency in Bigcity	Mean	14 years	13.8 years
	Standard deviation	Unknown	3.0
% living below poverty level		29.0%	33.1%

14. Follow the instructions of exercise 13 to answer the following:

   a. Is this sample representative of Bigcity's population with respect to years of residency?

   b. Is this sample representative of Bigcity's population with respect to the percentage living below the poverty level ?

Optional Computer Applications for Chapter 10

If your class uses the optional computer applications that accompany this text, open the Chapter 10 exercises on the *Computer Applications for The Statistical Imagination* compact disk. The exercises focus on (1) running single-sample hypothesis tests in *SPSS for Windows*, (2) using single-sample hypothesis tests to test target parameters, and (3) using single-sample hypothesis tests to examine the representativeness of samples.

CHAPTER 11

BIVARIATE RELATIONSHIPS: *t*-TEST FOR COMPARING THE MEANS OF TWO GROUPS

Introduction: Bivariate Analysis

As we noted in Chapter 6, prediction provides the connection between statistical analysis and probability theory. The ability to predict sampling outcomes and other future events is a valuable skill. Making predictions is an important part of science, marketing, finance, manufacturing, medical and social services, gambling, and every other endeavor that uses statistics.

The statistical imagination goes beyond predicting merely for the sake of anticipating what will happen: Prediction also assists in understanding. Scientific predictions depend on measuring several phenomena and tying those measurements together in a meaningful way. With the assistance of well-organized ideas (i.e., theory), prediction enhances understanding and vice versa. For example, in studying psychological depression, if we can determine what triggers depression, we can identify the "populations at risk" and institute preventive measures. For instance, research shows that people who experience multiple life crises—several "stressful life events" in a short period—are at greater risk of experiencing depression. The knowledge that such crises foster depressive symptoms has fueled a movement toward organizing crisis clinics and self-help groups. Simply put, there is a relationship between stressful life events and becoming depressed.

Bivariate (or two-variable) analysis involves searching for statistical relationships between two variables. A **statistical relationship** between two variables asserts that *the measurements of one variable tend to consistently change with the measurements of the other, making one variable a good predictor of the other*. In scientific research we call the *predictor* variable the independent variable and the *predicted* variable the dependent variable. How a relationship is measured depends on the levels of measurement of the two variables. There are three common approaches to measuring statistical relationships:

1. *Difference of means testing:* comparing means of an interval/ratio or interval-like ordinal variable among the categories or groups of a nominal/ordinal variable

2. *Counting the frequencies of joint occurrences* of attributes of two nominal variables

3. *Measuring the correlation* between two interval/ratio variables or between two ordinal variables

These approaches are summarized in Table 11–1. This chapter focuses on the difference of means approach, but let us begin by exploring all three approaches briefly.

A Statistical Relationship

The measurements of one variable tend to consistently change with the measurements of another, making one variable a good predictor of the other.

Difference of Means Tests

In hypothesizing a relationship between a dependent interval/ratio or interval-like ordinal variable and an independent dichotomous (i.e., two-group) nominal/ordinal variable, we use the difference of means approach. The hypothesis test for this relationship is called a two-group difference of means test, the topic of this chapter. For example, advertisers may wish to see if there is a rela-

---

TABLE 11–1   Common Approaches to Measuring the Statistical Relationship between Two Variables

Levels of Measurement of the Two Variables		Approach to Measuring the Statistical Relationship Between the Two Variables
Independent Variable	*Dependent Variable*	
Nominal or ordinal	Interval or ratio	Compare differences of means of the interval/ratio variable among the categories of a nominal or ordinal variable (Chapters 11 and 12).
Nominal or ordinal	Nominal or ordinal	Count the frequencies of the joint occurrence of category attributes of two nominal/ordinal variables (Chapters 13 and 16).
Ordinal, interval, or ratio	Ordinal, interval, or ratio	Measure the correlation between the two variables (Chapters 14, 15, and 16).

tionship between the nominal variable *gender* and the interval/ratio variable *time spent watching sports programs on television*. To hypothesize this relationship is to assert that the mean of hours spent watching is higher for men than for women. If this is found to be true, advertisements for male products such as mustache trimmers may be placed in sports programs.

To test for a difference among three or more means, we use a procedure called analysis of variance (ANOVA). See Chapter 12. With ANOVA, group means are compared indirectly by determining how much of the variance in the interval/ratio variable is explained by group membership. Suppose, for example, we have an interval/ratio variable called "favorableness to team concept" for hospital care, a measurement scale that consists of 40 questionnaire items. It discerns whether a hospital's medical professionals believe in sharing authority for patient care. A theory about interprofessional relationships might raise the question: Do physicians treat nurses, pharmacists, and physical therapists as coprofessionals, part of a team of relative equals, or as subordinates, underlings who are to be bossed around? The ANOVA test would compare the mean favorableness to team concept scores for these four groups to see whether physicians are less favorable. In terms of establishing a relationship between two variables, ANOVA is similar to the two-group difference of means test; both involve comparing means (of an interval/ratio or interval-like ordinal variable) among the groups or categories of a nominal/ordinal variable.

Joint Occurrences of Attributes

A second way to view the relationship between two variables pertains to two nominal variables with a focus on the *joint occurrence* of attributes. An attribute is some quality or characteristic of a subject that is conveyed in the category names of a nominal/ordinal variable. For gender there are the attributes male and female; for race, there are the attributes of white, African-American, and Hispanic; and so on. A joint occurrence of attributes involves two variables *for a single individual*, with pairings of attributes of the two variables. For instance, Mary Smith is a "white female"; she has the joint occurrence of the attributes white and female. Similarly, John Jones is an "African-American male."

An example of a research question about the relationship between two nominal/ordinal variables is: Is there a relationship between gender (male versus female) and support for government-subsidized child care services (yes versus no)? Put another way, do the joint occurrences of the attributes female–yes and male–no occur more often than expected? Simply put, are women more likely than men to support such services? If this is the case, knowing the gender makeup of a community allows better predictions of whether that community will support tax-subsidized child care services. We use a chi-square test (Chapter 13) to determine relationships between nominal variables and a gamma test for two ordinal variables (Chapter 16).

Correlation

A relationship between two interval/ratio or interval-like ordinal variables indicates that scores on one variable tend to change consistently, or *correlate*, with scores on the other. For example, there is a correlation between the variables frequent experience of stressful life events (such as death of a loved one, a divorce, or the loss of a job) and psychological depression. To say that these two variables are correlated is to say that individuals who experience very few stressful life events are likely to score low on measures of psychological depression, while those who experience a large number of these events are likely to score high on depression measures. Correlation statistics are discussed in Chapters 14 and 15.

For two ordinal level variables, we use a "rank-order correlation" test (Chapter 16). This involves seeing whether those study subjects who rank high on one measure also tend to rank high on another. For example, in comparing the 50 states, is there a correlation between a state's ranking on poverty level and its ranking on crime rates? Put simply, among the 50 states, if a state ranks in the top 10 in poverty, does it also rank in the top 10 in crime rates?

In all research questions on the relationship between two variables, we hypothesize a relationship between an independent variable and a dependent variable (review Chapter 1). The dependent variable is the one of main interest—the variable we are attempting to explain—and the independent variable is the one used to predict scores of the dependent variable. For example, do stressful life circumstances (independent variable) cause psychological depression (dependent variable)? Do poverty conditions (independent variable) contribute to the incidence of criminal acts (dependent variable)? This text deals only with two-variable cases, or bivariate statistical tests. The relationships among three or more variables are the topics of advanced *multivariate* statistics texts. Let us focus on the difference of means approach for the two-group case.

Two-Group Difference of Means Test (*t*-Test) for Independent Samples

A two-group difference of means test simply compares the means of an interval/ratio or interval-like ordinal variable for two groups or categories of a nominal/ordinal variable. For example, we may be interested in whether mean college admissions test scores are higher for students at City University than for students at State University. Or we may want to prove that there is no difference in the mean energy levels of subjects in an experimental group taking a multivitamin pill and control group subjects who are given placebos (fake pills).

Of course, the variable on which the mean is computed must be an interval/ratio or interval-like ordinal variable. Moreover, in this two-group means test, this variable is typically the dependent variable.

The two comparison groups of the independent variable may come from separate populations, such as City University and State University. The same test can be used, however, if the two groups are categories of a dichotomous nominal/ordinal variable from a single population (such as the variable gender, with the categories male and female). In such a situation we compare the separate populations of men and women within the total population.

To illustrate a two-group difference of means test, suppose we have gotten into an argument with a friend over whether men or women get better grades at Faroff University, a campus with approximately 9,000 students. We argue that there is no difference in the mean grade point averages (GPAs) of these two categories of students. Our friend, who has been influenced by traditional myths that women are intellectually inferior to men, bets us $10 that men do better than women. We feel that he is unaware of how markedly gender roles have changed. For example, while the college campus was once a bastion of male dominance, today women outnumber men in U.S. colleges. Thus, we take his bet.

To resolve the issue of GPAs, we randomly select the records of 208 students, 102 males and 106 females. We find that the mean GPA for males is 2.70 GPA points with a standard deviation of .65; for females the mean is 2.63 GPA points with a standard deviation of .71. Our friend says: "See. I told you. Pay up, sucker!" We respond: "Wait a minute. Sample differences do not always imply population differences." We then attempt to explain to our friend that it is necessary to test the hypothesis that there is a significant difference between the GPAs of men and women students *in the total population* of Faroff University students. We must convince our friend that the .07 difference between GPAs found in the samples may be due to sampling error.

In this hypothesis test, GPA is the dependent variable and gender is the independent variable because we are interested in whether gender predicts GPA. Our concern, of course, is with the population of Faroff University students. To keep our focus on the population, in doing a two-group means test it is good to view the subgroups in the context of their separate populations. In other words, imagine males and females as two distinct populations on the campus, as depicted in Figure 11–1.

The research question deals with the two groups' populations and inquires whether their parameters for mean GPA (i.e., μ_{X_i}) are different. The statistical hypothesis, however, is that the two μ_X's are the same, because it is this hypothesis that provides us with fixed, expected outcomes in sampling. Specifically, if the parameters of the two populations are equal, we should expect the two sample means to have a difference of zero—give or take a little sampling error. That is, if $\mu_{X_1} = \mu_{X_2}$, then by subtracting μ_{X_2} from both sides of this equation, we obtain $\mu_{X_1} - \mu_{X_2} = 0$.

Figure 11–1 shows that "$\mu_X = ?$" for each population, meaning that we do not know the actual mean GPA for either males or females. This highlights an interesting point: Unlike the single-sample means test in Chapter 10, with a two-group difference of means test it is *not* necessary to have a target value for

FIGURE 11–1

Testing the equality of two population means (μ_X)

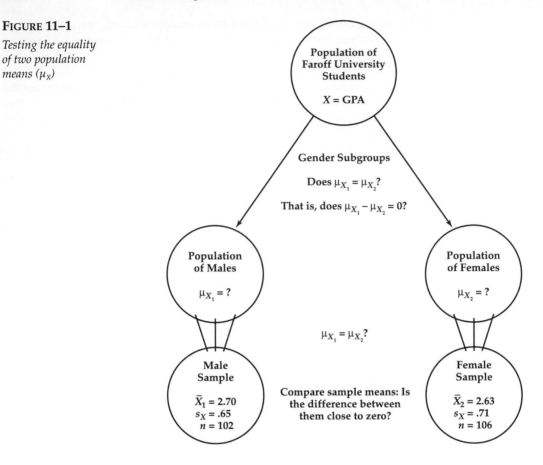

a parameter of X for the entire population or its subgroups. For all hypothesis tests, however, we must be able to predict a parameter and describe the sampling distribution around it. The known parameter required for the two-group difference of means test is zero. Regardless of the actual values of the mean GPAs of male and female students, if these values are equal, their difference is zero. It is zero, the "difference of means," not the means themselves, that is the target value of this hypothesis test.

The two-group difference of means is a *t*-test. It focuses on the computed difference between two sample means, $\bar{X}_1 - \bar{X}_2$, where $\bar{X}_1$ and $\bar{X}_2$ are the means of groups 1 and 2, respectively. In describing the sampling distribution, we can predict that the difference between any two randomly drawn sample means is zero, give or take expected sampling error. The test addresses the question of whether the observed difference between these sample means for our single observation of data reflects a real difference in the population means of the subgroups or simply is due to sampling error. In other words, we determine whether the effect of the test is statistically significant. For example, if we find a significant difference in GPAs between male and female college students, we will conclude that that difference is an effect of gender.

The *t*-test of differences between two means is used when the following criteria are met:

When to Use a Two-Group Difference of Means Test (*t*-Test) for Independent Groups (*t*-Distribution)

In general: Testing a hypothesis between a dichotomous nominal/ordinal independent variable and an interval/ratio dependent variable.

1. There are two variables from one population and sample, where one variable is of interval/ratio or interval-like ordinal level of measurement and the other is a dichotomous nominal/ordinal variable, *or* there are two populations and samples and one interval/ratio or interval-like ordinal variable; the samples are representative of their populations.

2. The interval/ratio or interval-like ordinal variable is the dependent variable.

3. The two groups are independent of one another; that is, they do not consist of the same subjects.

4. For the interval/ratio or interval-like ordinal variable, the variances (or standard deviations) in the *populations* from which the two groups come must be assumed to be equal to one another and must appear so in the sample variances. If *in the samples* the variance of one group is more than twice the size of the variance of the other, adjustments are required in the calculation of the standard error of the sampling distribution.

The third criterion—the independence of groups—distinguishes this statistical test from one in which the same group of subjects is being compared on two variables or at two different times on one variable. Later in this chapter we will learn about the *t*-test for a difference in means of "nonindependent" groups.

In statistics texts, the fourth criterion is called the assumption of equal variances (or equal standard deviations, keeping in mind that the variance is the standard deviation squared). If population variances are not equal, adjustments must be made to the statistical test. That is, slightly different *t*-test statistical formulas are used depending on whether the variances (or standard deviations) in the *populations* from which the two groups came are equal to one another. We will begin by illustrating the statistical test when the variances are equal. Later we will discuss why the test must be adjusted when the variances of the two groups are not equal.

The Standard Error and Sampling Distribution for the t-*Test of the Difference between Two Means*

To grasp how the sampling distribution for a two-group difference of means test is shaped, let us imagine that we are to do bean counting, repeatedly sampling from two populations with the same means for some interval/ratio variable X. For each sample we will compute the mean of X and subtract these two sample means to get the difference of means: $\bar{X}_1 - \bar{X}_2$. With the subscripts 1 and 2 representing the two groups, computations will fall in the positive or negative directions as follows:

- When $\bar{X}_1 > \bar{X}_2$, the difference will be positive.
- When $\bar{X}_1 < \bar{X}_2$, the difference will be negative.
- When $\bar{X}_1 = \bar{X}_2$, the difference will be zero.

If the statistical hypothesis that the two populations' means are equal is true, in repeated sampling we expect to miss on the high (positive) side just as often as we miss on the low (negative) side. Thus, the sampling distribution of a large number of sample mean differences is symmetrical and centers on zero. The shape is an approximately normal t-distribution, and the t-distribution table (Table C in Appendix B) is used to obtain the p-value: the probability of the sampling outcome assuming that the two population means are equal.

The sampling distribution centers on a difference of zero between the two population means (i.e., the difference between parameters: $\mu_{X_1} - \mu_{X_2}$). The standard error of the sampling distribution is estimated by using the variances (i.e., the squared standard deviations) and sample sizes of the two samples. When one sample variance is no larger than twice the size of the other, this suggests that the two population variances are equal and we "assume equality of variances." (Equality of variances also is referred to as *homogeneity of variances* or *homoscedasticity*. When variances are found to be unequal, the respective terms are *heterogeneity of variances* and *heteroscedasticity*.)

In this situation where equal variances are assumed, the standard error of the difference of means is computed by averaging the two variances. This is called a pooled variance estimate of the standard error, and it has the following formula.

Calculating the Standard Error of the Differences between Two Means (pooled variance estimate, used when the two population variances appear equal)

$$s_{\bar{X}_1 - \bar{X}_2} = \sqrt{\frac{(n_1 - 1)s_{X_1}{}^2 + (n_2 - 1)s_{X_2}{}^2}{n_1 + n_2 - 2}} \sqrt{\frac{n_1 + n_2}{n_1 n_2}}$$

(continued)

(concluded)

with $df = n_1 + n_2 - 2$

where

$s_{\bar{X}_1 - \bar{X}_2}$ = pooled variance estimate of the standard error of the difference between
        two means
n_1 = sample size of group 1
n_2 – sample size of group 2
$s_{X_1}^2$ = variance of group 1
$s_{X_2}^2$ = variance of group 2

Note that the *subscript* of the symbol for this standard error formula is $\bar{X}_1 - \bar{X}_2$. This standard error is the standard deviation of the distribution of *differences* between two sample means.

The *t*-test statistic is computed as follows:

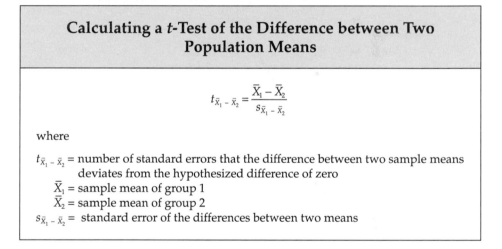

Calculating a *t*-Test of the Difference between Two Population Means

$$t_{\bar{X}_1 - \bar{X}_2} = \frac{\bar{X}_1 - \bar{X}_2}{s_{\bar{X}_1 - \bar{X}_2}}$$

where

$t_{\bar{X}_1 - \bar{X}_2}$ = number of standard errors that the difference between two sample means
        deviates from the hypothesized difference of zero
$\bar{X}_1$ = sample mean of group 1
$\bar{X}_2$ = sample mean of group 2
$s_{\bar{X}_1 - \bar{X}_2}$ = standard error of the differences between two means

This test statistic, like all statistical tests, is designed to answer questions about parameters. The statistical hypothesis for this test will always be that the two population means are equal. That is:

$$\text{Stat. } H: \mu_{X_1} = \mu_{X_2}$$

That is, there is no difference between the two population means.

Note, however, that the parameters μ_{X_1} and μ_{X_2} do not appear in the *t*-test formula. This is the case because when the two population means are equal, the difference between them is zero, which cancels out of the formula. In fact, the complete formula for the test statistic $t_{\bar{X}_1 - \bar{X}_2}$ is reduced to the formula above as follows:

$$t_{\bar{X}_1 - \bar{X}_2} = \frac{(\bar{X}_1 - \bar{X}_2) - (\mu_{X_1} - \mu_{X_2})}{s_{\bar{X}_1 - \bar{X}_2}}$$

$$= \frac{(\bar{X}_1 - \bar{X}_2) - 0}{s_{\bar{X}_1 - \bar{X}_2}} = \frac{\bar{X}_1 - \bar{X}_2}{s_{\bar{X}_1 - \bar{X}_2}}$$

This is consistent with all our test statistics. The numerator is a computation of the effect of the test, the difference between what we observe in the sample and what is expected when the statistical hypothesis is true. Here we observe $\bar{X}_1 - \bar{X}_2$ and expect zero because $\mu_{X_1} - \mu_{X_2} = 0$ when the population means are equal. When computed, the test statistic simply leaves off the zero because it is redundant. (Incidentally, this statistical hypothesis of "no difference" constitutes a true null hypothesis. If we choose, we can call it a null hypothesis.)

A look at the terms of this formula in relation to the distribution curve reveals that it is yet another distribution that measures how far off from an expected statistic the observed sample statistic falls. Any Z-distribution or *t*-distribution curve has a mean and a standard deviation (SD), and an interval/ratio score is measured across its horizontal axis as follows:

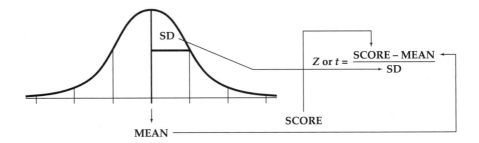

When the interval/ratio measurement is a raw score X, then Z_x is computed, as in Chapter 6.

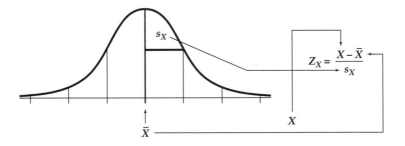

In the case of the sampling distribution for the difference of means, the formula takes shape in the same way, but with the standard deviation being the standard error (SE) of the difference between two means, as follows:

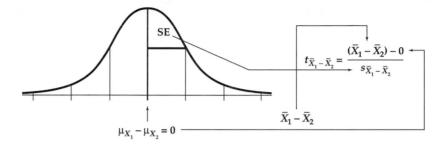

Now let us proceed with the six steps of statistical inference for the two-group difference of means test.

The Six Steps of Statistical Inference for the Two-Group Difference of Means Test

---

Brief Checklist for the Six Steps of Statistical Inference

Test Preparation

State the research question; list givens, including variables (e.g., $X = ...$, $Y = ...$), their levels of measurement, the population(s) under study, and sample(s) and sample size(s); select the statistical test; provide observations of statistics and parameters; and draw a conceptual diagram.

Six Steps

Using the symbol H for *hypothesis*:

1. State the statistical H and the alternative H and stipulate test direction.
2. Describe the sampling distribution.
3. State the level of significance (α) and specify the critical test value.
4. Observe the actual sample outcomes and compute the test effects, the test statistic, and the p-value.
5. Make the rejection decision.
6. Interpret and apply best estimates in everyday terms.

Test Preparation

Research question: The $10 bet with our friend hinges on the question: Is the average GPA of male students at Faroff University higher than that of female students? *Givens:* Variable: $X = $ GPA; interval/ratio level. *Population:* Faroff University, viewing the populations of men and women students separately.

Sample: 208 students. *Statistical procedure:* t-test of difference between two population means; t-distribution; assume equal variances of GPA in the populations of men and women.

Observation:

Male sample (group 1):

$$\bar{X}_1 = 2.70 \text{ GPA points}$$

$$s_{X_1} = .65 \text{ GPA point}$$

$$n_1 = 102 \text{ men}$$

Female sample (group 2)

$$\bar{X}_2 = 2.63 \text{ GPA points}$$

$$s_{X_2} = .71 \text{ GPA point}$$

$$n_2 = 106 \text{ women}$$

(This test is graphically depicted in Figure 11–1.)

Six Steps

1. *Stat. H:* μ_{X_1} $=$ μ_{X_2} (or $\mu_{X_1} - \mu_{X_2} = 0$)
   (male students)   (female students)

That is, there is no difference in the average GPAs of male and female students.

Alt. H: μ_{X_1} $>$ μ_{X_2} (or $\mu_{X_1} - \mu_{X_2} > 0$)
(male students)   (female students)   One-tailed

That is, male students have a higher average GPA than do female students.

2. *Sampling distribution.* If Stat. H is true and samples of 102 male and 106 female students are drawn repeatedly from their separate populations at Faroff University, differences between sample means, $\bar{X}_1 - \bar{X}_2$, will center on zero as an approximately normal t-distribution $df = n_1 + n_2 - 2 = 206$ with a standard error as follows. (This equation assumes that the population variances are equal.)

$$s_{\bar{X}_1 - \bar{X}_2} = \sqrt{\frac{(n_1 - 1)s_{X_1}^2 + (n_2 - 1)s_{X_2}^2}{n_1 + n_2 - 2}} \sqrt{\frac{n_1 + n_2}{n_1 n_2}}$$

$$= \sqrt{\frac{(101).65^2 + (105).71^2}{102 + 106 - 2}} \sqrt{\frac{102 + 106}{(102)(106)}} = .09$$

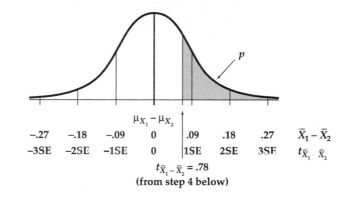

			$\mu_{X_1} - \mu_{X_2}$				
−.27	−.18	−.09	0	.09	.18	.27	$\bar{X}_1 - \bar{X}_2$
−3SE	−2SE	−1SE	0	1SE	2SE	3SE	$t_{\bar{X}_1 \bar{X}_2}$

$$t_{\bar{X}_1 - \bar{X}_2} = .78$$
(from step 4 below)

3. *Level of significance:* $\alpha = .05$. One-tailed. Critical test score = $t_\alpha = 1.64$.
4. *Observation:*

$$\bar{X}_1 = 2.70 \text{ GPA points}$$

$$s_{X_1} = .65 \text{ GPA point}$$

$$n_1 = 102 \text{ men}$$

$$\bar{X}_2 = 2.63 \text{ GPA points}$$

$$s_{X_2} = .71 \text{ GPA point}$$

$$n_2 = 106 \text{ women}$$

Test effect = $\bar{X}_1 - \bar{X}_2 = .07$ GPA point

Test statistic:

$$t_{\bar{X}_1 - \bar{X}_2} = \frac{\bar{X}_1 - \bar{X}_2}{s_{\bar{X}_1 - \bar{X}_2}} = \frac{2.70 - 2.63}{.09} = \frac{.07}{.09} = .78 \text{ SE}$$

p-value: *p* [drawing sample means ($\bar{X}$) with a difference as unusual as or more unusual than .07 when the difference in the population means (μ_X's) is zero] > .05. (This *p*-value is shaded on the curve in step 2.)

5. *Rejection decision:* $|t_{\bar{X}_1 - \bar{X}_2}| < |t_\alpha|$ (i.e., .78 < 1.64); thus, $p > \alpha$, (i.e., $p > .05$). Do not reject Stat. H.
6. *Interpretation:* There is not a real difference in the average GPAs of male and female students at Faroff University. *Best estimate:* The mean GPAs are the same. The difference of .07 GPA point observed in the samples resulted from normal, expected sampling error. *Answer:* The GPA of the men is not higher than that of the women. Our friend must pay up!

Some comments about the two-group difference of means test are in order.

- In step 1 we stated the Stat. H as "the means are equal." As indicated, we could have stated it as "the difference between the means is zero." It is zero that centers the curve of step 2.

- In step 2, in calculating the standard error, take care to distinguish the standard deviation from the variance. If a problem provides the standard deviation, the standard deviation must be squared to obtain the variance. If, however, a problem provides the variance, no squaring is necessary.
- In step 2 the degrees of freedom are computed as $df = n_1 + n_2 - 2$. One degree of freedom "is lost" in the calculation of each sample mean. (Recall that in the calculation of a single-sample t-test, $df = n - 1$. See Chapter 10.)
- In step 3 notice that we observed the t-distribution table to obtain the critical t-value (i.e., t_α), the value of t past which the critical region falls. Given the sample sizes and standard deviations for the two groups, t_α is the number of standard errors from zero that the calculated difference of sample means must be before we begin to suspect that the two populations' means are not equal. In other words, with repeated sampling, a difference between means that is 1.64 standard errors away from the hypothesized value of zero occurs less than 5 times out of 100 samples drawn. An observed, computed t-value (i.e., $t_{\bar{X}_1 - \bar{X}_2}$) equal to or larger than 1.64 would be unusual in populations with equal means. In this example, our observed t-value ($t_{\bar{X}_1 - \bar{X}_2}$) of .78 is not that large; it is less than 1.64. Thus, the .07 difference between sample means is not significantly different from the hypothesized value of zero. We conclude that this test effect is not unusual and simply is due to sampling error; therefore, we allow the statistical hypothesis to stand. Remember that there is an inverse relationship between the value of a test statistic and the likelihood of rejecting the statistical hypothesis. The larger the calculated t-value is, the more likely we are to reject the hypothesis of equal means.
- In step 5 we *fail to reject* the statistical hypothesis of equal means in the populations of the two groups. We demonstrate that the difference observed in the samples, given sample sizes of 102 and 106, is very slight and can be expected to occur quite frequently in estimating the difference using sample data.

When the Population Variances (or Standard Deviations) Appear Radically Different

As we noted above, the t-test of differences of means uses the above formulas only if the variances in the populations are equal. Adjustments to the t-test formula are necessary if these variances are radically different. A rule of thumb is that we may assume that the *population* variances are equal if the *sample* variance of one group is no more than twice the size of that of the other group. If this limit is exceeded, a different standard error formula may be needed, as is described below. The use of this modified formula, however, depends on several other factors, such as how large the samples are, whether they are of similar sizes, the sizes of the standard deviations relative to their means, and whether either of their distributions is skewed. These complications can be avoided by using the computer to do the calculations. Computer programs run the *t*-test both ways and provide guidelines for choosing the appropriate output. Given the complexities involved, we infrequently hand calculate *t*-tests for populations with unequal variances. Still, to enhance proportional and linear thinking, it is worthwhile to discuss the meaning of the assumption of equal variances and the consequences that arise when this assumption cannot be made.

Why must we know that the variances (or standard deviations) of the two populations are equal? With the standard error of any test we are estimating sampling error. As it turns out, if the population variances are *not* equal, the outcomes of repeated sampling will be more spread out. Sampling error will be larger. The calculation of the standard error for unequal variances takes this into account. If we ignore this extra error, we may incorrectly conclude that there is a difference of means between the two populations when in fact a large *observed* difference in the sample means is due to the large difference in variances.

To illustrate this, suppose we have two populations with equal mean intelligence quotient (IQ) test scores. One population is an upper-middle-class preparatory high school whose students have a mean IQ of 120 IQ score points with a standard deviation of 6; thus, the variance is $6^2 = 36$. IQ scores are normally distributed, and so we can expect almost all these students to fall within 3 standard deviations of 120; thus, the raw scores range from about 102 to 138. Repeated sampling from this population will result in a sampling distribution of means with a relatively small standard error, and most sample means will fall rather close to 120. Suppose a researcher named Carl samples this population once to test the hypothesis that the mean is equal to 120 IQ points. He obtains a sample mean of 120.4. This group 1 mean is very close to 120. It is within expected sampling error, and so he correctly concludes that the population mean is 120.

The second sample is a suburban high school that also has a mean IQ of 120, but this population has more diversity—its scores are more spread out. It has a standard deviation of 15 IQ score points with a range from about 75 to 165; thus, its variance is $15^2 = 225$—a variance over six times the size of that of the other high school (that is, the ratio of 225 to 36 is 6.25). If we *repeatedly sample* this population, the means in this sampling distribution also will center on 120 but the observations will have a larger spread. Sample means, being sensitive to extreme scores, frequently will calculate farther from 120. The standard error of this sampling distribution will be large. Suppose another researcher, Carolyn, samples this population once to test the hypothesis that the mean IQ of this school is 120. She obtains a sample mean of 118 IQ points. Since the variance and the standard error in her group 2 population are so large, it turns out that this sample mean, although a full 2 points from 120, is not unusual in repeated sampling, given the broad spread in the scores. Thus, Carolyn correctly concludes that her population, like Carl's, has a mean of 120 IQ points.

Suppose now that Carl hears about Carolyn's exercise and inquires about her results. She simply says that she found a mean of 118. Carl fails to ask about the size of the variance and falsely assumes that it is equal to that of his population. He compares their results and finds a difference between means of 2.4 IQ points:

$$\bar{X}_1 - \bar{X}_2 = 120.4 - 118 = 2.4 \text{ IQ points}$$

This difference appears very large to Carl because Carolyn's result appears quite far removed from 120 using Carl's small standard error. He concludes that Carolyn's population mean is different from 120 and therefore significantly different from his single-sample mean of 120.4. Unfortunately, Carl is drawing the wrong conclusion. The two separate tests each found correctly that the population means were no different from 120 and therefore were no different from one another. But in comparing the two means, Carl misread the large spread in Carolyn's population and sampling distribution to reveal a significant difference in means. In actuality, it was the large difference in variances that produced the spread of 2.4 IQ points between the two sample means. If Carl conducted a difference of means test using the pooled variance estimate of the standard error and incorrectly assumed that the variances were equal, he would incorrectly conclude that his sample mean was significantly different from Carolyn's. Even when two populations have the same means, when group variances differ, large differences *in observed sample means* can be due to a large difference in variances. Mistaken interpretations can result.

Being aware of this potential pitfall, when one population variance is much larger than the other, we make adjustments in the calculation of both the standard error and the degrees of freedom of the *t*-test. The standard error for unequal variances is called a *separate variance estimate* of the standard error of the differences between means. We subscript the symbol for this formula with *separate* to indicate that we are aware that the assumption of equal variances does not hold. Except for the notation that a separate variance estimate is used, the *t*-test formula *will appear* the same as that using the pooled variance estimate of the standard error.

Calculating the Standard Error of the Differences between Two Means (separate estimate, used when the two population variances appear unequal)

$$s_{\bar{X}_1 - \bar{X}_{2\,(separate)}} = \sqrt{\frac{s_{X_1}^2}{n_1 - 1} + \frac{s_{X_2}^2}{n_2 - 1}}$$

(continued)

(concluded)

with

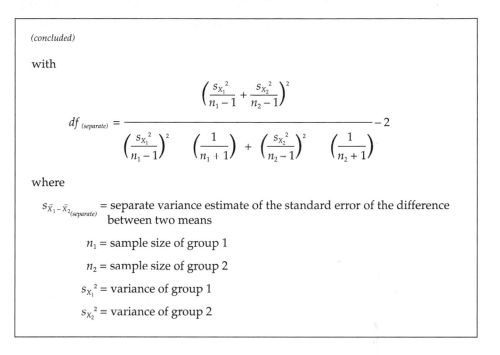

$$df_{(separate)} = \frac{\left(\dfrac{s_{X_1}{}^2}{n_1 - 1} + \dfrac{s_{X_2}{}^2}{n_2 - 1}\right)^2}{\left(\dfrac{s_{X_1}{}^2}{n_1 - 1}\right)^2 \left(\dfrac{1}{n_1 + 1}\right) + \left(\dfrac{s_{X_2}{}^2}{n_2 - 1}\right)^2 \left(\dfrac{1}{n_2 + 1}\right)} - 2$$

where

$s_{\bar{X}_1 - \bar{X}_{2(separate)}}$ = separate variance estimate of the standard error of the difference between two means

n_1 = sample size of group 1

n_2 = sample size of group 2

$s_{X_1}{}^2$ = variance of group 1

$s_{X_2}{}^2$ = variance of group 2

A true determination of whether the population variances are equal requires testing a separate hypothesis before we even calculate the *t*-test of the differences between the means. This extra test, along with the complicated calculation of degrees of freedom shown above, complicates things to a point where it is more sensible to rely on a computer. The *t*-test procedure in the software that accompanies this text is designed to test the assumption of equality of variances before the *t*-test is run for differences of means. It is advisable to use a computer when variances appear unequal. Nonetheless, gaining an understanding of the principles behind the assumption of equality of variances is an important exercise in proportional thinking.

The Two-Group Difference of Means Test for Nonindependent or Matched-Pair Samples

Sometimes there is a need to compare the statistics of two sets of scores from the same individuals. For example, we may wish to compare a sample of subjects who have completed two measurement scales that are scored the same way. Suppose we have questionnaire scales measuring marital happiness and overall life satisfaction for a sample of recently married women. The two scales are scored between 1 and 100, with high scores indicating high marital happiness or high life satisfaction. We might wish to determine whether there is a significant difference between the two scale scores matched for each individual in the sample. We have two "groups" or sets of scores, but we do not have two groups of individuals. Furthermore, the scores on the two scales are not independent of one another. How a subject scores on marital happiness is likely to be a good predictor of how that subject scores on overall life satisfaction. Thus, we refer to these sets of scores as *nonindependent* of one another. We call the sample a nonindependent, matched-pair sample.

A common matched-pair sample design is a "before-after" or "test-retest" experimental design in which a variable is measured twice for the same individuals, with some type of intervention employed between tests. Suppose, for example, a corporation is concerned with whether its workplaces are "hostile environments" for female workers because of sexual innuendo, obscene remarks, and "dirty" jokes on the part of the male employees. To make the place more comfortable for female employees and to avoid sexual harassment lawsuits, the company institutes a worker sensitivity program aimed at teaching the men about this problem. The program runs six months and requires all male employees to attend periodic discussion sessions at which female employees relate some of their negative experiences with gender discrimination. The overall objective of the training is to teach both men and women that sexual harassment has more to do with power and male dominance than with sexuality per se. If the program is effective, the gender sensitivity training should affect the attitudes of the men in a positive way by sensitizing them to the harm that sexual remarks can inflict on their female coworkers.

To evaluate the effectiveness of the training program we select a random sample of 15 male employees. We use a gender sensitivity scale that consists of 20 questionnaire items, with the respondents being asked to score each item from strongly disagree to strongly agree. The scale has an interval level of measurement, and scores range from zero to 100, with higher scores indicating high sensitivity. The scale is administered to the 15 employees on "day 1" of the training program—before any sensitivity sessions are held. These "before-treatment" scores provide baseline data. A month after the completion of training sessions the gender sensitivity scale is administered to these 15 men again. This retest measurement constitutes the "after-treatment" score. We then subtract the before-treatment from the after-treatment scores to measure improvement from baseline. If there is significant improvement, this suggests that sensitivity training has a positive effect on male attitudes.

Since we observe only 15 employees out of the larger population, any difference we obtain between the before and after measurements may simply be due to sampling error. If in fact the training did nothing to improve attitudes, the second measurement will be equivalent to drawing a second sample from the population. The difference between before-treatment and after-treatment scores will be zero. But slightly different scores can be expected in repeated sampling. Thus, we must test a hypothesis to determine whether any difference between measurements is simply due to sampling error.

We might be tempted to compute an *independent* groups *t*-test of the difference between mean gender sensitivity scores before and after training. But we do not have 30 subjects, only 15, and therefore we do not have 28 degrees of freedom. The subjects of the two groups are not independent of one another—

they are the same individuals. How they score the second time is likely to depend on how they scored the first time. That is, if a man scored high the first time, he is likely to do so the second time. What we are truly interested in is whether each score has changed and whether the difference between before and after scores is in the positive direction (i.e., the subjects have become more, not less, sensitive). Thus, we will acknowledge that the true sample size is 15 and treat each subject as a single case with a matched pair of test scores.

To state a statistical hypothesis—one that allows us to predict sampling outcomes when it is true—we focus on the difference between the before- and after-training sensitivity scores. Our statistical hypothesis is that the gender sensitivity training has *no* effect. (This may be called a null hypothesis.) If the statistical hypothesis is true, we can predict no change in scores and expect the mean of the differences between before and after scores to be zero. Where D represents the difference between the before and after scores, our statistical hypothesis is that the mean of differences is zero:

$$\text{Stat. } H: \mu_D = 0$$

That is, in the population of male workers there is no difference in mean sensitivity training scores in the before and after measurements. The training has no effect.

Note that this statement is like a single-sample means test in that it has a target value of zero. In actuality, then, this is a single-sample means test, but it involves two "groups" of scores. It is a test of whether *the mean of the differences* between matched scores is significantly different from zero.

Table 11–2 presents the computational spreadsheet for computing the mean of the differences between matched-pair scores. For this example of 15 cases, the test is essentially a single-sample means test (as illustrated in Chapter 10).

The criteria for using this test are as follows:

When to Use a Two-Group Difference of Means Test (*t*-Test) for Nonindependent or Matched-Pair Samples (*t*-distribution, $df = n - 1$)

In general: Testing the hypothesis that the scores of an interval/ratio or interval-like ordinal variable differ at two points in time for the same subjects.

1. There is one population with a representative sample from it.
2. There are two interval/ratio or interval-like ordinal variables with the same score design or a single variable measured twice for the same sample subjects.
3. There is a target value of the variable to which we may compare the mean of the differences between the two sets of scores. (This target value usually will be zero for a test of no difference between the two scores.)

TABLE 11–2   Computational Spreadsheet for Calculating the Mean and Standard Deviation of the Differences between Matched-Pair Scores

X = Gender Sensitivity Scale Score

	Givens		Calculations		
Subject Number	(A) Before-Training Score	(B) After-Training Score	D (difference = B − A)	$(D - \bar{D})$	$(D - \bar{D})^2$
1	47	53	6	.73	.53
2	39	38	−1	−6.27	39.31
3	52	54	2	−3.27	10.69
4	48	56	8	2.73	7.45
5	45	49	4	−1.27	1.61
6	42	51	9	3.73	13.91
7	48	54	6	.73	.53
8	50	56	6	.73	.53
9	45	54	9	3.73	13.91
10	44	51	7	1.73	2.99
11	46	44	−2	−7.27	52.85
12	45	54	9	3.73	13.91
13	43	53	10	4.73	22.37
14	47	55	8	2.73	7.45
15	41	39	−2	−7.27	52.85
$n = 15$				$\Sigma(D - \bar{D}) = .05^*$	
			$\Sigma D = 79$		$\Sigma(D - \bar{D})^2 = 240.89$

* Not equal to zero due to rounding error.

Computation of the mean and the standard deviation of the differences between scores proceeds as follows:

$$\bar{D} = \frac{\Sigma D}{n} = \frac{79}{15} = 5.27 \text{ sensitivity scale points}$$

$$s_D = \sqrt{\frac{\Sigma(D - \bar{D})^2}{n - 1}} = \sqrt{\frac{240.89}{14}} = 4.15 \text{ sensitivity scale points}$$

The test statistic is the same as that for a one-sample t-test except that the symbols correspond to the calculation of differences (D). In the following box, note that the calculation of the standard error and t-test statistic parallel the formulas used for a single-sample means test (Chapter 10).

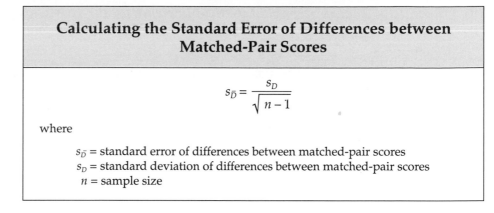

Calculating the Standard Error of Differences between Matched-Pair Scores

$$s_{\bar{D}} = \frac{s_D}{\sqrt{n-1}}$$

where

$s_{\bar{D}}$ = standard error of differences between matched-pair scores
s_D = standard deviation of differences between matched-pair scores
n = sample size

The effect of this test, like that of any hypothesis test, is the difference between the observed sample observation and the hypothesized parameter, in this case. $\bar{D} - \mu_D$. Since the hypothesized parameter difference is zero, this test effect reduces to $\bar{D}$, and this is the way the effect appears in the numerator of the test statistic.

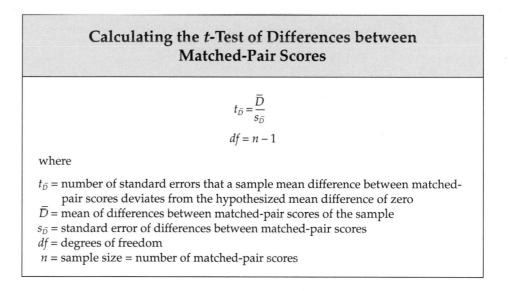

Calculating the *t*-Test of Differences between Matched-Pair Scores

$$t_{\bar{D}} = \frac{\bar{D}}{s_{\bar{D}}}$$

$$df = n - 1$$

where

$t_{\bar{D}}$ = number of standard errors that a sample mean difference between matched-pair scores deviates from the hypothesized mean difference of zero
$\bar{D}$ = mean of differences between matched-pair scores of the sample
$s_{\bar{D}}$ = standard error of differences between matched-pair scores
df = degrees of freedom
n = sample size = number of matched-pair scores

Let us use the data and calculations in Table 11–2 and follow the six steps of statistical inference.

The Six Steps of Statistical Inference for the Two-Group Difference of Means Test for Nonindependent or Matched-Pair Samples

---

Brief Checklist for the Six Steps of Statistical Inference

Test Preparation

State the research question; list givens, including variables (e.g., $X =...$, $Y =...$), their levels of measurement, the population(s) under study, and sample(s) and sample size(s); select the statistical test; provide observations of statistics and parameters; and draw a conceptual diagram.

Six Steps

Using the symbol H for *hypothesis:*

1. State the statistical H and the alternative H and stipulate test direction.
2. Describe the sampling distribution.
3. State the level of significance (α) and specify the critical test value.
4. Observe the actual sample outcomes and compute the test effects, the test statistic, and the p-value.
5. Make the rejection decision.
6. Interpret and apply best estimates in everyday terms.

Test Preparation

Research question: Did gender sensitivity scores improve significantly after sensitivity training sessions? Were the sessions effective? Should the program be instituted for all male employees? *Givens:* Variable: X = gender sensitivity score; interval level; D = the difference in a subject's X-scores before and after gender sensitivity training sessions. *Population:* male employees of a company. *Sample:* $n = 15$ randomly selected male employees. *Statistical procedure:* t-test of differences between matched-pair scores.

Observation:

$$\bar{D} = 5.27 \text{ gender sensitivity scale points.}$$

$$s_D = 4.15 \text{ gender sensitivity scale points.}$$

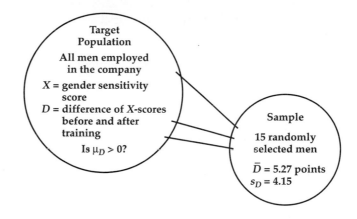

Six Steps

1. *Stat. H:* μ_D (all male employees taking training) $= 0$ (i.e., the difference in scores if training is ineffective)

That is, the gender sensitivity training is ineffective; there is no improvement in gender sensitivity scores after training.

Alt. *H:* μ_D (all male employees taking training) > 0. One-tailed

That is, the gender sensitivity training is effective; gender training results in an improvement in gender sensitivity scores.

2. *Sampling distribution:* If Stat. *H* is true and samples of size 15 are drawn repeatedly from the population of all male employees who are undergoing training, the sample means of the differences between matched-pair scores ($\bar{D}$s) will center on zero as an approximately normal *t*-distribution, $df = n - 1 = 14$, with a standard error:

$$s_{\bar{D}} = \frac{s_D}{\sqrt{n-1}} = \frac{4.15}{\sqrt{14}} = 1.11 \text{ sensitivity scale points}$$

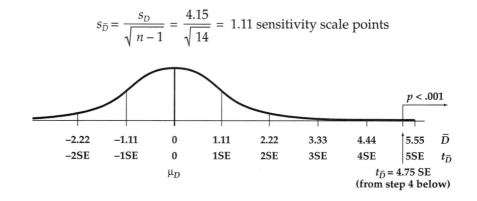

3. *Level of significance:* $\alpha = .05$. One-tailed. Critical test score $= t_\alpha = 1.76$.
4. *Observation:*

$$\bar{D} = 5.27 \text{ gender sensitivity scale points}$$

$$s_D = 4.15 \qquad n = 15 \text{ male employees.}$$

Test effect $= \bar{D} - \mu_D = 5.27 - 0 = 5.27$ sensitivity scale points

Test statistic $=$

$$t_{\bar{D}} = \frac{\bar{D}}{s_{\bar{D}}} = \frac{5.27}{1.11} = 4.75 \text{ SE}$$

p-value: p [drawing a sample with a mean difference between scores ($\bar{D}$) as unusual as or more unusual than 5.27 points when the true population mean of differences (μ_D) is 0] $< .001$. (This *p*-value is noted in the curve in step 2.)

5. *Rejection decision:* $|t_{\bar{D}}| > |t_\alpha|$ (i.e., $4.75 > 1.76$); thus, $p < \alpha$, (i.e., $p < .05$). Reject the Stat. *H* and accept the Alt. *H* at the 95 percent level of confidence.

6. *Interpretation:* The gender sensitivity training does appear to be effective. *Best estimate of the effect:* Gender sensitivity training sessions result in an average improvement of 5.27 points on the gender sensitivity scores. *Answer:* The program should be instituted for all male employees.

Practical versus Statistical Significance

The problem involving gender sensitivity training that was just described highlights an important point about statistical hypothesis testing. This hypothesis test focuses on whether to attribute a difference in sample data to sampling error or to a true effect of training on the population. In this example we did conclude—with 95 percent confidence—that the difference of 5.27 gender sensitivity scale points between before- and after-treatment measurements was so great that it probably was not due to expected sampling error. But is this difference of 5.27 points meaningful in practical terms? The gender sensitivity scale had a possible score range of 100 points. At baseline—before sensitivity training—the mean scale score was 45.47 points. The men appeared to be only moderately sensitive at that time. After the training the mean score was 50.73 points. The men were still only moderately sensitive. Moreover, with a 20-item questionnaire, a subject could pick up the average 5-point difference by moving up one level of agreement on only 5 of the 20 items. Is this enough to make a difference in behavior of men in the office? Perhaps not. This 5-point increase in sensitivity may have no influence on behavior. Additional research would be required, perhaps analyzing reports of harassment and data on female perceptions of it. *A hypothesis test determines significance in terms of likely sampling error. It simply tells us whether a sample difference is so large that there probably is a difference in the populations.* It does not guarantee that the difference is meaningful or significant in practical terms. Any statistical results must be weighed against well-thought-out theoretical ideas and practical circumstances. Practical significance, theoretical significance (i.e., whether the results support a theory), and statistical significance are separate issues.

The Four Aspects of Statistical Relationships

The ultimate goal of scientific research is to produce empirically tested statements that explain a phenomenon by giving us an understanding of how it relates to other phenomena. These statements take the form of a theory which describes the interrelationships among measured variables. A theory, along with its list of hypotheses, is tested by making predictions that assert that the measurements made on one variable are somehow related to the measurements made on others. As we noted above, these relationships can take the form of higher means being statistically related to one group or another, a high frequency of joint occurrences for two nominal variables, or a correlation between two interval/ratio variables or two ordinal variables. Once we conclude that two variables are related, we can say more about the relationship between them. An exhaustive analysis of statistical findings addresses four "aspects of a relationship" between variables. We address these four aspects in step 6 of the six steps of statistical inference.

Existence of a Relationship

The first aspect of a statistical relationship is *existence*. The existence of a relationship answers the question: On the basis of the statistical analysis of a sample, can we conclude that a relationship exists between two variables among all subjects *in the population?* For instance, among Americans, does a relationship exist between religious preference and amount of time spent in prayer? Is there a relationship between poverty levels and crime rates in American cities? Is there a relationship between the amount of time spent watching television and grade point average among college students? The existence of a relationship pertains to the *population* of study subjects. Keep in mind that sample data and the statistics computed from them provide only estimates of population parameters. Basically, determining whether a relationship exists establishes that sample statistical findings are not simply due to sampling error. In other words, the existence of a relationship is determined by hypothesis testing. It is when we make the rejection decision in a hypothesis test (step 5 of the six steps of statistical inference) that we decide whether a relationship exists between two variables. The first thing we say in step 6 is whether a relationship exists.

Direction of the Relationship

The second aspect of a relationship between two variables is *direction*, although this aspect does not apply to all bivariate analyses. The direction of a relationship addresses the question: When the independent variable increases, does the dependent variable increase or decrease? We use the terms *positive* and *negative* here. A positive relationship is one in which an increase in one variable is related to an increase in the other. For instance, there is a positive relationship between family income and the receipt of preventive dental care: *The higher* the family income is, *the more* preventive dental care is received by the family members. A negative relationship is one in which an increase in one variable is related to a decrease in the other. For example, there is a negative relationship between the income levels of neighborhoods and their crime rates: *The higher* the income, *the lower* the crime rate. Direction is specified in the alternative hypothesis as a one-tailed test. Direction is a very straightforward issue for the relationship between two interval/ratio variables, a topic thoroughly examined in Chapter 15.

Strength of the Relationship, Predictive Power, and Proportional Reduction in Error

The third aspect of a statistical relationship is *strength*. The strength of a relationship between two variables establishes the extent to which errors are reduced in predicting the scores of a dependent variable. A measurement of the strength of a relationship gives us an indication of **predictive power,** how well the independent variable predicts the outcomes of a dependent variable. Does the related variable explain a lot or very little about the dependent variable? For example, how good is high school GPA at predicting college GPA? Is it a strong indicator, say, accurate 50 percent of the time, or a weak one, accurate only 10 percent of the time? Do other variables, such as reading comprehension level, predict college GPA better? A focus on the strength of a relationship is useful for comparing the relative effects of several independent variables on a dependent variable.

Another way to view the predictive power of an independent variable on the scores of a dependent variable is to inquire: To what extent is error in the scores of the dependent variable reduced by knowledge of scores in the independent variable? This approach is referred to as proportional reduction in error (PRE). It is most useful with an interval/ratio dependent variable on which the mean has been calculated. Recall that the difference between the mean and any individual score in a distribution of scores is the deviation score. For example, let X = salary of middle-level managers in a company. The mean is $50,000. If someone challenged us to guess Jacob Smith's salary, our best estimate would be the mean of $50,000. But suppose we find out that he makes $60,000. We erred by $10,000, which is Jacob's deviation from the overall company mean. How can we explain this deviation score of $10,000? Can we find variables that allow us to reduce the error in making a best estimate of salary? Perhaps Jacob's "high-side" salary is related to his being with the company longer than other middle-level managers have been employed there. We test a hypothesis that length of service with the company is related to salary level. Using a difference of means test, we compare the mean salaries of "long-timers" to those more recently hired. Suppose the long-timers average $58,000—$8,000 more than the overall company average. Since Jacob is a long-timer, we can now make a better estimate of his salary—$58,000—the company mean of $50,000 plus $8,000 for length of service. By estimating his salary at $58,000 we deviate from his true salary of $60,000 by only $2,000. We have explained $8,000 of Jacob's $10,000 deviation from the mean of $50,000. Knowledge of the relationship between length of service (an independent variable) and salary (the dependent variable), allowed us to reduce error in prediction by 80 percent (i.e., $8,000/$10,000).

For an entire sample, PRE depends on finding relationships that explain the variance in the sample—the average of the sum of squared deviation scores (review Chapter 5). In chapter 12 we will show how we can explain parts of the dependent variable's variance by identifying related independent variables. We ask: What proportion of the variance is explained by knowing about the relationship? The explained amount of variance constitutes a proportional reduction in error. As we will see in Chapter 15, when both the independent variable and the dependent variable are of interval/ratio levels of measurement, PRE can be calculated very precisely.

Nature of the Relationship

The fourth aspect of a relationship between two variables is its *nature*. This involves describing how knowledge of a relationship between two variables helps us both understand a phenomenon and apply the results to practical circumstances. In describing the nature of a relationship, we avoid statistical jargon by presenting research findings in everyday language, especially when we present them to a public audience. A description of the nature of the relationship amounts to translating statistical gobbledygook into English. We bring our findings to life by revealing their worth for improving society or the lives of individuals. We answer the questions: So what? and Now that a statistical relationship has been found, what is this knowledge good for?

A scientific finding is especially worthwhile if it can change the lives of people. The nature of the relationship focuses on exactly how scientific knowledge can be applied in such a way that one variable predicts the other. Under the best circumstances, the relationship is shown to be "causal." That is, altering an independent variable can be shown to result directly in a change in the dependent variable. Where a causal relationship exists, the nature describes exactly how much change in the score of an independent variable causes how much change in the score of the dependent variable. For example, for the relationship between taking aspirin and reducing joint swelling, how much aspirin brings about how much reduction in swelling? Causation is best established with longitudinal data—data collected over time. This is the case because logically, X can cause Y only if it occurs before Y. Our nonindependent two-group test of the effectiveness of sensitivity training on gender attitudes is a situation where we could make a case for causation. Most social science research, however, relies on cross-sectional survey data—data collected at one point in time. Although causal relationships often are asserted for findings from cross-sectional data, such interpretations must be made carefully.

In circumstances where a statistical relationship is found to exist but causation is not clear, in describing the nature of the relationship we simply present the substance of the findings by providing specific empirical information. For example, if we find a relationship between gender and a preference for R-rated movies, what does this say in everyday terms? Is it males or females who are more interested in these movies? (You can guess the answer.) We report precisely those percentages of men and women in a sample expressing great interest in R-rated movies. In doing so, we are providing the best estimates available of how a dependent variable may be adjusted for the effects of an independent variable. The effect of the test (i.e., the difference between what is observed and what is statistically hypothesized) is typically the most meaningful component in describing the nature of the relationship. To remind us of this important practical side of testing a hypothesis, in the sixth step of statistical inference we not only make a general statement that the relationship exists but also provide best estimates based on computations of statistical test effects.

The Four Aspects of a Relationship between Two Variables

Existence: On the basis of statistical analysis of a sample, can we conclude that a relationship exists between two variables among all subjects in the population?

Direction: Can the dependent variable be expected to increase or decrease as the independent variable increases?

Strength: To what extent are errors reduced in predicting the scores of a dependent variable when an independent variable is used as a predictor?

Nature: In practical, everyday terms, how does knowledge of a relationship between two variables help us understand and predict outcomes of the dependent variable?

When to Apply the Various Aspects of Relationships

Testing a hypothesis to establish the existence of a relationship is the first step in any analysis. If a relationship is found *not* to exist between two variables, the other three aspects of a relationship are irrelevant; obviously, if no relationship exits, then the relationship has no direction, strength, or nature. Moreover, even when a relationship is found between two variables, the strength and direction may not be meaningful or useful. As we proceed through the remaining chapters, we will point out which aspects of a relationship are useful for each bivariate test.

Relevant Aspects of a Relationship for Two-Group Difference of Means Tests

With either the independent or the nonindependent two-group difference of means test, only two aspects of a relationship apply: existence and nature. The *existence* of a relationship between a dichotomous independent variable and an interval/ratio or interval-like ordinal dependent variable is established by using one of the *t*-tests described in this chapter. When the statistical hypothesis of no difference in means is rejected, we may conclude that a relationship exists.

Existence of a Relationship Using Two-Group Differences of Means Tests

Test the statistical hypothesis that $\mu_{X_1} = \mu_{X_2}$ (where X is an interval/ratio variable and 1 and 2 designate groups 1 and 2, respectively). That is, there is no difference between the means in the two populations. Use the test statistic:

Independent groups	Matched pairs

$$t_{\bar{X}_1 - \bar{X}_2} = \frac{\bar{X}_1 - \bar{X}_2}{s_{\bar{X}_1 - \bar{X}_2}} \qquad t_{\bar{D}} = \frac{\bar{D}}{s_{\bar{D}}}$$

When the Stat. H is rejected, we assert that a relationship exists.

With the *t*-test of independent groups, the *direction* of the relationship is not relevant. For example, if a difference is found between the mean incomes of men and women in a corporation, we would *not* say that an increase in maleness is related to an increase in income, because a person is either male or female, not more or less of one or the other. (Having said this, we should point out that some researchers use the phrasing "in the direction of males" to indicate that males have the higher income.) In a nonindependent groups matched-pair test, however, we may assert that we observed an effect of treatment that was positive—in the direction of improvement. This is what we did in the gender sensitivity example above, using a one-tailed test.

The *strength* of the relationship for the *t*-test does not apply either. It can be computed, but the simplicity of the two-group difference of means test is such that typically we do not bother.

Direction and Strength of a Relationship Using Two-Group Differences of Means Tests

Not applicable.

For any statistical test the nature of the relationship depends on our describing the effect of the test. Typically, the effect of a test is found in the numerator of the test statistic. For a two-group difference of means test, the effect is the difference between sample means. That is, the effect of the independent variable on the dependent variable = $\bar{X}_1 - \bar{X}_2$. When a relationship is found to exist, this difference between the sample means is treated as an estimate of the difference between population means. This amount is often called the effect of group membership. For example, suppose we test the statistical hypothesis that the mean weights of men and women are equal. We find a 25-pound difference in the mean weights and reject the statistical hypothesis. We may then conclude that the effect on bodily weight of being male is 25 pounds: On average, men tend to weigh 25 pounds more than women.

Nature of a Relationship Using Two-Group Differences of Means Tests

Describe the effect of the test in everyday terms, where the effect of the independent variable on the dependent variable is as follows:

Independent groups	Matched pairs
$\bar{X}_1 - \bar{X}_2$	$\bar{D}$

To summarize, only two aspects of a relationship typically are reported for a two-group difference of means test: existence and nature. Remember that if the statistical hypothesis of no difference between means is not rejected, no relationship exists between two variables. When this is the case, nature is irrelevant. By letting the statistical hypothesis stand, we are asserting that the effect of the test is not real in the populations and that the observed difference between sample means is simply due to sampling error.

☹   **STATISTICAL FOLLIES AND FALLACIES**   ☹

Fixating on Differences of Means While Ignoring Differences in Variances

---

Differences of means tests are used very frequently. Even in multivariate analysis, bivariate tests such as the ones presented in this chapter constitute the first step in getting a good grasp of the nature of data. Unfortunately, an emphasis on searching for differences between means can override a concern with differences in the spreads of scores between two groups. As we have seen in this chapter, it is important to look for differences in spread because unequal variances in comparison groups create additional sampling error and require adjustments in describing the sampling distribution. However, aside from this statistical necessity, much can be learned about the nature of two groups when their variances are found to be different.

Suppose we compare the educational levels of homeless men and homeless women and find no difference in the mean years of education. Suppose, however, we do find a significant difference in the variances, with women tending to have a greater spread in their education levels. Like the men, many of the women have about 6 to 14 years of schooling, but among the women there are more with meager educations (less than 6 years) but also more with college educations (16-plus years). This difference in spreads of the distributions is very informative. Why are there more meagerly educated individuals among the homeless women? Because many of them come from families that relied on family assistance from the government. In their struggle for economic survival, they left school early for low-paying jobs or because of pregnancy or other circumstances. This puts women at great risk of becoming homeless. Men growing up in these circumstances have other opportunities (such as construction work) that are more economically lucrative and steer them away from becoming homeless. But why are there more highly educated homeless women than men? Because many of these women are victims of spousal abuse, and this phenomenon is not uncommon even among college-educated women. There may be other reasons for differing variances in the educational levels of homeless men and women. If a researcher fixates on observing and interpreting only differences between means, he or she may miss an opportunity to better understand the true nature of the relationship between two variables. Paying close attention to differences in variances as well as differences in means is an important guide to the next level of research.

Statistical Procedures Covered to Here

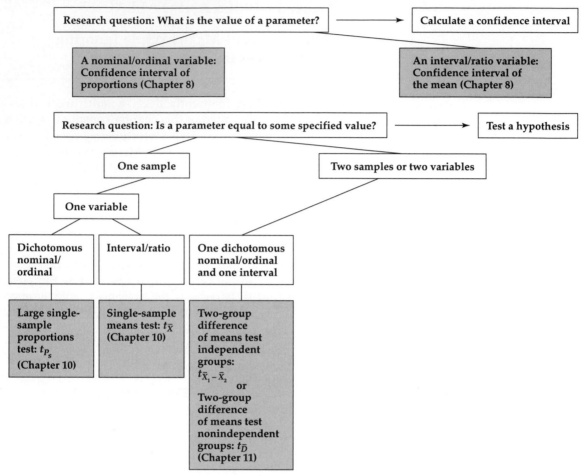

Formulas in Chapter 11

Two-group difference of means test (*t*-test) for independent groups:

> *Given:* An interval/ratio or interval-like ordinal dependent variable X compared for two groups that consist of different subjects (i.e., independent groups) obtained from either (1) a dichotomous nominal/ordinal variable from one sample and population or (2) two populations and samples.

> *Research question:* Are the means of X in populations of the two groups different?

> *Stat. H:* $\mu_{X_1} = \mu_{X_2}$ (i.e., $\mu_{X_1} - \mu_{X_2} = 0$)

Sampling distribution: t-distribution; standard error estimated one of two ways depending on whether variances of the two populations appear equal.

Standard error: If variances of the two populations appear equal, use the pooled variance estimate of the standard error:

$$s_{\bar{X}_1 - \bar{X}_2} = \sqrt{\frac{(n_1 - 1)s_{X_1}^2 + (n_2 - 1)s_{X_2}^2}{n_1 + n_2 - 2}} \sqrt{\frac{n_1 + n_2}{n_1 n_2}}$$

with

$$df = n_1 + n_2 - 2$$

If variances of the two populations appear unequal (i.e., the variance of one group is twice as large as that of the other), use the separate variance estimate of the standard error:

$$s_{\bar{X}_1 - \bar{X}_{2\,(separate)}} = \sqrt{\frac{s_{X_1}^2}{n_1 - 1} + \frac{s_{X_2}^2}{n_2 - 1}}$$

$$df_{(separate)} = \frac{\left(\frac{s_{X_1}^2}{n_1 - 1} + \frac{s_{X_2}^2}{n_2 - 1}\right)^2}{\left(\frac{s_{X_1}^2}{n_1 - 1}\right)^2 \left(\frac{1}{n_1 + 1}\right) + \left(\frac{s_{X_2}^2}{n_2 - 1}\right)^2 \left(\frac{1}{n_2 + 1}\right)} - 2$$

Test effect: $\bar{X}_1 - \bar{X}_2$

Test statistic [for use with the approximately normal t-distribution table (Statistical Table C in Appendix B)] determines whether a relationship exists:

$$t_{\bar{X}_1 - \bar{X}_2} = \frac{\bar{X}_1 - \bar{X}_2}{s_{\bar{X}_1 - \bar{X}_2}}$$

Addressing the aspects of a relationship:

Direction: Usually not applicable

Strength: Not applicable

Nature: Specify the difference between group means:

$$\bar{X}_1 - \bar{X}_2$$

Two-group difference of means test (t-test) for nonindependent or matched-pair samples:

Given: (1) Two interval/ratio or interval-like ordinal variables with the same score design measured on the same subjects or (2) a single interval/ratio or interval-like ordinal variable measured twice for the same sample subjects (i.e., nonindependent groups).

Research question: Are the means of X different for the two variables or two measurements?

Stat. H: $\mu_D = 0$

Sampling distribution: t-distribution of the distribution of mean differences, $\bar{D}$, with $df = n - 1$)

Standard error:

$$s_{\bar{D}} = \frac{s_D}{\sqrt{n - 1}}$$

Test effect: $\bar{D}$ (i.e., $\bar{D} - \mu_D = \bar{D} - 0 = \bar{D}$)

Test statistic [for use with the approximately normal t-distribution table, (Statistical Table C in Appendix B)]: determines whether a relationship exists):

$$t_{\bar{D}} = \frac{\bar{D}}{s_{\bar{D}}}$$

$$df = n - 1$$

Addressing the aspects of a relationship:

> Direction: Usually not applicable
> Strength: Not applicable
> Nature: Report the mean difference $\bar{D}$

Questions for Chapter 11

1. Study Table 11–1 until you are able to reproduce it.
2. Describe the situation where we use a "two-group difference of means test" for independent groups.
3. With a two-group difference of means test, we must assume equality of variances. Why must this be considered?
4. Explain the distinction between independent and nonindependent groups two-group difference of means tests.
5. How is the statistical (or *null*) hypothesis stated for a two-group difference of means test? Why must it be stated this way?
6. Statistical test effects involve both sample statistics and population parameters. The effect of the test is found in the numerator of the test statistic. For two-group difference of means tests, why do parameters *not* appear in the formulas for the test statistics?
7. With a two-group difference of means test for independent groups where

equal population variances are assumed, why are degrees of freedom calculated as follows?

$$df = n_1 + n_2 - 2$$

8. The existence of a relationship between two variables determines the following: On the basis of the statistical analysis of a _____, can we conclude that a relationship exists between two variables among all subjects in the _____?

9. The existence of a relationship is determined by hypothesis testing, which establishes whether sample statistical findings are due to __ _____ error.

10. Regarding the direction of a relationship, a positive relationship is one in which an increase in one variable is related to an _____ in the other. A negative relationship is one in which an increase in one variable is related to a _____ in the other.

11. The _____ of a relationship between two variables establishes the extent to which errors are reduced in predicting the scores of a dependent variable. This measurement gives us an indication of _____ _____, how well the independent variable predicts outcomes of a dependent variable.

12. The _____ of the relationship involves describing how knowledge of a relationship between two variables helps us understand a phenomenon and apply the results to practical circumstances.

13. In describing the _____ of a relationship, we avoid statistical jargon by presenting research findings in everyday language, especially when we present the results to a public audience.

14. A _____ statistical test is useful for "before-after" or "test-retest" experimental design, where a variable is measured twice for the same individuals with some type of intervention between the tests.

15. Distinguish statistical significance from practical difference. Give examples.

16. For the two-group difference of means test, which aspects of a relationship are relevant? How are these aspects addressed?

17. Match the following:

a. $s_{\bar{X}_1 - \bar{X}_2}$ _____ The number of standard errors that independent sample mean differences deviate from the hypothesized mean difference of zero

b. $t_{\bar{D}}$ _____ The standard error of differences between matched-pair scores

c. $t_{\bar{X}_1 - \bar{X}_2}$ _____ The number of standard errors that a sample mean difference between matched-pair scores deviates from the hypothesized mean difference of zero

d. $s_{\bar{D}}$ _____ The pooled variance estimate of the standard error of the difference between two means

Exercises for Chapter 11

General instructions: On all hypotheses tests, follow the six steps of statistical inference, including test preparation, a conceptual diagram, probability curves, and appropriate aspects of a relationship. For consistency, round standard errors to two decimal places. Use $\alpha = .05$ unless otherwise stipulated.

1. A restaurant conducts a random survey of two groups of women: those working inside the home and those working elsewhere. The survey inquires about how many times in the past two weeks they prepared meals at home. Using the (fictional) responses below, determine whether women who work outside the home prepare meals less often than do those who work at home. Assume equality of population variances.

Work Situation	Number of At-home Meals in Past Two Weeks
At home	9
At home	10
At home	11
At home	8
At home	9
At home	12
At home	14
At home	10
At home	12
At home	13
At home	9
At home	10
At home	12
At home	14
At home	10
Outside home	8
Outside home	10
Outside home	8
Outside home	7
Outside home	9
Outside home	9
Outside home	12
Outside home	8
Outside home	10
Outside home	10
Outside home	7
Outside home	12
Outside home	6
Outside home	10
Outside home	9
Outside home	8
Outside home	10
Outside home	9

2. Two social movement organizations that arose in the 1980s to increase public awareness of the dangers of drinking before driving were Mothers Against Drunk Driving (MADD) and Remove Intoxicated Drivers (RID) (McCarthy and Wolfson 1996). Suppose the following are survey data of a random sample of chapter presidents of the two organizations. X = the number of public appearances in the past year. Is there a significant difference in the means of X? Assume equality of population variances.

President's Organization	X
MADD	41
MADD	29
RID	10
MADD	33
RID	24
RID	26
MADD	45
MADD	39
MADD	33
RID	26
MADD	28
RID	23
MADD	45
RID	10
MADD	26
RID	19
MADD	37
RID	15
MADD	32
MADD	42
RID	20
RID	14
MADD	36
MADD	38
RID	24

3. Suppose two random samples of 40 companies each were selected to compare the mean hourly incomes of union workers and nonunion workers. The 40 nonunion companies offered a mean wage of $10.80 with a variance of $2.50, while the 40 unionized companies offered a mean wage of $11.90 with a variance of $2.50. Do these data present sufficient evidence to indicate that a worker is better off with a unionized company? Assume equality of population variances.

4. Random samples of 100 adults selected from two ethnic groups in a large city were questioned concerning the number of years they attended public schools. See if there is a significant difference in the two population means. Assume equality of population variances.

	Ethnic Group 1	Ethnic Group 2
Mean	7.4 years	8.2 years
Standard deviation	2.1 years	2.4 years
n	100	100

5. For a random survey of 641 adults, determine if there is a gender difference in degree of support for gun control. Support is measured with an attitudes toward gun control scale (X) that has an interval level of measurement (fictional data). A high score indicates a more favorable attitude toward gun control. Assume equality of population variances.

$\bar{X}_1$ $\bar{X}_2$

Men	Women
$\bar{X} = 6.2$	$\bar{X} = 6.5$
$s_X = 1.3$	$s_X = 1.4$
$n = 324$	$n = 317$

6. Orbuch and Eyster (1997) asked the wives of black couples and white couples to rate the husband's participation in traditionally feminine tasks such as preparing meals, dish washing, housecleaning, laundry, and child care. They used a six-item scale with a high score indicating that the husband is perceived to do more. Previous studies showed that black husbands do more. Is this born out in the Orbuch and Eyster data? Assume equality of population variances. X = husband participation score.

Blacks	Whites
$\bar{X} = 1.54$	$\bar{X} = 1.47$
$s_X = .36$	$s_X = .37$
$n = 199$	$n = 174$

7. A comparison of life expectancy in random samples of 40 less developed countries and 31 industrialized countries reveals the following (fictional) data. The standard deviations are significantly different from one another. Is there a significant difference in mean life expectancy between countries with these two levels of economic development? X = life expectancy of a resident at birth.

Less Developed Countries	Industrialized Countries
$\bar{X} = 66.1$ years	$\bar{X} = 76.7$ years
$s_X = 28.9$ years	$s_X = 4.2$ years
$n = 40$	$n = 31$

8. An upstart electronics company has been test marketing two models of compact disc (CD) players, one with a rotary disc changer and the other with a stacked changer. Random samples of recent purchasers returned questionnaires with a multi-item satisfaction scale that is of an interval level of measurement. The standard deviations are significantly different from one another. Is there a significant difference in mean purchaser satisfaction for the two models? Y = score on product satisfaction scale.

Purchasers of Rotary Model	Purchasers of Stack Model
$\bar{Y} = 31.1$	$\bar{Y} = 28.1$
$s_Y = 2.4$	$s_Y = 4.2$
$n = 149$	$n = 167$

9. Rotator cuff injuries to the arm and shoulder are common among athletes. A sports medicine institute is testing the effectiveness of a new therapy for improving arm range of motion (ROM). The new therapy is administered to an experimental treatment group, and traditional treatments are given to a control group. Subjects are randomly assigned to each group, and ROM is measured on a device scaled in centimeters. The experimental treatment regimen involved sessions three times per week for six weeks with measurements at time 1 (i.e., start of treatment) and time 2 (i.e., end of treatment). The (fictional) results are in the following table. Test hypotheses to answer questions (*a*) through (*c*) and then answer (*d*). Take care to use matched-pair tests when appropriate. Use $\alpha = .01$ and assume that the population variances are equal. Y – range of motion (ROM) of arm.

   a. If the members of the two groups were truly randomly assigned, then there should be no significant difference in ROM at time 1. Was this the case?
   b. Was there a significant difference between the experimental and control groups at time 2?
   c. Was there a significant difference in ROM at times 1 and 2 for the experimental subjects?

　　　　d. Considering the results of (*a*) through (*c*), does the new treatment appear to be an improvement over traditional treatment?

	Control Group (n = 35)	Experimental Treatment Group (n = 35)
Time 1	$\bar{Y}$ = 16.9 cm s_Y = 3.6 cm	$\bar{Y}$ = 17.1 cm s_Y = 3.7 cm
Time 2	$\bar{Y}$ = 32.1 cm s_Y = 3.4 cm	$\bar{Y}$ = 35.5 cm s_Y = 3.4 cm
Mean difference per subject	$\bar{D}$ = 14.7 cm s_D = 3.1 cm	$\bar{D}$ = 18.2 cm s_D = 3.0 cm

10. At the start of a weight-loss program, participants were asked to identify on a checklist foods that are high in saturated fat (i.e., HSF foods). After the nutritional education program, the same participants were administered the checklist again. Was the educational program effective in increasing the participants' knowledge about HSF foods? Assume that the population variances are equal. X = number of HSF foods correctly identified on a checklist (fictional data).

	Number of HSF Foods Identified	
Subject	Before Program	After Program
1	7	11
2	4	9
3	8	14
4	7	12
5	5	11
6	2	7
7	6	15
8	5	12
9	7	10
10	8	13
11	5	11
12	4	10
13	7	13
14	6	10
15	8	12
16	4	8
17	7	14
18	6	11
19	6	10
20	8	13

Optional Computer Applications for Chapter 11

If your class uses the optional computer applications that accompany this text, open the Chapter 11 exercises on the *Computer Applications for The Statistical Imagination* compact disk. The exercises for the two-group difference of means test in *SPSS for Windows* focus on choosing the appropriate test command sequences and correctly interpreting the output. Of particular interest is distinguishing output from equal and unequal variance tests.

ANALYSIS OF VARIANCE: DIFFERENCES AMONG MEANS OF THREE OR MORE GROUPS

Introduction

Just before the turn of the millennium, a nationwide movement began in the United States to reduce government assistance to poor single mothers and encourage them to seek employment. In most states, family assistance has never been sufficient to push all families out of poverty; it is a stopgap measure used by most recipients for a short time. Yet in the heat of political rhetoric, some politicians and citizens have come to believe that living "on welfare" is a paid long-term vacation of sorts.

Social researchers and social workers familiar with state assistance programs are skeptical of this public stereotype. In fact, a close look at the everyday lives of recipients of family assistance reveals a lifestyle characterized by a struggle for economic survival. For example, using a sample of 214 welfare-reliant mothers in four cities, Edin and Lein (1997) measured "monthly entertainment expenses" (MEES) to see how "lavishly" these mothers live. They found a mean MEES of only $22. This low average expenditure challenged the stereotype that welfare recipients are on an extended holiday.

The main purpose of Edin and Lein's study, however, was to see whether the average MEES differed from city to city. The cost of living varied among the cities, suggesting that entertainment costs also would vary. In theoretical terms, the research question was: Is there a relationship between the city in which a welfare-reliant mother resides and her MEES? City of residence is one variable, X, with a nominal level of measurement. MEES is the second variable, Y, and it is of ratio level. It is also the dependent variable, and the focus is on its mean.

The statistical design for comparing three or more group means is one-way analysis of variance (ANOVA). ANOVA is an extension of the two-group difference of means test (*t*-test) covered in Chapter 11, but with ANOVA we take a slightly different approach. To illustrate how ANOVA works, let us use data similar to those of Edin and Lein. To simplify, we will examine a sample of only 15 mothers from three cities. Our interest, of course, is in whether the mean MEES (μ_Y's) differ *in the populations* of welfare-reliant mothers in the three cities. That is, do their parameters, μ_Y, differ, where Y = MEES? This research question is graphically illustrated in Figure 12–1.

The data are presented in Table 12–1, where Y = MEES and X is the city of residence. In the lower right-hand corner of Table 12–1 we find that the mean MEES of all 15 mothers is $22. This overall, total sample mean is called the

FIGURE 12–1

Are the mean monthly entertainment expenses the same in the populations of welfare-reliant mothers in three cities?

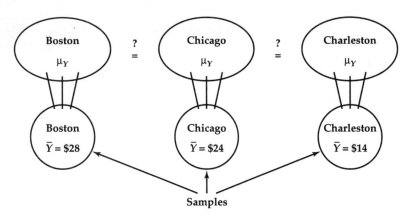

Populations: welfare-reliant mothers in three cities

Y = monthly entertainment expenses (MEES)

Samples

TABLE 12–1 Computational Spreadsheet of Monthly Entertainment Expenses (MEES) for 15 Welfare-Reliant Mothers from Three Cities

	Givens		Calculations		
Case	*City (X)*	*MEES (Y)*	$(Y_{(each\ case)} - \bar{Y}_{(grand)})$ *(deviation score)*	$(Y_{(each\ case)} - \bar{Y}_{(grand)})^2$	*Group Means*
1	Boston	$33	$ 11	$121	
2	Boston	30	8	64	
3	Boston	28	6	36	$\bar{Y}_{(Bos.)} = \dfrac{\Sigma Y}{n} = \dfrac{140}{5} = \$28$
4	Boston	26	4	16	
5	Boston	23	1	1	
6	Chicago	26	4	16	
7	Chicago	19	− 3	9	
8	Chicago	24	2	4	$\bar{Y}_{(Chic.)} = \dfrac{\Sigma Y}{n} = \dfrac{120}{5} = \$24$
9	Chicago	22	0	0	
10	Chicago	29	7	49	
11	Charleston	14	− 8	64	
12	Charleston	19	− 3	9	
13	Charleston	16	− 6	36	$\bar{Y}_{(Char.)} = \dfrac{\Sigma Y}{n} = \dfrac{70}{5} = \$14$
14	Charleston	12	− 10	100	
15	Charleston	9	− 13	169	

$$\Sigma Y_{(grand)} = \$330$$

$$\Sigma (Y_{(each\ case)} - \bar{Y}_{(grand)})^2 = \$694$$

$n = 15$

$$\Sigma (Y_{(each\ case)} - \bar{Y}_{(grand)}) = \$0$$

$$\bar{Y}_{(grand)} = \dfrac{\Sigma Y_{(grand)}}{n} = \dfrac{330}{15} = \$22$$

grand mean. Above the grand mean are the means for the three cities: Boston ($28), Chicago ($24), and Charleston ($14); these are called group means.

To test for differences among the means of the three cities, we could use *t*-tests (Chapter 11), but the process would require three tests, one for each of the following pairs of cities: Boston–Chicago, Boston–Charleston, and Chicago–Charleston. Comparing the means of, say, six cities would be even messier, requiring 15 *t*-tests. The cumbersome nature of calculating large sets of *t*-tests challenged statisticians to develop ANOVA, an extension of the *t*-test.

Like the *t*-test, with ANOVA the statistical hypothesis is stated as: There are no differences among group means. For our welfare-reliant mothers, we state the statistical hypothesis as follows:

$$\text{Stat. } H: \mu_{Y(Boston)} = \mu_{Y(Chicago)} = \mu_{Y(Charleston)}$$

where Y = MEES. This statement meets the requirements of a statistical hypothesis. When it is true, the differences among the three means will be zero, give or take some predictable sampling error.

Calculating Main Effects

Although the statement of the statistical hypothesis is essentially the same as it is with the *t*-test, with ANOVA we take a slightly different approach. Instead of comparing each group mean to the others, ANOVA compares each group mean to the grand mean. This makes sense. If the population means are equal for the three groups, the mean of all cases combined will be the same. Thus, the statistical hypothesis can be restated as

$$\text{Stat. } H: \mu_{Y(Boston)} = \mu_{Y(Chicago)} = \mu_{Y(Charleston)} = \mu_{Y(grand)}$$

Moreover, if the three means each equal the grand mean, the difference between any group mean and the grand mean is zero. In ANOVA, these *differences between each group mean and the grand mean* are the test effects, which for ANOVA are called **main effects.**

Calculating the Main Effect of a Group Mean

Main effect of a group mean = $\bar{Y}_{(group)} - \bar{Y}_{(grand)}$
= difference between a group's mean and mean of all scores in the sample

where

Y = an interval/ratio level variable

$\bar{Y}_{(group)}$ = mean of Y for a group (i.e., category of the nominal level variable)

$\bar{Y}_{(grand)}$ = mean of all scores in the sample

Recall that the test effect of a variable is the difference between what is observed in the sample (in step 4 of the six steps of statistical inference) and what is statistically hypothesized (in step 1 of the six steps). When the statistical hypothesis is true, there is no difference between the means of the three cities and the grand mean. The mean MEES of each city would be $22, and *all main effects would be zero*. Thus, the statistical hypothesis can be viewed in yet another way:

$$\text{Stat. } H: \overline{Y}_{(any \, group)} - \overline{Y}_{(grand)} = 0$$

(This can also be called a *null* hypothesis because it states *no* difference among the means.)

We can see, however, in Table 12–1 that the *sample* means from the three cities are not the same. Indeed, for the populations of welfare-reliant mothers of the three cities, the alternative hypothesis is that the mean MEES are not the same (i.e., the main effects are not zero). For our welfare-reliant mothers, the main effects are as follows:

Main effect on MEES of living in Boston = $\overline{Y}_{(Boston)} - \overline{Y}_{(grand)}$ = \$28 – \$22 = \$6

Main effect on MEES of living in Chicago = $\overline{Y}_{(Chicago)} - \overline{Y}_{(grand)}$ = \$24 – \$22 = \$2

Main effect on MEES of living in Charleston = $\overline{Y}_{(Charleston)} - \overline{Y}_{(grand)}$ = \$14 – \$22 = –\$8

Focusing on the grand mean and comparing each city's mean to it is a roundabout way of testing the difference among any number of group means. Using ANOVA, we can determine whether the main effects are significantly different from zero. This test hinges on whether the observed main effects are so great that they are unlikely to be due to sampling error.

In mathematical terms, then, with ANOVA the statistical hypothesis can be stated in any of several ways that convey the same meaning: There is no difference among group means, all means are equal, all means are equal to the grand mean, and all main effects are zero. If we reject the statistical hypothesis and accept the alternative hypothesis, we are asserting that some or all of the main effects are significantly different from zero. This in turn indicates that *at least two* of the population means differ. Moreover, accepting the alternative hypothesis asserts that there is a relationship between the nominal/ordinal level independent variable and the interval/ratio level dependent variable.

The General Additive-Effects Model: Testing the Statistical Significance of Main Effects

As it turns out, Edin and Lein found that there was indeed a relationship between city of residence and MEES. The effects of city of residence on MEES were significantly different from zero. They concluded that on average, *the populations* of welfare-reliant mothers in Boston had entertainment expenses that were \$6 greater than the grand mean of \$22; in Chicago, the expenses were \$2 greater; and in Charleston, they were \$8 less.

How are these effects used to come to this conclusion? The answer to this question lies in showing that the individual MEES scores in the sample are determined partly by the main effect of a subject's city of residence. This is done by focusing on individual deviations from the grand mean and seeing how much of this deviation is due to the effect of city of residence. Recall from Chapter 5 that a deviation score is the difference between an individual's score and the grand mean.

Calculating a Deviation Score

Deviation score for a case $= Y_{(each\ case)} - \bar{Y}_{(grand)}$
$\qquad\qquad\qquad$ = difference between the score of a case and the mean of all scores in the sample

where

$$Y = \text{an interval/ratio level variable}$$

$$Y_{(each\ case)} = Y\text{-score of an individual case}$$

$$\bar{Y}_{(grand)} = \text{mean of all scores in the sample}$$

Let us examine the deviation score of case 1 in Table 12–1, a Ms. Jones. With $Y =$ monthly entertainment expenses (MEES), her MEES or Y-score is $33. Therefore, her deviation score is

$$\text{Ms. Jones's deviation score} = Y_{(Ms.\ Jones)} - \bar{Y}_{(grand)} = \$33 - \$22 = \$11$$

Why does Ms. Jones spend $11 more than the average on entertainment? If MEES is related to city of residence, we can argue that $6 of this $11 deviation is "explained" by the differences in mean MEES among city of residence groups. Ms. Jones's group membership is Boston. The difference between the mean MEES in Boston and the grand mean is $6. This is the main effect for Boston, the "extra cost" of MEES of living in Boston. For Ms. Jones, $6 is the part of her $11 deviation that is explained by differences between group means. This is Ms. Jones's "between-group deviation." It is the same for all mothers in the Boston group and is equal to the main effect for Boston:

$$\text{Ms. Jones's between-group deviation} = \text{main effect on MEES of living in Boston}$$

$$= \bar{Y}_{(Boston)} - \bar{Y}_{(grand)} = \$28 - \$22 = \$6$$

While living in Boston explains $6 of Ms. Jones's $11 deviation score, this leaves an additional $5 that cannot be explained by city of residence. This is the difference between Ms. Jones's Y-score and the mean for Boston. This amount is called the within-group deviation because even within her Boston group Ms. Jones spends $5 more than the average. The within-group deviation accounts for why an individual does not score the mean within his or her group. It is the difference between an individual's Y-score and the mean of that individual's group. Whereas the *between*-group deviation is the same for all cases in a group, the *within*-group deviation varies among group members:

Calculating the Within-Group Deviation Score of a Case

$$\text{Within-group deviation} = Y_{(a\ group's\ case)} - \overline{Y}_{(group)}$$

$$= \text{difference between the score of a case and the mean of all scores in its group}$$

where

$$Y = \text{an interval/ratio level or interval-like ordinal variable}$$

$$Y_{(a\ group's\ case)} = Y\text{-score of an individual case in a group}$$

$$\overline{Y}_{(group)} = \text{mean of all scores in that case's group}$$

Thus:

$$\text{Within group deviation}_{(Ms.\ Jones)} = Y_{(Ms.\ Jones)} - \overline{Y}_{(Boston)} = \$33 - \$28 = \$5$$

The within-group deviation is also referred to as the "unexplained" deviation. While we can explain that $6 of Ms. Jones's $11 above-average MEES is due to her Boston residence, we do not know why she spends an extra $5 beyond the Boston average. It could be due to transportation costs, having kids who are big eaters, or some other reason. For the time being these other variables are unmeasured, and therefore, Ms. Jones's within-group deviation is left unexplained.

When all is said and done, we cannot explain every dollar of Ms. Jones's $33 expenditure for entertainment. We can, however, *account for it* by focusing on her $11 deviation score and isolating the parts explained and unexplained by her Boston residence:

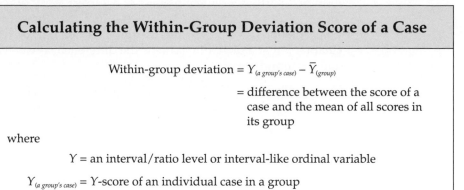

$$Y_{(Ms.\ Jones)} = \$33 = \overline{Y}_{(grand)} \quad + \quad \textit{her deviation score}$$

$$= \overline{Y}_{(grand)} \quad + \quad [Y_{(Ms.\ Jones)} - \overline{Y}_{(grand)}]$$

$$= \overline{Y}_{(grand)} \quad + \quad [\overline{Y}_{(Boston)} - \overline{Y}_{(grand)}] \quad + \quad [Y_{(Ms.\ Jones)} - \overline{Y}_{(Boston)}]$$

$$= \$22 \quad + \quad \$6 \quad + \quad \$5$$

↑	↑
Explained between-group deviation (that part of deviation score explained by Boston residence)	Unexplained within-group deviation (that part of deviation score explained by other unmeasured variables)

In this fashion, we can account for the Y-scores (i.e., MEES) of all cases in a sample. For instance, for case 15, a welfare-reliant mother from Charleston:

$$Y_{(case\ 15)} = \$9 = \bar{Y}_{(grand)} + [\bar{Y}_{(Charleston)} - \bar{Y}_{(grand)}] + [Y_{(case\ 15)} - \bar{Y}_{(Charleston)}]$$

$$= \$22 + (-\$8) + (-\$5)$$

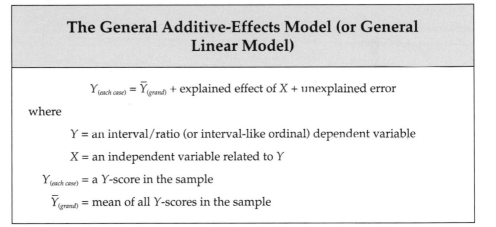

Explained deviation	Unexplained deviation
(effect of Charleston)	(effect of other variables)

This approach to analysis, which focuses on deviations from the mean of a dependent variable Y and explains its deviation scores $Y - \bar{Y}$, is called the general linear model, or, more aptly, the general additive-effects model. It simply states that the best prediction of any dependent variable Y is its mean plus the effects of an independent variable X. Whether for ANOVA or for any other statistical procedure, the general additive-effects model is mathematically represented as follows:

The General Additive-Effects Model (or General Linear Model)

$$Y_{(each\ case)} = \bar{Y}_{(grand)} + \text{explained effect of } X + \text{unexplained error}$$

where

Y = an interval/ratio (or interval-like ordinal) dependent variable

X = an independent variable related to Y

$Y_{(each\ case)}$ = a Y-score in the sample

$\bar{Y}_{(grand)}$ = mean of all Y-scores in the sample

The general additive-effects model breaks apart (or "decomposes") each Y-score into three parts:

1. The "amount of the Y-score explained by the grand mean" (i.e., the mean of all Y-scores)
2. The "amount of its deviation score explained by X" (i.e., the main effect for the category of X)
3. The "amount of its deviation score unexplained by X" (i.e., error)

Table 12–2 provides a breakdown of each of the 15 cases of our sample of welfare-reliant mothers in terms of these three parts. This type of table is called a decomposition table. For each city of residence, column (A) is the part of a Y-score explained by the grand mean. Column (B) is the main effect of the group: that part of the deviation score explained by city of residence (X).

TABLE 12–2   **Decomposition of Effects of City of Residence (X) on Total Monthly Entertainment Expenses [MEES (Y)] of Welfare-Reliant Mothers, n = 15**

All Columns (A): Grand Mean = $Y_{(grand)} = \dfrac{\Sigma Y}{n} = \dfrac{330}{15} = \$22$

Boston			Chicago			Charleston		
(A)	(B) Main Effect	(C)	(A)	(B) Main Effect	(C)	(A)	(B) Main Effect	(C)
$Y = \bar{Y}_{(grand)} +$	of X	+ Error	$Y = \bar{Y}_{(grand)} +$	of X	+ Error	$Y = \bar{Y}_{(grand)} +$	of X	+ Error
$\$33 = 22 +$	6	+ 5	$\$26 = 22 +$	2	+ 2	$\$14 = 22 +$	(−8)	+ 0
$\$30 = 22 +$	6	+ 2	$\$19 = 22 +$	2	+ (−5)	$\$19 = 22 +$	(−8)	+ 5
$\$28 = 22 +$	6	+ 0	$\$24 = 22 +$	2	+ 0	$\$16 = 22 +$	(−8)	+ 2
$\$26 = 22 +$	6	+ (−2)	$\$22 = 22 +$	2	+ (−2)	$\$12 = 22 +$	(−8)	+ (−2)
$\$23 = 22 +$	6	+ (−5)	$\$29 = 22 +$	2	+ 5	$\$ 9 = 22 +$	(−8)	+ (−5)

$$\bar{Y}_{(Bos.)} = \frac{\Sigma Y}{n} = \frac{140}{5} = \$28 \qquad \bar{Y}_{(Chic.)} = \frac{\Sigma Y}{n} = \frac{120}{5} = \$24 \qquad \bar{Y}_{(Char.)} = \frac{\Sigma Y}{n} = \frac{70}{5} = \$14$$

Column (B):

Between-group deviation = main effect for Boston

$\bar{Y}_{(Bos.)} - \bar{Y}_{(grand)} = \$28 - \$22 = \$6$

Column (C):

Within-group deviation = error

$= Y - \bar{Y}_{(Bos.)}$

Column (B):

Between-group deviation = main effect for Chicago

$\bar{Y}_{(Chic)} - \bar{Y}_{(grand)} = \$24 - \$22 = \$2$

Column (C):

Within-group deviation = error

$= Y - \bar{Y}_{(Chic.)}$

Column (B):

Between-group deviation = main effect for Charleston

$\bar{Y}_{(Char.)} - \bar{Y}_{(grand)} = \$14 - \$22 = -\$8$

Column (C):

Within-group deviation = error

$= Y - \bar{Y}_{(Char.)}$

Column (C) lists that part of each individual's Y-score that is not explained by city of residence—unexplained error.

Determining the Statistical Significance of Main Effects Using ANOVA

How do we determine that the $6 difference between the mean MEES of Boston residents and the grand mean is not simply due to sampling error? Is it not possible that in repeated sampling the mean of another Boston sample would be different? In other words, how do we determine that main effects, and therefore the differences among group means, are statistically significant? Is there truly a relationship between city of residence and MEES in the populations under study, or would a second sample produce radically different main effects?

To test whether the effects of city of residence are real in these populations, we must provide a summary measure—a statistic—that accounts for variation in all cases. If there are real differences between group means, as a general rule, welfare-reliant Boston mothers should have MEES about $6 above the grand mean. Similarly, the effects of Chicago and Charleston should be reflected in the pattern of MEES scores for subjects from those cities. With ANOVA, we are asserting that *the spread of scores*—Boston on the high end and Charleston on the low end—is due to the effects of residing in those different cities. The overall pattern of spread of scores should show a clustering of cases based on city of residence. This is depicted in Figure 12–2A, where the MEES scores of Charleston residents cluster $8 below the grand mean of $22 and those of Chicago and Boston residents cluster $2 above and $6 above, respectively.

When clustering does occur among cases from each city, as in Figure

FIGURE 12–2

Comparison of the spread of score distributions when main effects of groups are large (A) and small (B)

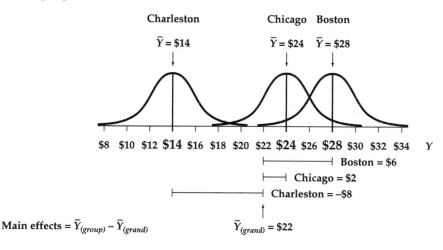

(A) When means are significantly different: Main effects are relatively large; scores cluster around group means.

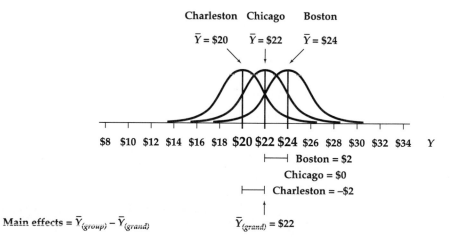

(B) When means are not significantly different: Main effects are relatively small; scores cluster around the grand mean.

12–2A, this indicates that the deviations of individual scores in a group (i.e., city) are due mostly to group membership. A group's cases vary about its group mean.

When the clustering does not occur in a pattern related to group membership, as in Figure 12–2B, scores simply vary around the grand mean. Deviations from the grand mean are random—occurring in either direction—uninfluenced by group membership. In other words, this is what happens when the statistical hypothesis of no differences between means is true. ANOVA is the statistical test that establishes whether the pattern of clustering is more like Figure 12–2A, where group scores are bunched around different means, or Figure 12–2B, where all scores regardless of city of residence tend to cluster around the grand mean.

As the name implies, ANOVA focuses on the variances of scores. Recall once again (see Chapter 5) that a deviation score for an individual case is the difference between its score and the grand mean. To obtain a summary measure for the entire sample, however, we must square the deviation scores. This is the case because the sum of (nonsquared) deviations is always zero, as is the case in Table 12–1. The sum of squared deviation scores is the *variation*, or "sum of squares." Finally, recall that the *variance* is the variation divided by sample size to produce an average of the variation. Deviation scores, the variation, and the variance all gauge how scores are spread about the mean. ANOVA focuses on the variation and then the variance of the sample as a whole. It then establishes whether those measures of spread are explained by differences in mean MEES among the three cities or simply result from random sampling error.

Just as we decomposed Ms. Jones's deviation score, ANOVA summarizes the decomposition for the entire sample. Let us compare the individual decomposition to the summary decomposition:

Explaining the individual case as an effect of group membership:

$$\text{Ms. Jones's deviation score} = Y_{(\text{Ms. Jones})} - \bar{Y}_{(\text{grand})}$$

$$= (\bar{Y}_{(\text{Boston})} - \bar{Y}_{(\text{grand})}) \quad + \quad (Y_{(\text{Ms. Jones})} - \bar{Y}_{(\text{Boston})})$$

$$\uparrow \qquad\qquad\qquad\qquad \uparrow$$

Explained deviation Unexplained deviation

Explaining the deviations of all cases taken together:

$$\text{Total variation} = \text{total sum of squares}$$

$$= \Sigma(Y_{(\text{each case})} - \bar{Y}_{(\text{grand})})^2$$

$$= \Sigma(\bar{Y}_{(\text{group})} - \bar{Y}_{(\text{grand})})^2 \quad + \quad \Sigma(Y_{(\text{each case})} - \bar{Y}_{(\text{group})})^2$$

$$\uparrow \qquad\qquad\qquad\qquad \uparrow$$

Explained variation   Unexplained variation

Note that in these summary measurements we calculate three types of sums of squares: the total sum of squares (SS_T), the between-group or "explained" sum of squares (SS_B), and the within-group or "unexplained" sum of squares (SS_W).

Types of Variation or "Sums of Squares"

SS_T = total variation = total sum of squares

$$= \Sigma(Y_{(each\ case)} - \bar{Y}_{(grand)})^2$$

SS_B = between-group sum of squares

$$= \Sigma(\bar{Y}_{(group)} - \bar{Y}_{(grand)})^2$$

= explained variation (i.e., that explained by group effects)

SS_W = within-group sum of squares

$$= \Sigma(Y_{(each\ case\ of\ group)} - \bar{Y}_{(group)})^2$$

= unexplained variation or error (i.e., variation not explained by group membership but by other unmeasured variables)

The calculations of the explained variation and the unexplained variation are made with the data in Tables 12–1 and 12–2. The *total variation*, or "total sum of squares" (SS_T), is the same calculation we made in Chapter 5 in calculating the standard deviation. For the data in Table 12–1 we see that SS_T is $694. For purposes of illustration, let us examine how this total accumulated:

$$SS_T = \Sigma(Y_{(each\ case)} - \bar{Y}_{(grand)})^2$$

Boston   Chicago
├ – – – – – – – – – – – – –┤ ├ – – – – – – – – – – – – – –┤
$$= 11^2 + 8^2 + 6^2 + 4^2 + 1^2 + 4^2 + (-3)^2 + 2^2 + 0^2 + 7^2$$

$$+ (-8^2) + (-3^2) + (-6^2) + (-10^2) + (-13^2) = 694$$

├ –┤
Charleston

Note that Boston residents tend to deviate in the positive direction and that Charleston residents deviate in the negative direction.

The part of the SS_T explained by group effects (i.e., city of residence) is called the explained sum of squares. This is calculated as the sum of squared group effects. The explained sum of squares also is called the between-group sum of squares (SS_B), because it is due to differences between group means.

Because every individual within a group (i.e., city) has the same effect score, calculating the SS_B is rather straightforward. These are the test effects listed under column (B) for each city in Table 12–2. Thus, for all welfare-reliant mothers in Boston, the squared effect is $\$6^2$; for those in Chicago, it is $\$2^2$; and for those in Charleston, it is $-\$8^2$. Thus, for the whole sample, the computation of the explained sum of squares is

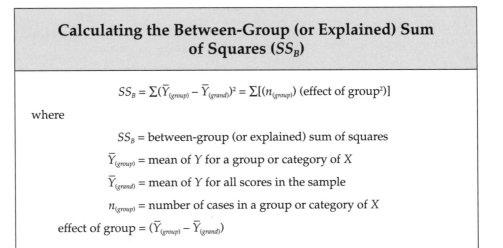

$$SS_B = \Sigma(\bar{Y}_{(group)} - \bar{Y}_{(grand)})^2$$

Boston   Chicago

$$= 6^2 + 6^2 + 6^2 + 6^2 + 6^2 + 2^2 + 2^2 + 2^2 + 2^2 + 2^2$$

$$+ (-8^2) + (-8^2) + (-8^2) + (-8^2) + (-8^2) = 520$$

Charleston

These calculations can be abbreviated since every case in a group has the same effect.

Calculating the Between-Group (or Explained) Sum of Squares (SS_B)

$$SS_B = \Sigma(\bar{Y}_{(group)} - \bar{Y}_{(grand)})^2 = \Sigma[(n_{(group)}) \text{ (effect of group}^2)]$$

where

SS_B = between-group (or explained) sum of squares

$\bar{Y}_{(group)}$ = mean of Y for a group or category of X

$\bar{Y}_{(grand)}$ = mean of Y for all scores in the sample

$n_{(group)}$ = number of cases in a group or category of X

effect of group = $(\bar{Y}_{(group)} - \bar{Y}_{(grand)})$

Thus, for the sample of welfare-reliant mothers:

$$SS_B = \Sigma(\bar{Y}_{(group)} - \bar{Y}_{(grand)})^2 = \Sigma[(n_{(group)}) \text{ (effect of group}^2)]$$

$$= (5) (6^2) + (5) (2^2) + (5) (-8^2) = 180 + 20 + 320 = 520$$

In column (C) of Table 12–2 we list the part of each individual's Y-score that is not explained by city of residence. This is the within-group deviation, the difference between an individual's Y-score and the mean of that individual's group. These within-group deviations are also squared and summed to obtain the "within-group sum of squares," or SS_W. For the welfare-reliant mothers' MEES scores in Table 12–2,

$$\text{Boston}$$
$$\vdash - - - - - - - - - - - - - - - \dashv$$

$$SS_W = \Sigma(Y_{(each\ case\ of\ group)} - \overline{Y}_{(group)})^2 = 5^2 + 2^2 + 0^2 + (-2^2) + (-5^2)$$
$$+ 2^2 + (-5^2) + 0^2 + (-2^2) + 5^2 + 0^2 + 5^2 + 2^2 + (-2^2) + (-5^2) = 174$$
$$\vdash - - - - - - - - - - - - - - \dashv \quad \vdash - - - - - - - - - - - - - - \dashv$$
$$\text{Chicago} \qquad\qquad\qquad \text{Charleston}$$

As we can see, calculation of the SS_W is somewhat cumbersome. However, there is a less complicated way to obtain this sum. Note that the between-group sum of squares and the within-group sum of squares are equal to the total sum of squares:

$$SS_T = SS_B + SS_W$$

That is, $694 = 520 + 174$. Therefore, once we have calculated the SS_T and SS_B, we can quickly compute the SS_W.

Calculation of the Within-Group (or Unexplained) Sum of Squares (SS_W)

$$SS_W = SS_T - SS_B$$

where

SS_W = within-group (or unexplained) sum of squares of Y

SS_T = total sum of squares (or variation) of Y

SS_B = between-group (or explained) sum of squares of Y

Thus, for the sample of welfare-reliant mothers,

$$SS_W = SS_T - SS_B = 694 - 520 = 174$$

What do the relative sizes of these sums tell us? If the group means differ, the effects of city of residence, and therefore the SS_B, will be large. How large is a statistically significant SS_B? In testing a statistical hypothesis of equal group means, it is not enough to simply observe the size of the SS_B, because that size depends greatly on the total number of cases in a sample (n). That is, regardless of whether group means differ, the more cases that are used in calculations, the greater will be all three types of sums of squares. Similarly, the number of groups (K) affects computations of the sums of squares; that is, the more groups being hypothesized, the more test effects to be computed, squared, and summed. Thus, we must account for sample size and the number of groups; therefore, variances are computed by dividing these sums of squares by their respective degrees of freedom. In ANOVA the resulting variances are called mean square variances. The between-group degrees of freedom (df_B) are $K - 1$; the within-group degrees of freedom (df_W) are $n - K$. The df_B is $K - 1$, because once the means and effects are calculated for all but one group, the last group's mean and effect are fixed. (Note in Table 12–2 that the effects sum to zero; if two effects are known, the other is mathematically fixed.) The df_W reflects the fact that when all but one case is known *within a group*, the last case is mathematically fixed. Thus, 1 degree of freedom is lost for each group. For the between-group sum of squares the mean square variance is as follows:

Calculating the Mean Square Variance between Groups (i.e., the Explained Variance)

$$MSV_B = \frac{SS_B}{df_B} = \frac{SS_B}{K-1}$$

where

MSV_B = mean square variance between groups, or "explained variance"

SS_B = between-group sums of squares (i.e., the explained variation)

df_B = degrees of freedom between groups

K = number of groups being compared

For the sample of welfare-reliant mothers,

$$MSV_B = \frac{SS_B}{df_B} = \frac{SS_B}{K-1} = \frac{520}{2} = 260$$

For the within-group sum of squares, the mean square variance within groups is as follows:

Calculating the Mean Square Variance within Groups (i.e., the Unexplained Variance)

$$MSV_W = \frac{SS_W}{df_W} = \frac{SS_W}{n-K}$$

where

MSV_W = mean square variance within groups, or the "unexplained variance"

SS_W = within-group sums of squares (i.e., the unexplained variation)

df_W = degrees of freedom within groups

n = total sample size

K = number of groups being compared

For the sample of welfare-reliant mothers,

$$MSV_W = \frac{SS_W}{df_W} = \frac{SS_W}{n - K} = \frac{174}{12} = 14.50$$

The F-Ratio Test Statistic

In ANOVA, the test formula for computing the probability of sample outcomes involves taking the ratio of explained *mean square variance* to unexplained *mean square variance*. This is called the **F-ratio statistic,** and its formula is as follows:

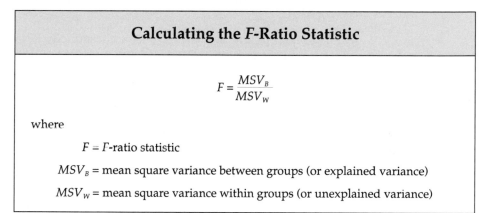

Calculating the *F*-Ratio Statistic

$$F = \frac{MSV_B}{MSV_W}$$

where

$F = F$-ratio statistic

MSV_B = mean square variance between groups (or explained variance)

MSV_W = mean square variance within groups (or unexplained variance)

For the sample of welfare-reliant mothers,

$$F = \frac{MSV_B}{MSV_W} = \frac{260}{14.50} = 17.93$$

A computed *F*-ratio will always be positive because squaring the numerator and denominator eliminates negative signs. To organize these calculations, the *F*-ratio is commonly presented in a "source table" which distinguishes the between-group, within-group, and total sums of squares. Table 12–3 is the source table for the MEES of welfare-reliant mothers.

TABLE 12–3   **Analysis of Variance Source Table for Data in Table 12–2**

Source of Variation	SS	df	Mean Square Variance: $MSV = SS/df$	$F = \frac{MSV_B}{MSV_W}$
Between groups (SS_B)	520	$K - 1 = 2$	260	17.93
Within groups (SS_W)	174	$n - K = 12$	14.50	
Total (SS_T)	694	$n - 1 = 14$	49.57	

Just as t-tests measure the significance of test effects, the F-ratio gauges whether observed main effects of sampled group means are significantly different from zero, the hypothesized effects. When the main effects are large, the SS_B and the MSV_B are large. Since MSV_B is in the numerator, when it is large, the F-ratio statistic will be large. The larger the F-ratio, the greater the chance that the statistical hypothesis will be rejected. As we will demonstrate when we do ANOVA with the six steps of statistical inference, an F-ratio of 17.93 is quite large. We will conclude that there is a significant difference in the mean MEES of at least two cities.

How the F-Ratio Turns Out When Group Means Are Not Significantly Different

Before completing the hypothesis test for the sample of welfare-reliant mothers, let us get a better sense of proportion about ANOVA and the F-ratio. Let us examine the case where group means are found *not* to be significantly dif-

TABLE 12–4   **Decomposition of Effects of City of Residence (X) on Total Monthly Entertainment Expenses [MEES (Y)] for the Hypothetical Example of Insignificant Group Differences (Welfare-Reliant Mothers, $n = 15$)**

$$\text{All Columns (A): Grand Mean} = \overline{Y}_{(grand)} = \frac{\Sigma Y}{n} = \frac{330}{15} = \$22$$

Boston			Chicago			Charleston		
(A)	(B) Main Effect	(C)	(A)	(B) Main Effect	(C)	(A)	(B) Main Effect	(C)
$Y = \overline{Y}_{(grand)} +$	of X	+ Error	$Y = \overline{Y}_{(grand)} +$	of X	+ Error	$Y = \overline{Y}_{(grand)} +$	of X	+ Error
$\$22 = 22 +$	2	$+ (-2)$	$\$27 = 22 +$	0	$+ 5$	$\$25 = 22 +$	(-2)	$+ 5$
$\$26 = 22 +$	2	$+ 2$	$\$24 = 22 +$	0	$+ 2$	$\$22 = 22 +$	(-2)	$+ 2$
$\$24 = 22 +$	2	$+ 0$	$\$22 = 22 +$	0	$+ 0$	$\$20 = 22 +$	(-2)	$+ 0$
$\$19 = 22 +$	2	$+ (-5)$	$\$20 = 22 +$	0	$+ (-2)$	$\$18 = 22 +$	(-2)	$+ (-2)$
$\$29 = 22 +$	2	$+ 5$	$\$17 = 22 +$	0	$+ (-5)$	$\$15 = 22 +$	(-2)	$+ (-5)$

$$\overline{Y}_{(Bos.)} = \frac{\Sigma Y}{n} = \frac{120}{5} = \$24 \qquad \overline{Y}_{(Chic.)} = \frac{\Sigma Y}{n} = \frac{110}{5} = \$22 \qquad \overline{Y}_{(Char.)} = \frac{\Sigma Y}{n} = \frac{100}{5} = \$20$$

Column (B):

Between-group deviation
= main effect for Boston

$$\overline{Y}_{(Bos.)} - \overline{Y}_{(grand)} = \$24 - \$22 = \$2$$

Column (C):

Within-group deviation = error

$$= Y - \overline{Y}_{(Bos.)}$$

Column (B):

Between-group deviation
= main effect for Chicago

$$\overline{Y}_{(Chic.)} - \overline{Y}_{(grand)} = \$22 - \$22 = \$0$$

Column (C):

Within-group deviation = error

$$= Y - \overline{Y}_{(Chic.)}$$

Column (B):

Between-group deviation
= main effect for Charleston

$$\overline{Y}_{(Char.)} - \overline{Y}_{(grand)} = \$20 - \$22 = -\$2$$

Column (C):

Within-group deviation = error

$$= Y - \overline{Y}_{(Char.)}$$

TABLE 12–5   **Analysis of Variance Source Table for Data in Table 12–4 Where Differences among Means Are Not Significant**

Source of Variation	SS	df	Mean Square Variance: $MSV = SS/df$	$F = \dfrac{MSV_B}{MSV_W}$
Between groups (SS_B)	40	$K - 1 = 2$	20	1.38
Within groups (SS_W)	174	$n - K = 12$	14.50	
Total (SS_T)	214	$n - 1 = 14$	15.29	

ferent. In other words, what is the value of F when the statistical hypothesis of equal population means is not rejected?

Table 12–4 presents such a scenario, with the grand mean of MEES still $22 but with the group means not significantly different from $22. Note in the distributions of MEES of the three groups that all the scores are in a similar range from the upper teens to the upper twenties. The means are quite close, and this suggests that the scores may have come from the same population (i.e., a national sample of welfare-reliant mothers whose average MEES is $22). With these new data the main effects of city of residence [Column (B)] are small compared to the within-group effects [Column (C)]. Table 12–5 presents the source table for the data in Table 12–4. With the small main effects, the F-ratio is only 1.39 compared to an F-ratio of 17.93 with the original data in Table 12–2.

The source table reveals that when the means are not significantly different, the between-group sum of squares (SS_B) is relatively small. This in turn results in a small F-ratio score. Note also that since all 15 scores are closely bunched together around the grand mean of $22, the total sum of squares is relatively small.

Return to Figure 12–2 above. Figure 12-2B provides a graphical illustration of the data in Table 12–4. The small main effects *in the sample* suggest that in fact the group *population means* are the same and are equal to the grand mean of $22. There is no clear clustering of scores. The minor differences in the cities' mean MEES is due to sampling error.

The F-Ratio as a Sampling Distribution

As we noted above, the F-ratio is used to determine statistical significance with ANOVA. The F-ratio is a sampling distribution and can be depicted with a curve such as the one in Figure 12–3. With repeated sampling, the F-ratio can be calculated for all possible sampling outcomes *when the statistical hypothesis is true*. These outcomes are represented by the area under the curve, which, like the normal and t-distribution curves, totals to 1.00, or 100 percent. Note that the F-distribution curve is skewed and that all scores are positive. This is due to the squaring in the F-ratio equation.

FIGURE 12–3

*Critical values of
the F-distribution
for 2 and 12
degrees of freedom
at the .05 and .01
levels of
significance*

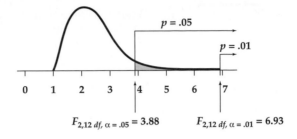

$F_{2,12\,df,\,\alpha\,=\,.05} = 3.88$ $F_{2,12\,df,\,\alpha\,=\,.01} = 6.93$

With ANOVA, the statistical hypothesis is that group population means are equal. When the statistical hypothesis is indeed true and we sample repeatedly, sample group means will differ little and the computed main effects will be small. These small main effects—which are due to random sampling error—result in a small F-ratio calculation. In the F-distribution curve, this high frequency of small F-scores is apparent in the lumping of sampling outcomes toward the low end of the curve (resulting in the right skew in Figure 12–3).

For our samples of welfare-reliant mothers, the statistical hypothesis is that mothers in Charleston, Chicago, and Boston all average the same MEES. If this is true, repeated sampling will provide a description of the sizes of sample means and differences of means that occur, say, 95 percent of the time. With repeated sampling, sometimes Boston will come out slightly on top as we frame our illustrations. Other times Charleston or Chicago will have slightly larger *sample* means. If the statistical hypothesis of no difference in means is true, most of the time all three group means will be close to the grand mean. As we repeatedly calculate main effects, sums of squares, and F-ratios, the results will show that the distribution of F-ratios has a lower limit of 1.00 and no upper limit.

We have noted, however, that the size of the F-ratio is influenced by degrees of freedom—sample size and the number of groups. Thus, a sampling distribution of F-ratios is shaped in accordance with its degrees of freedom. Statistical Tables D and E in Appendix B present F-ratio values for specified degrees of freedom for the .05 and .01 levels of significance, respectively. The bodies of the tables provide critical values of the F-ratio. Across the top are degrees of freedom for the MSV_B, the numerator of the F-ratio. Down the left side are degrees of freedom for the MSV_W, the denominator of the F-ratio. The F-ratio values in the table are like t-scores; they are critical values of F for the .05 and .01 levels of significance. For example, for our data in Tables 12–2 and 12–4, we have $(K - 1) = 2$ degrees of freedom between groups and $(n - K) = 12$ degrees of freedom within groups. From Statistical Table D the critical F-ratio value for 2 and 12 degrees of freedom at the .05 level is

$$\text{Critical } F_{2,\,12\,df,\,\alpha\,=\,.05} = 3.88$$

This means that when the statistical hypothesis of equal group means is true, with repeated sampling, calculations of the F-ratio will equal or exceed 3.88

only 5 percent of the time. From Statistical Table E in Appendix B, the corresponding critical value of the F-ratio at the .01 level of significance is 6.93. Figure 12–3 identifies the critical regions and illustrates the shape of the F-ratio distribution for 2 and 12 degrees of freedom.

For our original data in Table 12–2 we obtained an F-ratio of 17.93. This is larger than the critical value of the F-ratio at the .01 level, a value of 6.93. Thus, for step 4 of the six steps of statistical inference, the calculated p-value would be $p < .01$. And if we are testing at the .05 level of significance, the statistical hypothesis is rejected because

$$\mid F_{observed} \mid > \mid F_{\alpha} \mid \text{ (i.e., } 17.93 > 3.88)$$

Thus, $p < \alpha$ (i.e., $p < .05$).

However, for our hypothetical example of no significant differences (Tables 12–4 and 12–5) we would not reject the statistical hypothesis because

$$\mid F_{observed} \mid < \mid F_{\alpha} \mid \text{ (i.e., } 1.39 < 3.88)$$

Thus, $p > \alpha$ (i.e., $p > .05$).

These "nonsignificant" data illustrate that it is not unusual in repeated sampling to get main effects of $2, $0, and –$2 when there are indeed no differences in the Boston, Chicago, and Charleston population means.

Relevant Aspects of the Relationship for ANOVA

Existence of the Relationship

The existence of the relationship for ANOVA is determined by using the F-ratio to test the statistical hypothesis of equal group means, as was just described. (The complete six steps of statistical inference are presented below.) The alternative hypothesis is that the group means are not equal. If the statistical hypothesis is rejected and the alternative hypothesis is accepted, there is a relationship between city of residence and MEES.

Existence of a Relationship Using ANOVA

Test the statistical hypothesis:

$$\text{Stat. } H: \bar{Y}_{(group\ 1)} = \bar{Y}_{(group\ 2)} = \bar{Y}_{(group\ 3)} = \ldots = \bar{Y}_{(grand)}$$

and therefore main effects = 0. That is, there is no relationship between X and Y. Use the F-ratio test statistic:

$$F = \frac{MSV_B}{MSV_W}$$

Direction of the Relationship

Keep in mind that we address the direction, strength, and nature of a relationship between variables only when that relationship exists. Since the independent variable in ANOVA is typically of the nominal level of measurement, direction is meaningless. For example, it is meaningless to say that Ms. Jones is more in the direction of Boston than in that of Chicago or Charleston. Either she is from Boston or she is not. This absence of meaning for direction also is implied by the fact that the F-ratio statistic is always one-tailed yet nondirectional, because its calculations involve squaring away negative signs. Thus, a correct way to report the direction of an ANOVA test is to say that it is not applicable.

Direction of a Relationship Using ANOVA

Not applicable.

Strength of the Relationship

With ANOVA, if a relationship is found in a sample, this simply indicates that the main effects are significantly different from zero in the population. The strength of the relationship lies in the separate question: How large are these main effects in practical terms? Do the group means in the population differ only a little or a lot? For example, if city of residence is related to MEES, does this improve our understanding and prediction of MEES a little or a lot?

A strong relationship is one in which knowing group main effects allows us to make very precise predictions of the dependent variable. For example, suppose all welfare-reliant mothers in Boston spend exactly $28 on MEES, all in Chicago spend exactly $24, and all in Charleston spend exactly $14. The variances or spreads of scores around group means (i.e., the within-group variances) would be zero. Knowing city of residence would be a perfect predictor of MEES, and there would be no error in predictions of an individual welfare-reliant mother's MEES. In such an unlikely case, if we are given a mother's city of residence, we can perfectly predict her MEES: The main effects will explain all the total variance in MEES. A strong relationship is one in which a high proportion of the total variance in the dependent, interval/ratio variable is accounted for by the group variable.

There are several measures of the strength of the relationship for ANOVA, but often none is reported because each one must be used with caution. Any single measure may be biased by sample size and other issues related to sampling error. One conservative measure, however, is the *correlation ratio*, ε^2 (pronounced "epsilon squared") (Blalock 1979: 373–74). Keeping in mind that we are using sample data, ε^2 is conservative in that it is unlikely to overinflate the strength of the relationship in the population. The correlation ratio is a proportional reduction in error (PRE) measure. It provides a sense of how much more accurately the dependent variable (in this case MEES) can be predicted by using knowledge of the independent variable (in this case city of residence). Its formula is as follows:

Calculating the Correlation Ratio ε^2 to Measure the Strength of a Relationship Using ANOVA

$$\varepsilon^2 = 1 - \frac{MSV_W}{MSV_T}$$

where

ε^2 = correlation ratio of the strength of the relationship

MSV_T = total mean square variance

MSV_W = mean square variance within groups (or unexplained variance)

Note that this formula does not measure the proportion of explained variance (i.e., MSV_B) directly because the MSV_B depends heavily on the number of groups used in its calculation. Instead, it treats a proportion of 1 (or 100 percent) as the total variance to be explained and subtracts from it the proportion that is unexplained (i.e., MSV_W/MSV_T). Moreover, with this formula, the correlation ratio ε^2 has defined limits; it ranges from zero to 1.00 and thus is always positive. When the main effects of city of residence completely explain variance in MEES, within-group effects will be zero, leaving MSV_W at zero and producing an ε^2 of 1:

$$\varepsilon^2 = 1 - \frac{MSV_W}{MSV_T} = 1 - \frac{0}{MSV_T} = 1 - 0 = 1$$

At the other extreme, when group effects are zero, the unlikely case in which all the subjects score the grand mean of $22 on MEES, the MSV_B will be zero. This will leave the MSV_W equal to the MSV_T. Thus,

$$\varepsilon^2 = 1 - \frac{MSV_W}{MSV_T} = 1 - 1 = 0$$

In real situations, we seldom have perfect relationships between variables. An ε^2 will fall between zero and 1.00, and the larger it is, the stronger the relationship is. For instance, using data from Table 12–3, the source table for our sample of welfare-reliant mothers,

$$\varepsilon^2 = 1 - \frac{MSV_W}{MSV_T} = 1 - \frac{14.50}{49.57} = 1 - .2935 = .7065$$

As a percentage, this is $(.7065)(100) = 70.65$ percent. We conclude that 70.65 percent of the variance in MEES is explained by city of residence. Unfortunately, the interpretation of ε^2 must be made with caution. *In fact, it should not be computed and reported unless all groups have about the same number of cases and the variances within each group are about the same.*

Strength of a Relationship Using ANOVA

Calculate the percent of the variance in Y explained by knowledge of X by using the correlation ratio:

$$\varepsilon^2 = 1 - \frac{MSV_W}{MSV_T}$$

Nature of the Relationship

If a relationship between variables is found to exist, we may describe its nature. With the nature of the relationship we focus on substance—welfare-reliant mothers, their cities of residence, and their MEES—and provide best estimates of the dependent variable. Simply put, how does knowledge of a relationship between city of residence and MEES lead to improved predictions of the MEES of welfare-reliant mothers?

First, we make best estimates at the group level by reporting the grand mean, group means, and main effects. Second, we provide examples of best estimates for individuals. Finally, we specify which group means are significantly different from others. This requires the additional computation of what is called a range test.

Range Tests. Range tests are a necessary additional step with ANOVA because with ANOVA the rejection of the statistical hypothesis merely indicates that *at least two* of the group means are significantly different from each other. Especially in dealing with a large number of groups, range tests provide a quicker way than do a series of t-tests to identify which group means are significantly different from others.

A range test determines how much of a difference between means (i.e., a range of differences) is statistically significant. If the sample sizes and standard deviations of group means are not very different, we can start by assuming that the smallest and largest group means are significantly different—for the MEES example, those of Charleston and Boston. But perhaps other differences are also significant, such as that between Charleston and Chicago. A range test tells us how far apart two group means must be before we can assume that they are different in the populations. Range tests are also called multiple comparison tests.

There are several range tests. A conservative one is Tukey's highly significant difference formula, the HSD (Tukey 1953). The HSD formula is conservative because it is unlikely to mistakenly tell us that a difference exists when in fact it does not.

Since range tests compare each group to the others, we start by constructing a tree diagram that orders the means from lowest to highest and indicates the differences between group means (Table 12–6). In Table 12–6 we see that the difference between Charleston and Chicago is $10, that between Charleston and Boston is $14, and that between Chicago and Boston is $4. The HSD tells us exactly how large the difference between two sample means must be for us to assume that a difference truly exists between the means of the two populations. For instance, is a $4 difference statistically significant? The HSD formula is as follows:

Calculating Tukey's Highly Significant Difference (HSD) Range Test

$$HSD = q \sqrt{\frac{MSV_W}{n_{(per\ group)}}}$$

where

HSD = highly significant difference range test value: how large the difference between two sample means must be for us to assume that the difference truly exists between the population means

q = a critical value of the range test from Statistical Table F in Appendix B for a specified level of significance and degrees of freedom

MSV_W = mean square variance within groups

$n_{(per\ group)}$ = sample size of the groups (assuming sample n's are equal); if the sample sizes are not the same for all groups, complicated calculations must be made to arrive at an average group size

Degrees of Freedom (for Use with Statistical Table F in Appendix B)

df for the $MSV_W = n_{(total)} - K$ (listed down the left side of Statistical Table F)

where

$n_{(total)}$ = total sample size

K = number of groups

df for $n_{(per\ group)}$ = K (listed across the top of the Statistical Table F as "number of groups")

where K = number of groups

TABLE 12–6   **Tree Diagram of Differences between Means for Range Test Comparisons**

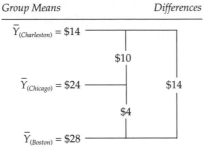

Group Means		Differences
$\bar{Y}_{(Charleston)} = \$14$		
	$\$10$	
$\bar{Y}_{(Chicago)} = \$24$		$\$14$
	$\$4$	
$\bar{Y}_{(Boston)} = \$28$		

Statistical Table F in Appendix B provides the values of q—critical values for the .05 and .01 levels of significance. To obtain q for the problem at hand, let us choose the .05 level of significance. We calculated degrees of freedom for the MSV_W when we did the F-ratio test, and in this case there are 12. There are 3 degrees of freedom for $n_{(per\ group)}$. Observing the table, for 12 and 3 degrees of freedom the q-value is 3.77. The calculation of HSD then is

$$HSD = q \sqrt{\frac{MSV_W}{n_{(per\ group)}}} = 3.77 \sqrt{\frac{14.50}{5}} = 6.42$$

Thus, a difference of at least $6.42 between any two means is statistically significant. From Table 12–6 we see that the mean MEES is significantly different between Charleston and Chicago (i.e., $10 > $6.42) and between Charleston and Boston (i.e., $14 > $6.42). The mean MEES of Chicago and Boston are not significantly different (i.e., $4 < $6.42). With the calculation of the range test, we have everything we need to address the nature of the relationship between city of residence and MEES. Now let us follow the six steps of statistical inference.

Nature of a Relationship Using ANOVA

1. Provide best estimates of the grand mean, group means, and main effects.
2. Provide examples of best estimates of Y for individual cases in the population:

$$Y'_{(each\ case)} = \bar{Y}_{(grand)} + \text{(explained) effect of } X$$
$$= \bar{Y}_{(grand)} + \text{main effect of the } X\text{-group}$$

(continued)

(concluded)

3. Use range tests to determine which group means are significantly different from one another.

The Six Steps of Statistical Inference for One-Way ANOVA

Now that we have acquired a sense of the logic of one-way ANOVA, let us follow the six steps of statistical inference. First we review the criteria for selecting ANOVA.

When to Use One-Way Analysis of Variance (ANOVA) to Test Differences of Means among Three or More Groups (*F*-distribution)

In general: Testing a hypothesis between a nominal/ordinal independent variable with three or more categories and an interval/ratio or interval-like ordinal dependent variable.

1. Number of variables, samples, and populations: (a) One population with a single interval/ratio dependent variable, comparing means for three or more groups of a single nominal/ordinal independent variable. Each group's sample must be representative of its subpopulation. Or, (b) a single interval/ratio dependent variable whose mean is compared for three or more populations using representative samples.
2. Sample size. Generally no requirements. However, the dependent interval/ratio variable should not be highly skewed within any group sample. Moreover, range tests are unreliable unless the sample sizes of groups are about equal. These restrictions are less important when group sample sizes are large.
3. Variances (and standard deviations) of the groups are equal. This is the same constraint used for the *t*-test (see the material on equality of variances in Chapter 11).

The requirement of equality of variances is necessary in any difference of means test, including the *t*-test and the *F*-ratio test. A large spread of scores in one group may mislead us into believing that a difference of means exists when in fact this is not the case. Recall from Chapter 11 that when there is a large difference between group variances (and therefore between the standard deviations), degrees of freedom must be adjusted. With ANOVA this is a difficult chore that is best left to a computer. Fortunately, however, with ANOVA and the *F*-ratio test, if the samples are large (each group > 30), unequal variances are less likely to affect the results of the test.

Brief Checklist for the Six Steps of Statistical Inference

Test Preparation

State the research question; list givens, including variables (e.g., $X = ...$, $Y = ...$), their levels of measurement, the population(s) under study, and sample(s) and sample size(s); select the statistical test; provide observations of statistics and parameters; and draw a conceptual diagram.

Six Steps

Using the symbol H for *hypothesis:*

1. State the statistical H and the alternative H and stipulate test direction.
2. Describe the sampling distribution.
3. State the level of significance (α) and specify the critical test value.
4. Observe the actual sample outcomes and compute the test effects, the test statistic, and the p-value.
5. Make the rejection decision.
6. Interpret and apply best estimates in everyday terms.

Test Preparation

Research question: Is there a relationship between city of residence and monthly entertainment expenses (MEES)? That is, are there significant differences among the mean MEES of welfare-reliant mothers in Boston, Chicago, and Charleston? *Givens:* Variables: Y = MEES, the dependent variable, ratio level; X = city of residence, a nominal variable with three categories. *Population:* welfare-reliant mothers in three cities. *Sample:* $n = 15$ welfare-reliant mothers in Boston ($n = 5$), Chicago ($n = 5$), and Charleston ($n = 5$). *Statistical procedure:* One-way ANOVA, F-test of difference among three or more sample means; assumes equal variances of MEES in the subpopulations of the cities. *Observation:* Data in Table 12–1. The research question is depicted in Figure 12–1.

Six Steps

1. *Stat. H:*

$$\mu_{Y(Boston)} = \mu_{Y(Chicago)} = \mu_{Y(Charleston)} = \mu_{Y(grand)}$$

Therefore, main effects = 0.
That is, there is no relationship between city of residence and MEES.

Alt. H:

$$\mu_{Y(Boston)} \neq \mu_{Y(Chicago)} \neq \mu_{Y(Charleston)} \neq \mu_{Y(grand)}$$

Therefore, main effects $\neq 0$.

That is, there is a relationship between city of residence and MEES.

2. *Sampling distribution:* If the Stat. *H* is true and samples of size 5 are drawn repeatedly from the populations of welfare-reliant mothers in the three cities, the sampling distribution will take the shape of the *F*-distribution with

$$df_B = K - 1 = 3 - 1 = 2$$

and

$$df_W = n - K = 15 - 3 = 12$$

$p < .01$

$F_{2,12\ df,\ observed} = 17.93$
(from step 4 below)

3. *Level of significance:* $\alpha = .05$ (nondirectional). Critical $F_\alpha = 3.88$ (for 2 and 12 *df*, from Statistical Table D in Appendix B).

4. *Observations:* From spreadsheet in Table 12–1.

Test effects: First, calculate means and the total variation:

$$\text{Grand mean} = \bar{Y}_{(grand)} = \$22$$

Group means:
$$\bar{Y}_{(Boston)} = \$28 \qquad \bar{Y}_{(Chicago)} = \$24 \qquad \bar{Y}_{(Charleston)} = \$14$$

$$\text{Total variation} = SS_T = \Sigma(Y_{(each\ case)} - \bar{Y}_{(grand)})^2 = 694$$

Second, calculate main effects:

Main effect for Boston $= \bar{Y}_{(Boston)} - \bar{Y}_{(grand)} = \$28 - \$22 = \$6$

Main effect for Chicago $= \bar{Y}_{(Chicago)} - \bar{Y}_{(grand)} = \$24 - \$22 = \$2$

Main effect for Charleston $= \bar{Y}_{(Charleston)} - \bar{Y}_{(grand)} = \$14 - \$22 = -\$8$

Third, calculate between-group and within-group sums of squares:

Between group sum of squares $= SS_B = \Sigma(\bar{Y}_{(group)} - \bar{Y}_{(grand)})^2$

$$= \Sigma[(n_{(group)})\ (\text{effect of group}^2)]$$
$$= (5)\ (6^2) + (5)\ (2^2) + (5)\ (-8^2)$$
$$= 180 + 20 + 320 = 520$$

Within-group sum of squares $= SS_W = SS_T - SS_B = 694 - 520 = 174$

Fourth, calculate mean square variances (using degrees of freedom from step 2):

$$\text{Mean square variance between groups} = MSV_B = \frac{SS_B}{K-1} = \frac{520}{2} = 260$$

$$\text{Mean square variance within groups} = MSV_W = \frac{SS_W}{n-K} = \frac{174}{12} = 14.5$$

Fifth, calculate the test statistic:

$$\text{Test statistic} = F = \frac{MSV_B}{MSV_W} = \frac{260}{14.50} = 17.93$$

Sixth, summarize in a source table:

Source of Variation	SS	df	Mean Square Variance: $MSV = SS/df$	$F = \dfrac{MSV_B}{MSV_W}$
Between groups (SS_B)	520	$K - 1 = 2$	260	17.93
Within groups (SS_W)	174	$n - K = 12$	14.50	
Total (SS_T)	694	$n - 1 = 14$	49.57	

Seventh, compute the *p*-value (using Statistical Tables D and E in Appendix B): *p-value: p* [main effects as unusual as or more unusual than those observed when in fact there are no differences among group means] < .01. (This *p*-value is noted on the curve in step 2.)

5. *Rejection decision:* $|F_{observed}| > |F_{\alpha}|$ (i.e., 17.93 > 3.88).
   Thus, $p < \alpha$ (i.e., $p < .05$). Reject the Stat. *H* and accept the Alt. *H* at the 95 percent level of confidence.

6. *Interpretation:* Aspects of relationship and best estimates.
   Existence: There is a relationship between city of residence and MEES; *F*-ratio = 17.93; $p < .01$.
   Direction: Not applicable.
   Strength:

$$\varepsilon^2 = 1 - \frac{MSV_W}{MSV_T} = 1 - \frac{14.50}{49.57} = 1 - .2935 = .7065$$

(.7065) (100) = 70.65 percent.
Thus, 70.65 percent of the variance in MEES is explained by knowledge of city of residence.

Nature: a. Means and main effects: grand mean = $22; group means: Boston = $28, Chicago = $24, and Charleston = $14. Main effects: Boston = $6, Chicago = $2, Charleston = –$8.

b. Best estimate of the MEES of a welfare-reliant mother is

$$Y'_{(each\ case)} = \overline{Y}_{(grand)} + (explained)\ effect\ of\ X$$

$$= \$22 + main\ effect\ of\ the\ X\text{-group}$$

(where Y' is a calculated estimate of Y).

For example, the best estimate of MEES for Ms. Jones of Boston is $22 + effect of Boston = $22 + $6 = $28.

c. Range test: The mean MEES of welfare-reliant mothers in Charleston is significantly different from those of mothers in Boston and Chicago (based on Tukey's HSD and Table 12–6 above).

Answer to research question: There is a relationship between city of residence and monthly entertainment expenses among welfare-reliant mothers. Welfare-reliant mothers in Boston and Chicago have higher average monthly entertainment expenses than do those in Charleston.

Tabular Presentation of Results

In a real-life study such as that of Edin and Lein (1997), the results of ANOVA can be presented to public or professional audiences in a format like that of Table 12–7. This format highlights a comparison of groups, and the table includes several dependent variables. Groups are listed across the top, and vari-

TABLE 12–7   Monthly Welfare Incomes, Selected Monthly Expenses, and Budget Deficits of Welfare-Reliant Mothers in Three Cities

Average Monthly Expenses/Income	Boston n = 75	Chicago n = 75	Charleston n = 75	Significance
Mean monthly welfare income	$696	$599	$493	†
Mean total expenses	$927	$1,003	$891	†
Housing	239	289	224	†
Food	217	288	249	†
Other essential expenses	372	365	372	*
Entertainment	28	24	14	†
Other nonessential expenses	70	37	31	†
Mean monthly budget deficit	–$231	–$404	–$398	†

Note: Expenses are in 1991 dollars. Subcategories may not sum to total because of rounding error.
* $p < .05$.
† $p < .01$.
Nondirectional F-tests of differences between means.
SOURCE: Modified from Edin and Lein (1997).

ables are listed down the left column. Although some of the figures correspond to those of Edin and Lein, Table 12–7 uses fictitious data.

Multivariate Applications of the General Additive-Effects Model

Although the calculations are beyond the scope of this text, it is worthwhile to point out how useful the general additive-effects model is for proportional reduction in error when several independent variables are used to explain a dependent interval/ratio variable. Each additional independent variable increases the precision of best estimates of the dependent variable and reduces predictive error. Suppose, for example, we have additional data on Ms. Jones, the welfare-reliant mother in Boston. We find that she has no personal transportation and that her children are big eaters, two variables known to affect a household's MEES. She has an especially high MEES. With the additional data, we explain this high Y-score as follows:

$$Y_{(Ms. Jones)} = \overline{Y}_{(grand)} + [Y_{(Ms. Jones)} - \overline{Y}_{(grand)}]$$

$$= \overline{Y}_{(grand)} + \text{effect of } X_1 + \text{effect of } X_2 + \text{effect of } X_3 + \text{error}$$

That is,

$$\$33 = \$22 + \$6 + \$2 + \$1 + \$2$$

$$= \$22 + \$9 + \$2$$

where Y = MEES; X_1 = city of residence, main effect of Boston = \$6; X_2 = personal transportation, main effect of having none = \$2; and X_3 = children are big eaters, main effect of yes = \$1. These effects combined account for \$9 of her \$11 deviation above the grand mean. Only \$2 of Ms. Jones's MEES of \$33 is left unexplained. Ideally, if all the variables that affect MEES are identified, we can perfectly explain and predict every welfare-reliant mother's MEES, thereby reducing predictive error to zero.

When we have more than one predictor variable to consider, the strength of a relationship becomes especially important. By comparing the strengths of various relationships, we establish which predictor variables are better. We found that city of residence improves predictions of MEES, but there may be other variables that characterize welfare-reliant mothers' lives that are better at improving predictions. For example, MEES may be related to income, amount of assistance received from the state, health insurance coverage, and other benefits. As we noted above, the calculation of strength of relationship for city of residence in predicting MEES is not especially valuable by itself. The correlation ratio, ε^2 is most useful when it is computed and compared for several independent variables.

Multivariate analysis also takes into account interrelationships among independent variables. Suppose, for instance, that not only Ms. Jones but nearly all the Boston mothers lack transportation. This effect is already combined in the $6 effect of Boston. Multivariate analysis helps separate out the test effects of various independent variables even when some are related to others.

Similarities between the *t*-Test and the *F*-Ratio Test

Both the *t*-test and the *F*-ratio test compare group means. In fact, even a two-group comparison of means can be tested with the *F*-ratio statistic instead of a *t*-test. As we have emphasized in this chapter, the *F*-ratio test weighs explained variance against unexplained variance:

$$F = \frac{\text{explained variance}}{\text{unexplained variance}}$$

When the statistical hypothesis is true (i.e., there is no significant difference between means), the unexplained variance in the denominator is essentially a standard error. It describes the variance in sampling error that can be expected when the independent variable has no effect. Similarly, in the *t*-test, the denominator of the test statistic is a standard error which describes variation in error when the statistical hypothesis is true. Moreover, variation in differences between means are calculated in the numerator of both tests, although in slightly different ways. These mathematical similarities are such that an *F*-ratio test *for a two-group comparison* is equal to the square of *t*-test results, and therefore, *t* is equal to the square-root of the *F*-ratio. Thus,

$$F = t^2 \quad t = \sqrt{F}$$

This consistency between measures also reveals that the *F*-ratio distribution is another approximately normal one, reflecting the natural tendency for sampling outcomes to take a predictable shape.

☹   **STATISTICAL FOLLIES AND FALLACIES**   ☹

Individualizing Group Findings

Comparing means from several groups is very informative. Care must be taken, however, to remember that the results are statistical generalizations—statements that apply to populations and subgroups, not to individuals (see Chapter 2). Our analysis focuses on averages between groups. We should avoid treating the results in a stereotypical fashion by assuming, for instance, that every welfare-reliant mother in Boston spends more than does every mother in the other cities. In fact, for the individual scores in Table 12–1, one of the mothers in Charleston had the same MEES as did one in Chicago.

Although the means are significantly different, there is some overlap in the score distributions of the three cities. Statistical analysis is more aptly applied to groups than to individuals.

The statistical imagination emphasizes seeing the broad picture—seeing the forest (the group) as well as the trees (individuals). Analyzing a single hypothesis, alone and outside the context of a broader theory, is only a preliminary step toward understanding. Multivariate analysis, the next stage of study beyond this course, is essential to gaining a complete understanding. When other variables are considered and controlled, the focus shifts from individuals to larger social systems. For instance, the results of our ANOVA of MEES, when coupled with other results, tell us as much about the cities as they do about the welfare-reliant residents. Note, for example, that in Table 12–7, in addition to expenses, we included monthly incomes and budget deficits (the shortfall between expenses and incomes). The total expenses are low for Charleston, but so is total welfare income. We could hypothesize that the low MEES of Charleston mothers is a combination of lower-cost entertainment and less income to spend on it. How much a mother spends on entertainment may have little to do with her attitudes toward having fun or her frugality in managing the family's meager budget. Instead, the differences we found among the three cities may have to do with the characteristics of the cities, not those of the mothers.

Another issue related to correct interpretation is avoiding the "ecological fallacy." This is the mistake of drawing conclusions about individual behavior on the basis of an analysis of groups such as families, communities, states, and nations. Ecology is the study of the environment, the reality outside individual human beings. Ecological analysis produces conclusions about these large entities, not necessarily about the individuals who compose them. Emile Durkheim, one of the first scientifically oriented sociologists, did an excellent ecological study of suicide rates over a hundred years ago (Durkheim 1951 [1897]). He found that predominantly Catholic counties in Europe had lower suicide rates than did predominantly Protestant counties. A first look at these data suggests that (1) Catholics commit suicide at a lower rate and (2) religious prohibitions against suicide in Catholic theology discourage this action. These conclusions, however, focus on individual choice, and they may be fallacious or wrong. In fact, it could be that Catholics actually commit suicide at a higher rate. Perhaps Catholics in predominantly Protestant counties commit suicide to escape oppression. The low suicide rates in the Catholic counties may simply indicate lack of oppression.

To avoid the ecological fallacy, Durkheim carefully interpreted his findings and focused on the social systems of the counties, not the individual characteristics of suicide victims. Through careful control of many variables, Durkheim's study avoids the ecological fallacy. He made a convincing argument that suicide rates are influenced not so much by the perspective of individuals but by the social systems in which individuals reside. He argued that Catholic religion, with its emphasis on community interests over those of individuals, encouraged social solidarity and provided a social support network that assisted individuals in hard times. His main point was that suicide is not an individual act but a social phenomenon.

The statistical imagination requires that conclusions always take into account the bigger picture. Stereotypical conclusions must be avoided. Statistical generalizations must be interpreted for what they are: averages, summary statements about a group or category of people. ANOVA, with its emphasis on variance both between and within groups, clearly reveals that an average is only one aspect of basic statistical work. Individuals vary around averages, and to ignore this variation is to be statistically unimaginative.

Statistical Procedures Covered to Here

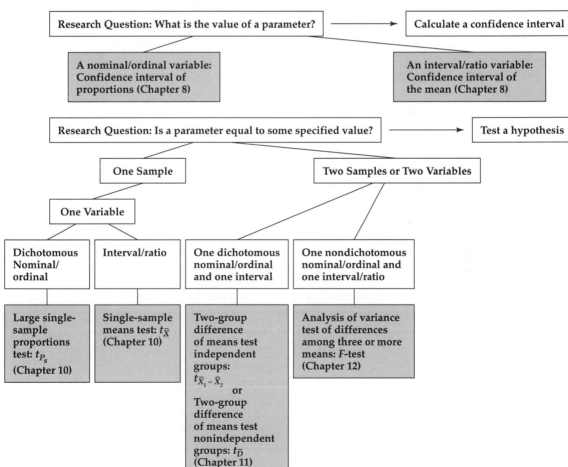

Formulas in Chapter 12

One-way analysis of variance (ANOVA), *F*-test of difference of means among three or more groups:

Given: An interval/ratio or interval-like ordinal dependent variable Y compared for three or more groups obtained from either (1) the categories of a nominal/ordinal variable X from one sample and population or (2) three or more populations and samples.

Research question: Are the means of Y in the populations of the groups different?

Note: A complete illustration of the test is presented in this chapter.

$$\text{Stat. } H: \mu_{Y_1} = \mu_{Y_2} = \mu_{Y_3} = ... = \mu_{Y_{(grand)}}$$

Sampling distribution: F-distribution with $df_B = K - 1$ and $df_W = n - K$

Test effects: Calculate main effects:

$$\text{Main effect of a group mean} = \bar{Y}_{(group)} - \bar{Y}_{(grand)}$$

Test statistic: The *F*-ratio statistic [for use with the *F*-table (Statistical Tables D and E in Appendix B); determines whether a relationship exists]:

Calculations for producing a source table with the *F*-ratio statistic:

Calculating sums of squares:

$$SS_T = \Sigma[Y_{(each\ case)} - \bar{Y}_{(grand)}]^2$$

$$SS_B = \Sigma(\bar{Y}_{(group)} - \bar{Y}_{(grand)})^2 = \Sigma[n_{(group)}) \text{ (effect of group}^2)]$$

$$SS_W = SS_T - SS_B$$

Calculating mean square variances:

$$MSV_B = \frac{SS_B}{df_B} = \frac{SS_B}{K-1}$$

$$MSV_W = \frac{SS_W}{df_W} = \frac{SS_W}{n-K}$$

The *F*-ratio statistic itself:

$$F = \frac{MSV_B}{MSV_W}$$

Source table:

Source of Variation	SS	df	Mean Square Variance: $MSV = SS/df$	$F = \dfrac{MSV_B}{MSV_W}$
Between groups	SS_B	$K-1$	MSV_B	
Within groups	SS_W	$n-K$	MSV_W	$F = \dfrac{MSV_B}{MSV_W}$
Total	SS_T	$n-1$	MSV_T	

Addressing the aspects of a relationship:
    Existence: the F-ratio test
    Direction: usually not applicable
    Strength: the correlation ratio ε^2:

$$\varepsilon^2 = 1 - \frac{MSV_W}{MSV_T}$$

Nature: 1. Report group means and main effects
       2. Best estimate of Y:

$$Y'_{(each\ case)} = \bar{Y}_{(grand)} + \text{the (explained) effect of } X$$

       3. Tukey's HSD range tests to determine which group means are different from one another:

$$HSD = q\sqrt{\frac{MSV_W}{n_{(per\ group)}}}$$

Questions for Chapter 12

1. Both the t test (Chapter 11) and the analysis of variance (ANOVA) test are used to establish differences among means. Explain the difference in approach between these two statistical tests.
2. Specify the formula for the general additive-effects model. Explain what each part of this model means.
3. Describe at least three ways in which the statistical hypothesis may be stated for an ANOVA test.
4. What are main effects in an ANOVA test? For what aspect of a relationship are they important?
5. In plain language, explain what within-group and between-group variations are.
6. Suppose we test a hypothesis that the means of a variable differ among four populations and then reject the statistical (null) hypothesis. Does this assure us that each of the four means is significantly different from the other three? Explain.
7. What is the ecological fallacy? Give an example.

Exercises for Chapter 12

General instructions: On all hypotheses tests, follow the six steps of statistical inference, including test preparation, a conceptual diagram, probability curves, and appropriate aspects of a relationship. For consistency, round calculations to two decimal places. Use $\alpha = .05$ unless otherwise stipulated.

1. With the following data, calculate the main effects of academic school on grade point average (GPA). Show symbols and formulas.

Academic School of Students	Mean GPA
Arts and sciences	2.74
Engineering	2.54
Business	2.62
Overall	2.63

2. Arthur and Graziano (1996) examined personality predictors of vehicle crash involvement. One interval level measure was overall conscientiousness: the dependability and feeling of an obligation to follow social norms in all aspects of life. With the modified data below, calculate the main effects of vehicle crash involvement on conscientiousness. Show symbols and formulas.

Vehicle Crash Involvement	Mean Conscientiousness
Crash but not at fault	122.70
Crash and at fault	109.41
No crash	134.63
Overall	123.11

3. The general additive-effects model arranges the individual scores of an interval/ratio dependent variable (Y) into parts that are and parts that are not explained by an independent variable (X). With the following statistics, use this model to explain the individual scores listed. Y = months served in prison; X = type of crime.

$$\bar{Y}_{(grand)} = 55 \text{ months} \qquad \bar{Y}_{(armed\ robbery)} = 71 \text{ months}$$

$$\bar{Y}_{(felony\ theft)} = 27 \text{ months} \qquad \bar{Y}_{(homicide)} = 133 \text{ months}$$

Inmate ID Number	X	Y
1	Felony theft	22
2	Homicide	156
3	Armed robbery	79
4	Homicide	131
5	Armed robbery	67
6	Felony theft	37

4. The general additive-effects model arranges the individual scores of an interval/ratio dependent variable (Y) into parts that are and parts that are not explained by an independent variable (X). With the following statistics, use this model to explain the individual scores listed. Y =

frequent flyer miles accumulated by employees of ACME, Inc.; $X =$ employee job classification.

$$\bar{Y}_{(grand)} = 16,489 \text{ miles}$$
$$\bar{Y}_{(vice\ presidents)} = 9,737 \text{ miles}$$
$$\bar{Y}_{(sales\ representatives)} = 26,391 \text{ miles}$$
$$\bar{Y}_{(engineers)} = 13,655 \text{ miles}$$

Case	X	Y
John Callahan	Vice president of finance	3,248
Michael Windom	Vice president of manufacturing	11,522
Antonio Williams	Materials engineer	21,467
Arlene Slater	Chemical engineer	2,487
Kathy Schaefer	East Coast sales representative	24,829
Charles Brown	Southwest sales representative	35,663

5. Political ideology often is measured with a conservative-liberal scale. Suppose you have an interval level ideology scale with scores ranging from zero (extremely conservative) to 15 (extremely liberal). With the following survey data, test the hypothesis that various racial/ethnic categories differ in political ideology. Assume equality of population variances.

Racial/Ethnic Category	Conservative-Liberal Ideology Score
Anglo-American	7
Anglo-American	8
Anglo-American	7
Anglo-American	5
Anglo-American	4
Anglo-American	8
Anglo-American	4
African-American	10
African-American	10
African-American	7
African-American	8
African-American	9
African-American	8
African-American	10
Hispanic	8
Hispanic	7
Hispanic	10
Hispanic	9
Hispanic	8
Hispanic	12
Hispanic	11

6. Searching for the dangers of caffeine, a researcher adds two types of caffeine (those found in coffee and chocolate) to the water supply of groups of laboratory-bred rats. This species ordinarily survives about 13 months. The water supply of a control group of rats was not fortified. Does caffeine affect the life span of rats? Test a hypothesis with the following data. Assume equality of population variances.

Treatment Group	Days Rat Lived
Coffee caffeine	398
Coffee caffeine	372
Coffee caffeine	413
Coffee caffeine	419
Coffee caffeine	408
Coffee caffeine	393
Coffee caffeine	387
Coffee caffeine	414
Chocolate caffeine	401
Chocolate caffeine	389
Chocolate caffeine	413
Chocolate caffeine	396
Chocolate caffeine	406
Chocolate caffeine	378
Chocolate caffeine	382
Chocolate caffeine	417
Control (no caffeine)	412
Control (no caffeine)	386
Control (no caffeine)	394
Control (no caffeine)	409
Control (no caffeine)	415
Control (no caffeine)	401
Control (no caffeine)	384
Control (no caffeine)	398

7. In the United States about one in four people is obese—seriously overweight to the extent that a person is at risk of adverse physical health effects such as diabetes and heart disease. Obesity also has adverse psychological effects, such as causing its victims to feel bad about how their bodies appear to others (Freidman and Brownell 1995). Suppose we compare three weight groups on a Body Dissatisfaction Scale, an interval/ratio level survey instrument with scores ranging from zero to 30. Taking into account height, gender, and body build, subjects are classified as normal, borderline obese (20 to 30 percent over normal weight), and obese (more than 30 percent over normal weight). Does obesity affect one's satisfaction with one's bodily appearance? Assume equality of population variances.

Weight Group	Body Dissatisfaction Scale Score
Normal range	11
Borderline obese	15
Borderline obese	13
Obese	16
Normal range	9
Borderline obese	14
Obese	19
Obese	17
Normal range	13
Borderline obese	16
Obese	15
Normal range	12
Borderline obese	11
Obese	15
Normal range	10

8. Like Guth et al. (1995), we are to examine whether religious ideas affect a person's views on the environment. We compare clergy of three types—Evangelical, mainline Protestant, and Catholic—with the assumption that religious leaders of a particular denomination have similar religious beliefs. Our dependent variable is an interval/ratio scale that measures positive attitudes toward environmentalism—support of government efforts to control pollution. (A high score indicates high support.) Is there a relationship between religious beliefs and environmentalism? Assume equality of population variances.

Clergy	Environmentalism Scale
Mainline Protestant minister	26
Catholic priest	30
Mainline Protestant minister	24
Evangelical minister	14
Catholic priest	25
Evangelical minister	12
Mainline Protestant minister	31
Catholic priest	34
Mainline Protestant minister	22
Evangelical minister	23
Mainline Protestant minister	28
Catholic priest	28
Catholic priest	24
Evangelical minister	17
Mainline Protestant minister	32
Catholic priest	25
Evangelical minister	22
Evangelical minister	19

9. In most prisons there are a variety of treatment and rehabilitation programs, such as substance abuse and psychological and spiritual counseling, as well as academic and vocational education programs. An interesting question is whether corrections officers of various races are more likely to oppose such inmate programs and take a punitive attitude toward doing time (Jackson and Ammen 1996). Using the following statistics, test the hypothesis that there are differences on a punitive attitude scale among Whites, African-American, and Hispanic corrections officers. Assume equality of population variances.

Race	Mean	Standard Deviation	n
White	27.90	3.09	30
African-American	21.77	3.39	30
Hispanic	25.58	3.03	30
Total	25.08	4.03	90

Source of Variation	SS	df	Mean Square Variance: $MSV = SS/df$	$F = \dfrac{MSV_B}{MSV_W}$
Between groups (SS_B)	567.12	$K - 1 = 2$	283.56	28.19
Within groups (SS_W)	875.60	$n - K = 87$	10.06	
Total (SS_T)	1,442.72	$n - 1 = 89$	16.21	

Tukey's HSD at the .05 level of significance = 1.95 punitive attitude scale points.

10. The Environmental Protection Agency monitors the toxic risk of counties by keeping records on the number of times chemicals are released into the air or streams by industries (Rogge 1996). Suppose we have the following data on the number of toxic releases last year for 60 counties with low, moderate, and high median incomes. Is the income level of a county related to the toxic risk experienced by its population? Assume equality of population variances.

Income Level of County	Mean Number of Toxic Releases in 1996	Standard Deviation	n
Low	252.65	19.68	20
Moderate	159.10	17.87	20
High	129.95	27.49	20
Total	180.57	57.07	60

Source of Variation	SS	df	Mean Square Variance: $MSV = SS/df$	$F = \dfrac{MSV_B}{MSV_W}$
Between groups (SS_B)	164,377.43	$K - 1 = 2$	82,188.72	168.63
Within groups (SS_W)	27,781.30	$n - K = 57$	487.39	
Total (SS_T)	192,158.73	$n - 1 = 59$		

Tukey's HSD at the .05 level of significance = 17.67 toxic releases.

Optional Computer Applications for Chapter 12

If your class is using the *Computer Applications for The Statistical Imagination* compact disk, open the Chapter 12 exercises to learn about one-way ANOVA in *SPSS for Windows*. The exercises emphasize proper interpretation of output for ANOVA and ways to address the aspects of the relationship.

NOMINAL VARIABLES: THE CHI-SQUARE AND BINOMIAL DISTRIBUTIONS

Introduction: Proportional Thinking about Social Status

In social and behavioral science research, variables with nominal and ordinal levels of measurement are used frequently. In particular, much research is done on how individuals' social status in groups and societies affects their opportunities in everyday life. Social positions have *status*, a Greek word meaning "rank or position within a group." Social status defines the relative amounts of privilege and authority awarded to any person occupying a social position within a group, community, or society. A person occupying a high-status position, such as a corporation president, is afforded more rights, rewards, and privileges than are given to individuals in lower-ranking positions, such as computer programmers.

Every individual occupies an assortment of statuses, such as student, spouse, parent, club treasurer, and office secretary. Some social statuses are open for the choosing and can be earned, although competition for them may be stiff. These are called achieved statuses, and they include positions such as husband, doctor, and bank vice president. Other status positions are ascribed—assigned or "stamped onto" individuals at birth. For example, being male and white has its privileges in American society, but (short of undergoing a sex or color change) these statuses are fixed and not chosen. Ascribed statuses are easily identifiable because of physical markers such as skin color and the distinctive biological traits of sex or ethnic heritage. Biological research is unclear about the effects of ascribed statuses on behavior. For example, it is not clear whether women are truly more emotional than men. But it is important to understand the effects of ascribed statuses because they are consequential for individuals. Whether men or women are more emotional is beside the point, if the myth that it is women who are, is widely believed. Ascribed statuses are social markers that affect how, for instance, women and minority group members are treated. Statuses limit opportunities for those occupying minority positions, as is evident in light of racism and sexism. On a positive note, since ascribed statuses often are visible, they are convenient for targeting products and focusing social interventions. For instance, golf clubs are advertised in male-oriented magazines, and breast cancer screening in female-oriented magazines.

Because of the importance of status, social research often begins by determining the effects of status variables on the dependent variables of a study. For example, in studies of criminal behavior, the first hypotheses to be tested probably will pertain to demographic relationships. (Demography is the study of a society's population.) Are criminal acts more likely to be committed by men or women, young or old, in rural areas or urban areas, and so on? Once statistics are computed, it is vital that they be interpreted statistically—as percentages of a group of observations—rather than individualistically. For instance, U.S. Department of Justice statistics consistently reveal that men are arrested for nearly 90 percent of violent crimes. However, this does not mean that every man is a potential criminal or that women do not commit crimes. A proper interpretation is that men have a higher probability of committing a violent crime. To interpret the data otherwise is to stereotype—to apply a statistical generalization to an individual. Stereotypes are common within every society and lead to prejudice and injustice. For instance, if a police officer apprehended a man and a woman alleged to have robbed a bank, could the woman not perhaps have been the mastermind and the leader of the plot? The tendency is to assume that the man is.

Research on status has the potential of reinforcing stereotypes, and therefore, care must be taken to avoid this pitfall. When statistics are reported as characterizations of individuals rather than as probabilistic generalizations, misunderstanding of data abounds. For example, in a demographic profile of homeless persons in Midcity, U.S.A., data may reveal that 70 percent of homeless persons in the community are male, 60 percent are African-American, and 50 percent are substance abusers. It would be wrong to report that the typical homeless person in Midcity is an African-American male who is addicted to drugs or alcohol. In fact, it may be that the homeless women are more likely to be substance abusers because women who are destitute but not addicted are more likely to be taken in by relatives. Scientific researchers must take care not to reinforce stereotypes. The key feature of the statistical imagination is to view isolated observations in relation to a larger whole.

This chapter focuses heavily on nominal variables, many of which are status markers. We start with the chi-square test of a relationship between two nominal variables. We will carefully interpret findings by using the language of proportions and percentages of the whole group. Conclusions will be about the category (i.e., the group), not the individual. Moreover, the findings will accurately portray the complex relationships among variables. These precautions are in order because in the popular press so much is made of relationships between status markers such as gender, race, and ethnic identity and other consequential phenomena such as crime rates. The failure to present results in a proportional manner adds to the disadvantages of minority statuses such as African-American, Arab-American, and female. In other words, popular reports often lack the statistical imagination. This chapter also covers the binomial distribution test, which is a small-sample proportions test.

The Chi-Square Test: Focusing on the Frequencies of Joint Occurrences

In examining the relationship between two nominal variables, the focus is on the frequency of joint occurrences of attributes. The existence of a relationship between the variables is established with a hypothesis test called the chi-square test.

Recall that an attribute is some quality or characteristic of a subject that is conveyed as category names of a nominal variable. For gender there are the attributes male and female; for race, the attributes might be coded as white, African-American, Asian-American, and so on; for political party preference, the attributes could be Democrat, Republican, and independent. A joint occurrence of attributes involves two variables *for a single individual,* with pairings of attributes from the two variables. For example, the possible pairings of attributes for the variables race and political party preference are white-Democrat, white-independent, African-American–Democrat, white-Republican, African-American–Republican, and African-American–independent. If there is a relationship between race and political party affiliation, we expect to find that higher proportions of one race prefer one party affiliation to another. We might hypothesize that higher proportions of African-Americans identify themselves as Democrats. If this is true, in a random sample of American adults we expect to find especially high frequencies of the joint occurrence African-American–Democrat.

The relationship between two nominal variables is analyzed by using a cross-tabulation (crosstab) table which reports frequencies (not proportions) of joint occurrences of attributes. Crosstab tables were introduced in Chapter 2 (it might be worthwhile to review Table 2–9). For hypothesis tests we put the attributes of the independent variable in the columns and those of the dependent variable in the rows. In the following crosstab table (Table 13–1, fictional data), the predictor variable is race, with the two categories of white and African-American. The dependent variable is political party preference, with the categories Democratic, Republican, and Independent/Other/None. We

TABLE 13–1   Political Party Preference by Race (Expected Cell Frequencies in Parentheses)

Political Party (Y)	Race (X) → White	African- American	Row Totals
Democrat	96 (112.5)	54 (37.5)	150
Republican	123 (112.5)	27 (37.5)	150
Independent/Other/None	81 (75.0)	19 (25.0)	100
Column totals	300 (300)	100 (100)	400

call this a 2 × 3 (stated "two-by-three") table to indicate the number of categories of each variable.

The squares in the heart of the table are called *cells,* and the numbers in them are called *joint frequencies* or *cell frequencies.* The cells in the margins on the right side and the bottom present *marginal totals,* the total number of subjects fitting a category. The total sample size, or *grand total,* is 400, which is reported in the bottom right cell. The marginal totals on the right indicate row totals, with 150 cases in each of the Democratic and Republican parties and 100 in the Independent/Other/None category for a grand total of 400 respondents. The marginal totals at the bottom indicate column totals, with 300 of the sample subjects being white and 100 being African-American, again summing to the grand total of 400. The cells in the heart of the crosstab table are joint frequencies of the categories above and across from the cell. For example, 96 sample subjects are both white and Democrat, 123 are both white and Republican, 54 are both African-American and Democrat, and so forth.

We can say, then, that the joint frequency of white-Democrat is 96 cases, the joint frequency of white-Republican is 123 cases, and so on. The number of rows times the number of columns is the number of joint frequency cells, with six in a 2 × 3 table.

As with any hypothesis test, the hypothesis must be stated in a way that allows us to know what sampling outcomes to expect when the hypothesis is true. With the chi-square test, we state our statistical hypothesis as one of "no relationship" between the two variables. (This can be called a *null* hypothesis since it states *no* relationship.) As we will see in a moment, when this is the case, the chi-square statistic will compute to zero within sampling error. Thus, we state our statistical hypothesis as follows:

$$\text{Stat. } H: \chi^2 = 0$$

That is, there is no relationship between race and political party preference.

$$\text{Alt. } H: \chi^2 > 0$$

That is, there is a relationship between race and political party preference. One-tailed but nondirectional.

As with any statistical hypothesis, this statement allows predictions of outcomes with repeated sampling. In this case, assuming no relationship, we can use the marginal frequencies to predict the *expected frequencies* of each cell. We then compare these expected frequencies to our *observed frequencies,* the joint frequencies actually found in the sample data and presented in the crosstab table. If the observed frequencies are about equal to the expected ones, give or take a little sampling error, we allow the hypothesis of "no relationship" to stand and conclude that race has nothing to do with political party preference. If, however, there is a large difference between observed and expected frequencies, we begin to suspect that there is a relationship between the variables. The chi-square hypothesis test tells us whether the summed differences between the observed and expected cell frequencies are so great that they are not simply the result of sampling error. As we will discuss in detail later, the test is nondirectional. Any chi-square test, however, is one-tailed because this statistic is based on squared numbers, which are always positive.

A Note to the Especially Inquisitive

Unlike the previous tests we have studied, the statistical hypothesis for chi-square does not directly state a value of a population parameter. This test, however, does assert that certain measures—joint frequencies—have specific values in the population: those of the expected frequencies.

Calculating Expected Frequencies

How are expected frequencies computed? In Table 13–1 we can see that three-fourths (300 of 400) of the sample subjects are white. We can predict that *if race has nothing to do with political party preference, that is, if there is no relationship between race and political party preference,* we can expect three-fourths of Democrats, three-fourths of Republicans, and three-fourths of Independent/Other/None to be white. In other words, whites will be represented among the political parties in proportion to their numbers in the general population. Similarly, given that one-fourth of the sample is African-American, we can expect one-fourth of each of the political party categories to be African-American. The expected cell frequencies tell us how many cases should fall in a cell if each cell is proportional to the marginal frequencies—the situation where the two variables are unrelated and thus the cells are filled randomly.

The expected cell frequency, *E,* for each cell is computed precisely with the following formula:

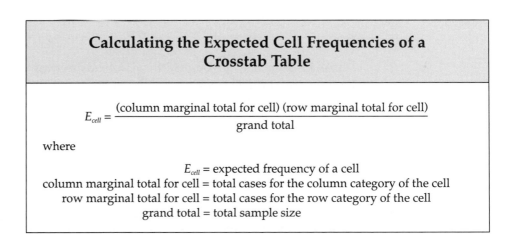

Calculating the Expected Cell Frequencies of a Crosstab Table

$$E_{cell} = \frac{(\text{column marginal total for cell}) \, (\text{row marginal total for cell})}{\text{grand total}}$$

where

E_{cell} = expected frequency of a cell
column marginal total for cell = total cases for the column category of the cell
row marginal total for cell = total cases for the row category of the cell
grand total = total sample size

For example, the expected frequency of white Democrats is

$$E_{(white\text{-}Dem)} = \frac{(\text{total number of whites})\,(\text{total number of democrats})}{\text{grand total}}$$

$$= \frac{(300)\,(150)}{(400)} = 112.5 \text{ cases}$$

Differences between Observed and Expected Cell Frequencies

With all hypothesis tests, the difference between what is observed in the actual sample data and what is hypothesized for the statistical hypothesis constitutes the "effect" of the test. The calculation of the chi-square statistic is based on measuring the differences between the observed frequencies and the expected frequencies, with the expected frequencies being the joint frequencies that will occur in repeated sampling when there is *no* relationship between the two variables. As in many statistical formulas, these differences are in the numerator of the test statistic. Similarly, the denominator of most test statistics is a measure of normal sampling error when the statistical hypothesis is true. Thus, the expected frequencies are used in the denominator.

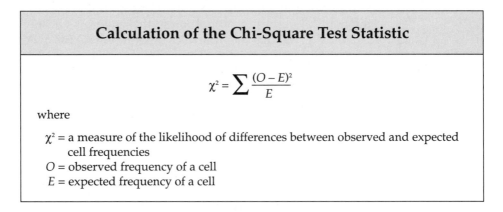

Calculation of the Chi-Square Test Statistic

$$\chi^2 = \sum \frac{(O-E)^2}{E}$$

where

χ^2 = a measure of the likelihood of differences between observed and expected cell frequencies
O = observed frequency of a cell
E = expected frequency of a cell

Table 13–2 presents a computational spreadsheet for computing the chi-square statistic. The data come from Table 13–1.

A close look at this formula provides a sense of proportion on how its values relate to real statistical outcomes. When the effects (i.e., the differences between observed and expected frequencies) are large, this suggests that the cases are not randomly distributed among the cells and that the statistical hypothesis should be rejected. Large differences appear when some of the cells (often the cells in opposite diagonal corners) "load up" because of a relationship between the two variables. Let us examine one of the cell differences more closely. The actual "observed frequency" of white Democrats is 96 cases. The difference between this observed frequency of 96 and the expected fre-

TABLE 13–2   **Computational Spreadsheet for Calculating the Chi-Square Statistic Using the Data from Table 13–1**

Givens		Calculations			
Cell (X, Y)	*O*	*E*	*(O – E)*	*(O – E)²*	*[(O – E)²/E]*
White Democrat	96	112.5	–16.5	272.25	2.42
African American Democrat	54	37.5	16.5	272.25	7.26
White Republican	123	112.5	10.5	110.25	.98
African-American Republican	27	37.5	–10.5	110.25	2.94
White Independent	81	75.0	6.0	36.0	.48
African-American Independent	19	25.0	–6.0	36.0	1.44
Totals	400	400.0	0.0		$\chi^2 = 15.52$

quency of 112.5 is –16.5 cases (i.e., about 17 fewer than expected given the overall numbers of Democrats and whites). It appears that whites are underrepresented among Democrats in proportion to their numbers in the general population. As we shall see below, similar effects of race on political party preference appear in other cells.

We must consider, however, the possibility that differences for this cell and the others result from chance sampling error. Even if there is no relationship between race and political party preference, in repeated sampling we will obtain a variety of cell distributions. A first sample might pick up slightly fewer white Democrats than expected, but the next sample might pick up slightly more. These fluctuations from one sample to the next would result from normal, expected sampling error. Our hypothesis test of the relationship between race and political party preference depends on the single sample we actually draw. The chi-square test answers the question: In repeated sampling, how unusual is it to see gaps between observed and expected frequencies when race has nothing to do with political party preference? In other words, are the effects of race on political party preference significant? A random distribution of cell frequencies—in proportion to marginal totals—is what occurs in sampling when there is no relationship between the two variables. The alternative hypothesis is likely to be accepted when the effects of the test are large (i.e., when there are large differences between the observed and expected frequencies).

The chi-square statistic and the chi-square table (Statistical Table G in Appendix B) allow us to compute the exact probability (the *p*-value) of the differences between observed and expected cell frequencies when the statistical hypothesis of "no relationship" is true. Comparing this probability to our alpha level, we either reject the statistical hypothesis or fail to reject it. If we fail to reject it, we conclude that there is no reason to believe that race and political party preference are related, that the differences between observed and expected cell frequencies result from sampling error. If we reject the statistical hypothesis, however, we conclude that there is a relationship between race and political party preference. We would also describe the nature of this relationship, pointing out strong effects—cells where large discrepancies exist between observed and expected frequencies. For example, we would point out that a disproportionately low percentage of whites identify themselves as Democrats in contrast to a disproportionately high percentage of African-Americans.

Degrees of Freedom for the Chi-Square Test

To read the chi-square distribution table (Statistical Table G in Appendix B) we must compute the chi-square test statistic and the appropriate degrees of freedom. For the chi-square test, degrees of freedom are determined by the number of columns and rows in the crosstab table.

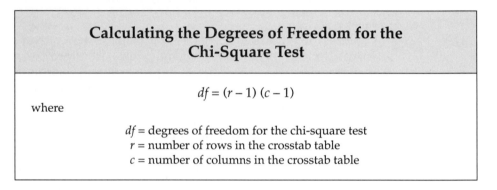

Calculating the Degrees of Freedom for the Chi-Square Test

$$df = (r - 1)(c - 1)$$

where

df = degrees of freedom for the chi-square test
r = number of rows in the crosstab table
c = number of columns in the crosstab table

For a 2×3 crosstab table such as Table 13–1 on race and party preference,

$$df = (r - 1)(c - 1) = (3 - 1)(2 - 1) = 2$$

Recall that degrees of freedom are the number of opportunities in sampling to compensate for limitations in a statistic or a statistical test. For example, in Chapter 10 we noted that with means tests, extreme scores tend to pull the mean of a sample away from the true parameter. For the chi-square test, as its df formula suggests, the number of cells in a crosstab table influences the size of the calculated statistic. A crosstab table can be distorted if, just by chance in this particular sampling, one cell is over- or underloaded in frequency compared to its true occurrence in the population. For example, suppose that in the population there are many white Democrats but this sample just happened to miss them. Just as an extreme score "distorts" a mean, one or more randomly over- or underloaded cells in a crosstab table can distort the computation of the chi-square test statistic. Calculation of degrees of freedom compensates for this tendency. Close examination of the df formula for the chi-square statistic reveals that the more categories the two variables of the crosstab table have, the higher the degrees of freedom are. Conversely, tables with few cells, such as 2×2 and 2×3 tables, have few degrees of freedom. With these small tables, if by chance the sample incurs an inaccurately over- or underloaded cell, there are few opportunities (i.e., other cells) to balance out this unlucky sampling event. Repeated sampling tells us that over time, when a large number of samples are drawn, we sometimes oversample one cell and at other times oversample another. With only four cells, an oversampling in only one cell can distort the outcomes. In fact, if we know the expected frequency of one cell in a 2×2 crosstab table, we can use the marginal totals to compute the other three. In other words, only one cell is free to vary independently of the way the statistic is calculated; hence, there is only 1 degree of freedom.

Minimum Cell Frequency Requirement. With chi-square, an increase in degrees of freedom is not always a blessing, however. This test statistic has a shortcoming that restricts the number of categories used. The expected frequency of each cell in a crosstab table must equal at least five, or adjustments must be made in the calculation of the chi-square statistic. Small cells introduce additional sampling error that can lead to an incorrect rejection decision and a wrong conclusion. When cell sizes come up short, we call this cell depletion. The practical experience of the author suggests that to avoid cell depletion, the overall sample size should be equal to the number of cells times 12. Thus, for a simple 2×2 table, we need about 48 cases; for a 2×3 table, 72 cases; and so on. Even with a large overall sample size, however, cell depletion can be a problem for some variables. For instance, with the variable religious preference we may have a sample of 100 but only six Muslims. If we attempt to break out this variable by, say, gender, there is no possibility that the joint frequencies of male-Muslim and female-Muslim will both have the required minimum of five cases.

When there is a shortage of cases in a cell, several corrections can be made. First, the number of cells can be reduced by eliminating sparse categories. For instance, for religious preference, the Muslim category might be dropped or folded into an "other" category with other religions with low frequencies, such as Hindu. This, of course, requires that the results be reported as having these modifications. A second alternative to dealing with cell depletion is to absorb the small-frequency category into another category that is theoretically meaningful. For example, for the variable race, the "other" category could be combined with African-American to create a new category called "nonwhite." This is appropriate if the race variable is essentially a proxy (or substitute) for majority-minority status. A third alternative is to make a correction in the computation of chi-square by subtracting 0.5 from each calculation of the difference between the observed and the expected frequencies. This is called Yates's correction for continuity; it adjusts for inconsistency in the sizes of cells. A fourth alternative is to use another statistical test called Fisher's exact test (Blalock 1979: 292). This is useful in situations where there are many cell frequencies less than five but none can be justifiably eliminated or combined.

Yates's correction and Fisher's exact test complicate calculations to the point where the time spent learning them would be better used learning how to calculate crosstab statistics on a computer. Computer crosstab programs typically provide a count of cells with small frequencies. Then the programs present a Yates's corrected chi-square and a Fisher's exact test along with the chi-square statistic so that they may be substituted when appropriate. A comparison of these statistics in the computer output will reveal that when the sample size is quite large, a few small-frequency cells have little impact on the resulting chi-square statistic. In other words, with large samples the corrected chi-square value will be about the same as the uncorrected value and both statistics will have the same *p*-values.

The Chi-Square Sampling Distribution and Its Critical Regions

The chi-square formula was derived by an early 20th-century statistician named Karl Pearson who also is noted for developing the statistics in Chapters 14 and 15. Most likely he figured out this formula mathematically, but let us imagine how he might have determined the formula empirically—through repeated sampling as was done by the bean counters of old. He takes a large box full of equal numbers of assorted beans—a population of beans. He treats white beans as white Democrats, red beans as African-American Democrats, spotted beans as white independents, and so on. He draws a random sample of 400 beans and counts each type to obtain the observed frequencies of the crosstab table. After calculating the expected frequencies, for each cell he subtracts the observed and expected frequencies, squares the result, and divides it by the expected frequency. Then he sums these quotients to obtain the χ^2 statistic. He does this, say, 10,000 times and plots the resulting calculations as a probability curve—a smoothed-out histogram. The shape of this probability distribution is presented in Figure 13–1. Note that it is one-tailed. This will always be the case, because squaring removes any negative signs. The test, however, is nondirectional, as we will discuss later.

As we noted earlier, the particular shape of the chi-square distribution for a given problem depends on the number of degrees of freedom, which is determined by the number of cells in the crosstab table. Figure 13–1 presents the critical values of chi-square for a level of significance of .05 with 2 degrees of freedom. This critical value means that if there is no relationship between the

FIGURE 13–1

The shape of the chi-square probability distribution curve with the critical region for $\alpha = .05$ and 2 degrees of freedom

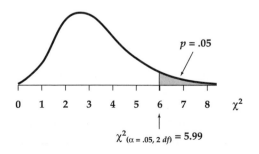

$p = .05$

0   1   2   3   4   5   6   7   8 χ^2

$\chi^2_{(\alpha = .05, \, 2 \, df)} = 5.99$

two variables, with repeated sampling the chi-square statistic will compute as high as or higher than 5.99 only 5 percent of the time. The other 95 percent of the time chi-square will compute below 5.99, with most outcomes falling just above zero; this is just what we expect when the observed and expected frequencies are the same within sampling error.

The chi-square test is used in the following circumstances:

When to Use the Chi-Square Test of a Relationship between Two Nominal Variables

In general: Testing a hypothesis of a relationship between two nominal variables.

1. There is one population with a representative sample from it.
2. There are two variables, both of a nominal/ordinal level of measurement.
3. The expected frequency of each cell in the crosstab table is at least five.

The Six Steps of Statistical Inference for the Chi-Square Test

Let us use the data in Table 13–1 and its spreadsheet (Table 13–2) to answer the research question of whether there is a relationship between race and political party preference. The statistical hypothesis is that there is no relationship. Since both variables are nominal and the expected frequencies are all above five, we may use the chi-square test.

Brief Checklist for the Six Steps of Statistical Inference

Test Preparation

State the research question; list givens, including variables (e.g., $X = ...$, $Y = ...$), their levels of measurement, the population(s) under study, and sample(s) and sample size(s); select the statistical test; provide observations of statistics and parameters; and draw a conceptual diagram.

Six Steps

Using the symbol H for *hypothesis:*

1. State the statistical H and the alternative H and stipulate test direction.
2. Describe the sampling distribution.
3. State the level of significance (α) and specify the critical test value.
4. Observe the actual sample outcomes and compute the test effects, the test statistic, and the p-value.
5. Make the rejection decision.
6. Interpret and apply best estimates in everyday terms.

Test Preparation

Research question: Are certain races more likely to favor certain political parties? That is, is there a relationship between race and political party preference? *Givens:* Variables: X = race, nominal level; Y = political party preference, nominal level. *Population:* The American adult population. *Sample:* $n = 400$ adults. *Statistical procedure:* Chi-square test of a relationship between two nominal variables. *Observation:* Observed frequencies and computed expected frequencies (E_{cell}), where:

$$E_{cell} = \frac{\text{(column marginal total for cell) (row marginal total for cell)}}{\text{grand total}}$$

Political Party (Y)	Race (X) → White	African-American	Row Totals
Democrat	96 (112.5)	54 (37.5)	150
Republican	123 (112.5)	27 (37.5)	150
Independent/Other/None	81 (75.0)	19 (25.0)	100
Column totals	300 (300)	100 (100)	400

Six Steps

1. *Stat. H:* $\chi^2 = 0$

   That is, there is no relationship between race and political party preference.

   Alt. H: $\chi^2 > 0$

   That is, there is a relationship between race and political party preference. One-tailed test but nondirectional.

2. *Sampling distribution:*

$$\chi^2 = \sum \frac{(O - E)^2}{E}$$

$$df = (r - 1)\,(c - 1) = (3 - 1)\,(2 - 1) = 2$$

   If the Stat. H is true and samples of size 400 are drawn repeatedly from the population and cross-tabulated for race and political preference, the calculations of the chi-square statistic will produce the following chi-square distribution:

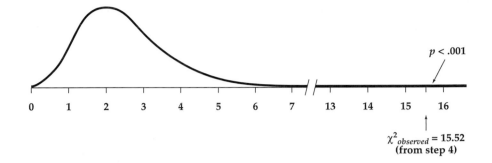

$p < .001$

$\chi^2_{observed} = 15.52$
(from step 4)

3. *Level of significance:* $\alpha = .05$ (nondirectional). One-tailed $df = 2$. Critical test score $= \chi^2_\alpha = 5.99$ (from Statistical Table G in Appendix B).

4. *Observations:*

   Test effects and test statistic:

Cell (X, Y)	O	E	(O – E)	(O – E)²	[(O – E)²/E]
White Democrat	96	112.5	–16.5	272.25	2.42
African-American Democrat	54	37.5	16.5	272.25	7.26
White Republican	123	112.5	10.5	110.25	.98
African-American Republican	27	37.5	–10.5	110.25	2.94
White Independent	81	75.0	6.0	36.0	.48
African-American Independent	19	25.0	–6.0	36.0	1.44
Totals	400	400.0	0.0		$\chi^2 = 15.52$

   p-value: p [drawing a sample with differences between observed and expected frequencies as unusual as or more unusual than those observed when in fact there is no relationship between the variables] < .001 (area noted on curve in step 2).

5. *Rejection decision:* $|\chi^2_{observed}| > |\chi^2_\alpha|$ (i.e., 15.52 > 5.99); $p < \alpha$; .001 < .05. Reject Stat. *H* and accept the Alt. *H* at the 95 percent level of confidence.

6. *Interpretation:* Aspects of relationship and best estimates.
   Existence: There is a relationship between race and political party preference; $\chi^2 = 15.52$, $p < .001$.
   Nature: A disproportionately high number of African-Americans prefer the Democratic party. *Best estimates:* Fifty-four percent of African-Americans are Democrats compared with 32 percent of whites. Only 27

percent of African-Americans are Republicans compared with 41 percent of whites.

Relevant Aspects of a Relationship for the Chi-Square Test

Note that in the last step of the hypothesis test only two of the four aspects of a relationship are readily addressed: existence and nature. The existence of a relationship is established with the chi-square test formula, testing the hypothesis of no relationship between the two nominal variables. If a relationship is found, we describe its nature by reporting the "effects" (i.e., the differences between the observed and expected cell frequencies) of noteworthy cells in the crosstab table. In everyday terms we report best estimates by calculating column percentages for selected cells. Recall from Chapter 2 that a column percentage is *a cell's frequency as a percentage of the column marginal total:*

$$\text{Column \% [of joint frequency]} = \frac{\text{\# in a cell}}{\text{total \# in column}} \times 100$$

To calculate the percentage of African-Americans who are Democrats:

$$\begin{array}{l}\text{\% [of African-Americans} \\ \text{who are Democrats]}\end{array} = \frac{\text{\# of African-American Democrats}}{\text{total \# of African-Americans}} \times 100$$

$$= \frac{54}{100} \times 100 = 54\%$$

Similar calculations of column percentages are made for the white-Democrat, African-American–Republican and white-Republican. We report the column percentages that make relevant points, in this case that one major political party is disproportionately African-American and the other is disproportionately white.

The direction of a test is meaningless for nominal variables. For example, with the variable gender, it is meaningless to say that males are more "positive" or "negative"; one is either male or female. (Chi-square can be used with ordinal variables, and in that situation direction sometimes does make sense.)

Measures of the strength of a relationship for the chi-square test statistic exist. Those measures are seldom reported, however, because such reports are fraught with potential error. Each measure requires very careful use and applies only in very specific circumstances (see Lee and Maykovich 1995: 129).

Aspects of a Relationship Using the Chi-Square Statistic

Existence: Test the statistical hypothesis that $\chi^2 = 0$; that is, there is no relationship between X and Y.

(continued)

(concluded)

Use the chi-square test statistic:

$$\chi^2 = \sum \frac{(O - E)^2}{E}$$

$$df = (r - 1)(c - 1)$$

Direction: not applicable.
Strength: Usually not reported.
Nature: Report column percentages for selected cells that accurately convey the substance of findings.

Using Chi-Square as a Difference of Proportions Test

As we learned in Chapter 2, when the joint frequencies of two nominal variables are presented in a crosstab table, it is very easy to calculate their percentages. For example, suppose we have the data in Table 13–3. The data come from a study of elderly patients seeing physicians at clinics for the first time. Each patient is accompanied by a caregiver, usually a family member, particularly a wife or daughter. Some of the patients and caregivers attend a regular primary care clinic that provides services to people of all ages. The others go to a geriatric clinic that specializes in providing care to elderly patients. Because caregivers often are stressed out, the geriatric clinic claims to include them in the treatment process and to provide assistance, such as referrals to caregiver support groups.

To evaluate this claim, we interview random samples of caregivers at both clinics. The data in Table 13–3 compare the numbers of caregivers at each clinic who are referred to support groups. One nominal variable, then, is clinic type, and the other is referral to support groups. We can investigate the research question that there is a relationship between type of clinic and likelihood of

TABLE 13–3   **Type of Clinic by Whether Caregiver Is Referred to a Support Group (Expected Cell Frequencies in Parentheses)**

Referred to Support Group	*Type of Clinic →*	*Primary Care*	*Geriatric*	*Row Totals*
Yes		7 (15.83)	23 (14.17)	30
No		50 (41.17)	28 (36.83)	78
Column totals		57 (57.00)	51 (51.00)	108

referral to a support group. If a geriatric clinic's patients are referred at a significantly higher rate, that clinic's claims are justified.

In Table 13–3 let us focus on the percentage of geriatric clinic caregivers referred to support groups by calculating the column percentage:

$$\text{\% [of geriatric clinic caregivers referred to support group]} = \frac{\text{\# in geriatric-yes cell}}{\text{total \# for geriatric clinic}} \times 100$$

$$= \frac{23}{51}(100) = 45.10\%$$

Similarly, the column percentage of primary care clinic caregivers being referred to support groups is 12.28 percent [i.e., (7/57) (100)]. On the face of it, there is a large difference in these two percentages. We must remember, however, that these are sample data. Any difference between the two percentages may be due to sampling error. Thus, we must test a hypothesis to determine whether these percentages are significantly different for the caregiver populations of the two clinics. Conceptually, this research problem may be conceived as it is in Figure 13–2. Although we multiplied the fractions by 100 to get column percentages, for consistency we call this a proportions test and use the symbol P_u in Figure 13–2. Let us proceed with the six steps of statistical inference and the chi-square test to address the research question.

Brief Checklist for the Six Steps of Statistical Inference

Test Preparation

State the research question; list givens, including variables (e.g., $X = ...$, $Y = ...$), their levels of measurement, the population(s) under study, and sample(s) and sample size(s); select the statistical test; provide observations of statistics and parameters; and draw a conceptual diagram.

Six Steps

Using the symbol H, for *hypothesis:*

1. State the statistical H and the alternative H and stipulate test direction.
2. Describe the sampling distribution.
3. State the level of significance (α) and specify the critical test value.
4. Observe the actual sample outcomes and compute the test effects, the test statistic, and the p-value.
5. Make the rejection decision.
6. Interpret and apply best estimates in everyday terms.

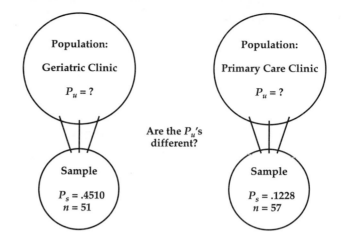

Test Preparation

Research question: Is there a significant difference in the percentages of caregivers referred to support groups by type of clinic? Put another way, is there a relationship between type of clinic and the likelihood of referral to a support group? *Givens:* Variables: X = type of clinic, nominal level; Y = referred to support groups, nominal level. *Population:* Caregivers at primary care and geriatric care clinics. *Sample:* n =108 caregivers (57 from primary care clinic and 51 from geriatric clinic). *Statistical procedure:* Chi-square test of a relationship between two nominal variables. Research question is graphically presented in Figure 13–2.

Observation:

Observed frequencies, computed expected frequencies (E_{cell} in parentheses), and column percentages (column %) where

$$E_{cell} = \frac{(\text{column marginal total for cell}) (\text{row marginal total for cell})}{\text{grand total}}$$

and

$$\text{Column \% [of joint frequency]} = \frac{\text{\# in a cell}}{\text{total \# in column}} \times 100$$

Referred to Support Group	Type of Clinic →	Primary Care	Geriatric	Row Totals
Yes		7 (15.83) Column % 12.28	23 (14.17) Column % 45.10	30
No		50 (41.17) Column % 87.72	28 (36.83) Column % 54.90	78
Column totals		57 (57.00)	51 (51.00)	108

Six Steps

1. *Stat. H:* $\chi^2 = 0$

   That is, there is no relationship between type of clinic and percentage of referrals to a support group.

   Alt. H: $\chi^2 > 0$

   That is, there is a relationship between type of clinic and percentage of referrals to a support group. One-tailed but nondirectional.

2. *Sampling distribution:*

$$\chi^2 = \sum \frac{(O - E)^2}{E}$$

$$df = (r - 1)(c - 1) = (2 - 1)(2 - 1) = 1$$

   If the Stat. *H* is true and samples of sizes 57 and 51 caregivers are drawn repeatedly from the clinic populations and cross-tabulated for type of clinic and percentage of referrals to a support group, the calculations of the chi-square statistic will produce the following chi-square distribution:

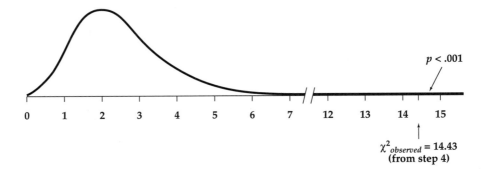

3. *Level of significance:* $\alpha = .05$ (nondirectional); one-tailed; $df = 1$. Critical test score = $\chi^2_\alpha = 3.84$ (from Statistical Table G in Appendix B).

4. *Observations:*

   Test effects and test statistic:

Cell (X, Y)	O	E	$(O - E)$	$(O - E)^2$	$[(O - E)^2/E]$
Primary Care Clinic–No referral	50	41.17	8.83	77.97	1.89
Primary Care Clinic–Yes referral	7	15.83	–8.83	77.97	4.92
Geriatric Clinic–No referral	28	36.83	–8.83	77.97	2.12
Geriatric Clinic–Yes referral	23	14.17	8.83	77.97	5.50
Totals	108	108	0.00		$\chi^2 = 14.43$

p-value: *p* [drawing a sample with differences between observed and expected frequencies as unusual as or more unusual than those observed when in fact there is no relationship between the variables] < .001 (area noted on curve in step 2).

5. *Rejection decision:* $|\chi^2_{observed}| > |\chi^2_{\alpha}|$ (i.e., 14.43 > 3.84); $p < \alpha$; .001 < .05. Reject Stat. *H* and accept the Alt. *H* at the 95 percent level of confidence.

6. *Interpretation:* Aspects of relationship and best estimates.
   Existence: There is a relationship between type of clinic and percentage of referrals to a support group; $\chi^2 = 14.43$, $p < .001$.
   Nature: Caregivers at geriatric clinics are more likely to be referred to support groups. *Best estimates:* 45.10 percent of caregivers. accompanying patients to the geriatric clinic are referred to support groups compared to only 12.28 percent of caregivers accompanying patients to the primary care clinic.
   Answer: Caregivers assisting patients at the geriatric clinic are more likely to be referred to a support group. The clinic's claims are justified.

Small Single-Sample Proportions Test: The Binomial Distribution

A "small single-sample proportions test," as the word *proportion* implies, is used with one nominal level variable, where $P = p$ [of the success category] of the variable and $Q = p$ [of the failure category(ies)]. This test is used when the smaller of P_u and Q_u times n is less than 5 (i.e., $[(p_{smaller})(n)] < 5$). Recall from Chapter 10 that when $[(p_{smaller})(n)] \geq 5$, we use the large single-sample proportions test.

The test statistic for the small single-sample proportions test is called the binomial distribution test. The term *binomial* means "two-number," and this test is used with very common dichotomous variables—those with only two categories. Examples of dichotomous variables are gender (male/female), majority-minority race classification (white/nonwhite), a coin toss (heads/

tails), attitude toward an issue (for/against), existence of an attribute (present/absent), outcome of an experiment (effect/no effect), effectiveness of treatment (effective/not effective), and outcomes for at-risk groups such as heart attack victims (survived/died). It also should be noted that with variables of any level of measurement, we often "dichotomize" by collapsing scores into two groups. For example, in a study of retirees it may be useful to compare those who retired before and after age 65 years (the age at which full Social Security benefits are attainable).

The binomial distribution is especially useful in laboratory experiments with few subjects. For example, suppose previous research reveals that one-half (a proportion of .5000) of all patients receiving chemotherapy can be expected to experience nausea. We have a sample of eight patients and expect four to experience nausea. We administer a new nausea-reducing drug. If it is effective, *significantly fewer* than four patients should experience nausea. Suppose only one of the eight (12.50 percent) experiences nausea with the new drug. This is three fewer nausea cases than expected with no drug, suggesting that the drug is effective. But does it truly mean that the drug is effective? Could this apparently favorable outcome have resulted from random sampling error? In other words, in a second group of eight patients receiving the new drug seven could experience nausea. In a third group some other random number may experience nausea. A hypothesis test would resolve the question of how unusual the outcome is in repeated sampling. The binomial distribution provides a quick way to determine this *p*-value and establish whether the observed reduction in the number of nauseated patients is statistically significant. This hypothesis test would lead to one of the following conclusions:

1. The drug is effective and reduces nausea in an additional three of eight cases.
2. The drug is not effective. The reduction in nausea cases is due to sampling error.

When to Use a Small Single-Sample Proportions Test (the Binomial Distribution)

In general: One dichotomous nominal/ordinal variable and one sample.

1. There is only one nominal variable that is dichotomous (i.e., it has *only two* categories, where $P = p$ [of the success category] and $Q = p$ [of the failure category]).
2. There is a single, representative sample from one population.
3. The sample size is such that $[(p_{smaller}) (n)] < 5$, where $p_{smaller}$ = the smaller of P_u and Q_u.
4. There is a target value of the variable to which we may compare the sample proportion.

FIGURE 13–3

Possible outcomes of two flipped coins

First Coin   **Second Coin**

The Binomial Distribution Equation

To illustrate how sampling outcomes are predicted for dichotomous variables, let us take the example of flipping two coins. In Chapter 6, when we discussed probabilities, we noted that with repeated tossing, the outcomes of two flipped coins are predictable, as is shown in Figure 13–3.

Early mathematician bean counters, or in this case coin flippers, surely used coin tosses to discover the predictability of sampling events. They probably tossed two coins over and over while recording the frequency of outcomes of heads and tails. Then they did the same for three coins, four coins, and so on. After noting a pattern or "law of nature," these mathematicians proceeded to develop a formula that readily calculates outcomes. For dichotomous outcomes such as heads and tails, yes and no, present and absent, and the like, the binomial equation quickly describes all possible outcomes and the probability of each one. This equation, then, can be used as a sampling distribution.

A binomial distribution is an expansion of the following general binomial equation:

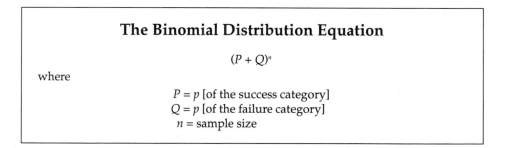

The Binomial Distribution Equation

$$(P + Q)^n$$

where

$P = p$ [of the success category]
$Q = p$ [of the failure category]
n = sample size

Recall that $P + Q = 1$; therefore, $Q = 1 - P$ and $P = 1 - Q$. To expand the equation is to raise it to the designated power of n. For example, if n is 2, then $(P + Q)$ is raised to the power of 2 (or simply squared):

$$(P + Q)^2 = (P + Q)(P + Q) = (P)(P) + (P)(Q) + (Q)(P) + (Q)(Q)$$
$$= P^2 + 2PQ + Q^2$$

For tossing two coins, let us define heads as success and tails as failure: $P = p$ [of heads] and $Q = p$ [of tails]. The sample size is $n = 2$, since only two coins are tossed. The expanded equation gives all possible outcomes and the probability of each one by delineating all possible heads-tails combinations that match Figure 13–3:

$$(P + Q)^2 = \quad P^2 \quad + \quad 2PQ \quad + \quad Q^2$$
$$= \text{heads, heads} + (2) \text{ heads, tails} + \text{tails, tails}$$

The coefficients of the equation (1, 2, and 1) represent how often each combination occurs in a large number of trials or samples. (Note that we did not write the coefficient 1, as this is redundant and unnecessary.) Since p [of heads] $= .5$ and p [of tails] $= .5$, both P and $Q = .5$. Thus, the sampling distribution of the tossing of two coins is

$$(P + Q)^2 = P^2 \quad + \quad 2PQ \quad + \quad Q^2$$
$$= (.5)^2 + 2\,(.5)\,(.5) + (.5)^2$$
$$= .25 + \quad .5 \quad + .25$$
$$= \frac{1}{4} + \quad \frac{2}{4} \quad + \frac{1}{4}$$

In other words, as is evident in Figure 13–3, when two coins are tossed, "double heads" occurs one in four times; the combination "heads-tails" occurs two in four times, or half the time; and "double tails" occurs one in four times.

Shortcut Formula for Expanding the Binomial Equation

Expanding the binomial equation is a difficult task. For example, to describe the sampling distribution for the tossing of four coins, we confront this:

$$(P + Q)^4 = (P + Q)(P + Q)(P + Q)(P + Q), \text{ etc.}$$

Fortunately, mathematicians value parsimony, *the preference for economy and simplicity over complexity.* This attitude is exemplified in the statement "The simplest solution is the best," and mathematicians spend lots of time simplifying calculations. Blaise Pascal (1623–1662) developed a shortcut method for expanding the binomial equation. First, he noted that once it is expanded, any binomial equation has $n + 1$ terms, where each term represents a combination of P and Q outcomes. For instance in the tossing of three coins, we have four terms or combinations: (1) all three heads, (2) one heads and two tails, (3) one tails and two heads, and (4) all three tails. Second, Pascal discovered that the equation's coefficients—the numbers that tell us how often a combination occurs—follow a predictable pattern. This discovery is called Pascal's triangle

TABLE 13–4   Pascal's Triangle of Coefficients of Binomial Equations for Sample Sizes 1 to 10

n	Coefficients	Sum of Coefficients (= 2 to the nth power)*
	1	
1	1 1	2
2	1 2 1	4
3	1 3 3 1	8
4	1 4 6 4 1	16
5	1 5 10 10 5 1	32
6	1 6 15 20 15 6 1	64
7	1 7 21 35 35 21 7 1	128
8	1 8 28 56 70 56 28 8 1	256
9	1 9 36 84 126 126 84 36 9 1	512
10	1 10 45 120 210 252 210 120 45 10 1	1024
Etc.		

* Use this sum of coefficients as a denominator of probabilities only when $P = Q = .5$.

(Table 13–4). For dichotomous variables, Pascal's triangle allows a quick computation of the probabilities of all possible outcomes. For any sample size n, by adding coefficients as we move down, the triangle provides the coefficients of the outcomes. Moreover, in the very common instance when P and Q are equal, in other words, when $P = .5$ and $Q = .5$, the sum of the coefficients provides the total number of outcome combinations and therefore the denominator for computing probabilities.

Again, let us illustrate with two coins, using the coefficients for $n = 2$ from Table 13–4:

$$(P + Q)^2 = P^2 + 2PQ + Q^2$$

From Pascal's triangle: 1 (heads, heads) + 2 (heads, tails) + 1 (tails, tails). Since P and Q are equal for coins, the probability of an outcome is quickly computed by dividing the coefficient for any combination by the sum of coefficients for the equation. Thus,

$$p \text{ [of heads and heads]} = P^2 = \frac{1}{4}$$

With a few steps, we can use Pascal's triangle to quickly compute the probabilities of outcomes. Let us illustrate for the tossing of five coins, $(P + Q)^5$, where $P = p$ [of heads] and $Q = p$ [of tails] and $n = 5$ (for five coins).

1. Since $n + 1 = 6$, write out the term "$PQ +$" six times to obtain the following partially completed equation:

$$(P + Q)^5 = PQ + PQ + PQ + PQ + PQ + PQ$$

2. Specify the exponent for each term, which will represent possible outcomes (possible combinations of heads and tails). At most, we can obtain five heads, and this occurs with no tails. Thus, the exponents for *P*s begin with 5 (i.e., the value of *n*) and then decrease to zero as we move across. The exponents for *Q*'s begin with zero and increase to the value of *n* as we move across. Therefore, start with the *P*s, putting the exponents 5, then 4, and so on, from left to right. Similarly, insert zero for the first *Q*, and so on, to obtain the following partially completed equation:

$$(P + Q)^5 = P^5Q^0 + P^4Q^1 + P^3Q^2 + P^2Q^3 + P^1Q^4 + P^0Q^5$$

Since any number raised to the power of zero = 1, this equation can be simplified by removing such terms to obtain the following partially completed equation:

$$(P + Q)^5 = P^5 + P^4Q^1 + P^3Q^2 + P^2Q^3 + P^1Q^4 + Q^5$$

This provides all combinations: P^5 represents the combination five heads and no tails, P^4Q^1 represents four heads and one tails, and so on, over to Q^5, which represents no heads and five tails.

3. Use Pascal's triangle (Table 13–4) to obtain coefficients for each term. Once these coefficients are inserted, we have the complete expanded binomial equation for $n = 5$:

$$(P + Q)^5 = P^5 + 5P^4Q^1 + 10P^3Q^2 + 10P^2Q^3 + 5P^1Q^4 + Q^5$$

4. Finally, since *P* and *Q* are equal, from the right column of Pascal's triangle (Table 13–4) obtain the sum of coefficients for a sample of $n = 5$ and divide this into each coefficient to obtain the probabilities of each outcome:

$$(P + Q)^5 = P^5 + 5P^4Q^1 + 10P^3Q^2 + 10P^2Q^3 + 5P^1Q^4 + Q^5$$
$$= \frac{1}{32} + \frac{5}{32} + \frac{10}{32} + \frac{10}{32} + \frac{5}{32} + \frac{1}{32}$$

Thus, the probability of tossing five coins and getting all heads is 1 in 32; four heads and one tails, 5 in 32; three heads and two tails, 10 in 32, and so forth.

With a little experience, Pascal's triangle is very efficient, especially when *P* and *Q* are equal. To illustrate, the following answers may be quickly taken from Table 13–4 without the need to construct the equations:

1. *p* [of flipping a coin 7 times and getting all heads] $= \dfrac{1}{128} = .0078$

2. *p* [of flipping 9 coins and getting 7 heads and 2 tails] $= \dfrac{36}{512} = .0703$

In instances where *P* and *Q* are *not* equal, Pascal's triangle still can be used to obtain coefficients. The sums on the right side of the table, however, do not apply, and the terms of the equation must be multiplied out. For example, suppose a room full of people is 70 percent male ($P = .7$) and 30 percent female ($Q = .3$). If three persons are randomly selected from the room, what possible male-female combinations will occur and with what probabilities? We observe Pascal's triangle to construct the equation and then insert values of .7 and .3 to solve for the probabilities of each combination:

$$(P + Q)^3 = P^3 + 3P^2Q^1 + 3P^1Q^2 + Q^3$$
$$= (.7^3) + 3 (.7^2) (.3) + 3 (.7) (.3^2) + (.3^3)$$
$$= .343 + .441 + .189 + .027$$

Note that the four probabilities sum to 1.0. Note also that the two predominantly male combinations on the left side of the equation occur much more frequently than do the two predominantly female combinations. This makes sense because the proportion of men in the room is much larger than the proportion of women. Indeed, Pascal's triangle is a handy device!

The Six Steps of Statistical Inference for a Small Single-Sample Proportions Test: The Binomial Distribution Test

Now let us use the binomial equation as a sampling distribution for hypothesis tests. Suppose that at the fictional Berry College the issue of date rape has become a hot topic. In response to pressure from students and parents, Berry's president announces that he will convene a focus group to begin discussing date rape and what can be done to eliminate it. Some outspoken students suspect that to minimize negative publicity about the college, the president wants a focus group to say that date rape is not a problem. They eagerly watch to see who the president selects for the focus group. They anticipate that he will load it with males, who are assumed to be less sympathetic to the problem than are females.

The proportion of males and females on campus is equal. The president announces his selection, and it is a group of eight students, six of whom are male. The outspoken students accuse him of loading the group with males. The president has stated publicly that he simply made a random selection of students by using a computer program and student records. Is the president of the college lying?

How can the binomial distribution be used here? Since the proportion of males and females is equal on the campus, each sex has an equal chance of being selected, just as a coin has an equal chance of coming up heads or tails. Thus, making a truly random selection of students is like tossing eight coins with, say, male as heads and female as tails. This does not mean, however, that a random selection of eight persons will always result in four males and four females. In tossing eight coins, there are nine possible outcomes, ranging from all heads to all tails. We would expect nevertheless to obtain balanced combinations such as four heads and four tails, five and three, or three and five, because these combinations occur more frequently in repeated tossing. Used along with Pascal's triangle (Table 13–4), the binomial distribution provides a description of all possible combinations of males and females for a group of eight and the probability of each combination *if the selection is indeed a random one.*

As with any hypothesis test, we must state a hypothesis so that it predicts sampling outcomes. The binomial distribution provides predictable outcomes for a random selection, one in which males and females have an equal chance of selection and "the coins" are not weighted in either's favor. Therefore, we can state the statistical hypothesis as: The president is not a liar; the focus group was chosen randomly. (This also can be called a *null* hypothesis because it tests *no* bias.) If we find that the president's outcome is common with a random or "blindfold" selection, we will stick with this statistical hypothesis of no bias. The alternative hypothesis is that the president intentionally loaded the focus group with males and lied when he said he made a random selection. The effect of the test is the difference between the observed number in the category, P, and the expected number, assuming no bias (i.e., assuming that P_u is true). This is a one-tailed test because it states that males had a *greater* chance of selection. Our rejection decision hinges on whether a combination as unusual as or more unusual than six males and two females is unlikely to happen by chance. Is the effect of having two more males than predicted by a 50–50 split due to random sampling error or to bias on the part of the university president? Put another way, in repeatedly tossing eight coins, is it unusual to get six heads or more? Does this occur quite frequently, say, more than .05 of the time, or is this an unlikely event? Let us frame this problem by using the six steps of statistical inference.

Brief Checklist for the Six Steps of Statistical Inference

Test Preparation

State the research question; list givens, including variables (e.g., $X = ...$, $Y = ...$), their levels of measurement, the population(s) under study, and sample(s) and sample size(s); select the statistical test; provide observations of statistics and parameters; and draw a conceptual diagram.

Six Steps

Using the symbol H for *hypothesis:*

1. State the statistical H and the alternative H and stipulate test direction.
2. Describe the sampling distribution.
3. State the level of significance (α) and specify the critical test value.
4. Observe the actual sample outcomes and compute the test effects, the test statistic, and the *p*-value.
5. Make the rejection decision.
6. Interpret and apply best estimates in everyday terms.

Test Preparation

Research question: Is the president of Berry College truthful in saying that his focus group was randomly selected (i.e., males and females had an equal chance of selection)? *Givens:* Variable: X = gender; nominal level, dichotomous; $P = p$ [of males]; $Q = p$ [of females], nominal level. *Population:* Berry College student body with equal proportions of men and women students. *Sample:* eight students. *Statistical procedure:* small single-sample proportions test, binomial distribution; target value: $P_u = .50$ (the known, true proportion of male students in the Berry College student population). *Observation:* $n = 8$. Six males and two females were selected for focus group (which is the binomial formula term P^6Q^2).

$$\text{As a proportion, } P_s = \frac{\text{\# males}}{n} = \frac{6}{8} = .75.$$

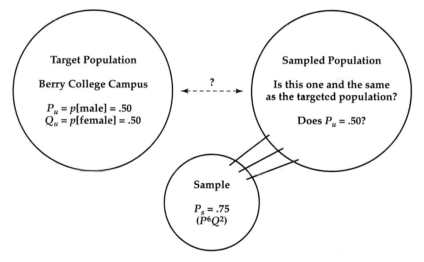

Six Steps

1. *Stat. H:* P_u (sampled population) $= .50$ (the known proportion of males (P_u) in the targeted Berry College population)

   That is, the president is not a liar; the focus group was chosen randomly.

   Alt. H: P_u (sampled population) $> .50$ (the known proportion of males (P_u) in the targeted Berry College population). One-tailed

   That is, the president is a liar. Males are overrepresented, suggesting that the focus group was loaded with males.

2. *Sampling distribution:* If Stat. *H* is true and samples of size 8 are drawn repeatedly from the Berry College student population, combinations of males and females will fit the binomial distribution with $P = .5$, $Q = .5$, $n = 8$ and coefficients from Pascal's triangle (Table 13–4):

$$(P + Q)^8 = P^8 + 8P^7Q^1 + 28P^6Q^2 + 56P^5Q^3 + 70P^4Q^4 + 56P^3Q^5 + 28P^2Q^6 + 8P^1Q^7 + Q^8$$

3. *Level of significance:* $\alpha = .05$. One-tailed

4. *Observation:* $n = 8$;

Test effect: Six males and two females; two more males than expected.

Test statistic $= (P + Q)^8 = P^8 + 8P^7Q^1 + 28P^6Q^2 + 56P^5Q^3 + 70P^4Q^4 + 56P^3Q^5 + 28P^2Q^6 + 8P^1Q^7 + Q^8$

$$= \frac{1}{256} + \frac{8}{256} + \frac{28}{256} + \frac{56}{256} + \frac{70}{256} + \frac{56}{256} + \frac{28}{256} + \frac{8}{256} + \frac{1}{256}$$

$$\overbrace{\qquad\qquad\qquad}$$
$$\downarrow$$
$$37/256 = .1445$$

p-value: *p* [observing a sample outcome as unusual as or more unusual than six males and two females when the true population proportion P_u is .50] = .1445.

5. *Rejection decision:* $p > \alpha$, .1445 > .05. Do not reject the Stat. *H*.

6. *Interpretation existence:* The president appears not to be a liar; the focus group could have been chosen randomly. *Best estimates:* The apparent overrepresentation of males in the focus group could easily have resulted from random sampling error. A combination as extreme as or more extreme than six males and two females occurs over 14 percent of the time in such random selections. *Answer:* We have no reason to believe that the president is a liar.

Some things of note about this hypothesis test:

- In step 2 note the efficiency of the binomial equation. Unlike the Z-test, *t*-test, and *F*-ratio test, this sampling distribution is not described with a frequency curve. This means that a frequency curve table (such as the *t*-distribution table) is not required. This concise equation alone meets the requirements of describing the sampling distribution. It describes all possible combinations of males and females for a group of eight and the probability of each combination occurring in repeated sampling.

- In step 4, in the binomial equation the term P^6Q^2 represents the combination of six males and two females, our sampling outcome. When "honest" sampling occurs, it would be more unusual to have drawn seven males and one female or eight males and no females. Thus, the *p*-value for the sampling outcome includes the probabilities of P^7Q^1 and P8. We added the probabilities of all terms in the "tail" of the equation—those as unusual as or more unusual than P^6Q^2.

- In step 4, *if we had done a two-tailed test,* we also would have included the probabilities of P^2Q^6, P^1Q^7, and Q^8, because it would have been just as unusual to randomly select these female-biased combinations as to select the male-biased combinations. The *p*-value would have been computed by adding the probabilities of both "tails" of the equation as follows:

$$(P + Q)^8 = P^8 + 8P^7Q^1 + 28P^6Q^2 + 56P^5Q^3 + 70P^4Q^4 + 56P^3Q^5 + 28P^2Q^6 + 8P^1Q^7 + Q^8$$

$$= \frac{1}{256} + \frac{8}{256} + \frac{28}{256} + \frac{56}{256} + \frac{70}{256} + \frac{56}{256} + \frac{28}{256} + \frac{8}{256} + \frac{1}{256}$$

$$\downarrow \qquad\qquad\qquad\qquad\qquad\qquad \downarrow$$

$$37/256 = .1445 \qquad\qquad\qquad\qquad 37/256 = .1445$$

In other words, since the equation is symmetrical when P and Q are equal (i.e., combinations are balanced on both sides), the *p*-value is doubled and computes to (2) (.1445) = .2890.

- In steps 5 and 6 in this example we failed to reject the statistical hypothesis. In situations in which the statistical hypothesis is rejected, provide best estimates of P_u and/or Q_u by reporting which category is overrepresented; for instance, "men are overrepresented."

Tabular Presentation of Data

As has been noted in several chapters, the main goal of research usually is to explain variation in an outcome variable—a single dependent variable. Sometimes, however, the focus is on a single independent nominal/ordinal variable—two or more groups—and the groups are compared for several dependent variables. For example, in the illustration of the chi-square test of differences of proportions we compared two groups of caregivers. Table 13–5 presents additional data comparing these two groups. The statistical significance of differences between percentages was determined with chi-square tests. This table also compares these two groups on some interval/ratio variables (i.e., differences of means) by using independent sample *t*-tests (Chapter 11).

A table such as Table 13–5 packs a lot of information on one page. First, it appears that the geriatric clinic is much more involved with its patients' caregivers. Nearly half the caregivers there indicate that they are referred to support groups, counseling services, and community agencies, and about half are advised on home safety, an important concern among elderly persons. In the primary care clinic very small percentages are advised on these things. Second, the data in the lower part of the table—based on *t*-tests—is important for guiding additional multivariate analysis. The caregivers of the geriatric clinic patients have a higher mean age of about six years. Although the rate of psychological depression is not statistically different between the groups, the geriatric clinic caregivers are found to experience a greater burden in the caregiver role. These findings may help explain why more of the geriatric clinic caregivers are being sent to counseling and support groups. Perhaps their patients are sicker, creating greater burdens for the caregivers. And perhaps the lack of caregiver services at the primary care clinic results from the fact that especially ill patients are referred to the geriatric clinic. Clearly, additional analysis is in order with controls for severity of patient condition, age of caregiver, and other variables. One of the main functions of bivariate analysis—such as that reported in Table 13–5—is to guide the research process into the next stage.

A couple of technical comments are in order in regard to how Table 13–5

TABLE 13–5   A Comparison of Primary Care and Geriatric Clinic Caregivers on Services Received, Demographic Variables, and Stress Outcomes (*n* = 108)

		Caregivers Accompanying Patients to		
Variables		*Primary Care Clinic (n = 57)*	*Geriatric Clinic (n = 51)*	*Significance*
Services received				
Percent referred to support groups		12.28%	45.10%	‡
Percent told of counseling services		5.26	43.14	‡
Percent told of community agencies that assist caregivers		14.04	45.10	‡
Percent referred to legal counsel		1.75	23.53	†
Percent advised on home safety		10.53	52.94	‡
Demographics				
Caregiver age	Mean	55.1 years	61.2 years	*
	Standard deviation	12.5	12.1	
Years of education	Mean	10.6 years	11.1 years	NS
	Standard deviation	3.1	3.2	
Stress outcomes				
Caregiver burden	Mean	17.2	21.2	‡
	Standard deviation	4.7	6.5	‡
Psychological depression	Mean	17.0	18.7	NS
	Standard deviation	11.2	11.5	

NS = not significant.
*$p < .05$.
†$p < .01$.
‡$p < .001$.
Source: Clair, Ritchey, and Allman 1993.

was designed. Note that at the primary care clinic, only about 2 percent of caregivers were referred to legal counsel and only 5 percent were told about other counseling services. These small percentages required Yates's correction in the calculation of the chi-square statistic. Finally, note that for the variable caregiver burden, not only the group means but also the group standard deviations were significantly different. There was a significantly wider distributional spread in the burden scores of caregivers at the geriatric clinic. The *t*-test of the differences in means for the burden variable required the separate variance estimate of the standard error because of the inequality of variances (or standard deviations). Some scientific journals require table footnotes to specify these fine statistical points, while others presume that their readers will assume that such corrections were made. For a public audience there is no point discussing statistical procedures. The data are accepted on the authority of the presenter. Moreover, pictorial presentations, especially bar graphs, are a more appropriate device for communicating a sense of proportion to a public audience.

☹   STATISTICAL FOLLIES AND FALLACIES   ☹

Low Statistical Power When the Sample Size Is Small

In our illustration of the binomial equation we found that even though his focus group appeared to be weighted in favor of males, we "have no reason to believe" that the president of Berry College lied when he said the group was randomly selected. While we gave him the benefit of the doubt, it is still possible that he loaded the focus group with males.

For one thing, in testing the statistical hypothesis that he was *not* a liar, we used the .05 level of significance. This kept the chance of a type I error (i.e., rejecting the statistical hypothesis when in fact it is true) at a moderately low level. In other words, we took only a 5 percent chance of calling him a liar if in fact he was not. The outspoken students who accuse him of bias might prefer a higher level of significance (say, .20) because they are viewing things politically, not scientifically. They might argue that we made it almost impossible to reject the statistical hypothesis because a *p*-value less than .05 could be obtained only if the president had selected seven males and one female or eight males:

$$(P +Q)^8 = P^8 + 8P^7Q^1 + 28P^6Q^2 + 56P^5Q^3 + 70P^4Q^4 + 56P^3Q^5 + 28P^2Q^6 + 8P^1Q^7 + Q^8$$

$$= \frac{1}{256} + \frac{8}{256} + \frac{28}{256} + \frac{56}{256} + \frac{70}{256} + \frac{56}{256} + \frac{28}{256} + \frac{8}{256} + \frac{1}{256}$$

$$\underset{\downarrow}{\overline{}}$$

9/256 = .0352 (which is less than α = .05, one-tailed)

These students would protest that the president would have had to select not one, not two, but three too many males to be called a liar with such a low alpha level.

What these students are actually expressing is their suspicion that a type II error occurred (see Chapter 9). Recall that a type II error occurs when a statistical test fails to reject a false statistical hypothesis. Recall also that β is the probability of making a type II error and that it is inversely related to α; as α increases, β decreases, and vice versa. In this case, a type II error would have occurred if the president actually had lied, but we concluded the opposite.

By setting the level of significance (α) higher, we could reduce β—the chance of making a type II error. For instance, if we had used $\alpha = .20$, we would have rejected the president's honesty when he selected six males and two females because the *p*-value that we had for the test was .1445, which is less than .20. If we had done this, however, the president could have accused us of bias in favor of the outspoken students. What this conundrum illustrates is that a small sample size is a rather weak device for determining whether observed facts are due to sampling error. Because the binomial equation is used with small samples, its results are rather tenuous. In statistical language we say that such a limited statistic has low statistical power. **Statistical power** refers to *a test statistic's probability of not incurring a type II error for a given level of significance*. Mathematically,

$$\text{Power of a test} = 1 - \beta = 1 - p \text{ [of a type II error]}$$

As we noted in Chapter 9, calculating the power of a statistical test is quite complicated and is beyond the scope of this text. Nevertheless, with the binomial equation it is easy to see that small sample test statistics are limited.

A simpler case may help us remember this limitation. Suppose the college president had chosen only three students for the focus group. At the .05 level of significance, would it even be possible to reject the statistical hypothesis that he lied? The answer is no. Even in the worst-case scenario that all three selected students turned out to be male, there would be no way to reject the statistical hypothesis. Using Pascal's triangle, with three persons randomly chosen, the probability of selecting all males is one in eight, or .1250. That is, this worst-case scenario with its *p*-value of .1250 is greater than .05. There would be no way to reject the statistical hypothesis using such a small, low-power sample and the binomial equation. Even an all-male result would not be unusual in an honest random selection of three students.

There is a second reason to be skeptical of the conclusion we drew that the president was not lying. As we discussed in Chapter 1, statistical work occurs within a larger political and cultural context. It is subject to distortion by dishonest users. Our hypothesis test simply determined that this president was in a position to assert that his selection was random. In fact, he could have placed six males on the focus group intentionally. Perhaps he knew that that was the maximum number of males that could be in the group without having a statistical hypothesis rejected at the .05 level of significance. Statistical conclusions based on small samples are not absolutely certain even when statistical test conclusions support a position. This is why the ethics of science is an important part of statistical work. An honest statistician would not support the president's position without noting that it is hard to draw a firm conclusion with a small sample.

Assuming that indeed the president of Berry College is honest, he could have prevented student protest by using gender quotas in forming the focus group. That is, he could have randomly selected exactly four males and four females—the correct proportions of gender representation in the student population. This would have saved him a lot of headaches.

Statistical Procedures Covered to Here

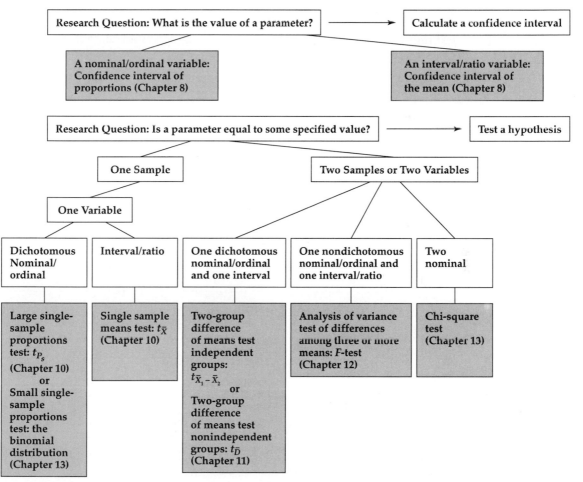

Formulas in Chapter 13

Chi-square test of a relationship between two nominal variables:

Given: two nominal/ordinal variables X and Y or a nominal/ordinal variable for two groups. A crosstab table of the variables reveals at least five cases per cell.

Research question: Is there a relationship between the two nominal/ordinal variables? Or is there a difference between two groups in the proportions of a category of a nominal/ordinal variable?

Stat. H: $\chi^2 = 0$

Sampling distribution: The chi-square distribution with

$$df = (r - 1)(c - 1)$$

Test effects: Differences between observed and expected frequencies, $O - E$, best illustrated with column percentages.

Test statistic: Chi-square [for use with the chi-square table (Statistical Table G in Appendix B); determines if a relationship exists]:

Calculations for producing the chi-square test statistic:

1. Organize data in a crosstab table and calculate the expected cell frequencies:

$$E_{cell} = \frac{(\text{column marginal total for cell})(\text{row marginal total for cell})}{\text{grand total}}$$

2. Insert observed and expected cell frequencies into this spreadsheet:

Givens			Calculations		
Cell (X, Y)	O	E	$(O - E)$	$(O - E)^2$	$[(O - E)^2/E]$
X–Y cell	...	...	...	...	...
X–Y cell	...	...	...	...	...
X–Y cell	...	...	...	...	...
X–Y cell	...	...	...	...	...
Totals	n	n	0.0		$\chi^2 = ...$

3. Calculate the chi-square statistic (from the right lower corner of the spreadsheet):

$$\chi^2 = \sum \frac{(O - E)^2}{E}$$

Addressing the aspects of a relationship:

Direction: Usually not applicable
Strength: Not applicable
Nature: Calculate column percentages of interesting cells:

$$\text{Column \% [of joint frequency]} = \frac{\text{\# in a cell}}{\text{total \# in column}} \times 100$$

Small single-sample proportions test (the binomial distribution):

Given: one nominal dichotomous variable where $P - p$ [of the success category] and $Q = p$ [of the failure category]; a single representative sample from one population; the sample size is such that $[(p_{\text{smaller}})\,(n)] < 5$, where $p_{\text{smaller}} =$ the smaller of P_u and Q_u, and there is a target value of the variable to which we may compare the sample proportion.

Research question: Is P_u, the proportion of cases in the success category, significantly different from a target value?

Stat. H: $P_{u\ \text{(sampled population)}} = $ = known target value

Sampling distribution: The binomial distribution

Test effect: The difference between the observed number in the category, P, and the expected number, assuming P_u is true

Test statistic: The binomial distribution equation, $(P + Q)^n$

Calculations for getting a *p*-value using the binomial equation:

1. Determine whether the binomial equation is appropriate by seeing that

$$[(p_{\text{smaller}})\,(n)] < 5$$

   (If $[(p_{\text{smaller}})\,(n)] \geq 5$, then use the large single-sample proportions test in Chapter 10.)

2. Expand the formula $(P + Q)^n$ by:

   a. Listing the term "*PQ*" $n + 1$ times.
   b. Specifying exponents for each term (to represent possible outcomes).
   c. Using Pascal's triangle (Table 13–4) to obtain coefficients for each term and inserting these coefficients to complete the expanded binomial equation.
   d. Calculate the *p*-value = *p* [combinations as unusual as or more unusual than the combination observed] by adding probabilities in the appropriate tail(s) of the equation.

Questions for Chapter 13

1. An attribute is a quality or characteristic of a subject that is conveyed in the names of categories of a nominal/ordinal variable. To the best of your knowledge, identify the attributes of the following variables:

    a. College grade level
    b. Hair color
    c. Religious preference
    d. Physician's medical specialty

2. For a single individual, the pairing of attributes from two variables is called a joint attribute. The joint attribute female-surgeon represents which two variables?

3. Choose two nominal variables, create some fictional data, and set up a crosstab table to depict joint frequencies. Label the parts of the table (cells, totals, etc.) to illustrate that you know how to read such tables (review Table 2–9 in Chapter 2).

4. Variables of what level of measurement are appropriate for using the chi-square test?

5. In a chi-square test, what does it indicate when the observed and expected frequencies are equal?

6. Variables of what level of measurement are appropriate for using the small single-sample proportions test, and what is this test called?

7. What does the term *binomial* mean? Must a variable necessarily be dichotomous in order to use the binomial distribution? Explain.

8. What is statistical power? Provide an example of an incorrect conclusion based on a sample with low statistical power.

Exercises for Chapter 13

General instructions: On all hypotheses tests, follow the six steps of statistical inference, including test preparation, a conceptual diagram, probability curves, and appropriate aspects of a relationship. Use $\alpha = .05$ unless otherwise stipulated.

1. The following crosstab table is from a random sample of physicians. The row variable distinguishes whether a physician is a member of a medical specialty with a high risk of being sued for medical malpractice (e.g., obstetrics or neurosurgery). The column variable, practice location, indicates rural (i.e., a county not adjacent to a metropolitan area), urban community (i.e., a metropolitan area but not affiliated with a medical school), or academic health science center (i.e., medical center attached to a medical school). Compute column percentages for all joint frequency cells.

Risk of Suit ↓	*Practice Location* → *Rural County*	*Urban Community*	*Academic Health Science Center*	*Totals*
High-risk specialty	100	462	77	
Low-risk specialty	42	279	23	
Totals				

2. The following crosstab table is from a random sample of employees of a city government. The column variable is job sector classification, and the row variable is *has earned a college degree*. Compute column percentages for all joint frequency cells.

College Degree	*Job Sector* → *Service*	*Staff Support*	*Managerial/ Administrative*	*Totals*
Yes	6	57	29	
No	41	29	5	
Totals				

3. Among 43 professors and 55 students surveyed, 25 professors and 18 students preferred the quarter system to the semester system. Present these data in a crosstab table. Test the hypothesis that there is a relationship between organizational status and preferred type of academic system.

4. In a local taste test between vanilla ice cream and vanilla yogurt, 41 of 69 men surveyed preferred ice cream. Among 75 women surveyed, 62 preferred ice cream. Construct a crosstab table. Is there a relationship between gender and dessert choice?

5. Use the data below from the 1994 General Social Survey to test the hypothesis that those who marry at a young age are more likely to divorce.

	Married when Under 20	*Married when 20 or Older*
Divorced	27	52
Never divorced	59	244

6. A campus student art council proposes to exhibit the work of a controversial artist known for his violent and sexual depictions of religious figures. The council surveys both students and alumni to assess opposition to the exhibit. Using the following fictional data, determine if there is a significant difference in the proportions of students and alumni opposing the exhibit.

	Students	Alumni
Supports the exhibit	172	278
Opposes the exhibit	60	170

7. Organize the following spreadsheet data into a crosstab table. Test the hypothesis that there is a significant difference between city center residents and suburban residents in terms of support of a tax increase for expanding the size of the police department.

Residence Location	Supports Tax Increase
Suburban	No
City center	Yes
Suburban	No
Suburban	Yes
City center	No
City center	Yes
Suburban	No
City center	Yes
City center	Yes
Suburban	Yes
City center	Yes
City center	No
Suburban	No
City center	Yes
City center	Yes
Suburban	Yes
City center	Yes
Suburban	No
Suburban	No
City center	No
City center	Yes
Suburban	Yes
City center	Yes
City center	No
Suburban	No
City center	Yes
Suburban	No
City center	Yes
City center	Yes

(handwritten note: ADD · 18 rural people too / 6 yes / 12 no*)*

Residence Location	Supports Tax Increase
Suburban	Yes
City center	Yes
Suburban	Yes
City center	Yes
Suburban	No
City center	No

8. Organize the following spreadsheet data into a crosstab table. Test the hypothesis that there is a significant difference in support for privatizing public schools between those who voted for Republicans and those who voted for Democrats in the last election (fictional data).

How Voted in Last Presidential Election	Supports Privatizing Schools?
Republican	Yes
Republican	No
Democrat	No
Democrat	No
Republican	No
Republican	Yes
Democrat	No
Republican	Yes
Republican	Yes
Democrat	Yes
Republican	Yes
Republican	No
Democrat	No
Republican	Yes
Republican	Yes
Democrat	No
Republican	Yes
Democrat	No
Democrat	Yes
Republican	No
Republican	Yes
Democrat	Yes
Republican	Yes
Republican	No
Democrat	No
Republican	Yes
Democrat	No
Republican	Yes
Democrat	No
Republican	Yes
Democrat	Yes
Democrat	No

How Voted in Last Presidential Election	Supports Privatizing Schools?
Republican	Yes
Democrat	Yes
Republican	Yes
Democrat	Yes
Democrat	No
Republican	Yes

9. Use Pascal's triangle to quickly report the following probabilities for the tosses of coins. For this exercise, it is not necessary to write out the equations.

    a. p [of tossing nine coins and getting all heads]
    b. p [of tossing four coins and getting one heads and three tails]
    c. p [of tossing six coins and getting three heads and three tails]

10. As parents of the baby boom generation, Phillip and Kitty had seven children—all boys. Assuming that for a single birth the probability of having a boy and that of having a girl are the same, what is the probability of a seven-child family being all male? Use Pascal's triangle. For this exercise it is not necessary to write out the equations.

11. Micro-Medication Corporation is testing a new cancer drug on genetically infected mice. Previous research in their laboratories shows that 50 percent of these mice survive six months without any treatment. Eight mice are administered the drug. Six survive for six months. Test the hypothesis that the drug treatment results in a better survival rate than does no drug at all. Use $\alpha = .001$.

12. Micro-Medication Corporation is testing another new cancer drug on genetically infected mice. Previous research in their labs shows that 50 percent of these mice survive six months without any treatment. Ten mice are administered this drug treatment. Six survive for six months. Test the hypothesis that the drug treatment results in a better survival rate than does no drug at all. Use $\alpha = .05$ since this drug is known to be safe.

13. A fertility clinic claims to have a procedure for selecting the gender of a child. Among nine randomly selected couples who wished to have girls, seven got the intended result. Test a hypothesis to determine if the procedure does better than chance.

14. A consumer watch group claims that most charity organizations spend over half their contributions on fund-raising activities. You examine the public disclosure forms of 10 randomly selected charity organizations and find that 6 fit the watch group's criticism. Test a hypothesis to determine whether the watch group's conclusion is correct.

15. Suppose you intend to use the binomial distribution to test a hypothesis at the .01 level of significance with a two-tailed test. What minimum sample size would be required for you to possibly reject the statistical hypothesis? Show calculations.

16. Suppose you intend to use the binomial distribution to test a hypothesis at the .05 level of significance with a one-tailed test. What minimum sample size would be required for you to possibly reject the statistical hypothesis? Show calculations.

Optional Computer Applications for Chapter 13

If your class uses the optional computer applications that accompany this text, open the Chapter 13 exercises on the *Computer Applications for The Statistical Imagination* compact disk. The exercises focus on running crosstabs and binomial procedures in *SPSS for Windows* and properly interpreting the output.

CORRELATION
AND REGRESSION
Part 1: Concepts and Calculations

Introduction: Improving Best Estimates of a Dependent Variable

Statisticians often are criticized for using jargon and being concerned with theory rather than practical results. A good researcher, whether testing theory or not, places much value in the practical aspects of analysis—making predictions about how the things around us work. In testing hypotheses about relationships between variables, practical questions are answered when the nature of the relationship is described. This is the final step of analysis, where we answer the questions: So what? What does all this gobbledygook about statistical hypotheses, levels of significance and confidence, and *p*-values mean in the real world? Our responses to these questions should be phrased in down-to-earth language and provide the nitty-gritty details of how findings can be applied to everyday situations. Putting our efforts into practice allows us to contribute to the welfare of society (e.g., improving the delivery of services) or its individuals (e.g., giving advice on stock investments).

The simple idea of making best estimates is a valuable one in applying the findings of statistical work. Especially valuable is the use of predictor (i.e., independent) variables to improve best estimates of a dependent variable of particular interest. Best estimates are directed toward the future. They are based on probabilities that establish confidence in what we are doing. Throughout this textbook we have emphasized that a key ingredient of the statistical imagination is the analysis of causes and consequences with the goal of predicting future events. Making a best estimate focuses our analysis on the practical side. Best estimates allow us to produce results that matter.

Let us retrace our experiences with making best estimates. Suppose, for example, we wish to estimate the mean weight of a population of seventh-graders. In dealing with this single variable, the best estimate of its parameter is a confidence interval—a point estimate such as the mean weight of a sample plus or minus a span of predictable error. If we find a sample mean of, say, 90 pounds, a 95 percent confidence interval may allow us to conclude that the mean weight is between 85 and 95 pounds. But what if we wish to make an estimate of the weight of an *unseen* individual in this population? Here we are left with a very gross estimate—the sample mean weight of 90 pounds—a point estimate. We make this estimate grudgingly because we know that not every seventh-grader weighs exactly 90 pounds. *Without any other information about the individual*, this is the best we can do.

From our experience with two variables, however, we know that the best estimate of a dependent variable can be improved if we can identify independent variables—predictor variables—and extend the analysis to the bivariate level. Suppose, for example, Doug is a seventh-grade boy and we know that boys tend to weigh on average 10 pounds more than the mean weight of seventh-graders as a whole. As we learned in Chapter 11, given this effect of male gender, we can now improve our best estimate of Doug's weight by adding 10 pounds to the mean of 90 to get a best estimate of 100 pounds—the mean weight of seventh-grade boys. By introducing a predictor or independent variable, X = gender, we improve estimates of the dependent variable, Y = weight. Knowledge about X is used to adjust the precision of best estimates of Y.

A Correlation between Interval/Ratio Variables

With a nominal independent variable such as gender, estimates of Y can be adjusted for only two "scores"—the "X-categories" of male and female. In examining the relationship between two interval/ratio or interval-like ordinal variables, however, we must deal with a large number of scores. For a sample of adults, with an independent variable X such as height, there are as many as 25 "height membership categories"—scores ranging from about 56 inches (4 feet, 8 inches tall) to about 80 inches (6 feet, 8 inches tall). We could test for differences of means among 25 height categories, but this would be cumbersome and would require a very large sample.

Fortunately, it is not necessary to think of each inch as a separate height category or X-category. Instead we treat each inch of height as an X-score, an increment along its interval/ratio unit of measure. If we are attempting to estimate weight (Y), we can seek to improve our estimates *for each additional inch* of height (X) from a low of 56 inches to a high of 80 inches. Because we know that taller people tend to be heavier, we search for a way to determine how much weight should be added *for each additional inch of height*. The statistical imagination beckons us to ask: What is the effect on weight of a one-inch increase in height? Informed by such knowledge, we can quickly make very fine, one-inch height adjustments to best estimates of weight.

How are these fine adjustments made? Interval/ratio variables, with their set units of measurement, offer many mathematical and geometric advantages. Whereas with earlier statistical tests we were unable to address all four aspects of a relationship, with two interval/ratio variables we are able to do that quite precisely by using the mathematical qualities of a straight line to estimate Y for given quantities of X. This straight-line, or "linear," geometry can be used when two variables are correlated. A **correlation** is *a systematic change in the scores of two interval/ratio variables (or interval-like ordinal variables)*.

A Correlation

A systematic change in the scores of two interval/ratio variables.

Two interval/ratio variables correlate (or "co-relate") when the measurements of one variable change in tandem with the measurements of the other. For example, there is a correlation between height (X) and weight (Y). Measurements of lots of inches (tallness) tend to coincide with measurements of lots of pounds (heaviness). Thus, to estimate weight, if someone is tall, add some pounds, or if that person is short, subtract some. Correlations between two interval/ratio variables are very common, and therefore, the idea of correlation is intuitively appealing. For example, in a population of adults, a correlation exists between age and the number of times a doctor is seen in a year; that is, older adults tend to go to the doctor more. Among college students, time spent reading is correlated with grade point average (GPA); the more time spent reading, the better the grades. Using slightly different terminology, we can say that educational level is "a correlate of" income; the higher the educational level, the higher the income. Two variables are correlated if their measurements consistently change together from case to case. We say that the measurements are ordered together or coordinated—or, simply, correlated.

Identifying a Linear Relationship

With two interval/ratio variables, the procedure for improving best estimates of a dependent variable (Y) by accounting for its relationship with an independent variable (X) is called *simple linear correlation and regression analysis*. (*Simple* refers to the two-variable case. With three or more variables we say *multiple correlation and regression analysis*, which is beyond the scope of this text.) The central idea behind simple linear correlation and regression is to use the formula for a straight line to obtain a best estimate of Y (e.g., weight in pounds) for any given value of X (e.g., any height in inches). We use the symbol $\acute{Y}$ (Y-cap) to refer to this estimated value of Y.

Central Idea behind Simple Linear Correlation and Regression Analysis

To use the formula for a straight line to improve best estimates of an interval/ratio dependent variable (Y) for all values of an interval/ratio independent variable (X).

The formula for a straight line to estimate Y is

$$\acute{Y} = a + bX$$

(You may have seen different symbols in geometry texts, where the straight-line formula is often presented as $\acute{Y} = mx + b$.) Before describing what each of the symbols in the formula signifies, we must grasp the circumstances in which this formula can be used accurately. First of all, this formula applies only when both variables are of interval/ratio or interval-like ordinal levels of measurement. Second, the formula can be used appropriately only when there is a linear relationship between X and Y on a scatterplot, a graphical representation of data. A **scatterplot** is *a two-dimensional grid* (like the lines on graph paper) *of the coordinates of two interval/ratio variables, X and Y. A* **coordinate** *is a point on a scatterplot where the values of X and Y are plotted for a case.* The statistics that accompany scatterplots apply only to situations in which the coordinates fall into a **linear pattern**—*one where the coordinates of the scatterplot fall into a cigar-shaped pattern that approximates the shape of a straight line.*

Graphical Representation of the Relationship between Two Interval/Ratio Variables

Scatterplot: A two-dimensional grid of the coordinates of two interval/ratio variables, X and Y.

Coordinate: A point on a scatterplot where the values of X and Y are plotted for a case.

Linear pattern: One where the coordinates of the scatterplot fall into a cigar-shaped pattern that approximates the shape of a straight line.

Drawing the Scatterplot

Table 14–1 presents data on the heights (X) and weights (Y) of 16 male high school seniors. Figure 14–1 presents the scatterplot of height (X) as a predictor of weight (Y). (For clarity, we do not draw the grid lines on the scatterplot; we simply imagine that they are there.) The coordinates of students 2 and 16 are highlighted in the table and the figure. A scatterplot is similar to a histogram; on both, the horizontal axis provides values of the interval/ratio variable X, and we call this the X-axis. The vertical axes of the two graphs are different, however. Recall that on a histogram, the vertical axis represents the frequency of occurrence (f) for a given value of X. But *on a scatterplot the vertical axis represents values of a second interval/ratio variable Y*, and we call this the Y-axis. Traditionally, X symbolizes the predictor (or independent) variable and Y symbolizes the dependent variable, the one we desire to explain.

TABLE 14–1   **Heights and Weights for 16 Male High School Seniors**

Student	Height (in inches) (X)	Weight (in pounds) (Y)
1	65	140
2	**66**	**144**
3	66	150
4	67	145
5	67	155
6	68	149
7	68	154
8	68	160
9	69	155
10	69	164
11	70	159
12	70	164
13	70	170
14	71	164
15	71	170
16	**72**	**176**

Coordinates are plotted by finding an *X*-score on the *X*-axis and a *Y*-score on the *Y*-axis and then locating the coordinate in the grid. For instance, student 16's *X,Y*-coordinate is $X = 72$ inches, $Y = 176$ pounds, or simply (72,176). It is plotted by moving over to 72 inches on the *X*-axis and then moving upward to 176 pounds on the *Y*-axis.

FIGURE 14–1

Scatterplot of height (X) as a predictor of weight (Y)

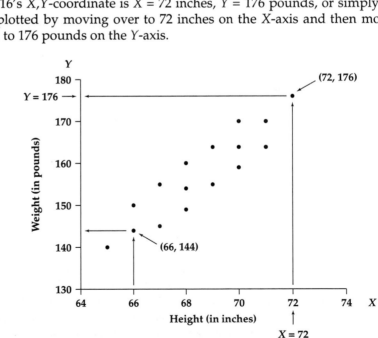

Identifying a Linear Pattern

On a scatterplot, a linear relationship is present if the coordinates fall into an elongated, cigar-shaped pattern that slopes up or down. The data in Figure 14–1 appear to fit an upward-sloping pattern. To get a sense of proportion about linear relationships, observe the actual numbers in Table 14–1, where the values of X and Y are rank-ordered from the shortest to the tallest heights. Note that as we move down the table column for heights, weights also tend to increase. This is an indication that the sizes of X and Y systematically change; that is, they shift upward together. In the scatterplot of Figure 14–1 this shift is apparent in the steady upward rise of the coordinates from left to right. The coordinates fit rather well into a cigar-shaped, linear pattern. As we increase height by moving over on the X-axis, the scores of Y (weight) also increase upward along the Y-axis. When both variables increase in tandem, we call this a positive relationship.

A Positive Correlation

An increase in X is related to an increase in Y. (As X increases, Y has a tendency to increase.)

The scatterplot in Figure 14–2 presents a negative relationship between two interval/ratio variables. The coordinates fit a cigar-shaped, linear pattern, but with a steady downward drop in the positions of the coordinates from left to right. An increase in caregiver role strain is related to a decrease in caregiver satisfaction with physician communication. As the X-scores go up, the Y-scores go down.

A Negative Correlation

An increase in X is related to a decrease in Y. (As X increases, Y has a tendency to decrease.)

Finally, what can we expect of a scatterplot if two variables are unrelated; that is, what if X is not a good predictor of Y? This is illustrated in Figure 14–3, where X is a caregiver's education and Y is the degree to which a patient can function without the caregiver's help. This scatterplot reveals no relationship between X and Y. The pattern of coordinates lacks an elongated, sloped cigar shape. When no correlation exists between X and Y, the mean of Y remains the best estimate of Y for all values of X. In other words, knowing a caregiver's education does not give us any information on how to improve a best estimate

FIGURE 14–2

Scatterplot of the negative relationship of caregiver satisfaction with physician communication regressed on caregiving role strain: As caregiving role strain increases, caregiver satisfaction with physician communication decreases

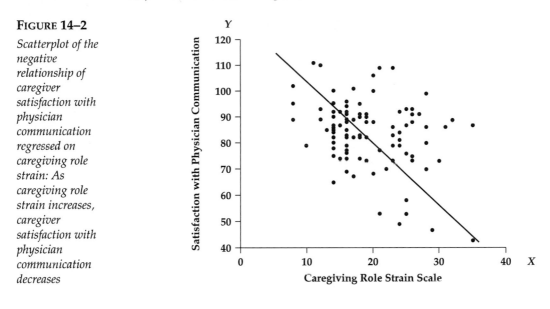

of a patient's ability to function without help. The medical condition of the patient has nothing to do with the educational level of the caregiver.

No Correlation

An increase in X is unrelated to the scores of Y. (As X increases, Y-scores vary randomly.)

FIGURE 14–3

Scatterplot of patient's ability to function without help regressed on caregiver education (shows no relationship between the two variables): Caregiver's educational level does not predict patient's ability to function

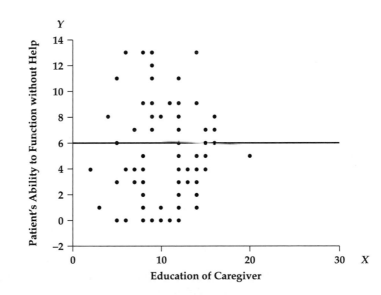

As you may have surmised, when we address the four aspects of a relationship in Chapter 15, the slope of pattern of coordinates in a scatterplot will convey the direction of a relationship.

Using the Linear Regression Equation to Measure the Effects of X on Y

When we find a distinctive linear pattern in the coordinates of a scatterplot, this tells us that the scores of a dependent variable Y follow those of an independent variable X either upward or downward. With knowledge of this predictable pattern we are equipped to adjust estimates of Y. For example, in Figure 14–1 we appear to have a positive relationship between height (X) and weight (Y). Thus, we know to provide a high estimate of weight if height is high (i.e., tall) and provide a low estimate of weight if height is low (i.e, on the shorter side). In fact, linear correlation and regression analysis allows us to make very fine mathematical adjustments in these estimates.

How can we make highly precise adjustments? If the scatterplot reveals a cigar-shaped, linear pattern of coordinates, a straight line can be drawn to "fit" the pattern of coordinates. This line is the *one that falls as close to every coordinate as possible* and is called the "best-fitting" line or, technically, the **regression line**. *Regression* means falling back or "gravitating" toward a point or having a tendency to move in a direction. For instance, we would predict that taller people tend to move in the heavy direction on weight. It is customary to say that the dependent variable (Y) "is regressed on" the independent variable (X). In this example we would say that weight is regressed on height.

The Regression Line

The best-fitting straight line plotted through the X,Y-coordinates of a scatterplot of two interval-ratio variables.

Figure 14–4 shows Figure 14–1 with the regression line drawn in. (We will discuss how to determine the precise location of this line below.) Once we have located this line, we can use coordinates on it to identify *the best estimate* of weight ($\acute{Y}$) for any amount of height (X). In Figure 14–4, two coordinates on the regression line, (67,150.23) and (72,173.33), are highlighted to show how X (height) is used to estimate Y (weight). The best estimate of the weight of a 67-inch-tall senior is 150.23 pounds; that of a 72-inch-tall senior, 173.33 pounds. In fact, we can use this line to estimate the weight of individuals of any height. We move over to a value of X on the X-axis and draw a perpendicular line up to the regression line. Then we draw a line from there over to the Y-axis; our best estimate of weight is the point where this line crosses the Y-axis. These values of X and Y will be coordinates that sit on the regression line. Note care-

FIGURE 14–4

Illustration of the regression line for height as a predictor of weight, that is, weight regressed on height

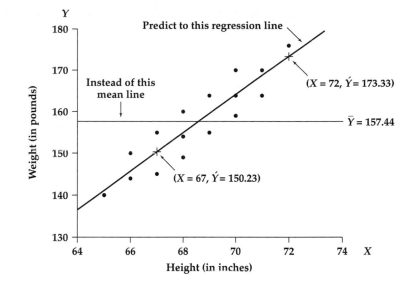

Predict to this regression line

Instead of this mean line

$(X = 72, \hat{Y} = 173.33)$

$\bar{Y} = 157.44$

$(X = 67, \hat{Y} = 150.23)$

Weight (in pounds)

Height (in inches)

fully that we call this estimate of weight the predicted Y and use the symbol $\hat{Y}$ to distinguish it from the actual observed weight of $Y = 164$ pounds. The $\hat{Y}$ is a "knowledgeable" estimate—*one based on knowing the precise relationship between height and weight.*

The key benefit of regression analysis is the ability to improve estimates of Y in a population by using the regression line instead of merely reporting the sample mean of Y. Remember that if we know nothing but the mean of Y, this mean is the best we can do in predicting weight. In Figure 14–4 note that we also drew the line representing the mean of Y. When we do not know a person's height, we always predict to this mean line for weight. Once we add the knowledge of a relationship with height, however, we can predict to a value of Y on the regression line—the $\hat{Y}$ that corresponds to a subject's X-score. Essentially, what linear regression analysis does is allow us to predict to the regression line rather than to the flat line that represents the mean of Y. When we do this, the resulting estimates are closer to the true values of Y. This can be observed in the scatterplot (Figure 14–4). The regression line is intentionally designed to get as close to the actual coordinates as possible. This line is the best fit.

Benefit of Regression Analysis for Improving Best Estimates of a Dependent Variable Y

Allows us to use an $X,\hat{Y}$-coordinate point on the regression line as a prediction of Y (in place of simply reporting the mean of Y).
$\hat{Y}$ = value of Y predicted by the regression line ($\hat{Y}$ is a knowledgeable estimate of Y based on knowing that Y is related to X)

For instance, if we are asked to estimate the weight of a high school senior *without* knowing his or her height, our best estimate would be 157.44 pounds—the total sample mean of Y computed from the data in Table 14–1. But if we know that height and weight are "linearly" related, we can place a straight line through the coordinates on the scatterplot and estimate a weight (Y) by finding its $X,\hat{Y}$-coordinate on this regression line. For instance, if this senior is rather tall at 72 inches, we will estimate his weight to be 173.33 pounds. In so doing, we are adding 15.89 pounds to the mean of 157.44 pounds to account for his above-average height.

Another way to look at the improvement in prediction is to view it in terms of proportional reduction in the error (PRE) of prediction. Suppose our 72-inch-tall student is named Christopher. Without knowledge of his height we would have had to predict his weight to be the mean of 157.44 pounds. Later, we find that he is case 16 in Table 14–1 with an actual weight of 176 pounds. The estimate "to the mean" misses his true weight by 18.56 pounds on the low side. (Recall from Chapter 6 that this amount is his deviation score.)

$$\text{Christopher's deviation score} = \text{error in estimating to the mean}$$
$$= Y_{(Christopher)} - \overline{Y} = 176 - 157.44 = 18.56 \text{ pounds}$$

Suppose that we have the opportunity to predict his weight again, but with knowledge of the relationship of height to weight. Instead of predicting to the mean, we predict "to the regression line" (Figure 14–4). The best estimate of a 72-inch-tall student is the $\hat{Y}$-score of 173.33. Using this as a knowledgeable estimate of Christopher's weight results in considerably less error—only 2.67 pounds compared to the error of 18.56 pounds when we predict to the mean:

$$\text{Error in estimating Christopher's weight to the regression line}$$
$$= Y_{(Christopher)} - \hat{Y}_{(X=72)} = 176 - 173.33 = 2.67 \text{ pounds}$$

We have improved this estimate of weight (Y) by a considerable amount by taking into account the fact that weight is correlated with height (X). As we can see by observing the scatterplot in Figure 14–4, error in predictions for the whole sample (and population) is reduced greatly if predictions are made to the regression line instead of the mean line.

In summary, when a relationship is found to exist between two interval/ratio variables, make best estimates by using the regression line rather than the mean. Knowledgeable estimates of Y—those taking into account X—reduce errors in predictions. This is the essence of correlation and regression analysis.

Pearson's *r* Correlation Coefficient

On a scatterplot, the tighter the fit of data coordinates around the regression line is, the stronger the correlation between X and Y is and the more precisely Y is estimated for any value of X. Pearson's r is a widely used correlation coefficient that measures tightness of fit of X,Y-coordinates around the regression line. The formula for Pearson's r is as follows:

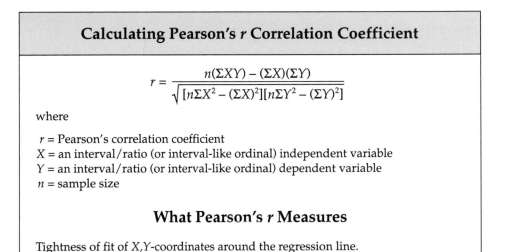

Calculating Pearson's r Correlation Coefficient

$$r = \frac{n(\Sigma XY) - (\Sigma X)(\Sigma Y)}{\sqrt{[n\Sigma X^2 - (\Sigma X)^2][n\Sigma Y^2 - (\Sigma Y)^2]}}$$

where

r = Pearson's correlation coefficient
X = an interval/ratio (or interval-like ordinal) independent variable
Y = an interval/ratio (or interval-like ordinal) dependent variable
n = sample size

What Pearson's r Measures

Tightness of fit of X,Y-coordinates around the regression line.

An Easy Computational Spreadsheet

To compute the statistics for this chapter, the following statistics and sums are needed:

$$n, X, Y, \Sigma X, \Sigma Y, \Sigma X^2, \Sigma Y^2, \Sigma XY$$

Using the data on heights and weights in Table 14–1, we can quickly compute these elements of the equations with the computational spreadsheet in Table 14–2.

The calculations and sums in the spreadsheet in Table 14–2 provide what is needed to compute Pearson's r for our data on the heights and weights of male high school seniors:

$$r = \frac{n(\Sigma XY) - (\Sigma X)(\Sigma Y)}{\sqrt{[n\Sigma X^2 - (\Sigma X)^2][n\Sigma Y^2 - (\Sigma Y)^2]}}$$

$$= \frac{16(172,995) - (1,097)(2,519)}{\sqrt{[16(75,275) - (1,097)^2][16(398,173) - (2,519)^2]}} = .91$$

Characteristics of the Pearson's r Correlation Coefficient

Computed values of Pearson's r can range from –1.0 to +1.0. The sign (+ or –) of r indicates the direction of a relationship. For the example in Figure 14–4 on the relationship between height and weight, we can see that the regression line

TABLE 14–2   **Spreadsheet for Computing Correlation and Regression Statistics: Heights and Weights for 16 Male High School Seniors**

| | Givens | | Calculations | | |
| | Height (in inches) | Weight (in pounds) | | | |
Student	X	Y	X^2	Y^2	XY
1	65	140	4,225	19,600	9,100
2	66	144	4,356	20,736	9,504
3	66	150	4,356	22,500	9,900
4	67	145	4,489	21,025	9,715
5	67	155	4,489	24,025	10,385
6	68	149	4,624	22,201	10,132
7	68	154	4,624	23,716	10,472
8	68	160	4,624	25,600	10,880
9	69	155	4,761	24,025	10,695
10	69	164	4,761	26,896	11,316
11	70	159	4,900	25,281	11,130
12	70	164	4,900	26,896	11,480
13	70	170	4,900	28,900	11,900
14	71	164	5,041	26,896	11,644
15	71	170	5,041	28,900	12,070
16	72	176	5,184	30,976	12,672

$\Sigma X = 1,097$ $\Sigma X^2 = 75,275$ $\Sigma XY = 172,995$

$n = 16$ $\Sigma Y = 2,519$ $\Sigma Y^2 = 398,173$

slopes upward: Low values of X correspond with low values of Y, and high values of X correspond with high values of Y. The upward slope indicates that the direction of the relationship is positive, and the Pearson's r calculates to a positive value. When r = +1.0, this is a (very unusual) perfect positive correlation, meaning that X is a perfect predictor of Y and that as X increases, Y increases. With a perfect positive correlation, every coordinate of the scatterplot rests on the regression line itself, and the line slopes upward.

When X and Y are correlated in the negative direction, the regression line of the scatterplot slopes downward so that as X increases, Y decreases. Pearson's r will calculate to a negative value. For example, the greater the number of poor people living in a community (X), the lower the rate of home ownership (Y). When r = –1.0, we have a (very unusual) perfect negative correlation, meaning that X is a perfect predictor of Y and that as X increases, Y decreases. With a perfect negative correlation, every coordinate of the scatterplot rests on the downward-sloping regression line. Perfect correlations in either the positive or the negative direction are unusual, especially in the social sciences.

The absolute value of Pearson's r (its size, ignoring its sign) indicates the tightness of fit of coordinates around the regression line of a scatterplot. The larger the absolute value of Pearson's *r* is, the closer coordinates cling to the line. For the plot of Figure 14–4 the coordinates fit rather tightly around the regression line, as reflected in the rather large Pearson's *r* of .91.

As we noted above, when we have *no correlation* between *X* and *Y*, knowing the values of *X* does not improve estimates of *Y*. This is the case in Figure 14–3. With no correlation, *r* = 0. Another example of no correlation is weight as a predictor of GPA; knowing how much people weigh tells us nothing about their GPAs.

The characteristics of Pearson's *r* can be summarized as follows:

Characteristics of the Pearson's *r* Correlation Coefficient

1. Computed values of Pearson's *r* can range from –1.0 to +1.0.
2. The larger the absolute value of Pearson's *r*, the tighter the fit of *X,Y*-coordinates around the regression line.
3. When the regression line slopes upward, we have a positive correlation: An *increase* in the level of *X*-scores is related to an *increase* in the level of *Y*-scores. Pearson's *r* will be positive up to a value of +1.00.
4. When the regression line slopes downward, we have a negative correlation: An *increase* in the level of *X*-scores is related to a *decrease* in the level of *Y*-scores. Pearson's *r* will be negative down to a value of –1.00.
5. When the regression line is flat (i.e., has no slope), we have no correlation and Pearson's *r* = 0. An *increase* in the level of *X*-scores is *not* related to a change in the level of *Y*-scores. That is, knowing an *X*-score does not improve an estimate of *Y*-scores.

Regression Statistics

Now that we have a general idea of how a straight line in a scatterplot can be used to make better estimates of *Y* if we know *X*, let us discuss how to make precise mathematical calculations of these estimates. For instance, let us continue to examine the correlation between height and weight by using the spreadsheet in Table 14–2 and the scatterplot of Figure 14–4. Now that we know that height and weight are related, we can adjust estimates of weight by taking into account the fact that taller boys are heavier than shorter boys. We can answer the question: In general, how many extra pounds should be added or subtracted to any estimate of weight for a particular height? Specifically, what are the best estimates of weight for male high school seniors of various heights? Answers are established with the following formula for a straight line:

Linear Equation Formula (or Regression Line Formula) for the Relationship between Two Interval/Ratio Variables

$$\hat{Y} = a + bX$$

where

$\hat{Y}$ = "the predicted Y" (an estimate of the dependent variable Y computed for a given value of the independent variable X)

a = Y-intercept, the point at which the regression line intersects the Y-axis when $X = 0$

b = slope of the regression line (called the regression coefficient)

To use this formula, we start by calculating the values of a and b. Once a and b are plugged into the formula, any number of inches of height, or X-scores, can be substituted for X in the formula. Then we solve for $\hat{Y}$—the best estimate of weight for that number of inches of height. The resulting $X,\hat{Y}$-coordinates will fit onto a straight line that best fits the pattern of coordinates on the scatterplot. Before calculating the elements of this formula, let us examine each term.

The Regression Coefficient or Slope, b

In the regression equation $\hat{Y} = a + bX$, b is the *slope* of the regression line and is called the *regression coefficient*. The regression coefficient tells us how many pounds to add to an estimate of weight for each additional one-inch increase in height.

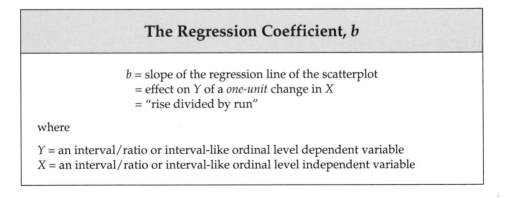

The Regression Coefficient, *b*

b = slope of the regression line of the scatterplot

  = effect on Y of a *one-unit* change in X

  = "rise divided by run"

where

Y = an interval/ratio or interval-like ordinal level dependent variable

X = an interval/ratio or interval-like ordinal level independent variable

---

What does the slope convey? For our data on the heights and weights of high school senior boys, $b = 4.62$ pounds per inch. A one-unit change in X would be one inch. To interpret this slope we would say that "a one-inch increase in the level of height is related to a 4.62-pound increase in the level of weight."

As with jogging up or down a hill, the slope tells us how much rise (a vertical gain of b on Y) we accomplish when we run one mile (a horizontal gain or "run" of one unit on X). For example, if the slope of a mountainside road is 300 feet per mile, for every mile we jog, we rise 300 feet in elevation. The larger the value of b, the steeper the slope. If a jogger elsewhere is rising 600 feet per mile, he or she is running up a much steeper hill. Figure 14–5 illustrates how the size of b conveys the steepness of the slope.

The Y-intercept, a

The Y-intercept, a, in the regression equation $\acute{Y} = a + bX$ is the value of Y when $X = 0$. The Y-intercept is called the *constant* of the equation. Whereas the equation multiplies the slope b by different X-scores, we add the same (a constant)

FIGURE 14–5

Illustration of the slope as the ratio of a vertical change in Y to a horizontal change of one unit in X

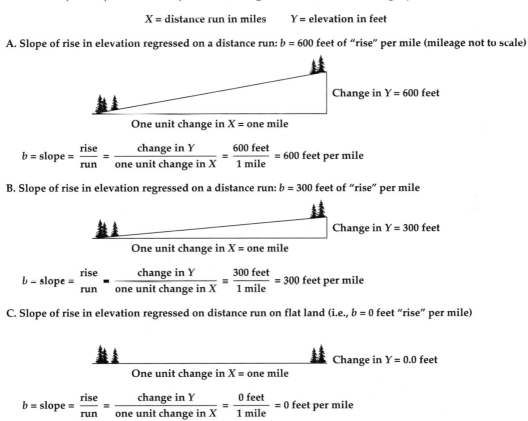

X = distance run in miles Y = elevation in feet

A. Slope of rise in elevation regressed on a distance run: b = 600 feet of "rise" per mile (mileage not to scale)

Change in Y = 600 feet

One unit change in X = one mile

$$b = \text{slope} = \frac{\text{rise}}{\text{run}} = \frac{\text{change in } Y}{\text{one unit change in } X} = \frac{600 \text{ feet}}{1 \text{ mile}} = 600 \text{ feet per mile}$$

B. Slope of rise in elevation regressed on a distance run: b = 300 feet of "rise" per mile

Change in Y = 300 feet

One unit change in X = one mile

$$b = \text{slope} = \frac{\text{rise}}{\text{run}} = \frac{\text{change in } Y}{\text{one unit change in } X} = \frac{300 \text{ feet}}{1 \text{ mile}} = 300 \text{ feet per mile}$$

C. Slope of rise in elevation regressed on distance run on flat land (i.e., b = 0 feet "rise" per mile)

Change in Y = 0.0 feet

One unit change in X = one mile

$$b = \text{slope} = \frac{\text{rise}}{\text{run}} = \frac{\text{change in } Y}{\text{one unit change in } X} = \frac{0 \text{ feet}}{1 \text{ mile}} = 0 \text{ feet per mile}$$

amount of *a* to each calculation. As we will calculate below, for our data on heights and weights, $a = -159.31$ pounds. We may view this quantity as a starting point from which to add or subtract amounts of bX.

What does *a* do? It anchors the regression line to the *Y*-axis. This is necessary because there can be any number of independent variables (*X*'s) that correlate with *Y and* have the same slope but different magnitudes of *Y*. Or there can be different populations with the same slopes but different *Y*-intercepts. Having the same slopes, *b*, these regression lines would be parallel to one another on a scatterplot and would be distinguishable only by their constants, *a*. Finally, note that the *Y*-intercept is often a hypothetical point because there may be no case where $X = 0$. For example, no one in a population can have a height of zero. Thus, it is not unusual for *a* to calculate to an impractical value such as *minus* 159.31 pounds.

The *Y*-intercept, *a* (the constant of the regression equation)

a = *Y*-intercept of the regression line of a scatterplot
= the point where the regression line intersects the *Y*-axis when $X = 0$
= the predicted value of *Y* when $X = 0$ (i.e., $\acute{Y}_{(X=0)}$)

where

Y = an interval/ratio or interval-like ordinal level dependent variable
X = an interval/ratio or interval-like ordinal level independent variable.

Calculating the Terms of the Regression Line Formula

To compile the linear equation formula $\acute{Y} = a + bX$, we first compute *b* as follows:

Calculating the Regression Coefficient *b*, the Slope of the Regression Line

$$b = \frac{n(\Sigma XY) - (\Sigma X)(\Sigma Y)}{n\Sigma X^2 - (\Sigma X)^2}$$

where

b = regression coefficient (the slope of the regression line)
X = an interval/ratio (or interval-like ordinal) level independent variable
Y = an interval/ratio (or interval-like ordinal) level dependent variable
n = sample size

We then compute a by substituting the calculated value of b into the equation $\hat{Y} = a + bX$. But in order to solve for a, we must stipulate known values of X and Y. As it turns out, on any regression line, the coordinate of the means of X and Y will fall on the line. Thus, we can substitute the means of X and Y, along with b, and solve for a. The means of X and Y are computed as follows:

$$\bar{X} = \frac{\Sigma X}{n}$$

$$\bar{Y} = \frac{\Sigma Y}{n}$$

Once b, $\bar{X}$, and $\bar{Y}$ have been computed, we solve for a as follows:

Calculating the Y-intercept, *a*

$$a = \bar{Y} - b\bar{X}$$

where

a = Y-intercept
$\bar{Y}$ = mean of the dependent variable
b = regression coefficient (the slope of the regression line)
$\bar{X}$ = mean of the independent variable.

Finally, we insert a and b into the regression line formula:

$$\hat{Y} = a + bX$$

Let us now compute the regression line statistics for weight regressed on height (Figure 14–4). Taking sums from the computational spreadsheet in Table 14–2, we first compute b:

$$b = \frac{n(\Sigma XY) - (\Sigma X)(\Sigma Y)}{n\Sigma X^2 - (\Sigma X)^2}$$

$$= \frac{16(172,995) - (1,097)(2,519)}{16(75,275) - (1,097)^2} = 4.62 \text{ pounds per inch}$$

Next we compute $\bar{X}$ and $\bar{Y}$:

$$\bar{X} = \frac{\Sigma X}{n} = \frac{1,097}{16} = 68.56 \text{ inches}$$

$$\bar{Y} = \frac{\Sigma Y}{n} = \frac{2,519}{16} = 157.44 \text{ pounds}$$

Next we use $\bar{X}, \bar{Y}$ and b to compute a:

$$a = \bar{Y} - b\bar{X} = 157.44 - (4.62)(68.56) = -159.31 \text{ pounds}$$

Finally, we specify the precise equation for the regression line that fits the scatterplot of weight regressed on height by substituting the computed values of a and b (Figure 14–4):

$$\hat{Y} = a + bX = -159.31 + (4.62)X$$

This regression equation now may be used to calculate $\hat{Y}$, the "best estimate" of Y (weight) for any value of X (height). We insert a few X-scores into the equation and solve for $\hat{Y}$ to get the results in Table 14–3.

We plot the regression line by marking two or more of these $X, \hat{Y}$-coordinates on the scatterplot and drawing a straight line between them. This is shown above in Figure 14–4, where the coordinates (67,150.23) and (72,173.33) are used as reference points for the line. Double-check the accuracy of the line by finding on Figure 14–4 the other $X, \hat{Y}$-coordinates computed in Table 14–3. These coordinates will fall in a straight line. Note also that although the Y-intercept is *minus* 159.31 pounds, the regression line crosses the Y-axis at about a positive 140 pounds. This discrepancy is due to the fact that the values of X and Y where their axes intersect are not zeros. Instead, the X and Y axes, as drawn, start at about 65 inches and 130 pounds, respectively. This is not a mistake. The axes of the plot have been "truncated" (or shortened) for clarity of presentation.

TABLE 14–3   **$X, \hat{Y}$-Coordinates: Best Estimates of Weights ($\hat{Y}$) of the Population of Male High School Seniors Based on Heights (X)**

Givens	Calculations	
X *(height in inches)*	$\hat{Y}(= a + bX)$ *(best estimate of weight in pounds)*	*Important Points about the Characteristics of the Linear Equation $\hat{Y} = a + bX$*
0	−159.31 ←	The Y-intercept is sometimes a computational
65	140.99	abstraction; it may not exist in reality.
66	145.61	
67	150.23	
68	154.85	
68.56	157.44 ←	The coordinate ($\bar{X}, \bar{Y}$) will always be on the
69	159.47	regression line.
70	164.09	
	> ←	The difference in weight (Y) between any two
71	168.71	heights (X) that are one inch apart is the slope, b
	> ←	= 4.62 pounds.
72	173.33	
73	177.95	

FIGURE 14–6

*A scatterplot
lacking truncated
axes: Height as a
predictor of weight*

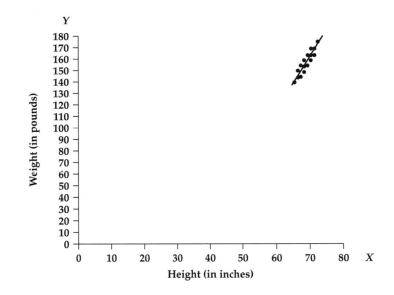

Why Truncate the Axes of the Scatterplot? Sometimes the interval/ratio variables of a scatterplot have many values that are impractical. For our illustration using the variables height and weight, no high school seniors are, say, 19 inches tall or weigh only 30 pounds. In the scatterplots of weight regressed on height we truncated, or shortened, the axes for each variable to make the scatterplot appear balanced on the page. Figure 14–6 presents the scatterplot for the data in Figure 14–4 without truncating the axes. The value of truncating should be obvious when Figures 14–4 and 14–6 are compared.

The "Formulas" section at the end of this chapter provides a step-by-step procedure for calculating correlation and regression statistics. In Chapter 15 we will use correlation and regression statistics to test hypotheses about the relationship between two interval/ratio variables.

☹   STATISTICAL FOLLIES AND FALLACIES   ☹

The Failure to Observe a Scatterplot before Calculating Pearson's *r*

Linear Equations Work Only with a Linear Pattern in the Scatterplot

Eager to see his or her results, a researcher may be tempted to skip the tedious task of drawing and observing scatterplots. Even with computers this task is somewhat time-consuming. It is a mistake, however, to proceed without observing a scatterplot. Linear regression statistics are based on predicting from the straight line produced by the formula $\hat{Y} = a + bX$. If the coordinates do not fit around a straight line, the predictions of Y based on X (i.e., the $\hat{Y}$s) will not be close to the observed values of Y. Simply put, the line will not fit the pattern of coordinates; therefore, predictions made by using such a misplaced line will be erroneous. Linear regression statistics are not appropriate for nonlinear (or curvilinear) relationships such as the one shown in Figure 14–7. In Figure 14–7, each dot (coordinate) represents a neighborhood (using fictional data). The position on the X-axis indicates the percentage of the neighborhood's population that is of minority status (i.e., African-American, Asian-American, Native American, and Hispanic racial/ethnic classifications). The position on the Y-axis represents the number of hate crimes occurring in the neighborhood over a period of time. This curvilinear plot tells us that hate crimes occur *in*frequently when the size of the minority population is either very low or very high. When the minority population is very low, it poses no threat to the majority white population. When the minority population is very high, hate-filled whites feel outnumbered and are afraid to act on their feelings. Hate crimes are highest when minority and white populations are roughly equal and are "contesting for control" of the neighborhood. The shape of this curve is an inverted parabola, and its equation—not the equation for a straight line—would be used to estimate the number of hate crimes based on the size of the minority population. [The equation for an inverted parabola is $\hat{Y} = [-c_1(X + c_2)^2] + c_3$, where the c's symbolize constants that establish the width of the parabola and the location of its vortex (i.e., its peak).] If the linear equation is used mistakenly, the resulting linear regression line (indicated in Figure 14–7) is a poor fit to the pattern of coordinates. Estimates made from this line will be erroneous.

FIGURE 14–7

Scatterplot of incidence of hate crimes against minority members of neighborhoods regressed on percentage of minority population in neighborhood (shows nonlinear relationship)

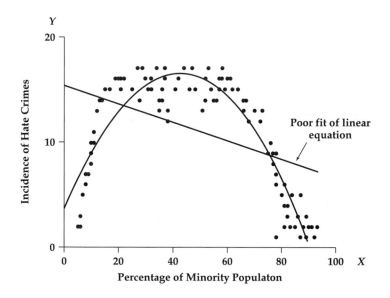

Analysis of curvilinear relationships is beyond the scope of this text. If the coordinates in a scatterplot do not fit the cigar-shaped, linear pattern, the statistics in this chapter do not apply. Fortunately, a linear pattern between interval/ratio variables is extremely common. It is important, however, to observe a scatterplot for nonlinear patterns such as that in Figure 14–7.

Outlier Coordinates and the Attenuation and Inflation of Correlation Coefficients

Note that we used the means of X and Y to calculate the correlation coefficient r and the regression line equation. All these statistics are "mean-based." As we discussed in Chapter 4, the mean is susceptible to distortion by extreme scores, or "outliers," in a variable's score distribution. Similarly, in the coordinates of a scatterplot, a few extreme or **outlier coordinates**—*ones that fall way outside the overall pattern of the scatterplot*—may distort correlation and regression coefficients. If they are significant, these distortions can cause the regression line to misfit the data on the scatterplot. Outlier coordinates may weaken or "attenuate" the correlation and regression coefficients computed with them.

Attenuation of correlation is *the weakening or reduction of correlation and regression coefficients*. An attenuated correlation will produce a small Pearson's r and therefore may cause us to conclude that a relationship between two interval/ratio variables does not exist when in fact it does.

Attenuation of Correlation

The weakening or reduction of correlation and regression coefficients (often as a result of the presence of outlier coordinates).

The following scatterplot illustrates attenuation resulting from an outlier coordinate for the weights and heights of male high school seniors. Suppose that unintentionally a member of the basketball team is included in our sample. This player is a tall, skinny guy with a height of 73 inches but a weight of only 146 pounds. Figure 14–8 shows the scatterplot of the new data. The basketball player's X,Y-coordinate (73,146) is an outlier coordinate, and regression lines are presented with and without it. The different locations of the regression lines reveal that the addition of this single outlier shifts the regression line away from the linear pattern found in the remaining cases. This attenuated regression line is not useful in predicting weights from heights. Moreover, the addition of this single outlier coordinate reduces or "attenuates" the correlation coefficient from our original value of .91 to a mere .64 (calculations not shown). The potential for attenuation of correlation is another important reason for observing the scatterplot before proceeding with correlational analysis.

FIGURE 14–8

Illustration of attenuation resulting from outlier coordinates: weight (Y) regressed on height (X)

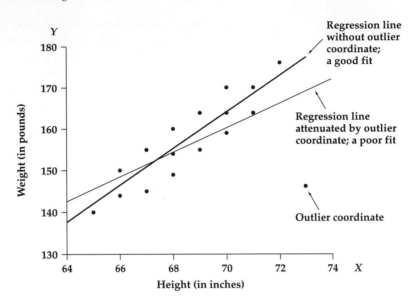

Just as an outlier coordinate may weaken coefficients, they also may inflate them. We found in Figure 14–3 that there was no relationship between a caregiver's education and a patient's ability to function without help. Suppose now that the sample included the three outlier coordinates in Figure 14–9. These outliers pull the calculated regression line upward, giving it a positive slope. Moreover, the Pearson's *r* increases from zero (i.e., no relationship) to .46 (i.e., a positive relationship; calculations not shown). Outlier coordinates

FIGURE 14–9

*Illustration of inflation of Pearson's **r** as a result of outlier coordinates: patient's ability to function independently (Y) regressed on caregiver's education (X) (compare to Figure 14–3)*

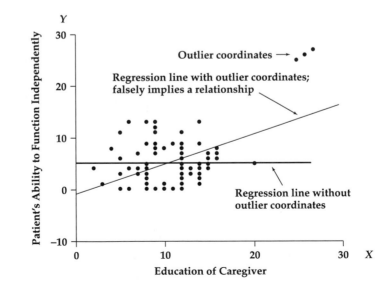

that inflate correlation and regression coefficients lead to the false conclusion that a relationship exists when in fact it does not.

How can we avoid attenuation or inflation of coefficients? Often one or two outlier coordinates can be explained by circumstances and can be justifiably excluded from the analysis. In the attenuation case in Figure 14–8, we could eliminate the basketball player and report the stronger correlation of $r = .91$. Our report would say that except for especially tall thin seniors such as basketball players, height is a moderately strong predictor of weight for male high school seniors. Similarly, for the inflated coefficients of the caregiver example (Figure 14–9) we might declare that the outlier coordinates are random cases that do not fit the overall pattern. In either figure, the scatterplot reveals that using the regression lines based on these outlier data would not provide good estimates.

In everyday research circumstances, much potential exists for attenuation or inflation of correlation, especially if the researcher is not savvy about the makeup of his or her data and its population of origin. For example, in a study of factory workers and the relationship of time employed (X) to pay scale (Y), it would be a mistake to mix managers (who are highly paid) and assembly line workers in the same sample. Managers who have been employed for even a short time may have very high salaries, and their coordinates will land high up in the left-hand side of a scatterplot.

A second example would be a study of states and the relationship of population size (X) to divorce rates (Y). The inclusion of Nevada with its exorbitantly high divorce rates would greatly distort the results. Most divorces in Nevada are for people from other states. In recognition of this commonly known fact, Nevada could be excluded and the results could be reported as "with the exception of Nevada."

Finally, the potential for attenuation or inflation of correlation and regression coefficients highlights the desirability of a large sample. As with any mean-based statistics, the more opportunities in sampling to compensate for the effect of outlier coordinates, the weaker their effects on predictions of Y based on knowing X. In other words, it is desirable to have many degrees of freedom.

Statistical Procedures Covered to Here

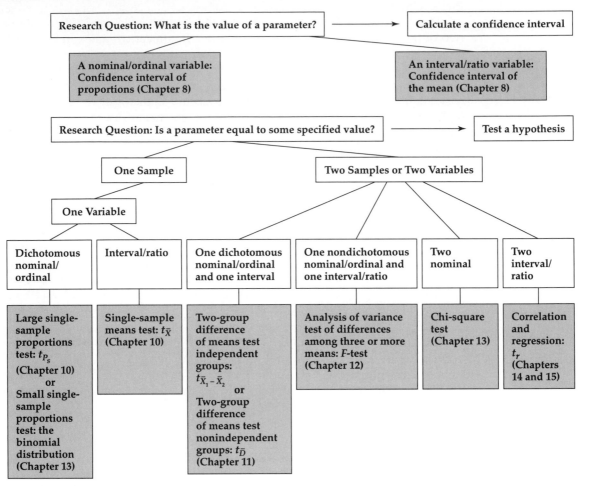

Formulas in Chapter 14

Calculation of statistics for examining the relationship between two interval/ratio variables (see formulas in Chapter 15 for the hypothesis test):

Given: Two interval/ratio or interval-like ordinal variables

1. Determine which of the two variables is the dependent variable (Y) and which is the independent variable (X).
2. Organize a spreadsheet of X,Y-coordinates and compute the sums:

	Givens			Calculations	
Case	X	Y	X^2	Y^2	XY
1	...	...	...	...	...
2	...	...	...	...	...
.	...	...	...	...	...
n	...	...	...	...	...
	$\Sigma X = ...$		$\Sigma X^2 = ...$		$\Sigma XY = ...$
$n = ...$		$\Sigma Y = ...$		$\Sigma Y^2 = ...$	

3. Draw a scatterplot to see if a linear pattern is present in the X,Y-coordinates.

4. Compute the Pearson's r correlation coefficient:

$$r = \frac{n(\Sigma XY) - (\Sigma X)(\Sigma Y)}{\sqrt{[n\Sigma X^2 - (\Sigma X)^2][n\Sigma Y^2 - (\Sigma Y)^2]}}$$

5. Compute the regression coefficient b:

$$b = \frac{n(\Sigma XY) - (\Sigma X)(\Sigma Y)}{n\Sigma X^2 - (\Sigma X)^2}$$

6. Compute the means of X and Y:

$$\bar{X} = \frac{\Sigma X}{n}$$

$$\bar{Y} = \frac{\Sigma Y}{n}$$

7. Use $\bar{X}$, $\bar{Y}$, and b to compute the Y-intercept, a:

$$a = \bar{Y} - b\bar{X}$$

8. Specify the precise regression line equation for calculating $\acute{Y}$'s (i.e., predicted values of Y) by substituting the computed values of a and b:

$$\acute{Y} = a + bX$$

9. Insert two or three values of X into the regression equation and solve for $\acute{Y}$. Use the resulting $X,\acute{Y}$-coordinates to plot the regression line on the scatterplot.

Questions for Chapter 14

1. With the help of a hand-sketched scatterplot and the regression equation $\acute{Y}$ = $a + bX$, explain the central idea behind regression analysis.

2. With the help of hand-sketched scatterplots, illustrate why linear correlation and regression analysis apply only when there is a cigar-shaped, linear pattern of coordinates.

3. With the help of hand-sketched scatterplots, illustrate the pattern of coordinates for positive, negative, and no relationships between X and Y.

4. With the help of hand-sketched scatterplots, illustrate why it sometimes is necessary to truncate the axis of a scatterplot.

5. What does Pearson's r correlation coefficient measure?

6. What does the regression coefficient b measure?

7. On the regression line, the Y-intercept, a, is the value of $\acute{Y}$ where $X =$ _____ .

8. With a linear relationship between two interval/ratio variables, what is the X,Y-coordinate that will always fall on the regression line?

9. Match the following regarding the direction of correlations:

   a. A positive correlation _____ The regression line has no slope; $r = 0$ and $b = 0$

   b. No correlation _____ The regression line slopes downward; r and b have a negative sign; an increase in X is related to a decrease in Y

   c. A negative correlation _____ The regression line slopes upward; r and b have a positive sign; an increase in X is related to an increase in Y.

10. Attenuation or inflation of the calculation of correlation and regression coefficients can result from the presence of _____ in the scatterplot.

Exercises for Chapter 14

General instructions: Show all sums and formulas.

1. An instructor with 16 students gives midterm and final examinations. She is interested in whether the midterm score is a good predictor of the final exam score. Her data are listed below.

   a. Decide which variable is independent and which is dependent and draw the scatterplot.

   b. Calculate the regression line statistics and plot the line.

   c. Calculate the Pearson's r correlation coefficient.

   d. Does there appear to be a linear relationship in the pattern of test score coordinates?

Midterm Exam Score	Final Exam Score
78	83
91	82
95	91
74	81
87	85
83	87
89	83
92	97
94	98
58	66
71	79
76	84
87	91
91	92
77	75
85	89

2. As the personnel director of a company, it is your responsibility to assure merit-based equity in salary levels. In other words, salary level should roughly parallel educational qualifications. The following are the salary levels and years of education of 15 employees who have been with the company for five years.

   a. Decide which variable is independent and which is dependent and draw the scatterplot.
   b. Calculate the regression line statistics and plot the line. To simplify, calculate salary in thousands of dollars (e.g., $22,500 = 22.5).
   c. Calculate the Pearson's r correlation coefficient.
   d. Does there appear to be a linear relationship in the pattern of coordinates?

Years of Education	Salary
12	$22,500
12	17,900
11	16,500
16	29,600
16	34,500
18	42,600
17	45,800
16	24,000
12	22,300
10	14,000
12	13,700
19	54,000
18	34,000
14	25,000
13	21,400

3. The following are data from a sample of 23 underclass students (first year students and sophomores) at Tuffstuff University.

 a. Draw the scatterplot for GPA (*Y*) regressed on reading comprehension score (*X*).
 b. *Without making any computations*, draw what appears to be the best-fitting straight line through the plot of the coordinates.
 c. *Without making any calculations*, estimate *a* and *b* in the regression equation $\hat{Y} = a + bX$.
 d. Now compute the regression statistics for the relationship of reading comprehension to GPA and plot the regression line.
 e. Compare your computed statistics to those you estimated in parts (*a*) and (*b*) to make sure you understand what each statistic means.

Student	GPA	Reading Comprehension Score	Hours of Study per Class Session
1	0.90	2	2.00
2	1.12	3	1.25
3	1.46	2	2.50
4	1.93	4	5.00
5	2.00	3	3.00
6	2.16	3	4.15
7	2.18	2	4.72
8	2.21	3	5.75
9	2.33	4	6.13
10	2.39	6	4.75
11	2.46	5	4.25
12	2.54	6	4.84
13	2.68	5	5.75
14	2.73	4	6.00
15	2.85	7	5.89
16	2.87	6	6.37
17	2.93	8	6.50
18	2.99	7	7.00
19	3.04	9	6.00
20	3.14	8	6.93
21	3.22	9	7.16
22	3.27	9	6.94
23	3.28	8	8.10

4. For the data in the table in exercise 3, hours of study per class session was measured by equipping students with an electronic time counter that could be turned on and off as a student studied.

 a. Draw the scatterplot for GPA (*Y*) regressed on hours of study per class session (*X*).
 b. *Without making any computations*, draw what appears to be the best-fitting straight line through the plot of the coordinates.

     c. Without making any calculations, estimate *a* and *b* in the regression
       equation $\hat{Y} = a + bX$.
     d. Now compute the regression statistics for the relationship of hours
       of study to GPA and plot the regression line.
     e. Compare your computed statistics to those you estimated in parts
       (*a*) and (*b*) to make sure you understand what each statistic means.

5. As an employee of a health consumer watchdog agency, you track the
activities of health maintenance organizations (HMOs). HMOs have been
criticized for pushing people too quickly out of hospitals to save money
and increase profits. You examine angioplasty procedures done at
hospitals owned by 12 HMOs. The fictional data below are the average
reductions in the length of stay for these patients in days and the
percentage increase in profits for the HMOs over the past year.

     a. Draw the scatterplot for percentage increase in profits (*Y*) regressed
       on reduction in length of stay (*X*).
     b. Compute the regression statistics and plot the regression line.
     c. Calculate Pearson's *r* correlation coefficient.
     d. Does there appear to be a linear relationship in the pattern of
       coordinates?

Average Reduction in Length of Stay (days)	Percentage Increase in Profits
1.3	2.9
2.2	15.3
2.3	13.9
1.7	6.3
1.9	10.4
1.0	.8
2.1	15.3
1.6	13.1
2.2	8.9
1.4	6.8
1.3	11.5
1.9	11.4

6. Disability days are the number of days individuals are unable to engage in
their regular activities because of illness or injury. Disability days are
related to risks in workplace and home environments, which in turn are
closely related to income levels. The following data are indicative of the
pattern of disability days per year as they relate to total family income (in
thousands of dollars).

     a. Draw the scatterplot for total family income (*Y*) regressed on
       disability days (*X*).
     b. Compute the regression statistics and plot the regression line.

c. Calculate Pearson's *r* correlation coefficient.

d. Does there appear to be a linear relationship in the pattern of coordinates?

Family Income	Disability Days
5	27
15	19
28	14
40	10
6	29
14	21
26	13
37	6

7. One measure of the poverty level of a county is the percentage of children who qualify for free lunches at school. The following spreadsheet includes this "% pupils with free lunch" variable (*X*) as well as a composite measure of how well the county's pupils scored on the SAT college entrance examination (average system SAT) (*Y*).

a. Draw the scatterplot for *Y* regressed on *X*.

b. Calculate Pearson's *r* correlation coefficient.

c. Note the outlier coordinates in the scatterplot. Identify them in the spreadsheet.

d. Recalculate Pearson's *r* without these outlier coordinates.

e. Comment on the effect of the outlier coordinates on the calculation of Pearson's *r* correlation coefficient.

Average System SAT	% Pupils with Free Lunch
68	34
71	15
56	37
61	33
39	75
65	73
47	59
57	40
43	79
69	69
54	59
55	38
70	17
63	36

8. Suppose you are studying skill development among 14-year-old pianists in a city music club and wonder if time of membership in the club (X) is related to the number of awards and trophies won (Y) in recital competitions.

    a. Draw the scatterplot for Y regressed on X.

    b. Calculate Pearson's *r* correlation coefficient.

    c. Note the outlier coordinate in the scatterplot. Identify it in the spreadsheet.

    d. Recalculate Pearson's *r* without this outlier coordinate.

    e. Comment on the effect of an outlier coordinate on the calculation of Pearson's *r* correlation coefficient.

Years in Music Club	*Merit Awards and Trophies*
4	5
6	6
2	1
3	4
2	7
1	2
3	3
5	4
4	4

Optional Computer Applications for Chapter 14

If your class uses the optional computer applications that accompany this text, open the Chapter 14 exercises on the *Computer Applications for The Statistical Imagination* compact disk. With instructions on producing scatterplots and correlation-regression statistics, these exercises emphasize understanding the relationship between the shape of a scatterplot and the size of Pearson's *r*.

CORRELATION AND REGRESSION

Part 2: Hypothesis Testing and Aspects of a Relationship

Introduction: Hypothesis Test and Aspects of a Relationship between Two Interval/Ratio Variables

In Chapter 14 we introduced the basic ideas behind correlation and regression analysis and the computation of coefficients. In this chapter we will use those statistics to test hypotheses about the relationship between two interval/ratio or interval-like ordinal variables.

To illustrate the hypothesis test, let us examine the relationship between level of education and acceptance of "lowbrow" music—styles associated with political protest, the lower classes, and ethnic and racial minorities (Bryson 1996, Peterson and Kern 1996). This type of music stands in contrast to "highbrow" music such as classical symphonic, chamber, and opera music; swing; show tunes; easy listening; "soft rock"; and popular music that is light on sexuality. The styles of music favored by a society are viewed by some individuals as symbolic of that society's moral character. A small but vocal minority points to lowbrow music as a form of deviance and a clear sign of moral decline. Even the middle class in American society takes issue with musical forms that have countercultural elements that challenge the dominant social, moral, and political systems. Some parents fear that heavy metal and politically charged rap music will corrupt the morals of their children. Other popular musical styles—those associated with the lower classes and ethnic minorities—evoke class prejudices and racist sentiments among some people. Such styles include rap, reggae, blues, rhythm and blues, rock and roll, alternative rock, heavy metal, country and western, Latin, contemporary jazz, and nontraditional contemporary Christian music.

What accounts for differences in how people evaluate and accept various forms of music? Among the predictor variables typically examined are age, race, gender, marital status, political opinions, religious affiliation, and education (Bryson 1996, Peterson and Kern 1996). One research hypothesis is that better-educated persons are more accepting—more tolerant—of lowbrow musical styles.

Organizing Data for the Hypothesis Test

Suppose we investigate this hypothesis by using questionnaire data from a sample of 12 mothers of high school students. These parents are asked to rate assorted musical styles. We then sum up the number of lowbrow styles each mother tolerates (i.e., considers acceptable for her teenage children) and call this variable lowbrow tolerance. The higher the score is, the more favorable a mother is toward lowbrow styles. The educational level of the mothers is operationalized as the number of years of formal schooling completed.

Let us follow the "Formulas" section toward the end of Chapter 14. We start by establishing which is the independent variable and which is the dependent variable. In this case we are interested in explaining lowbrow

TABLE 15–1   **Spreadsheet for Computing Correlation and Regression Statistics: Education Levels and Lowbrow Tolerance of 12 Mothers of High School Students (*X* = education level in years of education, *Y* = number of lowbrow styles tolerated)**

	Givens		Calculations		
Mother	*X*	*Y*	*X²*	*Y²*	*XY*
1	9	3	81	9	27
2	10	4	100	16	40
3	10	5	100	25	50
4	11	4	121	16	44
5	12	4	144	16	48
6	12	6	144	36	72
7	12	7	144	49	84
8	13	6	169	36	78
9	14	6	196	36	84
10	15	6	225	36	90
11	16	7	256	49	112
12	16	8	256	64	128
	$\Sigma X = 150$		$\Sigma X^2 = 1{,}936$		$\Sigma XY = 857$
$n = 12$		$\Sigma Y = 66$		$\Sigma Y^2 = 388$	

tolerance by mothers; thus, this is the dependent variable, to be designated as *Y*. We are hypothesizing that educational level is a predictor of lowbrow tolerance. Thus, education level is the independent variable *X*.

Next we organize the data into a computational spreadsheet. Table 15–1 presents the data on educational level and lowbrow tolerance along with the sums required for computing correlation and regression statistics.

Before we compute linear regression statistics, we must make sure they apply to these data; that is, we must observe a scatterplot to determine whether the data appear to fit the cigar-shaped pattern approximating a straight line. Figure 15–1 presents the scatterplot for the data in Table 15–1. Indeed, the data appear linear. Moreover, the slope is positive; that is, the coordinates of the scatterplot extend upward from left to right. Thus, we may proceed to calculate correlation and regression statistics.

Let us calculate the Pearson's *r* correlation coefficient:

$$r = \frac{n(\Sigma XY) - (\Sigma X)(\Sigma Y)}{\sqrt{[n\Sigma X^2 - (\Sigma X)^2][n\Sigma Y^2 - (\Sigma Y)^2]}}$$

$$= \frac{12(857) - (150)(66)}{\sqrt{[12(1{,}936) - (150)^2][12(388) - (66)^2]}} = .82$$

FIGURE 15–1

Scatterplot of educational level as a predictor of lowbrow tolerance among 12 mothers of high school students

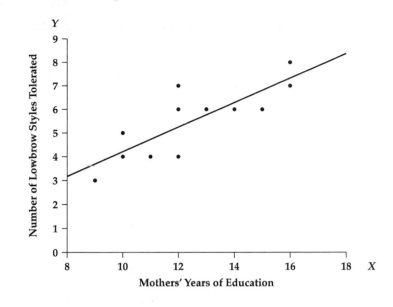

Next we compute the regression coefficient, b:

$$b = \frac{n(\Sigma XY) - (\Sigma X)(\Sigma Y)}{n\Sigma X^2 - (\Sigma X)^2} = \frac{12(857) - (150)(66)}{12(1,936) - (150)^2}$$

$$= .52 \text{ style tolerated per year of education}$$

Next we compute $\bar{X}$ and $\bar{Y}$:

$$\bar{X} = \frac{\Sigma X}{n} = \frac{150}{12} = 12.50 \text{ years}$$

$$\bar{Y} = \frac{\Sigma Y}{n} = \frac{66}{12} = 5.50 \text{ styles}$$

Next we use $\bar{X}$, $\bar{Y}$, and b to compute a:

$$a = \bar{Y} - b\bar{X} = 5.50 - (.52)(12.50) = -1.00 \text{ styles}$$

Next we specify the precise regression line equation for calculating $\acute{Y}$'s (i.e., predicted values of Y) by substituting the computed values of a and b:

$$\acute{Y} = a + bX = -1.00 + (.52)X$$

Finally, we insert a few values of X into the regression equation and solve for $\acute{Y}$. It is best to use low, medium, and high values of X. Thus,

X	$\acute{Y}$
9	3.68
12	5.24
16	7.32

Thus, the best estimate of lowbrow tolerance for a mother with nine years of education is acceptance of 3.68 music styles; for a mother with 12 years of education, 5.24 music styles; and so on. Using the resulting $X,\hat{Y}$-coordinates, we plot the regression line on the scatterplot (Figure 15–1).

The Six Steps of Statistical Inference and the Four Aspects of a Relationship

Pearson's r correlation coefficient is the statistic we use to test the hypothesis of the existence of a relationship between two interval/ratio variables, an independent variable X and a dependent variable Y. The following criteria must be met for us to be able to use linear correlation and regression statistics:

When to Test a Hypothesis Using Correlation and Regression Analysis (t-distribution, $df = n - 2$)

In general: Testing a hypothesis that a relationship exists between two interval/ratio or interval-like ordinal variables.

1. There is one representative sample from a single population.
2. There are two interval/ratio and/or interval-like ordinal variables.
3. There are no restrictions on sample size, but generally, the larger the n, the better.
4. A scatterplot of the coordinates of the two variables fits a linear pattern.

Existence of a Relationship

In our example of mothers of high school students, we used a sample of 12. Of course, with sample data the results may be due to sampling error. Although the data in the scatterplot of Figure 15–1 appear to be linear, it is possible that these sample coordinates poorly represent the coordinates *for the population* of all mothers of high school students. The linear pattern of the sample may simply be the result of sampling error. Especially with such a small sample size, drawing second, third, fourth, fifth, and sixth samples will produce different scatterplots each time. Some may appear linear, while others may not.

When we use sample data, then, we must address this question: Does a linear relationship between X and Y truly exist *in the population,* or is the linear pattern in this sample the result of sampling error? In practical terms, we are interested in the question: For *all* mothers, is there a relationship between educational level and lowbrow tolerance, or is the apparent linear pattern a chance occurrence in our sample? As with any hypothesis test, the real interest lies in the parameter, the summary measurement that applies to the entire population.

The Pearson's r correlation coefficient allows us to test a hypothesis to answer this question. Pearson's r is a statistic, a measure of the tightness of fit of coordinates around the regression line *for the sample. For the population* the corresponding parameter is symbolized by the Greek letter *rho* (ρ). *Rho* is the correlation coefficient that would be obtained if Pearson's correlation coefficient were computed for the entire population. It would measure the tightness of fit of X,Y-coordinates if they were plotted for all mothers, not just those in the sample.

As we noted in Chapter 14, Pearson's correlation coefficient computes to zero when there is no relationship between X and Y. Knowing this, we can state a statistical hypothesis—one that tells us what to expect of statistical calculations in repeated sampling when this statement is true. If there is no relationship between educational level and lowbrow tolerance *in the population of mothers,* then *rho* equals zero and sample Pearson's r's will compute to zero, give or take a little sampling error. The alternative hypothesis is that rho is *not* zero. The hypothesis test hinges on whether the observed sample Pearson's r is "significantly different" from zero.

As with any hypothesis test, the *effect* of the test is the difference between an observed sample statistic and the expected parameter when the statistical hypothesis is true. For a correlation hypothesis, the effect is the difference between the observed sample Pearson's r and the expected *rho* of zero. This difference calculates to the value of r:

$$\text{Test effect for a Pearson's correlation} = r - \rho = r - 0 = r$$

The hypothesis test determines whether this effect found in a sample is real for the population. Is the absolute value of the sample r so large that we are led to believe that ρ is not zero and that this effect is not simply the result of sampling error?

In general, for any hypothesis about the relationship between two interval/ratio variables, the statistical hypothesis is stated as

$$\text{Stat. } H: \rho = 0$$

That is, there is no relationship between X and Y.

The statement of the alternative hypothesis can be two-tailed, nondirectional (i.e., $\rho \neq 0$; there *is* a relationship), one-tailed in the negative direction (i.e., $\rho < 0$; there *is* a negative relationship), or one-tailed in the positive direction (i.e., $\rho > 0$; there *is* a positive relationship).

Existence of a Relationship between Two Interval/Ratio and/or Interval-Like Ordinal Variables

Test the statistical hypothesis that there is no relationship between X and Y:

$$\text{Stat. } H: \rho = 0$$

That is, there is *no* relationship between X and Y.

In step 2 of the six steps of statistical inference we project the size of the sampling error by describing the sampling distribution. In this case, if rho is indeed equal to zero and we repeatedly draw samples of size 12 from the population of mothers, what sample correlations (r's) will we obtain? Pearson's r's will center on zero in an approximately normal t-distribution. Calculation of the standard error for this test is very cumbersome. Fortunately, the test statistic is designed so that calculation of the standard error is unnecessary. We can say, however, that the standard error is inversely related to sample size. That is, the larger the sample size, the smaller the standard error. The test statistic for this hypothesis test is as follows:

The t-Test Formula for Testing the Significance of Pearson's r Correlation Coefficient

$$t_r = r \sqrt{\frac{n-2}{1-r^2}}$$

with $df = n - 2$

where

t_r = the t-test for Pearson's r correlation coefficient
r = Pearson's r correlation coefficient calculated on a sample
n = sample size
df = degrees of freedom

Let us proceed to test the statistical hypothesis of no relationship between X (educational level) and Y (lowbrow tolerance). We will go ahead and complete all four aspects of a relationship; then we will discuss the details of each step and each aspect.

Brief Checklist for the Six Steps of Statistical Inference

Test Preparation

State the research question; list givens, including variables (e.g., X =..., Y =...), their levels of measurement, the population(s) under study, and sample(s) and sample size(s); select the statistical test; provide observations of statistics and parameters; and draw a conceptual diagram.

(continued)

(concluded)

Six Steps

Using the symbol *H* for *hypothesis:*

1. State the statistical *H* and the alternative *H* and stipulate test direction.
2. Describe the sampling distribution.
3. State the level of significance (α) and specify the critical test value.
4. Observe the actual sample outcomes and compute the test effects, the test statistic, and the *p*-value.
5. Make the rejection decision.
6. Interpret and apply best estimates in everyday terms.

Test Preparation

Research question: Is there a relationship between educational level and lowbrow tolerance among mothers of high school students? *Givens:* Variables: *X* = educational level, *Y* = lowbrow tolerance = the number of music styles accepted; both are interval/ratio variables. *Population:* Mothers of high school students. *Sample:* One sample of 12 mothers. *Statistical procedure:* *t*-test for the significance of Pearson's *r* correlation coefficient; *t*-distribution. *Observations:* Scatterplot (Figure 15–1) suggests a linear relationship; data and computations from the spreadsheet in Table 15–1 are as follows:

$$r = .82 \qquad \hat{Y} = a + bX = -1.00 + (.52)X \qquad n = 12$$

This research question may be visualized graphically as follows:

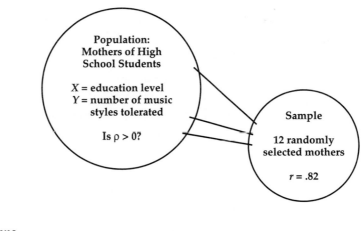

Six Steps

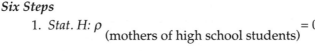

1. *Stat. H:* $\rho_{(\text{mothers of high school students})} = 0$

That is, there is *no* relationship between educational level and low-brow tolerance.

Alt. *H:* $\rho_{\text{(mothers of high school students)}} > 0$

That is, there *is* a positive relationship between educational level and lowbrow tolerance. One-tailed.

2. *Sampling distribution:* Approximately normal, *t*-distribution, *df* = *n* − 2 = 10. If the Stat. *H* is true and samples of size 12 are drawn repeatedly from the population of high school mothers, sample *r*'s will center on zero with a standard error inversely related to sample size (i.e., the larger the sample size, the smaller the standard error).

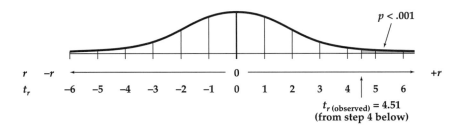

3. *Level of significance:* α = .05, one-tailed; critical value t_α = 1.812 [from the *t*-distribution table (Statistical Table C in Appendix B].
4. *Observation:* test effects, test statistic, and *p*-value.
   Scatterplot reveals a linear relationship, *r* = .82, *n* = 12.
   Test effect = .82 (i.e., effect = *r* − *ρ* = *r* − 0 = .82 − 0 = .82).
   Test statistic:

$$t_r = r\sqrt{\frac{n-2}{1-r^2}} = .82\sqrt{\frac{10}{1-.67}} = 4.51 \text{ SE}$$

From the *t*-table (Statistical Table C in Appendix B):
p-value: *p* [observing an *r* as unusual as or more unusual than .82 when *ρ* = 0] < .001 (area noted on curve in step 2).

5. *Rejection decision:* |t_r| > |t_α| (i.e., 4.51 > 1.812); thus, *p* < α, (i.e., *p* < .05). Reject Stat. *H* and accept Alt. *H* at the 95 percent level of confidence.
6. *Interpret results* (addressing the four aspects of a relationship) and make best estimates (details to be discussed below).
   Existence: There is a relationship between educational level and tolerance of lowbrow music among mothers of high school students; *r* =.82, *p* < .001.
   Direction: Positive. As the level of education increases, the number of music styles tolerated tends to increase.

Strength: $r^2 = .82^2 = .6724$; (100) (.6724) = 67.24 percent; thus, 67.24 percent of the variation in the number of lowbrow music styles tolerated is explained by knowledge of educational level.

Nature: (Interpret the slope of the regression line): $b = .52$ styles per year of education; a one-year increase in educational level is related to a .52 increase in the number of music styles tolerated.

Best estimates (use $X,\hat{Y}$-coordinates to illustrate the usefulness of knowing about the relationship between educational level and number of music styles tolerated):

$$\hat{Y} = a + bX = -1.00 + (.52)X$$

Thus, for example, the best estimate of the number of music styles tolerated by mothers with a high school education (12 years) is 5.24 styles, and with a college education (16 years) it is 7.32 styles.

We will comment further on the strength, direction, and nature of the relationship below. First, let us note some things about this hypothesis test:

- In step 1 we used a one-tailed test, but *not* because we saw a positive relationship in the scatterplot. This pattern could have occurred by chance. We did this because even before the sample was drawn, we posed the research question of whether *better*-educated mothers are more tolerant of diverse musical styles.

- In step 2, as we noted earlier, for the sake of computational simplicity, we use the test statistic t_r. This saves us from having to compute a very complicated standard error. Once t_r is computed, however, the standard error can be calculated quite easily. We now know that the Pearson's r quantity of .82 is 4.51 standard errors from a rho of zero. Thus, the width of one standard error is

$$s_{t_r} = \frac{.82}{4.51} = .18$$

where s_{t_r} is the estimated standard error of the t-distribution for Pearson's r (estimated because it is based on the sample r). Insert this value on the curve, and its fit will become apparent. Of further note, because regression statistics are based on deviations from the mean of Y, just as analysis of variance (ANOVA) statistics are, we could have used an F-ratio test. (Recall from Chapter 12 that the square root of the F-ratio test statistic is equal to the t-test statistic.) This, however, would require many more computations.

- In step 2 note that on the t-distribution curve, sample r's near zero occur frequently when the statistical hypothesis is true and large sample r's occur infrequently. That is, if rho is indeed zero, large absolute values of r are unusual in repeated sampling. Thus, when a significantly large r does occur, we reject the assumption that ρ is zero.

- In step 2, 2 degrees of freedom are lost because Pearson's r is computed from the sample means and variances of X and Y. The computation of each mean results in a loss of 1 degree of freedom (see Chapter 10).
- This hypothesis test, through "existence" in step 6, simply establishes whether a correlation exists between X and Y. If this is found to be true (i.e., *if we reject* the statistical hypothesis that $\rho = 0$), we can address the other aspects of relationship. However, *if we fail to reject the statistical hypothesis, these other aspects are irrelevant.* We simply conclude that there is no relationship and do not mention direction, strength, and nature. Since we did reject the statistical hypothesis, we will now discuss the direction, strength, and nature of a relationship for two interval/ratio variables.

Direction of the Relationship

The direction of a relationship between two interval/ratio or interval-like ordinal variables is ascertained by the sign of r and b, the slope of the regression line. An upward slope is positive, and a downward slope is negative. The direction of the slope for a truly linear, moderately strong relationship will be apparent in the scatterplot. The direction of the relationship can be observed directly in the signs (+ or –) of b and Pearson's r, which will always be the same. (*Thought question:* Observe the formulas for b and r. Why will they always have the same sign?) As part of our interpretation in step 6 of the hypothesis test, the direction of the relationship for educational level and lowbrow tolerance is revealed in the sign of r, with $r = +.82$. Therefore, the direction of the relationship is positive and is described as follows:

Positive: As education level increases, the number of music styles tolerated tends to increase.

Direction of a Relationship between Two Interval/Ratio Variables

Observe the sign (+ or –) of b and Pearson's r. Also observe the slope (or lean) of the pattern of coordinates in a scatterplot.

Strength of the Relationship

The correlation of educational level with lowbrow tolerance asserts that some part of the differences in the number of music styles tolerated (Y) by mothers is due to differences in their education levels—the effects of X. In Chapter 14 we observed that when these differences are systematic and X,Y-coordinates on a scatterplot have a linear pattern, we can improve best estimates of Y by estimating to the regression line rather than to the "mean line." The regression line is the one that is as close as possible to all X,Y-coordinates. By predicting to the regression line, we reduce error in predictions.

Let us apply these ideas to the population of mothers of high school students. From the data in Table 15–1 we found that the mean number of lowbrow music styles tolerated by these mothers is 5.50 styles. If we were asked to estimate the number for any mother *without any other knowledge* about her, 5.50 would be our best estimate—a prediction to the mean line of the scatterplot. How good is this *un*knowledgeable estimate? Mother 12 tolerates eight lowbrow musical styles. If we had estimated her Y-score to the mean of 5.50, we would have erred by 2.50 styles. Recall from Chapter 6 that this amount—the difference between a score and the mean of scores—is her deviation score:

Mother 12's deviation score = error in estimating to the mean

$$= Y_{(mother\ 12)} - \overline{Y} = 8 - 5.50 = 2.50 \text{ music styles}$$

Suppose we now follow a different course of action. In this scenario we are given the opportunity to predict her music tolerance level with the knowledge that educational level and lowbrow tolerance are correlated. Instead of predicting to the mean, we predict "to the regression line" (Figure 15–1), which we know is close to the observed X,Y-coordinates. The best estimate of styles tolerated for mother 12 with her 16 years of education is now more accurately estimated by the regression line equation. Based on her 16 years of education, her predicted $\hat{Y}$-score of 7.32 styles is

$$\hat{Y}_{(X = 16\ years)} = a + bX = -1.00 + (.52)16 = 7.32 \text{ music styles}$$

Using this as *a knowledgeable estimate*—a coordinate point on the regression line—we now estimate mother 12's tolerance level as being much closer to her true tolerance level. The error in this knowledgeable estimate is only .68 styles:

Error in estimating mother 12's music tolerance level when predicting to the
regression line = $Y_{(mother\ 12)} - \hat{Y}_{(X = 16\ years)} = 8 - 7.32 = .68$ music style

This estimate is a considerable improvement over the one made to the mean. Error is reduced from 2.50 styles to .68 style. To determine how much of an improvement this is, we take the difference between the knowledgeable estimate ($\hat{Y}$ predicted for 16 years of education) and the unknowledgeable estimate (i.e., $\overline{Y}$, the mean of Y):

Improvement in estimating Y using knowledge that it is related to X =
$\hat{Y}_{(X = 16\ years)} - \overline{Y} = 7.32 - 5.50 = 1.82$ music styles

This reduction in error of 1.82 styles is the part of the error "explained" by level of education. In predicting to the regression line we explain 1.82 of mother 12's 2.50 deviation score. We attribute the 1.82 styles above the mean of 5.50 to her higher educational level.

The strength of a relationship between two interval/ratio variables is a measure of just how much improvement occurs in making these estimates for the sample (and population) as a whole. For a summary statistic that applies to the entire sample, we must calculate the best estimates of every case and compare these knowledgeable estimates to the unknowledgeable estimates based on the mean. A measure of the total strength for the sample must assess how much of the total error—the sum of deviation scores—can be eliminated by using the regression line instead of the mean line as a basis for predicting lowbrow tolerance.

There is, however, an additional step required in making these summary calculations. We cannot simply sum deviation scores, because they always sum to zero. Thus, the deviation scores must be squared. Recall that the sum of squared deviation scores for an entire sample is called the total variation:

$$\text{Total variation in } Y = \Sigma(Y_{(each\ case)} - \bar{Y})^2$$

The variation is the total amount of squared deviations from the mean *that is in need of being explained*. Why is one mother two styles tolerant over the mean while another mother is one style under it? If the relationship between educational level and tolerance of lowbrow musical styles is strong, educational level will explain a large *proportion of the total variation* in lowbrow tolerance. A large amount of each subject's lowbrow tolerance deviation score could be attributed to her educational level. Thus, we must determine *what proportion of the total variation in Y can be explained by X.*

Let us make the extra calculation of squaring for mother 12. Again, we find that her deviation score is 2.50 styles. Her squared deviation is $(2.50)^2 = 6.25$. What proportion of this *squared* deviation is explained by her education?

Amount of mother 12's squared deviation explained by her educational level

$$= \frac{\text{squared improvement using knowledgeable estimate}}{\text{squared deviation score}}$$

$$= \frac{(\hat{Y}_{(X=16\ years)} - \bar{Y})^2}{(Y_{(mother\ 12)} - \bar{Y})^2} = \frac{1.82^2}{2.50^2} = .5296$$

Thus, the proportion of mother 12's *squared* deviation in lowbrow tolerance (Y) explained by her 16 years of education (X) is .5296, or 52.96 percent.

To obtain the total amount of variation in Y explained by X for the whole sample, we make these calculations for every individual in the sample and sum the calculations. This is a cumbersome process. Fortunately, there is a shortcut method for obtaining the proportion of the total variation in Y explained by X.

Shortcut Method for Computing the Strength of the Relationship.   Mathematically, the proportion of the total variation in Y explained by X can be obtained quickly by squaring Pearson's r correlation coefficient. That is, the statistic r^2 readily provides this proportion, and it is a measure of the strength of the relationship between X and Y.

$$r^2 = \text{proportion of variation in } Y \text{ explained by } X$$

$$= \frac{\sum(\hat{Y}_{(each\ case)} - \bar{Y})^2}{\sum(Y_{(each\ case)} - \bar{Y})^2}$$

Strength of a Relationship between Two Interval/Ratio Variables

r^2 = proportion of the variation in Y explained by knowing that it is related to X.

For the hypothesis on educational level and lowbrow tolerance, $r^2 = (.82)^2 = .6724$; $(100)\ (.6724) = 67.24$ percent. Thus, 67.24 percent of the variation in the number of musical styles tolerated is explained by knowing educational levels.

When there is a strong relationship between two interval/ratio variables, the X,Y-coordinates on the scatterplot will fit tightly around the regression line. The tighter the fit, the larger the value of Pearson's r and therefore the larger the value of r^2. And when the fit is tight, best estimates to the regression line are close to the actual observed Y-scores, just as in the case of mother 12. Error in predictions of Y taking into account its relationship with X will be small, and the proportional reduction in error (PRE) will be great. This means that X-scores are good, strong predictors of Y-scores. In other words, the relationship is strong.

Focus on r^2, not r. In interpreting the strength of a relationship, we focus on r^2 rather than r because both the sign of r and its size can be misleading. The sign of r has nothing to do with the strength of relationship; it merely indicates the direction of the relationship. Moreover, whether the relationship is positive or negative, squaring the r always results in a positive "proportion of variation explained" because squaring removes any negative signs. With respect to the size of r, squaring reveals the true strength of a relationship—the amount of PRE in predicting the dependent variable Y that is due to its correlation with the independent variable X.

Observing r directly (i.e., without squaring) encourages an overestimation of the strength of the relationship. This is revealed in Table 15–2. For instance, directly observing, say, $r = .50$ could lead to the incorrect conclusion that we are "halfway there" in reducing errors in prediction. In fact, we are only a quarter of the way there because $r^2 = (.50)^2 = .25$; that is, only 25 percent of the variation in Y is explained by X. Remember, it is r^2, not r, that establishes the strength of a relationship between two interval/ratio variables.

The General Additive-Effects Model Applied to Correlation and Regression Analysis. Examining the amount of variation explained should be familiar to those who have covered the material in Chapter 12 on ANOVA. There we used

TABLE 15–2 Comparing r to r^2: The Importance of Focusing on r^2 to Assess the Strength of a Relationship

r	r^2	Proportion and Percentage of Variation in Y Explained by X		Strength of the Relationship
		p	%	
1.00	1.00	1.00	100%	Perfect positive relationship
.90	.81	.81	81	Very strong positive
.80	.64	.64	64	
.70	.49	.49	49	Moderately strong positive
.60	.36	.36	36	
.50	.25	.25	25	
.40	.16	.16	16	Moderately weak positive
.30	.09	.09	9	
.20	.04	.04	4	
.10	.01	.01	1	Very weak positive
.00	**.00**	**.00**	**0%**	**No relationship**
−.10	.01	.01	1	Very weak negative
−.20	.04	.04	4	
−.30	.09	.09	9	
−.40	.16	.16	16	Moderately weak negative
−.50	.25	.25	25	
−.60	.36	.36	36	
−.70	.49	.49	49	Moderately strong negative
−.80	.64	.64	64	
−.90	.81	.81	81	Very strong negative
−1.00	1.00	1.00	100%	Perfect negative relationship

the general additive-effects model by decomposing the Y-scores of a sample into their parts explained by the mean of Y, the effects of X, and the effects of other unmeasured variables (i.e., remaining error). The same approach may be applied to regression analysis. For instance, we can decompose mother 12's lowbrow music tolerance score into those parts explained and those parts unexplained by educational level:

$$
\begin{aligned}
Y_{(mother\ 12)} &= \text{mean of } Y \; + \; \text{mother 12's deviation score} \\
&= \bar{Y} \; + \; (Y_{(mother\ 12)} - \bar{Y}) \\
&= \bar{Y} \; + \; (\hat{Y}_{(X = 16\ years)} - \bar{Y}) \; + \; (Y_{(mother\ 12)} - \hat{Y}_{(X = 16\ years)})
\end{aligned}
$$

Thus:

$$
\begin{aligned}
8 \text{ styles} &= 5.50 \text{ styles} \; + \; 2.5 \text{ styles} \\
&= 5.50 \text{ styles} \; + \; 1.82 \text{ styles} \qquad\qquad\; + \; .68 \text{ styles} \\[2ex]
&= \text{the mean} \; + \; \begin{array}{l}\text{amount explained} \\ \text{by 16 years of} \\ \text{education}\end{array} \; + \; \begin{array}{l}\text{error—the amount} \\ \text{explained by other} \\ \text{variables}\end{array}
\end{aligned}
$$

This illustrates that the general additive-effects model works whenever we have an interval/ratio dependent variable (Y) on which we are computing its mean. Measures of the strength of a relationship in both ANOVA and regression analysis simply sum up the amount of explained variation in Y and calculate the proportion of the total variation that this amount constitutes.

Nature of the Relationship

Keep in mind that the nature of the relationship provides a down-to-earth description of the results—in everyday terms to the extent possible. For two interval/ratio and/or interval-like ordinal variables we start with a general description of how to estimate the number of musical styles tolerated when we know the educational level. This general description is simply an interpretation of the regression coefficient b, the slope of the regression line. Recall from Chapter 14 that in general

$$b = \text{slope of the regression line of the scatterplot}$$
$$= \text{effect on } Y \text{ of a } \textit{one-unit} \text{ change in } X$$

The slope of the regression line in the scatterplot tells us how much vertical rise occurs with a one-unit horizontal run (see Figure 14–5 in the previous chapter). In Chapter 14 we stated that Pearson's r is a measure of the effect of X on Y. In fact, r and b are both measures of slope, but in different ways. (Pearson's r is a standardized slope, the slope as a number of standard deviations. It tells us how many standard deviations rise in Y can be expected with a 1 standard deviation run on X.) This connection between the two statistics also means that b is a measure of the effect of X on Y.

For our sample of mothers a general description of the nature of the relationship between educational level and number of musical styles tolerated would be stated as follows:

$$b = .52 \text{ styles per year of education}$$

A one-year increase in education level is related to a .52 increase in number of lowbrow musical styles tolerated. Put another way, add .52 to the estimates of musical styles tolerated with the addition of each year of education. If Ms. Franklin has one year of education more than Ms. Curry does, estimate Ms. Franklin's lowbrow tolerance as .52 style higher.

In describing the nature of the relationship, after reporting the slope, we provide examples of "best estimates" (i.e., $\hat{Y}$s) of the number of musical styles tolerated for a few selected educational levels (X). Specific examples are especially meaningful to a public audience. These best estimates are calculated from the regression equation $\hat{Y} = a + bX$. We insert chosen values of X and compute $\hat{Y}$s. It is useful to choose a low value and a high value of X or a number of years of education that is especially meaningful, such as 12 years (i.e., high school graduate) or 16 years (i.e., college graduate). Thus, we make the following calculations:

$$\hat{Y} = a + bX = -1.00 + (.52)X$$

$$\hat{Y}_{(X = 12)} = -1.00 + (.52)12 = 5.24 \text{ styles}$$

$$\hat{Y}_{(X = 16)} = -1.00 + (.52)16 = 7.32 \text{ styles}$$

In reporting these best estimates we state that

$$\hat{Y} = a + bX = -1.00 + (.52)X$$

Thus, for example, the best estimate of the number of musical styles tolerated by mothers with a high school education (12 years) is 5.24 styles, and among mothers with a college education (16 years) it is 7.32 styles.

Nature of a Relationship between Two Interval/Ratio Variables

In general, describe the slope of the regression line of the scatterplot:

b = effect on Y of a one-unit change in X

Provide best estimates using the regression line equation:

$$\hat{Y} = a + bX$$

Insert chosen values of X, compute $\hat{Y}$'s, and interpret them in everyday language.

Careful Interpretation of Correlation and Regression Statistics

Correlations Apply to a Population, Not to an Individual

A key facet of the statistical imagination is interpreting data in relation to a whole—a population—rather than with respect to a single individual or case. Statements about an individual case are weak estimates because individuals are highly complex. Statements about a population based on a sample are also estimates. Proper interpretation of data requires a clear understanding of the application of estimates. Does an estimate apply to an individual or to the group to which that individual belongs?

This distinction between an individual and a group is important in the interpretation of correlation statistics. The interpretation is limited by the fact that for most studies, data on subjects are collected only once. *Data collected at one point in time for each person in a sample* are called **cross-sectional data,** and the sample is called a cross-sectional sample. For example, every data set mentioned in this text is cross-sectional. *Data collected over a period of time with multiple contacts with subjects* are called **longitudinal data,** and the sample is called a longitudinal sample. For example, we might study the effects of a new prescription drug for high blood pressure for a one-year period by examining the same sample of patients every two months.

Interpretation of regression statistics differs for these two types of data. For the cross-sectional data in this text, estimates cannot be made about changes over time. Interpretation of the slope applies to a single point in time. For example, when we say that a one-year change in educational level is related to a .52 increase in lowbrow musical styles tolerated, we do not mean that a mother will necessarily become more tolerant by picking up an additional year of education. Instead, we are saying that within the sample and as an estimate for the population, .52 style is the difference *in the mean number of musical styles tolerated* between two categories that are one year apart in education level. We are comparing levels of education among sampled individuals at one point in time.

This distinction is illustrated by the *negative* correlation between age and educational level. In a cross-sectional sample of adults who have *already finished* their schooling (say, people age 25 and older) an increase in age is related to a *decrease* in education; that is, the correlation is in the negative direction. Does this mean that people lose education as they age? Of course not. The data are cross-sectional; we did not track people over time. We are comparing distinct individuals at different age levels, say, 30, 40, 50, and 60 years, at one point in time. The negative correlation simply indicates that people in older age groups have fewer years of education. For instance, members of your grandparents' generation typically acquired only a high school diploma. A correct interpretation would be that an increase in *the level of age within the population* is related to a decrease in *the level of* education. Furthermore, suppose we use a regression equation to calculate a best estimate of Grandfather Parker's educational level. We determine that his age is 76 years and predict an educational level of 10.5 years of schooling. This does not mean that he quit school in the middle of his junior year of high school. Rather, this estimate is the mean education level of all 76-year-olds. The best estimate is based on an X-score. It applies to the X-score of all 76-year-olds. Short of a multivariate analysis that takes into account a large number of predictor variables, this estimate must do. But not too much should be made of estimates of Y based on X unless the correlation is very strong, say, .9 or higher. Unless the correlation is perfect, there will still be error in estimates of Y based on knowing X.

Careful Interpretation of the Slope, b

Correlation and regression analysis has much in common with analysis of variance (see Chapter 12). In both procedures we examine the variation around the mean of an interval/ratio dependent variable Y. With ANOVA, we examine differences in means among three or more *groups or categories*. For example, is there a difference in the mean incomes of Catholic, Protestant, and Jewish households, and if so, what are the best estimates of the dollar amount differences in income? Similarly, with correlation and regression analysis we indirectly focus on the mean because deviation scores are distances from the mean. This is an important point: Correlation and regression statistics are based on the means of X and Y, and it is the mean of Y about which we are making estimates. When we estimate that a mother with 12 years of education tolerates 5.24 lowbrow styles of music, we are not asserting that every mother at this educational level scores 5.24 styles. What we are saying is that the best estimate *of the mean* number of musical styles tolerated by *all mothers with 12 years of education* is 5.24 styles. Just as with ANOVA, we are basing best estimates of an individual on the mean of his or her group. In the case of these mothers, the group is an X-score on an interval/ratio measure.

Distinguishing Statistical Significance from Practical Significance

Statistical significance demonstrates that a measured test effect for a sample is so large that it indicates a real effect in the population and is not merely the result of random sampling error. As we noted in Chapters 11 and 12 in discussing difference of means tests, with a large sample a small difference may be found to be statistically significant. For example, with a very large sample we may find a $10 difference in mean annual salaries of men and women in a corporation. Using a *t*-test, we conclude that the $10 difference between the sample means reflects a real $10 difference in the populations of men and women.

But does $10 suggest rampant gender discrimination? For 250 working days in a year, a $10 difference comes out to 4 cents per day, or less than a penny per hour. In practical terms the difference is meaningless. Statistical significance and practical significance are separate issues.

In all hypotheses tests, a large sample size reduces the standard error of the sampling distribution. This makes the test more sensitive in detecting statistical significance even if the effect of the test is small. With simple correlation and regression analysis, Pearson's r is the measure of the effect of the test. With large samples, even a small r will produce a large *t*-test statistic. This in turn may result in a small p-value and lead to a rejection of the statistical hypothesis. The size of the standard error—and therefore the size of the p-value—is greatly influenced by sample size. All else being equal, the larger the sample size is, the smaller the p-value is and the more likely it is that the statistical hypothesis will be rejected. This is illustrated with *t*-tests for two samples, one quite small and the other quite large, where Pearson's r came out the same:

Illustration 1: Sample size, $n = 16$; $r = .10$; one-tailed test, $\alpha = .05$, $df = n - 2 = 14$.

$$t_r = r\sqrt{\frac{n-2}{1-r^2}} = .10\sqrt{\frac{14}{1-.01}} = .38 \text{ SE}$$

From the *t*-distribution table (Statistical Table C in Appendix B): *p*-value: *p* [observing an *r* as unusual as or more unusual than .10 when $\rho = 0$] > .05.

  Conclusion: Not statistically significant.

Illustration 2: Sample size, $n = 2002$; $r = .10$; one-tailed test, $\alpha = .05$. $df = n - 2 = 2,000$.

$$t_r = r\sqrt{\frac{n-2}{1-r^2}} = .10\sqrt{\frac{2000}{1-.01}} = 4.49 \text{ SE}$$

From the *t*-distribution table (Statistical Table C in Appendix B): *p*-value: *p* [observing an *r* as unusual as or more unusual than .10 when $\rho = 0$] < .001.

  Conclusion: Statistically significant at the .05 level of significance.

Even though the *r*'s are the same in both illustrations, different conclusions are drawn. In Illustration 2 we conclude that the sample correlation *r* indicates a real correlation in the population.

  But is an *r* of .10 meaningful? The strength of the relationship is measured with r^2. For illustration 2: $r^2 = (.10)^2 = .01$ (or 1 percent). Thus, 1 percent of the variation in the dependent variable *Y* is explained by knowledge of the independent variable *X*.

  The effect is real in the population, as we established with 95 percent confidence when we rejected the statistical hypothesis of no relationship. The effect, however, is so weak as perhaps to be meaningless. In a sense, a large sample can be overly sensitive to small test effects. The determination of statistical significance is not the only consideration. Strength also must be considered.

  Of course, because they are insensitive to even large test effects, small samples present a different problem. With a small sample, we may conclude that a large Pearson's *r* is not statistically different from zero. If it turns out that there truly is a relationship in the population but we simply missed it, then we have made a type II error: failing to reject a false statistical hypothesis (see Chapter 9). Another illustration reveals that even an apparently strong relationship can be missed when we use a small sample:

Illustration 3: Sample size, $n = 5$; $r = .70$; one-tailed test, $\alpha = .05$. $df = n - 2 = 3$.

$$t_r = r\sqrt{\frac{n-2}{1-r^2}} = .70\sqrt{\frac{3}{1-.49}} = 1.69 \text{ SE}$$

From the *t*-distribution table (Statistical Table C in Appendix B): *p*-value: *p* [observing an *r* as unusual as or more unusual than .70 when $\rho = 0$] > .05.

  Conclusion: Not statistically significant.

In this illustration, the strength of the relationship would be $r^2 = (.70)^2 = .49$ (or 49 percent). Thus, it appears that 49 percent of the variation in the dependent variable *Y* is explained by knowledge of the independent variable *X*. We must conclude, however, that there is no relationship between the variables, and given the small sample size, this is all we can do. This raises the suspicion, however, that we have made a type II error. The relationship may or may not exist, but with such a small sample we may never know. This illustration highlights the importance of having a large enough sample to avoid type II errors. In "Statistical Follies and Fallacies" in Chapter 13 we addressed this issue as one of statistical power. Small samples have low statistical power.

These illustrations of the influence of sample size on statistical testing also highlight the importance of not treating the *p*-value of a statistical test as a measure of the strength of the relationship. If one correlation is found significant at the .001 level of significance and a second at the .05 level, this does not mean that the first correlation is necessarily stronger than the second. The *p*-values of Illustrations 1 and 2 above are radically different, yet the strength of the relationship is the same. The existence and strength of the relationship are separate issues.

Tabular Presentation: Correlation Tables

Correlations often are presented in tables as matrices with a diagonal shape. Table 15–3 is an example. It presents aggregate data—data based on groups—for students in 76 randomly selected school districts. The mean Stanford Admissions Test (SAT) score for the district is correlated with the percentage of families in the district with only one parent and the percentage of students in the district who receive free school lunches. The last variable is a common measure of poverty in a residential area.

The table is designed so that quick comparisons can be made among correlations. First, note that the correlation of a variable with itself is perfect (i.e., *r* = 1.00). Of course, a variable is a perfect predictor of itself. Second, correlations are presented on only one cornered side, or "diagonal," of the table because it is redundant to repeat them on the other side. Third, the *p*-values for significant *r*'s are presented by footnoted asterisks. The signs of the correlation coef-

TABLE 15–3   **Correlations among Mean Stanford Admissions Test (SAT) Scores, Percentage of One-Parent Families, and Percentage of Students Receiving Free Lunches for 76 School Districts (fictional data)**

	1	*2*	*3*
1 Mean SAT score	1.00		
2 Percent one-parent families	−.61***	1.00	
3 Percent students receiving free school lunches	−.91***	.63***	1.00

* $p < .05$. ** $p < .01$. *** $p < .001$. One-tailed tests.

ficients provide information on the direction of the relationship, and by squaring a coefficient we can estimate the proportion and percentage of variation explained by a chosen independent variable.

The statistics in the table reveal that average test performance in a school district is moderately related to the percentage of one-parent families (Pearson's $r = -.61$; $p < .001$). This moderate strength is determined by squaring $-.61$ and seeing that about 36 percent of the variance is explained by this family structure variable. The negative sign tells us that the higher the percentage of one-parent families in a district, the lower the mean SAT score.

The mean SAT score in a district also has a strong negative correlation with the percentage of students receiving free lunches: $r = -.91$; $p < .001$; r^2 equal about 82 percent. The higher the percentage of students in a district relying on the school for free lunches, the lower the mean SAT score in the district.

We also can see that the percentage of one-parent families is related to poverty; that is, the correlation between one-parent families and free lunches is a moderate, positive one: $r = .63$; $p < .001$; r^2 equal about 40 percent. As one can imagine, a correlation table with a large number of variables packs a lot of information onto one page.

☹   STATISTICAL FOLLIES AND FALLACIES   ☹

Correlation Does Not Always Indicate Causation

In attempting to explain a phenomenon of interest (i.e., our dependent variable Y), we search for a correlated variable X. Finding a correlation, however, does not necessarily mean that X causes Y. The existence of a correlation simply denotes that the scores of the two variables systematically change together in a predictable pattern. This discovery by itself does not establish causation between the variables. Many correlations are spurious.

A **spurious correlation** is *one that is conceptually false, nonsensical, or theoretically meaningless*. This is illustrated by the correlation between ice cream consumption (X) and the rape rate (Y) over time. As ice cream consumption goes up, the rape rate increases. Many spurious correlations are like this one. The simultaneous increases and decreases in the rates of these two variables are explained by a third variable—seasonal change. As it turns out, people eat more ice cream in warm weather, and for reasons related to victim availability, more rapes occur during the warm summer months. Thus, although changes in the rates of one have nothing to do with changes in the rates of the other, ice cream consumption and rape rates go up and down together as the seasons change. To imply a meaningful connection between the two behaviors, however, is nonsensical.

> # Spurious Correlation
>
> A correlation between two variables that is conceptually false, nonsensical, or theoretically meaningless.

Another spurious correlation concerns the relationship between crime rates in city neighborhoods and the racial makeup of a community. There is a positive correlation between the percentage of the minority population (e.g., African-Americans) living in neighborhoods and crime rates. That is, for a sample of communities, those with a high percentage of African-Americans tend to have high rates of crime. On the face of it, this suggests that African-Americans are more prone to criminal behavior, and indeed, racists often quote this statistic. This correlation, however, is spurious. Crime rates are high in *poor* neighborhoods regardless of their racial makeup, and a disproportionate share of minority neighborhoods are poor. Moreover, the relationship between poverty and racial makeup is due to racism, not biological race. That is, being poor has nothing to do with genetics. It is the racist heritage of the United States that contributes to the fact that a disproportionate share of African-Americans live in poverty, which in turn is a good predictor of crime rates.

How do we prove this point to a racist? Examine only wealthy neighborhoods, some that are predominantly white and some that are predominantly African-American. Regardless of racial predominance, these neighborhoods will have low crime rates. Moreover, *within* a sample of wealthy neighborhoods, the correlation between percentage minority and crime rate will be zero. Similarly, in poor neighborhoods—regardless of racial makeup—crime rates are relatively high and a zero correlation is found between poverty and racial makeup. This approach of focusing on a constant level for a third variable, such as the socioeconomic status of a neighborhood, is called *holding that variable constant*. When we hold socioeconomic status constant, its effects on the crime rate are eliminated, and thus this variable no longer produces the spurious relationship between X (percentage minority population) and Y (crime rate). Calculating correlation and regression statistics to control for additional variables is called *multiple correlation and regression,* a topic covered in advanced statistics texts. Nonetheless, these illustrations of spurious effects underscore the importance of interpreting statistical findings with a great deal of caution.

Spurious correlations are not unusual. This is due partly to the fact that many things, such as the size of the earth's population, continually increase. Any other thing that continually increases (such as the growth of gargantuan underground mushrooms) will be positively correlated with population size. Similarly, any other variable that continually decreases (such as the size of ice shelves on the continent of Antarctica or the percentage of American adults smoking cigarettes) will be negatively correlated with population size. Recall from Chapter 1 that a good scientific theory has two elements: a sense of understanding and the ability to provide empirical predictions. Spurious correlations allow for predictions but fail to provide a sense of understanding. In fact, they often confuse a situation.

Statistical Procedures Covered to Here

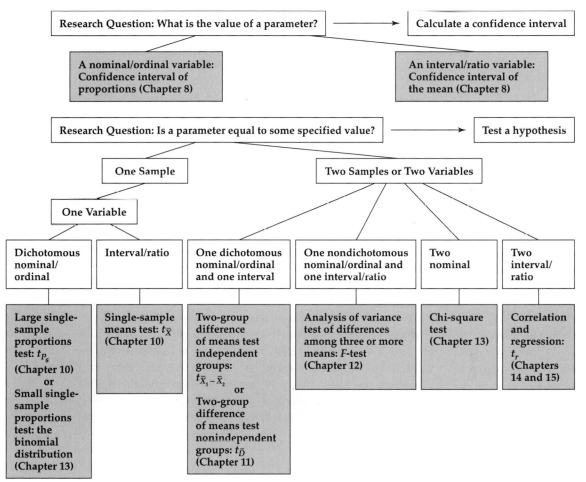

Summary of the Six Steps of Statistical Inference for Testing a Relationship between Two Interval/Ratio Variables

---

> ## Brief Checklist for the Six Steps of Statistical Inference
>
> ### Test Preparation
>
> State the research question; list givens, including variables (e.g., X =..., Y =...), their levels of measurement, the population(s) under study, and sample(s) and sample size(s); select the statistical test; provide observations of statistics and parameters; and draw a conceptual diagram.
>
> ### Six Steps
>
> Using the symbol H for *hypothesis:*
>
> 1. State the statistical H and the alternative H and stipulate test direction.
> 2. Describe the sampling distribution.
> 3. State the level of significance (α) and specify the critical test value.
> 4. Observe the actual sample outcomes and compute the test effects, the test statistic, and the *p*-value.
> 5. Make the rejection decision.
> 6. Interpret and apply best estimates in everyday terms.

Test Preparation

1. *Research question: Givens:* Variables: [determine which of the two interval/ratio variables is the dependent variable (Y) and which is the independent variable (X)]. X = ... (independent variable), Y = ... (dependent variable). *Population:...* *Sample:* ... *Statistical procedure: t*-test for the significance of Pearson's *r* correlation coefficient.

2. Following the formulas in Chapter 14, organize a spreadsheet of X,Y-coordinates (as in Table 15–1 or use a computer program), compute sums and calculate Pearson's *r* and the statistics for the regression equation:

$$\acute{Y} = a + bX$$

3. Draw a scatterplot to see whether a linear pattern is present in the X,Y-coordinates. If so, proceed.

4. Using the symbol H for *hypothesis*, complete the six steps of statistical inference and the four aspects of a relationship.

Six Steps

1. State the statistical H and the alternative H and stipulate the direction of the test. For this test, the Stat. H is always stated as *Stat. H: p = 0.* There is no relationship between X and Y.

Options on the alternative hypothesis (use one of the three):

Alt. *H: ρ ≠ 0.* There *is* a relationship between X and Y. Two-tailed.
Alt. *H: ρ > 0.* There *is* a positive relationship between X and Y. One-tailed.
Alt. *H: ρ < 0.* There *is* a negative relationship between X and Y. One-tailed.

2. *Sampling distribution:* Approximately normal, *t*-distribution, $df = n - 2$. If the Stat. H is true and samples of size n are drawn repeatedly, sample r's will center on zero with a standard error inversely related to sample size (i.e., the larger the sample size, the smaller the standard error). Draw the *t*-distribution curve and mark the *p*-value.

3. *Level of significance* (α): Specify the critical *t*-value.

4. *Observations:* Test effects, test statistic, and *p*-value. Observe r and n.
Test effect $= r$.

$$\text{Test statistic} = t_r = r\sqrt{\frac{n-2}{1-r^2}}$$

From the *t*-distribution table (Statistical Table C in Appendix B) determine the *p*-value: *p* [observing an r as unusual as or more unusual than the one observed when $\rho = 0$].

5. *Rejection decision:* Compare the *p*-value to α and make the rejection decision.

6. *Interpret results and make best estimates* (using the four aspects of a relationship).

If the Stat. H is not rejected, simply state that there is no relationship between X and Y. (Do not address the other aspects of relationship; they are irrelevant.)
If the Stat. H is rejected, address the four aspects of a relationship:

Existence: There appears to be a relationship between X and Y; $r = ..., p < ....$
Direction: Observe the sign of r and b. If it is positive, an increase in X is related to an increase in Y. If it is negative, an increase in X is related to a decrease in Y.
Strength: $r^2 = $ the proportion of variation in Y explained by knowledge of X.

Nature:

Nature: Interpret the slope of the regression line b. The effect of a one-unit change in X is a b-units change in Y.

Best estimates: To illustrate the usefulness of knowing about the relationship between X and Y, use the regression equation:

$$\hat{Y} = a + bX$$

Compute and interpret some examples by inserting chosen values of X and solving for $\hat{Y}$.

Questions for Chapter 15

1. For Pearson's r correlation coefficient, draw a conceptual diagram depicting a population and a sample and insert the appropriate statistics and parameters. Stipulate how the statistical hypothesis is stated for the hypothesis test.

2. For a hypothesis test of the relationship between two interval/ratio and/or interval-like ordinal variables, what is the shape of the sampling distribution and what test statistic is used?

3. In testing a hypothesis between two interval/ratio variables, the direction of the test is stated in the alternative hypothesis. For the general case of Y regressed on X, show how the alternative hypothesis is stated when the direction is hypothesized to be positive. Indicate the shape of the pattern of coordinates of a scatterplot when this is the case. Do the same for a negative relationship.

4. Observe the formulas for the Pearson's r correlation coefficient and the regression coefficient b and explain why these two coefficients always have the same directional sign (+ or –).

5. Explain what r^2 tells us.

6. In ascertaining the strength of a relationship between two interval/ratio variables, what is the danger in relying solely on an interpretation of the absolute value of Pearson's r? Explain.

7. Provide a one-word answer to this question: When no relationship is found between X and Y, what do we say about the other aspects of a relationship?

8. Match the following with regard to the relationship between two interval/ratio variables:

    a. Pearson's r _____ The Y-intercept; the value of Y when $X = 0$

    b. a   _____ The proportion of variation in Y explained by knowledge of X; a measure of the strength of the relationship

c. r^2 _____ Slope of the regression line; the effect on Y of a one-unit change in X; a measure of the nature of the relationship

d. b   _____ Predicted value of Y; best estimate of Y for a given value of X; used to describe the nature of the relationship

e. $\acute{Y}$ _____ Measures how tightly X,Y-coordinates fit around the regression line; used to describe the existence and direction of a relationship

9. Explain the difference between cross-sectional data and longitudinal data.

10. Using cross-sectional data, a researcher finds a negative relationship between age and knowledge about personal computers. Does this mean that as people age, they lose this knowledge? Explain.

11. Mathematically, there is a positive correlation between shoe size and the ability to do complicated mathematical problems. Is this really meaningful? Explain.

12. Mathematically, there is a negative correlation between the number of movies being produced in Hollywood each year and the size of the Amazon rain forests. Is this really meaningful? Explain.

Exercises for Chapter 15

General instructions: On all hypotheses tests, follow the six steps of statistical inference, including test preparation, a conceptual diagram, probability curves, and appropriate aspects of a relationship. For consistency, round calculations to two decimal places. Use $\alpha = .05$ unless otherwise stipulated.

1. Interpret the following Pearson's r's with regard to the direction of the relationship (fictional data).

X	Y	r
a. Yearly income	Dollar value of long-term investments	.69
b. Literacy rate of the population	Extent to which a government is democratic	.73
c. Age	Number of movies seen in past six months	−.45
d. Traffic citations and accidents in the past three years	Cost of automobile insurance premiums	.87

2. Interpret the following Pearson's r's with regard to the direction of the relationship (fictional data).

X	Y	r
a. High school grade point average	College grade point average	.57
b. Number of previous convictions	Length of prison sentence	.38
c. Socioeconomic status of a convicted felon	Length of prison sentence	−.71
d. Socioeconomic status of a neighborhood	Percentage of high school graduates attending college	.68

3. You are conducting a "couch potato" study of young teenagers at risk of developing obesity. For a sample of adolescent males in one of the 14 experimental groups from seven cities, the fictional data below indicate the number of hours a subject watches television per week, age, weight, height, and number of fast-food meals consumed in the past week.

   a. Draw a scatterplot of weight regressed on TV hours per week.
   b. Compute Pearson's r correlation coefficient for these two variables as well as the regression equation $\hat{Y} = a + bX$.
   c. Test the hypothesis that there is a relationship between these two variables. If there is, address the other aspects of the relationship.
   d. Age and height are roughly equal among the subjects. In fact, these variables were intentionally "held constant." Why is it wise to do this in testing for a relationship between the amount of time subjects watch TV and their weights?

Subject	TV Hours per Week	Age (years)	Weight (pounds)	Height (inches)	Number of Fast-food Meals in Past Week
1	9	12	112	65	2
2	14	13	131	66	2
3	20	12	171	66	5
4	18	14	160	66	2
5	16	13	182	67	4
6	14	14	165	66	3
7	19	13	149	67	3
8	12	13	137	66	2

4. The table for exercise 3 presents fictional data for a study of young teenagers at risk of developing obesity. For these data, do the following.

   a. Draw a scatterplot of weight regressed on the number of fast-food meals consumed in the past week.
   b. Compute Pearson's r correlation coefficient for these two variables as well as the regression equation $\hat{Y} = a + bX$.
   c. Test the hypothesis that there is a relationship between these two variables. If there is, address the other aspects of the relationship.
   d. Age and height are roughly equal among the subjects. In fact, these variables were intentionally "held constant." Why is it wise to do this in testing for a relationship between the number of fast-food meals consumed in the past week and weight?

5. Imagine that you are an admissions officer at a university. For a random sample of 114 sophomores, you compare current college grade point average (GPA) to high school GPA (data not shown). A computer-generated scatterplot reveals a linear relationship between these variables. Computer output gives you the following: Pearson's $r = .47$, $b = .73$, and the Y-intercept, $a = .80$. Test the hypothesis that students who did well in high school also do well in college.

6. Survey measures of religiosity gauge the extent to which an individual believes, prays, attends church, and follows the morals set down by a religion. The variable life satisfaction is a perception of how well things are going in a person's life at present. A computer-generated scatterplot reveals a linear relationship between these variables. Computer output gives you the following (fictional) results: $n = 14$ adults, Pearson's $r = .48$, $b = .78$, and the Y-intercept, $a = 6.24$. Test the hypothesis that religious persons tend to have greater life satisfaction.

7. The following are interval/ratio level variables with appropriate statistics computed for a sample of adult males (fictional data). All the coefficients are statistically significant at the .05 level.

   a. Which is the stronger relationship, that between age and occupational prestige score or that between age and educational level? Why?
   b. Interpret b_{zx}.
   c. Interpret the direction of r_{zx}.
   d. Organize the correlation coefficients into a correlation table.

X = age	Y = occupational prestige score	Z = educational level
	$r_{yx} = .24$ $r_{zx} = -.32$	$r_{zy} = .31$
	$b_{yx} = 2$ $b_{zx} = -.3$ year	$b_{zy} = 6$

8. The following are interval/ratio level variables with appropriate statistics computed for a sample of 100 Internet users (fictional data). All the coefficients are statistically significant at the .05 level.

   a. Which is the stronger relationship, that between age and hours connected or that between political conservatism and hours connected? Why?
   b. Interpret b_{zx}.
   c. Interpret the direction of r_{zx}.
   d. Organize the correlation coefficients into a correlation table.

X = age Y = political conservatism
Z = hours connected (to the Internet—World Wide Web—per month)

$r_{yx} = .19$	$r_{zx} = -.26$	$r_{zy} = .25$
$b_{yx} = .35$ conservatism scale point	$b_{zx} = -1.10$ hours	$b_{zy} = .79$ hour

---

9. The following are fictional data from 12 randomly selected cities. Is there a relationship between the level of education of a city (i.e., median years of education of adult household heads) and fire and burn fatalities per 100,000 population?

Fire/Burn Deaths per 100,000	Median Level of Education
2.3	11.7
1.5	12.2
2.1	11.3
2.3	11.1
1.4	12.2
1.9	12.0
1.6	12.3
1.7	12.4
1.5	12.5
1.7	11.6
2.2	10.9
2.1	12.1

10. An interesting psychological trait is openness to experience: a willingness to try new things and keep an open mind (McCrae 1996). Another often researched trait is authoritarianism: a general belief that society is better off with strongly enforced laws and punitive parents and bosses to keep people in line. Is there a relationship between these two traits for a group of randomly selected adults?

Openness to Experience Scale	Authoritarianism Scale
9	31
12	20
17	15
16	14
15	12
13	26
10	28
7	34
11	27
9	24
10	22
6	33
7	27
13	22
15	17

Optional Computer Applications for Chapter 15

If your class uses the optional computer applications that accompany this text, open the Chapter 15 exercises on the *Computer Applications for The Statistical Imagination* compact disk. The exercises involve using *SPSS for Windows* to obtain statistics to test hypotheses and address the four aspects of relationship for two interval/ratio variables.

RANK-ORDER CORRELATION BETWEEN TWO ORDINAL VARIABLES

Introduction: Spearman's rho Rank-Order Correlation Coefficient

To this point in the text, there has been little discussion of statistical procedures designed for variables with an ordinal level of measurement. Although ordinal variables are used infrequently in scientific research, rank ordering is common in political polls as well as athletic and academic competitions.

Suppose, for example, we wish to determine whether the physiological characteristics required for running track events differ by type of event. There are several types of runners: sprinters, who run in 40-,100-, and 200-meter races; intermediate distance runners for the 400-, 800-, and 1,500-meter races; and long-distance runners, who compete in cross-country and marathon races. Some runners, however, compete in more than one event. An interesting question is: Do these runners tend to do better in one event than they do in another? If this is true, the types of events are fundamentally different in terms of the talents, skills, and training they require. Common experience suggests that sprinters train to produce short bursts of speed while distance runners train to develop muscular and aerobic endurance.

We could answer this question partially by comparing the ranks of finish in a couple of these races for athletes who compete in both. We could test the research question that there is an inverse relationship between rank of finish in short sprint races and that in, say, longer intermediate-distance races. That is, do runners who place high in one race tend to place low in the other? This calls for a hypothesis test about the relationship between two ordinal variables.

Having the same runners compete in several events is a common practice at the high school level. Table 16–1 presents fictional data for a sample of 10 girls who run both the 100-meter and 800-meter races for a high school track team. These results suggest that there may be a difference in how the races are run. Coming out on top in the 100-meter sprint appears not to guarantee success in the 800-meter race. To measure the similarity of rankings of the two events we can correlate ranks by using a correlation coefficient designed for ordinal variables: the Spearman's rho rank-order correlation coefficient, r_s. The calculations needed to compute it are also shown in Table 16–1.

The formula for Spearman's rank-order correlation coefficient follows. Note that we use an English symbol (r_s) because we are treating our 10 female

TABLE 16–1   **Computational Spreadsheet for Computing Spearman's rho Rank-Order Correlation Coefficient: Rank of Finish for 100-Meter and 800-Meter Races, n = 10 High School Girls**

	Givens		Calculations	
Runner	*Rank of Finish in the 100-Meter Race*	*Rank of Finish in the 800-Meter Race*	*D*	*D²*
Bartlett	1	9	−8	64
Franks	2	7	−5	25
Hallman	3	8	−5	25
Schultz	4	10	−6	36
Brown	5	6	−1	1
Cutter	6	5	1	1
Anderson	7	1	6	36
Williams	8	3	5	25
Baldone	9	2	7	49
Gupta	10	4	6	36
$n = 10$			$\Sigma D = 0$	$\Sigma D^2 = 298$

runners as a sample of the population of all female high school runners. The formula is based on squaring the differences between ranks on the two ordinal variables. Squaring is necessary because the sum of the differences in ranks will always equal zero. In its denominator the formula accounts for sample size. This formula is most appropriate when the sample size is 10 or more and there are very few ties in the ranks (i.e., several individuals at the same rank) of either ordinal variable.

Computing Spearman's rho Rank-Order Correlation Coefficient (rho-distribution)

$$r_s = 1 - \frac{6\Sigma D^2}{n(n^2 - 1)}$$

where

r_s = Spearman's rank-order correlation coefficient
D = difference in rank between the two ordinal variables
n = sample size

Let us get a sense of proportion about this formula. Like Pearson's r in Chapter 15, it produces coefficients that range from −1.00 to zero to +1.00. A coefficient of zero indicates that there is no relationship between the ranked scores of the two variables: Knowing how a runner finishes in one type of event does not help to predict how she will finish in the other. A coefficient of 1.00 is a perfect positive relationship in which the ranks match exactly for the two races. This occurs when all differences in ranks (i.e., D's) are zero, resulting in $\Sigma D^2 = 0$; then $r_s = 1 - 0 = 1$. A coefficient of -1.00 indicates a perfect negative relationship in which ranks between the two races are reversed (i.e., 1 comes in tenth in the second race, 2 comes in ninth, 3 comes in eighth, etc.).

For the data in Table 16–1, there are substantial differences in order of finish for the two races and the ranking is reversed to some degree. Given this pattern, intuition tells us that the r_s should be quite large and negative. Thus,

$$r_s = 1 - \frac{6\Sigma D^2}{n\,(n^2 - 1)}$$

$$= 1 - \frac{(6)(298)}{10\,(100 - 1)} = 1 - 1.81 = -.81$$

Indeed, this is the case. The negative value of r_s shows that there is a reverse relationship in rank of finish between the 100-meter and 800-meter races. The runners who are good at sprinting short distances tend to do poorly in longer races requiring endurance. Of course, this is only a sample. We must test a hypothesis to establish whether these results are generalizable to all female high school track team members.

Hypothesis Test and Aspects of a Relationship for Spearman's rho

Existence and Direction of the Relationship for Spearman's rho

If our sample of track runners is representative of the population of all female team members, we can use it to determine whether these results are generalizable to this population. Our research question is: Is there a negative relationship between ranks of finish in 100-meter and 800-meter races? To establish whether this relationship exists, we test the statistical hypothesis that the population rank-order correlation coefficient ρ_s is zero. In general, the statement of the statistical hypothesis for the Spearman's test is Stat. *H:* $\rho_s = 0$. There is *no* relationship between ranks of the two variables. When $\rho_s = 0$, the correspondence between ranks is poor, indicating no relationship between rankings. The alternative hypothesis can be nondirectional, two-tailed (i.e., there is a relationship between ranks of the two variables), one-tailed positive (i.e., there is a positive relationship between ranks of the two variables), or one-tailed negative (i.e., there is a negative relationship between ranks of the two variables). For our track team sample the alternative hypothesis is that $\rho_s < 0$, that there is a negative relationship between rank of finish in the two races. This asserts that those who finish high in one race will finish low in the other, suggesting that training must differ for the two events.

Existence of a Relationship Using Spearman's rho

Test the statistical hypothesis that $\rho_s = 0$ (i.e., that there is no relationship between the ranks of the two ordinal variables) by using the test statistic:

$$r_s = 1 - \frac{6\sum D^2}{n(n^2 - 1)}$$

The sampling distribution for this statistical test is the Spearman's rho rank-order correlation distribution. Critical values for the .05 and .01 levels of significance for this distribution are presented in Statistical Table H in Appendix B. This table is set up to allow direct comparison of r_s's. As in the t-distribution table, these critical values are given only for the positive direction but may be applied for the negative direction. In other words, for negative r_s's imagine a minus sign in front of the numbers. Like any critical values in a table, for a given sample size the figures in this table tell how large a computed sample r_s must be to reject the statistical hypothesis.

As with any hypothesis test, the *effect* of the test is the difference between an observed sample statistic and the expected parameter when the statistical hypothesis is true. For Spearman's rho rank-order correlation, the test effect is the difference between the observed, sample r_s and the hypothesized ρ_s of zero. This difference calculates to the value of r_s:

Test effect for Spearman's rho rank-order correlation $= r_s - \rho_s = r_s - 0 = r_s$

The hypothesis test determines whether the effect found in a sample is real for the population. Is the absolute value of the sample r_s so different from zero that we can conclude that ρ_s is not zero and that this effect is not the result of sampling error?

For our sample of 10 high school runners, the critical value of r_s at the .05 level one-tailed is −.564. Since our observed r_s of −.81 is farther from zero than −.564 is, we reject the statistical hypothesis at the .05 level. We conclude that indeed, a negative relationship exists: The observed r_s of −.81 is so large that it did not result from sampling error. Sprinters in the 100-meter race tend not to do well in endurance events such as the 800-meter race, and vice versa.

Direction of a Relationship Using Spearman's rho

Observe the sign (+ or −) of r_s.

Strength of the Relationship for Spearman's rho

Regarding the strength of a relationship for two ordinal variables, just as with Pearson's r, Spearman's r_s can be squared to determine *the proportion of variation in ranks* of a dependent variable Y that is explained *by the ranks* of an independent variable X. Multiplying this proportion by 100 provides the percentage of variation that is explained. If we view the 100-meter race as X and the 800-meter race as Y, the strength of the relationship is as follows:

$$r_s^2 = -.81^2 = .6561; \% = (.6561)(100) = 65.61\%$$

Therefore, 65.61 percent of the variation in rank of finish in the 800-meter race (Y) is explained by knowing the rank of finish in the 100-meter race (X).

For predicting success in the 800-meter race, this is a considerable proportional reduction in error (PRE). Knowing that a runner did well in the 100-meter race allows us to predict that she will do relatively poorly in the 800-meter race. The prediction will not be perfect, however; other variables, such as individual talent, humidity, and wind speed, explain the remaining variation in rankings in the 800-meter race.

Strength of a Relationship Using Spearman's rho

r_s^2 = proportion of variation in rank of Y explained by knowing the rank of X

Nature of the Relationship for Spearman's rho

Ordinal variables, of course, do not have a set unit of measure. Therefore, it would be inaccurate to presume that precise best estimates can be provided. For example, it would be a strain to claim that a second-place finish in the 100-meter race will result in a seventh-place finish in the 800-meter race. Thus, in describing the nature of a relationship for ordinal data, it is best to provide only generalities. Describe whether subjects who rank toward the top on X rank toward the top or bottom on Y. In other words, emphasize the direction of the test. We could safely assert for this sample: If a runner ranks high in the 100-meter race, she is unlikely to do so in the 800-meter race, and vice versa. Now let us follow the six steps of statistical inference.

Nature of a Relationship Using Spearman's rho

Provide an illustration of correspondence between ranks, emphasizing the direction of the relationship. Describe whether a subject with a high rank on X has a high or low rank on Y.

The Six Steps of Statistical Inference for Spearman's rho

When to Use Spearman's rho Rank-Order Correlation Coefficient

In general: To test a hypothesis of a relationship between two ordinal variables with many ranks and few ties.

1. There are two ordinal variables.
2. There is a single representative sample from one population.
3. The sample size is 10 or more.
4. There are very few ties in the ranks of either variable (i.e., several observations do not fall at the same rank on a variable).

Brief Checklist for the Six Steps of Statistical Inference

Test Preparation

State the research question; list givens, including variables (e.g., $X =...$, $Y =...$), their levels of measurement, the population(s) under study, and sample(s) and sample size(s); select the statistical test; provide observations of statistics and parameters; and draw a conceptual diagram.

Six Steps

Using the symbol H for *hypothesis:*

1. State the statistical H and the alternative H and stipulate test direction.
2. Describe the sampling distribution.
3. State the level of significance (α) and specify the critical test value.
4. Observe the actual sample outcomes and compute the test effects, the test statistic, and the *p*-value.
5. Make the rejection decision.
6. Interpret and apply best estimates in everyday terms.

Test Preparation

Research question: Is there a negative relationship between rank of finish in 100-meter and 800-meter events for female high school track athletes, indicating that the races require different skills and training? *Givens:* Variables: X = rank of finish in the 100-meter race, Y = rank of finish in the 800-meter race; both are ordinal variables. *Population:* female high school track athletes. *Sample:* 10

members of the girls' track team who run in both events. *Statistical procedure:* Spearman's rho rank-order correlation coefficient; rho-distribution.

Observations: Ranks of finish for the two races and calculations of ΣD^2 are listed in Table 16–1.

$$r_s = 1 - \frac{6\Sigma D^2}{n(n^2 - 1)} = 1 - \frac{(6)(298)}{10\,(100 - 1)} = 1 - 1.81 = -.81$$

$n = 10$.

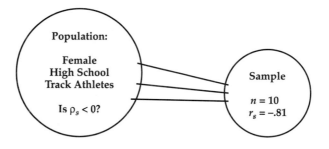

Six Steps

1. *Stat. H:* $\rho_{s\ \text{(high school track athletes)}} = 0$.

   That is, there is *no* relationship between ranks of finish in 100-meter and 800-meter races.

   Alt. H: $\rho_{s\ \text{(high school track athletes)}} < 0$.

   There *is* a negative relationship. One-tailed.

2. *Sampling distribution:* Spearman's rho rank-order correlation distribution for $n = 10$. If the Stat. *H* is true and samples of 10 female high school track athletes are drawn repeatedly, sample r_s's will center on zero with a standard error that is inversely related to sample size (i.e., the larger the sample, the smaller the standard error).

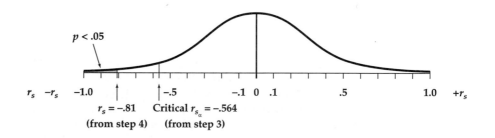

3. *Level of significance:* $\alpha = .05$, one-tailed; critical $r_{s_a} = -.564$ (from Statistical Table H in Appendix B).

4. *Observations:* Test effects, test statistic, and *p*-value.

   Test statistic: $r_s = -.81$
   Test effect $= r_s = -.81$ (i.e., effect $= r_s - \rho_s = r_s - 0 = -.81$)
   p-value: p [observing an r_s as unusual as or more unusual than $-.81$ when $\rho_s = 0$] $< .01$.

5. *Rejection decision:* $|r_{s_{(observed)}}| > |r_{s_\alpha}|$ (i.e., $|-.81| > |-.564|$) ; thus, $p < \alpha$. Reject Stat. *H* and accept Alt. *H* at the 95 percent level of confidence.

6. *Interpret results* (four aspects of a relationship and best estimates).

   Existence: There appears to be a relationship between ranks of finish in 100-meter and 800-meter races. $r_s = -.81$, p $< .01$.

   Direction: Negative: A high ranking in the 100-meter race is related to a low ranking in the 800-meter race.

   Strength: $r_s^2 = -.81^2 = .6561$; $\% = (.6561)(100)$. Thus, 65.61 percent of the variation in rank of finish in the 800-meter race (*Y*) is explained by knowing the rank of finish in the 100-meter race (*X*).

   Nature: If a runner ranks high in the 100-meter race, she is unlikely to do so in the 800-meter race, and vice versa.

   Answer: The talents, skills, and training required for one type of race are different from those required for the other.

Computing Spearman's rho When Ranks Are Tied

In everyday events, it is not uncommon for ranks to be tied. For example, in golf tournaments, often several people make the same score. Suppose we are comparing the rank of finish in two golf tournaments where 12 golfers competed. Table 16–2 provides the spreadsheet for these data. In tournament 1, three golfers tied for second and two tied for seventh. In tournament 2, two tied for third. In calculating r_s, we must account for all 12 ranks. In tournament 1, the three tying for second account for ranks 2, 3, and 4. We adjust these three ranks by averaging them:

$$\text{Adjusted rank for ties} = \frac{\Sigma \text{ ranks taken by ties}}{\# \text{ ties}} = \frac{2 + 3 + 4}{3} = 3$$

These adjusted ranks are indicated in parentheses in Table 16–2. Similar averaging is done for the seventh-place and third-place ties in tournament 2. Note in tournament 1 that the adjusted ranks for the ties for second are lower than "second," reflecting the fact that tying is not as distinctive as placing all alone. (Professional golfers know this well because tying reduces their winnings. When three golfers tie for second, the prize money for ranks 2, 3, and 4 is averaged and distributed among them.)

TABLE 16–2   Ranks of Finish for Two Golf Tournaments, $n = 12$

	Givens						Calculations	
Golfer	Golf Score, Rank of Finish, and (adjusted rank) in Tournament 1			Golf Score, Rank of Finish, and (adjusted rank) in Tournament 2			D	D^2
DuBose	69	1	(1)	68	2	(2)	−1	1
Bowden	71	Tie 2	(3)	67	1	(1)	2	4
Hernandez	71	Tie 2	(3)	73	6	(6)	−3	9
Carlton	71	Tie 2	(3)	69	Tie 3	(3.5)	−.5	.25
Jones	72	5	(5)	71	5	(5)	0	0
Bovey	73	6	(6)	69	Tie 3	(3.5)	2.5	6.25
McDuff	74	Tie 7	(7.5)	77	9	(9)	−1.5	2.25
Jenkins	74	Tie 7	(7.5)	74	7	(7)	.5	.25
Nickeless	75	9	(9)	76	8	(8)	1	1
Armstrong	76	10	(10)	80	10	(10)	0	0
Pearlman	78	11	(11)	81	11	(11)	0	0
Ryan	84	12	(12)	85	12	(12)	0	0
$n = 12$							$\Sigma D = 0$	$\Sigma D^2 = 24$

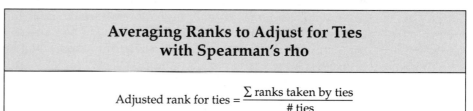

**Averaging Ranks to Adjust for Ties
with Spearman's rho**

$$\text{Adjusted rank for ties} = \frac{\Sigma \text{ ranks taken by ties}}{\# \text{ ties}}$$

Even before calculating r_s we should suspect that its value will be relatively large because the same six golfers placed high in both tournaments. The ranks of the two tournaments correspond rather well. Using ΣD^2 and n, we calculate r_s:

$$r_s = 1 - \frac{6\Sigma D^2}{n(n^2 - 1)} = 1 - \frac{(6)(24)}{12(144 - 1)} = .92$$

Indeed, the correlation is rather high. Using Statistical Table H, we compare this observed r_s of .92 to the critical r_{s_α} of .506 (for the .05 level of significance, one-tailed, $n = 12$). Since $.92 > .506$, $p < .05$. We accept the alternative hypothesis that there is a positive relationship between ranks of finish in golf tournaments.

Gamma: Relationships between Ordinal Variables with Few Ranks and Many Ties

Often ordinal variables have many tied scores; that is, there are only a few crude ranks, such as low, medium, and high, and there are many sample subjects in each category. Spearman's rho rank-order correlation does not apply with such variables. Instead, a statistic called Goodman and Kruskal's gamma is used. Table 16–3 presents fictional data for 115 married men so that we can test the hypothesis that overall life satisfaction (Y) is influenced greatly by marital happiness (X). This is a crosstab table, but with ordinal data, and it is arranged so that the variable categories go from low to high across and up like the score order of the axes of a scatterplot (see Chapter 14). Recall that in a crosstab table the cells record the joint frequencies of occurrence of cases. For example, in the lower left-hand cell there are 18 married men who rank low on marital happiness and low on life satisfaction; for X and Y, then, this is cell LL for "low-low." The LM cell above LL contains eight cases that rank low on marital happiness and moderate on life satisfaction. The cell to the right of LM is MM, which contains 24 men who are moderate on both variables, and so on. As with the chi-square procedure discussed in Chapter 13, the expected frequencies of these tables are predictable, and in fact, the chi-square test could be used here. If there is *no* relationship between X and Y, the observed cases will be distributed randomly according to the expected frequencies (see Chapter 13). By contrast, if those high on one variable rank similarly on the other, diagonal cells will have higher than expected frequencies.

A perfect positive relationship between X and Y would assert that as X increases, Y increases. For the sample at hand, subjects ranking low on marital

TABLE 16–3   Crosstab Table for Marital Happiness (X) as a Predictor of Life Satisfaction (Y)

Life Satisfaction (Y) ↓	$X \rightarrow$ Marital Happiness			
	Low (L)	*Moderate (M)*	*High (H)*	*Totals*
High (H)	LH 6	MH 9	HH 22	37
Moderate (M)	LM 8	MM 24	HM 11	43
Low (L)	LL 18	ML 10	HL 7	35
Totals	32	43	40	115

TABLE 16–4   Distribution of Cases When There Is a Perfect Positive Relationship between X and Y

Y $X \rightarrow$	*Low (L)*	*Moderate (M)*	*High (H)*
High (H)	LH	MH	**HH**
	0	0	**40**
Moderate (M)	LM	**MM**	HM
	0	**43**	0
Low (L)	**LL**	ML	HL
	32	0	0

---

happiness also would rank low on life satisfaction, those moderate on marital happiness would rank moderate on life satisfaction, and those high on marital happiness would rank high on life satisfaction. Such a perfect positive relationship is depicted in Table 16–4, where the cases fall in an upward diagonal pattern reminiscent of the upward-sloping regression line on a scatterplot. A perfect negative relationship, in which an increase in X is related to a decrease in Y, is depicted in the downward-sloping diagonal cells of Table 16–5. In reality we seldom encounter perfect relationships. Instead, data fall out as in Table 16–3 and indicate a less than perfect relationship.

With two crudely measured ordinal level variables, Goodman and Kruskal's gamma is a useful statistic and is preferable to the chi-square statistic. While both statistics are based on crosstab tables, gamma does not involve directly comparing observed frequencies to expected frequencies. Instead, gamma measures rank ordering by asking whether sample subjects are falling in the right order *for both variables*. To ascertain this, gamma compares each

---

TABLE 16–5   Distribution of Cases When There Is a Perfect Negative Relationship between X and Y

Y $X \rightarrow$	*Low (L)*	*Moderate (M)*	*High (H)*
High (H)	**LH**	MH	HH
	32	0	0
Moderate (M)	LM	**MM**	HM
	0	**43**	0
Low (L)	LL	ML	**HL**
	0	0	**40**

---

joint frequency to every other joint frequency. These comparisons are called case pairings.

To illustrate case pairings, let us observe Table 16–3 closely. Suppose Bob is a married man low on X, marital happiness, and Bill is a man moderate on X. If there is a positive relationship between X and Y, we would expect Bob to also be low on Y but Bill to be moderate or high on Y. Suppose that indeed Bob is an LL and Bill is an MM. When a comparison occurs that way, suggesting a positive relationship between the variables, we say that there is *an agreement* between Bob and Bill. A **case pairing with agreement** occurs when *a case ranks lower than another case on both variables.*

If it turns out, however, that Bill is not moderate or high on Y, we have a case pairing called *an inversion*. A **case pairing with inversion** occurs when *a case is ranked higher on one variable but lower on the other compared to another case.* An example of an inversion is a comparison between someone who scores LH and someone who scores HL. Such case pairings suggest a negative relationship.

For the perfect positive relationship in Table 16–4 note that every LL case is in agreement—lower on both X and Y than are the cases in MM and HH—and every case in MM is in agreement with HH. In other words, a perfect positive relationship has 100 percent agreement between all case pairings. Similarly, for the perfect negative relationship in Table 16–5 all case pairings are inverted. Gamma is calculated in a way that determines the extent of agreement or inversion in the case pairings in the crosstab table. The formula for gamma is as follows:

Calculation of Goodman and Kruskal's Gamma for Two Ordinal Variables

$$G = \frac{\Sigma f_a - \Sigma f_i}{\Sigma f_a + \Sigma f_i}$$

where

G = gamma computed on a sample
Σf_a = sum of agreements
Σf_i = sum of inversions

Let us obtain a sense of proportion about this formula. The denominator is simply the total of all case pairings in agreement and inversion. When there are complete agreements and no inversions, the relationship between the variables will be a perfect positive one, as in Table 16–4. When that happens, the sum of inversions (Σf_i) will be zero in both the numerator and the denominator and gamma will compute to +1.0:

$$G = \frac{\Sigma f_a - \Sigma f_i}{\Sigma f_a + \Sigma f_i}$$

$$= \frac{\Sigma f_a - 0}{\Sigma f_a + 0} = 1.0 = \text{perfect positive relationship}$$

In contrast, when there are only inversions, we have a perfect negative relationship, as in Table 16–5. The sum of agreements (Σf_a) will equal zero and gamma will compute to –1.0:

$$G = \frac{\Sigma f_a - \Sigma f_i}{\Sigma f_a + \Sigma f_i}$$

$$= \frac{0 - \Sigma f_i}{0 + \Sigma f_i} = 1.0 = \text{perfect negative relationship}$$

When there is no relationship between X and Y, agreements and inversions will be equal. This reduces the numerator ($\Sigma f_a - \Sigma f_i$) to zero and results in a gamma of zero:

$$G = \frac{\Sigma f_a - \Sigma f_i}{\Sigma f_a + \Sigma f_i} = \frac{0}{\Sigma f_a + \Sigma f_i} = 0.0 = \text{no relationship}$$

Thus, gamma ranges from –1.0 to zero to +1.0.

Calculating and Interpreting Gamma

Let us return to Table 16–3 and measure gamma for the relationship between marital happiness and life satisfaction. To calculate gamma, we must compute the sum of agreements (Σf_a) and the sum of inversions (Σf_i).

Summing the Agreements. To obtain the sum of agreements, start by focusing on the LL cases. The 18 cases in LL will be in agreement with all the cases in any cell where both X and Y are higher. These cells consist of the following boldface entries:

LH 6	**MH 9**	**HH 22**
LM 8	**MM 24**	**HM 11**
Compare LL 18	ML 10	HL 7

With 18 individuals in LL and 24 in MM, there are 18 times 24 case pairings (i.e., each case in LL is paired with each of the 24 cases in MM). Similarly, comparing the 18 LL cases to the 11 in HM, there are 18 times 11 case pairings. Additional LL agreements are for comparisons with MH (18 times 9) and HH (18 times 22). In other words, the frequency of agreements for the 18 cases in LL is

$$f_a \text{ for LL case pairings} = 18 (24 + 11 + 9 + 22) = 1{,}188$$

Three additional cells in the table (ML, LM, and MM) can be in agreement (i.e., situated so that both X and Y are higher in other cells). Along with LL, these constitute the four comparisons cells for which agreements are possible in a 3×3 table. The calculation of the frequency of case pairings in agreement for these three additional comparison cells is as follows:

LH 6	MH 9	**HH** **22**
LM 8	MM 24	**HM** **11**
LL 18	**Compare** **ML 10**	HL 7

Thus,

$$f_a \text{ for ML case pairings} = 10 (11 + 22) = 330$$

LH 6	**MH** **9**	**HH** **22**
Compare **LM 8**	MM 24	HM 11
LL 18	ML 10	HL 7

Thus,

$$f_a \text{ for LM case pairings} = 8 (9 + 22) = 248$$

LH 6	MH 9	**HH** **22**
LM 8	**Compare** **MM 24**	HM 11
LL 18	ML 10	HL 7

Thus,

$$f_a \text{ for MM case pairings} = 24\ (22) = 528$$

The total number of case pairings in agreement in the table is

$$\Sigma f_a = f_a \text{ for LL case pairings} + f_a \text{ for ML case pairings}$$

$$+ f_a \text{ for LM case pairings} + f_a \text{ for MM case pairings}$$

$$= 1{,}188 + 330 + 248 + 528 = 2{,}294$$

Note that the four comparison cells used in computing agreements are all in the lower left-hand corner of the crosstab table. The cells to which they are compared are in the upper right-hand corner. This structure in the case-cell pairings fits the diagonal of the perfect positive relationship in Table 16–4.

Summing the Inversions.   There are also four comparison cells for case pairings where X and Y are inverted. The following comparisons are needed to sum the inversions.

LH 6	MH 9	HH 22
LM 8	MM 24	HM 11
LL 18	ML 10	Compare HL 7

Thus,

$$f_i \text{ for HL case pairings} = 7\ (8 + 24 + 6 + 9) = 329$$

LH 6	MH 9	HH 22
LM 8	MM 24	Compare HM 11
LL 18	ML 10	HL 7

Thus,

$$f_i \text{ for HM pairings} = 11 \, (6 + 9) = 165$$

LH 6	MH 9	HH 22
LM 8	MM 24	HM 11
LL 18	**Compare ML 10**	HL 7

Thus,

$$f_i \text{ for ML case pairings} = 10 \, (8 + 6) = 140$$

LH 6	MH 9	HH 22
LM 8	**Compare MM 24**	HM 11
LL 18	ML 10	HL 7

Thus,

$$f_i \text{ for MM case pairings} = 24 \, (6) = 144$$

The total number of case pairings in inversion in the table is

$$\Sigma f_i = f_i \text{ for HL case pairings} + f_i \text{ for HM case pairings}$$

$$+ \, f_i \text{ for ML case pairings} + f_i \text{ for MM case pairings}$$

$$= 329 + 165 + 140 + 144 = 778$$

Note that the four comparison cells used in computing inversions are all in the lower right-hand corner and the cells to which they are compared are in the upper left-hand corner of the table. This structure in the case-cell pairings fits the diagonal of a perfect negative relationship (Table 16–5).

Calculating Gamma. Now that we have the sums of agreements and inversions, we can calculate gamma:

$$G = \frac{\Sigma f_a - \Sigma f_i}{\Sigma f_a + \Sigma f_i} = \frac{2{,}294 - 778}{2{,}294 + 778} = \frac{1{,}516}{3{,}072} = .49$$

What does this tell us? First, the result is positive. There is a relative over-supply of agreements, reflecting an overload of cases in the cells running from lower left to upper right. In other words, there is a tendency for a subject's rank on Y to be equal to or higher than his rank on X. An increase in marital happiness is related to an increase in life satisfaction. Since terms are not squared and the same terms are used in both the numerator and the denominator, the interpretation of gamma is that it is a straightforward proportion. In the situation of this positive relationship, we can see that 1,516 of the 3,072 case pairings are in agreement beyond the 778 in disagreement. Thus, .49, or 49 percent, of the case pairings favor agreement, suggesting a moderately strong relationship between marital happiness and life satisfaction.

Existence of the Relationship for Gamma

Of course, the distribution of joint frequencies in Table 16–3 could be the result of sampling error. Repeated sampling from the same population will produce slightly different patterns of cell frequencies and case pairings even when there is no relationship between ranks of the two variables. Thus, we must test the hypothesis that a gamma of .49 is significantly different from zero. In other words, our statistical hypothesis is that there is no relationship between marital happiness and life satisfaction in the population, or that the parameter $\gamma = 0$. (This may legitimately be called a null hypothesis.) Our alternative hypothesis asserts a positive relationship (i.e., $\gamma > 0$).

The sampling distribution for gamma is a normal one, and therefore, the test statistic is a Z-score. That is, if the statistical hypothesis that $\gamma = 0$ is true and we draw a large number of samples of size 115, sample G's will be normally distributed around zero. Since the standard error for gamma is very complicated, conventionally the Z-score to measure the deviation of the observed sample from zero is simplified. As we did for the sampling distribution of Pearson's r in Chapter 15, we state that the standard error is inversely related to sample size (i.e., the larger the sample size, the smaller the standard error). The formula gives the number of standard errors a computed gamma deviates from the hypothesized parameter of zero. For the relationship between marital happiness and life satisfaction,

$$Z_G = G \sqrt{\frac{\Sigma f_a + \Sigma f_i}{n(1 - G^2)}} = .49 \sqrt{\frac{3072}{115(1 - .49^2)}} = 2.91$$

Using the normal curve table (Statistical Table B in Appendix B), we calculate the p-value by locating the Z-score in column A and the area in the tail of the distribution curve in column C. Thus,

p-value: p [observing a G as unusual as or more unusual than .49 when $\gamma = 0$] = .0018

At the .05 level of significance for a one-tailed test, we reject the statistical hypothesis and accept the alternative hypothesis at the 95 percent level of confidence. Since we found a relationship between marital happiness and life satisfaction, we may address the other aspects of relationships.

Existence of a Relationship Using Gamma (*G*)

Test the statistical hypothesis that $\gamma = 0$ using the test statistic:

$$Z_G = G \sqrt{\frac{\Sigma f_a + \Sigma f_i}{n(1 - G^2)}}$$

Direction of the Relationship for Gamma

The direction of the relationship depends on the sign of gamma. For the data in Table 16–3 we would say that there is a positive relationship between marital happiness and life satisfaction. That is, an increase in rank on marital happiness is related to an increase in rank on life satisfaction.

Direction of a Relationship Using Gamma (*G*)

Observe the sign (+ or –) of *G*.

Strength of the Relationship for Gamma

The strength of the relationship is described by interpreting the magnitude of gamma as a percentage of the case pairings favoring agreement (or inversion):

Percentage of the case pairings favoring agreement = (*G*) (100)

For the relationship between marital happiness and life satisfaction, the strength is described as follows: "Forty-nine percent of the case pairings favored agreement, suggesting a moderately strong relationship." Keep in mind that unlike Pearson's *r* and Spearman's rho, we do not need to square gamma.

Strength of a Relationship Using Gamma (*G*)

Interpret gamma as the percentage of case pairings favoring agreement:

Percentage of case pairings favoring agreement = (*G*) (100)

Nature of the Relationship for Gamma

The nature of the relationship describes substance. In general, we may state: Married men tend to rank about the same on both marital happiness and life satisfaction, suggesting the marital happiness is an important factor in overall life satisfaction. In addition, we may point to one or two of the cells in the crosstab table to convey a best estimate. Cells in the corners are especially informative because they convey extreme lows and highs. Typically, comparing the HH cell to the LH cell is informative. To do this we compute the column percentage for HH, the percentage of cases high on X that also are high on Y. In Table 16–3 there are a total of 40 subjects who ranked high on X, marital happiness; this is the column total for high. Of these 40 cases, 22 also ranked high on Y, life satisfaction; this is the cell frequency for HH. Thus, 22 of 40, or 55 percent, of those high on marital happiness also rank high on life satisfaction. Similarly, for the LH cell, 6 of 32, or only about 19 percent, of subjects rank low on X, marital happiness, but rank high on Y, life satisfaction. Thus, we describe the particulars of the nature of the relationship as follows: Among married men, 55 percent with high marital happiness also have high life satisfaction but only 19 percent of those with low marital happiness have high life satisfaction. This could be followed with the comment that nearly three times the percentage (the ratio of 55 percent to 19 percent) of happily married men have high life satisfaction. If Table 16–3 is presented to a public audience, additional comparisons can be made, for instance, between the LL and LH cells.

Nature of a Relationship Using Gamma (*G*)

Provide best estimates by computing column percentages for one or two informative cells in the crosstab table (usually corner cells that convey extreme lows and highs).

Summary Guide for Calculating Gamma

As a guide to calculations, Table 16–6 summarizes the steps for calculating gamma for a 3×3 ordinal crosstab table. The case pairings we described above are identified for obtaining Σf_a and Σf_i. Note again that in the agreements pairings, the four comparison cells (LL, ML, LM, and MM) are in the lower left-hand corner of the crosstab table and the cells to which they are compared are in the upper right-hand corner. This will always be the case when X goes from low to moderate to high across and Y goes from low to moderate to high upward on a 3×3 crosstab table. The calculation of agreements follows the positive relationship diagonal (Table 16–4), and the sum will be large when frequencies are heavily loaded along this diagonal.

Similarly, the calculation of inversions involves the four comparison cells in the lower right-hand corner (HL, HM, ML, and MM) and case-cell comparisons follow the negative relationship diagonal (Table 16–6). The sum of inversions will be large when frequencies are heavily loaded along the negative diagonal.

TABLE 16–6   Guide for Calculating Gamma (G) for a 3×3 Ordinal Crosstab Table

A. Calculating the sum of agreements Σf_a (where f = frequency)
Identify the case pairings that are in agreement:

$Y \uparrow X \rightarrow$

	MH	HH			HH		MH	HH			HH
	MM	HM			HM	Compare LM				Compare MM	
Compare LL				Compare ML							

Cells for LL case pairings   Cells for ML case pairings   Cells for LM case pairings   Cells for MM case pairings

Calculate the frequency of agreements:

$$f_a \text{ for LL case pairings} = f_{LL}(f_{MM} + f_{HM} + f_{MH} + f_{HH})$$
$$f_a \text{ for ML case pairings} = f_{ML}(f_{HM} + f_{HH})$$
$$f_a \text{ for LM case pairings} = f_{LM}(f_{MH} + f_{HH})$$
$$f_a \text{ for MM case pairings} = f_{MM}(f_{HH})$$
$$\Sigma f_a = f_a \text{ for LL case pairings} + f_a \text{ for ML case pairings}$$
$$+\, f_a \text{ for LM case pairings} + f_a \text{ for MM case pairings}$$

B. Calculating the sum of inversions Σf_i (where f = frequency)
Identify the case pairings that are inverted:

$Y \uparrow X \rightarrow$

LH	MH		LH	MH		LH			LH		
LM	MM				Compare HM	LM				Compare MM	
		Compare HL					Compare ML				

Cells for HL case pairings   Cells for HM case pairings   Cells for ML case pairings   Cells for MM case pairings

Calculate the frequency of inversions:

$$f_i \text{ for HL case pairings} = f_{HL}(f_{LM} + f_{MM} + f_{LH} + f_{MH})$$
$$f_i \text{ for HM case pairings} = f_{HM}(f_{LH} + f_{MH})$$

$$f_i \text{ for ML case pairings} = f_{ML} \, (f_{LM} + f_{LH})$$

$$f_i \text{ for MM case pairings} = f_{MM} \, (f_{LH})$$

$$\Sigma f_i = f_i \text{ for HL case pairings} + f_i \text{ for HM case pairings}$$

$$+ f_i \text{ for ML case pairings} + f_i \text{ for MM case pairings}$$

C. Calculating gamma (G):

$$G = \frac{\Sigma f_a - \Sigma f_i}{\Sigma f_a + \Sigma f_i}$$

D. Calculating the test statistic Z_G:

$$Z_G = G \sqrt{\frac{\Sigma f_a + \Sigma f_i}{n(1 - G^2)}}$$

When to Use Goodman and Kruskal's Gamma for Two Ordinal Variables (normal distribution)

In general: To test a hypothesis of a relationship between two ordinal variables with few ranked categories for each variable (tied scores are expected).

1. There are two ordinal variables.
2. There is a single representative sample from one population.
3. The sample size is 10 or more.
4. There are few ranked categories for each variable (tied scores are expected).

Sample Problem Using the Six Steps of Statistical Inference for Gamma

For the sake of variety and to see how gamma works for a negative relationship, let us illustrate the six steps of statistical inference for a new problem that deals with labor force participation. This is an important concern for economists and sociologists, who often study the obstacles to acquiring and keeping gainful employment. For example, Browne (1997) examines labor force participation among women who head households. One obstacle to obtaining gainful employment among some of these women is parenting responsibilities, which depend, among other things, on the ages of their children. Table 16–7 presents crosstab data from a fictional random sample similar to Browne's. Is labor force participation lower for women with greater parenting responsibilities?

TABLE 16–7   Degree of Labor Force Participation (*Y*) by Extent of Parenting Responsibilities (*X*)

Degree of Labor Force Participation	Extent of Parenting Responsibilities			Totals
	Low (no children)	*Moderate (child 6–18 years)*	*High (child under 6 years)*	
High (employed full time)	54	23	19	96
Moderate (employed part time)	5	20	7	32
Low (no regular employment)	4	8	18	30
Totals	63	51	44	158

Brief Checklist for the Six Steps of Statistical Inference

Test Preparation

State the research question; list givens, including variables (e.g., $X =...$, $Y =...$), their levels of measurement, the population(s) under study, and sample(s) and sample size(s); select the statistical test; provide observations of statistics and parameters; and draw a conceptual diagram.

Six Steps

Using the symbol *H* for *hypothesis:*

1. State the statistical *H* and the alternative *H* and stipulate test direction.
2. Describe the sampling distribution.
3. State the level of significance (α) and specify the critical test value.
4. Observe the actual sample outcomes and compute the test effects, the test statistic, and the *p*-value.
5. Make the rejection decision.
6. Interpret and apply best estimates in everyday terms.

Test Preparation

Research question: Is labor force participation lower for women with greater parenting responsibilities? In other words, is there a negative relationship between extent of parenting responsibilities and degree of labor participation?

Givens: Variables: X = extent of parenting responsibilities and Y = degree of labor force participation; both are ordinal level variables. *Population:* women who are heads of households. *Sample:* 158 women. *Statistical procedure:* Goodman and Kruskal's gamma (normal distribution). *Observations:* Data in Table 16–7 (gamma and Z-score are calculated below).

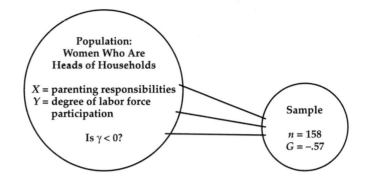

Six Steps

1. *Stat. H:* $\gamma_{(\text{female heads of households})} = 0$

   That is, there is *no* relationship between extent of parenting responsibilities and degree of labor force participation for female heads of households.

   Alt. H: $\gamma_{(\text{female heads of households})} < 0$

   That is, there *is* a negative relationship. One-tailed. As parenting responsibilities increase, the degree of labor force participation decreases.

2. *Sampling distribution:* Normal distribution. If the Stat. H is true and samples of size 158 are drawn repeatedly from the population of female heads of households, sample gamma coefficients (G's) will center on zero with a standard error inversely related to sample size.

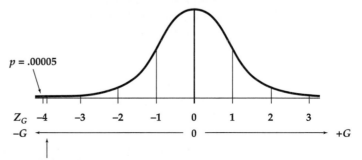

3. *Level of significance:* $\alpha = .05$, one-tailed. Critical $Z_\alpha = -1.64$.

4. *Observations:* Test effects, test statistic, and p-value. Using Table 16–6 as a guide to calculate gamma (G) for the data in Table 16–7:

$$f_a \text{ for LL case pairings} = 4\ (20 + 7 + 23 + 19) = 276$$

$$f_a \text{ for ML case pairings} = 8\ (7 + 19) = 208$$

$$f_a \text{ for LM case pairings} = 5\ (23 + 19) = 210$$

$$f_a \text{ for MM case pairings} = 20\ (19) = 380$$

$$\Sigma f_a = 276 + 208 + 210 + 380 = 1{,}074$$

$$f_i \text{ for HL case pairings} = 18\ (5 + 20 + 54 + 23) = 1{,}836$$

$$f_i \text{ for HM case pairings} = 7\ (54 + 23) = 539$$

$$f_i \text{ for ML case pairings} = 8\ (5 + 54) = 472$$

$$f_i \text{ for MM case pairings} = 20\ (54) = 1{,}080$$

$$\Sigma f_i = 1{,}836 + 539 + 472 + 1{,}080 = 3{,}927$$

$$G = \frac{\Sigma f_a - \Sigma f_i}{\Sigma f_a + \Sigma f_i} = \frac{1{,}074 - 3{,}927}{1{,}074 + 3{,}927} = \frac{-2{,}853}{5{,}001} = -.57$$

Test effect: The difference between the observed G and the hypothesized γ of 0 is $-.57$.

Test statistic:

$$Z_G = G \sqrt{\frac{\Sigma f_a + \Sigma f_i}{n(1 - G^2)}} = -.57 \sqrt{\frac{5{,}001}{158[1 - (-.57)^2]}} = -3.89 \text{ SE}$$

p-value: p [observing a G as unusual as or more unusual than $-.57$ when $\gamma = 0$] $= .00005$ (from the normal curve table and diagrammed on the curve in step 2 above).

5. *Rejection decision:* $|Z_G| > |Z_a|$ (i.e., $|-3.89| > |-1.64|$); thus, $p < \alpha$; $.00005 < .05$. Reject Stat. H and accept Alt. H at the 95 percent level of confidence.

6. *Interpretation* (aspects of relationship and best estimates).

   Existence: There appears to be a relationship between extent of parenting responsibilities and degree of labor force participation for female heads of households: $G = -.57$, $p = .00005$.

   Direction: Negative. As the extent of parenting responsibilities increases, the degree of labor force participation decreases.

Strength: $G = -.57$; 57 percent of the case pairings favored inversion, suggesting a moderately strong negative relationship.

Nature: In general, individuals with low parenting responsibilities tend to rank low on labor force participation.

Best estimates: While 86 percent of the women with no children are employed full time, only 43 percent of the women with children under six years of age are employed full time.

Answer: Labor force participation is lower for women with greater parenting responsibilities.

Some things of note about this hypothesis test:

- In step 2, to avoid a truly cumbersome calculation of an estimated standard error of gamma, we simply describe the sampling distribution's spread as being "inversely related to sample size." Once G is computed, however, the standard error can be calculated quite easily. We now know that the quantity .57 is 3.89 standard errors. Thus,

$$s_G = \frac{-.57}{-3.89} = .15$$

where s_G is the estimated standard error of the gamma distribution (estimated because it is based on this sample). Insert this value on the curve, and its fit will become apparent.

- In step 4, after calculating G, we note that it constitutes a test effect, the difference between the observed sample statistic G and the hypothesized parameter $\gamma = 0$. Remember that G essentially measures how well cell frequencies fit a diagonal of the crosstab table. The stronger the effect of X (parenting responsibilities) on Y (labor force participation), the larger the absolute value of the observed gamma (G).

- In step 6 the best estimates are column percentages for cells LH and HH, which are obtained by dividing the cell frequency by the column total and multiplying by 100. Note the "down-to-earth" tone of the description of these percentages. Best estimates are especially valuable for public audiences, where the discussion should stick to women who head households, the number of children they have, and the nature of their employment or lack of employment. In describing the nature of a relationship, technical language such as gamma, *p*-value, and case pairings should be avoided as much as possible.

- The pencil-and-paper formula for calculating the test statistic Z_G is one that bypasses having to calculate a very complex standard error. The results we obtain from this formula, however, will differ slightly from the results obtained from the *SPSS* computer software that accompanies this text. The pencil-and-paper formula is a conservative one in that it produces the minimum value of Z and, therefore, the maximum *p*-value for the sample outcome. The *SPSS* computer output will likely produce a smaller *p*-value increasing the chance of rejecting the statistical hypothesis and making a Type I error. Taking this into account, experienced researchers weigh gamma computer output against other computed statistics as described in the next section.

Other Rank-Order Correlation Statistics

Several other statistics measure rank-order correlation between two ordinal variables, including Somer's *d* and Kendall's tau-*b* and tau-*c* (see Lee and Maykovich 1995: 149–53). We will not describe them in detail here. We note, however, that the calculated values and interpretation of these statistics are similar to those of gamma in that each one (1) uses sums and ratios of agreements and inversions, (2) has a value between –1.0 and 1.0, and (3) requires a representative sample. Why are these additional statistics used in some circumstances? Note in Table 16–6 that we did not use every possible case pairing (and cell comparison) in calculating gamma. In calculating agreements, we include only the cells in which both *X* and *Y* increase. We ignore ties in ranks. For example, we did not compare LL to LM even though Y increases. We did this because the subjects in LL and LM are tied on *X*. Similar ties occur with *Y*. Somer's *d* is calculated taking into account ties on one of the variables. Kendall's tau takes into account ties on both variables. These statistics, like gamma, hinge on the difference between agreements and inversions. They differ from gamma in that the number of tied case pairings is added to the denominator. Since the denominators with Somer's *d* and Kendall's tau are larger, these statistics provide *smaller* values than does gamma.

To acquire a good understanding of the logic of gamma and similar statistics and to obtain a good sense of proportion about ranks and case pairings, it is important to do some pencil and paper calculations. The particulars of calculating gamma-type statistics, however, have led researchers to rely heavily on computers. One advantage of the computer is that a variety of coefficients (gamma, Somer's *d*, and Kendall's tau-*b* and tau-*c*) can be requested at once. In many circumstances, the results of the various statistics are the same (except that gamma typically is larger). However, when differences *are* detected among the statistics, this provides a warning that there are peculiarities in the data (such as a large number of tied case pairings). The time spent calculating more than just a few gamma-type coefficients by hand can better be used in learning about statistical computer software.

Unfortunately, interpretation of rank-order statistics is constrained by the level of measurement; that is, care must be taken in describing the strength and nature of the relationship. For this reason and others, statisticians often treat ordinal level variables as though they had interval/ratio level qualities and use interval/ratio variable techniques such as correlation and regression.

Using Ordinal Variables with Interval/Ratio Techniques

Statistical Robustness

Most research involves multivariate statistics—examining how several independent variables, taken together, account for a PRE in predicting the scores of a single dependent variable. PRE is most meaningful when the dependent variable is of interval/ratio level of measurement. In these situations, correlation and regression (Chapters 14 and 15) and analysis of variance (ANOVA) (Chapter 12) are widely utilized. Although this text does not cover multivariate procedures, it is worth noting that ordinal level independent variables sometimes complicate the use of these interval/ratio techniques.

In general, interval/ratio procedures provide more thorough information. For example, Pearson's correlation coefficient (r) is superior to Spearman's rho rank-order coefficient (r_s) in terms of providing precise best estimates in describing the nature of a relationship. Thus, attempts are made to determine whether an ordinal variable qualifies as "interval-like" so that it can be used with Pearson's r or ANOVA. Interval/ratio techniques, of course, work under the assumption that variables have a set interval. However, exceptions can be made to this assumption because the t-test and F-ratio tests used for Pearson's r and ANOVA frequently produce the same statistical results that are produced by ordinal techniques such as Spearman's test. This is the case, for instance, for the data in Table 16–2 on the rankings of finish for 12 golfers in two tournament appearances. When the scores adjusted for ties are used, the Pearson's r computes to .91 compared to the Spearman's calculation of .92. In both tests, the statistical hypothesis of no relationship is rejected and the alternative hypothesis of a positive relationship is accepted. The interpretation is essentially the same, although "rank" instead of "score" is what is described in the aspects of the relationship. Although an assumption of the Pearson's coefficient test is that the variable will be of interval/ratio level, the t-test still works. *Statistical tests that work even when all assumptions are not met* are called **robust statistical tests.**

How is it determined that an ordinal variable can be treated as interval/ratio? One way is to test the hypothesis by using both ordinal and interval techniques. If the same results are found, the variable can be treated as interval thereafter. This is useful especially if the variable is to be combined with others in a multivariate model. As was noted in Chapter 2, typically the results will be the same for an ordinal variable when (1) it has at least seven ranked categories or scores and (2) the score distribution is not skewed or bimodal. The latter criterion means that the scores can be either normally distributed or rectangularly distributed (i.e. evenly distributed across their range with about the same frequency at each score; see "Statistical Follies and Fallacies," below).

When an ordinal variable has fewer than seven ranks, it often will fail to produce good results with Pearson's *r*. In these situations, the ranked categories of the variable may be collapsed into a dummy variable, a dichotomous variable with scores of 0 and 1. For example, a variable with the ranked categories scored 1 = strongly disagree, 2 = disagree, 3 = agree, and 4 = strongly agree might be recoded so that 0 = disagree (i.e., recode 1 and 2 to 0) and 1 = agree (i.e., recode 3 and 4 to 1). However, when dummy variables are used in correlation and regression techniques they must be interpreted carefully. In any case, if you go beyond this course into multivariate statistics, you will often encounter ordinal variables being treated as though they were interval/ratio variables. Do this only if it is appropriate, and use care in the interpretation.

Finally, the use of an ordinal variable as the dependent variable is especially limiting. In research design it is wise to construct measurement instruments (such as questionnaires) with important variables at an interval/ratio level. This goal can be accomplished by using summary measurement scales—in which responses to a series of nominal/ordinal questionnaire items are summed.

☹   STATISTICAL FOLLIES AND FALLACIES   ☹

When Ordinal Variables with Many Ranks Are Actually Dichotomous Nominal Variables

---

In Chapter 2 we noted that the first step in data analysis is to observe the raw frequency distributions of variables. One reason for doing this is to identify and confirm the level of measurement of each variable to assist in choosing appropriate statistical techniques. This exercise in error control often reveals that an intended multiple-category ordinal variable is actually a dichotomous (two-category) variable. This situation is recognizable when the score frequency distribution is bimodal. This often occurs with survey items that measure attitudes on controversial topics about which respondents tend to hold either strongly positive or strongly negative opinions.

Suppose, for example, we wish to measure opinions on physician-assisted suicide, the situation in which physicians help terminally ill patients end their lives. One of our questionnaire items may read: Physician-assisted suicide should be an option for patients who are terminally ill and suffering great pain. We may design responses in a Likert format in which the respondent answers strongly disagree, disagree, agree, or strongly agree. After gathering data, suppose we find the following frequency distribution for this variable.

Code	Response Value	f	Percent
1	Strongly disagree	76	55.9%
2	Disagree	12	8.8
3	Agree	9	6.6
4	Strongly agree	39	28.7
Totals		136	100.0%

Although we scored this in four categories, the loading of responses on the extremes essentially reveals two clusters of opinion: those who disagree and those who agree. If ordinal data techniques are used, because the disagree and agree categories are sparsely populated, there will be many cells that are nearly empty and many ties for the extreme response categories. If we use interval/ratio techniques—all based on computations of means and standard deviations—the extreme scores will inflate the values of these statistics. In this type of situation the variable should be recognized for what it is: a dichotomous nominal variable. Codes 1 and 2 would be recoded to zero for disagree; codes 3 and 4 would be recoded to 1 for agree. This will provide a truer representation of the distribution of scores with the following frequency distribution.

Code	Response Value	f	Percent
0	Disagree	88	64.7%
1	Agree	48	35.3
Totals		136	100.0%

Statistical Procedures Covered to Here

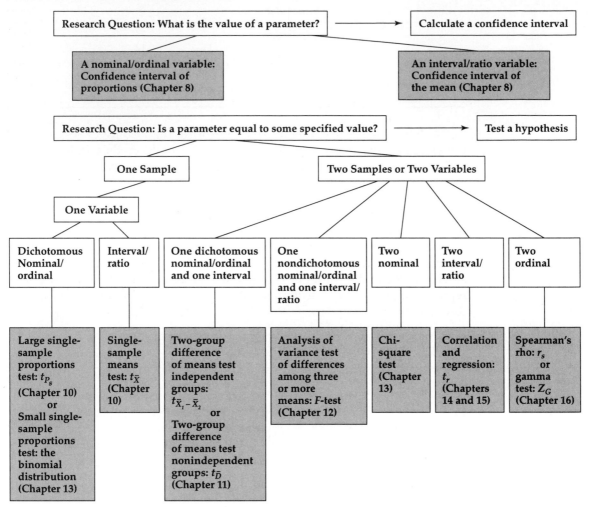

Formulas in Chapter 16

Spearman's rho rank-order correlation coefficient for testing the relationship between two ordinal variables:

Given: Two ordinal variables X and Y with many ranks. Order the data in a spreadsheet:

	Givens		Calculations	
Subject	*Rank on X*	*Rank on Y*	*D*	*D²*
...	...	...	...	...
...	...	...	...	...
...	...	...	...	...
$n = ...$			$\Sigma D = 0$	$\Sigma D^2 = ...$

Research question: Is there a relationship between the variables? Do the subjects who rank high on X rank high (or low) on Y?

Stat. H: $\rho_s = 0$.

Sampling distribution: Spearman's rho rank-order correlation distribution.
Test effect:

$$r_s - \rho_s = r_s - 0 = r_s$$

Test statistic:

$$r_s = 1 - \frac{6\Sigma D^2}{n(n^2 - 1)}$$

Addressing the aspects of the relationship:

Direction: Observe the sign of r_s.
Strength: r_s^2 = proportion of variation in rank of Y explained by knowing the rank of X (multiply r_s^2 by 100 to express this as a percentage).
Nature: Describe the direction, specifying whether those ranking high on X rank high or low on Y.

Averaging ranks to adjust for ties with Spearman's rho:

$$\text{Adjusted rank for ties} = \frac{\Sigma \text{ ranks taken by ties}}{\# \text{ ties}}$$

Goodman and Kruskal's gamma for testing the relationship between two ordinal variables with few ranks and many ties:

Given: Two ordinal variables X and Y with few ranks and many ties (arranged in a crosstab table).
Research question: Is there a relationship between the variables?

Stat. H: $\gamma = 0$.

Sampling distribution: the normal distribution.
Test effect: $G - \gamma = G - 0 = G$.
　　Follow Table 16–6 to make calculations of Σf_a and Σf_i:

$$G = \frac{\Sigma f_a - \Sigma f_i}{\Sigma f_a + \Sigma f_i}$$

Test statistic:

$$Z_G = G \sqrt{\frac{\Sigma f_a + \Sigma f_i}{n(1 - G^2)}}$$

Addressing the aspects of the relationship:
　　Direction: Observe the sign of G.
　　Strength: Interpret gamma as the percentage of case pairings favoring agreement: percentage of the case pairings favoring agreement = $(G)(100)$.
　　Nature: Provide best estimates by computing column percentages for one or two informative cells in the crosstab table (usually corner cells that convey extreme lows and highs).

Questions for Chapter 16

1. Under what circumstances is the Spearman's rho rank-order correlation coefficient used to test a hypothesis?

2. For Spearman's rho rank-order correlation coefficient, draw a conceptual diagram depicting a population and a sample and insert the appropriate statistics and parameters. Stipulate how the statistical hypothesis is stated for the hypothesis test.

3. How is the test effect calculated for the Spearman's rho rank-order correlation? Describe the relationship between the size of the test effect and the likelihood of rejecting the statistical hypothesis.

4. In testing a hypothesis of a relationship between two ordinal variables using the Spearman's rho rank-order correlation coefficient, how is the strength of the relationship calculated and interpreted? How does this interpretation differ from that of Pearson's r (Chapter 15)?

5. For Goodman and Kruskal's gamma, draw a conceptual diagram depicting a population and a sample and insert the appropriate statistics and parameters. Stipulate how the statistical hypothesis is stated for the hypothesis test.

6. When is it appropriate to use Goodman and Kruskal's gamma to test a hypothesis about a relationship between two variables?

7. Describe what case pairings with agreement and case pairings with inversion are. Explain how these ideas are used with the gamma statistic.

8. What is a robust statistical test? Why is this sometimes an issue with hypothesis testing?

Exercises for Chapter 16

General instructions: On all hypothesis tests follow the six steps of statistical inference, including test preparation, a conceptual diagram, probability curves, and appropriate aspects of a relationship. For consistency, round calculations to two decimal places. Use $\alpha = .05$ unless otherwise stipulated.

1. Critics assert that modern election campaigns often center more on a candidate's ability to raise funds than on the candidate's positions on issues. Is this belief supported by the following fictional data from a city council election?

Rank of Finish in the Election	Rank in Terms of Campaign Expenditures
1	1
2	3
3	2
4	4
5	6
6	5

2. The Social Science Citation Index (SSCI) Factor Score is a measure of the frequency with which a research article is cited by other scientists. It sometimes is used by college administrators in making promotion decisions. Critics argue that these scores can be misleading because the frequency of citation depends on how many scientists are available to cite the work (i.e., the size of the discipline).
Is this criticism justified?

Discipline	Ranking of Discipline by Number of Members	Ranking of Discipline in Terms of How Frequently its Leading Journal is Cited
Psychology	1	1
Law	2	2
Justice sciences	3	5
Political science	4	4
History	5	6
Sociology	6	3
Anthropology	7	7

3. Elementary and secondary schools are funded primarily from local property taxes, not state funds. This suggests that a high educational expenditure by a state government is an attempt to make up for poor local property values. In other words, the more a state government spends compared to localities, the less well funded its schools are. Do the following fictional data for a random sample of nine states bear this out?

State's Rank on Per Capita Educational Expenditures	State's Rank on Total per Student Funding
1	7
2	6
3	9
4	4
5	8
6	2
7	3
8	1
9	5

4. As airports become more crowded, airline companies worry that flight delays may reduce overall customer satisfaction to the same extent as do ticket price, food quality, and route availability problems. Suppose we have ranks of percentage of on-time flights and customer satisfaction. Need airlines with lots of flight delays worry about overall customer satisfaction?

Airline's Rank on Percentage of On-Time Flights	Airline's Rank on Customer Satisfaction
1	4
2	5
3	7
4	2
5	8
6	10
7	1
8	3
9	6
10	9

5. A factor that influences whether a worker feels safe from becoming a victim of crime while at work is low target attractiveness: the presence of

workplace security such as guarded gate entry, alarm systems, security cameras, and guard dogs (Madriz 1996). With the following fictional data, test the hypothesis that workers in secure environments feel safer from crime.

| | X → | Level of Workplace Security | | |
Considers Work-place Safe? (Y) ↓	*Low*	*Moderate*	*High*	*Totals*
Fairly safe	6	6	12	24
Fairly unsafe	7	16	8	31
Very unsafe	11	5	5	21
Totals	24	27	25	76

6. Social workers play several roles in the health care system. In small towns they assist physicians by arranging home health services, mental health counseling, and nursing home placement. Badger et al. (1997) examined whether physicians' ratings of social workers (X) are correlated with physicians' interest in hiring social workers for their medical practices (Y). They obtained the following crosstab data, $n = 85$. Are physicians who rate social workers positively also more likely to hire them? Provide theoretical and practical speculations on why your answer came out as it did.

| | Rating of Social Workers | | |
Physicians' Interest in Hiring Social Workers	*Poor*	*Good*	*Excellent*
Yes	5	4	18
Maybe	3	16	11
No	5	12	11

7. Gibbs and Beitel (1995: 133) note that the "ability to understand proverbial sayings such as *a rolling stone gathers no moss* has been of great interest to researchers in many areas of psychology." Are those who are good at deciphering such sayings better able to think abstractly? Answer this research question with the following fictional data.

X →	Ability to Understand Proverbial Sayings			
Ability to Think Abstractly (Y) ↓	*Poor*	*Average*	*High*	*Totals*
High	11	15	13	39
Average	14	11	14	39
Poor	13	16	12	41
Totals	38	42	39	119

8. Social surveys carried out by the National Opinion Research Center assess the confidence individuals have in social institutions. For the data in the following crosstab table, test a hypothesis to determine whether individuals who have confidence in financial institutions tend to have less confidence in the press. (Source of data: selected cases from the 1994 General Social Survey, www.icpsr.umich.edu/gss/codebook.)

X →	Confidence in Banks and Financial Institutions			
Confidence in the Press (Y) ↓	*Little*	*Some*	*A Lot*	*Totals*
A lot	20	30	5	55
Some	41	157	47	245
Little	25	121	47	193
Totals	86	308	99	493

9. The consumption of tobacco is a widely recognized health risk factor. For the following fictional data, is there a relationship between cigarette consumption and a person's self-rating of health?

	X →	**Smokes Cigarettes?**		
Self-Assessment of Health (Y) ↓	*No*	*Less Than a Pack per Day*	*Pack per Day or More*	*Totals*
Excellent or Good	79	23	10	112
Fair	44	26	24	94
Poor	11	7	9	27
Totals	134	56	43	233

10. The Glasgow Coma Scale is used to measure the severity of head injuries, with a score of 7 or below being severe (Kaiser and Pfenninger 1984). Imagine that the following data are Glasgow measurements made at the time of injury and that recovery is assessed two years later. Is the scale a good predictor of recovery?

	X →	**Glasgow Coma Scale**		
Recovery Status after 2 Years (Y) ↓	*Not Severe (> 7)*	*Severe (3–7)*	*Very Severe (0–2)*	*Totals*
Full recovery	17	6	2	25
Partial recovery	9	16	11	36
Died	1	3	9	13
Totals	27	25	22	74

Optional Computer Applications for Chapter 16

If your class uses the optional computer applications that accompany this text, open the Chapter 16 exercises on the *Computer Applications for The Statistical Imagination* compact disk. The exercises focus on running Spearman's rho and gamma procedures in *SPSS for Windows* and properly interpreting the output.

REVIEW OF BASIC MATHEMATICAL OPERATIONS

This appendix does not provide a thorough lesson in mathematical computations. It merely provides review examples to assist students in recalling the basic mathematical operations typically encountered in statistical calculations. After each review section, problems are provided; the answers appear at the end of this appendix.

Basic Mathematical Symbols and Terms

$\pm$	Plus or minus	$\div$ or $/$	Divided by
$<$	Less than	$\times$ or $\cdot$ or $(...)$	Multiplied by
$>$	Greater than	$\leq$	Less than or equal to
$\geq$	Greater than or equal to	∞	Infinity
$\approx$	Approximately equal	$\neq$	Not equal
$\vert\ \vert$	Absolute value of (e.g., $\vert -15 \vert = 15$)	$\sqrt{}$	Square root (reviewed below)

A *sum* is the answer to an addition or subtraction problem.
A *product* is the answer to a multiplication problem.
A *quotient* is the answer to a division problem.

Order of Mathematical Operations

In calculating the parts of a formula, follow these rules:

1. Work inside each set of parentheses before moving outside them. If sets of parentheses are bracketed, work inside each set of brackets before moving outside them.
2. Terms are parts of an equation separated by addition and subtraction signs. Before adding and subtracting terms, complete any multiplications and divisions within each term.
3. With division problems, complete all calculations above and below the division sign before dividing.
4. Treat a radical sign (i.e., the square root sign) as a large set of brackets; that is, complete all calculations under the radical sign before taking the square root.

Exponents: Squaring and Square Roots

Exponents: Raising to a Power.   An exponent is the number of times a base number is multiplied by itself. When we make such calculations, we say that we "raise the base number to a power." To "square" a base number is to raise it to the power of 2. For example, 4 to the power of 2 is 4^2 (i.e., 4 squared), or 4 multiplied by itself:

$$4^2 = (4)\,(4) = 16$$

A base number raised to the first power is the base number itself, and we do not bother to place the exponent 1 in the notation: $4^1 = 4$. In general, for any number a: $a^1 = a$.

Any number raised to the exponent of zero equals 1: $4^0 = 1$, $7^0 = 1$. In general, $a^0 = 1$.

A base number raised to the power of 3 is "cubed." Thus, four cubed is

$$4^3 = (4)\,(4)\,(4) = 64$$

Similarly, 5 raised to the fifth power is

$$5^5 = (5)\,(5)\,(5)\,(5)\,(5) = 3{,}125$$

Note that 5^5 is equal to 5 squared times 5 cubed, or 5 to the fourth power times 5. That is, when a base number raised to a power is multiplied by the same base number raised to a power, the result is equal to the base number raised to the sum of the exponents:

$$5^5 = (5^2)\,(5^3) = (25)\,(125) = 3{,}125, \text{ or } 5^5 = (5^1)\,(5^4) = (5)\,(625) = 3{,}125$$

This is called the product rule for exponents. In general, it states that for any positive integers, m and n,

$$(a^m)\,(a^n) = a^{m+n}$$

There are several general *power rules for exponents*. For any positive integers m and n,

$$(a^m)^n = a^{mn}; \text{ for example, } (6^2)^3 = 6^6 = 46{,}656$$

$$(ab)^m = a^m b^m; \text{ for example, } (2 \cdot 3)^2 = (2^2)\,(3^2) = 4 \cdot 9 = 36$$

$$(a/b)^m = \frac{a^m}{b^m}; \text{ for example, } (4/2)^3 = \frac{4^3}{2^3} = \frac{64}{8} = 8$$

The quotient rule for exponents states that

$$\frac{a^m}{a^n} = a^{m-n}; \text{ for example, } \frac{3^4}{3^2} = 3^{(4-2)} = 3^2 = 9$$

Review Problems

1. $7^2 =$ 2. $21^2 =$ 3. $21^3 =$ 4. $19^2 =$ 5. $9^4 =$

6. $10^3 =$ 7. $(2^2)\,(2^5) =$ 8. $(3^2)^4$ 9. $100^2 \div 10^2 =$

10. $10^4 \div 10^3 =$

Square Roots   Taking the square root is the inverse of squaring. Thus, the square root of 16 is 4:

$$\sqrt{16} = 4$$

To check the accuracy of taking a square root, square the result to see if the number under the radical reappears. Similarly, when a number is squared, take the square root of the result to see if the base number reappears. This means that the square root of a number squared is equal to the number:

$$\sqrt{16} = \sqrt{4^2} = 4$$

In general, $\sqrt{a^2} = a$ where a is some base number.

Review Problems

Note the pattern of answers for items 11 through 16.

11.	$\sqrt{8.1} =$	12.	$\sqrt{81} =$
13.	$\sqrt{810} =$	14.	$\sqrt{8,100} =$
15.	$\sqrt{81,000}$	16.	$\sqrt{810,000} =$
17.	$\sqrt{7.568} =$	18.	$\sqrt{100}$
19.	$\sqrt{10^2} =$	20.	$\sqrt{41^2}$

Summation Notation

The Greek letter sigma (Σ) is used to mean "sum of." Care must be taken to sum the proper terms of an equation.

Illustration: The variable X = age. John is 32, Kirk is 40, and Jim is 24.

Example 1: Their average or "mean" age is "the sum of X" divided by 3:

$$\bar{X} = \frac{\Sigma X}{3} = \frac{(32 + 40 + 24)}{3} = 32 \text{ years}$$

where the symbol $\bar{X}$ is read "mean" (see Chapter 4).

Example 2: To calculate the *sum of ages squared*, first square each X-score and then sum:

$$\Sigma X^2 = (32^2 + 40^2 + 24^2) = 1,024 + 1,600 + 576 = 3,200 \text{ squared years}$$

Example 3: To calculate the *sum of ages* squared, first sum the ages and then square the result:

$$(\Sigma X)^2 = 96^2 = 9,216 \text{ squared years}$$

Summations are facilitated when the data are organized into spreadsheets with variables in columns and cases in rows. The following spreadsheet provides ages (X) and weights (Y) for four cases or subjects. Use this spreadsheet for review problems 21 through 26.

Case/Subject	X (age)	X^2	Y (weight)	Y^2
John	32	1,024	169	28,561
Kirk	40	1,600	191	36,481
Jim	24	576	157	24,649
Carl	44	1,936	212	44,944

Review Problems

21. $\sum X =$ 22. $\sum X^2 =$ 23. $(\sum X)^2 =$ 24. $\sum Y =$
25. $\sum Y^2 =$ 26. $(\sum Y)^2 =$

Fractions and Common Denominators

Before fractions can be added or divided, they must have common denominators. An easy way to determine a common denominator is to multiply the denominators. (This method works, although it does not always result in the "lowest common denominator.") Once a common denominator is found, the numerators are added or subtracted.

Example:

$$\frac{1}{2}+\frac{1}{3}=\frac{3}{6}+\frac{2}{6}=\frac{5}{6}$$

Example:

$$\frac{1}{2}-\frac{1}{3}=\frac{3}{6}-\frac{2}{6}=\frac{1}{6}$$

Multiplication of fractions is straightforward: We simply multiply numerators and denominators. Again, the answer to a multiplication problem is called the *product*.

Example 1: The product of one-half of one-third is one-sixth.

$$\frac{1}{2}\cdot\frac{1}{3}=\frac{1}{6}$$

Example 2:

$$\frac{3}{52}\cdot\frac{4}{51}=\frac{12}{2,652}$$

In general, to multiply fractions,

$$\frac{a}{b}\cdot\frac{c}{d}=\frac{a\cdot c}{b\cdot d}$$

In dividing fractions, we refer to the answer as a *quotient*. In general,

$$\frac{a}{b}\div\frac{c}{d}=\frac{a\cdot d}{b\cdot c}$$

For example, the quotient of three-fourths divided by two-thirds is one and one-eighth:

$$\frac{3}{4} \div \frac{2}{3} = \frac{3 \cdot 3}{4 \cdot 2} = \frac{9}{8} = 1\frac{1}{8}$$

An easier way to deal with fractions is to transform them into decimal numbers. This is illustrated below.

Review Problems

27. $\frac{5}{8} + \frac{3}{12} =$

28. $\frac{13}{22} - \frac{7}{49} =$

29. $\frac{6}{11} + \frac{2}{3} - \frac{1}{8} =$

30. $\frac{10}{12} \cdot \frac{4}{5} =$

31. $\frac{13}{25} \cdot \frac{6}{14} \cdot \frac{2}{5} =$

32. $\frac{16}{18} \div \frac{5}{6} =$

Decimals and Decimal Place Locations

Deci- means 10, and the decimal system of numbers is based on multiples of 10. Figure A–1 stipulates decimal place locations. When a number is multiplied by a multiple of 10, the decimal point is simply moved the appropriate number of places to the right. When a number is divided by a multiple of 10, the decimal point is moved to the left. Decimal place location also may be conceived in terms of raising 10 to a power or whole-number exponent. For instance,

$$10^1 = 10, 10^2 = 100, 10^3 = 1{,}000, 10^4 = 10{,}000, \text{etc.}$$

In multiplying by 10, move the decimal point one place to the right; by 100, two places; and so on:

$$(98.49)(1{,}000) = 98{,}490 \qquad (.3587)(100) = 35.87$$

Negative exponents imply division. Thus, $10^{-1} = .1$, $10^{-2} = .01$, $10^{-3} = .001$, $10^{-4} = .0001$, and so on. In dividing by 10, move the decimal point one place to the left; by 100, two places; and so on:

$$(45.91)/100 = .4591$$

$$(.0083)/1{,}000 = .0000083$$

FIGURE A–1
Decimal place locations

Decimal Places

Millions	Hundred thousands	Ten thousands	Thousands	Hundreds	Tens	Ones (integer)	Decimal point	Tenths	Hundredths	Thousandths	Ten-thousandths	Hundred-thousandths	Millionths	Ten-millionths
X	X	X	X	X	X	X	•	X	X	X	X	X	X	X

Review Problems

Round answers to four decimal places.

33. 29.869/1,000 = 34. (.0388) (10,000) = 35. 4/1,000 =
36. (1.957) (100) = 37. (3.503) (10^{-3}) = 38. (3.503) (10^{3}) =

As we discussed in Chapter 1, fractions are easier to deal with in decimal form. A fraction is "decimalized" simply by dividing the numerator by the denominator. To transform this quotient into a percentage, move the decimal point two places to the right, which is simply a matter of multiplying by 100.

Care must be taken in using various decimal places in a single problem. Test your ability to keep track of decimal places with the following review problems.

Review Problems

39. (0.15) (4) = 40. (2.0) (.3) = 41. (.024 – .03) =
42. (.05 + 235.44) = 43. (34.076 – 6.3) = 44. (4.141 – .09) =

The Relationship of the Numerator to the Denominator

Having a feel for the relative size of fractions, percentages, and proportions is important in statistics, because every statistical procedure uses fractions. *Percent* means "per hundred." If the term *percent* does not convey a sense of proportion for you, take 100 pennies and toss them on the bed. Then compute the percentage of heads by simply counting the number of heads.

Mathematical proportions are derived from fractions, and understanding the dynamics of fractions goes a long way toward helping one get a feel for statistics. Let us study these dynamics by comparing the relative sizes of the numerator and denominator of fractions and see how these sizes affect quotients. Such a study reveals the following:

1. When the numerator is small in comparison to the denominator, the quotient will be small. As an example, compare 1/567 to 439/567 by dividing each of these fractions to obtain their proportions in decimal form.

2. When the numerator is at least half the size of the denominator, the quotient will be above 50 percent, and this constitutes a simple majority. For example, in a runoff election for sorority president, if Nancy gets 51 of the 100 votes, she wins.

3. When the numerator is almost as large as the denominator, the quotient will be close to a proportion of 1.0 and a percentage of 100 percent. For example, if 222 out of 236 students pass a course,

$$p \text{ [of students in a course who passed]} = \frac{\text{\# passed}}{\text{total class size}} = \frac{222}{236} = .9407$$

% [of students in a course who passed] = $(p)(100) = 94.07\%$

That is, for every 100 students, about 94 pass.

4. When the numerator is larger than the denominator, the quotient will be greater than 1.

5. In summary, the larger the numerator in relation to the denominator, the larger the quotient.

Basic Algebraic Solutions

Algebra involves the use of symbols, such as letters, to represent a general mathematical case. Specific numbers then may be substituted for symbols to arrive at a specific answer. For example, we might define X as height and Y as weight and understand that weight is a function of height: The taller a person is, the more that person tends to weigh. To estimate weight for a given height, we may substitute values of X into an appropriate equation and solve for Y. For instance,

$$Y = -159.31 + (4.62)X$$

If X is 68 inches, the best estimate of that person's weight is 154.85 pounds:

$$Y = -159.31 + (4.62)(68) = 154.85 \text{ pounds}$$

Basic Rules of Arithmetic and Algebra

In multiplying or dividing two numbers, the product, or quotient, is positive if both numbers have the same sign but negative if the two numbers have different signs:

$$(4)(3) = 12 \qquad (-4)(3) = -12$$
$$(-4)(-3) = 12 \qquad (4)(-3) = -12$$

$$\frac{4}{3} = 1.25 \qquad \frac{-4}{3} = -1.25 \qquad \frac{4}{-3} = -1.25$$

In general, any number times zero is zero. Any number times 1 is that number. Zero divided by any number is zero. Division by zero is not permitted (because it results in an undefined quotient). Thus,

$$0 \cdot a = 0; \text{ for example, } 0 \cdot 25 = 0 \text{ and } (0)\,(4{,}500) = 0$$
$$1 \cdot a = a; \text{ for example, } 1 \cdot 25 = 25 \text{ and } (1)\,(4{,}500) = 4{,}500$$
$$0 \div a = 0; \text{ for example, } 0 \div 25 = 0 \text{ and } (0/4{,}500) = 0$$
$$a \div 0 = \text{undefined (because something cannot be divided by nothing)}$$

Any number divided by itself equals 1. In general,

$$\frac{a}{a} = 1; \quad \text{for example, } \frac{34}{34} = 1 \quad \text{and } \frac{3}{3} = 1$$

The *multiplicative inverse* of a number is equal to 1 divided by that number. A number times its multiplicative inverse equals 1:

$$a \cdot \frac{1}{a} = 1; \quad \text{for example, } 3 \cdot \frac{1}{3} = 1$$

Terms may be simplified by using *commutative and distributive properties*. In general,

$$(a + b) = (b + a); \quad \text{for example, } (2 + 3) = (3 + 2) = 5$$
$$(ab) = (ba); \quad \text{for example, } (2 \cdot 3) = (3 \cdot 2) = 6$$
$$a(b + c) = ab + ac; \quad \text{for example, } 6(2 + 3) = 6(2) + 6(3) = 30$$
$$a(b - c) = ab - ac; \quad \text{for example, } 6(3 - 2) = 6(3) - 6(2) = 6$$

Consistent with algebraic properties and rules, exponential equations may be "expanded" into a set of terms. For example,

$$(a + b)^3 = (a + b)\,(a + b)\,(a + b) = a^3 + 3a^2b + 3ab^2 + b^3$$

There is a simple method of expanding such equations when they have only two base numbers, a and b (see "The Binomial Distribution Equation" in Chapter 13).

Solving for an Unknown Quantity

A common mathematical problem involves solving an equation for an unknown variable or function. For example, we might be told that some quantity X is such that 3 times that quantity plus 30 is equal to 100, minus 6 times the quantity, plus 2 times the quantity. In symbolic form,

$$3X + 30 = 100 - 6X + 2X$$

We are asked to determine the quantity; that is, we are asked to "solve for X." These types of solutions depend on *mathematical equivalency*. That is, the equals sign must be respected so that quantities on both sides of the equal sign remain the same. Any mathematical operation performed on one side of the equation must be performed on the other side to maintain mathematical equivalency. Solutions are arrived at by combining like terms and performing mathematical operations on each side of the equation. To solve for X, we select mathematical operations that "isolate" X to one side of the equation. Thus,

We start with:	$3X + 30 = 100 - 6X + 2X$
Simplify by combining like terms to obtain:	$3X + 30 = 100 - 4X$
Add $4X$ to both sides of the equation:	$3X + 30 + 4X = 100 - 4X + 4X$
To obtain:	$7X + 30 = 100$
Subtract 30 from both sides:	$7X + 30 - 30 = 100 - 30$
To obtain:	$7X = 70$
Divide both sides by 7:	$\dfrac{7X}{7} = \dfrac{70}{7}$
To obtain:	$X = 10$

Check the accuracy of the answer by substituting 10 for X in the original equation:

	$3X + 30 = 100 - 6X + 2X$
Substituting 10 for X:	$3(10) + 30 = 100 - 6(10) + 2(10)$
Solve:	$60 = 60$

Thus, we know that 10 is a correct solution because its substitution for X maintains mathematical equivalency.

Review Problems

45. *Given:* $Y = a + bX$, $a = 17$, $b = 5$, and $X = -2$. Solve for Y.

46. If $a = 3$, solve the equation $(4a^2)(6a^3) =$

47. Given: $8 - 3X = 4X - 6$. Solve for X.

48. Given: $7X - 5X - 4 = 4X - 10$. Solve for X.

49. $a = \dfrac{b}{c}$. Solve for c.

50. Expand the equation $(a + b)^2 =$

Answers

1. 49   2. 441   3. 9,261   4. 361   5. 6,561   6. 1,000   7. 128   8. 6,561   9. 100   10. 10   11. 2.85   12. 9   13. 28.46   14. 90   15. 284.60   16. 900   17. 2.75   18. 10   19. 10   20. 41   21. 140 years   22. 5,136 squared years   23. 19,600 squared years   24. 729 pounds   25. 134,635 squared pounds   26. 531,441 squared pounds   27. 21/24 = .8750   28. 483/1,078 = .4480   29. 287/264 = 1.0871   30. 2/3 = .6667   31. 156/1,750 = .0891   32. 96/90 = 1.0667   33. .0299   34. 388   35. .0040   36. 195.7   37. .0035   38. 3,503   39. .60   40. .6   41. −.006   42. 235.49   43. 27.776   44. 4.051   45. $Y = 7$ 46. 5,832   47. $X = 2$ 48. $X = 3$ 49. $c = b/a$ 50. $a^2 + 2ab + b^2$

APPENDIX B
STATISTICAL PROBABILITY TABLES

STATISTICAL TABLE A   Random Number Table

```
9 5 7 3 4 3 9 3 1 1 1 5 6 7 8 2 9 3 5 3 2 5 0 1 4 8 2 4 3 7 3 2 4 2 8
5 7 9 4 6 5 7 5 9 3 6 5 8 5 3 7 2 4 9 3 7 7 5 2 6 1 5 1 6 5 2 6 0 9 4
3 9 9 2 6 8 1 4 8 1 8 7 1 8 3 5 0 7 9 6 0 8 2 2 5 1 8 7 7 3 7 3 1 3 7
3 6 1 4 3 4 8 4 9 7 0 3 1 8 3 6 8 0 9 2 4 9 5 3 8 9 2 9 6 7 3 7 5 1 1
3 2 7 6 1 8 7 3 2 2 2 9 8 4 0 5 4 0 5 7 3 3 2 7 2 8 4 7 0 5 9 3 8 1 1
5 8 3 7 5 7 2 0 1 9 4 9 4 1 8 7 0 4 4 9 1 3 5 9 3 1 1 8 5 0 1 7 8 2 8
6 6 7 9 7 5 5 9 0 8 7 4 1 1 1 6 4 9 3 5 1 0 0 6 0 2 7 9 6 2 5 9 8 3 7
1 0 9 6 5 4 0 7 6 1 2 1 6 0 2 1 5 8 4 1 3 5 0 7 6 9 0 8 1 6 0 8 2 5 9
2 0 8 5 1 0 4 4 0 7 6 2 2 5 5 9 4 6 6 7 4 0 2 5 9 3 5 8 3 9 5 7 6 7 0
0 4 2 5 8 3 4 3 3 5 3 6 3 1 8 7 9 1 1 7 5 6 8 5 9 3 9 3 8 7 7 9 5 2 6
0 5 7 5 5 2 6 0 4 5 0 9 8 6 2 2 3 2 0 8 5 6 4 8 9 7 9 7 6 5 6 2 0 9 5
2 3 8 8 4 9 4 2 2 0 0 8 2 0 4 1 8 6 3 9 6 0 7 2 4 7 7 9 5 9 9 6 9 2 8
1 4 0 2 8 2 5 7 0 2 2 5 6 9 6 5 9 3 2 9 8 1 1 7 8 5 1 2 1 8 9 0 6 5 4
1 6 8 2 3 7 6 4 0 5 9 3 4 7 8 9 0 4 9 0 8 3 4 3 6 6 1 1 4 7 0 8 7 9 6
3 6 9 5 8 1 1 5 3 1 1 3 0 8 4 7 8 5 7 7 0 2 2 4 0 2 1 8 2 1 9 3 1 8 2
1 2 2 3 9 4 2 4 0 1 8 1 0 2 1 1 7 3 6 8 9 8 3 8 7 8 0 2 4 9 0 4 8 8 4
9 3 4 4 9 2 2 5 9 3 3 4 8 0 9 0 6 2 2 4 5 7 6 2 8 0 7 9 2 4 1 5 0 4 7
9 4 5 9 6 9 2 4 1 8 1 3 2 9 7 6 3 0 0 5 6 8 9 1 4 4 2 6 0 8 1 5 3 1 5
1 4 6 4 5 4 2 4 3 6 7 1 4 3 9 4 4 0 5 7 4 0 3 9 0 7 9 5 3 6 6 0 1 6 7
6 8 0 5 5 2 3 5 8 6 4 4 1 0 7 5 5 7 0 3 1 9 6 9 8 6 1 3 4 4 6 9 5 7 9
2 1 7 4 7 0 5 3 6 7 8 6 5 0 6 4 7 6 0 6 2 5 2 7 1 8 3 6 1 8 7 1 2 1 5
3 9 1 8 7 0 5 6 6 7 3 3 0 4 0 2 4 3 5 7 7 3 7 7 1 8 4 2 4 0 9 4 8 3 0
4 8 2 8 4 0 2 7 9 8 6 7 1 0 4 6 1 6 9 7 0 9 1 7 6 6 4 3 8 6 5 9 6 0 9
5 1 9 8 4 8 4 6 4 1 4 0 1 8 2 3 7 5 3 0 7 9 5 1 3 8 0 1 6 8 9 2 0 6 5
3 7 4 9 7 9 4 4 7 2 3 9 3 8 4 9 2 2 1 8 5 9 7 7 1 0 6 0 2 0 7 8 0 5 6
5 9 1 1 0 6 5 5 0 4 7 8 6 8 7 8 8 6 3 1 3 1 4 6 0 8 5 5 2 8 9 7 4 6 0
2 2 6 4 9 7 8 8 4 3 6 9 6 3 7 6 3 1 2 5 4 3 0 5 1 1 5 6 6 6 1 2 9 4 1
6 5 2 2 5 3 4 3 3 9 1 3 4 2 2 0 7 5 1 9 2 7 9 5 6 0 9 4 9 4 6 0 3 3 3
1 7 1 4 3 3 3 4 8 7 8 2 2 8 3 9 3 2 4 1 6 5 1 6 5 7 5 5 9 9 5 6 1 4 5
9 6 7 5 3 4 9 2 2 8 1 5 0 1 9 3 8 4 5 4 6 3 4 3 4 4 5 8 4 2 9 3 3 7 3
5 0 4 1 9 6 3 9 2 3 2 5 7 8 9 2 8 0 6 3 6 0 6 7 4 6 3 8 0 8 9 4 2 9 5
9 5 6 8 8 4 0 2 8 9 3 9 7 5 3 9 1 7 3 9 3 2 7 8 3 4 7 3 0 8 0 5 1 4 2
1 9 4 6 0 7 1 9 6 6 2 9 8 0 4 8 7 4 6 4 7 4 8 2 9 6 1 5 0 8 0 8 3 6 7
9 3 0 9 9 7 0 5 5 7 3 4 5 5 0 3 0 2 8 4 7 4 6 2 1 9 4 1 9 6 2 8 3 3 4
6 7 6 6 1 2 7 5 4 5 6 7 5 9 5 3 4 2 4 0 1 0 3 8 7 5 9 5 2 3 7 1 0 0 0
3 8 7 5 1 2 2 0 1 3 5 2 2 5 5 0 4 8 0 8 9 7 6 4 3 7 9 5 0 2 9 6 7 2 1
3 9 3 2 4 1 1 1 6 5 7 4 2 6 5 0 0 2 2 0 0 1 5 0 2 1 6 8 6 7 9 7 3 2 5
```

STATISTICAL TABLE B   Normal Distribution Table

Specified areas under the normal curve (columns B and C) for stipulated Z-scores (column A)

(A) +Z or –Z	(B)	(C)	(A) +Z or –Z	(B)	(C)	(A) +Z or –Z	(B)	(C)
0.00	.0000	.5000	0.55	.2088	.2912	1.10	.3643	.1357
0.01	.0040	.4960	0.56	.2123	.2877	1.11	.3665	.1335
0.02	.0080	.4920	0.57	.2157	.2843	1.12	.3686	.1314
0.03	.0120	.4880	0.58	.2190	.2810	1.13	.3708	.1292
0.04	.0160	.4840	0.59	.2224	.2776	1.14	.3729	.1271
0.05	.0199	.4801	0.60	.2257	.2743	1.15	.3749	.1251
0.06	.0239	.4761	0.61	.2291	.2709	1.16	.3770	.1230
0.07	.0279	.4721	0.62	.2324	.2676	1.17	.3790	.1210
0.08	.0319	.4681	0.63	.2357	.2643	1.18	.3810	.1190
0.09	.0359	.4641	0.64	.2389	.2611	1.19	.3830	.1170
0.10	.0398	.4602	0.65	.2422	.2578	1.20	.3849	.1151
0.11	.0438	.4562	0.66	.2454	.2546	1.21	.3869	.1131
0.12	.0478	.4522	0.67	.2486	.2514	1.22	.3888	.1112
0.13	.0517	.4483	0.68	.2517	.2483	1.23	.3907	.1093
0.14	.0557	.4443	0.69	.2549	.2451	1.24	.3925	.1075
0.15	.0596	.4404	0.70	.2580	.2420	1.25	.3944	.1056
0.16	.0636	.4364	0.71	.2611	.2389	1.26	.3962	.1038
0.17	.0675	.4325	0.72	.2642	.2358	1.27	.3980	.1020
0.18	.0714	.4286	0.73	.2673	.2327	1.28	.3997	.1003
0.19	.0753	.4247	0.74	.2704	.2296	1.29	.4015	.0985
0.20	.0793	.4207	0.75	.2734	.2266	1.30	.4032	.0968
0.21	.0832	.4168	0.76	.2764	.2236	1.31	.4049	.0951
0.22	.0871	.4129	0.77	.2794	.2206	1.32	.4066	.0934
0.23	.0910	.4090	0.78	.2823	.2177	1.33	.4082	.0918
0.24	.0948	.4052	0.79	.2852	.2148	1.34	.4099	.0901
0.25	.0987	.4013	0.80	.2881	.2119	1.35	.4115	.0885
0.26	.1026	.3974	0.81	.2910	.2090	1.36	.4131	.0869
0.27	.1064	.3936	0.82	.2939	.2061	1.37	.4147	.0853
0.28	.1103	.3897	0.83	.2967	.2033	1.38	.4162	.0838
0.29	.1141	.3859	0.84	.2995	.2005	1.39	.4177	.0823
0.30	.1179	.3821	0.85	.3023	.1977	1.40	.4192	.0808
0.31	.1217	.3783	0.86	.3051	.1949	1.41	.4207	.0793
0.32	.1255	.3745	0.87	.3078	.1922	1.42	.4222	.0778
0.33	.1293	.3707	0.88	.3106	.1894	1.43	.4236	.0764
0.34	.1331	.3669	0.89	.3133	.1867	1.44	.4251	.0749
0.35	.1368	.3632	0.90	.3159	.1841	1.45	.4265	.0735
0.36	.1406	.3594	0.91	.3186	.1814	1.46	.4279	.0721
0.37	.1443	.3557	0.92	.3212	.1788	1.47	.4292	.0708
0.38	.1480	.3520	0.93	.3238	.1762	1.48	.4306	.0694
0.39	.1517	.3483	0.94	.3264	.1739	1.49	.4319	.0681
0.40	.1554	.3446	0.95	.3289	.1711	1.50	.4332	.0668
0.41	.1591	.3409	0.96	.3315	.1685	1.51	.4345	.0655
0.42	.1628	.3372	0.97	.3340	.1660	1.52	.4357	.0643
0.43	.1664	.3336	0.98	.3365	.1635	1.53	.4370	.0630
0.44	.1700	.3300	0.99	.3389	.1611	1.54	.4382	.0618
0.45	.1736	.3264	1.00	.3413	.1587	1.55	.4394	.0606
0.46	.1772	.3228	1.01	.3438	.1562	1.56	.4406	.0594
0.47	.1808	.3192	1.02	.3461	.1539	1.57	.4418	.0582
0.48	.1844	.3156	1.03	.3485	.1515	1.58	.4429	.0571
0.49	.1879	.3121	1.04	.3508	.1492	1.59	.4441	.0559
0.50	.1915	.3085	1.05	.3531	.1469	1.60	4452	.0548
0.51	.1950	.3050	1.06	.3554	.1446	1.61	.4463	.0537
0.52	.1985	.3015	1.07	.3577	.1423	1.62	.4474	.0526
0.53	.2019	.2981	1.08	.3599	.1401	1.63	.4484	.0516
0.54	.2054	.2946	1.09	.3621	.1379	1.64	.4495	.0505

(A) +Z or −Z	(B)	(C)	(A) +Z or −Z	(B)	(C)	(A) +Z or −Z	(B)	(C)
1.65	.4505	.0495	2.22	.4868	.0132	2.79	.4974	.0026
1.66	.4515	.0485	2.23	.4871	.0129	2.80	.4974	.0026
1.67	.4525	.0475	2.24	.4875	.0125	2.81	.4975	.0025
1.68	.4535	.0465	2.25	.4878	.0122	2.82	.4976	.0024
1.69	.4545	.0455	2.26	.4881	.0119	2.83	.4977	.0023
1.70	.4554	.0446	2.27	.4884	.0116	2.84	.4977	.0023
1.71	.4564	.0436	2.28	.4887	.0113	2.85	.4978	.0022
1.72	.4573	.0427	2.29	.4890	.0110	2.86	.4979	.0021
1.73	.4582	.0418	2.30	.4893	.0107	2.87	.4979	.0021
1.74	.4591	.0409	2.31	.4896	.0104	2.88	.4980	.0020
1.75	.4599	.0401	2.32	.4898	.0102	2.89	.4981	.0019
1.76	.4608	.0392	2.33	.4901	.0099	2.90	.4981	.0019
1.77	.4616	.0384	2.34	.4904	.0096	2.91	.4982	.0018
1.78	.4625	.0375	2.35	.4906	.0094	2.92	.4982	.0018
1.79	.4633	.0367	2.36	.4909	.0091	2.93	.4983	.0017
1.80	.4641	.0359	2.37	.4911	.0089	2.94	.4984	.0016
1.81	.4649	.0351	2.38	.4913	.0087	2.95	.4984	.0016
1.82	.4656	.0344	2.39	.4916	.0084	2.96	.4985	.0015
1.83	.4664	.0336	2.40	.4918	.0082	2.97	.4985	.0015
1.84	.4671	.0329	2.41	.4920	.0080	2.98	.4986	.0014
1.85	.4678	.0322	2.42	.4922	.0078	2.99	.4986	.0014
1.86	.4686	.0314	2.43	.4925	.0075	3.00	.4987	.0013
1.87	.4693	.0307	2.44	.4927	.0073	3.01	.4987	.0013
1.88	.4699	.0301	2.45	.4929	.0071	3.02	.4987	.0013
1.89	.4706	.0294	2.46	.4931	.0069	3.03	.4988	.0012
1.90	.4713	.0287	2.47	.4932	.0068	3.04	.4988	.0012
1.91	.4719	.0281	2.48	.4934	.0066	3.05	.4989	.0011
1.92	.4726	.0274	2.49	.4936	.0064	3.06	.4989	.0011
1.93	.4732	.0268	2.50	.4938	.0062	3.07	.4989	.0011
1.94	.4738	.0262	2.51	.4940	.0060	3.08	.4990	.0010
1.95	.4744	.0256	2.52	.4941	.0059	3.09	.4990	.0010
1.96	.4750	.0250	2.53	.4943	.0057	3.10	.4990	.0010
1.97	.4756	.0244	2.54	.4945	.0055	3.11	.4991	.0009
1.98	.4761	.0239	2.55	.4946	.0054	3.12	.4991	.0009
1.99	.4767	.0233	2.56	.4948	.0052	3.13	.4991	.0009
2.00	.4772	.0228	2.57	.4949	.0051	3.14	.4992	.0008
2.01	.4778	.0222	2.58	.4951	.0049	3.15	.4992	.0008
2.02	.4783	.0217	2.59	.4952	.0048	3.16	.4992	.0008
2.03	.4788	.0212	2.60	.4953	.0047	3.17	.4992	.0008
2.04	.4793	.0207	2.61	.4955	.0045	3.18	.4993	.0007
2.05	.4798	.0202	2.62	.4956	.0044	3.19	.4993	.0007
2.06	.4803	.0197	2.63	.4957	.0043	3.20	.4993	.0007
2.07	.4808	.0192	2.64	.4959	.0041	3.21	.4993	.0007
2.08	.4812	.0188	2.65	.4960	.0040	3.22	.4994	.0006
2.09	.4817	.0183	2.66	.4961	.0039	3.23	.4994	.0006
2.10	.4821	.0179	2.67	.4962	.0038	3.24	.4994	.0006
2.11	.4826	.0174	2.68	.4963	.0037	3.25	.4994	.0006
2.12	.4830	.0170	2.69	.4964	.0036	3.30	.4995	.0005
2.13	.4834	.0166	2.70	.4965	.0035	3.35	.4996	.0004
2.14	.4838	.0162	2.71	.4966	.0034	3.40	.4997	.0003
2.15	.4842	.0158	2.72	.4967	.0033	3.45	.4997	.0003
2.16	.4846	.0154	2.73	.4968	.0032	3.50	.4998	.0002
2.17	.4850	.0150	2.74	.4969	.0031	3.60	.4998	.0002
2.18	.4854	.0146	2.75	.4970	.0030	3.70	.4999	.0001
2.19	.4857	.0143	2.76	.4971	.0029	3.80	.4999	.0001
2.20	.4861	.0139	2.77	.4972	.0028	3.90	.49995	.00005
2.21	.4864	.0136	2.78	.4973	.0027	4.0	.49997	.00003

Source: Table III, page 45 of *Statistical Tables for Biological, Agricultural and Medical Research*. Copyright 1963. R.A. Fisher and S. Yates. Reprinted by permission of Addison Wesley Longman Ltd.

STATISTICAL TABLE C   *t*-Distribution Table
Critical values of *t* (*t*α) for specified levels of significance and degrees of freedom

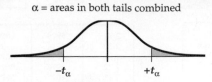

α = areas in both tails combined	α = areas in one tail of curve
−*t*α +*t*α	−*t*α +*t*α
Two-tailed or nondirectional test	One-tailed or directional test
Level of Significance	**Level of Significance**

df	α = .05	α = .01	α = .001	df	α = .05	α = .01	α = .001
1	12.706	63.657	636.62	1	6.314	31.821	318.31
2	4.303	9.925	31.598	2	2.920	6.965	22.326
3	3.182	5.841	12.924	3	2.353	4.541	10.213
4	2.776	4.604	8.610	4	2.132	3.747	7.173
5	2.571	4.032	6.869	5	2.015	3.365	5.893
6	2.447	3.707	5.959	6	1.943	3.143	5.208
7	2.365	3.499	5.408	7	1.895	2.998	4.785
8	2.306	3.335	5.041	8	1.860	2.896	4.501
9	2.262	3.250	4.781	9	1.833	2.821	4.297
10	2.228	3.169	4.587	10	1.812	2.764	4.144
11	2.201	3.105	4.437	11	1.796	2.718	4.025
12	2.179	3.055	4.318	12	1.782	2.681	3.930
13	2.160	3.012	4.221	13	1.771	2.650	3.852
14	2.145	2.977	4.140	14	1.761	2.624	3.787
15	2.131	2.947	4.073	15	1.753	2.602	3.733
16	2.120	2.921	4.015	16	1.746	2.583	3.686
17	2.110	2.898	3.965	17	1.740	2.567	3.646
18	2.101	2.878	3.922	18	1.734	2.552	3.610
19	2.093	2.861	3.883	19	1.729	2.539	3.579
20	2.086	2.845	3.850	20	1.725	2.528	3.552
21	2.080	2.831	3.819	21	1.721	2.518	3.527
22	2.074	2.819	3.792	22	1.717	2.508	3.505
23	2.069	2.807	3.767	23	1.714	2.500	3.485
24	2.064	2.797	3.745	24	1.711	2.492	3.467
25	2.060	2.787	3.725	25	1.706	2.485	3.450
26	2.056	2.779	3.707	26	1.705	2.479	3.435
27	2.052	2.771	3.690	27	1.703	2.473	3.421
28	2.048	2.763	3.674	28	1.701	2.467	3.408
29	2.045	2.756	3.659	29	1.699	2.462	3.396
30	2.042	2.750	3.646	30	1.697	2.457	3.385
40	2.021	2.704	3.551	40	1.684	2.423	3.307
60	2.000	2.660	3.460	60	1.671	2.390	3.232
120	1.980	2.617	3.373	120	1.658	2.358	3.160
∞	1.96	2.58	3.30	∞	1.64	2.33	3.096

Source: Table III, page 46 of *Statistical Tables for Biological, Agricultural and Medical Research*. Copyright 1963. R.A. Fisher and S. Yates. Reprinted by permission of Addison Wesley Longman Ltd.

STATISTICAL TABLE D   Critical Values of the *F*-Ratio Distribution at the .05 Level of Significance

$p = .05$

F_α

df for the Denominator

df for the numerator $\alpha = .05$

$K-1 \rightarrow$

	1	2	3	4	5	6	8	12
1	161.4	199.5	215.7	224.6	230.2	234.0	238.9	243.9
2	18.51	19.00	19.16	19.25	19.30	19.33	19.37	19.41
3	10.13	9.55	9.28	9.12	9.01	8.94	8.84	8.74
4	7.71	6.94	6.59	6.39	6.26	6.16	6.04	5.91
5	6.61	5.79	5.41	5.19	5.05	4.95	4.82	4.68
6	5.99	5.14	4.76	4.53	4.39	4.28	4.15	4.00
7	5.59	4.74	4.35	4.12	3.97	3.87	3.73	3.57
8	5.32	4.46	4.07	3.84	3.69	3.58	3.44	3.28
9	5.12	4.26	3.86	3.63	3.48	3.37	3.23	3.07
10	4.96	4.10	3.71	3.48	3.33	3.22	3.07	2.91
11	4.84	3.98	3.59	3.36	3.20	3.09	2.95	2.79
12	4.75	3.88	3.49	3.26	3.11	3.00	2.85	2.69
13	4.67	3.80	3.41	3.18	3.02	2.92	2.77	2.60
14	4.60	3.74	3.34	3.11	2.96	2.85	2.70	2.53
15	4.54	3.68	3.29	3.06	2.90	2.79	2.64	2.48
16	4.49	3.63	3.24	3.01	2.85	2.74	2.59	2.42
17	4.45	3.59	3.20	2.96	2.81	2.70	2.55	2.38
18	4.41	3.55	3.16	2.93	2.77	2.66	2.51	2.34
19	4.38	3.52	3.13	2.90	2.74	2.63	2.48	2.31
20	4.35	3.49	3.10	2.87	2.71	2.60	2.45	2.28
21	4.32	3.47	3.07	2.84	2.68	2.57	2.42	2.25
22	4.30	3.44	3.05	2.82	2.66	2.55	2.40	2.23
23	4.28	3.42	3.03	2.80	2.64	2.53	2.38	2.20
24	4.26	3.40	3.01	2.78	2.62	2.51	2.36	2.18
25	4.24	3.38	2.99	2.76	2.60	2.49	2.34	2.16
26	4.22	3.37	2.98	2.74	2.59	2.47	2.32	2.15
27	4.21	3.35	2.96	2.73	2.57	2.46	2.30	2.13
28	4.20	3.34	2.95	2.71	2.56	2.44	2.29	2.12
29	4.18	3.33	2.93	2.70	2.54	2.43	2.28	2.10
30	4.17	3.32	2.92	2.69	2.53	2.42	2.27	2.09
40	4.08	3.23	2.84	2.61	2.45	2.34	2.18	2.00
60	4.00	3.15	2.76	2.52	2.37	2.25	2.10	1.92
120	3.92	3.07	2.68	2.45	2.29	2.17	2.02	1.83
∞	3.84	3.00	2.60	2.37	2.21	2.10	1.94	1.75

Source: From Table 18 of Pearson and Hartley (1976: 171), *Biometrika Tables for Statisticians*, volume 1. London: Biometrika Trust. By permission of Oxford University Press.

STATISTICAL TABLE E Critical Values of the *F*-Ratio Distribution at the .01 Level of Significance

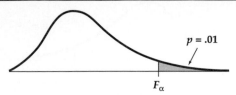

$p = .01$

F_α

df for the
Denominator

df for the numerator $\alpha = .01$

$K-1 =$	1	2	3	4	5	6	8	12
1	4052	4999.5	5403	5625	5764	5859	5981	6106
2	98.49	90.01	99.17	99.25	99.30	99.33	99.36	99.42
3	34.12	30.81	29.46	28.71	28.24	27.91	27.49	27.05
4	21.20	18.00	16.69	15.98	15.52	15.21	14.80	14.37
5	16.26	13.27	12.06	11.39	10.97	10.67	10.27	9.89
6	13.74	10.92	9.78	9.15	8.75	8.47	8.10	7.72
7	12.25	9.55	8.45	7.85	7.46	7.19	6.84	6.47
8	11.26	8.65	7.59	7.01	6.63	6.37	6.03	5.67
9	10.56	8.02	6.99	6.42	6.06	5.80	5.47	5.11
10	10.04	7.56	6.55	5.99	5.64	5.39	5.06	4.71
11	9.65	7.20	6.22	5.67	5.32	5.07	4.74	4.40
12	9.33	6.93	5.95	5.41	5.06	4.82	4.50	4.16
13	9.07	6.70	5.74	5.20	4.86	4.62	4.30	3.96
14	8.86	6.51	5.56	5.03	4.69	4.46	4.14	3.80
15	8.68	6.36	5.42	4.89	4.56	4.32	4.00	3.67
16	8.53	6.23	5.29	4.77	4.44	4.20	3.89	3.55
17	8.40	6.11	5.18	4.67	4.34	4.10	3.79	3.45
18	8.28	6.01	5.09	4.58	4.25	4.01	3.71	3.37
19	8.18	5.93	5.01	4.50	4.17	3.94	3.63	3.30
20	8.10	5.85	4.94	4.43	4.10	3.87	3.56	3.23
21	8.02	5.78	4.87	4.37	4.04	3.81	3.51	3.17
22	7.94	5.72	4.82	4.31	3.99	3.76	3.45	3.12
23	7.88	5.66	4.76	4.26	3.94	3.71	3.41	3.07
24	7.82	5.61	4.72	4.22	3.90	3.67	3.36	3.03
25	7.77	5.57	4.68	4.18	3.86	3.63	3.32	2.99
26	7.72	5.53	4.64	4.14	3.82	3.59	3.29	2.96
27	7.68	5.49	4.60	4.11	3.78	3.56	3.26	2.93
28	7.64	5.45	4.57	4.01	3.75	3.53	3.23	2.90
29	7.60	5.42	4.54	4.04	3.73	3.50	3.20	2.87
30	7.56	5.39	4.51	4.02	3.70	3.47	3.17	2.84
40	7.31	5.18	4.31	3.83	3.51	3.29	2.99	2.66
60	7.08	4.98	4.13	3.65	3.34	3.12	2.82	2.50
120	6.85	4.79	3.95	6.48	3.17	2.96	2.66	2.34
∞	6.63	4.61	3.78	3.32	3.02	2.80	2.51	2.18

$n-k$

Source: From Table 18 of Pearson and Hartley (1976: 173), *Biometrika Tables for Statisticians*, volume 1. London: Biometrika Trust. By permission of Oxford University Press.

df for MSV_W $(n-k)$	Level of Significance	\multicolumn{10}{c}{k = Number of Group Means Compared}									
	α	2	3	4	5	6	7	8	9	10	11
5	.05	3.64	4.60	5.22	5.67	6.03	6.33	6.58	6.80	6.99	7.17
	.01	5.70	6.98	7.80	8.42	8.91	9.32	9.67	9.97	10.24	10.48
6	.05	3.46	4.34	4.90	5.30	5.63	5.90	6.12	6.32	6.49	6.65
	.01	5.24	6.33	7.03	7.56	7.97	8.32	8.61	8.87	9.10	9.30
7	.05	3.34	4.16	4.68	5.06	5.36	5.61	5.82	6.00	6.16	6.30
	.01	4.95	5.92	6.54	7.01	7.37	7.68	7.94	8.17	8.37	8.55
8	.05	3.26	4.04	4.53	4.89	5.17	5.40	5.60	5.77	5.92	6.05
	.01	4.75	5.64	6.20	6.62	6.96	7.24	7.47	7.68	7.86	8.03
9	.05	3.20	3.95	4.41	4.76	5.02	5.24	5.43	5.59	5.74	5.87
	.01	4.60	5.43	5.96	6.35	6.66	6.91	7.13	7.33	7.49	7.65
10	.05	3.15	3.88	4.33	4.65	4.91	5.12	5.30	5.46	5.60	5.72
	.01	4.48	5.27	5.77	6.14	6.43	6.67	6.87	7.05	7.21	7.36
11	.05	3.11	3.82	4.26	4.57	4.82	5.03	5.20	5.35	5.49	5.61
	.01	4.36	5.15	5.62	5.97	6.25	6.48	6.67	6.84	6.99	7.13
12	.05	3.08	3.77	4.20	4.51	4.75	4.95	5.12	5.27	5.39	5.51
	.01	4.32	5.05	5.50	5.84	6.10	6.32	6.51	6.67	6.81	6.94
13	.05	3.06	3.73	4.15	4.45	4.69	4.88	5.05	5.19	5.32	5.43
	.01	4.26	4.96	5.40	5.73	5.98	6.19	6.37	6.53	6.67	6.79
14	.05	3.03	3.70	4.11	4.41	4.64	4.83	4.99	5.13	5.25	5.36
	.01	4.21	4.89	5.32	5.63	5.88	6.08	6.26	6.41	6.54	6.66
15	.05	3.01	3.67	4.08	4.37	4.59	4.78	4.94	5.08	5.20	5.31
	.01	4.17	4.84	5.25	5.56	5.80	5.99	6.16	6.31	6.44	6.55
16	.05	3.00	3.65	4.05	4.33	4.56	4.74	4.90	5.03	5.15	5.26
	.01	4.13	4.79	5.19	5.49	5.72	5.92	6.08	6.22	6.35	6.46
17	.05	2.98	3.63	4.02	4.30	4.52	4.70	4.86	4.99	5.11	5.21
	.01	4.10	4.74	5.14	5.43	5.66	5.85	6.01	6.15	6.27	6.38
18	.05	2.97	3.61	4.00	4.28	4.49	4.67	4.82	4.96	5.07	5.17
	.01	4.07	4.70	5.09	5.38	5.60	5.79	5.94	6.08	6.20	6.31
19	.05	2.96	3.59	3.98	4.25	4.47	4.65	4.79	4.92	5.04	5.14
	.01	4.05	4.67	5.05	5.33	5.55	5.73	5.89	6.02	6.14	6.25
20	.05	2.95	3.58	3.96	4.23	4.45	4.62	4.77	4.90	5.01	5.11
	.01	4.02	4.64	5.02	5.29	5.51	5.69	5.84	5.97	6.09	6.19
24	.05	2.92	3.53	3.90	4.17	4.37	4.54	4.68	4.81	4.92	5.01
	.01	3.96	4.55	4.91	5.17	5.37	5.54	5.69	5.81	5.92	6.02
30	.05	2.89	3.49	9.85	4.10	4.30	4.46	4.60	4.72	4.82	4.92
	.01	3.89	4.45	4.80	5.05	5.24	5.40	5.54	5.65	5.76	5.85
40	.05	2.86	3.44	3.79	4.04	4.23	4.39	4.52	4.63	4.73	4.82
	.01	3.82	4.37	4.70	4.93	5.11	5.26	5.39	5.50	5.60	5.69
60	.05	2.83	3.40	3.74	3.98	4.16	4.31	4.44	4.55	4.65	4.73
	.01	3.76	4.28	4.59	4.82	4.99	5.13	5.25	5.36	5.45	5.53
120	.05	2.80	3.36	3.68	3.92	4.10	4.24	4.36	4.47	4.56	4.64
	.01	3.70	4.20	4.50	4.71	4.87	5.01	5.12	5.21	5.30	5.37
∞	.05	2.77	3.31	3.63	3.86	4.03	4.17	4.29	4.39	4.47	4.55
	.01	3.64	4.12	4.40	4.60	4.76	4.88	4.99	5.08	5.16	5.23

Source: From Table 29 of Pearson and Hartley (1976: 192–3), *Biometrika Tables for Statisticians*, volume 1. London: Biometrika Trust. By permission of Oxford University Press.

STATISTICAL TABLE G Critical Values of the Chi-Square Distribution

Level of Significance

df	Critical χ^2, $\alpha = .10$	Critical χ^2, $\alpha = .05$	Critical χ^2, $\alpha = .01$	Critical χ^2, $\alpha = .001$
1	2.71	3.84	6.64	10.83
2	4.50	5.99	9.21	13.82
3	6.25	7.81	11.34	16.27
4	7.78	9.49	13.28	18.47
5	9.24	11.07	15.09	20.52
6	10.64	12.59	16.81	22.46
7	12.02	14.07	18.48	24.32
8	13.36	15.51	20.09	26.12
9	14.68	16.92	21.67	27.88
10	15.99	18.31	23.21	29.59
11	17.28	19.68	24.72	31.26
12	18.55	21.03	26.22	32.91
13	19.81	22.36	27.69	34.53
14	21.06	23.68	29.14	36.12
15	22.31	25.00	30.58	37.70
16	23.54	26.30	32.00	39.25
17	24.77	27.59	33.41	40.79
18	25.99	28.87	34.80	42.31
19	27.20	30.14	36.19	43.82
20	28.41	31.41	37.57	45.32
21	29.62	32.67	38.93	46.80
22	30.81	33.92	40.29	48.27
23	32.01	35.17	41.64	49.73
24	33.20	36.42	42.98	51.18
25	34.38	37.65	44.31	52.62
26	35.56	38.88	45.64	54.05
27	36.74	40.11	45.96	55.48
28	37.92	41.34	48.28	56.89
29	39.09	42.56	49.59	58.30
30	40.25	43.77	50.89	59.70
40	51.80	55.76	63.69	73.40
50	63.17	67.50	75.15	86.66
60	74.40	79.08	88.38	99.61
70	85.53	90.53	100.42	112.32

Source: From Table 8 of Pearson and Hartley (1976: 137), *Biometrika Tables for Statisticians,* volume 1. London: Biometrika Trust. By permission of Oxford University Press.

STATISTICAL TABLE H **Critical Values of Spearman's Rank-Order Coefficient r_s at the .05 and .01 Levels of Significance, α**

Sample Size	Level of Significance (α)			
	Critical r_s, $\alpha = .05$		Critical r_s, $\alpha = .01$	
n	Two-tailed	One-tailed	Two-tailed	One-tailed
5	1.000	.900	—	1.000
6	.886	.829	1.000	.943
7	.786	.714	.929	.893
8	.738	.643	.881	.833
9	.683	.600	.833	.783
10	.648	.564	.794	.746
12	.591	.506	.777	.712
14	.544	.456	.714	.645
16	.506	.425	.665	.601
18	.475	.399	.625	.564
20	.450	.377	.591	.534
22	.428	.359	.562	.508
24	.409	.343	.537	.485
26	.392	.329	.515	.465
28	.377	.317	.496	.448
30	.364	.306	.478	.432

Source: From Table G of R. P. Runyon, A. Haber, D. J. Pittenger and K. A. Coleman (1996: 654), *Fundamentals of Behavioral Statistics*, 8 ed. New York: McGraw-Hill, 1996, p. 654. By permission of The McGraw-Hill Companies.

THESE ARE PARTIAL ANSWERS. BE SURE TO SHOW ALL WORK AND FORMULAS.

Chapter 1

1. *a.* 40.76%   *e.* $\dfrac{2,322}{10,000}$, .2322   2. *a.* 20.31%   *e.* $\dfrac{4,550}{10,000}$, .4550

3. Anne: $p = .5924$ 4. Slam Dunk Williams; $p = .5385$ 5. 55 days
6. For Scott, $p = .4054$ 7. For males in the 21–30 age group, $p = .0992$; # to attend = 5; for females in the 41–50 age group, $p = .2876$; # to attend = 14
8. For Los Angeles, from the personnel department, $p = .1558$; # to attend = 6; for New York, in the marketing department, $p = .3286$; # to attend = 13
9. .7859   10. 351   11. Bellingham, Washington, 1,254
12. Burlington, North Carolina, 1,070   13. *b.* 65.39%   *d.* 70.78%
14. *a.* Women (14.23%)   *b.* Women (72.97%)   15. *a.* 22.22%   *c.* .0019 = 2 per thousand   16. Muslims, .1801; 18.01%   17. Abilene, TX, .8947, .0971, .0082   18. Battle Creek, MI, .7000, .2792, .0208

Chapter 2

1. *a.* ratio   2. *a.* ratio   3. *a.* ratio   4. *a.* ordinal
5. *a.* Not inclusive; no place to score a response of Muslim, Hindu, etc. To improve, add an "other" category. Not exclusive; a Baptist could be classified as either Protestant or Baptist. To improve, organize the question as presented in Table 2–5

6. *c.* Not inclusive; no place for scores of 5 or scores greater than 15. To improve, change 0–4 to 0–5. Not exclusive; someone with a score of "none" could also mark 0–4

7 *a.* 28.3   *c.* 600   8. *a.* 5.5   *f.* 500,000

9. *a.* 3.95 to 4.05   *f.* 3,355 to 3,365

10. *a.* 4.995 to 5.005   *e.* 70,950 to 71,050

11. 8.25:1   12. 2.82:1   13. *b.* 75th   14. *b.* 16th

15. *a.* 29.93%   *c.* Col. % of Belgium, very important = 23.16

16. *a.* 59.28%   *c.* Col. % of working class, no. = 70.54

17. Proportional frequency of vanilla = .3000

18. Proportional frequency of Democratic = .4615

19. *a.* 45.00%   *d.* 45.45%   20. *a.* 55.00%   *d.* 63.64%

Chapter 3

1. Calculation spreadsheet follows. See chart for exercise 2 for additional hints.

Category	%	p	pX360°
Income taxes	30%	.3000	108.0
Gasoline taxes	12	.1200	43.2
Sales taxes	21	.2100	75.6
Other taxes and fees	24	.2400	86.4
Other sources	13	.1300	46.8
Totals	100%	1.0000	360.0

2. Calculation spreadsheet and pie chart:

Task	Time (in hours)	p	pX360°	%
Cooking and feeding	1.6	.2000	72.0	20%
Etc.				

CHART 2

Time spent on various tasks

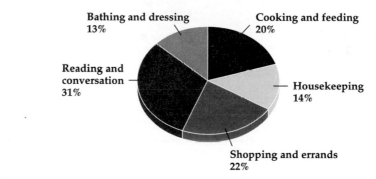

Bathing and dressing 13%

Cooking and feeding 20%

Reading and conversation 31%

Housekeeping 14%

Shopping and errands 22%

3. Bar chart:

CHART 3

Percentage of gross domestic product spent on health care in selected European countries

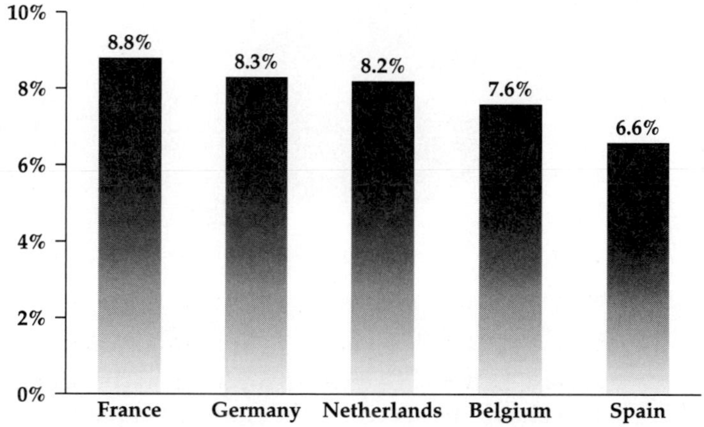

8.8% France
8.3% Germany
8.2% Netherlands
7.6% Belgium
6.6% Spain

4. See chart in exercise 3 for hints.
5. See chart in exercise 6 for hints.
6. Clustered bar chart:

CHART 6

Parents' levels of education

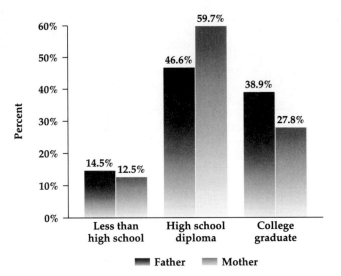

7. *a*. Pie charts:

CHART 7A

Makeup of white ethnic neighborhoods in New York City, 1980 and 1990

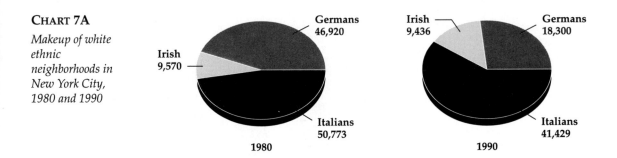

b. See Chart 8B in exercise 8 for hints on constructing Chart 7B.   *c.* For reasons that should be specified, the clustered bar chart is better.

8. *a.* See Chart 7A in exercise 7 for hints on constructing Chart 8A.
b. Clustered bar chart:

CHART 8B

Types of weight control advertisements in Ladies Home Journal *in the 1980s and 1990s*

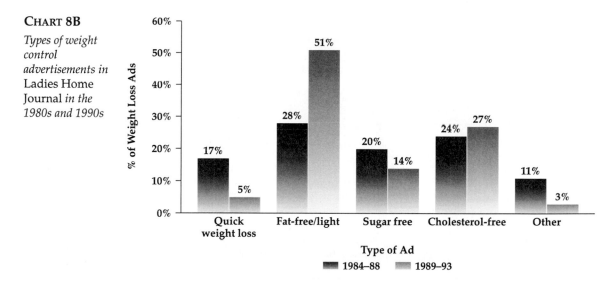

c. For reasons that should be specified, the clustered bar chart is better.

9. *a.* Frequency histogram:

CHART 9A

Ages of students on a college debating team

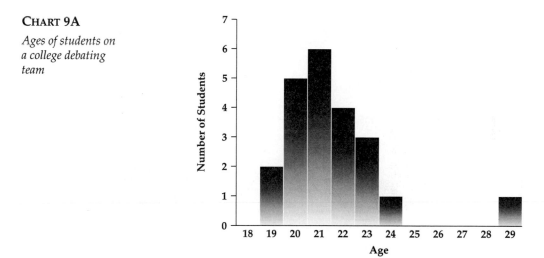

b. See exercise 10*b* for hints   *c.* Probably the histogram. With a small sample size such as this and the small range of scores, it is easier on the histogram to match frequency (number of students) with each age.   *d.* There is an outlier.

10. For parts *a.*, *c.*, and *d.*, see answers to exercise 9 for hints.
    b. Frequency polygon:

CHART 10B

Participation in campus events

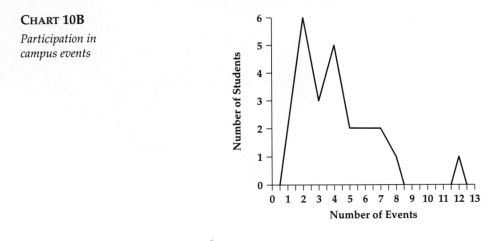

11. *a.* Calculation spreadsheet and polygons:

Kilometers	Suburban			Rural		
	f	p	%	f	p	%
1	2	.0298	3%	0	.0000	0%
2	4	.0597	6	1	.0090	1
Etc.						

CHART 11

A comparison of distances traveled to school by suburban and rural students

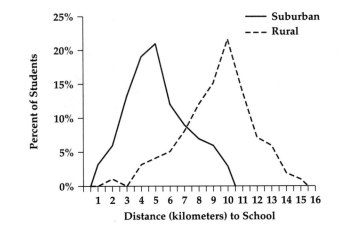

12. See answer to exercise 11 for hints.

Chapter 4

1. Calculation spreadsheet:

X	X(cont.)	X(ranked)	X(ranked cont.)
...	...	...	...

Mo = 19 years; Mdn = 19 years; mean = 18.9 years   2. See answer to exercise 1 for hints. Mdn = 9.5 miles; mean = 9 miles   3. *a.* Modal position = 3; Mdn position = 3; mean position = 2.82   4. *a.* Modal position = 2; Mdn position = 2; mean position = 2.25   5. Mo = 3 pounds; Mdn = 3 pounds; mean = 3.43 pounds   6. Mean = 631 points; Mdn = 625
7. *a.*

$$\text{Speed}_{(Terry)} = \frac{\text{distance}}{\text{time}} = \frac{2 \text{ miles}}{4/60 \text{ hours}} = \frac{2 \text{ miles}}{.067 \text{ hour}} = 30 \text{ mph}$$

b. 60 mph   *c.* No. (Explain why short distances do not allow enough time to be saved.)   8. *a.* 202.33 pins per game   9. *a.* Frequency curves:

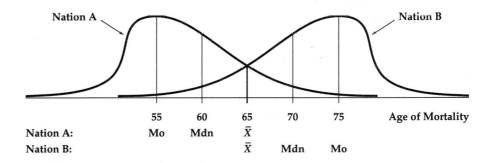

	55	60	65	70	75	**Age of Mortality**
Nation A:	Mo	Mdn	$\bar{X}$			
Nation B:			$\bar{X}$	Mdn	Mo	

b. See answer to exercise 10*b* for hints.   10. *a.* See answer to exercise 9*a* for hints   *b.* City A   11. *a.* Mean = \$12.73   *d.* Adjusted mean = \$8.41
12. *a.* Mean = 2.39 GPA points   *d.* Adjusted mean = 2.13 GPA points
13. 55.71 years   14. 34.82 years   15. *a.* X = chicken reaction times; partial spreadsheet:

X	f	f(X)
.88	1	.88
...	...	...
1.45	1	1.45
	n = ...	$\Sigma f(X)$= ...

b. $\bar{X} = \ldots = 1.03$ seconds   *c.* See answer to exercise 16 for hints   16. *a.* See answer to exercise 15*a* for hints   *b.* Mdn = .355; Mo = .360   *c.* Left skew
17. The shape of the curve of household size is a right skew
18. The shape of the curve of grocery budget is a right skew

Chapter 5

1. Partial answer:

Sum of Squares	n	Variance	Standard Deviation
893.49	30	30.81	5.55
43,128.90	347	124.65	11.16

2. Partial answer:

Sum of Squares	n	Variance	Standard Deviation
38.76	7	6.46	2.54
347,295.92	1,041	333.94	18.27

3. *a.* $\bar{X} = \ldots = 78.43$ years   *c.* $s_x = \ldots = 3.05$ years
4. *a.* $\bar{X} = \ldots = 7.86$ visits   *c.* $s_x = \ldots = 3.18$ visits
5. *a.* Mdn = $2,347, Mo = indeterminable   *b.* Estimate of s_x based on the range
= ... = $262   *c.* $s_x = \ldots = $356.53
6. *a.* Mdn = 8 case contacts   *b.* Range = ... = 10 case contacts   *c.* $s_x = \ldots$ 3.54 case contacts
7. 42.86%   8. 28.57%

9. *b.* $\bar{X} = \dfrac{\Sigma fX}{n} = \dfrac{204}{10} = 20.40$ years; $s_x = \ldots = 3.31$ years

c. $\bar{X} = \ldots = 19.44$ years; $s_x = \ldots = 1.43$ years

10. *b.* $\bar{X} = \dfrac{\Sigma fX}{n} = \dfrac{29}{8} = 3.62$ GPA points;

$$s_X = \sqrt{\frac{\Sigma f(X - \bar{X})^2}{n-1}} = \sqrt{\frac{1.29}{7}} = .43 \text{ GPA points}$$

c. $\bar{X} = 3.77$ GPA points; $s_x = .25$ GPA points

11. Partial answer:

Case	Y *(cigarettes per day)*	$Y - \bar{Y}$ *(deviation score)*	Z_Y *(standardized score)*
Bob Smith	17 cigarettes	2 cigarettes	+ .4 SD

12. Partial answer:

State	Y *(hate crimes)*	$Y - \bar{Y}$ *(deviation score)*	Z_Y *(standardized score)*
Florida	1.15 hate crimes	− .04 hate crimes	− .12 SD

13. Partial answer:

X *(pounds)*	*Sight Estimate of Z-Score (SD)*	*Computed Z-Score (SD)*
128		−2.28
192	≈ 1.2	

14. Partial answer:

X *(acts)*	*Sight Estimate of Z-Score (SD)*	*Computed Z-Score (SD)*
9		−1.77
12	≈ −1.1	

Chapter 6

1. *a*. .1667   *b*. .3333   *c*. .0046   2. *a*. .1667   *b*. .0278   *c*. .5000
3. *a*. .0628   *b*. .0625   *c*. .0316   4. *a*. .0314   *b*. .0667   *c*. .0144
5. *a*. .5000   *b*. .2500   *c*. .1250   6. *a*. .5000   *b*. .2500   *c*. .1250
7. *a*. .0769   *b*. .1538   *c*. .3077   8. *a*. .0769   *b*. .1538   *c*. .3077   *d*. .0090
9. With   10. Without   11. 56.52%   12. .0168   13. *a*. .0228
b. .0606   *c*. .6687   *d*. 24.56   14. *a*. .0668   *b*. .0994   *c*. .7745.   *d*. 91.2
15. *a*. .8413   *b*. .0359   *c*. 31.3   16. *a*. .6826   *b*. .1336   *c*. 19.44
17. *a*. 2.33   *b*. 2.58   18. *a*. 3.08   *b*. 3.30   19. 99   20. Caroline is
only one percentile rank higher than Michelle

Chapter 7

1. .11   2. .22   3. *a.* $57.47   *b.* .19 years   *e.* .02   4. *a.* .25 years
c. .02   15. *a.* No; $Q_s = .1$; $p_{smaller}(n) < .5$ *b.* 50   16. *a.* No; $Q_s = .2$; $p_{smaller}$
$(n) < .5$ *b.* 25

Chapter 8

1. 55.71 to 58.29 years   2. 173.02 to 174.98 pounds   3. 55.30 to 58.70
years   4. 172.71 to 175.29 pounds   5. $42,723.61 to $44,418.39
6. 56.81 to 61.19   7. 29.65% to 40.35%   8. No. His support could be as
low as 40.67%   9. 2,400   10. 1,508   11. 46   12. 30

Chapter 9

1. *a.* If we repeatedly sampled the campus population, sample means for age
would center on 21 years   *b.* If we repeatedly sampled Fortune 500
corporations, sample proportions of female corporate board members would
center on .20   2. *a.* If we repeatedly sampled the viewing public, sample
proportions of those watching a network nightly news program would center
on .50   3. *a.* Alt. *H*   4. *c.* Alt. *H*   5. *a.* One-tailed, positive; >
6. *c.* Two-tailed, nondirectional; ≠   7. *b.* One-tailed because of *below*
c. Reject   8. *b.* One-tailed because of *more*   *c.* Fail to reject   9. *a.* Reject
b. Fail to reject   10. *c.* Reject   *e.* Fail to reject   11. *a.* .00002
12. *b.* .0006

Chapter 10

1. *a.* –.6 years   *b.* –.06   2. *a.* 13 ears per bushel   *c.* 19 stolen cars
3. *a.* $t_\alpha = 1.761$; $.05 > p > .01$; reject   *b.* $t_\alpha = -3.355$; $.05 > p > .01$; fail to reject
4. *a.* $t_\alpha = 2.074$; $p > .05$; fail to reject   *b.* $t_\alpha = -2.896$; $.01 > p > .001$; reject
5. *a.* $t_{p_s} = 1.20$; $p > .05$; no   6. $t_{\bar{X}} = 2.73$; $.01 > p > .001$; reject; no
7. $t_{\bar{X}} = -1.76$; $.05 > p > .01$; reject; yes   8. $t_{p_s} = 2.00$ 9. $t_{p_s} = -1.25$; $p > .05$;
fail to reject; yes   10. $t_{\bar{X}} = -1.86$; $p < .05$; mean GPA is less than 3.0
11. $t_{\bar{X}} = 2.23$; yes   12. $t_{\bar{X}} = -1.76$; since $t_{\bar{X}}$ is in the opposite direction of that
hypothesized, $p > .50$, as illustrated on this curve:

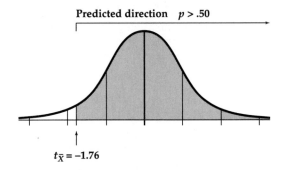

Predicted direction $p > .50$

$t_{\bar{X}} = -1.76$

13. *a.* $t_{\bar{X}} = -2.86$; no   *b.* $t_{p_s} = .63$; yes   14. *a.* $t_{\bar{X}} = -1.18$; yes   *b.* $t_{p_s} = 1.37$; yes

Chapter 11

1. $t_{\bar{X}_1 - \bar{X}_2} = -3.07$; $p < .01$; yes
2. $t_{\bar{X}_1 - \bar{X}_2} = 6.89$; $p < .001$; yes
3. $t_{\bar{X}_1 - \bar{X}_2} = 3.14$; $p < .01$; yes
4. $t_{\bar{X}_1 - \bar{X}_2} = -2.50$; $p < .05$; yes
5. $t_{\bar{X}_1 - \bar{X}_2} = -2.73$; $p < .01$; yes
6. $t_{\bar{X}_1 - \bar{X}_2} = 1.75$; $p < .05$, one-tailed; yes
7. $t_{\bar{X}_1 - \bar{X}_2} = -2.26$; $p < .05$; yes
8. $t_{\bar{X}_1 - \bar{X}_2} = 7.69$; $p < .001$
9. *a.* $t_{\bar{X}_1 - \bar{X}_2} = -.23$; $p > 05$; yes
b. $t_{\bar{X}_1 - \bar{X}_2} = -4.20$; $p < .001$, one-tailed; yes
c. $t_{\bar{D}} = 35.68$; $p < .001$; yes
10. $t_{\bar{D}} = 16.56$; $p < .001$; yes

Chapter 12

1. Main effect of arts and sciences = .11   2. Main effect of crash but not at fault = −.41   3. $Y_{(Inmate\ 1)} = \$22 = \$55 + (-\$28) + (-\$5)$
4. $Y_{(Kathy\ Schaefer)} = 24{,}829$ miles $= 16{,}489 + 9.902 + (-1{,}562)$
5. $F = 7.76$; $p < .01$; yes; Anglo-Americans are significantly less liberal (or more conservative) than African-Americans and Hispanics   6. $F = .08$; $p > .05$; no   7. $F = 12.16$; $p < .01$; yes   8. $F = 11.27$; $p < .01$; yes. Evangelical ministers are significantly less supportive of the government's efforts to control pollution   9. Main effect of white = 2.82 punitive attitude scale points; $p < .01$; reject   10. Main effect of low income = 72.08 toxic releases; $p < .01$; the mean number of toxic releases of each income level is significantly different from the others

Chapter 13

1. % [of rural county physicians in high risk specialty] = 70.42%   2. % [of service employees with college degree] = 12.77%   3. $\chi^2 = 6.33$; $p < .05$; reject   4. $\chi^2 = 9.53$; $p < .01$; yes   5. $\chi^2 = 7.77$; $p < .01$; reject
6. $\chi^2 = 9.97$; $p < .01$; reject   7. $\chi^2 = 4.38$; $p < .05$; reject   9. *c.* .3125
10. .0078   11. $p = .1445$; no   12. $p = .3769$; not any better
13. $p = .0898$; not any better   14. $p = .3769$; conclusion is not correct
15. Minimum $n = 8$ 16. Minimum $n = 5$

Chapter 14

1. *b.* $\hat{Y} = 27.92 + (.69)X$ *c.* $r = .85$
2. *b.* $\hat{Y} = -\$26{,}413.60 + (\$3{,}768.54)X$ *c.* $r = .90$
3. *d.* $\hat{Y} = 1.23 + (.23)X$
4. *d.* $\hat{Y} = .63 + (.35)X$
5. *b.* $\hat{Y} = -4.64 + (8.24)X$ *c.* $r = .74$
6. *b.* $\hat{Y} = 49.19 - 1.60X$ *c.* $r = -.96$
7. *b.* $r = -.61$ *d.* $r = -.94$
8. *b.* $r = .46$ *d.* $r = .86$

Chapter 15

1. *b.* The higher the literacy rate of a country, the greater the extent of democratization (positive relationship)   2. *b.* The greater the number of

previous convictions, the longer the prison sentence (positive relationship)
3. b. $r = .71$; $\hat{Y} = 83.32 + 4.43X$ c. $t_r = 2.47$; $p < .05$ 4. b. $r = .74$; $\hat{Y} = 107.18 +$
15.20X c. $t_r = 2.68$; $p < .05$ 5. $t_r = 5.63$; $p < .001$ 6. $t_r = 1.89$; $p < .05$
7. Age and education level   8. Age and hours connected   9. $r = -.75$; t_r
$= -3.61$; $p < .01$; yes   10. $r = -.88$; $t_r = -6.68$; $p < .001$; yes

Chapter 16

1. $r_s = .89$; $p < .01$; yes   2. $r_s = .75$; $p < .05$; yes   3. $r_s = -.62$; $p < .05$; yes
4. $r_s = .19$; $p > .05$; no   5. $G = .34$; $Z_G = 1.51$; $p = .0655$; fail to reject
6. $G = .24$; $Z_G = 1.05$; $p = .1469$; no   7. $G = .05$; $Z_G = .26$; $p = .3974$; no
8. $G = -.26$; $Z_G = -2.37$; $p = .0089$; yes   9. $G = -.41$; $Z_G = -2.98$; $p = .0014$; yes
10. $G = -.71$; $Z_G = -4.08$; $p = .00003$; yes

References

Alba, Richard D., John R. Logan, and Kyle Crowder. 1997. "White Ethnic Neighborhoods and Assimilation: The Greater New York Region, 1980–1990." *Social Forces* 75:883–909.

American Medical Association. 1982. *Physician Characteristics and Distribution in the U.S.* Chicago: American Medical Association.

———. 1997. *Physician Characteristics and Distribution in the U.S., 1996–97.* Chicago: American Medical Association.

Arthur, Winfred, Jr., and William G. Graziano. 1996. "The Five-Factor Model, Conscientiousness, and Driving Accident Involvement." *Journal of Personality* 64(3):593–615.

Asbjörnsen, P. C. 1986. "Chicken Licken." In DePaola, Tomie, *Tomie dePaola's Favorite Nursery Tales.* New York: G. P. Putnam's Sons, pp. 105–11.

Babbie, Earl. 1992. *The Practice of Social Research,* 6th ed. New York: Wadsworth.

Badger, Lee W., Barry Ackerson, Frederick Buttell, and Elizabeth H. Rand. 1997. "The Case for Integration of Social Work Psychosocial Services into Rural Primary Care Practice." *Health and Social Work* 22:20–9.

Bailey, Kenneth D. 1978. *Methods of Social Research.* New York: Free Press.

Blalock, Hubert M. 1979. *Social Statistics,* 3rd ed. New York: McGraw-Hill.

Browne, Irene. 1997. "Explaining the Black-White Gap in Labor Force Participation among Women Heading Households." *American Sociological Review* 62:236–52.

Bryson, Bethany. 1996. "'Anything but Heavy Metal': Symbolic Exclusion and Musical Dislikes." *American Sociological Review* 61:884–99.

Clair, Jeffrey M., Ferris J. Ritchey, and Richard M. Allman. 1993. "Satisfaction with Medical Encounters among Caregivers of Geriatric Outpatients." *Sociological Practice* 11:139–57.

David, F. N. 1962. *Games, Gods and Gambling.* London: Charles Griffen and Company.

Durkheim, Emile. 1951 [1897]. *Suicide: A Study in Sociology.* Translated by John A. Spaulding and George Simpson. Glencoe, IL: Free Press.

Edin, Kathryn, and Laura Lein. 1997. "Work, Welfare, and Single Mothers' Economic Survival Strategies." *American Sociological Review* 61:253–66.

Ensminger, Margaret E. 1995. "Welfare and Psychological Distress: A Longitudinal Study of African American Urban Mothers." *Journal of Health and Social Behavior* 36:346–59.

Fisher, Ronald A., and Frank Yates. 1963. *Statistical Tables for Biological, Agricultural and Medical Research.* London: Addison Wesley Longman Ltd.

Freund, John E., and Gary A. Simon. 1991. *Statistics: A First Course,* 5th ed. Englewood Cliffs, NJ: Prentice Hall.

Friedman, Michael A., and Kelly D. Brownell. 1995. "Psychological Correlates of Obesity: Moving to the Next Research Generation." *Psychological Bulletin* 117:3–20.

Gibbs, Raymond W., and Dinara Beitel. 1995. "What Proverbial Understanding Reveals about How People Think." *Psychological Bulletin* 118:133–54.

Gillings, Richard J. 1972. *Mathematics in the Time of the Pharaohs.* Cambridge, MA: MIT Press.

Guth, James L., John C. Green, Lyman A. Kellstedt, and Corwin E. Smidt. 1995. "Faith and the Environment: Religious Beliefs and Attitudes on Environmental Policy." *American Journal of Political Science* 39:364–82.

Haub, Carl, and Machiko Yanagishita. 1993. *World Population Data Sheet,* 1993. Washington, DC: Population Reference Bureau.

Jackson, Jerome E., and Sue Ammen. 1996. "Race and Correctional Officers' Punitive Attitudes toward Treatment Programs for Inmates." *Journal of Criminal Justice* 24:153–66.

Johnson, Elmer H. 1973. *Social Problems of Urban Man*. Homewood, IL: Dorsey Press.

Kaiser, G., and J. Pfenninger. 1984. "Effect of Neurointensive Care upon Outcome Following Severe Head Injuries in Childhood—A Preliminary Report." *Neuropediatrics* 15:68–75.

Lee, Ivy, and Minako Maykovich. 1995. *Statistics: A Tool for Understanding Society*. Needham Heights, MA: Allyn and Bacon.

Likert, Rensis. 1932. "A Technique for the Measurement of Attitudes." *Archives of Psychology* 21, monograph no. 140.

Lueschen, Guenther, William Cockerham, Jouke van der Zee, Fred Stevens, Jos Diederiks, Manuel Garcia Ferrando, Alphonse d'Houtaud, Ruud Peeters, Thomes Abel, and Steffen Niemann. 1995. *Health Systems in the European Union: Diversity, Convergence, and Integration*. Munich: Oldenbourg.

Madriz, Esther. 1996. "The Perception of Risk in the Workplace: A Test of Routine Activity Theory." *Journal of Criminal Justice* 24:407–18.

Marshall, Grant N., M. Audrey Burnam, Paul Koegel, Greer Sullivan, and Bernadette Benjamin. 1996. "Objective Life Circumstances and Life Satisfaction: Results from the Course of Homelessness Study." *Journal of Health and Social Behavior* 37:44–58.

McCarthy, John D., and Mark Wolfson. 1996. "Resource Mobilization by Local Social Movement Organizations: Agency, Strategy, and Organization in the Movement against Drinking and Driving." *American Sociological Review* 61:1070–88.

McCrae, Robert R. 1996. "Social Consequences of Experiential Openness." *Psychological Bulletin* 120:323–37.

Mills, C. Wright. 1959. *The Sociological Imagination*. New York: Oxford University Press.

National Advisory Commission on Civil Disorders. 1968. *Report of the National Advisory Commission on Civil Disorders*. Washington, DC: U.S. Government Printing Office.

National Opinion Research Center (NORC). 1994. *General Social Surveys, 1972–1994: Cumulative Codebook*. Chicago: University of Chicago (Internet access: www.icpsr.umich.edu/gss/codebook).

Neugebauer, O. 1962. *The Exact Sciences in Antiquity*. New York: Harper.

Orbuch, Terri L., and Sandra L. Eyster. 1997. "Division of Household Labor among Black Couples and White Couples." *Social Forces* 76:301–32.

Pearson, E. S., and H. O. Hartley. 1976. *Biometrika Tables for Statisticians*, volume 1. London: Biometrika Trust.

Pearson, Jane L., Andrea G. Hunter, Margaret E. Ensminger, and Sheppard G. Kellam. 1990. "Black Grandmothers in Multigenerational Households: Diversity in Family Structure and Parenting Involvement in the Woodlawn Community." *Child Development* 61:434–42.

Peterson, Richard A., and Roger M. Kern. 1996. "Changing Highbrow Taste: From Snob to Omnivore." *American Sociological Review* 61:900–7.

Rogge, Mary E. 1996. "Social Vulnerability to Toxic Risk." *Journal of Social Service Research* 22:109–29.

Runyon, R. P., A. Haber, D. J. Pittenger, and K. A. Coleman. 1996. *Fundamentals of Behavioral Statistics*, 8th ed. New York: McGraw-Hill.

Sagan, Carl. 1995a. "Crop Circles and Aliens: What's the Evidence?" *Parade*, December 3, pp. 10–3.

———. 1995b. *The Demon-Haunted World*. New York. Random House.

Sibicky, Mark E., David A. Schroeder, and John F. Dovidio. 1995. "Empathy and Helping: Considering the Consequences of Intervention." *Basic and Applied Psychology* 16:435–53.

Smetana, Judith G., and Pamela Asquith. 1994. "Adolescents' and Parents' Conceptions of Parental Authority and Personal Autonomy." *Child Development* 65:1147–62.

Snyder, Douglas K., Robert M. Willis, and Averta Grady-Fletcher. 1991. "Long-Term Effectiveness of Behavioral versus Insight-Oriented Marital Therapy: A 4-Year Follow-Up Study." *Journal of Consulting and Clinical Psychology* 59:138–41.

Struik, Dirk J. 1948. *A Concise History of Mathematics*. New York: Dover.

Tompkins, Peter. 1971. *Secrets of the Great Pyramid*. New York: Harper & Row.

Tukey, J. W. 1953. *The Problem of Multiple Comparisons*. Princeton, NJ: Princeton University, mimeographed monograph.

Turner, Jonathon B. 1995. "Economic Context and the Effects of Unemployment." *Journal of Health and Social Behavior* 36:213–29.

U.S. Bureau of the Census. 1990. *Census of the Population: General Population Characteristics*. Washington, DC: U.S. Government Printing Office.

———. 1993. *Poverty in the United States: 1992*. Washington, DC: U.S. Government Printing Office. Ser. P-60, no. 185, p. 132.

Williams, Robin M., Jr. 1970. *American Society*, 3rd ed. New York: Knopf.

INDEX

Guide: Where there are multiple page entries, definitions and basic information are noted with bold numbers.